KB084861

CEDU 쎄듀는 A Comprehensive English eDUcation(종합적 영어교육)의 약자입니다.

저자

김기훈

現 ㈜ 쎄듀 대표이사

現 메가스터디 영어영역 대표강사

前 서울특별시 교육청 외국어 교육정책자문위원회 위원

저서   천일문 / 천일문 Training Book / 천일문 GRAMMAR

첫단추 BASIC / 쎄듀 본영어 / 어휘끝 / 어법끝 / 문법의 골든룰 101

절대평가 PLAN A / 리딩 플랫폼 / ALL씀 서술형 시리즈

Reading Relay / The 리딩플레이어 / 빈칸백서 / 오답백서

첫단추 / 파워업 / 수능영어 절대유형 / 수능실감 등

쎄듀 영어교육연구센터

쎄듀 영어교육센터는 영어 콘텐츠에 대한 전문지식과 경험을 바탕으로

최고의 교육 콘텐츠를 만들고자 최선의 노력을 다하는 전문가 집단입니다.

오혜정 센터장 · **김진경** 전임연구원 · **손아영** 연구원

마케팅   콘텐츠 마케팅 사업본부

제작   정승호

영업   문병구

인디자인 편집   올댓에디팅

디자인   쎄듀 디자인팀

영문교열   Stephen Daniel White

실감하다

300제

PREFACE

수능 영어 독해 고득점을 목표로 하는 수험생들이 막연하게 많은 문제를 풀다보면 성적이 오르겠지 하는 생각으로 문제 풀이만 하는 경우가 종종 있습니다. 그러나 이런 양만을 중시하는 학습은 시험 일정이 정해진 수능 대비에 비효율적일 수 있습니다. 효과적인 학습을 위해서는 고난도 유형을 포함한 다양한 문제들을 접해보는 것이 우선입니다.

본 교재 〈실감하다 300제〉는 매일 일정한 양의 문제를 제대로 학습하는 것에 중점을 두었습니다. 고득점 달성을 위해 해결해야 하는 대의 파악, 밑줄 함의, 빈칸 추론, 문장 넣기, 무관 문장, 글의 순서, 요약문 완성, 장문 유형과 어법, 어휘 유형까지 다양한 유형의 문제를 풀며 실력을 향상시킬 수 있습니다.

매일 성실하게 문제를 풀다 보면 수능 영어 고득점이 여러분에게 찾아올 것을 믿어 의심치 않습니다. 〈실감하다 300제〉로 고득점을 위한 독해 문제 대비를 마쳤다면, 〈독해 최우수 문항 500제〉, 〈독해 모의고사 6회〉로 실전 대비 단계로 나아갈 것을 추천해 드립니다.

저자

CONTENTS

책속의 책 [정답 및 해설]

1. 다음 글에서 필자가 주장하는 바로 가장 적절한 것은?

Mark Twain observed, "We are all ignorant, but about different things." One mistake technical professionals make when writing for non-technical readers is assuming their readers are as knowledgeable as they are about the subject. This is a fatal assumption that will only result in confusion and frustration for your reader. Also, a great deal of your time will be spent generating additional messages to the reader trying to explain what should have been clear the first time. Just because it's clear to you does not make it clear to your reader. If you are an engineer or accountant writing to others in your field, then perhaps there will be less need to explain all aspects of your message. If you're writing to the senior vice president of marketing, who is not familiar with software applications, then you will need to "walk" that reader through your message. Remember that when it comes to technical knowledge, writers and readers are hardly equal.

① 전문 지식에 대한 글은 독자의 눈높이에 맞춰 써야 한다.
② 전문가들의 지식이라고 해서 언제나 정확한 것은 아니다.
③ 전문 지식을 비전문가들에게 완전히 이해시키기는 어렵다.
④ 전문 지식이 많다고 해서 글을 더 잘 쓸 수 있지는 않다.
⑤ 미래에는 각 분야의 전문 지식이 더 융합 발전될 것이다.

2. 다음 글에서 밑줄 친 breathe in the world가 의미하는 바로 가장 적절한 것은? [3점]

In cultures where circular time is given as much attention as linear time, people's lives are far more relaxed and stress-free. Most traditional aboriginal people work far fewer hours, at most two or three days out of each week. And this is not working as we understand it; they visit, hang out, talk and gossip, ensuring that the social cement that holds their society together is in good order. To live with circular time is to let go of deadlines. Circular time encourages meditation, idling, play. It is often one of the biggest surprises for people who take their foot off the pedal, to find a richer, simpler and more rewarding life. Their bodies are rested, they enjoy better health and they smile more. They're harmonious with the world, and breathe easier than people living with linear time. More often they create and play and remember what it was like to be a child, where the journey from A to B was seldom straight and never narrow. Their ability to access subtle details increases. They breathe in the world.

① focus on the future
② work well with others
③ endure stressful conditions
④ are able to enjoy their lives
⑤ are content with their routines

3. 다음 빈칸에 들어갈 말로 가장 적절한 것은?

Most often, you will find or meet people who introduce themselves in terms of their work or by what they spend time on. These people introduce themselves as a salesman or an executive. There is nothing criminal in doing this, but psychologically, we become what we believe. People who follow this practice tend to lose their individuality and begin to live with the notion that they are recognized by the job they do. However, jobs may not be permanent, and you may lose your job for a countless number of reasons, some of which you may not even be responsible for. In such cases, these people suffer from an inevitable social and mental trauma, leading to emotional stress and a feeling that all of a sudden they have been disassociated from what once was their _____.

① goal   ② property
③ identity   ④ background
⑤ capability

4. 주어진 글 다음에 이어질 글의 순서로 가장 적절한 것은?

Though economic considerations are of great importance, technological realities remain most important in determining how engineering shapes a product.

(A) Exploring such difficulties involving numerous opposing goals and seeing how engineers and others have wrestled with the problems helps us to better understand the interaction between engineering, economics, and the environment. A single aluminum can in isolation is one thing, but in the context of its billions of clones the aluminum can is quite another.

(B) For example, in designing a drink container, not only must engineers fashion a can that will hold the drink without contaminating it or allowing it to leak after rough shipping and handling, but they must also make the can easy to open and pour or drink from.

(C) Furthermore, while aluminum cans are a great convenience, they also represent an enormous potential waste of raw materials and energy, and getting rid of them raises significant issues of litter and waste disposal.

*contaminate: 오염시키다 **clone: 복제품

① (A) – (C) – (B)
② (B) – (A) – (C)
③ (B) – (C) – (A)
④ (C) – (A) – (B)
⑤ (C) – (B) – (A)

5. 글의 흐름으로 보아, 주어진 문장이 들어가기에 가장 적절한 곳은?

This is not to say, of course, that we regularly catalog all possible happenings in our minds before entering such situations, so that we are prepared for anything and everything.

Our knowledge of who is doing what in a situation allows us to make reasonably accurate guesses about the actual behavior of others. (①) We enter a doctor's examining room, for instance, knowing who is the patient, who is the doctor, and who is the nurse. (②) We know that medical talk and activity will take place, and that we may be asked to lie on a table or to take deep breaths. (③) We can prepare for what the doctor may ask us to do, what questions will be asked, and what her manner will be. (④) We do not, in fact, imagine everything that will take place, nor do we attempt to do so, nor could we do so. (⑤) But we do entertain at least a few thoughts about what may take place — we imagine what is going to happen — and we get our ideas about what may happen from our understanding of the perspectives provided by roles and situations.

1. 다음 글의 주제로 가장 적절한 것은?

Speaking is intrinsically social. Whether it comes from a person or a machine, speech activates a powerful and varied cognitive apparatus that is designed to express and recognize who a person is and what she or he is thinking and feeling. Although people have separate parts of the brain that are devoted to each social judgment and each aspect of speech production and understanding, people do not have separate parts of the brain for human speech and technology-generated speech. Even when voice interfaces exhibit all of the limitations associated with machines — including odd pronunciations, emotional ignorance, and chronic inconsistencies — they are not exempted from the social expectations that are activated by talking and listening. When technologies, regardless of quality, fail to conform to social norms, users experience confusion, frustration, and cognitive exhaustion and question the competence, utility, and enjoyability of the system. Socially inept interfaces suffer the same fate as socially inept individuals: they are ineffective, criticized, and shunned.

*shun: 피하다

① impact of technology-generated speech on the brain
② difficulties of communicating using machine-made speech
③ social norms of speech and listening in human interaction
④ differences between human speech and machine-made speech
⑤ reasons why human-machine interaction should follow social norms

2. 다음 글의 밑줄 친 부분 중, 어법상 틀린 것은?

People regularly do a kind of backwards thinking, and really believe it. One of the most famous examples in psychological research is cognitive dissonance. This is the idea ① that people don't like to hold two inconsistent ideas to be true at the same time. Studies ② conducted more than half a century ago find that when people are induced into behaviour that is inconsistent with their beliefs, they simply change their beliefs to match. It's like ③ when someone ends up spending too much on a new car. Instead of feeling bad about the clash between their original plan and what they've actually done, they prefer to convince ④ themselves that the car is worth the extra money. This is a result of our natural desire to maintain consistency between our thoughts and actions. We all want to be right, and one thing we should all be able to be right about ⑤ being ourselves. Backwards thinking allows us to do just that.

*dissonance: 부조화

3. 다음 빈칸에 들어갈 말로 가장 적절한 것은? [3점]

One of the most important goals you can have in the transition from high school to college is to sample widely from the academic offerings at your college. Even the most elite prep schools do not have the range of departments found at most colleges. Your high school probably didn't have a sociologist or an anthropologist on the faculty. But your ignorance about their disciplines, just from lack of exposure to them, could cost you. It's entirely possible that you'd be a happy and successful anthropology major, but since you don't know what that means, you don't bother exploring it. So, when you arrive on campus, make it a point to _____. You might find an academic home you never knew was there.

*prep school: 사립 고등학교

① make your major as enjoyable as possible
② learn about unfamiliar areas and disciplines
③ join a study group to improve your social skills
④ participate in many school events and activities
⑤ break down your studying into simple chunks

4. 다음 글에서 전체 흐름과 관계 없는 문장은?

It isn't hard to understand why our ancestors first became interested in harnessing the process of fermentation — it was a question of survival. ① If there is one thing our current love affair with seasonal eating has done successfully, it is to remind us of what our ancestors always knew. ② That is, if you are going to make it from one season to the next, you need to prepare. ③ As our ancestors developed beyond simple survival they began to ask questions about life and the world around them, the most fundamental of which was to understand the nature of matter. ④ You need a place to shelter you, clothes to keep you warm, and food to keep you strong, even when the wild game is gone, the cow has gone dry, and the fruit trees are finished producing. ⑤ This is our human heritage, passed down to us by those who learned to harness microbes and make milk into cheese, grapes into wine, and anchovies into fish sauce.

*harness: (자연력을) 활용하다 **fermentation: 발효

***anchovy: 멸치

5. 다음 글의 내용을 한 문장으로 요약하고자 한다. 빈칸 (A)와 (B)에 들어갈 말로 가장 적절한 것은?

In the less hierarchical and less bounded networked environment — where special knowledge is more in dispute than in the past and where relationships are less stable — there is more uncertainty about whom and what information sources to trust. The explosion of information and information sources has had the paradoxical impact of pushing people on the path of greater reliance on their networks. It might seem that the abundance of information that organizations provide on the Internet would prompt people to rely less on their friends and colleagues for facts and advice. Yet it turns out that the increasing amount of information pouring into people's lives leads them to turn to their social networks to make sense of it. The result is that as people gather information to help them make choices, they cycle back and forth between Internet searches and discussion with the members of their social networks, using in-person conversations, phone chats, and e-mails to exchange opinions and weigh options.

*paradoxical: 역설적인

↓

> As information is becoming increasingly ____(A)____ in today's world, people are turning away from organizations and toward social networks to ____(B)____ it.

	(A)		(B)
①	abundant	⋯⋯	produce
②	abundant	⋯⋯	interpret
③	technical	⋯⋯	criticize
④	biased	⋯⋯	produce
⑤	biased	⋯⋯	interpret

1. 다음 빈칸에 들어갈 말로 가장 적절한 것은?

Generalizations are similar to stereotypes. In the stereotype there exists one small kernel of truth, but that truth does not tell the whole tale. Relying on that one little truth to reach a conclusion distorts the whole truth. In writing, relying on broad generalizations alone _____. Oddly enough, in fact, generalizations are a necessary starting point for stating an overview of your basic message. For example: *There are indications that business is improving.* The challenge for this statement will be to add supporting facts consisting of numerical data, such as recent sales figures, surveys of consumer buying trends, and factual proof of additional or resurgent interest in your company's products or services (possibly including professional opinions from sales representatives and buyers to support sales or production data). So although generalizations can serve as initial foundations of thought, they can never serve as conclusive ones as well without hard, supporting evidence.

① is acceptable in some circumstances
② is likely to undermine your credibility
③ is important to make a specific point
④ is attempting to appeal to inappropriate authority
⑤ is guaranteed to deny the premise of your argument

2. 주어진 글 다음에 이어질 글의 순서로 가장 적절한 것은?

Increasing commercialization is the main cause of changing social structures. Consider traditional farmers, who see rice as a gift from the gods and the very support of life.

(A) Eventually, they adopt the same attitude as many farmers in industrialized nations who see producing food simply as a means to make money. A successful rice crop becomes nothing more than the result of spending money on fertilizers, pesticides, machinery or irrigation.

(B) When farmers start growing rice for profit rather than for themselves, they gradually become less inclined to spend resources such as time, money and rice to celebrate traditional religious beliefs.

(C) These farming communities organize their society and religious festivals around the annual cycle of rice growing. But commercialization breaks down this traditional culture bit by bit.

*irrigation: 관개, 물을 댐

① (A) – (C) – (B)　　② (B) – (A) – (C)
③ (B) – (C) – (A)　　④ (C) – (A) – (B)
⑤ (C) – (B) – (A)

3. 글의 흐름으로 보아, 주어진 문장이 들어가기에 가장 적절한 곳은?

Most of all, video games are excellent for developing visual awareness.

Some of the skills and abilities that are encouraged in video games are useful for many different purposes. (①) For example, recent studies show that they can significantly improve a surgeon's skill in using her hands when performing operations. (②) Also, playing video games has been shown to increase short-term memory of people in test groups. (③) The reason for this is that most games require players to spread their attention over the screen in order to quickly detect and react to changing events. (④) In fact, playing video games may trigger previously inactive genes that are important for developing neural pathways necessary for spatial attention. (⑤) Research is now suggesting that playing video games could even increase attention spans rather than reduce them.

[4~5] 다음 글을 읽고, 물음에 답하시오.

Today, digital technology has made it possible to collect, store, analyze, and distribute all kinds of information about you, ranging from your demographic profile to your driving record to a complete list of all your online activities. This so-called data mining — the 2010s buzzword for the trend toward collecting huge amounts of data about nearly every subject imaginable — exists because technology has made it nearly (a) <u>costless</u> to collect and store data. The easiest way to understand the capacity of digital data storage today is that a 1-terabyte disk drive holds more information than is (b) <u>housed</u> in an average research library. Such drives are readily available to consumers, (c) <u>fit</u> neatly in a large pants pocket or a small purse, and cost comfortably less than $100 — and the price is falling lower every year. The result is that today a company or an individual doesn't have to have the resources of a giant corporation to store a seemingly infinite amount of personal information about other individuals. This collapse in the price of storage allows nearly (d) <u>limited</u> data to be stored and processed in a way that was never previously possible.

Now that digital data storage is practically free, everything that can be will be collected and stored — permanently. In fact, it is fast becoming cheaper to keep large data sets than to try to figure out which data to delete. And once the data is available, you can bet somebody will find a use for it. As a result, (e) <u>massive</u> digital dossiers are being developed on every individual, right down to the websites you visit and the links you click on.

*buzzword: 유행어 **dossier: 서류[자료] 일체

4. 윗글의 제목으로 가장 적절한 것은?

① The Era of Ubiquitous Personal Information
② Don't Leave Your Footprints on the Web
③ The Outlook for Future Media Storage
④ The Shift from Mass Production to Customization
⑤ The Inequality in Information Caused by Digital Technology

5. 밑줄 친 (a)~(e) 중에서 문맥상 낱말의 쓰임이 적절하지 <u>않은</u> 것은?

① (a)　　② (b)　　③ (c)　　④ (d)　　⑤ (e)

1. 다음 글의 요지로 가장 적절한 것은?

To what extent is the human brain programmed for speech? The answer is unclear. Our brain is heavier than that of other animals, but size alone is not especially important. Elephants and whales have bigger brains than humans, but they do not talk. However, elephants and whales also have bigger bodies, so some people have suggested that it is the brain-body ratio which matters. At first sight, this seems a promising approach, especially when we find that the brain of an adult human is more than 2 percent of his or her total weight, while that of an adult chimp is less than 1 percent. But such ratios can be very misleading. Some animals are designed to carry around large reserves of energy which make their bodies enormously heavy. Camels, for example, are not necessarily more stupid than horses just because they have huge humps.

① 높은 지능이 말을 하기 위한 필수 조건은 아니다.
② 인간은 특수한 신체 구조로 인해 말을 할 수 있다.
③ 두뇌의 크기나 비율이 언어 능력을 담보하지 않는다.
④ 두뇌의 신체에 대한 비율이 크면 클수록 지능이 높다.
⑤ 신체에 예비 에너지를 축적하는 것은 생존에 필수적이다.

2. 다음 빈칸에 들어갈 말로 가장 적절한 것은?

In one study, psychologists Davis, Woolley, and Bruell presented children with a sequence of pictures illustrating a story about a girl, a bird, and a butterfly. The final picture depicted the girl with the bird nearby. The girl was waving her arms as if to fly, and a "thought bubble" above the girl's head indicated that she was thinking about the butterfly. Children were asked which of the two animals the girl was pretending to be. The girl's flying actions were consistent with both the bird and the butterfly, so if the children did not understand that pretending involves thinking about something, they should have chosen randomly between the two animals. However, even 3-year-olds were quite successful at this task, and 4- and 5-year-olds performed perfectly. This study suggests that by age 3, children have begun to

understand that the act of pretending involves _____. This understanding improves with age, and seems to be relatively well established by about age 5.

① communicative skills
② learning by imitation
③ background information
④ mental representation
⑤ real-life experience

3. 다음 글에서 전체 흐름과 관계 <u>없는</u> 문장은?

Why do insects become resistant to a particular pesticide? In any population of plants and insects there will always be that rare individual which survives exposure to a toxic agent. ① For example, if the pesticide works by blocking a specific enzyme, then it might be that this one individual has a slightly different arrangement of atoms around the enzyme's active site, and this prevents the toxin from gaining access. ② That being so, then its descendants will also have that protection and within a few years a significant population of resistant insects will defeat the efforts of the farmer to kill them off. ③ If the resistant gene is dominant enough, it will spread throughout the entire species of insect. ④ Moreover, pesticides have reduced the number of beneficial insects, such as bees and other pollinators, due to acute exposure to chemicals. ⑤ More worrying is that the resistant gene not only blocks this particular pesticide but may block other pesticides as well.

*enzyme: 효소 **active site: 활성 부위

4. 주어진 글 다음에 이어질 글의 순서로 가장 적절한 것은?

Empathy could be a highly generalized characteristic in that people who are empathic toward animals would be more likely to be empathic toward people.

(A) Unfortunately, however, a lack of empathy may also be a general characteristic of some people; little concern or care is shown toward victims of distress, human or animal. There is also the possibility that empathy is more specific.

(B) Some people may be highly empathic toward the suffering of other human beings but insensible to or unconcerned with animal distress. The opposite may also occur in cases where a person has great affection and empathy for animals but cares little for the concerns and welfare of other people.

(C) This inclination makes sense if we assume that many of the processes underlying empathy (a living creature is involved, distress cues can be perceived and correctly identified, relieving the distress of another is a valued trait) are applicable to both people and animals.

[3점]

① (A) – (C) – (B)　　② (B) – (A) – (C)
③ (B) – (C) – (A)　　④ (C) – (A) – (B)
⑤ (C) – (B) – (A)

5. 글의 흐름으로 보아, 주어진 문장이 들어가기에 가장 적절한 곳은?

By doing this, he was able to prove that all the people who had died of cholera had been drinking water from the same pump on Broad Street.

John Snow was a doctor who developed a link between cholera and dirty water in 1854. (①) He was not able to prove that dirty water caused cholera because germ theory hadn't been developed at that point. (②) Instead, he mapped out all the cases of cholera from the most recent outbreak and investigated the water supplies of homes and businesses where cholera had not caused any deaths. (③) For example, he discovered that all the workers at the local brewery drank beer or water from the brewery's own well, and none of them were affected by the cholera outbreak. (④) He insisted that the handle be removed from this pump to prevent anybody else from drinking from it. (⑤) After the removal of the handle, the cholera outbreak subsided, thus proving Snow's theory that it had been caused by the water in that particular well.

*brewery: 맥주 공장

1. 다음 글의 제목으로 가장 적절한 것은?

One day during the 1970s, a medium-sized demonstration outside the American Embassy in London suddenly grew into a massed uprising of many thousands of people, who crammed into the small square in front of the Embassy. Police on horses were holding the increasingly hostile crowd at bay. The mood began to get ugly, and people were beginning to panic. Suddenly, near the front, a young student climbed onto his friend's shoulders and began to entertain the crowd with witty comments and observations about what was going on. He performed like a stand-up comic. Everyone in the danger zone, including the police, was fascinated by his performance. The tension, the anger, and the fear decreased and a state of relative ease possessed the crowd. The young man continued for over half an hour, using a superb weapon, humor, to save his fellows from probable serious injury.

*cram into: (좁은 공간 속으로) 잔뜩 들어가다

① A Brave Action to Reject a Foreign Power
② Guarantee Freedom of Assembly and Association
③ The Power of Humor in Calming Down and Uniting People
④ The Unbearable Tension between England and America
⑤ Jokes: A Weapon Police Use to Suppress Protests

2. 다음 글의 밑줄 친 부분 중, 문맥상 낱말의 쓰임이 적절하지 않은 것은?

If an animal is innately programmed for some type of behavior, then there are ① likely to be biological clues. It is no accident that fish have bodies which are streamlined and smooth, with fins and a powerful tail. Their bodies are structurally ② adapted for moving fast through the water. Similarly, if you found a dead bird or mosquito, you could guess by looking at its wings that flying was its normal mode of ③ transport. However, we must not be over-optimistic. Biological clues are not essential. The extent to which they are found varies from animal to animal and from activity to activity. For example, it is impossible to guess from their bodies that birds make nests, and, sometimes, animals behave in a way quite ④ similar to what might be expected from their physical form: ghost spiders have tremendously long legs, yet they weave webs out of very short strands. To a human observer, their legs seem a great ⑤ hindrance as they spin and move about the web.

3. 다음 빈칸에 들어갈 말로 가장 적절한 것은?

What is the best order for a report, paper or other technical document? Of course, it must be logical; but that means simply that the paper must have connection and sequence, and a variety of orders are possible under this heading. Too many writers interpret the term *logical* to mean chronological, and it has become habitual to begin reports and papers with careful reviews of previous work. Usually, this is tactically weak. Most readers of reports and papers are reading the documents because they are interested in, and know something about, the subject. Therefore, to them the findings of previous work are _____. The interesting thing for them is the new information — the new findings and conclusions. So it is usually best to start with those pieces of information. To give a long chronological account of work or procedures is normally appropriate only when the essential point of the paper is the chronological sequence.

① creative outlets
② safety precautions
③ powerful motivators
④ a detailed summary
⑤ unnecessary reminders

4. 다음 글에서 전체 흐름과 관계 <u>없는</u> 문장은?

Streams generally contain an abundant supply of oxygen which is almost uniform throughout, even when there are no green plants, because of the large surface exposed to air and constant motion of water. This helps in easy respiration. ① Because of this reason, the animals in running water are sensitive to reduced oxygen content. ② Therefore, stream communities are especially sensitive to any type of organic pollution which reduces the oxygen supply. ③ Policy makers must constantly work to balance the concerns of a sensitive environment with those of developing economies struggling to compete globally. ④ When organic matter from sewage or waste from a paper mill is dumped in large quantities into streams, the oxygen in the water is consumed or used up in the bacterial decay process. ⑤ Stream pollution of this type is one of the most important problems in heavily populated and industrialized regions.

*respiration: 호흡

5. 다음 글의 내용을 한 문장으로 요약하고자 한다. 빈칸 (A)와 (B)에 들어갈 말로 가장 적절한 것은?

You can't have a democracy if you can't talk with your neighbors about matters of mutual interest or concern. Thomas Jefferson, who had an enduring interest in democracy, came to a similar conclusion. He was prescient in understanding the dangers of concentrated power, whether in corporations or in political leaders or exclusionary political institutions. Direct involvement of citizens was what had made the American Revolution possible and given the new republic vitality and hope for the future. Without that involvement, the republic would die. Eventually, he saw a need for the nation to be subdivided into "wards" — political units so small that everyone living there could participate directly in the political process. The representatives for each ward in the capital would have to be responsive to citizens organized in this way. A vibrant democracy conducted locally would then provide the active basic unit for the democratic life of the republic. With that kind of involvement, the republic might survive and prosper.

*prescient: 선견지명이 있는

↓

Thomas Jefferson argued for a form of ___(A)___ government that stressed ___(B)___ direct involvement in civic affairs.

	(A)		(B)
①	local	······	citizens'
②	local	······	representatives'
③	independent	······	ministers'
④	centralized	······	citizens'
⑤	centralized	······	representatives'

1. 다음 빈칸에 들어갈 말로 가장 적절한 것은?

Regardless of what Plato might have thought, there is no way that our minds have direct access to "eternal truths." Our senses, especially vision, hearing, and touch, are our only gates to reality. Essential as they are, however, our senses can also mislead us. Vision provides some good examples. "Seeing is believing," but what we see doesn't always produce a reliable belief. Errors can arise because what we think we see is influenced by what we already believe. We often "see" what we expect to see, and don't see what we don't anticipate. In a famous 1949 experiment, the psychologists Jerome Bruner and Leo Postman presented quick glimpses of pictures of trick playing cards to a group of subjects. Quite often the subjects said that a black three of hearts, for example, was either a normal three of spades (misperceiving the heart for a spade) or a normal three of hearts (misperceiving the black color for red). Expectations about the playing cards _____ _____.

① interfered with accurate perception
② decreased the confidence of the subjects
③ affected performance both positively and negatively
④ improved efficient and effective recognition
⑤ were not supported by their various senses

2. 주어진 글 다음에 이어질 글의 순서로 가장 적절한 것은?

The analogy below allows us to recognize that moral progress is possible. Before the invention of the microscope, people had no tools for seeing microscopic creatures and, consequently, made inaccurate judgments regarding the causes of disease.

(A) Similarly, in the moral sphere, when people don't have the tools needed for perceiving the rightness or wrongness of something, they make judgments that are less accurate than they would be if they had such tools.

(B) With the invention of the microscope, however, scientists were able to perceive entities they'd previously been unable to and, as a result, were able to make improved judgments — many of which we still accept today.

(C) We can see then, for instance, how the limited perspective of some people in 19th-century America led them to conclude that racism was acceptable and how our wider perspective these days enables us to recognize how terribly mistaken that earlier judgment was.

*analogy: 유추

① (A) – (C) – (B) 　② (B) – (A) – (C)
③ (B) – (C) – (A) 　④ (C) – (A) – (B)
⑤ (C) – (B) – (A)

3. 글의 흐름으로 보아, 주어진 문장이 들어가기에 가장 적절한 곳은?

All these changes allow the small-sized animal to survive long periods without any food and decrease the need for fuel.

Some animals hibernate to conserve energy and decrease the need for food. Prior to hibernation, an animal will generally feed to build up a store of fat. (①) When the animal hibernates, its body functions slow down considerably. (②) For example, the heartbeat of a dormouse, with body lengths of about 10cm, slows down to just a beat every few minutes. (③) Also, its breathing becomes slow and its body temperature drops to just a few degrees above the temperature of ground around it. (④) It would, however, be a mistake to think that all hibernating animals sleep for the whole winter. (⑤) In fact, many animals hibernate for short spurts during the winter, and they may wake for an interval of mild weather or as often as three or four times a day.

*hibernate: 동면하다 **dormouse: 겨울잠쥐

[4~5] 다음 글을 읽고, 물음에 답하시오.

Scientists are not, as many believe, primarily concerned about discovering and gathering facts. Rather, researchers ask crucial questions about the natural world and then try to answer them by proposing hypotheses — creative insights about what the (a) <u>truthful</u> responses to those questions might be. What really separates the scientific method from other ways of knowing is its (b) <u>reliance</u> on the rigorous testing of each hypothesis by experimentation or by the gathering of additional observations; the explicit intent of the test is to determine whether the hypothesis is false or true. If the test results (c) <u>agree</u> with the prediction, then the hypothesis being evaluated is disproved, meaning that it cannot be a legitimate account of reality. Then it is either (d) <u>modified</u> into a new hypothesis that is compatible with the test findings or discarded altogether and replaced by other, still-to-be-tested hypotheses. Keep in mind, however, that agreement between expected and experimental test results is not proof that the hypothesis is true. Rather, it means only that the hypothesis continues to be a valid version of reality for the time being. It may not survive the next test. If a hypothesis repeatedly (e) <u>avoids</u> disproof, then scientists regard it as a close approximation of reality.

4. 윗글의 제목으로 가장 적절한 것은?

① How to Make a Perfect Hypothesis
② Science: Not a Product but a Process
③ Science Offers Insights into the Future
④ Only Through Tests Can the Truth Be Revealed
⑤ Reality Can't Keep Up with the Science Anymore

5. 밑줄 친 (a)~(e) 중에서 문맥상 낱말의 쓰임이 적절하지 <u>않은</u> 것은?

① (a)　　② (b)　　③ (c)　　④ (d)　　⑤ (e)

1. 다음 글에서 필자가 주장하는 바로 가장 적절한 것은?

It is an unfortunate fact that many large companies do not conduct open interviews with students at the less well-established universities. If you are a student at one of these universities, keep in mind that these so called "milk-round interviews" are not out of your reach. It's not that employers do not want students from small schools, but merely that traditionally they have visited other universities and need a good reason to change their venue. Therefore, if you are interested in a company which has not visited your university, send an application form to head office or the company's recruitment center. You may then attend a milk-round interview at a nearby university or at the company's assessment center. The milk-round is like a giant melting pot into which all final-year undergraduates and all companies are thrown. Everyone is welcome.

*milk-round: 취업 설명회

① 고학생들은 자신의 전공을 잘 살릴 수 있는 직업을 찾아야 한다.
② 고용주는 구직자를 선발할 때 출신 대학으로 차별해선 안 된다.
③ 기업은 취업 면접 기회를 좀 더 많은 학생들에게 제공해야 한다.
④ 출신 대학에 구애받지 않고 적극적인 구직활동을 해야 한다.
⑤ 대학은 학생들을 위해 취업 설명회를 적극적으로 유치해야 한다.

2. 밑줄 친 "The roulette wheel does not remember its recent results."가 다음 글에서 의미하는 바로 가장 적절한 것은? [3점]

Laura is in a casino watching people play roulette. The 38 slots on the roulette wheel include 18 black numbers, 18 red numbers, and 2 green numbers. Hence, on any one spin, the probability of red or black is slightly less than 50-50 (47.4 to be exact). Although Laura hasn't been betting, she has been following the pattern of results in the game very carefully. The ball has landed on red seven times in a row. Laura concludes that black is long overdue and she jumps into the game, betting heavily on black. Do you agree with Laura's reasoning? A great many people tend to believe that Laura has made a good bet. However, they're wrong. People believe that the laws of probability should yield fair results and that a random process must be self-correcting. These aren't bad assumptions in the long run. However, they don't apply to individual, independent events. As statisticians say, "The roulette wheel does not remember its recent results."

① Fortune often favors one number over another.
② Each spin of the wheel is an independent event.
③ Knowing the future is correctly analyzing the present.
④ The roulette wheel doesn't select numbers randomly.
⑤ The odds of winning increase with every loss.

3. 다음 빈칸에 들어갈 말로 가장 적절한 것은?

A major economic motivation of balanced reciprocity is to exchange surplus goods and services for those that are in short supply. Shortfalls and surpluses can result from different levels of technology, environmental variations, or different production capacities. But whatever the cause, balanced reciprocity enables both parties in the exchange to maximize their consumption. The Indians of Oaxaca, Mexico exemplify balanced reciprocity in the exchange of both goods and services. According to social custom, a man is expected to sponsor at least one festival celebrating a major saint's day. Such an event, involving elaborate food, beverages, and entertainment, is almost always beyond the capacity of a man to provide by himself. Consequently, the man seeks the help of his relatives, friends, and neighbors, thereby mortgaging his future surpluses. Those who help out expect to be repaid in equivalent amounts when they sponsor a similar festival. In effect, the Indians of Oaxaca have created a kind of _____.

*reciprocity: 상호의 이익, 상호성 **mortgage: 저당 잡히다

① parasitic relationship
② traditional legal practice
③ mutual insurance system
④ complex social hierarchy
⑤ effective communication

4. 주어진 글 다음에 이어질 글의 순서로 가장 적절한 것은? [3점]

The modern, consumer-oriented society, with its urban lifestyle, expectations of high service levels, and understanding that everything is for sale, has a significant impact on tourism.

(A) It revitalizes local traditions and authenticity, promotes cultural awareness, and creates new systems of values and power. One must only know which elements of culture are for sale and tourist consumption, which are not, and which need to be preserved.

(B) And it is often believed that the resulting consumption-focused tourism is harmful and generates environmental and social problems such as traffic jams, overcrowding, and long lines at attractions, museums, and restaurants.

(C) However, these things are often accepted by tourists and seen as being an important part of their experience. Furthermore, high tourism consumption creates high demand for cultural preservation and conservation.

① (A) – (C) – (B)
② (B) – (A) – (C)
③ (B) – (C) – (A)
④ (C) – (A) – (B)
⑤ (C) – (B) – (A)

5. 글의 흐름으로 보아, 주어진 문장이 들어가기에 가장 적절한 곳은?

This does not, however, mean that drinking milk actually causes people to live longer.

The difficulty in determining whether correlation equals causation causes an enormous number of misunderstandings. (①) Until a specific mechanism demonstrating how A causes B is identified, it's best to assume that any correlation is accidental, or that both A and B relate independently to some third factor. (②) An example that highlights this is the correlation between drinking milk and cancer rates, which some groups use to argue that drinking milk causes cancer. (③) A more likely explanation is that cancer diagnoses and milk consumption both have a positive correlation with increased age. (④) On average, milk drinkers live longer than non-milk drinkers, and the older you are, the more likely you are to develop cancer. (⑤) It could be that people who drink milk have better access to high-quality health care or eat more healthily than those who do not.

*causation: 인과관계

1. 다음 글의 주제로 가장 적절한 것은?

Most linguists and local community members agree that education and literacy in the local language are necessary to maintain vitality, or to revitalize a language threatened with endangerment. Some local communities reject this notion, wanting to preserve their oral traditions and to rely solely on them. There is, however, a cost to this decision, as it limits the domains in which the language can be used. Regardless, most regard literacy as essential for local languages. Yet more than half of all languages have no written form, and so a writing system needs to be developed for them in order to use them in education and literacy programs. Basic pedagogical and reference materials are needed, including textbooks, dictionaries and usable descriptive grammars. Such materials are readily available for languages of wider communication, but not for the majority of local languages. In addition, reading material is needed for literacy as well.

① how to learn a local language quickly and efficiently
② the most essential step in learning a new local language
③ varied training for literacy development in the local language
④ the importance of saving local language for preserving a cultural identity
⑤ necessity of a writing system and educational materials for local language

2. 다음 글의 밑줄 친 부분 중, 어법상 틀린 것은?

Many of us tend to feel uncomfortable ① making requests of anyone beyond our "inner circle" of family and close friends. But in doing so we vastly underestimate the responsiveness of "weak ties" — our acquaintances and people we don't know very well. Weak ties are ② extremely valuable because they are the bridges between social circles. Novel information, new solutions to problems, and other resources travel across these bridges. We also vastly underestimate the responsiveness of "dormant ties" — the connections we once had ③ what we haven't maintained. For example, most people wouldn't even consider reaching out to a high school classmate they haven't seen in twenty-five years to ask for a job lead; we assume such attempts to reconnect would be rejected, or that our former classmate would resent our reaching out only ④ to ask for a favor. But most people in your past would actually welcome hearing from — and ⑤ helping — you, according to organizational researchers. The passage of time doesn't erase a shared history of understanding, emotions, and trust.

*dormant: 휴면기의, 활동을 중단한

3. 다음 빈칸에 들어갈 말로 가장 적절한 것은?

In modern economies, the distinction between goods and services itself is _____.
One aspect of this shift to a service economy is what has been called the 'servitization' of products. The notion is that, in a modern economy, products cannot exist on their own and some degree of service is needed to make those products useful. Consider the automobile, which is of course a real good. It is only useful, however, over an extended period of time if the owner submits it to continual checkups, fills it with gas and oil, and pays for insurance, registration, and taxes so that he can operate it on community roads. The car is a real good, but it is not necessarily useful unless one also includes the many services that accompany it.

① actually being obscured
② more apparent than ever before
③ a classification of specific ways of knowing
④ the key distinction in economic concepts
⑤ easier to explain than to apply

4. 다음 글에서 전체 흐름과 관계 없는 문장은?

The efficiency and beautiful simplicity of how a forest maintains its life force is always striking. ① Trees receive energy from the sun and combine this with the nutrients and water they draw up from the soil to create the bark, limbs and leaves that enable them to grow and thrive. ② The leaves drop off in autumn and fall to the ground, only to be decomposed by bacteria and converted back into the nutrients that again feed the tree. ③ When choosing trees for a harsh climate, the species' native environment must be considered carefully, otherwise many will not survive the winter. ④ The same process takes place when a branch falls off or when an entire tree dies, producing nutrient-rich soil and providing the nourishment for the next generation. ⑤ Given a fairly stable supply of water and sunshine, a forest can maintain itself for thousands of years without the need for any new outside resources.

*nourishment: 영양(분)

5. 다음 글의 내용을 한 문장으로 요약하고자 한다. 빈칸 (A)와 (B)에 들어갈 말로 가장 적절한 것은?

In practice in science, we stay with one hypothesis until we can reject it. Then we move on to a better one. In order to reject the hypothesis we carry out experiments with which we actually hope to confirm it (such is human nature and human ego needs). The problem with this approach is that the existing hypothesis determines our perceptions and the sort of evidence that we look for. Thus it often needs mistake, accident or chance to provide the intrusive evidence we could never have looked for when holding the orthodox hypothesis. So what should we do about it? The simple answer is to change the form of expression. Instead of just holding the best hypothesis, we should spend a lot of time generating alternatives — not in order to reject them in favor of the best one but to allow us to look at things more broadly.

*intrusive: 거슬리는, 침입하는 **orthodox: 전통적인, 정통의

↓

> When it comes to scientific hypotheses, a(n) _____(A)_____ attitude regarding possibilities is superior to focusing only on the _____(B)_____ theory.

	(A)		(B)
①	open	······	current
②	open	······	proven
③	restrictive	······	alternative
④	exclusive	······	current
⑤	exclusive	······	proven

1. 다음 빈칸에 들어갈 말로 가장 적절한 것은?

Doctors often find that people they see are more interested in getting pills and in removing their symptoms than in changing a stressful lifestyle. Some of these patients see themselves as victims of their complaints rather than as being responsible for them. Some physicians resist prescribing pills to relieve the symptoms of what they see as a problematic lifestyle. Psychologically oriented physicians emphasize the roles of choice and responsibility as critical determining factors of our physical and psychological well-being. In their practice these doctors challenge patients to look at what they are doing to their bodies through lack of exercise, the substances they take in, and other damaging behavior. Although they may prescribe medication to lower a person's extremely high blood pressure, they inform the patient that medications can do only so much and that what is needed is a fundamental change in lifestyle. The patient is encouraged to _____ _____.

① continue daily activities whenever possible
② give a full account of their symptoms to the physician
③ do what they want and trust physicians regarding health
④ share with the physician the responsibility for maintaining health
⑤ talk with their doctor about side effects expected from medication

2. 주어진 글 다음에 이어질 글의 순서로 가장 적절한 것은?

Humans have extraordinarily large brains compared to other animals. Mammals weighing sixty kilograms have an average brain size of 200 cubic centimeters. The earliest men and women had brains of about 600 cubic centimeters. Modern Homo sapiens sport a brain averaging 1,200-1,400 cubic centimeters.

(A) But if that were the case, the cat family would also have produced cats who could do calculus and frogs would by now have launched their own space programme. Why are giant brains so rare in the animal kingdom?

(B) That evolution should select for larger brains may seem to us like a natural choice. We are so fascinated by our high intelligence that we assume that when it comes to brain power, more must be better.

(C) It is because a jumbo brain makes our body exhausted. It's not easy to carry around, especially when wrapped inside a massive skull. It's even harder to fuel. In Homo sapiens, the brain accounts for about 2-3 per cent of total body weight, but it consumes 25 per cent of the body's energy when the body is at rest.

*cubic centimeter: 세제곱센티미터 **calculus: 미적분학

① (A) – (C) – (B)
② (B) – (A) – (C)
③ (B) – (C) – (A)
④ (C) – (A) – (B)
⑤ (C) – (B) – (A)

3. 글의 흐름으로 보아, 주어진 문장이 들어가기에 가장 적절한 곳은?

Both developed and developing countries have embraced the concept of sustainable development, but often in different ways.

Economic growth is almost universally considered a worthwhile goal. Ecological conservation and cultural preservation are also accepted as important. (①) These three large-scale systems are not independent, so one cannot focus on one goal while ignoring the other two. (②) The ever-expanding web of globalization and industrialization, partly caused by the expanding human population, further links these three systems. (③) In 1987, the term 'sustainable development' was brought into common use by the World Commission on Environment and Development. (④) The commission's report, *Our Common Future*, defined the term as a form of development that "meets the needs of the present without compromising the ability of future generations to meet their own needs." (⑤) The shared goal, however, is to maintain and improve the long-term welfare of both humans and ecosystems.

[4~5] 다음 글을 읽고, 물음에 답하시오.

For centuries researchers and the public have agreed on the rather (a) <u>unpleasant</u> "truth" that the only reason we humans tend to cooperate is self-interest. Now, happily, a much more complex, sophisticated, and positive picture is emerging from recent studies. Anthropologist Joseph Henrich of the University of Michigan, and his colleague Robert Boyd of the University of California in Los Angeles, studied the transmission of social behavior and culture among humans. They came to a startling conclusion: cooperation is not the result of (b) <u>selfishness</u>; it is the result of two major "Brain Tendencies." According to Henrich: "There are two elements of human psychology that we know about: one is that people have a tendency to copy the majority; the other is that people have a tendency to copy the most successful individual. What we are able to show is that because humans rely on copying the successful and the majority, this creates a stable cooperative equilibrium which doesn't (c) <u>exist</u> if those two cultural mechanisms aren't in place."

This double mimicking leads to a (d) <u>negative</u> spiral of success. Cooperation leads to a high probability of more food, better health, more creativity, and more general energy and therefore more powerful economic (e) <u>growth</u> for the community as a whole.

4. 윗글의 제목으로 가장 적절한 것은?

① What Motivates Us to Cooperate?
② How Does Self-interest Benefit Society?
③ When Is Selfishness Better Than Cooperation?
④ Why Do We Fall In Love with Successful People?
⑤ Where Does the Tendency to Copy Others Come from?

5. 밑줄 친 (a)~(e) 중에서 문맥상 낱말의 쓰임이 적절하지 <u>않은</u> 것은?

① (a) ② (b) ③ (c) ④ (d) ⑤ (e)

1. 다음 글의 요지로 가장 적절한 것은?

Life has rules and only the foolish person refuses to follow these rules at all. However, sometimes we expand this "rule" approach to life to such a degree that we get locked into patterns that are no longer applicable to life and our creative juices get squeezed out. Therefore, one way to enhance our creativity is to challenge the rules. In the movie IQ, Walter Matthau played the part of Einstein. Meg Ryan was Einstein's niece. At one point in the movie, Einstein said to his niece, "Question everything!" That's good advice. Every advance in history came from someone who challenged the rules. Columbus discovered America because he challenged the rules of navigation. Martin Luther started the Reformation because he challenged the rules of the church. Einstein discovered the theory of relativity because he challenged the rules of Newtonian physics. Sometimes creativity arises out of the awareness that we do not have to do things in the same way they have always been done.

*the Reformation: 종교 개혁

① 창의적이고 도전적인 사람들만이 역사의 진보를 앞당긴다.
② 창의력은 우연히 생긴 것이 아니고 꾸준한 노력의 산물이다.
③ 바람직한 사회적 규칙은 받아들이는 것이 창의력 신장에 좋다.
④ 기존의 규칙에 대해 의심하고 도전하는 것이 창의력을 높인다.
⑤ 창의력 증진을 위해 규칙에 대한 순응과 도전이 모두 필요하다.

2. 다음 빈칸에 들어갈 말로 가장 적절한 것은?

In her book *We Don't Play With Guns Here*, early years researcher Penny Holland argues that for younger children play fighting, gun play and rough-and-tumble play are neither primitive displays of animal aggression nor mindless imitations of yesterday's TV. Rather, they are outward signs of a sophisticated and largely unconscious learning process. According to psychologists, these forms of play allow children _____ in a context where real harm is not part of the game. For instance, they give children invaluable experience in reading facial expressions and body language, and they enable children to learn about their position and status in their peer group. What is more, researchers have known for years that most children quickly become skilled at reading the body language of play fighting — unlike adults, who can find it difficult to distinguish between play and the real thing.

*rough-and-tumble play: 거친 신체 놀이

① to release their flood of energy
② to reinforce and increase aggressive behavior
③ to solve conflicts through the use of violence
④ to teach themselves how to deal with anger
⑤ to perfect some important social skills

3. 다음 글에서 전체 흐름과 관계 <u>없는</u> 문장은?

Switching barriers, or artificially created financial penalties for switching to a competitor's product, can prevent the loss of customers by imposing a significant penalty for switching to a competitor. ① Switching barriers in the mobile phone industry take the form of penalties associated with the early cancelation of a contract. ② Similarly, many airlines now award air miles based on how much travelers paid for their ticket, not how far they're traveling. ③ In its earlier days, IBM was able to keep its control over the mainframe computer market by requiring that all hardware components, such as monitors and printers, be also made by IBM. ④ In so doing, IBM managed to tie its customers into its products, which made switching any part of the computing system to other companies' products inconvenient. ⑤ Another approach to creating switching barriers is to provide customer incentives to sign longer-term contracts, thereby locking out competitors for a longer period of time.

*mainframe computer: (다수의 사용자가 함께 쓸 수 있는) 대형 컴퓨터

4. 주어진 글 다음에 이어질 글의 순서로 가장 적절한 것은?

Most often, readers create mental images by retrieving pictures that are already stored in their memory. In other words, they make a connection with something they have seen or know about and that is what helps them to create the image.

(A) Readers who were first introduced to Hogwarts School of Witchcraft and Wizardry, for example, had never personally experienced it; however, J. K. Rowling's rich descriptions helped us all to "see" it with our imaginations.

(B) Our brains search through our files until we find an image we can use to support the text we are reading. When a reader has no specific experience or memory from which to draw, imagination can often support visualizing.

(C) It is more challenging to visualize things we have not personally experienced. This all happens in an instant, but if we were to slow it down, we might see it as similar to searching through archives of photo files to find a specific photo.

*retrieve: 생각해내다, 상기하다 **archive: 기록 보관소

① (A) – (C) – (B)　　② (B) – (A) – (C)
③ (B) – (C) – (A)　　④ (C) – (A) – (B)
⑤ (C) – (B) – (A)

5. 글의 흐름으로 보아, 주어진 문장이 들어가기에 가장 적절한 곳은?

Instead we should understand what living things or the life of living things means and that there are differences between the two worlds.

We should not forget that the integrated body possesses a wholeness. (①) If you analyze it, it can be reduced to cells and atoms and electrons, but the phenomena that these atoms or electrons express themselves cannot simulate what the integrated body expresses. (②) For instance, it is nonsense to explain why birds fly and fish swim in terms of cells which cannot fly or swim. (③) To put it concretely, one is the world of matter or cells which constitute living things or the life of living things, but they are on a lower level and in a different world from the other world of living things which is an integration of them. (④) Physics and chemistry, which deal with matter, developed earlier and independently of biology. (⑤) At present, cellular research is still included in biology, but in the future we may imagine that cytology will develop into a distinct interdisciplinary field that deals with an area somewhere between living things and matter.

*cytology: 세포학 **interdisciplinary: 여러 학문 분야가 관련된

1. 다음 글의 제목으로 가장 적절한 것은?

Research has shown that proactive people have more positive energy flowing through their systems than reactive or inactive types. And there is a direct correlation between the amount of energy flowing through your wires and your influence on those in your presence. Positive energy has a weird influence that defies the laws of physics. In *Positive Energy*, Judith Orloff wrote, "I believe that the most profound transformations can take place only on an energetic level." This psychiatrist discovered that "The more positive energy we give off, the more we'll magnetize to us. Ditto for negativity. It works like this: Passion attracts passion. Rage attracts rage. The explanation: We are all subtle energy transmitters." The moral is that life is way too short to spend with losers as they will influence us without us even knowing it. Those dark clouds hovering over negative types impact everything they touch and everyone that comes into their sphere of influence. Be careful. They rob others of their energy without them even knowing it.

*proactive: 상황을 앞서서 주도하는 **defy: 거스르다 ***ditto: 마찬가지이다

① You Have a Self-Starter. Try Using It!
② Change Your Attitude, Change Your Life!
③ Emotions Spread Quickly Among a Group of People
④ Energy Is Contagious! Choose Your Company Wisely!
⑤ Energy Can't Be Created or Destroyed, and It Flows

2. 다음 글의 밑줄 친 부분 중, 문맥상 낱말의 쓰임이 적절하지 않은 것은?

There are many creative domains that require individuals to insert as little of themselves as possible into the work. In translating a novel or poem into a different language, the translator is unavoidably creative; this is reflected by the fact that the translator receives ① recognition, and his or her name is published in the work next to that of the original author. But the ideal translator is one who most faithfully retains the creative spirit of the original, thereby keeping his or her own contribution to the translation as ② maximal as possible. Dubbing a foreign movie into one's own language requires that the translator develop a version of the ③ original line that can most easily be spoken in the time that the foreign actor's mouth is moving. It also requires the voice-over actors to ④ match their delivery to the moving image. Although these are unquestionably creative activities, they're activities in which individual inspiration and originality would be ⑤ harmful to the work.

3. 다음 빈칸에 들어갈 말로 가장 적절한 것은? [3점]

The spread of Western clothing to areas in which little or no clothing was worn in the past has sometimes _____. In many such cases, people took over only one part of the clothing complex, that is, the wearing of clothes. They knew nothing of the care of clothing and in many cases lacked the necessary equipment for such care. When they had worn no clothing, their bodies got a cleansing shower in the rain, and the bare skin dried quickly in the sun and air. When they obtained clothing, however, a shower meant wet clothes that did not dry so quickly as bare bodies, and pneumonia or other lung diseases sometimes resulted. Often they had little or no water for washing clothes, even if they had known how to do it. There were no fresh clothes to change into so people usually simply wore what they had until the clothes fell apart.

*pneumonia: 폐렴

① came into conflict with local valuation of cultural heritage
② brought about an unexpected and positive change in society
③ produced disastrous results in terms of health and cleanliness
④ provided opportunities for people to socialize with each other
⑤ influenced and accelerated the development of modern civilization

4. 다음 글에서 전체 흐름과 관계 <u>없는</u> 문장은?

Too often we overcome one resource limitation by stretching another. ① The effect, overall, can be likened to a rubber band that can stretch and then stretch some more. ② Frequently, our solution to local resource shortages is to transport the limited resource from an area where it is more abundant or to manufacture alternatives using additional energy and other resources. ③ While this process gives the impression of increasing abundance, like the rubber band that appears longer when stretched, continued expansion puts more tension on remaining resources. ④ With resource shortages inevitable, there has never been a better time to invest in the operation and maintenance of global transport networks. ⑤ At the present time, our capacity for moving resources around and for powering industrial processes is enormous, but, like the rubber band, there will be a point where further expansion will fail.

5. 다음 글의 내용을 한 문장으로 요약하고자 한다. 빈칸 (A), (B)에 들어갈 말로 가장 적절한 것은?

Imagine that a few bystanders (each walking alone) come upon a potential emergency at about the same time, such as a man lying on the ground. They need to decide what is going on and what they should do. Is the man sick? Is he drunk? Will he be angry if they ask him questions? One source of information they might use is how other people in the situation are responding: Do other people seem to think that this is an emergency requiring intervention? If they are not doing anything about the event, then perhaps it is not an emergency at all. Unfortunately for the victim, all of the bystanders may be looking at one another for cues about how to respond, with the result that no one does anything! Bystanders may misinterpret the situation as a non-emergency based on the inaction of other bystanders.

↓

When faced with a possible emergency, people _____(A)_____ to others to interpret the situation rather than using their own _____(B)_____.

     (A)   (B)
① turn   …… judgement
② turn   …… creativity
③ contribute …… morals
④ object   …… judgement
⑤ object   …… creativity

1. 다음 빈칸에 들어갈 말로 가장 적절한 것은? [3점]

If you want your children to be well-disciplined, then you have to be _____. If your children know that you're liable to overlook their bad behavior if you're tired, distracted, or because you sometimes just feel sorry for them, then they won't know how to properly act every time. Though it may be hard, this is the only way to ensure that you are taken seriously and that your child will understand your guidelines. For example, every time your child breaks a toy, then he/she has to earn a new one by helping out around the house — don't give in one time when he/she breaks a toy just because you really feel sorry for him/her on that particular day. If you normally don't let your child go to McDonald's more than once a week, don't let the child go just when he/she's throwing a public tantrum. Though it may be embarrassing to suffer through a public tantrum, it's better than teaching your child that he/she can always get what he/she wants if he/she just waits to throw a tantrum in public.

*tantrum: 짜증

① flexible   ② communicative
③ consistent   ④ challenging
⑤ generous

2. 주어진 글 다음에 이어질 글의 순서로 가장 적절한 것은?

The response to art is based on a number of objective and subjective factors.

(A) It would be impossible for them to respond to, experience, and look at art in the same way as someone from the 1500s or even the 1950s.

(B) These include knowledge, taste, values, and tradition, as well as gender, education, emotions, and many more. Most art in the world today was created in past centuries for audiences that differed substantially from contemporary ones. Although art from the past continues to intrigue modern spectators, it is impossible to respond to art in the same way as the original audience.

(C) This should not suggest that art from previous centuries cannot be fully understood or valued. Rather, it underlines that art is appreciated on terms compatible with contemporary culture. Today's viewers think, speak, and behave very differently not only from Renaissance but also early twentieth-century audiences.

① (A) – (C) – (B)   ② (B) – (A) – (C)
③ (B) – (C) – (A)   ④ (C) – (A) – (B)
⑤ (C) – (B) – (A)

3. 글의 흐름으로 보아, 주어진 문장이 들어가기에 가장 적절한 곳은?

Having an intuitive understanding of other people can help overcome these challenges.

In any organization, decision makers often find themselves working with simplified data that lacks any sort of context. (①) They often deal with information in the abstract instead of experiencing it for themselves. (②) In many cases, their disconnection from customers forces them to rely on so-called authorities who are anything but. (③) Empathy for the people you serve can make the abstract more grounded and immediate because that information is now connected to a real person you know. (④) It can provide context for the data we receive by incorporating factors left off the map. (⑤) And this kind of connection to other people can, over time, provide the kind of deep experience in a territory that people inside an organization need to identify new opportunities.

*off the map: 중요하지 않은, 잊혀진

[4~5] 다음 글을 읽고, 물음에 답하시오.

The patent system is one of the main instruments governments use to promote research and development. Patenting an idea gives its inventor a 20-year monopoly to exploit the fruit of his labor in the marketplace, in exchange for publishing a full account of how the new product, process, or material works. Most economists would argue that, without a patent system, even fewer inventions would lead to successful innovations. But what if patents actually (a) discourage the combining and recombining of inventions to yield new products and processes — as has happened in biotechnology, genetics, and other disciplines?

Unlike the informal system that scientists use for sharing intellectual credit, the patent system is winner take all. Whoever gets his or her application (b) approved first gets all the money. That creates an incentive for (c) concealment — if scientists' ideas leak out, someone else could file the patent more quickly. But secrecy is the (d) core of science. All really great breakthroughs are actually a chain of small discoveries. Each team of scientists eagerly reads the latest results from other labs and (e) adds some small but brilliant insights of their own. But if billion-dollar patents are at stake, universities — which end up owning much of the intellectual property that comes out of professors' discoveries — have a strong incentive to pressure their scholars to keep new findings and ideas under wraps. Hence, there is growing concern among academic scholars and policy makers that patent rights are themselves slowing innovation.

4. 윗글의 제목으로 가장 적절한 것은?

① Maximize Your Patent Value
② How Do Patent Laws Help Inventors?
③ Encourage Creative Ideas and Don't Punish Failure
④ The Road to Science Is to Ask a Question
⑤ Do Patents Truly Promote Innovation?

5. 밑줄 친 (a)~(e) 중에서 문맥상 낱말의 쓰임이 적절하지 <u>않은</u> 것은?

① (a)　　② (b)　　③ (c)　　④ (d)　　⑤ (e)

1. 다음 글에서 필자가 주장하는 바로 가장 적절한 것은?

If you were asked about your writing when you first start, you'd most likely excuse yourself with a lack of inspiration. But imagine yourself in a serious writing contest where you have made it to the final stage. Tell me, will you wait to be inspired by something before you kick off with whatever it is that you have to write? Maybe you won't wait, and you will still come up with a masterpiece. This only shows that you have a greater power over your muse than the other way round. The reason why you excuse yourself with the inspiration excuse is simply that you have too much time on your hands and you don't have a goal to meet. By creating a schedule to write, you give yourself a time-frame and target to work with. Set a smart schedule and don't just come up with a plan like "I will write 3 articles this week." You will likely find yourself on Friday evening, yet to complete the first paragraph of the first article.

① 글을 쓰는 첫걸음으로써 첫 단락부터 먼저 완성하라.
② 훌륭한 글을 쓰기 위해 영감이 떠오를 때까지 기다려라.
③ 한 번에 글을 완성하지 말고 오랜 시간에 걸쳐 수정하라.
④ 글쓰기 전 주제와 관련된 자료를 찾는 데 시간을 할애하라.
⑤ 글을 쓸 때는 명확한 목표를 부여하여 시간 계획을 세워라.

2. 밑줄 친 trade perfect recall for the ability to handle information이 다음 글에서 의미하는 바로 가장 적절한 것은?

Though human memory is distorted with time, if those distortions had proved detrimental to our ancestors' survival, our memory, and perhaps our species itself, would not have survived. Though our memory system is far from perfect, it is, in most situations, exactly what evolution requires: it is good enough. In fact, in the big picture, human memory is wonderfully efficient and accurate — sufficient to have enabled our ancestors to generally recognize the creatures they should avoid and those they should hunt down, where the best trout streams are, and the safest way back to camp. In modern terms, the starting point in understanding how memory works is that the mind is continuously bombarded by a quantity of data so vast that it cannot possibly handle all of it — roughly eleven million bits per second. And so we trade perfect recall for the ability to handle information.

① We rely on memories of the past to make decisions.
② We sort through the information to identify what matters.
③ We combine past experiences to predict what to do next.
④ We forget memories due to a processing malfunction.
⑤ We constantly take in information through our senses.

3. 다음 빈칸에 들어갈 말로 가장 적절한 것은?

Children often invent novel ways to express desired meanings. In her 1995 article, linguist Clark cited such examples as a 24-month-old saying, "There comes the rat-man" and a 25-month-old saying, "Mommy just fixed this spear-page." The "rat-man" was a colleague of her father's who worked with rats in a psychology laboratory; the "spear-page" was a torn picture of a jungle tribe holding spears that her mother had taped together. Clark also cited the example of a 28-month-old saying, "You're the sworder and I'm the gunner." As these examples suggest, children's innovative uses of language _____. They reflect rules for forming new words, such as combining words or other components that are meaningful in their own right and that, when put together, have an unambiguous meaning. Such linguistic creativity allows children to express meanings that are well beyond what their limited vocabularies would otherwise allow.

*spear: 창

① are made within families
② are perfectly consistent
③ are far from random
④ are bound up with mental acts
⑤ are actually accompanied by other gestures

4. 주어진 글 다음에 이어질 글의 순서로 가장 적절한 것은?

> Ethnic groups in the United States differ in their motivations for consuming coffee; for example, in the Philadelphia area, sensory (taste/smell) motivations are particularly important among Jews, whereas social factors seem more important among Italian Americans.

(A) In terms of such structure, coffee is more complex than many other foods. The motivation for consuming rice, fish, or chili pepper is less changeable, both among individuals within a culture and across cultures.

(B) The motivation for doing so is rather simple and uniform: to warm up in the morning. The point of this is that we must understand the motivational structure of consumption before attempting further analyses and general explanations.

(C) Cross-culturally, there are differences in both specific motivations and the complexity of the motivations. In a Mexican highland village weak but hot coffee is drunk once a day, an hour or so after awakening.

*chili pepper: 고추

① (A) – (C) – (B)　　② (B) – (A) – (C)
③ (B) – (C) – (A)　　④ (C) – (A) – (B)
⑤ (C) – (B) – (A)

5. 글의 흐름으로 보아, 주어진 문장이 들어가기에 가장 적절한 곳은?

> For example, European agricultural markets have a substantial amount of government control.

The proportions of the mixture of free-market determination and government control vary from economy to economy and over time. There is more free-market determination in the USA than in France. There is more free-market determination in the UK today than there was forty years ago. (①) The mix also varies from sector to sector within any one economy. (②) Under market determination, the average size of a farm would be much larger and agricultural prices much lower than they now are. (③) In contrast, the markets for information and computer technologies are largely free from government intervention. (④) Even the economies closest to free markets have a significant role for government. (⑤) So it appears that there is no real alternative to a mixed system with major reliance on markets but also with a substantial government presence in many aspects of the economy.

1. 다음 글의 주제로 가장 적절한 것은?

Bruce Abernethy, working with a group from Brunel University London, used fMRI (functional magnetic resonance imaging) to examine the brains of elite badminton players as they exercised their skills of anticipation. They scanned players of various skill levels as they watched occluded clips of shots being played (the video clips would cut off just before contact was made with the shuttlecock) and tried to predict in which area of the court the shots would land. The expert players showed more brain activity in areas of the brain associated with observing and understanding other people's actions. The more experience an athlete has, the better they are at doing this. A few years later, the same group at Brunel did a similar study with footballers, who watched occluded clips of an opponent running towards them with the ball. In some clips, the players would start a feint just before the video cut off, and the footballer in the scanner would have to predict whether they would go left or right. The earlier the clips were cut off, the bigger the difference in neural activity between semipro and novice footballers on fMRI scans.

*occlude: 차단하다

① effects of athletes' intelligence on performance prediction ability
② differences in performance prediction ability based on proficiency
③ importance of observing and analyzing opponents for optimal performance
④ factors affecting development and prediction ability of athletic performance
⑤ improvement in player's performance prediction occurring regardless of brain injury

2. 다음 글의 밑줄 친 부분 중, 어법상 틀린 것은?

Memories are known to be the sum of what people have thought and what they have been told. Cognitive psychologists have long known ① that memory, at least in significant part, is a reconstruction of events. When we remember something, say an event from several years ago, we do not replay in our minds a faithfully recorded version of ② it. We encode fragments of an experience — a sight, a sound, a feeling. When we access a memory, we may retrieve some accurate fragments but these have to ③ put back together again — the gaps between these fragments are filled using expectations, common sense, and logic. At times, the pieces ④ needed to reconstruct the memory may be missing or inaccurate, and the recollection becomes a reflection of what we expect rather than how things really were. This makes us feel as though the memory is accurate and true even though it is false, and this process occurs, without our awareness, ⑤ automatically.

3. 다음 빈칸에 들어갈 말로 가장 적절한 것은?

By their very nature, big data analysis projects involve large data sets. But that doesn't mean that all of a company's data sources, or all of the information within a relevant data source, will need to be analyzed. Organizations need to identify the strategic data that will lead to valuable analytical insights. For instance, what combination of data can help pinpoint key customer-retention factors? Or what data are required to uncover hidden patterns in stock market transactions? Focusing on a project's business goals in the planning stages can help an organization home in on the exact analytics that are required, after which it can — and should — look at the data needed to meet those business goals. In some cases, this will indeed mean including everything. In other cases, though, it means _____ _____ of the big data on hand.

*pinpoint: 정확히 찾아내다[보여 주다] **analytics: 분석된 정보

① using only a subset
② selling the concept
③ understanding the scale
④ pointing out incorrect analysis
⑤ creating reliable measurement

4. 다음 글에서 전체 흐름과 관계 <u>없는</u> 문장은?

Self-driving vehicles have the potential to completely change the way we think about cars, particularly in a city environment. ① Autonomous taxis may someday be parked on every street, in every city. ② When you want to go somewhere, you will be able to summon one using your mobile phone, and it will be parked outside your house ready for you by the time you have walked out of your front door. ③ Once it has taken you to your destination, it drives off for its next customers. ④ Despite the convenience of an autonomous taxi like this, there are also lots of problems to be solved as soon as possible. ⑤ Self-driving vehicles may be used to collect children from school, take elderly people to shops, and carry out all the usual, everyday journeys, all at a small percentage of the cost of what you would expect to pay to own a car.

*summon: 호출하다, 부르다

5. 다음 글의 내용을 한 문장으로 요약하고자 한다. 빈칸 (A), (B)에 들어갈 말로 가장 적절한 것은?

Politics cannot be suppressed, whichever policy process is employed and however sensitive and respectful of differences it might be. In other words, there is no end to politics. It is wrong to think that proper institutions, knowledge, methods of consultation, or participatory mechanisms can make disagreement go away. Theories of all sorts promote the view that there are ways by which disagreement can be processed or managed so as to make it disappear. The assumption behind those theories is that disagreement is wrong and consensus is the desirable state of things. In fact, consensus rarely comes without some forms of subtle coercion, and the absence of fear in expressing a disagreement is a source of genuine freedom. Debates cause disagreements to evolve, often for the better, but a positively evolving debate does not have to equal a reduction in disagreement. The suppression of disagreement should never be made into a goal in political deliberation. A defense is required against any suggestion that political disagreement is not the normal state of things.

*coercion: 강압 **deliberation: (신중한) 숙고

↓

It may be tempting to believe that total political ____(A)____ is desirable and achievable, but in reality dissent and debate are both desirable and ____(B)____.

	(A)		(B)
①	freedom	·····	inevitable
②	freedom	·····	rare
③	consensus	·····	avoidable
④	agreement	·····	rare
⑤	agreement	·····	inevitable

1. 다음 빈칸에 들어갈 말로 가장 적절한 것은?

Good writers are not passive; they don't simply record immediate responses. They *look closely, ask questions, analyze, make connections,* and *think.* Learning to see with a writer's eye benefits not just those who write for a living but all professionals. In any career you choose, success depends on _____.
A skilled physician detects minor symptoms in a physical or follows up on a patient's complaint and asks questions that lead to a diagnosis others might miss. A successful stockbroker observes overlooked trends and conducts research to detect new investment opportunities. A passerby might assume a busy store must be successful, but a retail analyst would observe what merchandise people are purchasing and how they are paying for it. If all the shoppers are buying discount items and paying with credit cards, the store could be losing money on the sales.

① countering trends and innovation
② keen observation and in-depth analysis
③ resource management and economic understanding
④ diverse circumstances and networking opportunities
⑤ literary attainments and cultured education

2. 주어진 글 다음에 이어질 글의 순서로 가장 적절한 것은?

One approach to human-wildlife conflicts is to create preserves, wildlife refuges, or parks where human impact on wildlife is minimized.

(A) There is also the problem that wildlife may not respect our boundary lines and will not stay inside parks. In fact, the vast majority of wildlife live outside parks — the same place people live. Wildlife populations thrive in our most densely settled cities.
(B) Clearly, if human-wildlife conflicts are going to be resolved, ways must be found for humans and wildlife to coexist harmoniously without either having an adverse impact on the other.

(C) Although this approach is well intended, it does little to resolve human-wildlife conflicts because societal demands for natural resources are so great that only a small fraction of the environment can ever be set aside in parks.

① (A) – (C) – (B)   ② (B) – (A) – (C)
③ (B) – (C) – (A)   ④ (C) – (A) – (B)
⑤ (C) – (B) – (A)

3. 글의 흐름으로 보아, 주어진 문장이 들어가기에 가장 적절한 곳은?

However, where the degree of competition is particularly intense a zero sum game can quickly become a negative sum game, in that everyone in the market is faced with additional costs.

In mature markets, breakthroughs that lead to a major change in competitive positions and to the growth of the market are rare. (①) Because of this, competition becomes a zero sum game in which one organization can only win at the expense of others. (②) As an example of this, when one of the major high street banks in Britain tried to gain a competitive advantage by opening on Saturday mornings, it attracted a number of new customers who found the traditional Monday-Friday bank opening hours to be a constraint. (③) However, faced with a loss of customers, the competition responded by opening on Saturdays as well. (④) The net effect of this was that, although customers benefited, the banks lost out as their costs increased but the total number of customers stayed the same. (⑤) In essence, this proved to be a negative sum game.

*high street: 시내 중심가

[4~5] 다음 글을 읽고, 물음에 답하시오.

Most dreams are not simple replays of our daily lives; those account for just about 1 to 2 percent of dreams. The rest of the time, our various thoughts and visualizations come together in new, often creative ways. Through dreams, the unconscious system in the brain provides us with an (a) alternative way of associating concepts, closed off from all the distractions of waking life. Ideas can dance freely through the mind. Perhaps that's why we think of great new ideas as we sleep.

What is it about the dreaming brain that makes our thoughts and experiences come together in unique ways? One explanation is that sleep protects us from external stimuli, preventing interference and allowing our imagination to (b) decline. Another possibility is that the prefrontal cortex is largely deactivated, so our more abstract, and even bizarre, thoughts can play freely without being subjected to our (c) usual judgmental analytic logic. There may be a third, more fundamental explanation for why dreams are so creative. Some neuroscientists theorize that during sleep the brain relaxes preformed synapses, (d) loosening connections between our memories and learned concepts. This is thought to enhance neuronal flexibility, allowing new pathways to form in the brain and fresh, creative ideas to burst forth. In fact, some studies show that the neurons that have worked together most extensively during the day are the most quiet as we sleep. The theory is that relaxing our synapses opens the door for dreaming. It creates the opportunity for novel connections between our thoughts to (e) emerge, allowing the brain to spin its stories.

*prefrontal cortex: 전두엽 **synapses: 신경 접합부, 시냅스

4. 윗글의 제목으로 가장 적절한 것은?

① Dreams Go Beyond the Brain Functions
② How to Turn Your Dreams Into a Story
③ Dreams Come True While You Are Awake
④ Magical Ways Dreams and Reality Intersect
⑤ How Dreams Guide Us to Creative Thoughts

5. 밑줄 친 (a)~(e) 중에서 문맥상 낱말의 쓰임이 적절하지 않은 것은?

① (a)　　② (b)　　③ (c)　　④ (d)　　⑤ (e)

1. 다음 글의 요지로 가장 적절한 것은?

As nature without human intervention, wilderness does not need nature conservation. When an active nature conservationist raves about wilderness, he must be aware that he is pulling the rug from under his own feet because for nature conservationists, wilderness means simply doing nothing. Anyone who wants wilderness in his garden fires his gardener. In many respects, nature conservation is the opposite of wilderness. In many cases, nature conservation requires the protection of a particular state of nature in an area (usually temporary and influenced by humans); but protection from the threat of a different, 'other nature'. This 'other nature' would gain a foothold in the area in question if man did not protect it from the 'other nature'. In extreme cases, nature conservation means the protection of the nature which dominates in one particular area against the penetration and domination of the wilderness.

*rave about: ~에 대해 극찬하다

① 자연은 회복력이 강해서 인위적인 보호는 필요가 없다.
② 진정한 의미의 자연 보호는 인간의 개입을 필요로 한다.
③ 자연 보호는 자연이 균형과 조화를 이루게 하려는 것이다.
④ 지역 특성에 맞도록 자연에 대한 통제가 이루어져야 한다.
⑤ 자연 보호의 실천을 위해 자연 보호의 중요성부터 인식해야 한다.

2. 다음 빈칸에 들어갈 말로 가장 적절한 것은?

Our world is changing at a rapid rate, and as concerned educators, we no longer can predict with confidence the kind of social ecology that our students will encounter as mature individuals. Our only adaptive recourse, therefore, is to prepare pupils not to be rigidly cooperative, competitive, or individualistic, but to be flexible — to recognize a broad range of social situations and the kinds of behaviors appropriate to each. There are situations in which competition is an adaptive strategy; there are other situations in which cooperation is adaptive; and there are yet other situations in which an individualistic approach is most successful. By including a variety of task and reward structures within the classroom, teachers can prepare their students to recognize a fuller range of environmental contingencies and _____.

*recourse: 의지할 수 있는 것, 방책 **contingency: 우발적인 사건

① to engage in cooperation without conflict
② to get rewards by trying every possible means
③ to choose the type of classroom best suited to their needs
④ to create the ideal foundation for healthy competition
⑤ to be able to adjust their behavior accordingly

3. 다음 글에서 전체 흐름과 관계 없는 문장은?

In sport, it has been assumed that the original form of the game is naturally attractive and therefore satisfies consumer needs. An analysis of sporting organisations in Australia shows this to be an outdated view. ① Many sports have modified rules to make their games more attractive, and in the case of cricket matches, which have traditionally been played for 4-5 days, one-day matches have become an important part of the range of product offerings. ② One-day international matches played throughout the Australian summer have more readily satisfied consumer need for compressed entertainment and a quick result. ③ Nowadays, many young cricket players who are very competitive and eager for fame are distinguishing themselves on the international scene. ④ At junior levels, many sports have been significantly modified to satisfy the desire of many more young people to participate in the game. ⑤ Inherent in this change has been the recognition that juniors wish to develop game skills through actual participation, to have fun, and in general to be with their friends in a sport setting.

*product offering: 제품[상품]군

4. 주어진 글 다음에 이어질 글의 순서로 가장 적절한 것은?

> Advertisers have hit on one particularly effective way of seeming to argue against their own interests. They mention a minor weakness or drawback of their product in the ads promoting it.

(A) Experiments have demonstrated that this tactic works. When jurors heard an attorney bring up a weakness in his own case first, jurors assigned him more honesty and were more favorable to his overall case in their final verdicts because of that perceived honesty.

(B) Attorneys are taught to "steal the opponent's thunder" by mentioning a weakness in their case before the opposing lawyer does, thereby establishing a perception of honesty in the eyes of jury members.

(C) That way, they create a perception of honesty from which they can be more persuasive about the strengths of the product. Advertisers are not alone in the use of this tactic.

① (A) – (C) – (B)
② (B) – (A) – (C)
③ (B) – (C) – (A)
④ (C) – (A) – (B)
⑤ (C) – (B) – (A)

5. 글의 흐름으로 보아, 주어진 문장이 들어가기에 가장 적절한 곳은?

> They've learned from experience that valuable insights often emerge when they get some distance from the work.

Successful scientists have learned how to structure their workday for maximum creativity. They shift from one project to another based on what they do most effectively at a given time of day. (①) Original, new, and conceptual work, problem-finding work, is best done first thing in the morning. (②) Many scientists also schedule their writing in the morning, because this involves creative conceptualization. (③) Scientists tend to schedule the concrete, hands-on laboratory work for late morning and after lunch. (④) Finally, many scientists report that they schedule some idle time in the late afternoon, after the concrete phase of hard work, perhaps taking a walk around campus or going for a cup of coffee. (⑤) Scientists then close the day by returning to writing and conceptual work, often continuing to work long after dinner.

1. 다음 글의 제목으로 가장 적절한 것은?

How much of our behavior is in fact influenced by nature, rather than nurture? Furthermore, are nature and nurture the only factors? Nature does not cover all the biological factors that may be at work before birth that are generally considered to constitute our make-up. Then are all our other traits and tendencies accounted for by nurture? Do not free will and contextual factors play a contributory role in determining action? While culture inevitably influences behavior, individual 'deviant' decision-makers over time affect culture. In any case, nature versus nurture is one of those fundamental questions that do not yield easy answers. As to the difficult issue of free will, *free will* is something most of us believe in because we have the conscious experience of deciding what we will do given the circumstances. It might be added that this conscious experience is in no way removed by knowing that environmental factors make it more than likely that we decide in the way we do.

*deviant: 벗어난, 일탈적인

① Is Our Free Will an Illusion?
② How Does Culture Affect Human Behavior?
③ What Is the Influence of Nature and Nurture?
④ Why Can't We Behave the Way We Choose?
⑤ What Makes Us Behave the Way We Do?

2. 다음 글의 밑줄 친 부분 중, 문맥상 낱말의 쓰임이 적절하지 않은 것은? [3점]

When you begin to tell a story again that you have retold many times, what you retrieve from memory is the index to the story itself. That index can be embellished in a variety of ways. Over time, even the embellishments become ① standardized. An old man's story that he has told hundreds of times shows little variation, and any variation that does exist becomes part of the story itself, regardless of its origin. People add details to their stories that may or may not have occurred. They are recalling indexes and ② reconstructing details. If at some point they add a nice detail, not really certain of its validity, telling the story with that same detail a few more times will ensure its ③ permanent place in the story index. In other words, the stories we tell time and again are identical to the memory we have of the events that the story relates. Stories ④ change over time because of the process of telling, due to the embellishments added by the teller. The actual events that gave rise to the story in the first place have long since been ⑤ strengthened.

*embellish: (이야기를) 꾸미다[윤색하다]

3. 다음 빈칸에 들어갈 말로 가장 적절한 것은?

Part of the challenge children face is in training their eyes to move from left to right across lines of print. The eye is controlled by small muscle movements, and for children small muscle movements are a challenge in and of themselves. When the eyes move across a line of print, they make a series of jumps, stopping briefly to focus. An experienced adult reader typically sees two letters to the left side of the point of focus and six to eight letters to the right. The inexperienced child reader, however, sees one letter to the left and one letter to the right of their point of focus. This physical reality explains why children learning to read find it easier to decode words made up of fewer than five letters. As their eye muscles begin to develop, they are gradually able to _____ and they can handle longer, unfamiliar words.

① reverse the side of the point of focus
② control the amount of information on both sides
③ take in much more on the right side of the point of focus
④ grasp the most essential parts of the words they see
⑤ balance the number of letters they see on both sides

4. 다음 글에서 전체 흐름과 관계 <u>없는</u> 문장은?

The distribution of health and ill health has been analyzed from a historical and social science perspective. ① Some have argued that medicine has not been as effective as is often claimed. ② The medical writer, Thomas McKeown, demonstrated that most of the fatal diseases of the 19th century had disappeared before the arrival of antibiotics or immunization programs. ③ He reasoned that social advances in overall living conditions, such as improved sanitation and better nutrition resulting from rising real wages, have been responsible for the majority of the reduction in mortality achieved during the last century. ④ According to this conclusion, public health improvements from major medical breakthroughs have fundamentally changed what it means to be human by drastically changing the conditions under which we live. ⑤ Although his assertion has been disputed, there is little disagreement that the contribution of medicine to reduced mortality has been minor, when compared with the impact of improved living conditions.

*sanitation: 위생 시설

5. 다음 글의 내용을 한 문장으로 요약하고자 한다. 빈칸 (A), (B)에 들어갈 말로 가장 적절한 것은?

Most of us are typically used to listening and being listened to on a fairly surface level. We don't pay much attention to what is not being said, pick up on subtle incongruities in speech, nor hear the emotion behind a person's words unless it is obvious and clear. Consider a client who tells us that she is excited to be moving house and living in a new city. We hear the words and respond accordingly, telling the person how happy we are for her and what a great adventure she will have. The active listener might hear between the words, noting the speaker's deep intake of breath before she responds, or slight shrug of the shoulders. They might hear the slightly pensive tone, or note the look in her eyes, which indicates that although the move might be exciting, there are other emotions at play — perhaps she is frightened about taking such a big step, or cautious about leaving friends and family behind. The active listener hears her words, and notes the other information she is communicating, and can therefore respond on a deeper level.

*incongruity: 부조화(한 것) **pensive: 침울한, 수심에 잠긴

↓

Unlike those who listen ___(A)___, the active listener is often able to ___(B)___ what has not been said.

	(A)		(B)
①	politely	......	detect
②	superficially	......	detect
③	superficially	......	disregard
④	attentively	......	disregard
⑤	attentively	......	perceive

1. 다음 빈칸에 들어갈 말로 가장 적절한 것은?

Perhaps the most famous case of _____ is that of the light bulb. Today, more than 150 years after the light bulb was invented, an average modern incandescent bulb lasts 750 hours. So why is there an incandescent light bulb in Livermore, California, that has been burning nonstop for 110 years? It's because in 1924 in Geneva, all the light bulb manufacturers got together and created a cartel, at the time called Phoebus, to cut the life of a light bulb. By making the filaments less stable than they needed to be, light bulbs would burn out quicker, and the cartel could sell more. It was so serious that manufacturers were fined if their light bulbs lasted more than 1,500 hours. Before 1924 the average bulb lasted about 2,500 hours. Within a decade it was at 1,500 hours and has since declined to today's 750.

*(incandescent) light bulb: 백열전구   **filament: (전구 안에 든) 필라멘트

① planned breakability
② competitive advantage
③ gradual improvement
④ stabilization testing
⑤ failed technology

2. 주어진 글 다음에 이어질 글의 순서로 가장 적절한 것은?

Interest in extremely long periods of time sets geology and astronomy apart from other sciences. Geologists think in terms of billions of years for the age of Earth and its oldest rocks — numbers that, like the national debt, are not easily understood.

(A) Likewise, understanding how climate has changed over millions of years is vital to properly assess current global warming trends. Fortunately, clues to past environmental change are well preserved in many different kinds of rocks.

(B) Nevertheless, the time scales of geological activity are important for environmental geologists because they provide a way to measure human impacts on the natural world.

(C) For example, we would like to know the rate of natural soil formation from solid rock to determine whether topsoil erosion from agriculture is too great.

*erosion: 부식, 침식

① (A) – (C) – (B)   ② (B) – (A) – (C)
③ (B) – (C) – (A)   ④ (C) – (A) – (B)
⑤ (C) – (B) – (A)

3. 글의 흐름으로 보아, 주어진 문장이 들어가기에 가장 적절한 곳은?

They likewise increase their intake of sweets and water when their energy and fluids become depleted.

Have humans evolved food preferences? Both humans and rats have evolved taste preferences for *sweet* foods, which provide rich sources of calories. A study of food preferences among the Hadza hunter-gatherers of Tanzania found that honey was the most highly preferred food item, the item that has the highest caloric value. (①) Human newborn infants also show a strong preference for sweet liquids. (②) Both humans and rats dislike *bitter* and *sour* foods, which tend to contain toxins. (③) They also adaptively adjust their eating behavior in response to deficits in water, calories, and salt. (④) Experiments show that rats display an immediate liking for salt the first time they experience a salt deficiency. (⑤) These appear to be specific evolved mechanisms, designed to deal with the adaptive problem of food selection and coordinate consumption patterns with physical needs.

[4~5] 다음 글을 읽고, 물음에 답하시오.

Today, people are constantly hammering away on a keyboard or texting on a smartphone. They are no longer writing by hand. Does this make penmanship an outdated and inefficient mode of communication or is there value in trying to keep it? At one time, writing clearly and quickly was essential to everything from public documents to personal letters. However, in the age of e-mail and text messages, most people (a) rarely need to write more than a shopping list or a short note.

Although handwritten communication is less (b) widespread than it once was, many people continue to believe that the art of penmanship must be protected. They suggest it's essential to reading handwritten documents and thus maintaining a direct connection with the past. For them, it's a tragedy that a person might one day find his grandmother's diary and be unable to read it. In addition, people note that a person's handwriting is (c) distinctive and can be as personal as his voice or laugh. By (d) terminating handwritten communication, they claim, we are also maintaining our connection with the individuality of the writer.

Interestingly, the development of technology has not completely removed the need to write by hand. In fact, it seems highly unlikely that handwritten communication will ever (e) disappear completely, since there is always the possibility of not having a computer available at a particular moment. Even in the digital age, the handwritten word is very much alive and well, and it looks like that isn't going to change.

4. 윗글의 제목으로 가장 적절한 것은?

① Understanding and Creating Digital Texts
② Will Handwriting Survive in the Digital Era?
③ The Death of Handwriting: Causes and Effects
④ Wireless Communications Vs. Handwritten Notes
⑤ What Are We Losing with the Death of Handwriting?

5. 밑줄 친 (a)~(e) 중에서 문맥상 낱말의 쓰임이 적절하지 않은 것은? [3점]

① (a)　　② (b)　　③ (c)　　④ (d)　　⑤ (e)

1. 다음 글에서 필자가 주장하는 바로 가장 적절한 것은?

One of the most important things on the part of the teacher is a willingness to show some humility, to reveal their struggles, and to attempt to make their life and their message congruent. They don't have to be perfect, but they'll be a better teacher if they are using their own life as a laboratory for their ideals and methods. The most superb teachers are the "wounded healers" — the ones whose wisdom is tested in reality. Good teachers are always learning themselves, adapting what they know to a world that keeps changing. There's nothing worse than listening to someone who has polished a personal growth speech or a spiritual sermon that remains static over the years. While religious or academic training, degrees, books, and previous teaching positions are credentials that may indicate a highly trained teacher or therapist, equally important are the ways in which this person continually tests her knowledge in the world around her.

*congruent: 일치하는 **credentials: 증명서

① 교사는 검증되지 않은 이론을 가르치는 것을 지양해야 한다.
② 교사는 표준적인 사회적 규범을 학생들에게 가르쳐야 한다.
③ 교사는 이상과 현실을 조화시키는 방법으로 교육해야 한다.
④ 훌륭한 교사가 되기 위해서는 끊임없이 배우려고 노력해야 한다.
⑤ 교사는 자신의 지식을 세상에 맞게 변화시키려고 노력해야 한다.

2. 밑줄 친 the iron cage가 다음 글에서 의미하는 바로 가장 적절한 것은?

Play is often discounted as something for children, because it does not deal with important survival processes, because it is useless. But this is a profound misunderstanding. Play is important *because* it is useless; because it allows us to act not because of necessity or convenience, but in order to freely express our being. The problem, however, starts again when play becomes a profession — with all the external rewards and responsibilities that this entails. Musicians playing for leading symphony orchestras, or athletes playing for multimillion contracts with elite teams, no longer feel that they play to express their being. Instead, they start feeling that their skill is being used by others for their own ends. When that happens, instead of allowing for the free flow of consciousness, even play becomes part of the iron cage.

① secret identity hidden behind a mask of iron
② a boring routine in which freedom is totally lost
③ work for life itself, but not a labor to make a living
④ the source of irritation that causes one to lose patience
⑤ worldly success as measured by other people's standards

3. 다음 빈칸에 들어갈 말로 가장 적절한 것은?

Until well into the modern era, textiles were the world's primary manufactured product. Often woven with silver, gold, and silk, they were also the chief form of stored wealth for both rich and poor; most families wore their estate on their backs and hung it on their walls and windows. More to the point, people inherited these textile treasures from their parents; fashions would remain relatively unchanged for centuries, and all but the wealthiest possessed only a few items. Styles during this period _____.
An inflexible social structure, reinforced by sumptuary laws, determined just who could wear what. In the mid-seventeenth century, however, the East India Company destroyed this age-old state of affairs, turning the worlds of English industry, trade, fashion, and social rank upside down in just a few decades. The Company's instrument in this commercial revolution was cotton.

*sumptuary law: 사치 금지법

① were readily influenced by external forces
② were a reflection of the preferences of the wealthiest
③ not only were static over time but were also rigidly divided by class
④ were determined not so much by social position as preference in style
⑤ were hard to change due to the revolutionary power inherent within them

4. 주어진 글 다음에 이어질 글의 순서로 가장 적절한 것은?

> Obviously, plants are not considered important enough to be classified properly. Even at a regular supermarket, one can see that other food departments have more detailed classifications.

(A) For example, placing starch roots in the same category with tomatoes could prompt customers to make improper food-combination choices, which can create fermentation and gas in our intestines.

(B) The meat department is divided into poultry, fish, and red meat. Nobody would ever classify cheese and meat together in one "sandwich food" department because it would be inconvenient and unclear.

(C) Yet, this kind of confusion and error continually occurs in the produce section. Some of these errors are quite serious — to such a degree that they could cause health problems.

*intestine: 장(腸), 창자

① (A) – (C) – (B)   ② (B) – (A) – (C)
③ (B) – (C) – (A)   ④ (C) – (A) – (B)
⑤ (C) – (B) – (A)

5. 글의 흐름으로 보아, 주어진 문장이 들어가기에 가장 적절한 곳은?

> This inherent conflict is probably what propelled our evolution into relatively small social groups; we needed social bonds, and yet we had to minimize our fear-arousing contact with strangers.

Human social life originates with the evolution of parental care and the mother-infant bond. The behavior between mother and infant, and later between father and infant, is the foundation stone for adult bonding, friendliness, and love, all of which are at the heart of social organization. (①) Unfortunately, all mammals, including humans, demonstrate ambivalence about other people. (②) As powerfully wired as we are for social contact, so too are we wired for "xenophobia" : the fear of strangers. (③) This fear begins during the second half of the first year of life, and although it is modifiable by culture, it is never totally absent from human social relationships. (④) Thus, the perfect solution is a fixed, relatively small group of familiar people. (⑤) Modern urban life, of course, poses serious problems in this regard.

*ambivalence: 모순된 감정 **xenophobia: 낯선 사람 공포증

1. 다음 글의 주제로 가장 적절한 것은?

It is not only in the realm of identity creation that consumption is of significance. The manner in which particular goods or services are culturally embedded in the individual consumer's social world, for example, may determine how or why they are consumed, and tourism is no exception. Once considered the preserve of the wealthy people, it has become 'democratized' — an accepted and, perhaps, expected element of contemporary social life. Moreover, tourism possesses different meanings to different consumers in relation to their personal cultural context; to some, for example, it may represent spiritual refreshment, to others the fulfillment of dreams or fantasies. Equally, tourism may be consumed as a means of experiencing a (temporary) social world with other tourists; it may be purposefully consumed in expectation of shared experiences.

① the necessity of reducing waste in tourism
② negative effects of tourism on local people
③ how tourism functions as a consumer good
④ why local identities are weakened by global tourism
⑤ the rapid growth of tourism due to economic success

2. 다음 글의 밑줄 친 부분 중, 어법상 틀린 것은?

Our insatiable appetite for seafood, coupled with the brutal efficiency of our industrial fishing technologies, ① has wreaked havoc. But above all, it has been a combination of government weakness, industrial greed and a scientific community ② lacking the courage to sound the alarm that has resulted in one of the greatest ecological tragedies of our time. Decision-makers have routinely ignored the warning signs. The reason is ③ that they have been frightened of upsetting the 'fishing lobby'. As a result, they have set hopelessly unrealistic quotas, and have gone out of their way to appease industrial fishing companies. For example, in November 2008, the inappropriately named International Commission for the Conservation of Atlantic Tuna (ICCAT) set a catch quota for bluefin tuna that is nearly 50 per cent higher than ④ its own scientists advise. Citing concern for jobs, livelihoods and consumer interest, politicians have brought fish stocks to the brink of collapse, and by their failure, they threaten the very people in ⑤ which interests they claim to be acting.

*insatiable: 만족할 줄 모르는 **wreak havoc: 많은 문제를 초래하다
***appease: 요구를 들어주다

3. 다음 빈칸에 들어갈 말로 가장 적절한 것은?

Many people I've met say they never write letters or anything at all because they've learned that they always make mistakes. Communication is not like cooking, where you only get one chance to get it right. In cooking, there is a recipe to follow and the food comes out bad if you stray from it. What those people I met didn't know until I told them this is that nobody gets it right the first time, or the second, or the third. Everybody needs to write and revise, then rewrite and revise again, and keep that process up until finally it's as good as it's going to get. The secret to writing letters, speeches, or any planned communication is to work at it until you have revised the whole thing at least seven times. The first draft of almost anything (letter, essay, speech, document), is never going to be your best work. Personal letters may be the exception in some cases, but even they often need to be rewritten before mailing. _____.

① Writers are similar to chefs
② Quality comes with rewriting
③ Writing requires special talent
④ Mistakes are the key to learning
⑤ The personal touch gets lost in editing

4. 다음 글에서 전체 흐름과 관계 없는 문장은?

Since the concept of a teddy bear is very obviously not a genetically inherited trait, we can be confident that we are looking at a cultural trait. However, it is a cultural trait that seems to be under the guidance of another, genuinely biological trait: the cues that attract us to babies (high foreheads and small faces). ① Cute, baby-like features are inherently appealing, producing a nurturing response in most humans. ② Teddy bears that had a more baby-like appearance — however slight this may have been initially — were thus more popular with customers. ③ Over time, however, there has been a change in the role of the teddy bear, as teddy bear makers expanded their targets to older customers through adding maturity to existing bears. ④ Teddy bear manufacturers obviously noticed which bears were selling best and so made more of these and fewer of the less popular models, to maximize their profits. ⑤ In this way, the selection pressure built up by the customers resulted in the evolution of a more baby-like bear by the manufacturers.

5. 다음 글의 내용을 한 문장으로 요약하고자 한다. 빈칸 (A)와 (B)에 들어갈 말로 가장 적절한 것은?

A large group of psychologists and architects conducted two experiments among eight thousand college students at three institutions in Massachusetts and Pennsylvania. Some of the students lived in high-density towers, some in medium-density apartment blocks, and others in lower-density halls of residence. The researchers began by scattering a series of stamped addressed envelopes inside the buildings, creating the sense that the letters had been lost on the way to the mailbox. When the researchers returned four hours later, they found that 100 percent of the letters in the low-density housing were posted, 87 percent were posted in the medium-density blocks, and only 63 percent were posted in the high-density towers. In a different set of apartment blocks that similarly varied in density, the researchers placed boxes asking residents to donate used milk cartons for an art project. Calculating the number of cartons that were used by the residents in the blocks, they found again that high-density dwellers were less helpful. Those in low-and medium-density housing contributed 55 percent of their cartons, whereas the students in high-density housing gave only 37 percent of their cartons.

↓

> According to the two experiments, we can assume that the more ____(A)____ the living environment is, the less ____(B)____ the residents are.

	(A)		(B)
①	packed	......	independent
②	packed	......	generous
③	convenient	......	independent
④	convenient	......	generous
⑤	eco-friendly	......	selfish

1. 다음 빈칸에 들어갈 말로 가장 적절한 것은?

The primary reason given by most regular exercisers for continuing their fitness activities is that they help them feel better on a day-to-day basis. It could be argued that the link between vigorous activity and mental health is just a function of genetic predispositions. However, there is evidence that regular exercise directly _____ _____. In a study with almost 2,000 adults, little or no recreational exercise was predictive of an increase in depressive symptoms eight years later. Men who had many depressive symptoms during the initial assessment usually remained feeling that way unless they began to regularly exercise. Sedentary women who originally showed few symptoms also manifested increased signs of depression at the eight-year follow-up.

*predisposition: 성향 **sedentary: 주로 앉아서 지내는

① fails as a substitute for social recreation
② corresponds to the health of one's genes
③ contributes to weight loss and muscle gain
④ reduces the risk of future psychological difficulties
⑤ leads to depression in otherwise healthy individuals

2. 주어진 글 다음에 이어질 글의 순서로 가장 적절한 것은?

There is no doubt that mountainous areas with low valleys among them tend to have higher species richness than surrounding areas of flat land.

(A) A similar diversity of species composition with elevation is found in the Siskiyou Mountains of Oregon, and in fact on almost any set of high mountains, simply because there is a wide range of climates there.
(B) For example, in the Santa Catalina Mountains of Arizona, many different plant species occur in the same mountains but at distinct altitudes, each species at its own climatic optimum.

(C) This is partly because there are more different environments, each with its own characteristic set of species. For one thing, there are different climate zones on a mountain, but only one climate in a flat lowland area.

*optimum: 최적 조건; 최적의

① (A) – (C) – (B)
② (B) – (A) – (C)
③ (B) – (C) – (A)
④ (C) – (A) – (B)
⑤ (C) – (B) – (A)

3. 글의 흐름으로 보아, 주어진 문장이 들어가기에 가장 적절한 곳은?

Successfully hunting such large animals usually takes more than one wolf, so it makes sense to suppose that wolf packs evolved because of the size of wolves' food.

The social lives of numerous animals are strongly shaped by affiliative and cooperative behavior. Consider wolves. (①) For a long time researchers thought that pack size was regulated by available food resources. (②) Wolves typically feed on animals such as elk and moose, both of which are bigger than an individual wolf. (③) However, long-term research by David Mech shows that pack size in wolves is regulated by social and not food-related factors. (④) Mech discovered that the number of wolves who can live together in a coordinated pack is governed by the number of wolves with whom individuals can closely bond balanced against the number of individuals from whom an individual can tolerate competition. (⑤) Packs and their codes of conduct break down when there are too many wolves.

*affiliative: 연합하는 **elk: 엘크 ((유럽·아시아의 큰 사슴))
***moose: 무스 ((캐나다·미국 북부의 큰 사슴))

[4~5] 다음 글을 읽고, 물음에 답하시오.

There are certain compelling features of the imagination. (a) Fictional people tend to be wittier and more clever than friends and family, and their adventures are usually much more interesting. I have contact with the lives of people around me, but this is a small slice of humanity, and perhaps not the most interesting slice. My real world doesn't include an emotionally wounded cop tracking down a serial killer, a shoplifter with a heart of gold, or a wisecracking vampire. But I can meet all of those people in imaginary worlds.

The technologies of the imagination provide any sensitive or private information that is (b) impossible to get in the real world. A novel can span birth to death and can show you how the person behaves in situations that you could never otherwise (c) observe. In reality you can never truly know what a person is thinking; in a story, the writer can tell you. Such psychic intimacy isn't (d) limited to the written word.

There are conventions in other artistic mediums that have been created for the same purpose. A character in a play might turn to the audience and begin a dramatic monologue that expresses what he or she is thinking. In a musical, the thoughts might be sung; on television and in the movies, a voiceover may be used. This is (e) uncommon now, but it must have been a revelation when the technique was first invented, and I wonder what young children think when they come across this for the first time, when they hear someone else's thoughts expressed aloud. It must be thrilling.

*voice-over: 보이스오버 ((영화 · 텔레비전에서 화면에 나타나지 않는 인물이 들려주는 정보))

4. 윗글의 제목으로 가장 적절한 것은?

① Fiction Can Be More Realistic Than Reality
② Why Are We So Attracted by Fictional Stories?
③ Reading Novels Is a Tool for Self-Improvement
④ Understanding Human Nature Through Reading
⑤ Our Brain Cannot Distinguish Fiction from Reality

5. 밑줄 친 (a)~(e) 중에서 문맥상 낱말의 쓰임이 적절하지 않은 것은?

① (a)　　② (b)　　③ (c)　　④ (d)　　⑤ (e)

1. 다음 글의 요지로 가장 적절한 것은?

World history teachers already grasp the fact that they could not hope to cover the history of the world without picking and choosing. Otherwise, they would have to devote perhaps 13 minutes to the history of Malaysia, 7 to Singapore, and 28 to Thailand — impossible! But in U.S. history, teachers still feel a compulsion to teach 4,444 twigs rather than a much smaller number of trees and only a handful of forests. Sometimes they feel compelled to do so by statewide "standardized" twig tests. Unfortunately, the more teachers cover, the less kids remember. Fragmenting history into unconnected "facts" practically guarantees that students will not be able to relate many of these terms to their own lives. As a professor who specializes in teaching first-year courses, I can guarantee that by the time they enter college, most students who were taught U.S. history the usual way have forgotten everything — except that World War I preceded World War II.

*twig: 잔가지

① 역사 교육은 국가별로 공평하게 시간이 배분되어야 한다.
② 역사 교육은 지엽적 사항보다는 큰 줄기를 가르쳐야 한다.
③ 역사 교육은 세계사보다 자국의 역사에 중점을 두어야 한다.
④ 역사 교육의 자료들은 최대한 사실에 근거한 것이어야 한다.
⑤ 세계사적인 주요 사건들에 대해서는 확실한 암기가 중요하다.

2. 다음 빈칸에 들어갈 말로 가장 적절한 것은?

With waiting lists for gardening spaces growing longer, many plots are being reduced in size, yet the desire to grow fruit and vegetables is stronger than ever. So what should you do if you just don't have acres of space or at least a full-size plot to grow on? How to use your plot should be based on the end product. The question should be "What do I like to eat?", not "What do I want to grow?" Visit some gardens in late winter or early spring and you will see half rotting cabbages and the general debris of winter. Go around in late spring and summer and you will often see runner beans that have grown several meters high. If they are not eaten, these are a waste of space. So the first rule of planning a garden is this: _____ has taken time, space, and energy that should have been spent on growing something else that finds a home in your stomach.

① everyone who has rented a plot
② anything that is not actually consumed
③ anyone who has focused on desirable food
④ everything that is currently grown in plots
⑤ anything that is planted out of season

3. 다음 글에서 전체 흐름과 관계 <u>없는</u> 문장은?

Being a "good team player" can have a downside, because the consensus of a group can sometimes be misguided or dangerous. Dissent might save the group from making mistakes, but the pressure to conform despite individual doubts — sometimes called *groupthink* — can lead to disaster. ① A natural predisposition to agree with others in a particular group can, however, assure an efficient and quick decision making process. ② For instance, groupthink was at work in high-level meetings preceding the space shuttle *Columbia* disaster in 2003. ③ Transcripts of those meetings at NASA show that the official who ran shuttle management meetings, a non-engineer, believed from the beginning that foam insulation debris could not damage the spacecraft. ④ When an engineer expressed his concerns, she dismissed the issue and cut off discussion. ⑤ The others present quickly fell into line with the person running the meeting. A few days later, damage caused by foam insulation debris caused *Columbia* to break apart on reentry into the Earth's atmosphere.

*foam insulation: 발포 단열재 **debris: 잔해

4. 주어진 글 다음에 이어질 글의 순서로 가장 적절한 것은? [3점]

In 1908 a cowboy named George McJunkin was riding near the small town of Folsom, New Mexico, searching for a lost cow.

(A) There they stayed until 1925, when they landed on the desk of Jesse Figgins of the Colorado Museum of Natural History. Figgins easily identified the bones as those of a long-extinct form of bison that had roamed the plains at the end of the Ice Age.

(B) But it was the stone spearpoints McJunkin had found beside the bones that had the more far-reaching implications. If these spearpoints were manmade weapons used to kill the bison, that meant humans had been hunting (and living) in America during the Ice Age.

(C) Instead, he came across some bones with stone spearpoints beside them. The bones were much too large to belong to a cow; intrigued, McJunkin took them back to the ranch house.

*bison: 들소

① (A) – (C) – (B)   ② (B) – (A) – (C)
③ (B) – (C) – (A)   ④ (C) – (A) – (B)
⑤ (C) – (B) – (A)

5. 글의 흐름으로 보아, 주어진 문장이 들어가기에 가장 적절한 곳은? [3점]

As a result, Poe chose to present the origination of *The Raven* in a contrary light.

In 1845 Edgar Allan Poe completed *The Raven*. One year later, Poe published the critical essay *The Philosophy of Composition*, which described the process by which this poem had been created. (①) We might have expected Poe, as a poet in the Romantic age, to talk about the flash of inspiration by which the entire poem appeared in an instant. (②) As Poe put it, "Most writers — poets especially — prefer having it understood that they compose through a type of intense frenzy — an ecstatic intuition." (③) Yet Poe always prided himself on his analytical powers. (④) "It is my intention to render it manifest that no one point in its composition is attributable either to accident or intuition — that the work proceeded, step by step, to its completion with the precision and rigid consequence of a mathematical problem." (⑤) He emphasized that logic drove every decision, from the poem's length and themes down to single words and images.

*frenzy: 극도의 흥분, 광란

1. 다음 글의 제목으로 가장 적절한 것은?

Even though science believes it is predicated on physical laws that describe objective processes, the historian of science Thomas Kuhn pointed out that scientific facts are instead embedded in cultural practices or paradigms. Science operates within the context of the culture it exists in; it does not exist in a vacuum where pure absolute objectivity prevails. In biomedicine, for example, physicians always base their diagnosis on assumptions within the context of their culture. In the United States, a reasonably healthy person with an enlarged spleen would be suspected of mononucleosis. In South America, this same person would be suspected of having Chagas' disease; in Ethiopia, Ewing's tumor. All these diagnoses would be correct. If an American physician were put in sub-Sahara Africa, or a Saudi physician in Nebraska, each would have trouble making proper diagnoses of their patients. Because biomedicine operates within the context of the culture of which it is part, these physicians would be like fish out of water and not fully cognizant of the cultural mores of their host land.

*predicate: 근거를 두다 **spleen: 비장(脾臟) ***mores: 관습

① Science Cannot Transcend Cultural Bias
② Scientific Knowledge and Cultural Diversity
③ The Key to Scientific Information: Cultural Context
④ Science: A Tool for Interpreting Cultural Differences
⑤ The Pursuit of Science Overcomes the Limitations of Culture

2. 다음 글의 밑줄 친 부분 중, 문맥상 낱말의 쓰임이 적절하지 않은 것은? [3점]

There is a growing body of research that shows that too much information can hinder behavior change. With apps monitoring sleep, heart rate, calories, exercise, steps, stairs, and breathing — not to mention spending and Internet use and other behaviors — we live in an age of personal ① quantification. We can instantly know how much of everything we're doing, have done, and should do. While it's great information to have, too much data can actually ② lessen the pleasure we get from even healthy activities, like exercise, sleep, diet, and savings. As data ③ accumulates, and as we have to make an effort to measure, track, and think about it, the activities themselves can move from "lifestyle" to "④ work." As a consequence, our motivation to engage in these healthy activities drops. So, even if the data would help us understand what we *should* do, too much data ⑤ fulfills our desire to do anything about it.

3. 다음 빈칸에 들어갈 말로 가장 적절한 것은? [3점]

Pamela Dalton, a psychologist at Monell Chemical Senses Center, proved that _____ actually change the perception of smell. The participants were divided into three groups, who sat down in a lab, and were then exposed to an odor that was neither pleasant nor unpleasant for 20 minutes. To one group, she did not say anything about the odor, while she told the second and the third groups that the odor was an industrial chemical that might be harmful and a distilled pure natural extract, respectively. The result was that the subjects who were either told nothing or positive information felt the odor to be weaker as time passed. In contrast, the subjects who were told negative information felt the odor became stronger as time passed. In other words, an odor that is thought to be good disappears from consciousness fast, while an odor thought to be harmful keeps our attention and remains strong. This experiment shows that prejudices are very effective at distorting the senses.

*distilled: 증류하여 얻은, 증류한

① desires
② interests
③ behaviors
④ experiences
⑤ expectations

4. 다음 글에서 전체 흐름과 관계 없는 문장은?

The title of a scientific article should be chosen with care because it provides the first basis on which a prospective reader can decide whether or not to go further in reading the article. ① It therefore should provide as much information as possible about the nature of the paper, without, however, exceeding the length limitations. ② In practice it will be the chief source on which indexers will rely. ③ Therefore, it is desirable, if possible, to get index words into the title, *i.e.,* words under which the paper should be listed in the subject index. ④ Consequently, a journal article usually runs from two to twenty printed pages, which forces its authors to compress into the limited space the information the reader needs. ⑤ For example, if a small number of chemical compounds were studied in some way, such that the article should be indexed under the names of the compounds, try to get the names in the title.

5. 다음 글의 내용을 한 문장으로 요약하고자 한다. 빈칸 (A)와 (B)에 들어갈 말로 가장 적절한 것은?

Why do some in society always want more? One obvious answer is the boredom of comfort. In a rich economy, material comfort is easily achieved. The pleasure of satisfying the simple wants, so difficult to do in a poor society, is removed. Every day is a feast day. Tensions are aroused by only the new and the novel. In an otherwise boring world, stimulation and arousal are sought through new and novel consumption experiences. Once incorporated into daily routines, the novelty of new consumer items wears off and the pleasure of acquiring and making use of them diminishes. Playing a new computer game sparks arousal and creates tension; learning to play the game and succeeding at it brings the pleasure of tension reduction. As the experience is repeated, the level of arousal diminishes, and so does pleasure.

↓

As an individual ____(A)____ the consumption of a new and novel product, the satisfaction or happiness derived by the consumption experiences eventually ____(B)____ .

	(A)		(B)
①	increases	……	equalizes
②	increases	……	declines
③	reduces	……	declines
④	reduces	……	reinforces
⑤	postpones	……	reinforces

1. 다음 빈칸에 들어갈 말로 가장 적절한 것은? [3점]

Humans are predisposed to _____
_____. We have all seen the shape of the Big Dipper among the stars at night, even though the only thing we have really seen are seven points of light. Humans infer meanings not only with visual perceptions but other information as well. Errors in logic are committed by drawing conclusions from a few facts when no such conclusion is warranted by the available evidence. Retailers know this when they announce low prices on a few very visible items, leading to the inference that overall prices are lower at that store. If one person wins the lottery with a ticket purchased at the local mini-mart, that becomes the lucky location to purchase tickets.

① comprehend the new by a closer study of the old
② see whole patterns from partial or random evidence
③ prefer simple answers that can be readily understood
④ ignore important evidence unless it supports existing beliefs
⑤ assume that two events that occur together must be related

2. 주어진 글 다음에 이어질 글의 순서로 가장 적절한 것은? [3점]

> The event that began the transition from Old English to Middle English was the Norman Conquest of 1066, when William the Conqueror invaded England from Normandy in northern France and the conquering Normans began their rule of it.

(A) On the other hand, the peasantry and lower classes (the vast majority of the population, an estimated 95%) continued to speak English, which was considered by the Normans a low-class, vulgar tongue. It is this mixture of Old English and French that is usually referred to as Middle English.

(B) French became the language of the kings and nobility of England for more than 300 years. While it was the verbal language of the court, administration, and culture, Latin was mostly used for written language, especially by the Church and in official records.

(C) They were themselves descended from Vikings who had settled in northern France about 200 years before. However, they had completely abandoned their own language and wholeheartedly adopted French to the extent that not a single Norman word survived in Normandy.

*vulgar: 저속한, 천박한

① (A) – (C) – (B)　　　② (B) – (A) – (C)
③ (B) – (C) – (A)　　　④ (C) – (A) – (B)
⑤ (C) – (B) – (A)

3. 글의 흐름으로 보아, 주어진 문장이 들어가기에 가장 적절한 곳은?

> Instead, he recognized the zigzag pattern separating the light and dark areas of the moon.

It's not just that a certain kind of original person seeks out exposure to the arts. (①) The arts also serve in turn as a powerful source of creative insight. (②) When Galileo made his astonishing discovery of mountains on the moon, his telescope didn't actually have enough magnifying power to support that finding. (③) Other astronomers were looking through similar telescopes, but only Galileo was able to appreciate the implications of the dark and light regions. (④) He had the necessary depth of experience in physics and astronomy, but also breadth of experience in painting and drawing. (⑤) Thanks to artistic training in a technique called *chiaroscuro*, which focuses on representations of light and shade, Galileo was able to detect mountains which others were not able to detect.

[4~5] 다음 글을 읽고, 물음에 답하시오.

Students who have a high level of self-control are especially effective at achieving health, wealth, and happiness. Their lives are marked by success on many fronts. We found that these individuals don't attain these admirable outcomes in the (a) expected way — by actively exerting willpower. Their success is not due to some superhuman ability to inhibit unwanted actions. People who score high on "self-control" scales have effective strategies. They aren't using control at all. Instead, they form habits to automate their behavior. Habits make it easy to accomplish their goals.

There's another important story of how people with high "self-control" are successful. It has to do with (b) contexts. It seems that the talents of high "self-control" people extend beyond just knowing how to form beneficial habits. In an online survey, individuals who scored high on a "self-control" scale also agreed with statements like "I choose friends who keep me on track to accomplishing my long-term goals," or "When I work or study, I deliberately seek out a place with no distractions," and "I (c) avoid situations in which I might be tempted to act immorally." These people understood the power of circumstances to make actions easy or difficult. They recognized that if they controlled their surroundings, they'd control their actions, too. Once someone understands this, it gets easier to form beneficial habits. Students who tested (d) low in "self-control" didn't agree as strongly with these statements. They weren't trying to make their lives easier by establishing the right (e) internal forces — ones to drive desired behaviors and put friction on undesired ones. High "self-control" people don't just say the right thing. They do it.

4. 윗글의 제목으로 가장 적절한 것은?

① The Psychological benefits of Self-Control
② When Do We Fail at Self-Control, and Why?
③ Making Good Habits and Building Willpower
④ How the Willpower Myth Is Holding You Back
⑤ Self-Control: Strategies Rather Than Willpower

5. 밑줄 친 (a)~(e) 중에서 문맥상 낱말의 쓰임이 적절하지 않은 것은? [3점]

① (a)　　② (b)　　③ (c)　　④ (d)　　⑤ (e)

1. 다음 글에서 필자가 주장하는 바로 가장 적절한 것은?

Parents should be firm but open to suggestions, i.e. authoritative but not a dictator. They also must be wary of giving too much freedom and independence to their children, as children are not aware of all the possible effects of their decisions. Hence, it is up to the parent to help children understand the possible consequences of their decisions. The duty of the parent is to give his or her child independence in thinking — let him think of the situations, what can happen, what won't happen, if there are options, what will work out best, etc. Let your children think of the impossible, let them dream, hope, and aspire! Let them challenge your beliefs — because from those will arise new answers and new beliefs!

① 부모는 자녀의 안전을 위하는 환경을 개선해야 한다.
② 부모는 때때로 자녀의 친구로서의 역할도 수행해야 한다.
③ 부모는 자녀가 독립적으로 사고할 수 있도록 지도해야 한다.
④ 부모는 자녀의 올바른 사회화를 위해 엄격하게 훈육해야 한다.
⑤ 부모는 자녀가 사회의 확립된 체계를 따르도록 교육해야 한다.

2. 밑줄 친 a carrot and stick approach가 다음 글에서 의미하는 바로 가장 적절한 것은?

Different bacterial species need different nutrients; some prefer sugar, and others live off fat. But they not only fight with one another for food, and to retain a foothold in the ecosystem. Your gut bugs often want different things than you do, and they're not shy about going after their goals. Your gut bugs have the ability to impact your behavior and mood by altering the neural signals in your vagus nerve. They change taste receptors and produce toxins to make you feel bad when you don't eat the things they want, or release chemical rewards to make you feel good when you *do*. So the bacteria inside your gut are actually manipulating you. It's important to understand this, because it's what makes it so hard to change your diet: the bugs inside you are playing you like a big marionette, trying to force you to give them what they crave. It's a carrot and stick approach.

*foothold: 발판, 기반 **vagus nerve: 미주 신경

***marionette: 꼭두각시

① Gut bacteria produces two kinds of chemicals for our health.
② Gut bacteria chooses and absorbs what it needs from our bodies.
③ Gut bacteria controls our bodies in many ways for its own purposes.
④ Gut bacteria helps our bodies stay in good shape to get what it wants.
⑤ Gut bacteria can have both beneficial and harmful effects on the human body.

3. 다음 빈칸에 들어갈 말로 가장 적절한 것은? [3점]

There is a point of similarity between texting and Egyptian writing: the notion of a *rebus*. A rebus is a message which, in its original definition, consists entirely of pictures that are used to represent the sounds of words, rather than the objects they refer to. They are known in Latin, and found in European art and literature. Leonardo da Vinci drew rebus puzzles. Ben Jonson ridiculed them in one of his plays. So there is actually nothing novel at all about such text messages as *c u l8r* ("see you later") in English. They are part of European linguistic tradition, and similar features can be found in all languages which have been written down. Individual texters may have devised some of the modern abbreviations without being aware of that tradition, but they are only doing what generations have done before them. And certainly there should be no reason for us to be taken aback when we encounter such forms in texting, for we have all seen them before. To suggest that they are part of a "code for initiates" is _____ .

*initiate: (비밀 의식을 통해 단체 · 조직에 가입한) 가입자

① to reveal their origin
② to distort the soul of wit
③ to pay respect to tradition
④ to think of them as cliché
⑤ to ignore linguistic history

4. 주어진 글 다음에 이어질 글의 순서로 가장 적절한 것은? [3점]

When Atlantic cod populations collapsed due to overfishing, the Canadian government suggested hunting expeditions to kill North Atlantic harp seals, because the seals were known to eat cod.

(A) The seals, for example, not only fed on cod but also on 150 other species, many of which also fed on cod! So there simply was no way of knowing in advance whether reducing the seal population would actually produce more cod or less cod.

(B) It was assumed that eliminating the seals, a principal cod predator, would allow the cod populations to rebound. What the government failed to realize was that the cod/seal relationship was affected by many other less prominent species in the system.

(C) In food webs involving as few as eight species, there can be more than 10 million distinct chains of cause and effect that would link the seal to the cod. How can we ever exercise effective control management in such complex, dynamic communities?

① (A) – (C) – (B) ② (B) – (A) – (C)
③ (B) – (C) – (A) ④ (C) – (A) – (B)
⑤ (C) – (B) – (A)

5. 글의 흐름으로 보아, 주어진 문장이 들어가기에 가장 적절한 곳은?

Subsequent to the trauma, individuals may rebuild their assumptions in ways that map more closely onto the world as it is for them now, and this, in turn, may facilitate future coping.

As individuals go through life, they build up sets of beliefs about who they are and how the world works. These sets might include specific beliefs such as "Heart trouble only affects people older than I." The problem, of course, is that events in the real world can challenge such beliefs. (①) When the challenge is great enough, individuals may be forced to drop their beliefs and develop new ones. (②) It is in this context that growth can occur. (③) Individuals may also be provided with opportunities they did not see before (e.g., new careers, new relationships). (④) In these ways, and others, it is possible for individuals to experience some growth alongside of, and because of, the loss and pain associated with the trauma. (⑤) The growth (e.g., improvements in social support) may in fact result from the individuals' attempts to deal with the trauma.

1. 다음 글의 주제로 가장 적절한 것은?

Slow ageing seeks to redefine ageing as a positive growth experience, rather than one linked with decrepitude, degeneration and decline. The anti-ageing movement generally seeks to position 'getting old' as something to be avoided at all costs. It feeds on people's fears and typically doesn't provide real solutions. This is unrealistic and unnecessary. We want to slow ageing, not fear it. Attitude is the single most important factor in healthy ageing. A positive attitude drives healthy behaviour and gives us control over our lives. It can more than compensate for a number of other things that may be failing. Ageing needs to be re-positioned as an experience of value, not only for ourselves as individuals, but for our society. It is possible to LOVE the ageing process, to re-frame ageing as a positive experience and take control so we age with pleasure, resilience and growth.

*decrepitude: 노쇠, 노후 **resilience: 회복

① biological causes of aging and age-related diseases
② importance of having positive attitudes towards ageing
③ effective strategies to help slow down the ageing process
④ knowledge and attitude towards ageing among elderly people
⑤ relationships between attitudes toward ageing and life satisfaction

2. 다음 글의 밑줄 친 부분 중, 어법상 틀린 것은? [3점]

The classic example of people focusing so much on rules that they forget ① to think is what happened in asbestos removal projects in the 1980s. The government issued a set of rules that was hundreds of pages thick ② describing every aspect of how to remove asbestos-containing materials from buildings. Most of the rules, such as those requiring that workers wear masks and that the asbestos ③ is wet to reduce the amount of airborne dust, were designed to prevent people from breathing asbestos fibers. People paid so much attention to following these rules and ④ avoiding breathing asbestos fibers that they forgot what happens when water (necessary to keep the asbestos wet) and electricity (necessary for lights and equipment) mix. Thus, a leading cause of injury at these sites ⑤ was electrocution. The rules were so thorough that people assumed they could ignore common sense and just follow the rules.

*asbestos: 석면 **electrocution: 감전

3. 다음 빈칸에 들어갈 말로 가장 적절한 것은? [3점]

When designing advanced resistance training programs, there are many variables that can be altered to enhance the difficulty and prolong the positive adaptations. One of the most important variables is variety. Most advanced training programs incorporate different styles of programs during various training periods. The rationale is that in order to continue to promote training adaptations, you must continually _____ the system. Individuals who have been training for long periods of time using identical training methods (i.e., order of exercises, types of exercise, workloads, intensities, etc.) do not experience as much adaptation. You must continually alter your program so the body does not become too accustomed to it. Therefore, you must increase the variety of your workouts to attain advanced training outcomes. That is not always as simple as adding more weight or changing the number of repetitions within a program. The advanced competitive individual might also add in specialized training to enhance speed, quickness, and agility to help accomplish their exercise-specific training goals.

*rationale: 근거, 이유 **agility: 민첩성

① simplify   ② overload
③ distribute   ④ undermine
⑤ standardize

4. 다음 글에서 전체 흐름과 관계 <u>없는</u> 문장은?

A biography tells an account of a person's life written in the third person in a narrative structure. Biographies can be studied to learn about how people reacted to, shaped, and constructed opportunities during historical periods and the cultural contexts in which they lived. ① They provide nonfiction information and communicate why a person's legacy is so important that it is documented. ② Reading biographies can help students reflect about how they should feel about historical people and events in terms of a dynamic process of continuity and change. ③ Moreover, people in history are humanized by biographies that allow students to be drawn close to the past as they experience specific personalities and realities. ④ A biographer inevitably finds it impossible to give a complete picture of his subject if he hesitates to present his subject as an imperfect human being. ⑤ Through this, biographies offer students a richer context of history, providing more opportunities for engagement as they connect with the people as well as the events of the times.

*legacy: 업적, 유산

5. 다음 글의 내용을 한 문장으로 요약하고자 한다. 빈칸 (A), (B)에 들어갈 말로 가장 적절한 것은?

Even very subtle manipulation of object-orientation in an ad design can impact purchase behavior. Advertisers can increase purchase intentions by facilitating mental simulation through their visual depictions of the product. They can do this simply by orienting a product (e.g., a cake with a fork) toward the right side. While this may not suit the smaller percentage of left-handers, the larger percentage of right-handers will have better mental product-interaction. These results also hold for shelf display design in retail environments. For example, a very slight change in display design of mugs in the window of a coffee shop could affect purchases with consumers imagining picking up that coffee mug and drinking from it. Including an instrument (e.g., a spoon for eating an advertised soup) that facilitates mental simulation should also increase purchase intentions. These consequences of visual depiction impact not just advertising design, but product packaging design and display design as well.

*object-orientation: 객체 지향 방법론

↓

> Subtle changes in the design of an ad ___(A)___ the mental simulation of the consumer, which may lead to an ___(B)___ in the intention of purchasing an item.

　　　(A)　　　　　　(B)
① assist ‥‥‥ elevation
② assist ‥‥‥ reduction
③ alleviate ‥‥‥ elevation
④ alleviate ‥‥‥ reduction
⑤ impede ‥‥‥ abatement

1. 다음 빈칸에 들어갈 말로 가장 적절한 것은? [3점]

Most of us are embarrassed to admit that our opinions can be strongly affected by an appeal to our emotions. We tend to take pride in our rationality and feel a bit ashamed of our emotions, as if rationality were more likely to be right and the emotions commensurately apt to be wrong. Where rationality is concerned, we feel in control; where emotions dominate, we feel out of control, as if our emotions have a life of their own and are even somewhat alien to us. This is a cultural prejudice. Our emotions, no less than our faculty of reason, are part of us, and there is nothing abnormal or regrettable, let alone shameful, about being moved by emotion. In fact, very few of the major decisions we make _____. Even the most rational of decisions typically have an important emotional component, and many emotionally motivated decisions are quite reasonable.

*commensurately: 비례하여, 상응하여

① set a higher value on emotion than reason
② are based purely on reason or purely on emotion
③ become either time-consuming or energy-intensive
④ take the environment into account first and foremost
⑤ have an emotional connection to what we've experienced

2. 주어진 글 다음에 이어질 글의 순서로 가장 적절한 것은? [3점]

Historians' approaches to the past vary enormously, but some common disciplinary features unite them.

(A) So all studies of history are driven by the discovery of evidence from the period being studied, and its analysis and interpretation. Historians aim to describe what happened, explain how and why it happened, and link past events to wider contexts and the passage of time.

(B) There are limits to what historians can study: they can study only parts of the past that left evidence behind and for which evidence has survived. The dominant type of evidence has been documentary: government archives, private papers, newspapers and published materials have long been the most consulted forms of source.

(C) The range has recently broadened, and many historians are now happy to use artefacts, buildings, visual evidence, oral testimony and many other non-written sources. However, regardless of the type of evidence, the point is that without evidence, historians cannot function.

*archive: 공적(公的) 기록, 공문서 **testimony: 증거, 증언

① (A) – (C) – (B)   ② (B) – (A) – (C)
③ (B) – (C) – (A)   ④ (C) – (A) – (B)
⑤ (C) – (B) – (A)

3. 글의 흐름으로 보아, 주어진 문장이 들어가기에 가장 적절한 곳은?

A better method, however, is to send a new copy of the survey questionnaire with the follow-up letter.

Due to the variability in responses for mail-in surveys, it's often necessary to send follow-up mailings. Such mailings may be administered in several ways. In the simplest, nonrespondents are simply sent a letter of additional encouragement to participate. (①) If potential respondents have not returned their questionnaires after two or three weeks, the questionnaires have probably been lost or misplaced. (②) Receiving a follow-up letter might encourage them to look for the original questionnaire, but if they can't find the questionnaire easily, the letter may be good for nothing. (③) The methodological literature strongly suggests that follow-up mailings provide an effective method for increasing return rates in mail surveys. (④) In general, the longer a potential respondent delays replying, the less likely he or she is to do so at all. (⑤) Properly timed follow-up mailings, then, provide additional stimuli to respond.

*mail-in: 우편에 의한

[4~5] 다음 글을 읽고, 물음에 답하시오.

Do you feel better after taking a walk in the park or watching a beautiful sunset? If so, you may be unknowingly using your own form of "ecotherapy," a type of therapy designed to (a) <u>improve</u> emotional health by reconnecting people with nature and the environment. The field of ecopsychology, which first became popular in the United States in the 1990s, claims that humans are an (b) <u>integral</u> part of the natural world and should not be separated from it. Their emotional health may suffer if they are cut off from nature by urbanization or other aspects of modern life. In addition, this alienation may cause emotional and physical (c) <u>comfort</u>.

Out of this movement grew ecotherapy, offering strategies to strengthen people's relationship with nature. These range from the sophisticated to the simple. For instance, learning to survive alone in the wilderness can build confidence, but even a simple walk outdoors can also be effective. Some therapies involve animals: swimming with dolphins, playing with your pet, or watching a tropical fish tank are all (d) <u>beneficial</u>. Even looking at a picture of an outdoor scene can help.

As a result, one UK mental-health charity is now proposing that ecotherapy be made more (e) <u>readily</u> available for mental-health patients, as it already is in Holland and Norway. So if you're feeling a bit down, you may not need anti-depressants or costly therapy. First, try riding your bike or walking on the beach. These activities will surely be good for your physical health, and may strengthen your spirits, too.

4. 윗글의 제목으로 가장 적절한 것은?

① How Can You Shake off Your Blues?
② Nature Is Neither Enemy nor Friend!
③ Leading Causes of Emotional Distress
④ Ways of Getting in Touch with Nature
⑤ Mother Nature: A Hospital Without Walls

5. 밑줄 친 (a)~(e) 중에서 문맥상 낱말의 쓰임이 적절하지 <u>않은</u> 것은? [3점]

① (a) ② (b) ③ (c) ④ (d) ⑤ (e)

1. 다음 글의 요지로 가장 적절한 것은?

Values and their supporting beliefs are lenses through which we see the world. The views that these lenses provide are often of what life *ought* to be like, not what it is. For example, Americans value individualism so highly that they tend to see almost everyone as free and equal in pursuing the goal of success. This value blinds them to the significance of the circumstances that keep people from achieving success. The dire consequences of family poverty, parents' low education, and dead-end jobs tend to drop from sight. Instead, Americans see the unsuccessful as not taking advantage of opportunities, or as having some inherent laziness or dull minds. And they "know" they are right, because the mass media dangle before their eyes enticing stories of individuals who have succeeded despite the greatest of handicaps.

*dire: 끔찍한, 심각한

**dangle: (상대방의 마음을 끌 수 있는 것을) 제시하다

① 객관적이고 중립적인 사회적 가치를 형성하는 것은 불가능하다.
② 사회적 가치는 소수의 여론 주도층에 의해 형성되는 경향이 있다.
③ 가치가 제공하는 견해는 현실을 보여주기보다는 당위와 관련된 것이다.
④ 가치는 사회적 환경에 의해 형성된 것으로 시대에 따라 변하기 마련이다.
⑤ 지배 계층은 자신의 견해를 모범적인 사회적 가치로 주장하는 경향이 있다.

2. 다음 빈칸에 들어갈 말로 가장 적절한 것은? [3점]

Your brain originally is like a little empty attic, and you have to stock it with such furniture as you choose. If the brain held on to everything that it received, it would have so many memories that it would soon run out of room, and could accept no more. A fool takes in all the furnishings of every sort that he comes across, so that the knowledge which might be useful to him gets crowded out, or at best is mixed up with a lot of other things, so that he has difficulty laying his hands on it. It is a mistake to think that the little room _____ _____. Depend upon this: there comes a time when for every addition of knowledge, you forget something that you knew before.

① will be messed up with every detail
② is not accessible without any permission
③ cannot be adjusted to whatever you need
④ has elastic walls and can stretch to any extent
⑤ is filled with forgettable things of all different shapes

3. 다음 글에서 전체 흐름과 관계 <u>없는</u> 문장은?

The obvious role of sugar in ice cream is to sweeten the product. However, sugar also plays a role in determining the textural characteristics of the frozen ice cream, because sugar causes the freezing temperature of the mixture to drop. ① In fact, a cup of sugar in a quart of an ice cream mixture will decrease the freezing point approximately 2°F. ② This means that the ice cream must be chilled below the normal freezing temperature of water if ice crystals are to form. ③ The flavor of ice cream can be enhanced by storing it at an extremely low temperature, which creates an outstanding cold sensation while the ice cream melts in your mouth. ④ The greater the content of sugar in an ice cream, the lower the freezing point. ⑤ This delayed freezing temperature helps to keep the size of crystals in the ice cream very small because a reasonable amount of stirring can be done during the freezing process to help break up any ice crystal aggregates as they slowly form.

*aggregate: 집합체

4. 주어진 글 다음에 이어질 글의 순서로 가장 적절한 것은?

For those of us who have lived through the invention of the Internet and mobile computing, it feels like digital technology has finally reached a mature phase. But as most tech experts will tell you, we've barely scratched the surface.

(A) It can send birthday greetings for us, nudge us when a friend posts troublesome news, and even remind us to dress appropriately tomorrow when it looks like it might rain.

(B) This modern digital world offers much to amuse, amaze, and delight us, enabling us to do things we didn't think possible just five years ago. For example, today we have the option of "hiring" an app as our personal assistant.

(C) Every day, tens of thousands of new apps are developed, and smarter, more powerful gadgets are designed to replace what's in our pockets and fill the gaps in our lives that have yet to be digitized.

*nudge: 주의를 환기시키다, 팔꿈치로 살짝 찌르다 **gadget: 장치, 도구

① (A) – (C) – (B)　　② (B) – (A) – (C)
③ (B) – (C) – (A)　　④ (C) – (A) – (B)
⑤ (C) – (B) – (A)

5. 글의 흐름으로 보아, 주어진 문장이 들어가기에 가장 적절한 곳은?

According to the historian E. H. Warmington, this absence of silver coins suggests a trade mainly in luxury goods during that period.

Local goods in India were purchased with durable gold and silver coins, each dated by the image of a Roman emperor. Caches of these coins are still being discovered in south India, offering us a glimpse of trade patterns two thousand years ago. (①) They include gold and silver coins from the reigns of Augustus and Tiberius (27 BC to AD 37), suggesting a vigorous trade in a large volume of goods. (②) After the death of Tiberius, the composition of the Indian coin caches changes. (③) Significant numbers of only gold, but not silver, coins bearing the heads of Caligula, Claudius, and Nero (AD 37-68) are found. (④) Few Roman coins of any type are found after the death of Marcus Aurelius in AD 180. (⑤) When Roman and Han authority finally collapsed around AD 200, trade with the East came to an almost complete standstill.

*cache: 은닉물, 저장물

1. 다음 글의 제목으로 가장 적절한 것은?

If we look at written Dutch and written German, or listen to these two languages as spoken on television or radio, we can see that they are clearly two separate languages. An average German speaker would not be able to understand Dutch and vice versa. Moreover, people living in a rural community on the Dutch side of the Dutch-German border would say that they are speaking Dutch. Inhabitants of a rural community a few miles away on the German side of the border would say that they are speaking German. Yet the languages they speak are very similar, and mutually intelligible. They are more similar to one another than they are to the respective written languages. One way of explaining this situation is to say that the inhabitants of these border communities are speaking 'varieties' or 'dialects' of German and Dutch. These 'dialects' are different from a 'standard' form of the language employed in writing or in formal spoken usage.

① Why Dutch Is So Close to German
② The More Globalized, the Fewer Languages
③ Language Standardization: A Modern Trend
④ Converging Communities, Diverging Languages
⑤ Border Dialects Find Common Language Ground

2. 다음 글의 밑줄 친 부분 중, 문맥상 낱말의 쓰임이 적절하지 않은 것은?

Most children develop an ability to manufacture facial expressions they don't feel, but not everyone does this equally well or believes it to be a good thing. Some children, for example, do not ① suppress anger with a smile. These children tend to be the ones who more generally have behavior problems. Psychologists have observed that unpopular children are more likely to frown and grimace when they lose at a game and less likely to ② contain their smiling when they win at a game than popular children. They will likely vent their "real" feelings and are ③ less likely to hold them back for the sake of others' feelings. Celebrating a win with an enormous grin is not likely to ④ endear you to others. Socially ⑤ incompetent children understand that there are times when hiding or disguising emotions is what friends do.

3. 다음 빈칸에 들어갈 말로 가장 적절한 것은? [3점]

In many domains, there are issues that have not yet been resolved, questions that have not yet been posed, and problems that have no obvious solution. These "ill-structured" problems require a creative approach. Paradoxically, when people are given free rein to solve a problem, they tend to be wholly uncreative, focusing on what's worked best in the past. This is due to the fundamental nature of human cognition: to imagine the future we generate what we already know from the past. Such freedom can hinder creativity, whereas the strategic use of constraints can promote creativity. By using constraints, reliable responses are precluded and novel surprising ones are encouraged. You'll be more creative if _____.

*preclude: 제외하다

① your mind is not allowed to roam free
② you keep exposing yourself to new experiences
③ your mind refers to the reaction of those around you
④ you don't allow yourself to fall for the easiest solution
⑤ you start questioning or being curious about everything

4. 다음 글에서 전체 흐름과 관계 없는 문장은?

Rap music flourished without access to the music establishment. Most rap is performed by artists in their own homes, using inexpensive, widely accessible equipment, in contrast to the sound studios and sophisticated recording equipment of other musical genres. ① Rap music is mainly disseminated on homemade cassettes and by locally owned independent record companies. ② For a decade, the major recording companies resisted rap, and even in the mid-1990s only a small portion of the music on the *Billboard* rap singles chart was produced by the major labels. ③ The radio industry (which usually makes or breaks the success of any piece of music) ignored rap because its audience is not a priority for radio advertisers to reach. ④ Radio ads are still a powerful and effective tool for your business — in fact, every week, over 90% of Americans listen to the radio. ⑤ For example, New York does not have a single rap station, although it has two full-time classical radio stations.

*disseminate: 보급하다, 널리 퍼뜨리다

5. 다음 글의 내용을 한 문장으로 요약하고자 한다. 빈칸 (A), (B)에 들어갈 말로 가장 적절한 것은?

In the early 1980s, Nancy Andreasen, a neuroscientist at the University of Iowa, interviewed several dozen successful writers from the Iowa Writers' Workshop about their mental history. Andreasen found that 80 percent of the writers were exceedingly worried and nervous. Why is severe mental burden so closely associated with creativity? Her explanation is straightforward: It's not easy to write a good novel. The process often requires years of careful attention as the artist fixes mistakes and corrects errors. As a result, the ability to stick with the process is extremely important. "Successful writers are like prizefighters who keep on getting hit but won't go down," Andreasen says. "They'll stick with it until it's right. And that seems to be what the mood disorders help with." A similar theme emerged from biographical studies of British novelists and poets done by Kay Redfield Jamison, a professor of psychiatry at Johns Hopkins. According to her data, successful writers were eight times as likely as people in the general population to suffer from feelings of severe despondency and dejection.

↓

One reason successful writers tend to suffer from ____(A)____ is because an important element of creative work is ____(B)____.

	(A)		(B)
①	publicity	……	novelty
②	depression	……	novelty
③	publicity	……	perseverance
④	depression	……	perseverance
⑤	competition	……	imitation

1. 다음 빈칸에 들어갈 말로 가장 적절한 것은? [3점]

An instrument is useless if you can't make a good connection between it and your soul. The music that we play on our musical instruments comes from our souls, our experience and our feelings. There are numerous ways to work on this. In most music institutes, people are attending the ear-training classes. Students learn to sight-read the written notes using their voices and their brain and not their instrument. This is a very convenient way to create a strong bond between you and your instrument, but not the only one. Guess what the best way is. Playing with a band and interacting with real musicians is the point. No matter how many exercises you do or how many ear-training sessions you are taking, you are never going to see any significant progress if you _____.

*sight-read: (악보를) 처음 보고 연주하다

① take part in contests
② know your place in life
③ keep playing in your room
④ see professional performances
⑤ love the music with all your heart

2. 주어진 글 다음에 이어질 글의 순서로 가장 적절한 것은? [3점]

The sun sends us more than heat and light; it sends lots of other energy and small particles our way. The protective magnetic field around Earth shields us from most of the energy and particles, and we don't even notice them.

(A) There, the particles interact with gases in the atmosphere resulting in beautiful displays of light in the sky called auroras. Oxygen gives off green and red light. Nitrogen glows blue and purple.

(B) When it comes toward Earth, some of the energy and small particles ionize the oxygen and nitrogen gas in the atmosphere. This usually happens around the poles of a planet where the magnetic field lines are concentrated and the atmosphere becomes thicker.

(C) But the sun doesn't send the same amount of energy all the time. During one kind of solar storm called a coronal mass ejection, the sun burps out a huge bubble of electrified gas that can travel through space at high speeds.

*coronal mass ejection: 코로나 질량 방출 **burp: 트림하다

① (A) – (C) – (B)   ② (B) – (A) – (C)
③ (B) – (C) – (A)   ④ (C) – (A) – (B)
⑤ (C) – (B) – (A)

3. 글의 흐름으로 보아, 주어진 문장이 들어가기에 가장 적절한 곳은?

For others, however, "mine is better" is not an attitude that everyone has about his or her things.

For most people in most cases, the "mine-is-better" tendency is balanced by the understanding that other people feel the same way about their things, and that it's an unavoidable part of being human to think like this. (①) In other words, most people realize that we all see ourselves in a special way, different from everything that is not ourselves, and that whatever we associate with ourselves becomes part of us in our minds. (②) Rather, it is a special, higher truth unique to their particular situation. (③) They believe they have the only correct answer and want to force all others to be like them. (④) Fortunately, most who think like this are able to control the tendency to dominate. (⑤) The problem is, some people cannot even understand that each person has a special viewpoint.

[4~5] 다음 글을 읽고, 물음에 답하시오.

Brilliant individuals, whether anthropologists, psychologists or economists, assume that brilliance is the key to human achievement. They vote for the smartest people to run governments, they ask the cleverest experts to devise plans for the economy, and they (a) credit the sharpest scientists with discoveries. They are all barking up the wrong tree. The key to human achievement is not (b) individual intelligence at all. Human achievement is entirely a networking phenomenon. It is by combining brainpower through the division of labor that human society happened upon a way to raise the living standards, technological virtuosity and knowledge base of the species. We can see this in all sorts of phenomena: the (c) advance of technology in people who became isolated, like native Tasmanians; the prosperity of trading city states in Greece, Italy, Holland and south-east Asia; the creative consequences of trade. Human achievement is rooted in collective intelligence — the nodes in the human neural network are people themselves. By each doing one thing and mastering it, then combining the results through (d) exchange, people become capable of doing things they do not even understand. As the economist Leonard Read pointed out in his essay "I, Pencil," no single person knows how to make even a pencil — the knowledge is (e) distributed in society among many thousands of graphite miners, lumberjacks, designers and factory workers.

4. 윗글의 제목으로 가장 적절한 것은?

① Brilliant People Accomplish Amazing Things
② Smart People Value Team Accomplishments
③ How Can We Maximize Collective Intelligence?
④ Individual Achievement vs. Collective Responsibility
⑤ Human Achievement: The Fruit of Collective Intelligence

5. 밑줄 친 (a)~(e) 중에서 문맥상 낱말의 쓰임이 적절하지 <u>않은</u> 것은? [3점]

① (a)　　② (b)　　③ (c)　　④ (d)　　⑤ (e)

1. 다음 글에서 필자가 주장하는 바로 가장 적절한 것은?

Advertising is a form of persuasion. This means that from square one, your goals and interests are often very different from those of the advertiser. Let's say your goal is to buy the best dishwashing machine you can afford. I don't have to be the first to break it to you that this is not the main concern of an advertising copywriter for a home appliance company. He's unlikely to suffer a single pang of failure upon finding out that, by buying the washer in his beautifully-crafted ad, you've passed up a wiser purchase. If you really want to read something that's written with your best interests in mind, you pick up a copy of *Consumer Reports* — you don't go flipping through *Good Housekeeping* to find that dishwasher ad you saw last week. When you do read the ad, you take it for granted that any comparisons it makes to the competition are not necessarily "fair and balanced."

*pang: 고통

① 제품의 광고를 볼 때 이면의 숨겨진 정보를 읽는 게 필요하다.
② 광고의 목적은 제품 판매에 있으므로 그대로 믿어서는 안 된다.
③ 현명한 구매를 위해 유사 제품의 광고를 비교하는 게 도움이 된다.
④ 광고되지 않았지만 좋은 제품을 소셜 미디어를 통해 구할 수 있다.
⑤ 경쟁사와의 비교 광고는 객관적이지 않다는 것을 알고 참고해야 한다.

2. 밑줄 친 allowing you to experience a second wind가 다음 글에서 의미하는 바로 가장 적절한 것은? [3점]

We often think we slow down and stop during athletic training because we run out of physiological energy — that it is the strength of our muscles or the oxygen in our blood that caps our maximum expenditure. Yet research finds that when individuals feel they've reached their physical limits, they actually have the capacity to go on for much longer. It isn't your body that shuts things down, it's your mind. The brain exercises a miserly control over the body's life-sustaining resources; it monitors the environment within and without, and when it feels there's a risk of your getting too fatigued and run-down, it puts the brakes on your efforts, throwing the switch far from the actual point at which you would become dangerously exhausted. But, when an unusual necessity compels you beyond this premature barrier — such as the pressures of competition — a surprising thing occurs: The power of the brain relents, allowing you to experience a second wind.

*relent: 약해지다

① you'll find new energy and strength to continue
② you'll feel more compelled to avoid the shame of losing
③ you'll control your brain by overcoming the physical limit
④ you'll be driven by genuine motivation and intrinsic desire
⑤ you'll be allowed to take a break from intense competition

3. 다음 빈칸에 들어갈 말로 가장 적절한 것은? [3점]

Harvard psychologist Felix Warneken had adults show elementary-aged children two pictures they drew — one pretty good, one terrible. If the adults didn't show any particular pride in the picture, the kids were truthful in saying whether it was good or bad. If the grown-up acted sad about being a bad artist, most of the kids would rush to reassure her that it wasn't too awful. In other words, they told a white lie; the older they were, the more likely the kids were to say a bad drawing was good. There were no negative consequences for telling the truth to these bad artists; the kids just wanted these strangers to feel better about themselves. In other words, says Warneken, it's a(n) _____ that drives children to tell white lies. In fact, children are trying to resolve two conflicting norms — honesty vs. kindness — and by about age seven, his studies suggest, they start consistently coming down on the side of kindness.

① strategy for avoiding conflict
② attempt to impress the artists
③ feeling of empathic connection
④ desire for getting fast attention
⑤ intention of pleasing themselves

4. 주어진 글 다음에 이어질 글의 순서로 가장 적절한 것은?

The electromagnetic force works between any two things that have electric charge. The more the charge, the stronger the force. And, like gravity, the force depends on the separation between the objects. The further they are apart, the weaker the force.

(A) This balance, the result of charge neutrality, can never happen with gravity. There being no negative mass, there is no possibility of a mass-neutral object. You can't neutralize gravity as you can the electromagnetic force. This is why it is ever-present in our experiences.

(B) But unlike gravity, electromagnetism can be both attractive and repulsive; it can pull things together and push them apart. Opposite charges, one positive the other negative, attract. Like charges, both positive or both negative, repel.

(C) This means that a composite object that has an equal amount of positive and negative charge will push and pull in equal amounts and consequently experience and exert no electromagnetic force at all.

① (A) – (C) – (B)　　② (B) – (A) – (C)
③ (B) – (C) – (A)　　④ (C) – (A) – (B)
⑤ (C) – (B) – (A)

5. 글의 흐름으로 보아, 주어진 문장이 들어가기에 가장 적절한 곳은?

Obviously, after repeatedly viewing and absorbing such observations, members of the public are likely to agree with this verdict, even if they may be less than susceptible to the pictures' affecting their beliefs or actions.

The public plays almost no expressive or even approving role in selecting "big pictures" of photojournalism (the exception being some contests to name "photo of the year"). (①) Editors do not poll the public before displaying images of the day's news and selecting those worthy of more extensive coverage and comment. (②) The Pulitzer Prize, too, is voted upon by journalistic elites. (③) Photographers and journalists (through prize committees), editors (through selection), and political and editorial elites (through notation and commentary) impose greatness and thus fame on images. (④) Historians and textbook companies, by reemploying or "quoting" such images for discussion or simply illustration, reaffirm that they are "great." (⑤) Elites, thus, largely set the agenda of greatness and establish the criteria for which images are judged great.

*verdict: 결정, 평결　**susceptible to: ~에 흔들리기 쉬운

1. 다음 글의 주제로 가장 적절한 것은?

Suppose four-year-old Sally is making a clay elephant and she uses a carrot as a trunk. Sally's mom explains that the carrot will be burnt in the kiln, or rot first. Sally agrees reluctantly and looks very disappointed. Too late her mom realizes what she has done. Sally is not interested in the finished product so much as the immediate effect, which she has achieved to her immense satisfaction. How tempting it is to give a hand to a struggling artist or sculptor! This kind of action lets the child feel that her version is inferior to ours and she is undermined. It is important not to impose our adult values on the child's creativity. This does not mean that we cannot show the child a variety of processes to choose from. But a child must feel free to develop them by himself or herself.

*kiln: (벽돌 등을 굽는) 가마

① necessity of giving a child greater creative autonomy
② reasons why art education is a really important subject
③ importance of artistic activities to promote learners' creativity
④ art education for fostering children's sense of independence
⑤ art education as a tool for developing children's personality

2. 다음 글의 밑줄 친 부분 중, 어법상 틀린 것은? [3점]

The most astonishing thing about trees is how social they are. The trees in a forest care for each other, sometimes even going so far as to nourish the stump of a felled tree for centuries by feeding it sugars and other nutrients, and so keeping it ① alive. A tree's most important means of staying connected to other trees is a "wood wide web" of soil fungi that connects vegetation in an intimate network. Scientific research aimed at understanding the astonishing abilities of this partnership between fungi and plants ② have only just begun. The reason trees share food and communicate is that they need each other. It takes a forest to create the unique atmospheric conditions ③ where trees can grow and thrive. So it's not surprising that isolated trees have far shorter lives than ④ those living together in forests. Perhaps the saddest plants of all are the plants we have enslaved in our agricultural systems. They seem ⑤ to have lost the ability to communicate a long time ago, and are thus rendered deaf and dumb.

*stump: (나무의) 그루터기

3. 다음 빈칸에 들어갈 말로 가장 적절한 것은? [3점]

"What is the sum of 5 plus 5?" "What two numbers add up to 10?" The first question has only one right answer, and the second question has an infinite number of solutions, including negative numbers and fractions. These two problems, which rely on simple addition, differ only in the way they are framed. In fact, all questions are the frame into which the answers fall. And as you can see, by changing the frame, you can dramatically change the range of possible solutions. Albert Einstein is quoted as saying, "If I had an hour to solve a problem and my life depended on the solution, I would spend the first fifty-five minutes determining the proper question to ask, for once I know the proper question, I could solve the problem in less than five minutes." _____ is an important tool for increasing your imagination because it unlocks a vast array of solutions.

① Letting your mind flow freely
② Being willing to learn new things
③ Removing stereotypes and prejudices
④ Mastering the ability to reframe problems
⑤ Expanding your interests by shifting your focus

4. 다음 글에서 전체 흐름과 관계 <u>없는</u> 문장은?

Observation can offer ethnographers solid evidence of demonstrated behaviors occurring within a specific environment at a specific time. ① Observational skills help, for instance, when we want to use people's actions to independently verify their spoken claims; describe and make sense of what is happening when no one can — or will — talk with us; and better capture higher-level patterns of behavior especially regarding objects and environments. ② Systematic, observation-based data can help us both find out what is actually going on and justify our claims to others. ③ But observation only gives clues and partial answers as to *why* things happen and the meanings actors attribute to them. ④ To avoid such an observational bias we have to carefully design the study questionnaire. ⑤ This is why direct observation should be combined with other methods of understanding to address most ethnographers' problems of interest.

*ethnographer: 민족지학자 ((민족학 연구와 관련된 자료를 수집·기록하는 학자))

**verify: 입증하다, (진실인지) 확인하다

5. 다음 글의 내용을 한 문장으로 요약하고자 한다. 빈칸 (A), (B)에 들어갈 말로 가장 적절한 것은?

In one study conducted by business school professor Frank Flynn and a former doctoral student, Vanessa Lake, participants were asked to estimate how many strangers they would need to approach in order to get 5 people to fill out a short questionnaire. The average estimate was about 20 people. When the participants actually tried to get people to fill out the short questionnaire, they only needed to approach about 10 people on average to get 5 to comply with the request. Asking for some small help from strangers was apparently so uncomfortable that about one in five of the study participants did not complete the task. This dropout rate is much higher than typical in experiments where almost everyone finishes once they agree to participate. In another study, people estimated they would need to approach 10 strangers to let them borrow their cell phone to make a short call — the actual number approached to reach the target of 3 acceptances was 6.2.

↓

> According to the study, people who are thinking of making a request have a tendency to ____(A)____ the likelihood that the recipient of their request will actually ____(B)____ it.

	(A)		(B)
①	maximize	......	deny
②	maximize	......	accept
③	underestimate	......	deny
④	underestimate	......	accept
⑤	predict	......	accept

1. 다음 빈칸에 들어갈 말로 가장 적절한 것은? [3점]

The intriguing thing about the effects of censoring information is not that audience members want to have the information more than they did before; that seems natural. Rather, it is that they come to believe in the information more, even though they haven't received it. For example, when University of North Carolina students learned that a speech opposing coed dorms on campus would be banned, they became more opposed to the idea of coed dorms. Thus, without ever hearing the speech, they became more sympathetic to its argument. This raises the worrisome possibility that especially clever individuals holding a weak or unpopular position can get us to agree with that position by _____ _____. The irony is that for such people — members of fringe political groups, for example — the most effective strategy may not be to publicize their unpopular views, but to get those views officially censored and then to publicize the censorship.

*coed dorm: (대학의) 남녀 공용 기숙사 **fringe: 비주류

① provoking sympathy for their weakness
② arranging to have their message restricted
③ setting forth their views as often as possible
④ providing enough evidence in their argument
⑤ forming public opinion to remove the censorship

2. 주어진 글 다음에 이어질 글의 순서로 가장 적절한 것은? [3점]

Much social life involves belonging to secondary groups without knowing or interacting with most group members. For an individual to interact with any more than a small fraction of the more than 300 million people living in the United States is impossible.

(A) It is formed because you cannot possibly meet most members of the group and can only speculate about what they must be like. It is nonetheless a community because people believe strongly in its existence and importance.

(B) Nonetheless, most Americans feel a strong emotional bond to their fellow citizens. Similarly, think about the students at your school. They know they belong to the same secondary group, and many of them are probably fiercely loyal to it.

(C) Yet, how many people at your school have you met? You have probably met no more than a small fraction of the total. One way to make sense of the paradox of intimacy despite distance is to think of your school or the United States as an "imagined community."

① (A) – (C) – (B)   ② (B) – (A) – (C)
③ (B) – (C) – (A)   ④ (C) – (A) – (B)
⑤ (C) – (B) – (A)

3. 글의 흐름으로 보아, 주어진 문장이 들어가기에 가장 적절한 곳은? [3점]

But they reduce the likelihood of accumulating greater benefits from exchange and cooperation with the same partner (and perhaps others) in the future.

Most people use reputation as a proxy for integrity. But there's a problem with such a strategy. Contrary to common belief, integrity isn't a stable trait: Someone who has been fair and honest in the past won't necessarily be fair and honest in the future. (①) To understand why, we need to abandon the notion that people wrestle with "good" and "evil" impulses. (②) Except in cases of serious psychopathology, their brains don't work that way, and, rather, they focus on two types of gains: short-term and long-term. (③) And it's the trade-off between them that typically dictates integrity at any given moment. (④) Individuals who break a trust — by promising work they won't or can't deliver, for instance — may reap an immediate reward. (⑤) Which outcome is better for them depends on the situation and the parties involved.

*proxy: 대리, 대용물

[4~5] 다음 글을 읽고, 물음에 답하시오.

Winning the lottery is a happy event, but the excitement does not last. On average, individuals with high income are in a better mood than those with lower income, but the difference is about a third as (a) large as most people predict. When you think of rich and poor people, your thoughts are naturally focused on income. But happiness depends on other factors more than it depends on income. This is a perfect example of the *focusing illusion*, which is the name given to the tendency of people to focus on one aspect of a product or situation. In this example, the idea of winning the lottery naturally leads people to think only about money, and obviously more is (b) better. Nevertheless, lottery winners still have to deal with health issues, relationships, boredom, etc., but the focusing illusion (c) blinds us to this.

Marketers (d) exploit the focusing illusion. Usually, they greatly exaggerate the difference that the good will make to the quality of a consumer's life. Marketers are skilled at making people think that a new smartphone will greatly (e) decrease their productivity, or that a new car will allow them a greater level of freedom that will in turn have a huge impact on their quality of life. For better or worse, these purchases will make a difference in the life of the consumer, but the difference will be smaller than predicted.

4. 윗글의 제목으로 가장 적절한 것은?

① Attack the Problem, Never the Person
② Be Satisfied With What You Have Achieved
③ Things More Important than Money in Life
④ Nothing in Life Is as Important as You Think
⑤ Everybody Remains the Same Without a Challenge

5. 밑줄 친 (a)~(e) 중에서 문맥상 낱말의 쓰임이 적절하지 않은 것은? [3점]

① (a)   ② (b)   ③ (c)   ④ (d)   ⑤ (e)

1. 다음 글의 요지로 가장 적절한 것은?

It's tempting to see a strong dividing line between philosophy and science. After all, science is precise and defined by proven, concrete facts, whereas philosophy goes beyond the facts and into areas of speculation that probably can never be proven. Still, there is considerable overlap. Science may rely on cold, hard facts, but its directions have been determined by philosophy more than by any other area of study. The scientific method itself grew out of philosophical inquiry into the natures of meaning, truth, and knowledge, and these inquiries continue today in the fields of philosophy. At the same time, the philosophy of ethics determines the types of experiments we allow our scientists to carry out. In the end, one may be concerned with observable data and the other with meanings and values, but neither science nor philosophy exists in a vacuum.

① 철학과 과학은 사회 발전을 견인한다.
② 철학과 과학은 서로 영향을 주고받는다.
③ 현대 철학은 예전의 방법론을 탈피해야 한다.
④ 철학적 방법론은 과학적 방법론에 비해 한계가 있다.
⑤ 철학이 없는 과학은 필연적으로 윤리적 문제를 야기한다.

2. 다음 빈칸에 들어갈 말로 가장 적절한 것은? [3점]

Each dolphin has its own vocalization that is referred to as a signature-whistle, and it will remain relatively unchanged throughout the animal's relatively long lifetime. Research has revealed that dolphins can remember at least eight different signature-whistles and playback experiments suggest that they can use them to reliably discriminate between individuals. The whistles are used in a variety of behavioral contexts, but during studies of captive animals Vincent Janik and Peter Slater have shown that they are particularly commonly heard in situations where an animal has become isolated from the other members of its pod. It is supposed that these animals effectively call out their "name" when they emit their signature-whistle and thereby broadcast their identity and give away their location. Once the separated animals are reunited signature-whistle broadcasting stops. So at least one function of the whistles is _____ _____.

*pod: (고래, 물개 등의) 작은 무리, 떼

① the warning of impending danger
② the defence of a group's territory
③ the maintenance of group cohesion
④ the signature of aggressive behavior
⑤ the strategy for dealing with alienation

3. 다음 글에서 전체 흐름과 관계 <u>없는</u> 문장은?

The strategies and responses of human populations to massive outbreaks of disease have been remarkably similar. ① Because illness was so often attributed to divine providence, many societies developed ceremonies, sacrifices, and processions designed to appease the gods. ② In Christian communities one of the most common responses to the appearance of epidemic disease was the organization of religious processions during which clergy and laypeople removed the images of saints from their churches and carried them through the streets of the community, praying for divine mercy. ③ During an epidemic in Paris in 1466, for example, thousands turned out to watch the remains of Saints Crepin and Crepinien being paraded through the streets. ④ Nevertheless, during times of widespread sickness, many people in Paris did flee, abandoning home and family in the process. ⑤ Ironically, bringing large numbers of people together for public gatherings actually facilitated the spread of contagious illnesses and may, in fact, have worsened epidemics in many cases.

*divine providence: 신의 섭리 **appease: 달래다

4. 주어진 글 다음에 이어질 글의 순서로 가장 적절한 것은?

Anyone who has ever stayed out in the rain too long or soaked for hours in a tub knows their hands and feet can become wrinkled. Conventional wisdom suggests it is little more than the skin absorbing water.

(A) Now a paper in the journal *Brain, Behavior and Evolution* offers evidence that wet wrinkles serve a purpose. Similar to the tread on a tire, they improve traction. In the study, an evolutionary neurobiologist and his co-authors examined 28 fingers wrinkled by water.

(B) They found that they all had a pattern of wrinkles that split like the branches of a tree. This branching pattern allows water to drain away from the fingertips, allowing for more skin contact and better grip.

(C) But a number of questions have puzzled scientists. Why do "wet wrinkles" appear only on the hands and feet? And why are the most prominent wrinkles at the ends of the digits?

*tread: (타이어의) 접지면 **traction: 견인력, 정지 마찰력

① (A) – (C) – (B)　　　② (B) – (A) – (C)
③ (B) – (C) – (A)　　　④ (C) – (A) – (B)
⑤ (C) – (B) – (A)

5. 글의 흐름으로 보아, 주어진 문장이 들어가기에 가장 적절한 곳은? [3점]

Negative affect thus improved the accurate distinction of truths from lies in the observed interviews.

To explore the effects of mood on communication, researchers asked either happy or sad participants to accept or reject the videotaped statements of targets who were questioned after a staged theft, and were either guilty, or not guilty. (①) The targets were instructed to either steal or leave in place a movie pass in an empty room, unobserved by anyone, and then deny taking the movie ticket. (②) So some targets were lying and some were telling the truth when denying the theft. (③) Those in a positive mood were more likely to accept denials as truthful. (④) Sad participants made significantly more guilty judgements, and were significantly better at correctly detecting deceptive (guilty) targets. (⑤) A signal detection analysis also confirmed that sad judges were more accurate in detecting deception (identifying guilty targets as guilty) than were neutral or happy judges, consistent with the predicted mood-induced processing differences.

*staged: 일부러 꾸민

1. 다음 글의 제목으로 가장 적절한 것은?

We all know from experience that some of our dreams seem to be related to daily problems, some are vague and incoherent, and some are anxiety dreams that occur when we are worried or depressed. But whatever the source of the images in our sleeping brains may be, we need to be cautious about interpreting our own dreams or anyone else's. A recent study of people showed that individuals are biased and self-serving in their dream interpretations, accepting those that fit in with their preexisting beliefs or needs and rejecting those that do not. For example, they will give more weight to a dream in which God commands them to take a year off to travel the world than one in which God commands them to take a year off to work in a relief camp. Our biased interpretations may tell us more about ourselves than do our actual dreams.

① Dreams: A Bridge Between Spirit and Ego
② Cognitive Patterns in Dreams and Daydreams
③ Our Dream Interpretation Is Affected by Our Ego
④ Dream Interpretation Offers Valuable Insight to Us
⑤ Methods of Dream Interpretation: What Do Dreams Mean?

2. 다음 글의 밑줄 친 부분 중, 문맥상 낱말의 쓰임이 적절하지 않은 것은?

Broadly speaking, art exists as a consequence of the universal human desire for sympathy. Man is forever endeavoring to break down the wall which ① separates him from his fellows. Whether we call it egotism or simply humanity, we all know the wish to make others ② appreciate our feelings; to show them how we suffer, how we enjoy. We batter our fellowmen with our opinions sufficiently often, but this is ③ nothing in comparison to the insistence with which we pour out our feelings. A friend is the most valued of earthly possessions largely because he is willing to receive without appearance of ④ patience the unending story of our mental sensations. We are all more or less conscious of the constant impulse which urges us on to ⑤ expression; of the inner necessity which moves us to continual endeavors to make others share our thoughts, our experiences, but most of all our emotions. It seems to me that if we trace this instinctive desire back far enough, we reach the beginnings of art.

*batter: 난타하다, 연타하다

3. 다음 빈칸에 들어갈 말로 가장 적절한 것은? [3점]

The thousands of infants who will be born today across the world will experience very different environments in their first two years. Some will be cared for by grandmothers or older sisters; some will attend day care centers; some will remain at home with their mothers. Some will have many toys; some will have not one. Some will spend the first year in a dark, quiet hut wrapped in old rags; some will crawl in brightly lit rooms full of toys, picture books, and television images. But despite these differences, excluding the small proportion with serious brain damage or a genetic defect, most will speak before they are two years old, become self-conscious by the third birthday, and be able to assume some family responsibilities by age seven. The psychological differences among these children _____. The prevalence of serious mental disorders like schizophrenia and depression, as well as the less impairing anxiety disorders, is surprisingly similar around the world, even though children are being reared in different environments.

*schizophrenia: 조현병

① make them the isolated from their community
② provoke many and varied emotional responses
③ give them opportunities to make relationships with peers
④ are trivial when compared with the long list of similarities
⑤ are reduced when the stimuli are more varied and complex

72

4. 다음 글에서 전체 흐름과 관계 <u>없는</u> 문장은?

While in animals, as in humans, the expression of emotions via facial expressions is more or less invariable, the context in which those emotions are triggered and expressed is very context specific, and relates to socialization, individual relationships, and other factors. ① For example, we are more able to read the facial expressions of those with whom we are intimate. ② Moreover, we humans can mask our emotions by using a false facial expression, and many animals can do this too, as is seen when an animal with a blank face surprises another while play fighting. ③ While there are some key traits that are unique to humans, like kinship, there are many important similarities that we share with nonhuman primates. ④ Finally, like humans, nonhuman animals — especially primate — can mimic the facial expressions of other animals. ⑤ Orangutans, for instance, when playing with other orangutans, will almost immediately react to a play-smile with one of their own.

5. 다음 글의 내용을 한 문장으로 요약하고자 한다. 빈칸 (A), (B)에 들어갈 말로 가장 적절한 것은?

Dove's Real Beauty Campaign began nearly a decade ago, and it's been selling a powerful message in various ways. On April 15, 2013, Dove launched a 3-minute video entitled "Dove Real Beauty Sketches." The video achieved instant popularity and has been watched millions of times — a successful viral campaign which has been widely talked about. In the video, a small group of women are asked to describe their faces to a person whom they cannot see. The person is a forensic artist who is there to draw pictures of the women based on their verbal descriptions. A curtain separates the artist and the women, and they never see each other. Before all this, each woman is asked to socialize with a stranger, who later separately describes the woman to the forensic artist. In the end, the women are shown the two drawings, one based on their own description, the other based on the stranger's description. Much to their amazement and delight, the women realize that the drawings based on strangers' descriptions depict much more beautiful women.

*forensic: 범죄 과학 수사의

↓

In a Dove campaign comparing how we view ourselves and how others see us, the participants' descriptions revealed that women are clearly their own _____(A)_____, while others think they are _____(B)_____.

	(A)		(B)
①	critics	......	attractive
②	critics	......	plain
③	supporters	......	appealing
④	supporters	......	plain
⑤	fans	......	attractive

1. 다음 빈칸에 들어갈 말로 가장 적절한 것은? [3점]

Over half the human population of the planet now lives in cities, and the proportion is likely to continue to increase in the foreseeable future. Building in cities is becoming more and more important, and urban form and urban architecture are the focus of much debate. Some architects have decided to respond to what they perceive to be the potentially formless and anonymous nature of the city by creating buildings that are obviously strange and are intended to become urban landmarks. One of the simplest ways of making a building look unusual is to break the normal rules of structure — or at least make it seem as if gravity is of no consequence. Such buildings make difficult demands on structural engineers, who have to _____ _____.

① design the buildings to be easily recognized from various angles
② negotiate the tension between practicality and beauty of a building
③ achieve anything that brings themselves both reputation and status
④ understand both the technological evolution and architectural aesthetics
⑤ make paradoxical forms work while concealing how the trick is pulled off

2. 주어진 글 다음에 이어질 글의 순서로 가장 적절한 것은? [3점]

The world has made huge investments in the facilities that extract fossil fuels from the ground and burn them — mines, oil wells, power stations, hundreds of thousands of ships and aircraft, a billion motor vehicles.

(A) If the world had the capacity to deliver one of the largest nuclear power plants ever built once a week, week in and week out, it would take 20 years to replace the current stock of coal-fired plants (at present, the world builds about three or four nuclear power plants a year, and retires old ones almost as quickly).

(B) Leaving aside the political lobbying power that such investment can command, there would be a limit to how quickly that much kit could be replaced even if there were perfect substitute technologies to hand that simply needed scaling up.

(C) To replace those coal plants with solar panels at the rate such panels were installed in 2013 would take about a century and a half. That is all before starting on replacing the gas and the oil, the cars, the furnaces and the ships.

① (A) – (C) – (B)　　② (B) – (A) – (C)
③ (B) – (C) – (A)　　④ (C) – (A) – (B)
⑤ (C) – (B) – (A)

3. 글의 흐름으로 보아, 주어진 문장이 들어가기에 가장 적절한 곳은?

An alternative is to connect a noisemaker to a motion detector, auditory sensor, or infrared sensor that activates the noisemaker whenever an animal is detected.

The more animals are exposed to a fear-provoking stimulus, the sooner they will become habituated to it. (①) For this reason, shell-crackers should be used sparingly and propane cannons should be set to fire only once or twice per hour. (②) Ideally, a propane cannon or other auditory stimuli should fire only when wildlife are close to it. (③) One way to accomplish this is to have the noisemaker remotely controlled by someone who fires it only when an animal is nearby. (④) This, however, is too labor-intensive to be practical for most wildlife control problems. (⑤) For instance, Belant et al. discovered that deer habituated less rapidly to motion-activated gas exploders than to those that fired at timed intervals.

*shell-cracker: (해로운 새나 야생 동물을 쫓을 때 사용하는) 폭죽

[4~5] 다음 글을 읽고, 물음에 답하시오.

As social psychologists have come to recognize that creativity can (a) change according to the situation and context, the interesting question has become: which circumstances make us creative? In a recent set of studies, psychologist Lile Jia at Indiana University looked into one possible factor influencing creativity. He randomly (b) divided a few dozen students into two groups, both of which were asked to name as many different modes of transportation as possible. (This is called a creative generation task.) One group of students was told that the task was developed by Indiana University students studying abroad in Greece, while the other group was told that the task was developed by Indiana University students studying in the state of Indiana.

At first glance, it seems (c) unlikely that such a difference would influence the performance of the subjects. Why would it matter where the task was developed? Nevertheless, Jia found a (d) striking difference between the two groups: when students were told that the task was brought over from Greece, they came up with significantly more transportation possibilities. They didn't just list buses, trains, and planes; they named horses, scooters, bicycles, and even spaceships. Because the source of the problem was far away, the subjects felt less (e) crowded by their local transport options; they didn't focus only on getting around in Indiana — they considered getting around all over the world and even in deep space.

4. 윗글의 제목으로 가장 적절한 것은?

① Repeated Research Makes People Creative
② Distance Leads to More Creative Thinking
③ Some Ways to Come Up with Creative Ideas
④ What Is the Most Effective Form of Transportation?
⑤ Travel to a Foreign Country Makes You More Creative

5. 밑줄 친 (a)~(e) 중에서 문맥상 낱말의 쓰임이 적절하지 않은 것은? [3점]

① (a) ② (b) ③ (c) ④ (d) ⑤ (e)

1. 다음 글에서 필자가 주장하는 바로 가장 적절한 것은?

Any good theory of argument must admit that emotional appeals and responses should be balanced against cognitive considerations. But on the other hand, in most of the major personal decisions in life, sensitivity to emotions and feelings of one's own, in addition to those of others, is extremely important. Any theory of argument that ignores such appeals altogether must be a very limited theory, inapplicable to many, significant everyday situations. Especially in common-sense reasoning, which is so common, for instance, in controversial political debates concerning choice of policy or candidate, instinct and emotional reaction, always subject to critical reflection, have an important place. To declare that any conclusion resulting even partly from an appeal to emotion must be false is an ineffective and even misguided approach.

① 논쟁 시에 감정적 요소를 개입시켜서는 안 된다.
② 논쟁에 감정이 개입하는 불가피성을 인정해야 한다.
③ 타인의 주장을 감정적 요소를 배제하고 판단해야 한다.
④ 감정적 논쟁을 사전에 막는 토론 장치를 만들어야 한다.
⑤ 논쟁의 여지가 많은 토론일수록 객관성을 견지해야 한다.

2. 밑줄 친 are 90 percent chimp and 10 percent bee가 다음 글에서 의미하는 바로 가장 적절한 것은?

My father was a basketball coach, so as a kid I accompanied him to practice every day. As I grew older, I was at the gym or on the sports field from dawn to dusk. This investment of time and energy eventually led to a basketball scholarship at a university in southern Ohio. As a basketball player, I learned very early about the paradox of team sports — the tension between individual and collective competition. During practice, athletes competed with fellow teammates for playing time, just as chimps fight fiercely to have a bigger share of food. When game day rolled around, however, teammates were required to put all of their individual rivalries aside and became like bees working for the sake of the hive. We came together as a cohesive unit for the higher purpose of defeating the opposing foe. While this is difficult to accomplish, humans possess the equipment to pull this off under the right conditions. We can do this because we are by nature 'homo duplex.' As Jonathan Haidt puts it, we are 90 percent chimp and 10 percent bee.

① are inherently social, but sometimes enjoy being alone
② are fundamentally greedy, yet benevolent to our families
③ are excellent in reasoning, but often make errors of judgment
④ are aggressive in nature, yet try to be friendly to others
⑤ are primarily self-serving, yet cooperative creatures

3. 다음 빈칸에 들어갈 말로 가장 적절한 것은? [3점]

Creativity is about "connecting the dots" — making connections between things that have never before been linked. It is the ability to recognize the possibilities that exist within any scenario and the opportunities in every situation. Changing the game starts with seeing the unseen within even the ordinary. Out of a plain slab of marble, Michelangelo carved his best work. German philosopher Arthur Schopenhauer once said, "Talent hits a target no one else can hit. Genius hits a target no one else can see." Creative solutions and breakthroughs come from viewing something differently and discovering what others have missed. Patents for novel ideas, processes and methodologies are simply the tangible results of someone seeing something differently than the world had ever seen it before. _____ _____ when people come along who see how to connect the dots, apply multiple perspectives and build a bridge between unrelated ideas.

*slab: 평판 **tangible: 실제적인

① Brains work
② Analyses start
③ Paradigms shift
④ Persistence pays
⑤ Enthusiasm retreats

4. 주어진 글 다음에 이어질 글의 순서로 가장 적절한 것은?

In 1890, Kodak introduced a cheap consumer camera that everyone could afford. This put the portrait studios out of business; the newly unemployed photographers needed a way to distinguish between what they did and this new popular photography.

(A) They presented their works in art galleries, next to paintings. The elements of an art world began to form: collegial groups called "photo clubs," a journal called *Camera Work*, and shows and openings.

(B) The movement of *pictorialism* was the response, with photographers attempting to imitate the artistic processes of painting; rather than reproducible photos, they worked directly on the negatives and other materials of the process.

(C) However, art photography remained marginalized; there were no markets, buyers, or collectors, and museums were not interested in adding photos to their collections. Pictorialism eventually died out with the outbreak of World War I.

*negative: (사진의) 원판

① (A) – (C) – (B)　　② (B) – (A) – (C)
③ (B) – (C) – (A)　　④ (C) – (A) – (B)
⑤ (C) – (B) – (A)

5. 글의 흐름으로 보아, 주어진 문장이 들어가기에 가장 적절한 곳은? [3점]

Initially, the group may simply go through the process of converting files or rewriting documents, rather than abandoning the program for one that is more appropriate.

Problem definition is affected by social context in any domain. Individuals can become unable to redefine problems or evaluate progress on current problems due to the attitudes of the group. (①) For example, in an office environment, individuals may be familiar with a particular computer application for word processing. (②) However, the program eventually may become outdated or unsupported. (③) Here the problem has become not word processing, but rather the word processing program itself. (④) The problem is not particularly difficult to spot, but the ways of the group may be so entrenched that changing programs becomes an unacceptable option. (⑤) In other words, the attitudes of a group can be pervasive in the decision process of the individual.

*entrenched: 깊게 뿌리박힌

1. 다음 글의 주제로 가장 적절한 것은?

Not everyone perceives the taste of apple pie the same way. There is considerable genetic variation among individuals in sensitivity to basic tastes. Tasting abilities may also vary within the individual, depending on a number of outside influences. One such factor affecting taste is the temperature of a food or beverage. Taste buds operate best at temperatures of around 30℃. As the temperature of foods or beverages goes below 20℃ or above 30℃, it becomes harder to distinguish their tastes accurately. For example, very hot coffee tastes less bitter, whereas slightly melted ice cream tastes sweeter. Psychological factors, such as preconceived ideas based on appearance or on previous experiences with a similar food, also affect a person's perception of taste. For instance, cherry-flavored foods are expected to be red, but if they are colored yellow, they become difficult to identify as cherry. Also, unpleasant experiences associated with a food may influence the perceived taste of that food in the future.

*taste bud(s): (혀의) 미뢰[맛봉오리]

① various factors that affect the perception of tastes
② reasons why taste buds are affected by temperature
③ the necessity to stop using artificial coloring in foods
④ the effect of climate on the development of preserved foods
⑤ the relationship between temperature and preference of tastes

2. 다음 글의 밑줄 친 부분 중, 어법상 틀린 것은? [3점]

Low self-esteem can make you feel as if you don't deserve success. Even if things are going well, you'll sabotage yourself just ① because of the mistaken belief you don't deserve to achieve your goal. Building self-esteem starts with self-awareness and self-monitoring. When you start monitoring your inner critic and replacing bad thoughts with positive ② ones, you'll be on your way to killing your self-critical voice. Making a list of positive attributes you believe you possess ③ is another useful technique to improve your self-esteem. The key is to be honest and write the list without any judgments. Once it's ready, re-read it every single day until you understand ④ what you're not as worthless as you think. Another useful method is to become kinder toward other people. When you treat other people well, they will return the favor, thus ⑤ making you feel better about yourself.

3. 다음 빈칸에 들어갈 말로 가장 적절한 것은? [3점]

The amount of distance between the teacher and his/her students and perceived or actual barriers can have a significant impact on communication. Teachers who stay securely ensconced behind the 'barricade' of their desk automatically create a boundary that blocks effective interpersonal contact and gives a territorial feel to the room. The use of proximity, on the other hand, can be a powerful behaviour management tool. Firm reminders and warnings are best conducted privately and discreetly (it reduces embarrassment or threat to the student and minimizes the spectator effect, both of which can fuel a challenge or counter-attack). Getting down to the student's eye level (and not towering over him/her in a threatening way) models consideration and invites the student to respond in an equally respectful way. However, unless the classroom is organized in such a way as _____ _____, this will be problematic and the teacher may resort to making public scolding.

*ensconce: 편히 앉히다 **proximity: 근접성

① to facilitate various types of group activities
② to encourage children to work independently
③ to take advantage of a child's innate curiosity
④ to promote positive interactions between children
⑤ to allow the teacher to access individual students

4. 다음 글에서 전체 흐름과 관계 없는 문장은?

Culture is the primary factor affecting the way in which man responds to the environment, and since there is a wide variety of cultures, there is a wide variety of cultural responses, even to the same environment. ① For example, in the Fijian Islands of the Pacific, two distinct cultures can be identified, each with a different relationship with the environment. ② On the one hand, there is the old Melanesian culture, whose members utilize the environment to grow a small range of subsistence crops and whose wants are very limited. ③ In contrast, there are the new Melanesians, largely Indian immigrants, who have a much more Westernized view of the environment, growing cash crops such as sugar cane for export. ④ Thus, all environments have both positive and negative features, and the most dangerous and unpredictable environments may be the most desirable. ⑤ Similar contrasts can be found throughout the world, between Chinese and Malay in Malaysia, African and European in Kenya, and Indian and Latino in Mexico.

*subsistence: 생계

5. 다음 글의 내용을 한 문장으로 요약하고자 한다. 빈칸 (A), (B)에 들어갈 말로 가장 적절한 것은?

Psychologist Ersner-Hershfield conducted an experiment attempting to learn how he could increase people's inclinations to delay gratification for the future. Before the experiment began, he took pictures of the participants and used software to create digital avatars of them. Half of the participants had avatars of their current selves, while the avatars for the other half were aged with wrinkles, and gray hair. The subjects then explored virtual environments as their avatars, eventually coming to a mirror reflecting either their current or future self. Following the virtual reality experience, participants were asked how they would allocate $1,000 given four options — buying a gift for somebody special, investing in a retirement fund, planning a fun event, or depositing the money into a checking account. Those that had seen an aged version of themselves reflected in the virtual mirror, which made that future self seem much less like a stranger, put nearly double the amount of money into the retirement fund than the other participants.

↓

> According to the experiment, ____(A)____ our future self helps to better connect ourselves to our future, and increases interest in setting ____(B)____ financial goals.

	(A)		(B)
①	judging	······	high-return
②	modifying	······	long-term
③	creating	······	high-return
④	visualizing	······	long-term
⑤	describing	······	low-risk

1. 다음 글의 빈칸에 들어갈 말로 가장 적절한 것은? [3점]

A curious fact about names based on places is that they are so often obscure — usually from places that few people have heard of. Why should there be so many more Middletons than Londons, so many more Worthingtons than Bristols? The main cities of medieval Britain — London, York, Norwich, Glasgow — are relatively uncommon as surnames even though many thousands of people called those places home. To understand this apparent paradox, you must keep in mind that the function of surnames is _____. If a person called himself Peter of London, he would be just one of hundreds of such Peters and anyone searching for him would be at a loss. So as a rule a person would earn the name Peter of London only if he moved to a rural location, where London would be a clear identifying feature.

① to emphasize the importance of class and status
② to highlight the most interesting feature of the person
③ to distinguish one person or family from all the others
④ to establish bonds among various community members
⑤ to identify an individual's place of birth and background

2. 주어진 글 다음에 이어질 글의 순서로 가장 적절한 것은?

An interesting question related to processing fluency in organizations concerns how organizations gauge their employees' and customers' opinions. Consider the following example.

(A) Will the vocal employee's frequent requests bias the manager's sense of how the rest of the people in the organization feel about the policy? Research by Weaver, Garcia, Schwartz, and Miller suggests the answer is yes.

(B) A manager consistently gets requests from one employee that a company policy be changed. From those requests, the manager must decide how the other people in the organization feel about the issue in question.

(C) In a series of six experiments, they demonstrated that people have a tendency to infer that a familiar opinion is a prevalent one, even if the perceived familiarity is the result of one particularly vocal group member.

*prevalent: 일반적인, 널리 퍼진

① (A) – (C) – (B)　　② (B) – (A) – (C)
③ (B) – (C) – (A)　　④ (C) – (A) – (B)
⑤ (C) – (B) – (A)

3. 글의 흐름으로 보아, 주어진 문장이 들어가기에 가장 적절한 곳은?

After a few years, however, the soil is compacted and needs breaking up, and weeds have proliferated.

One of the reasons that farming spreads quickly once it has begun is that the first few crops are both more productive and more easily grown than later crops, so farmers are always eager to move on to uncultivated land. (①) If you burn down a forest, you are left with fertile soil. (②) All you need to do is dig a small hole in the ground, plant a seed, and wait for it to grow. (③) If you now let the ground rest to allow the fertility to build up again, the tough roots of weeds need to be removed to make a good seedbed — and for that you need a plough and an ox to pull it. (④) But an ox must be fed, so you need pasture as well as cultivable land. (⑤) It's no surprise that shifting agriculture remains so popular with many tribal people in forests to this day.

*proliferate: 급증하다, (빠르게) 확산되다

[4~5] 다음 글을 읽고, 물음에 답하시오.

Audience tend to take film naturally, without suspicion, and feel at ease with its conventions. They sit in a comfortable, darkened theater, free from most distractions, giving (a) optimal attention to a flickering image on the screen that is often the only source of light. The dark environment has a tendency to (b) produce a lowered defense reaction and a heightened emotional reaction. Psychologists Gordon Globus and Roy Shulman studied the effects of the darkness on the audience in the movie theater and concluded, "The darkness, immobility, relative lack of distractions, and isolation from objective reality-oriented interpersonal events causes the self to not tell the (c) difference between the real and the unreal. Additionally there is an increase of emotional arousal, and more primitive defenses are also invoked."

Film also engages an audience physiologically, for it surrounds its audience with visual and aural stimuli that (d) block the senses. A film makes its statement through composition, color, sound, and rhythm. The visual picture and the sound track engulf the eyes, ears, and mind all at once. Research conducted at the Psychological Institute of the University of Rome has revealed that the motion of film (e) provokes kinesthetic responses in the audience such as muscular reflexes, motor impulses, increased pulse rate, and other metabolic behavior. Movie theater owners have known this without the benefit of experimental research, for when they show horror pictures, they are often asked to increase the amount of air conditioning due to the increased perspiration of the excited viewers.

*engulf: 에워싸다 **kinesthetic: 운동 감각의

4. 윗글의 제목으로 가장 적절한 것은?

① Questions to Ask When We Watch a Movie
② Movies in Mind: Our Addiction to the Screen
③ Watching a Movie: It's Not Just for Art's Sake
④ Why Are Movies So Compelling and Attractive?
⑤ What Happens to Us When We Watch a Movie?

5. 밑줄 친 (a)~(e) 중에서 문맥상 낱말의 쓰임이 적절하지 <u>않은</u> 것은? [3점]

① (a)　　② (b)　　③ (c)　　④ (d)　　⑤ (e)

1. 다음 글의 요지로 가장 적절한 것은?

Socrates said, "dura lex, sed lex," which means the law is harsh, but it is the law. However, obeying the law is not always the right thing to do. In history, there have been many people who refused to follow unjust laws. Two remarkable examples are Mahatma Gandhi and Martin Luther King. Both of these men believed that the laws of their time were not fair. Mahatma Gandhi was against the British rule of India; he believed that Indians should control their own country. Martin Luther King was against the laws that discriminated against black people in the United States. Both of these men broke the law because they wanted to change the system they felt was wrong. Consequently, they made big differences in the history of human rights.

① 법이 모든 사람에게 공평한 것은 아니다.
② 특정 집단의 이익을 위한 법은 악법이다.
③ 인종을 차별하는 법이 가장 악한 법이다.
④ 부당한 법에는 대항해 싸울 필요가 있다.
⑤ 법이 모든 요구사항을 반영할 수는 없다.

2. 다음 빈칸에 들어갈 말로 가장 적절한 것은? [3점]

The origins of contemporary Western thought can be traced back to the golden age of ancient Greece in the sixth and fifth centuries BCE, when Greek thinkers formulated the basis for modern Western politics, philosophy, science, and law. Their novel approach was to pursue rational inquiry through _____ _____: The best way to evaluate one set of ideas, they believed, was by testing it against another set of ideas. In the political sphere, the result was democracy, in which supporters of rival policies vied for rhetorical supremacy; in philosophy, it led to reasoned arguments and dialogues about the nature of the world; in science, it prompted the development of competing theories to try to explain natural phenomena; in the field of law, the result was prosecutors and defense attorneys. This approach forms the foundation of the modern Western way of life, in which politics, commerce, science, and law are all rooted in orderly competition.

*vie for: ~을 위해 경쟁하다, 다투다

① constant practice
② adversarial discussion
③ voluntary participation
④ traditional knowledge
⑤ critical thinking

3. 다음 글에서 전체 흐름과 관계 없는 문장은?

An experience can be a particularly useful tool, but overexposure to something can develop an individual's mental baggage. ① When mental baggage is prevalent it can be difficult to consider any creative direction other than that of the overfamiliar, and it can be arduous to persuade others to explore an alternative path when they also have a preconceived notion of what the product is. ② It is only when things can be thought of differently, without accustomed barriers, that it is plausible to innovate markets. ③ If the problem is not confronted with a 'why attitude', similar to a small child constantly asking questions about something, it is almost impossible to understand and solve. ④ Curious children are aware of what is going on around them and don't usually see themselves as the center of the universe, which means that they are less likely to be selfish and spoiled. ⑤ In the event that mental baggage can be broken down through repeated enquiry and probing, it is likely that a delightful and practical proposal can emerge and be accepted broadly.

*arduous: 힘든

4. 주어진 글 다음에 이어질 글의 순서로 가장 적절한 것은?

> Perhaps the only difference between categories like "living cell" and "species" is that grouping organisms into species demands more conscious effort, because the ways of classifying the living are practically infinite.

(A) Eventually, the majority of them agreed that such a system should reflect an organism's position on the tree of life, its evolutionary history. Such classification not only organizes what we know about the living but tells us whether two organisms belong on the same branch of life's tree.

(B) One could classify organisms by shape, color, or taste; by their ability to lay eggs; and so on. Naturalists worked for centuries to create the best system of organizing life's boundless diversity.

(C) It places apes closer to humans than, say, mice, flies, or bacteria, simply because the common ancestor of humans and apes lived more recently than that of humans and mice, flies, or bacteria. Organizing life around this tree, however, presents a challenge. It requires reconstructing the history of life itself.

① (A) – (C) – (B)　　② (B) – (A) – (C)
③ (B) – (C) – (A)　　④ (C) – (A) – (B)
⑤ (C) – (B) – (A)

5. 글의 흐름으로 보아, 주어진 문장이 들어가기에 가장 적절한 곳은? [3점]

> But coaches of the same sports at big universities can become national celebrities who earn more than $1 million a year, equal to the salaries of college presidents.

The process of job advancement in the field of sports is often compared to the shape of a pyramid. (①) At the wide base are many jobs with youth or high school athletic teams, while at the narrow tip are the few, highly-coveted jobs with professional organizations. (②) Thus there are many sports jobs in total, but the competition becomes increasingly tough as one works his or her way up. (③) The salaries of various positions correspond to this pyramid model. (④) For example, high school football and basketball coaches are often teachers who get paid a little extra for their after-class work. (⑤) One level higher up are the National Football League and the National Basketball Association, where head coaches often receive many times more than their best-paid campus counterparts.

*covet: 탐내다, 갈망하다

1. 다음 글의 제목으로 가장 적절한 것은?

You're walking towards a forest through a grassy plain, and when you step into this forest, all of a sudden, the temperature is cool and the air is damp. You have entered a microclimate! Climate describes the weather in a place over a long period of time. "Micro-" means "small," so a microclimate is the climate of a small, restricted area that is different than the climate around it. There are a few ways microclimates can be made. The shape of the land can impact the area's weather. It can be natural or changed by humans. Houses, rocks, and cars can all change the climate in a small area. Lakes, streams, and even the ocean can change the climate of the areas nearest to them. This is because water gains and loses heat more slowly than land does. Soil can shape climate, too. Soils that hold lots of water, like the rich soils in the jungle, make the air wet and humid. Dry soils, like desert sand, do not hold water in the same way.

① Creating and Utilizing Microclimates
② Microclimates: Definition and Causes
③ What Benefits Do Microclimates Bring?
④ Microclimate Formation and Its Significance
⑤ Microclimate: A Double-Edged Sword of Farming

2. 다음 글의 밑줄 친 부분 중, 문맥상 낱말의 쓰임이 적절하지 않은 것은?

A quality of the human brain is known as *induction*, how something positive generates a ① contrasting negative image in our mind. This is most obvious in our visual system. When we see some color — red or black, for instance — it tends to ② intensify our perception of the opposite color around us, in this case, green or white. As we look at the red object, we often can see a green halo forming around it. In general, the mind operates by contrasts. We are able to ③ transform concepts about something by becoming aware of its opposite. The brain is continually dredging up these contrasts. What this means is that whenever we see or imagine something, our minds cannot help but see or imagine the opposite. If we are ④ forbidden by our culture to think a particular thought or entertain a particular desire, that taboo instantly brings to mind the very thing we are prohibited from. Every no sparks a corresponding yes. We cannot control this vacillation in the mind between contrasts. This predisposes us to think about and then ⑤ desire exactly what we do not have.

*halo: 후광 **dredge up: ~을 떠올리다 ***vacillation: 동요, 흔들림

3. 다음 빈칸에 들어갈 말로 가장 적절한 것은? [3점]

We are obsessed with having as many irons as possible in the fire, ruling nothing out, and being open to everything. However, this can often get in the way of success. We must learn to close doors. A business strategy is first and foremost a statement on what not to engage in. Adopt a life strategy similar to a corporate strategy: Write down what not to pursue in your life. In other words, make deliberate decisions to disregard certain possibilities and when an option presents itself, test it against your not-to-pursue list. It will not only keep you from trouble but also save you lots of thinking time. Think hard once and then simply consult your list instead of needing to make up your mind whenever a new door cracks open. Most doors _____ _____, even when the handle seems to turn so effortlessly.

① aren't really closed
② are difficult to enter
③ are not worth entering
④ lead to opportunities
⑤ close in your face

4. 다음 글에서 전체 흐름과 관계 <u>없는</u> 문장은?

Have you ever been watching someone play golf on TV and found yourself involuntarily moving in the direction of his swing? ① Obviously, your conscious brain is aware that you are sitting on the couch eating potato chips, but another small part of your brain — the part where the mirror neurons reside — believes you are out on that green. ② Then, because mirror neurons are often just beside motor neurons in the brain, copied feelings result in copied actions — suddenly you are moving like you're swinging a golf club without even knowing it. ③ This is why smiles become contagious and why babies automatically mimic the funny faces their parents make. ④ It is not normally possible to study single neurons in the human brain, so most evidence for mirror neurons in humans is indirect. ⑤ And it's why watching someone get elbowed in the face in Brisbane immediately caused rugby fans in Sydney to reach toward their own faces in agony.

5. 다음 글의 내용을 한 문장으로 요약하고자 한다. 빈칸 (A)와 (B)에 들어갈 말로 가장 적절한 것은?

It is quite clear that technology choices are never made by determining, in a narrowly technical sense of 'best', which device best performs the task in question. The 'best' chosen is relative to all sorts of constraints other than those of performing a certain technical task as well as possible. This is another way of saying that the problems technology is introduced to solve are never purely technical problems. Technologies, to be widely adopted, have to be mass manufactured, marketed, purchased and used successfully. The extra constraints thus derive from the contexts in which the device is to be manufactured, purchased and used. Many of these have to do with material infrastructure and existing practices, which of course vary from one country to another and have a variety of relevant aspects.

↓

> Technologies are never adopted solely based on ____(A)____ properties; the adoption is also determined by a variety of other ____(B)____ surrounding the decision.

	(A)		(B)
①	technical	⋯⋯	restrictions
②	technical	⋯⋯	superpowers
③	economic	⋯⋯	innovations
④	cultural	⋯⋯	restrictions
⑤	cultural	⋯⋯	superpowers

1. 다음 빈칸에 들어갈 말로 가장 적절한 것은? [3점]

We make decisions based on our strongest inclination at the moment. This is a simple fact — try to think of a choice you have made that was not in accord with your strongest inclination. However, we sometimes get confused about this because we are assaulted with a wide variety of inclinations, and they _____ _____. For example, after finishing a large meal, it is easy to decide to go on a diet. After a few hours, however, we become hungry again and the desire for food grows. If our desire to eat some pie surpasses our desire to lose weight, we choose the pie over the diet. All things being equal, we may want to shed excess weight. We truly want to be slim, but that goal is in conflict with our love of culinary pleasures. The problem is that all things do not stay equal.

① consist of goals we've created
② grow in strength as time passes
③ conflict with our true objectives
④ hinder us from making decisions
⑤ change in intensity from time to time

2. 주어진 글 다음에 이어질 글의 순서로 가장 적절한 것은?

Adam Smith recommended the establishment of universal public schooling, largely at government expense, so that even the poor could acquire the essential skills of reading, writing, and arithmetic.

(A) Instead, he offered a plan to make it more accessible and more practical. He suggested offering support to encourage parents to have their children educated.
(B) This suggestion went against the prevailing wisdom of the dominant classes in Britain, who feared it would discourage deference. However, Smith did not advocate making schooling compulsory.

(C) Such incentives were necessary because, as Smith knew, the spread of manufacture supported by the division of labor, by making it possible for children to be employed at income-generating tasks, led many parents to send even very young children out to work.

*arithmetic: 연산, 산술, 계산 **deference: 복종, 존경, 경의

① (A) – (C) – (B)   ② (B) – (A) – (C)
③ (B) – (C) – (A)   ④ (C) – (A) – (B)
⑤ (C) – (B) – (A)

3. 글의 흐름으로 보아, 주어진 문장이 들어가기에 가장 적절한 곳은?

The Slow Food movement's prime concern is to protect the diverse, local traditions responsible for artisanal food production and encourage people to eat local ingredients.

Food politics is not a new phenomenon. (①) A battle over the production of bread in Paris was the occasion of Marie Antoinette's unfortunate remark about eating cake, and increases in prices or taxes on food have provoked revolt in countless countries including colonial America. (②) But in Europe in the twenty-first century, food politics is directed not at scarcity or justice but at identity. (③) The threatened loss of specific tastes and the local cultures that produce them animate this movement. (④) They deploy the aesthetic and symbolic content of food in a search for a more authentic lifestyle anchored in local traditions, which then becomes the idiom through which political mobilization occurs. (⑤) Thus, the Slow Food movement understands the food artisan, not as a conservative standing in the way of progress but as someone charged with the preservation of local heritage.

*artisanal: 장인의 **deploy: 활용하다

[4~5] 다음 글을 읽고, 물음에 답하시오.

Can creators ever be objective in judging their own ideas? One of my former students, Justin Berg, is now a successful young professor at Stanford who has spent years investigating this question. Berg specializes in creative forecasting, the art of predicting the success of novel ideas. In one study, he showed different groups of people videos of circus performances and asked them to make projections about how well each would do. Circus artists from *Cirque du Soleil* and other organizations submitted predictions about how popular their videos would be. Circus managers watched the videos and registered their predictions, too.

To test the (a) accuracy of their forecasts, Berg then measured the actual success of each performance by tracking how much general audience members liked, shared, and funded the videos. He invited over thirteen thousand people to (b) rate the videos; they also had a chance to share them via Facebook, Twitter, Google+, and email, and received a ten-cent bonus that they could donate to the performers.

The creators proved to be terrible at judging how their performances would do with the test audiences. On average, when ranking their videos against the performances of nine other circus artists, they put their own work two slots too (c) low. The managers were more realistic; they had some distance from the performances, which put them in a more (d) neutral position. Social scientists have long known that we tend to be overconfident when we (e) evaluate ourselves.

*Cirque du Soleil: 태양의 서커스 ((캐나다의 세계적 서커스단))

4. 윗글의 제목으로 가장 적절한 것은?

① We Are Blind to Ourselves
② Words of Praise Work Wonders
③ The More Realistic, The More Artistic
④ Low Self-Esteem Suppresses Creativity
⑤ Life Lessons We Can Learn From the Circus

5. 밑줄 친 (a)~(e) 중에서 문맥상 낱말의 쓰임이 적절하지 <u>않은</u> 것은? [3점]

① (a)　　② (b)　　③ (c)　　④ (d)　　⑤ (e)

1. 다음 글에서 필자가 주장하는 바로 가장 적절한 것은?

Our tendency to overlook habit can be explained by one aspect of habit itself: the way in which familiarity and repetition dull our senses. Marcel Proust describes habit as a 'heavy curtain' which 'conceals from us almost the whole universe, and prevents us from knowing ourselves.' Not only this: habit 'cuts off from things which we have witnessed a number of times the root of profound impression and of thought which gives them their real meaning.' Proust realized that an artist has to draw back, or tear open, this curtain of habit, so that the most familiar features of our world become visible, meaningful, and cause for wonder. But this is also the philosopher's task. Although it is often said — quoting Plato or Aristotle — that philosophy begins with wonder, the wondering state of mind is only reached by first penetrating the heavy curtain of habit.

*penetrate: 꿰뚫다, 뚫고 들어가다

① 각 분야에 맞는 체계적인 습관을 형성해야 한다.
② 가장 오래된 습관일수록 가장 먼저 버려야 한다.
③ 습관을 타파하는 일은 철학자들에게 맡겨야 한다.
④ 세상과 자신을 더 잘 이해하려면 습관을 버려야 한다.
⑤ 잘못된 습관을 없애려면 끊임없는 자기 성찰을 해야 한다.

2. 밑줄 친 <u>You only have to be wrong once before your genes are out of the gene pool</u>이 다음 글에서 의미하는 바로 가장 적절한 것은? [3점]

Consider: You are offered a bet on the toss of a coin. Heads, you win $150. Tails, you lose $100. How do you feel about it? Although the expected value is obviously positive (if you repeated the bet 100 times, you'd almost certainly make a profit), most people decline the bet. When asked, "What is the smallest gain that you need to balance an equal chance to lose $100?," most people answer $200 — twice as much as the loss. It means that people typically want to see not less than a 200% expected return to make the bet. This is a mentality from our evolutionary past. If a bush rustles as you walk across the African savannah and there's a 90% chance it's a delicious meal and a 10% chance that it's a hungry lion, you're better off not investigating. <u>You only have to be wrong once before your genes are out of the gene pool.</u> In the modern world alike, in cases where serious consequences are a real possibility, it can be an effective strategy.

① Your genes determine when you will die.
② Big returns don't come without taking big risks.
③ Everything in life happens based on your choices.
④ The fear of loss alters your behavioral patterns.
⑤ If you lose your bet, you can't escape death.

3. 다음 빈칸에 들어갈 말로 가장 적절한 것은? [3점]

External economies of scale result in large companies receiving preferential treatment from government or other external sources simply due to their size. For example, most states will lower taxes to attract large companies since they will provide jobs for their residents. Large companies can also benefit from joint research with universities, lowering their own research expenses. Small companies just don't have the leverage to take advantage of external economies of scale, and thus may find it difficult or at least more expensive to compete. However, they can take advantage of geographic economies of scale by _____ _____ in a small area. For example, artist lofts, galleries and restaurants in a downtown art district benefit from being near each other.

*leverage: 영향력

① diversifying local services
② subsidizing the art projects
③ clustering similar businesses
④ expanding towards other areas
⑤ highlighting regional characteristics

4. 주어진 글 다음에 이어질 글의 순서로 가장 적절한 것은?

> Amid the confusion and chaos of the natural environment, predators limit their search to specific details, ignoring everything else. There is a great benefit to this.

(A) When you specialize in searching for only a few things, even expertly hidden prey can seem obvious. But there is also a cost to paying too much attention to one thing, since you may become blind to the alternatives.

(B) At a minimum, even a minor delay due to clever coloration between the approach of a predator and its subsequent attack can help a prey animal escape. And at best, the prey will be completely ignored.

(C) When a bird searches intently for caterpillars that look like twigs, for example, it misses nearby moths that look like bark. The benefit of concealing coloration is not that it provides an absolute guarantee of survival, but that it consistently yields a small edge in the struggle to live through each successive threatening encounter.

① (A) – (C) – (B)
② (B) – (A) – (C)
③ (B) – (C) – (A)
④ (C) – (A) – (B)
⑤ (C) – (B) – (A)

5. 글의 흐름으로 보아, 주어진 문장이 들어가기에 가장 적절한 곳은?

> However, it gets a great deal of media publicity for innovation and forward thinking, particularly architects.

Like all sectors in mature industries, the construction sector is characterized by a relatively few leading thinkers who innovate and monitor trends and a larger group of technical experts who receive and disseminate innovation and new ideas. (①) This dissemination group consists of architects, consultants, designers, and engineers. (②) In the construction sector this dissemination group is very small, relatively conservative, and divided up into groups. (③) Yet for most construction work, such high levels of technical sophistication are not necessary and are not supported because it is costly. (④) Most buildings are built for functional purposes and not to advance or explore the limits of technology. (⑤) A practical building with a facade that is interesting or artful is more than sufficient for most purposes.

*disseminate: (정보·지식 등을) 전파하다 **facade: (건물의) 전면[앞면]

1. 다음 글의 주제로 가장 적절한 것은?

Several major studies in the UK have attempted to discover what patients find important about their care environment and how nurses and other healthcare staff can improve that environment. Patients consistently remark that they want greater control of their personal environment. For example, in a study by Douglas and Douglas, hospital inpatients reported that they desired a sense of control over their own activity. Patients interviewed explained that they wanted to be able to move freely about the ward area, open and close curtains, control lights and temperature, and access external areas of the building. These findings are supported by a previous study by Lawson and Phiri which also reported on the need to increase patients' personal control and how helping them to take responsibility for aspects of their care can reduce helplessness and aid recovery.

① the importance of empowering patients
② the relationship between patients and caregivers
③ reasons why cleanliness is important in hospitals
④ the effect of environment on the recovery of patients
⑤ the danger of patients' control over their environment

2. 다음 글의 밑줄 친 부분 중, 어법상 틀린 것은? [3점]

Whereas social networking systems allow users to stay ① connected to their friends, social bookmarking is a way of sharing bookmarks. That is, it is a way to share webpages you use either with your network of friends or with the world at large. Unlike filesharing, there is nothing illegal about social bookmarking because the only information that gets shared and downloaded ② is web addresses, not their actual content. It works by users bookmarking the sites they like and indexing them with subject tags ③ to enable others to search for popular sites on a given topic. In many ways, this is more effective for users than using conventional search engines to look for websites ④ in which they are interested. It's because the search tags are assigned by humans who understand the content of a web page rather than by computers that ⑤ aren't. Due to this effectiveness, social bookmarking systems are becoming more and more popular.

3. 다음 빈칸에 들어갈 말로 가장 적절한 것은? [3점]

Dan Ariely, a behavioral economist, did a series of experiments demonstrating that paying people for their services may _____ than asking them to do something for free, particularly if it's a good deed. He tells a real-life anecdote that illustrates his findings. The American Association of Retired Persons(AARP) asked a group of lawyers if they would be willing to provide legal services to needy retirees at a discounted rate of $30 an hour. The lawyers refused. Then the AARP asked if they would provide legal advice to the needy retirees for free. The lawyers agreed. Once it was clear they were being asked to engage in a charitable activity as opposed to a market transaction, the lawyers responded charitably.

① let them lose less face
② bring about better results
③ elicit less effort from them
④ induce more intrinsic interest
⑤ utilize more of their motivation

4. 다음 글에서 전체 흐름과 관계 <u>없는</u> 문장은?

There is real danger to the security of systems when a user leaves a terminal logged in to a system and the terminal is left unattended; this terminal is left open to use by unauthorized individuals. ① In such a situation, the unauthorized person can use the terminal and access the system, just as if the authorized user were present, without having to know or guess the authorized user's sign-on or password. ② For this reason, users must be reminded not to leave a terminal logged in, without use of a password-protected screen saver. ③ Viruses and other malicious software can cause a wide array of problems for your data, ranging from individual deleted files to drive partitions becoming unusable. ④ Some systems may themselves have a process whereby inactivity of the keyboard or mouse will automatically lock down the terminal unless the authorized user enters a password. ⑤ If such a process exists, company policy should explicitly require its use.

5. 다음 글의 내용을 한 문장으로 요약하고자 한다. 빈칸 (A)와 (B)에 들어갈 말로 가장 적절한 것은?

The anxiety many spectators experience when looking at and responding to art is well justified. Art is typically seen in its final resting place, in museums and galleries, disconnected from its original context. These passive displays conceal most of the history and processes that have determined the creation, meaning, and value of the work. The mandatory distance between viewers and art, rightfully observed by institutions, further heightens the mystery of art. Labels, statements, and other materials are useful aids. However, the information, presented as concluding statements rather than a starting point for critical inquiry, leaves many viewers with unanswered questions. How was the art made? Why is it so expensive? Why is it in a museum?

*mandatory: 의무적인

↓

Displaying art in settings that are _____(A)_____ from the art's creation leaves viewers with little room for personal _____(B)_____ with it.

	(A)		(B)
①	inspired	······	interaction
②	inspired	······	competition
③	disconnected	······	struggle
④	disconnected	······	interaction
⑤	disconnected	······	competition

1. 다음 빈칸에 들어갈 말로 가장 적절한 것은?

One strategy for studying behavior is to observe and record events as they naturally occur in life. Researchers utilizing this method, called naturalistic observation, do not bring their subjects into the laboratory and manipulate their behavior in any way. Nor do they choose groups of subjects or create different experimental conditions. Naturalistic observation is commonly used to study animal behavior, such as the hibernation habits of bears or the maternal behavior of hens. It is important, however, that the subject _____ _____. For example, a psychologist using naturalistic observation to study how children of various races play together would watch groups of children playing in the school yards or parks, but he would remain at a distance so as not to be detected. If the children noticed that a strange adult was watching, they might behave differently than they otherwise would.

*hibernation: 동면

① be chosen completely at random
② be comfortable in a laboratory setting
③ be unaware that he is being observed
④ be representative of the group being studied
⑤ be indifferent to taking part in an experiment

2. 주어진 글 다음에 이어질 글의 순서로 가장 적절한 것은?

When you watch a theatrical production, you engage in something called the "willing suspension of disbelief." That is, your conscious mind fully understands that the events being portrayed were written by a playwright and may never have truly taken place at all.

(A) But if, on the other hand, the actors have become complacent and the action is boring, you will not be able to fully suspend your disbelief, and you will have the uncomfortable awareness of watching actors who are merely reciting memorized lines.

(B) If the actors are succeeding at their job, you may, for a time, actually believe that what is taking place before you is real and that the events and interactions you are seeing are only just now taking place for the first time.

(C) Yet you willingly suspend your disbelief of the action onstage so that you may be drawn into the production and experience the story with all of your emotions.

① (A) – (C) – (B)
② (B) – (A) – (C)
③ (B) – (C) – (A)
④ (C) – (A) – (B)
⑤ (C) – (B) – (A)

3. 글의 흐름으로 보아, 주어진 문장이 들어가기에 가장 적절한 곳은? [3점]

This can be hard because some financial salespeople will rush to contact you in these circumstances.

The sooner you begin financial planning, the better prepared you'll be to adapt your plans when personal circumstances change. (①) Changing job status, relocating to a new state, getting married, having children, being in a serious car accident, retiring, and other stressful events are "financial shocks" that require reevaluation of your financial goals and plans. (②) However, it is important not to rush to make important financial decisions at these times, when you're most vulnerable. (③) Delay any action until you have had time to recover from the event and evaluate all your options carefully. (④) For example, when you have a child, you will find that insurance agents, financial planners, and stockbrokers actively encourage you to buy insurance and begin investing in a college fund. (⑤) Although these are valid objectives, don't be pressured into any expensive decisions.

[4~5] 다음 글을 읽고, 물음에 답하시오.

Richard Wiseman, of the University of Hertfordshire in the United Kingdom, handed test subjects in his laboratory a newspaper and asked each of them to count all the photos inside. Wiseman picked subjects for this experiment by recruiting individuals who (a) identified themselves as being either extremely lucky or terribly unlucky. He wanted to see whether those people whose lives are filled with good fortune actually see the world (b) differently than do those who are unlucky. What do you think happened?

In this experiment, the unlucky people took several minutes to count all the photos in the newspaper, and most came back with an incorrect answer. The lucky people, on the other hand, took only a few seconds to find an answer, and they were all correct. Why was this?

Wiseman designed special newspapers for this experiment. Inside the front cover of each newspaper there was a two-inch-high message that read, "STOP COUNTING. THERE ARE 43 PHOTOGRAPHS IN THIS NEWSPAPER." Both groups were looking for photos, as requested, but the lucky people also read this message and responded (c) accordingly. In contrast, the unlucky people were focused only on counting the photos — since that was their (d) specific assignment — and they didn't see the message with the answer they needed. This elegant experiment demonstrates beautifully that by (e) appreciating information in your environment, you miss important clues that are the keys to solving problems.

4. 윗글의 제목으로 가장 적절한 것은?

① Man Is What He Believes
② Are You Paying Attention?
③ Success Is Simply a Matter of Luck
④ Make It a Rule to Read a Newspaper
⑤ Don't Follow Others, Just Trust Yourself

5. 밑줄 친 (a)~(e) 중에서 문맥상 낱말의 쓰임이 적절하지 <u>않은</u> 것은? [3점]

① (a)　　② (b)　　③ (c)　　④ (d)　　⑤ (e)

1. 다음 글의 요지로 가장 적절한 것은?

Incompleteness represents instability to our brain. A basic illustration of this is the open-circle experiment. Draw a circle on a piece of paper, but leave a small gap such that the circle is not all the way closed. Now stare at it for a couple minutes and notice what happens — your brain wants to close the circle. For some people the urge to close it is so strong that they'll eventually pick up the pencil and draw it closed. The same dynamic can be applied to stop procrastination from burning you. The trick is simply to start whatever project is front of you — just start anywhere. Psychologists call this the Zeigarnik effect, named for the Russian psychologist who first documented the finding that when someone is faced with an overwhelming goal and is procrastinating as a result, getting started anywhere will launch motivation to finish what was started. When you start a project — even if you begin with the smallest, simplest part — you begin drawing the circle. Then move on to another part (draw more of the circle), and another (more circle), and so forth.

① 완벽주의 성향이면 목표 달성을 그르치기 쉽다.
② 마감 시간을 정하면 미루는 습관을 고칠 수 있다.
③ 일단 일을 시작하면 완료하게 될 가능성이 커진다.
④ 어려운 일은 조금씩 나누어서 하면 완료하기 쉽다.
⑤ 실현 가능한 일이 아니라면 착수하지 말아야 한다.

2. 다음 빈칸에 들어갈 말로 가장 적절한 것은?

Morality and the law do not always cover the same ground. In societies with some separation between the sacred and the secular, the law alone would be insufficient to maintain the cohesion of society: moral prescriptions are essential. Some actions that are generally considered as moral or immoral are outside the scope of the law. In general, the law is concerned with the more extreme examples of what one should not do, while morality emphasizes everyday misdeeds and what one should do. For instance, it is regarded as morally right to give to charity, but (in the UK) there is no law that one should. In this case, then, morality has regard for the common good, but the law at most encourages donations. Therefore, in normal circumstances and over trivial issues, taking more than one's share is _____.

*secular: 세속적인 **cohesion: 화합

① a moral but not a legal matter
② covered by ethics in all societies
③ encouraged morally but discouraged legally
④ an issue the law must soon address
⑤ a more common problem in the UK

3. 다음 글에서 전체 흐름과 관계 <u>없는</u> 문장은?

American music is intertwined with music from around the world, so it is neither possible nor desirable to draw firm lines around what "American music" is. ① It has been said that jazz is distinctly American, yet it has been influenced by music from all parts of the world. ② The distinction between jazz and blues, or jazz and rock for that matter, is fuzzy, as many artists mix genres to create their own unique sound. ③ Musicians who relocated to the United States, whether escaping from war and persecution or attempting to advance their careers, have also had a profound impact on American music and culture, bringing with them the influences of their home countries and cultures. ④ Composers like Aaron Copland tried to create a distinctly American music, yet his work was influenced by his studies with Nadia Boulanger in Paris; travels to work with composer Carlos Chávez in Mexico and to Africa and Europe; and interests in jazz and other forms of music. ⑤ American music is not created and does not exist in isolation from other parts of the world.

4. 주어진 글 다음에 이어질 글의 순서로 가장 적절한 것은?

> Many health education campaigns have tried to encourage people to change their behavior through fear or guilt. Anti-drinking and driving campaigns at Christmas depict the devastating effects on families of road-accident victims; smoking-prevention posters urge parents not to teach their children how to smoke.

(A) Although fear can encourage a negative attitude and even a desire to change, such feelings tend to disappear over time and when faced with a real decision-making situation.

(B) Increasingly, these hard-hitting campaigns are used amongst others to raise awareness of the consequences of heavy drinking, smoking, and drug use. Whether such campaigns are effective at shocking people into changing their behavior is the topic of ongoing debate.

(C) Being very frightened can also cause people to deny and avoid the message. Protection Motivation theory suggests that fear only works if the threat is seen as serious and likely to occur if the person does not follow the recommended advice.

① (A) – (C) – (B) ② (B) – (A) – (C)
③ (B) – (C) – (A) ④ (C) – (A) – (B)
⑤ (C) – (B) – (A)

5. 글의 흐름으로 보아, 주어진 문장이 들어가기에 가장 적절한 곳은?

> However, if you have selected a fairly uncommon subject on which little has been written, then it may be difficult to find sufficient material to review.

By the time you start your literature review, you will probably have decided upon the main theme for your investigation, and also upon the key research objectives. (①) To some extent, therefore, the essential task has been predetermined. (②) You may have selected a research topic or theme around which a great deal of research has been previously conducted. (③) If that is the case, it should not be difficult to find writing and research to review. (④) In fact, the main difficulty may be in selecting what you want to include, and what you wish to exclude. (⑤) You may have to consider including a discussion of material which only exists on the periphery of the subject chosen.

*literature review: 문헌 조사 **periphery: 주변

1. 다음 글의 제목으로 가장 적절한 것은?

French cognitive scientist Franck Ramus discovered that human infants raised in French-speaking households could distinguish other languages they heard over a loudspeaker. Ramus used the rate at which the babies sucked on their pacifiers as evidence of their level of interest. He found that after listening to sentences spoken in Dutch, they recognized a change in language had occurred when the loudspeaker switched to Japanese. But the startling finding was that the babies could not make this distinction if the recordings were played backward. In other words, the babies understood certain properties of language that the backward sentences lacked, and they took notice of the differences in the two languages accordingly.

① Proof of Universal Grammar
② Babies Can Tell Languages Apart
③ How to Fluently Speak Backwards
④ The Secret to Language Acquisition
⑤ What Makes a Language a Language?

2. 다음 글의 밑줄 친 부분 중, 문맥상 낱말의 쓰임이 적절하지 않은 것은?

The majority of medical errors are flaws in thinking rather than technical or implementation flaws. Through ample use of checklists and structured decision-making models, medical procedures are generally implemented with ① high precision. However, if a physician missed a presenting symptom or did not rule out alternate hypotheses, then the treatment would not ② meet the actual need of the patient, and the result would not be the desired one. A classic example of this is the ③ overuse of antibiotics. Antibiotics can be effective for treating bacterial infections, but they are useless for viral infections. There are certainly tests to help determine whether the source of a sinus infection is viral or bacterial. However, because the tests are costly and take time to produce results, many physicians used to ④ skip those tests, assume a bacterial infection, and prescribe antibiotics. Not only would the antibiotics be ⑤ effective for helping overcome viral infections, but the unintended consequence is that we have an increasing number of bacteria strains resistant to what were once useful medications.

*sinus infection: 축농증 **strain: (동식물·질병 등의) 종류[유형]

3. 다음 빈칸에 들어갈 말로 가장 적절한 것은? [3점]

Suppose you have a student who usually fails to complete his work. He manages to submit a project on time, although it's not very good. It's tempting to praise the student — after all, the fact that he submitted something is an improvement over his past performance. But consider the message that praising an ordinary project sends. You say "good job," but that really means "good job for someone like you." The student is probably not so naive as to think that his project is really all that great. By praising substandard work, you send the message that you have lower expectations for this student. If you want your compliment to take effect, your compliment must be _____. Better to say, "I appreciate that you finished the project on time, and I thought your opening paragraph was interesting, but I think you could have done a better job of organizing it. Let's talk about how."

*naive: 순진무구한

① made in person in public
② general rather than specific
③ expressed as promptly as possible
④ focused on the person's act or conduct
⑤ accompanied by what needs betterment

4. 다음 글에서 전체 흐름과 관계 <u>없는</u> 문장은?

Aging is universal, as is death. But how quickly you age is not. Nor is your own individual lifespan. ① Both the rate at which you age and your time on earth are under more control than you may dream — and than scientists imagined until recently. ② Exploding research into aging and related diseases is now producing some amazing prospects. ③ Recent discoveries are astonishing to scientists and us, as scientists enter territory never before explored, witnessing at ever closer range the ultimate biological mysteries of life and death. ④ Aging populations are not the main driver of the annual growth in national health spending, which is mainly due to rising incomes and costly new medical technology. ⑤ These new investigations, for the first time in human history, promise ways to extend our lifespan and overcome fear of aging.

5. 다음 글의 내용을 한 문장으로 요약하고자 한다. 빈칸 (A), (B)에 들어갈 말로 가장 적절한 것은?

If we can't find a product at all, we can't use it. And if a product is in easy reach everywhere, not only are we more likely to use it at all, but also if we are already using it we tend to use it more often. Supply doesn't only meet demand; supply stimulates demand. The demand it stimulates may be "impulsive demand," but it means sales (and consumption). That's not to say that supply determines demand. People do not have to consume products that are widely available; no one straps us down and shoves snack foods down our throats. But when products fill a basic biologic need or are tempting in other ways, we can be enticed to grab them whether we believe they are good for us or not. This effect matters so much to our health because whether or not we give in to our modern killers depends to such a great extent on the items we consume.

*entice: 유도하다

↓

The fact that the more (A) any consumer product is, the more we use it, drives us to consume food without regard to its (B) .

	(A)		(B)
①	accessible	······	flavor
②	accessible	······	wholesomeness
③	luxurious	······	appearance
④	desirable	······	flavor
⑤	desirable	······	wholesomeness

1. 다음 빈칸에 들어갈 말로 가장 적절한 것은? [3점]

Stanford University professor Baba Shiv's research demonstrates just how our willpower works. He split 165 undergraduate students, who were on a diet, into two groups and asked them to memorize either a two-digit or seven-digit number. Both tasks were well within the average person's cognitive abilities, and they could take as much time as they needed. When they were ready, students would then proceed to a second room where they would recite the number. Along the way, they were offered a snack for participating in the study. The two choices were chocolate cake or a bowl of fruit salad — guilty pleasure or healthy treat. Here's the kicker: students who had been given the seven-digit number were nearly twice as likely to choose cake. This tiny extra cognitive load was just enough to _____ _____. The implication is staggering: willpower is like a muscle that gets tired easily and needs rest.

① lead to better learning
② increase their willpower
③ result in more endurance
④ prevent a prudent choice
⑤ offset eating the sugar

2. 주어진 글 다음에 이어질 글의 순서로 가장 적절한 것은?

Our traditions encourage us to think of justice as an issue of equal opportunities for every individual to pursue whatever he or she desires. Equal opportunities are guaranteed by fair laws and political procedures — laws and procedures applied in the same way to all people.

(A) Thus, there could be great differences in the income given to people in different occupations in a just society so long as everyone had an equal chance of obtaining a well-paid job.

(B) But this way of thinking about justice does not in itself offer a vision of what the distribution of goods in a society would end up looking like if individuals had an equal chance to pursue their dreams.

(C) But if, as is now becoming painfully apparent, there are more qualified applicants than openings for the interesting jobs, is equal opportunity sufficient to ensure justice? What of the socially disadvantaged for whom a fair race is beyond reach since they are left well short of the starting line?

① (A) – (C) – (B)　　② (B) – (A) – (C)
③ (B) – (C) – (A)　　④ (C) – (A) – (B)
⑤ (C) – (B) – (A)

3. 글의 흐름으로 보아, 주어진 문장이 들어가기에 가장 적절한 곳은? [3점]

The name does not then have the same identifying function, though context can be used to partially bridge this gap.

Translators often leave foreign names unchanged, and this non-translation can have an alienating effect on the reader of the translation. (①) This sometimes makes it difficult for the reader to identify with the characters. (②) Moreover, original names that are too difficult to read may spoil the mere pleasure of reading. (③) If the name of a well-known person remains unchanged in the translation, the name will function differently if the reader of the translation is not familiar with the person to whom the name refers. (④) In *Juist en Tweemeter*, the Dutch translation of the work by Norwegian author Kjersti Wold, the context makes it clear to the reader of the translation that the character Ole Gunnar Solskjaer is a football player. (⑤) Still, the translation is likely to have a different emotional impact, because few Dutch-speaking children will associate the name Solskjaer with that of a national hero.

*alienate: 생경하게 만들다

[4~5] 다음 글을 읽고, 물음에 답하시오.

Some psychologists believe that if you are in a good mood and someone asks you to do something, you are likely to view the requester as truly in need of help. The favor seems (a) reasonable. Conversely, the theory suggests, when you are angry you perceive a requester as being manipulative. Dr. Sandra Milbery and Margaret Clark conducted an experiment that found the happier the subjects, the more likely they were to (b) yield to the wishes of another.

In another study, Alice Isen and Paul Levin set out to make us a little happier to see if we would be more willing to do good deeds for others. Alice and Paul chose a library. One of them randomly gave cookies to some of the people who visited the library. Later, in a seemingly (c) unrelated encounter, the other researcher asked the patrons for help on a task. You guessed it — the patrons who got a cookie were more willing to help out.

The experimenters then tried to (d) discard their findings by leaving dimes in public telephone booths. Some unwitting telephone users happened to get a little (e) profit while others found nothing. Shortly after either finding the dime or finding nothing, the subjects saw someone who had dropped a stack of papers. It turns out that significantly more of those who found the dime helped pick up the notes. If you can do something to make someone's day a little brighter, your generosity will pay you back for it.

4. 윗글의 제목으로 가장 적절한 것은?

① Does Mood Affect Helping?
② The Role of Incidents in Life
③ What Is It Like to Feel Accepted?
④ Are Experiments Valid Enough to Believe?
⑤ Where There Is Money, There Is Willingness

5. 밑줄 친 (a)~(e) 중에서 문맥상 낱말의 쓰임이 적절하지 <u>않은</u> 것은? [3점]

① (a)　　② (b)　　③ (c)　　④ (d)　　⑤ (e)

1. 다음 글에서 필자가 주장하는 바로 가장 적절한 것은?

Memory is like light. Unfocused, it is diffused and scattered. But a focused memory, much like the beam of a powerful laser, can cut through the barriers and limitations you may have inadvertently created in your mind about your memory. I know because for years I sabotaged my memory with such negative phrases as "I am always forgetting names" or that universal favorite, "Honey, have you seen my car keys?" The first step in your journey to that focused memory begins either on a piece of paper or on your computer screen. The best way to learn how you remember is to write down your experiences on a regular basis. When you sit down at the end of the day and write a bit about your experiences, you are mentally reconstructing the day. The first time you do this, some parts of the day will be startlingly clear.

① 기억력은 원래 어느 정도 타고나는 것이다.
② 반복해서 암기를 하면 잘 잊어버리지 않는다.
③ 기억하려는 의지가 기억하는 기간을 늘려준다.
④ 사람마다 경험을 기억하는 데는 큰 차이가 있다.
⑤ 경험을 정기적으로 기록하면 기억력 향상에 좋다.

2. 밑줄 친 If only Chukwu had had an SNS account가 다음 글에서 의미하는 바로 가장 적절한 것은?

Certain abilities that were considered divine for many millennia have today become so commonplace that people living in modern times hardly think about them. The average person now moves and communicates across distances much more easily than the Greek, Hindu, or African gods of old. For example, the Igbo people of Nigeria believe that the creator god Chukwu initially wanted to make people immortal. He sent a dog to tell humans that when someone dies, they should sprinkle ashes on the corpse, and the body will come back to life. Unfortunately, the dog was tired and he lingered on the way. The impatient Chukwu then sent a sheep, telling her to make haste with this important message. Alas, when the breathless sheep reached her destination, she garbled the instructions, and told the humans to bury their dead, thus making death permanent. If only Chukwu had had an SNS account!

*garble: 혼동하다, 잘못 이해하다

① Ancient gods were terrible at living in harmony.
② Both dogs and sheep disappear from the Igbo myth.
③ The message would have been distorted by the humans.
④ Communicative ability is becoming more and more significant.
⑤ Due to an ancient god's incompetence, we humans are mortal.

3. 다음 빈칸에 들어갈 말로 가장 적절한 것은? [3점]

Each child is unique. They have different backgrounds, different strengths, and different weaknesses. Some may be thrilled to be tutored; others may be suspicious. A tutor's conception of a student _____ _____. Tutors must be open to receiving and working with any students they are assigned. This can be challenging because our expectations are determined by our value systems, upbringing, and past experiences and can be vastly different from those of others. These expectations can become major sources of frustration when they conflict with others' behavior, such as that of our tutees. Therefore, it is advised to try to approach tutoring without any expectations at all. This, of course, includes giving up expectations you may have of your future students and their personalities, their academic skills or progress, and their motivation and attitude toward you.

① is at odds with reality
② can be formed by observation
③ should be a blank sheet of paper
④ is based on a faulty interpretation
⑤ should be his or her own idea

4. 주어진 글 다음에 이어질 글의 순서로 가장 적절한 것은? [3점]

> One of the stumbling blocks to enjoying the peace of a tranquil mind, according to Epicurus, is the fear of death, and this fear is heightened by the religious belief that you will be severely punished in the afterlife.

(A) To explain this, Epicurus starts from the assumption that the entire universe is made up of either atoms or empty space. Epicurus then reasons that the soul could not be empty space, because it operates dynamically with the body, so it must consist of atoms.

(B) But rather than countering this fear by suggesting an alternative state of immortality, Epicurus attempts to explain the nature of death itself. He begins by proposing that when we die, we have no awareness of our death, since our consciousness (our soul) ceases to exist at the moment of death.

(C) He describes these atoms of the soul as being distributed around the body, but as being so fragile that they dissipate when we die, and so we are no longer capable of sensing anything, mentally or physically. If you are unable to feel anything when you die, it is foolish to let the fear of death cause you pain while you are still alive.

① (A) – (C) – (B)   ② (B) – (A) – (C)
③ (B) – (C) – (A)   ④ (C) – (A) – (B)
⑤ (C) – (B) – (A)

5. 글의 흐름으로 보아, 주어진 문장이 들어가기에 가장 적절한 곳은? [3점]

> Although their original food customs may have been nutritionally adequate, their new environment may lead them to alter their eating habits.

When people move from one country to another or from one area to another, their economic status may change. (①) They will be exposed to new foods and new food customs. (②) For instance, if milk was a staple food in their diet prior to moving and is unusually expensive in the new environment, milk may be given up for a cheaper, nutritionally inferior beverage such as soda, coffee, or tea. (③) Candy, possibly a luxury in their former environment, may be inexpensive and widespread in their new environment. (④) As a result, a family might increase consumption of soda or candy and limit purchases of more nutritious foods. (⑤) Someone who is not familiar with the nutritive values of foods can easily make such mistakes when shopping.

*staple food: 주식(主食) **nutritive value: 영양가

1. 다음 글의 주제로 가장 적절한 것은?

There are a number of ways in which technology can be used to protect social network users from disclosure or privacy threats or violations. More drastic technical solutions involve disabling or banning social media/social networking. For example, some schools and workplaces place explicit restrictions or in some cases a complete ban on social networking sites and they are disabled at the IT level so that students or employees cannot access these sites. The problem with this solution is that the benefits of using these sites are also lost. Additionally, while this may prevent use of these sites during school or work hours, it has no impact on what is done after hours. The context collapse that occurs in an online environment blurs the line between people's professional and personal lives such that online information exchanges that occur outside of school or work hours impact people's lives at school or work. Therefore, employing these strategies is not necessarily effective in minimizing the potential risks overall.

*drastic: 철저한, 격렬한

① potential positive effects of social media in public
② some reasons to ban or restrict social media in certain settings
③ downside of controlling social networking sites for protecting users
④ social networking that blurs the boundary between work and home
⑤ necessity of restricting access to social networking in certain settings

2. 다음 글의 밑줄 친 부분 중, 어법상 틀린 것은?

A great change occurred with the arrival of the phonograph. Recorded music privatized and decontextualized ① what had often been a social event — and church music or sailors' songs could now be heard while dressing in the morning, while Beethoven was transformed into "wallpaper." At ② its simplest level music was *heard*, but performers were no longer *seen*. Sounds of all sorts could thus be integrated into everyday life as a kind of aural background — but more often to enhance a mood or ③ decorate some setting than as a focused object of attention. Claude Debussy in 1913 fretted that recorded music could be bought as ④ easy as "one can buy a glass of beer." And with no hint of irony, the first issue of *Gramophone* (1923) called for ⑤ listening to recorded music while shaving.

*decontextualize: 문맥에서 분리하다 **fret: 고민하다

3. 다음 빈칸에 들어갈 말로 가장 적절한 것은? [3점]

Before the invention of printing, we had a different technology for communicating ideas and information. It was called talking. It evolved over millions of years, and there is a lot more happening than just the words passing from brain to brain. There's modulation, tone, emphasis, and passion, each of which grabs the attention of the listener. She watches as well as listens. Subconsciously she notes the widening of the speaker's eyes, the movement of the hands, the swaying of the body, the responses of other listeners. When correctly employed by a speaker, this all makes a positive difference on the way the receiving brain categorizes and prioritizes the incoming information. By _____ _____, the speaker's lasting impact on the intellectual world of the listener may be far greater than the same words in print.

*modulation: 억양, 음성의 변화

① paying attention to verbal meanings
② defining effective communication skills
③ increasing the motivation to understand
④ playing important roles of listeners in communication
⑤ understanding the origin of the human capacity for speech

4. 다음 글에서 전체 흐름과 관계 <u>없는</u> 문장은?

When you find yourself saying "If only he would tell me what he's thinking," or "If only she didn't criticize so much," stop yourself and remind yourself to be realistic. ① If you want to bring about some changes in those relationships, you should put away these "if only's" and accept people as they are. ② Once you start to make changes in yourself, the other person is likely to begin to change. ③ Then you will be able to find out if you can accommodate to each other and get on. ④ The relationships you have with other people are projections of the relationships you feel society expects. ⑤ If after you have tried to change you still find the relationship is no better, and you still keep wishing the other person were different, then it might be better to end the relationship.

5. 다음 글의 내용을 한 문장으로 요약하고자 한다. 빈칸 (A)와 (B)에 들어갈 말로 가장 적절한 것은?

We have officially entered the era of technology in schools. As we move further into the 21st century, it is apparent that we need to take a close look at the way we are introducing new topics to students. We need to be sure that we are preparing our students to be productive members of society in the future. Although technology is a fantastic way to motivate students' learning, a study was conducted at Stanford University that revealed the negative side to introducing too much technology. Students' attention spans are being reduced; they often find it hard to focus in the classroom for prolonged periods of time. The study also found that students are using up memory portions of their brains that were previously used to store information learned in school. Technology is immediate and has given students the idea that learning can also be immediate. This, of course, is not the case, as we know learning takes practice and repetition.

↓

A study revealed that learning has become increasingly ____(A)____ for students, whose attention and memory have been ____(B)____ due to increases in technology use.

	(A)		(B)
①	important	······	assessed
②	important	······	altered
③	difficult	······	altered
④	difficult	······	assessed
⑤	widespread	······	limited

1. 다음 빈칸에 들어갈 말로 가장 적절한 것은? [3점]

It is sometimes difficult to say _____. Consider an individual who is forced to reflect and start over after a mild setback. In the period immediately following the setback, the individual is less content but acting with greater autonomy. To evaluate the change in the individual's state, we must treat the values of being content and being autonomous as commensurable, though many will believe that they are not. Evaluating a change in an entire society involves similar types of difficult comparisons, plus a whole collection of additional ones based on distributive concerns. For instance, what if a society becomes wealthier and less equal over time? Finally, even if we think that all states of affairs can be compared effectively, we might question the justification of violence or other catastrophes. Why should we be reconciled to a violent war just because it set the stage for institutional improvement?

*commensurable: 같은 단위로 잴 수 있는

① if freedom is more valuable than equality
② the individual is more important than the society
③ not only violence but also inaction is inexcusable
④ whether changes have been improvements or not
⑤ autonomy is essential for healthy human development

2. 주어진 글 다음에 이어질 글의 순서로 가장 적절한 것은?

Imagine finding a nail with two heads: one at the top of the spike and one to the side.

(A) This is the reflex we must overcome. Remember "function follows form"? That's how it should be. If we push ourselves to find a beneficial use for a nail with two heads, we may run across some ideas that are truly innovative.

(B) Immediately, it grabs our attention. Surely, it must be defective. Because of structural fixedness, our minds want to correct the oddity and restore the nail back to having just one head.

(C) For example, suppose a second head allows you to hold the nail in place as you hammer, so that you don't smash your thumb. "Function follows form" helps us break fixedness by taking odd configurations and imagining beneficial uses for them.

① (A) – (C) – (B)   ② (B) – (A) – (C)
③ (B) – (C) – (A)   ④ (C) – (A) – (B)
⑤ (C) – (B) – (A)

3. 글의 흐름으로 보아, 주어진 문장이 들어가기에 가장 적절한 곳은? [3점]

Rational individuals will seek perfect balance between freedom and security, but this balance varies among individuals, depending upon their ability to benefit from freedom and to bear the cost of insecurity.

Although the case for freedom is strong, this goal cannot be pursued without limit. Almost everyone admits that some restrictions are necessary when the exercise of individual freedom endangers others or imposes large external costs. (①) A more subtle but more pervasive limit to freedom arises when it conflicts with the individual's desire for security. (②) In the face of the complexities and uncertainties of modern life, many people willingly vote for programs that restrict freedom — their own and that of others — in exchange for the promise of greater security. (③) For instance, numerous laws deny consumers the freedom to buy products that have been judged to be dangerous. (④) But not everyone makes the same evaluation of the tradeoff. (⑤) This variation is the major reason why it is so difficult to reach agreement on this issue.

[4~5] 다음 글을 읽고, 물음에 답하시오.

On the surface, ceremonies may appear to be a waste of time, empty words said unthinkingly. But they do have a (a) deeper meaning. We use these rituals to create a sense of belonging. While the National Anthem is being sung before a baseball game, the crowd and the players are performing as a unit. In the same way, the congregation in a church become one when they sing a hymn or recite a prayer. Ceremonies serve to (b) unify the participants in an event.

Ceremonies are also used to (c) reinforce the atmosphere of an event. Couples who repeat wedding vows are making a public, solemn statement of their intention to live together permanently. Their decision seems much more significant than an offhand "Let's share an apartment" would be. Similarly, when a president swears in public that he will uphold the Constitution of the United States, the entire country realizes the importance of the job and of his commitment to it.

Finally, at a basic level, rituals give people a feeling of control. This function is particularly (d) vague in funerals. We can't prevent the death of a loved one, but we can organize a ceremony to help those grieving cope with loss, death, and tragedy. This ritual makes us feel that we are not entirely at the mercy of natural forces, resulting in a (e) calming of internal emotional chaos.

4. 윗글의 제목으로 가장 적절한 것은?

① Ceremony: Its Origin and Types
② How Do We Perform Ceremonies?
③ Ceremony: Its Meaning and Functions
④ The Wedding Ceremony and Its Symbolism
⑤ What's Wrong with the Change of a Ceremony?

5. 밑줄 친 (a)~(e) 중에서 문맥상 낱말의 쓰임이 적절하지 않은 것은? [3점]

① (a)　　② (b)　　③ (c)　　④ (d)　　⑤ (e)

1. 다음 글의 요지로 가장 적절한 것은?

You might have a bad interaction with a family member before getting to work. As the day wears on, you may interpret your negative feelings as frustration for the project you're working on rather than lingering negative effects from the events of the morning. Many people try to power through their negative feelings rather than attempt to understand them. But this is a lost opportunity. Emotions provide valuable information about the state of your motivational system. Ignoring them is like driving around lost, only refusing to ask for directions. You need to think about things that bother you in order to understand the source of your feelings. You can't manage feelings without thinking about them. Once you can better comprehend where your own feelings come from, you'll have a much better ability to deal with them.

① 먼저 부정적인 감정을 이해해야 그 감정을 다스릴 수 있다.
② 일과 삶을 분리하지 못하면 부정적인 감정에 휩싸이기 쉽다.
③ 부정적인 감정을 없애려면 가족 간의 원활한 소통이 필요하다.
④ 어떤 것에 대한 강한 동기는 부정적인 감정으로부터 시작된다.
⑤ 부정적인 감정을 무시함으로써 긍정적인 감정을 야기할 수 있다.

2. 다음 빈칸에 들어갈 말로 가장 적절한 것은? [3점]

I like to use the phrase *positive discipline* to refer to using your authority in positive ways, either to broaden your child's horizons or to reward good behavior. Let's imagine you are planning a family vacation. You and your spouse want to take a trip to Mexico, but your kids prefer Disney World. However, none of your kids have ever been to Mexico. In this situation, your kids don't get a choice. A well-run family is not a democracy. Asking your child whether she'd like to go to Mexico if she's never been there is no different from asking her whether she'd like curried chicken when she's never tried it. Her answer isn't based on experience.

Tell her: "We're going to Mexico, and you're coming along." Don't promise her that she'll love it, because she might not. Your job is not to guarantee your child's happiness, but to broaden her horizons. Those two objectives _____.

① do not always coincide
② thrive in fair conditions
③ affect each other positively
④ should be met simultaneously
⑤ cannot be achieved in a single attempt

3. 다음 글에서 전체 흐름과 관계 없는 문장은?

A former colleague of mine said that she thought it was now no longer important to teach Shakespeare because among other things he had a very feeble grasp of women. ① This means that, if taken seriously, nobody's place in the entire canon is very secure, that it's constantly changing. ② John Donne's position was, in the nineteenth century, of no consequence at all; *The Oxford Book of English Verse* contained only one poem of his. ③ And now, of course, he has been resurrected by Herbert Grierson and T. S. Eliot and he's one of the great figures of seventeenth-century poetry. ④ Another important theme in Donne's poetry is the idea of true religion, something that he spent much time considering and about which he often theorized. ⑤ Even the great Bach was relatively unpopular for two hundred years before being rediscovered by Mendelssohn, proving that even in music we are constantly reassessing the past.

*canon: 주요 문헌[작품] 목록 **resurrect: ~을 다시 살리다

4. 주어진 글 다음에 이어질 글의 순서로 가장 적절한 것은?

> Your body is not a vehicle you inhabit; it is a creation of your nonphysical being and therefore reflects your personality characteristics.

(A) When I was younger, I was quite rigid in my attitudes and physically inflexible as well. Not surprisingly, I disliked stretching exercises. Contrary to what is expected to occur as we age, my physical flexibility has increased considerably, and I now enjoy stretching exercises.

(B) Facial wrinkles (expression lines) may be an external manifestation of people's automatic reactions — habitually doing the same things and repeatedly making the same choices. An inflexible body can be a physical representation of becoming set in one's ways.

(C) Many people become less mentally flexible as they get older, hence the stiffness and loss of physical flexibility experienced by so many older adults. It can happen the other way around as well: if we become more mentally flexible, our physical flexibility can increase. I'm living proof that this is possible.

*manifestation: 징후, 표명

① (A) – (C) – (B)　　　② (B) – (A) – (C)
③ (B) – (C) – (A)　　　④ (C) – (A) – (B)
⑤ (C) – (B) – (A)

5. 글의 흐름으로 보아, 주어진 문장이 들어가기에 가장 적절한 곳은?

> Here spending money on luxury goods to publicly display economic power was a norm and expected.

In European cultures, the trend in food habits had always been towards sophistication in food preparation and consumption. (①) In contrast to the European cultures, developments in early American food habits have been more towards simplification of meal preparation methods rather than sophistication and expansion. (②) The European food habits of the 18th and 19th centuries were driven by the sophistication in cooking arts advanced by the chefs. (③) In contrast, American food habits of the 18th and 19th centuries were driven by simplicity in preparation and efficiency in mass production. (④) This was a reflection of the political system of the land. In early Europe, the political systems were feudalistic and ruled by the royal families. (⑤) The democratic political system of America did not encourage indulgence in excessive food consumption by its national leaders since it symbolized concentration of power.

*feudalistic: 봉건 제도의　**indulgence: 탐닉, 사치

1. 다음 글의 제목으로 가장 적절한 것은?

Poor students are seldom allowed to be the heroes in Hollywood films (adults always must "save" them) while middle-class students are almost always the heroes of the films in which they are featured (they are always more clever than the adults in the film). This double standard, I believe, reflects the middle-class bias of American culture. The middle-class perspective is always the predominant and heroic perspective in film. While it would be convenient to simply blame Hollywood for this double standard, the truth is that these distorted images of poor and middle-class teens are a reflection of the distorted image that Americans as a whole have of various social classes. These representations are a fantasy of the middle class (that poor students are troubled and middle-class students are wise), but it is an illusion that extends beyond the middle class because the middle-class perspective in American society is dominant.

① Teens versus Adults: A Hollywood Theme
② The Economic Perspective of Hollywood Movies
③ Hollywood's Contribution to American Culture Abroad
④ A Distorted Portrait: The Ethnic Minority in Hollywood Films
⑤ The Middle-Class Hollywood Hero: A Reflection of Widespread Bias

2. 다음 글의 밑줄 친 부분 중, 문맥상 낱말의 쓰임이 적절하지 않은 것은?

The mechanical thinker takes considerable pride in his opinions, which he believes to be "right." It is proper and necessary, he believes, for a person to "take a stand" on things — on just about everything, in fact. Each time he voices a sweeping generalization on some topic, he commits himself to adopt a rigid stand on similar topics. He must, above all, be ① "consistent." If you study the mechanical thinker closely, you will probably notice a singular lack of apparent ② curiosity. He seldom asks questions, and he seldom seeks ③ new information about his world. He would seldom ④ admit to having learned something from another person. He rarely reads books and certainly not nonfiction material. If a man, he may read the sports pages, which is acceptable behavior for a male in his society — or if a woman she may read the women's section of the paper. The mechanical thinker may reveal a noticeable uneasiness in ⑤ familiar situations and may be embarrassed when confronted with a fact that forces him to revise a strongly held opinion.

3. 다음 빈칸에 들어갈 말로 가장 적절한 것은? [3점]

It is interesting to note that all sources of energy can _____. For example, because of the way that uranium behaves in the environment, a large quantity of it can be found in coal. Consequently, burning coal can release uranium into the environment; the disposal of coal ash can also release radioactivity into the environment. The majority of fuel oil also contains small amounts of uranium, so extracting petroleum, refining it to form fuel oil, and then burning it releases radioactivity as well. It turns out that coal and fuel oil power plants, when added together, actually release more radioactivity into the environment than do all of the world's existing nuclear power plants. Natural gas also contains some radioactivity, but not as much as petroleum or coal. So while natural gas plants do release some radioactivity, the amount is less than that released by nuclear reactors.

*uranium: 우라늄 **radioactivity: 방사능

① lose a lot during the extraction process
② release radioactivity into the environment
③ pollute the environment more than we know
④ be used to eliminate hazards from radiation
⑤ help with managing radioactive waste

4. 다음 글에서 전체 흐름과 관계 <u>없는</u> 문장은?

In the physical sciences, it is usually the case that a handful of concepts can be applied to solve problems across a wide range of contexts. ① Research literature on the transfer of knowledge suggests that when people acquire knowledge in one context they can seldom apply this knowledge to situations in related contexts that look superficially different from the original context, but which are related by the major idea that could be applied to solve or analyze them. ② The implication is that students should learn to apply major concepts in multiple contexts in order to make the knowledge "fluid." ③ The more they know about, and focus on, their major area of study, the easier it is to transfer what students already know to problems in that area. ④ Other sciences that have larger sets of concepts also require practice for students to relate the concepts to new and varied situations. ⑤ To repeat what has been said before, providing practice exercises across a variety of contexts and situations is what makes learning last — it is the way to promote transfer of learning.

5. 다음 글의 내용을 한 문장으로 요약하고자 한다. 빈칸 (A)와 (B)에 들어갈 말로 가장 적절한 것은?

Anyone who can read can read a poem. Part of poetry's power is in the sound of the spoken word, so after you have read it silently, you have to read it again aloud. One time won't do it. More than one time reading aloud will put you on the right path. You will find upon re-reading a poem that you begin to convey meaning through vocal stress, that you begin to parse the poem's literal and figurative meanings, and that your imagination actively engages in associative feelings. It is actually like having a conversation with the poet, since what his artistic mind and ear created is interacting with your imaginative mind and ear. The more you read, the more you will realize that poems do not have just one meaning. Readers make subjective and imaginative choices when they read, and these can change upon re-reading a poem. A poem read just one time is not fully read.

*parse: (문장을) 분석하다 **figurative: 비유적인

↓

Repeatedly reading a poem aloud ____(A)____ your understanding of a poem's meaning, because the more you re-read its text, the more your interpretation of it can be ____(B)____.

(A)　　　　　　(B)
① restricts　……　altered
② restricts　……　objective
③ increases　……　altered
④ increases　……　objective
⑤ deepens　……　valid

1. 다음 빈칸에 들어갈 말로 가장 적절한 것은? [3점]

We need to understand health so much better than we do. What a world of difference there is between being ill in the eyes of your doctor and feeling sick when you get out of bed to face the day. In 1948, the founders of the World Health Organization (WHO) defined health as "physical, mental, and social well-being, not merely the absence of infirmity." John Kennedy and Dwight Eisenhower both battled serious illnesses; but nobody, including themselves, as they tirelessly bore the burden of the presidency, would have called them sick. For eight years, the crippled President Roosevelt was an active and cheerful president; yet some people half his age and in far better health spend most of their time unhappily in bed. Clearly, subjective health is _____ _____.

*infirmity: 질병, 질환

① influenced by good physical fitness
② as important as objective physical health
③ poorly understood by the healthy elderly
④ people's satisfaction with their medical treatment
⑤ known to have different meanings in different people

2. 주어진 글 다음에 이어질 글의 순서로 가장 적절한 것은?

When an underwater object is viewed from above the water, its appearance becomes distorted. This is because refraction changes the direction of the light rays that come from the object.

(A) You can easily observe this effect by looking at a straw in a glass of water. Light rays from the part of the straw that is underwater refract at the surfaces between the water and the glass, and between the glass and the air.

(B) The rays seem to come from closer to the surface than they are, and the straw looks bent. If the straw were viewed from underwater, the part above water would be distorted.

(C) When these rays find the eyes of an observer, nerves in the eyes send signals to the observer's brain. The brain then creates an image based on where the rays appear to have originated. It does this without taking into consideration the effects of refraction, so the object's appearance is distorted.

① (A) – (C) – (B)   ② (B) – (A) – (C)
③ (B) – (C) – (A)   ④ (C) – (A) – (B)
⑤ (C) – (B) – (A)

3. 글의 흐름으로 보아, 주어진 문장이 들어가기에 가장 적절한 곳은?

The man agreed and, according to Franklin, "when we next met in the House, he manifested a readiness to serve me on all occasions."

Eighteenth-century American politician Benjamin Franklin was once eager to gain the cooperation of a difficult and apathetic member of the Pennsylvania state legislature. (①) Rather than spend his time bowing and scraping to the man, Franklin decided on a completely different course of action. (②) He knew that the man had a copy of a rare book in his private library, and so Franklin asked whether he might be able to borrow it for a couple of days. (③) Franklin attributed that to a simple principle: "He that has once done you a kindness will be more ready to do you another than he whom you yourself have obliged." (④) In other words, to increase the likelihood that someone will like you, get that person to do you a favor. (⑤) A century later, Russian novelist Leo Tolstoy appeared to agree, writing, "We do not love people so much for the good they have done us, as for the good we do them."

[4~5] 다음 글을 읽고, 물음에 답하시오.

There's a group of Russian immigrants in Los Angeles who have a tradition of celebrating New Year's Eve on the afternoon of December 30th. When they were asked why, one of them said, "When we were young and didn't have much money, it was (a) cheaper to get a band on the afternoon of the 30th, rather than the next day. That's how our tradition started." The curious thing is that now most of these people could easily afford entertainment on New Year's Eve, but they still celebrate on the afternoon of the 30th. The point: once an attitude or belief gets established, it tends to (b) survive even though the original reason for its development no longer exists.

Every situation or problem has a little of this "people celebrating early" for (c) outdated reasons. It could be the age at which you decide to retire. Indeed, the retirement age for many western nations, 65, is a perfect example. Back in the 1870's, German chancellor Otto von Bismarck arbitrarily set 65 as the retirement age. This decision made good financial sense because average life expectancy then was far shorter than that. The problem is that life expectancy is currently much longer than 65, and yet that age (d) expires even though financial considerations might dictate otherwise.

To be effective in anything, you must always be looking for obsolete ideas and (e) deleting them. Indeed, this is a cornerstone of creative thinking.

4. 윗글의 제목으로 가장 적절한 것은?

① Don't Underestimate Yourself
② Learn from Traditional Customs
③ Be Ready for Unexpected Early Retirement
④ Constantly Re-examine Old Assumptions
⑤ Step Out of Your Danger Zone

5. 밑줄 친 (a)~(e) 중에서 문맥상 낱말의 쓰임이 적절하지 <u>않은</u> 것은? [3점]

① (a)　　② (b)　　③ (c)　　④ (d)　　⑤ (e)

1. 다음 글에서 필자가 주장하는 바로 가장 적절한 것은?

History tells us of people who reached their peak after middle age. Verdi wrote *Othello* when he was seventy-three. Cervantes wrote *Don Quixote* when in his middle years. Pearl Buck, a great writer, once talked about her eightieth birthday. She said that she became a far better person at eighty than she was at fifty or forty. She said that she had learned a great deal since she was seventy. She felt that she had learned more in those ten years than in any other ten-year period. In fact, Pearl Buck was right. Many studies show that smart people tend to get smarter as they grow older. So, don't think that old age is a cue to simply do nothing. Instead, keep developing your good qualities that can be used to help society and yourself.

① 노인들의 연륜과 지혜를 존중하면서 배워야 한다.
② 나이가 들어서도 계속해서 자기 계발을 해야 한다.
③ 노인들의 복지를 위한 사회 제도를 정비해야 한다.
④ 문학 작품을 쓰기 위해서 많은 경험을 해야 한다.
⑤ 인구 고령화로 인해 생기는 문제에 대처해야 한다.

2. 밑줄 친 the tub sinks가 다음 글에서 의미하는 바로 가장 적절한 것은?

Sometimes a novel thought long dead can come back to life, brush the dirt off its pages, and shuffle back into an author's career. And that's what happened to Michael Chabon and his novel *Fountain City*, which he killed after five and a half years' work in 1992. "It was erasing me, breaking me down, burying me alive, drowning me, kicking me down the stairs," he said about the novel's impact on him. Chabon, however, published the first four chapters of it in the literary magazine in 2010, completing the task of lifetime. And there's also Stephen King, whose recent novel *Under the Dome* is a complete rewrite of his unfinished novel from 30 years ago. "The character list kept growing, and the characters didn't connect, and I just got to a point where I dropped it," King recalled. But three decades later, a fresh shot at the concept worked at last. Writing a novel is like paddling from Boston to London in a bathtub. Sometimes the tub sinks. It's a wonder that most of them don't.

① The novel's deadline is missed.
② The novel receives critical acclaim.
③ The novel is abandoned by its writer.
④ The novel fails to balance fact and fiction.
⑤ The novel doesn't meet readers' expectations.

3. 다음 빈칸에 들어갈 말로 가장 적절한 것은? [3점]

A universal moment of truth for artists arrives when the destination for their work is suddenly removed. Consider an artist whose single-minded goal, for twenty years, was to land a one-man show at his city's major art museum. When he finally got it, he never produced a serious piece of art again. There's a painful irony to stories like that, to discovering how frequently and easily success leads to depression. Avoiding this fate has something to do with _____. With individual artworks it means leaving some unresolved issue to carry forward and explore in the next piece. And for a few physically risky art forms (like dance), it may even mean developing other interests in case of injury.

① trying to make many friends in various fields
② postponing arriving at the destination on purpose
③ not obsessing about the exhibition of your artwork
④ not letting your current goal become your only goal
⑤ cultivating a healthy balance between work and play

4. 주어진 글 다음에 이어질 글의 순서로 가장 적절한 것은?

> Although psychology and dog training may appear to be quite different professions, the philosophies of how we interact with dogs and with people in a positive way actually have much in common.

(A) You are probably aware that in previous generations the physical punishment of children was more acceptable, and the view that 'children should be seen but not heard' was much more common.

(B) Furthermore, the evolution of both dog and child psychology have followed similar paths. The concept of positive reinforcement has been around since the early twentieth century, but it has only been in recent years that so much emphasis has been placed on rewarding the good behavior of children and on maintaining their self-esteem.

(C) Similarly, traditional dog-training methods involved correction and punishment, with positive reinforcement virtually unheard of in dog-training circles until the Gentle Modern Method of Dog Training was introduced in the early 1970s.

① (A) – (C) – (B)　　　② (B) – (A) – (C)
③ (B) – (C) – (A)　　　④ (C) – (A) – (B)
⑤ (C) – (B) – (A)

5. 글의 흐름으로 보아, 주어진 문장이 들어가기에 가장 적절한 곳은?

> The major shortcoming of the traditional dictionary is that there is limited space available to give only a sampling of how words are used.

Our 21st century technologies, such as the World Wide Web, have profound implications for the way we define the words in our language. (①) In pre-Internet times, the hard copy dictionary always served as the final authority for what a word means and how it is used. (②) The authors of dictionaries (lexicographers) traditionally have arrived at their definitions by carefully analyzing as many examples as possible of how a particular word is used. (③) While some complex words found in any standard desk dictionary can have as many as nine or ten possible uses, even these definitions fail to cover all possible usages. (④) According to lexicographer Erin McKean, a recent study showed that in a set of randomly chosen passages from modern fiction, 13 percent of the nouns, verbs, and adjectives were used in ways not found in large desk dictionaries. (⑤) There are, in other words, many more contemporary usages that never make it into a standard dictionary because of the limitations of physical space.

*lexicographer: 사전 편찬자

1. 다음 글의 주제로 가장 적절한 것은?

A taste for Sauvignon Blanc and Chardonnay or a liking for Bordeaux or Zinfandel can indicate more than just a preference in wines. It could also reveal personality traits. New research by scientists in Australia and Britain showed that drinkers who preferred a sweet taste in wine were more likely to be impulsive, while those who chose dry varieties had greater openness. "Participants with a sweet taste preference were significantly higher in impulsiveness than their dry preference counterparts," Anthony J. Saliba, of Charles Sturt University in Wagga Wagga, Australia, and his colleagues said in the report. They said apart from impulsiveness and openness, no other personality trait was significantly different between the two groups.

① the impact of red wine on heart health
② reasons why people prefer wine over others
③ tips for selecting a good quality wine reliably
④ common roles of wine in human relationships
⑤ the correlation between personality and wine choice

2. 다음 글의 밑줄 친 부분 중, 어법상 틀린 것은?

Existing travel information systems, such as electronic signage on motorways, ① are designed to consider travellers as crowds, lacking any form of personalized information format and delivery. Moreover, most advanced traffic management systems rely on a ② centrally controlled infrastructure and information source. These two characteristics hinder the development of trust and credibility of the particular systems. Indeed, a travel information system that more often than not delivers information unrelated to someone's journey gradually ③ becoming 'noise' in the travellers' environment. According to experts in transportation research, the reaction of drivers to electronic signage messages ④ decreases over time, showing a potential distrust of the displayed messages. An information system that relies on a single source of information is at risk of becoming untrustworthy. Incidents ⑤ where wrong or inaccurate information is delivered by the single information source would damage trust levels in the system as a whole.

*electronic signage: 전광판

3. 다음 빈칸에 들어갈 말로 가장 적절한 것은? [3점]

A message is transferred from facts to language, from language to written words, from written words to language in another mind, and out of that language into stored information. Just how successful the process is at these stages no one knows. It would also be nearly impossible to devise an experiment to determine the efficiency. Nevertheless, in the real world, such transfers are never 100% efficient. If we allow them to be as good as 90%, losses at the four stages still reduce the overall efficiency to less than 65%. By a rough guess, only a little over half the original message reaches the reader's mind, and probably much less. Just think for a moment about the proportion of the total information you retain after reading a book or attending a lecture. Information transfer _____.

① is actually a losing business
② leads to mutually beneficial results
③ requires good communication skills
④ creates an effect of temporal uncertainty
⑤ occurs when there is real-time communication

4. 다음 글에서 전체 흐름과 관계 없는 문장은?

The massive tombs and ceremonial structures built from huge stones in the Neolithic period are known as megalithic architecture, from the Greek words for "large" (*megas*) and "stone" (*lithos*). ① Archaeologists disagree about the nature of the societies that created them. ② Some believe megalithic monuments reflect complex, stratified societies in which powerful religious or political leaders dictated their design and commanded the large workforce necessary to accomplish these ambitious engineering projects. ③ Other interpreters argue that these massive undertakings are clear evidence for cooperative collaboration within and among social groups, coalescing around a common project that fueled social cohesion without the controlling power of a ruling elite. ④ Tomb architecture was complex and its art in the form of painting, sculpture and script gives a glimpse into the beliefs and daily life of the ancient people. ⑤ Many megalithic structures are associated with death, and recent interpretations stress the fundamental role of death and burial as public theatrical performances in which individual and group identity, cohesion, and disputes were played out.

*stratified: 계층화된 **coalesce: 하나가 되다

5. 다음 글의 내용을 한 문장으로 요약하고자 한다. 빈칸 (A)와 (B)에 들어갈 말로 가장 적절한 것은?

Believe it or not, even in this computerized world there are still many situations where a sheet of paper and a pencil are the best tools for the music composer. Many important modern composers, especially those born before 1940, won't work with anything but paper and pencil. So, never think you are too advanced for these humble tools. Writing music with only paper and pencil has some amazing advantages to composing at a piano or other instrument. For one thing, many composers find the actual sound of the instrument itself interruptive to the composition process. Just imagine yourself deep in thought, hearing the perfect sequence of notes in your head, when suddenly, your finger touches the actual piano key, and it doesn't sound exactly like you imagined. Real sound is harsh, and hearing even the first note of your imagined phrase before you've written it down can cause you to lose an entire piece of music.

*phrase: 악구 ((악절을 이루는 한 부분으로, 음악 주제가 비교적 완성된 두 소절에서 네 소절 정도까지의 부분))

↓

Writing music with conventional tools like paper and a pencil is more ___(A)___ than with a musical instrument, because real sound can be ___(B)___ to the composition process.

	(A)		(B)
①	difficult	⋯⋯	similar
②	difficult	⋯⋯	disruptive
③	useful	⋯⋯	similar
④	useful	⋯⋯	disruptive
⑤	popular	⋯⋯	contradictory

1. 다음 빈칸에 들어갈 말로 가장 적절한 것은?

Humans are creatures of story, so story touches nearly every aspect of our lives. Archaeologists dig up clues in the stones and bones and piece them together into a story about the past. Historians, too, are storytellers. Some argue that many of the accounts in school textbooks, like the standard story of Columbus's discovery of America, are so full of distortions and omissions that they are closer to myth than history. Business executives are increasingly told that they must be creative storytellers: they have to spin compelling narratives about their products and brands that emotionally transport consumers. Political analysts see a presidential election not only as a contest between influential politicians and their ideas but also as _____. Legal scholars regard a trial as a story contest, too, in which opposing counsels construct narratives of guilt and innocence — arguing over who is the real protagonist.

*protagonist: (이야기의) 주인공

① a very important chance for people to exercise their rights

② a contest between political pledges to establish a national identity

③ a fierce conflict between a conservative right wing and a liberal left wing

④ an inevitable fight between government and opposition parties

⑤ a competition between conflicting stories about the nation

2. 주어진 글 다음에 이어질 글의 순서로 가장 적절한 것은?

In the 1980s, John Riskind chose to examine the effect of posture on persistence. Riskind placed participants in one of two positions. Half of the participants were placed in a slumped position, so that their backs were bent over, and heads dropped down.

(A) In fact, many of the puzzles were impossible to solve, and Riskind was only interested in how long the participants managed to carry on in the face of failure.

(B) Describing his findings in a paper, Riskind made a note of how the participants who had previously been sitting up straight endured for nearly twice as long as the slouchers.

(C) In contrast, the remaining participants were told to sit upright, with their shoulders pulled back and heads held high. After sitting stooped or upright for about three minutes, each participant was sent to another room and asked to try and solve several puzzles that involved tracing over a diagram without removing their pencil from the page.

*slump: 털썩 앉다; 푹 쓰러지다 **sloucher: 구부정한 자세로 앉은 사람

***stoop: 몸을 굽히다

① (A) – (C) – (B)　　② (B) – (A) – (C)

③ (B) – (C) – (A)　　④ (C) – (A) – (B)

⑤ (C) – (B) – (A)

3. 글의 흐름으로 보아, 주어진 문장이 들어가기에 가장 적절한 곳은?

In other words, a limited fluency in English is not a valid reason for putting off writing an article to announce a good piece of research.

Science has a language of its own that has nothing to do with the scientist's native tongue. (①) It is the language of logic, in which reasoned arguments are developed from well-presented evidence and lead to sound and consistent conclusions. (②) That language is the same regardless of the origin and preferred tongue of the person who writes it, and good scientific writing depends primarily on expressing the science precisely and clearly. (③) Subsequent editing by a native speaker to tidy up English expressions and comply with modern vernacular is relatively easy, and the article will be a good one. (④) If the expression of the science is poor, no amount of correction of the English can turn it into a satisfactory paper. (⑤) In fact, non-native English speakers often have unexpected advantages when it comes to writing science.

*vernacular: 일상적 표현

[4~5] 다음 글을 읽고, 물음에 답하시오.

When traveling, you learn to make friends out of strangers and get used to talking with new people. When I first started traveling, I was kind of an (a) introvert and uncomfortable talking to those I didn't know. Now, I'll gladly talk to strangers like we've known each other for years. Travel not only makes you comfortable talking to strangers, it makes you better at it too. After talking to people all the time, the usual questions become (b) boring. After a while, you don't care about where people are from, where they are going, how long they've been traveling, and so on. Those kinds of questions don't really tell you anything about the person. You'll get better at small talk and asking interesting questions — the ones that (c) matter and tell you something about the person. Unless you sit at a resort sipping frozen drinks, travel will teach you about the world.

You'll learn about people, history, and culture, and surprising facts about places some people could only dream about. That's something that can't be learned from books; you can only pick it up with on-the-road experience. In addition, travel teaches you to be (d) less materialistic. On the road, you learn just how little stuff you truly need. You'll realize that all those things they sell at the mall are pretty (e) useful in leading a happy life. Coming home, you'll find yourself a minimalist simply because you realize what you need to live and what you don't.

4. 윗글의 제목으로 가장 적절한 것은?

① Having More versus Being More
② Travel Abroad to Buy Experiences
③ Ways to Make Your Travel More Fun
④ Why Travel Makes You a Better Person
⑤ Travel Gives You Space to Take a Breath

5. 밑줄 친 (a)~(e) 중에서 문맥상 낱말의 쓰임이 적절하지 <u>않은</u> 것은? [3점]

① (a) ② (b) ③ (c) ④ (d) ⑤ (e)

1. 다음 글의 요지로 가장 적절한 것은?

Your brain is updated moment by moment and hour by hour. In essence, you frequently get a new processing system. Indeed, you have the potential to change your brain with everything you do that has some level of challenge, novelty, or variety. My research has found an interesting paradox: when one focuses on remembering the minute details, it may adversely affect the ability to engage in more strategic abstract thinking. In essence, trying to remember as many details as possible can actually work against being selective about what you let into your brain's attic. This pattern helps explain why access to more information is not, on its own, making us smarter. More likely, quite the opposite is true. Exposure to large volumes of information steals and freezes your brainpower.

① 올바른 정보와 잘못된 정보를 판별하는 능력이 필요하다.
② 많은 정보를 습득할수록 추상적인 사고 능력이 향상된다.
③ 두뇌의 능력은 매 순간 동일하지 않고 환경에 따라 변화한다.
④ 추상적인 것과 세부 사항을 기억하는 능력은 각각 구분된다.
⑤ 많은 정보를 기억하는 것은 지능 향상에 도움이 되지 않는다.

2. 다음 빈칸에 들어갈 말로 가장 적절한 것은?

Contemporary reading and writing practices are transforming before our eyes. Interactive reading and writing now increasingly engage us. One can read together with others remotely, commenting between the virtual lines and in the margins, reading each other's comments instantaneously, composing documents together in real time by adding words or sentences to those just composed by one's collaborators. The lines between one's own words and those of another's — let alone between whole sentences — become quickly blurred. Hyperlinking has encouraged reading not just *within* and then *between* discrete texts but much more robustly across texts, inter-referencing and interweaving insights and lines of referencing. How texts relate, as a consequence, has become dramatically _____, making visible what hitherto has been hidden largely from view.

*robustly: 활발하게 **hitherto: 지금까지

① trifling
② disregarded
③ magnified
④ impartial
⑤ invariable

3. 다음 글에서 전체 흐름과 관계 없는 문장은?

The innovativeness of cities is related directly to the quality of human talent. ① China's coastal cities have been quicker off the mark because they have been more successful in nurturing quality, retaining the most talented knowledge workers, and attracting the cream of the knowledge workers from other parts of the country. ② The coastal cities are also more open and accessible to outsiders and have integrated with global knowledge networks. ③ For smaller inland cities to become innovative smart cities, they will need to specialize and pull in some of the best brains in their fields of specialization from across the country. ④ Smart cities have become the most popular term for the future city, and it is becoming a globally recognized term, replacing with terms in other languages, such as the "sustainable city" and the "digital city." ⑤ Any serious attempt to become an innovative city built on the quality of talent, which after all is the life blood of innovation, will have to combine urban design and renewal with a focus on developing a few core areas of world-class expertise.

*the cream of: ~의 최고[정수]

4. 주어진 글 다음에 이어질 글의 순서로 가장 적절한 것은?

> Naturally, people eat many different kinds of meals and choose them with the intention of communicating the right message to the right audience.

(A) Equally, a meal of roast beef offered to a vegetarian might be construed as a calculated insult. As with all language, there can be miscommunication. Despite this, an outsider observing or commenting on an eating event can usually decode the intended message without too much difficulty.

(B) One would not reheat half-eaten leftovers when trying to impress a potential lover, just as one would not spend a fortune on extravagant ingredients for a hurried everyday meal eaten in solitude. Every meal has, in a sense, its own coded message.

(C) This is not to say, however, that it is always readily perceived or interpreted correctly by others. What may be intended as cozy informality to someone preparing a meal might be interpreted as laziness by an invited guest.

*construe: 해석하다 **decode: 해독하다

① (A) – (C) – (B)
② (B) – (A) – (C)
③ (B) – (C) – (A)
④ (C) – (A) – (B)
⑤ (C) – (B) – (A)

5. 글의 흐름으로 보아, 주어진 문장이 들어가기에 가장 적절한 곳은? [3점]

> But behind these is an unstated assumption: that it is one person's *ten unaided fingers* that produce the sounds.

To know whether an artistic performance succeeds or fails requires that we know what counts as success or failure in any performance context. Music critics will consider a pianist's tone, phrasing, tempo, accuracy, and ability to sustain a line or build to a climax. (①) Speed and brilliance may be important considerations, which is not to say the fastest performance will be the best. (②) The excitement a virtuoso pianist generates with a glittering shower of notes is intrinsically connected with this fact. (③) An aurally identical experience that is electronically synthesized can never dazzle us in the same way: sound synthesizers can produce individual notes as fast as you please, while pianists cannot. (④) Built into the thrill of hearing a virtuoso is admiration for what the performance represents as a human achievement. (⑤) Forgery and other forms of fakery in the arts misrepresent the nature of the performance and so misrepresent achievement.

*virtuoso: (예술의) 거장(의), 대가(의) **forgery: 위조

1. 다음 글의 제목으로 가장 적절한 것은?

Peter Gollwitzer, a psychologist at New York University, and colleague Veronika Brandstatter found that action triggers are quite effective in motivating action. In one study, they followed college students who had the chance to earn extra credit in a class by writing a paper about how they spent Christmas Eve. But there was a condition: To earn the credit, they had to turn in the paper by December 26. Most students had intentions of writing the paper, but only 33 percent of them ended up writing and submitting it. However, some students in the study were required to set action triggers — to record, in advance, exactly when and where they intended to write the report. Seventy-five percent of those students wrote the report. That's a fairly significant result for such a small mental investment.

① Don't Be a Talker, but a Doer
② Why Is It Always So Hard to Get Started?
③ Promise Only What You Can Definitely Do
④ Motivating Action: Write Down Your Resolution
⑤ Action Triggers Change Things When Change Is Hard

2. 다음 글의 밑줄 친 부분 중, 문맥상 낱말의 쓰임이 적절하지 않은 것은?

In new relationships, people often ① disclose themselves slowly, sharing only a few details at first, and offering more personal information only if they like and trust each other. When they started becoming friends, for instance, Deepak and Prasad shared mostly ② routine information with each other, such as where they grew up, what their favorite teams were, and what they did for a living. As they got to ③ trust each other more, they started sharing their opinions on things such as politics, relationships, and religion. Only after they had known each other for quite a while did they feel ④ uncomfortable talking about more personal things, such as Prasad's health problems or the challenges in Deepak's marriage. Although people in some relationships begin sharing ⑤ intimate information very quickly, self-disclosure usually moves in small increments.

*increment: 증가량

3. 다음 빈칸에 들어갈 말로 가장 적절한 것은?

When people don't trust their own judgments, they look to others for evidence of how to choose correctly. This self-doubt may come about because the situation is ambiguous, as it was in a classic series of experiments conducted by the Turkish social psychologist Muzafer Sherif. Sherif projected a dot of light on the wall of a darkened room and asked subjects to indicate how much the light moved while they watched it. Actually, the light never moved at all, but because of an optical illusion termed the *autokinetic effect*, it seemed to shift constantly about, although to a different extent for each subject. When participants announced their movement estimates in groups, these estimates were strongly influenced by what the other group members estimated; nearly everyone changed toward the group average. Sherif concluded that when there's _____, people are likely to doubt themselves and thus are especially likely to assume that the group must be right.

*optical illusion: 착시

**autokinetic effect: 자동운동 효과(시각적 자극 운동의 환상)

① little time to think and answer
② no objectively correct response
③ consistency of external messages
④ substantial evidence against them
⑤ any context announced in advance

4. 다음 글에서 전체 흐름과 관계 없는 문장은?

Findings from several studies on nonpatient groups such as university students suggest that simply looking at everyday nature, as compared to built scenes that lack nature, is significantly more effective in promoting restoration from stress. ① One early study focused on students who were experiencing mild stress because of a final course exam. ② A self-ratings questionnaire was used to assess restorative influences of viewing either a diverse slide sample of unblighted built settings lacking nature, or slides of undistinguished nature settings dominated by green vegetation. ③ Results suggested that the nature views fostered greater psychological restoration as indicated by larger reductions in negative feelings such as fear and anger/aggression and much higher levels of positive feelings. ④ The new-made views of concrete jungle selected to target these feelings directly helped to create an environment offering stress restoration. ⑤ Also, the scenes with vegetation sustained interest and attention more effectively than did the urban scenes without nature.

*built scene: 인공적인 경관 **unblighted: 손상되지 않은

5. 다음 글의 내용을 한 문장으로 요약하고자 한다. 빈칸 (A), (B)에 들어갈 말로 가장 적절한 것은?

Generations of kids have grown up with plump cartoon characters like Winnie the Pooh and Homer Simpson — and it may not be good for their diets. In an experiment, children between the ages of 6 and 14 years old viewed cartoon characters that were drawn to represent either normal weight or overweight physiques. After answering questions on the quality of the picture, they were offered candy or cookies. The kids ate almost twice as much candy or as many cookies when they saw the apparently overweight character as those exposed to a thinner cartoon character or no cartoon at all. In another study, kids were asked questions about their health knowledge before viewing the images of cartoon characters. This time, their eating choices were no longer impacted by seeing the overweight character.

↓

> Children exposed to obese cartoon characters are more likely to _____(A)_____ eating unhealthy diets, which can be _____(B)_____ by stimulating their health knowledge.

	(A)		(B)
①	indulge in	……	induced
②	indulge in	……	modified
③	be conscious of	……	reinforced
④	be resistant to	……	reduced
⑤	be resistant to	……	optimized

1. 다음 빈칸에 들어갈 말로 가장 적절한 것은? [3점]

Even though many of our memories are vivid and some may even be accurate, most of what we remember of our daily lives is neither exact nor rich in detail. There is overwhelming neuropsychological evidence that evolution did not design our memories to be video cameras faithfully and precisely recording our daily experiences. For example, a key memory system in the brain is specifically structured to extract from experience unconscious rules and abstractions that allow organisms to deal with the ever-changing world that surrounds them in an expedient and self-serving manner. There is also evidence that we may change our memories, if only a little, each time we recall them. The fluidity of memory may reflect the challenges inherent in engineering brains able to make life-and-death decisions at a moment's notice in noisy, uncertain, and ever-changing environments. Memory _____ _____.

*expedient: 편의주의적인

① is about survival, not accuracy
② notifies us of a potential danger
③ is distorted by misleading information
④ shows how past events are understood
⑤ changes based on our present experiences

2. 주어진 글 다음에 이어질 글의 순서로 가장 적절한 것은?

The idea that we are living moments of more and lives of less is supported by a recent study in which pairs of college-aged friends were asked to communicate in four different ways: face-to-face conversation, video chat, audio chat, and online instant messaging.

(A) The students had tried to "warm up" their digital messages by using emoticons, typing out the sounds of laughter ("Hahaha"), and using the forced urgency of TYPING IN ALL CAPS.

(B) But these techniques had not done the job. It is when we see each other's faces and hear each other's voices that we become most human to each other.

(C) Then, the degree of emotional bonding in these friendships was assessed both by asking how people felt and watching how they behaved toward each other. The results were clear: in-person conversation led to the most emotional connection and online messaging led to the least.

① (A) – (C) – (B)　　② (B) – (A) – (C)
③ (B) – (C) – (A)　　④ (C) – (A) – (B)
⑤ (C) – (B) – (A)

3. 글의 흐름으로 보아, 주어진 문장이 들어가기에 가장 적절한 곳은?

But they were a sign of our universe's astonishing capacity to build complex objects from simple building blocks.

In the first minutes of its existence, the universe cooled so rapidly that it was impossible to manufacture elements heavier or more complex than hydrogen, helium, and (in minute amounts) lithium. (①) In the heat and chaos of the early universe, nothing more complex could survive. (②) From a chemical point of view, the early universe was very simple, far too simple to create complex objects such as our earth or the living organisms that inhabit it. (③) The first stars and galaxies were constructed from little more than hydrogen and helium. (④) Once created, stars laid the foundations for even more complex entities, including living organisms, because in their fiery cores they practiced an alchemy that turned hydrogen and helium into all the other elements. (⑤)

*alchemy: 연금술

[4~5] 다음 글을 읽고, 물음에 답하시오.

In one study, social psychologists sprang a surprise memory test on shoppers who were leaving a small magazine shop in Sydney, Australia. Before the shoppers entered the shop, the researchers placed ten small ornamental objects on the shop counter — four plastic animals, a toy cannon, a piggy bank, and four Matchbox cars. After leaving the shop, the shoppers were asked to remember as many of the ten items as possible, and also to choose the ten items from a list of twenty that included the ten correct items and ten new items. The shoppers recalled three times as many items on the rainy days as on the sunny days, and they were approximately four times as accurate when identifying the ten objects from the longer list of twenty items. The researchers explained that (a) <u>gloomy</u> weather hampers our mood, which in turn makes us think more deeply and clearly.

Humans are biologically predisposed to avoid sadness, and they respond to sad moods by seeking opportunities for mood repair and vigilantly protecting themselves against whatever might be making them sad. In contrast, happiness sends a signal that everything is fine, the environment doesn't pose an imminent threat, and there's no need to think (b) <u>carefully</u>. These (c) <u>contrasting</u> mental approaches explain why the shoppers remembered the ten trinkets more accurately on rainy days. The rainy days induced a generally negative mood state, which the shoppers subconsciously tried to overcome by (d) <u>scanning</u> the environment for information that might have replaced their dampened sad moods with happier alternatives. If you think about it, this approach makes sense. Mood states are all-purpose measurement devices that tell us whether something in the environment needs to be (e) <u>uniform</u>.

4. 윗글의 제목으로 가장 적절한 것은?

① Sunny Days and Logical Thoughts
② How the Weather Can Affect Your Mood
③ Rainy Days Are Really Good for Shopping
④ Why Rainy Weather Helps Us Think More Clearly
⑤ We Tend to Distort Our Memories When We're Sad

5. 밑줄 친 (a)~(e) 중에서 문맥상 낱말의 쓰임이 적절하지 <u>않은</u> 것은? [3점]

① (a)　　② (b)　　③ (c)　　④ (d)　　⑤ (e)

● CHECK! 각 Day별 정답 개수를 기록해보세요.

Day 01	/ 5	Day 31	/ 5
Day 02	/ 5	Day 32	/ 5
Day 03	/ 5	Day 33	/ 5
Day 04	/ 5	Day 34	/ 5
Day 05	/ 5	Day 35	/ 5
Day 06	/ 5	Day 36	/ 5
Day 07	/ 5	Day 37	/ 5
Day 08	/ 5	Day 38	/ 5
Day 09	/ 5	Day 39	/ 5
Day 10	/ 5	Day 40	/ 5
Day 11	/ 5	Day 41	/ 5
Day 12	/ 5	Day 42	/ 5
Day 13	/ 5	Day 43	/ 5
Day 14	/ 5	Day 44	/ 5
Day 15	/ 5	Day 45	/ 5
Day 16	/ 5	Day 46	/ 5
Day 17	/ 5	Day 47	/ 5
Day 18	/ 5	Day 48	/ 5
Day 19	/ 5	Day 49	/ 5
Day 20	/ 5	Day 50	/ 5
Day 21	/ 5	Day 51	/ 5
Day 22	/ 5	Day 52	/ 5
Day 23	/ 5	Day 53	/ 5
Day 24	/ 5	Day 54	/ 5
Day 25	/ 5	Day 55	/ 5
Day 26	/ 5	Day 56	/ 5
Day 27	/ 5	Day 57	/ 5
Day 28	/ 5	Day 58	/ 5
Day 29	/ 5	Day 59	/ 5
Day 30	/ 5	Day 60	/ 5

① 구문 　판매 1위 '천일문' 콘텐츠를 활용하여 정확하고 다양한 구문 학습

(끊어읽기) (해석하기) (문장 구조 분석) (해설·해석 제공) (단어 스크램블링) (영작하기)

② 문법·서술형 　쎄듀의 모든 문법 문항을 활용하여 내신까지 해결하는 정교한 문법 유형 제공

(객관식과 주관식의 결합) (문법 포인트별 학습) (보기를 활용한 집합 문항) (내신대비 서술형) (어법+서술형 문제)

③ 어휘 　초·중·고·공무원까지 방대한 어휘량을 제공하며 오프라인 TEST 인쇄도 가능

(영단어 카드 학습) (단어 ↔ 뜻 유형) (예문 활용 유형) (단어 매칭 게임)

④ 선생님 보유 문항 이용

(Online Test) (OMR Test)

cafe.naver.com/cedulearnteacher

쎄듀런 학습 정보가 궁금하다면?

쎄듀런 Cafe

· 쎄듀런 사용법 안내 & 학습법 공유
· 공지 및 문의사항 QA
· 할인 쿠폰 증정 등 이벤트 진행

실감
하다

정답 및 해설

5문항 × 60 DAYS

300 제

실감하다

300제

정답 및 해설

1 필자 주장 　①

해설　필자는 기술 전문가들이 기술 전문가가 아닌 독자들을 대상으로 글을 쓸 때 독자의 지식 수준을 그 분야의 기술 전문가들만큼 높게 가정해서는 안 된다는 주장을 펼치고 있다.

해석　마크 트웨인은 "우리는 모두 무지하다. 다만 다른 것들에 대하여."라고 말했다. 기술 전문가들이 기술 전문가가 아닌 독자들을 위한 글을 쓸 때 저지르는 한 가지 실수는 독자들이 주제에 대하여 자신들만큼 지식이 있을 것이라고 가정하는 것이다. 이것은 독자에게 오로지 혼란과 좌절만을 초래할 치명적인 가정이다. 또한 애당초 명확했어야 할 것을 설명하려고 노력하며 독자에게 추가적인 메시지를 생성하는 데에 막대한 당신의 시간이 쓰이게 될 것이다. 단지 당신에게 명확하다는 이유로 독자에게도 명확해지는 것은 아니다. 당신이 당신 분야의 다른 사람들에게 글을 쓰는 엔지니어나 회계사라면 아마 당신의 메시지의 모든 측면을 설명할 필요성은 낮아질 것이다. 소프트웨어 어플리케이션을 잘 모르는 마케팅 부서의 상무에게 글을 쓴다면, 당신은 그 독자에게 당신의 메시지를 '차근차근 보여줄' 필요가 있을 것이다. 기술적 지식에 관해서는 필자와 독자가 동등한 일은 거의 없다는 점을 명심하라.

구문　[6행~9행] Also, a great deal of your time will be **spent** generating additional messages to the reader **trying** to explain **what should have been** clear the first time.

• 「spend [시간] v-ing (v하는 데 [시간]이 걸리다) 구문이 수동태로 「[시간] be spent v-ing (v하는 데 [시간]이 쓰이다)」의 형태로 쓰였다. trying 이하는 분사구문이고 what 이하는 to explain의 목적어이다. 「should have p.p.」는 '~했어야 했는데'의 뜻이다.

[9행~10행] **Just because** it's clear to you does not make it clear to your reader.

• Just because ~ to you 부분이 주어로, because절이 명사절로 사용되기도 한다. Just because는 '단지 ~라는 이유로'의 뜻이다.

어휘　observe (논평·의견을) 말하다　ignorant 무지한　knowledgeable 지식이 있는　fatal 치명적인　accountant 회계사　senior vice president (회사의) 상무　be familiar with ~을 잘 알다　walk A through A에게 ~을 차근차근 보여주다　when it comes to A A에 관한 한

2 밑줄 함의 　④

해설　밑줄 친 문장의 They는 순환적 시간을 사는 사람들을 뜻한다. 그들은 직선적 시간을 사는 사람보다 더 느긋하고 스트레스가 없으며 삶이 여러모로 더 풍요롭고 건강하다고 했다. 또한 세상과 조화를 이루고 더 편히 숨을 쉰다고 했다. 그러므로 밑줄 친 부분의 의미로 가장 적절한 것은 ④ '자신들의 삶을 즐길 수 있다'이다.
① 미래에 초점을 둔다
② 다른 사람들과 잘 일한다
③ 스트레스 상황을 견딘다
⑤ 일상적으로 하는 일들에 만족한다

해석　직선적 시간만큼 많은 관심을 순환적 시간에 기울이는 문화에서는 사람들의 생활이 훨씬 더 느긋하고 스트레스가 없다. 대부분의 전통적인 원주민들은 훨씬 더 적은 시간 동안, 기껏해야 한 주에 2~3일 일을 한다. 그런데 이것은 우리가 이해하고 있는 '일하기'가 아니다. 그들은 방문하여, 어울려 노닐며, 이야기를 하고 잡담을 하면서, 자신들의 사회를 한데 묶어주는 사회적 결속이 잘 유지되고 있는지 확인한

다. 순환적 시간에 맞추어 산다는 것은 기한을 버리는 것이다. 순환적 시간은 명상, 빈둥거림, 놀이를 권장한다. 페달에서 발을 뗄 때는 사람들이 더 풍요롭고, 더 단순하고, 더 보람 있는 삶을 발견한다는 것은 흔히 가장 큰 놀라움들 중 하나이다. 그들의 몸은 원기를 회복한 상태이며, 그들은 더 좋은 건강을 누리고 더 많이 웃는다. 그들은 세상과 조화를 이루고, 직선적인 시간을 가진 사람들보다 더 편히 숨을 쉰다. 더 자주 그들은 어린아이였을 때에 어땠는지를 만들어내고, 놀이를 하고, 그것을 기억하는데, 거기서는 A 지점에서 B 지점으로 가는 여정이 직선인 경우가 거의 없었으며 절대 좁지 않았다. 미묘한 세부 사항에 접근하는 그들의 능력은 증가한다. 그들은 세상 속에서 숨 쉰다.

구문　[1행~3행] In *cultures* [where circular time is given as much attention as linear time], people's lives are **far** more relaxed and stress-free.

• [ ] 부분은 관계사절로 앞에 나온 명사 cultures를 수식한다. 부사 far는 비교급을 강조하는 수식어로 하는 '훨씬'이라는 뜻이다.

어휘　circular 순환적인　linear 직선적인　relaxed 느긋한, 여유 있는　aboriginal 원주민　gossip 잡담을 하다　cement 결속시키는 것　let go of (생각·태도를) 버리다; (손에서) 놓다　deadline 기한, 데드라인　rewarding 보람 있는　harmonious 조화된　access 접근하다　subtle 미묘한
[선택지] endure 견디다, 인내하다

3 빈칸 추론 　③

해설　자신이 하는 일 또는 자신이 시간을 보내는 일의 측면에서 자기 자신을 소개하는 것은 직업으로 자신을 인정받는다는 것이고 이것은 곧 직업이 자기 자신, 즉 자신의 정체성이 된다는 것이다. 그런 사람이 실직을 하게 되면 자신들의 정체성으로부터 분리된 느낌을 받을 것이라는 점에서 빈칸에는 ③ '정체성'이 가장 적절하다.
① 목표 ② 재산 ④ 배경 ⑤ 능력

해석　아주 자주 여러분은 자신이 하는 일 또는 자신이 시간을 보내는 일로 자기 자신을 소개하는 사람들을 발견하거나 만날 것이다. 이러한 사람들은 자신을 영업 사원이나 경영 간부로서 소개한다. 이렇게 하는 것에 죄가 되는 것은 없지만, 심리적으로는, 우리는 우리가 (그렇다고) 믿는 것이 된다. 이러한 관행을 따르는 사람들은 자신들의 개성을 잃고 자기가 하는 직업에 의해 인정받는다는 개념을 용납하기 시작하는 경향이 있다. 그러나 직업은 영구적이지 않을 수도 있고, 여러분은 셀 수 없이 많은 이유로 실직할지도 모르는데, 그 이유 중 몇몇에 대해서는 아무런 책임이 없을 수도 있다. 그러한 경우, 이런 사람들은 피할 수 없는 사회적, 그리고 정신적 외상으로 고통을 받고 이것은 정서적 스트레스와 한때 그들의 정체성이었던 것과 자신이 갑자기 분리되었다는 느낌으로 이어진다.

구문　[9행~11행] ~ you may lose your job for *a countless number of reasons*, **some of which** you may not even be responsible for.

• some of which에서 계속적 용법의 관계대명사 which의 선행사는 a countless number of reasons이다.

어휘　in terms of ~의 면에서, ~에 관해　executive 경영 간부, 임원　criminal 범죄의, 죄 있는　psychologically 심리적으로　practice 관행　individuality 개성　live with 수용하다, 용납하다; 같이 살다　notion 개념　permanent 영구적인　countless 셀 수 없이 많은, 무수한　inevitable 피할 수 없는, 필연의　trauma 외상, 마음의 상처　disassociate 분리하다
[선택지] property 재산; 부동산　capability 능력, 역량

4 글의 순서 ③

해설 주어진 문장의 내용은 기술적 현실이 어떻게 제품을 만드는지를 결정하는 데 여전히 가장 중요하다는 것이므로, 이에 대한 예시에 해당하는 알루미늄 캔에 대한 (B)가 맨 먼저 나와야 한다. (C)는 (B)의 알루미늄 캔에 대한 추가적인 내용이므로 (B) 다음에 나와야 한다. (A)의 '그러한 어려움(such difficulties involving numerous opposing)'은 (B)와 (C)에서 언급된 서로 상충되는 여러 어려움들을 뜻하므로 마지막으로 위치해야 적절하다.

해석 경제적인 고려가 매우 중요하다 할지라도, 기술적 현실은 어떻게 공학이 하나의 제품을 만드는지를 결정하는 데 있어서 여전히 가장 중요하다.
(B) 예를 들면, 음료 용기를 제작할 때, 공학자는 음료를 오염시키지 않게, 혹은 거칠게 다루는 운송과 취급을 한 후에도 새지 않게 음료를 담을 캔을 만들어야 할 뿐만 아니라, 그 캔을 따서 따르거나 마시기 쉽게 만들어야 한다.
(C) 더욱이 알루미늄 캔은 매우 편리한 것인 반면에, 그것들은 또한 원료와 에너지의 엄청난 잠재적 낭비를 나타내며, 그것을 처리하는 것은 쓰레기와 폐품 처리라는 중대한 문제를 제기한다.
(A) 수많은 대립되는 목표들을 포함하는 그런 어려움을 탐구하는 것과, 공학자들과 다른 사람들이 어떻게 그 문제들을 해결하려고 애써왔는지를 알아보는 것은, 우리가 공학, 경제학, 그리고 환경 사이의 상호 작용을 더 잘 이해하도록 돕는다. 별개로 있는 하나의 알루미늄 캔과 그것의 복제품이 수십억 개나 있는 상황에서의 알루미늄 캔은 전혀 다른 문제이다.

구문 [5행~9행] **Exploring** such difficulties (involving numerous opposing goals) and **seeing** how engineers and others have wrestled with the problems / **helps** us to better understand the interaction (between engineering, economics, and the environment).

• Exploring ~ the problems 부분이 주어로서 동명사가 and로 연결되는 병렬구조이고 helps가 동사이다. 두 개의 동명사가 and로 연결된 경우 동사는 단수동사와 복수동사 모두 올 수 있다.

[9행~11행] *A single aluminum can in isolation* **is one thing**, but *in the context of its billions of clones the aluminum can* **is** quite **another**.

• 'A와 B는 전혀 다르다'는 뜻의 「A is one thing, B is another」 구문으로 '별개로 있는 하나의 알루미늄 캔'과 '복제품이 수십억 개나 있는 상황에서의 알루미늄 캔'은 전혀 다르다는 의미이다.

어휘 **consideration** 고려 사항; 사려, 숙고 **explore** 탐구하다, 조사하다 **numerous** 수많은 **opposing** 대립되는, 반대의 **wrestle with** ~을 해결하려고 애쓰다, ~와 씨름하다 **interaction** 상호 작용 **in isolation** 별개로, 홀로 **fashion** 만들다, 모양 짓다 **leak** 새다, 새어 나오다 **convenience** 편리한 것; 편리, 편의 **enormous** 엄청난 **raw material** 원료 **get rid of** ~을 처리하다[없애다] **litter** (길에 마구 버려진) 쓰레기 **disposal** 처리

5 문장 넣기 ④

해설 우리가 이러한 상황(such situations)에 들어서기 전에 모든 것을 예상한다는 것은 아니라는 내용의 주어진 문장에서 '이러한 상황'은 앞서 예로 들은 상황에 해당하므로 ④에 주어진 문장을 넣어야 한다.

해석 어떤 상황에서 누가 무엇을 하고 있는지를 우리가 알고 있으면 우리는 타인들의 실제 행동에 관해 꽤 정확한 추측을 할 수 있다. 예를 들어, 우리가 의사의 진찰실로 들어가면 누가 환자이고 누가 의사이고 누가 간호사인지를 안다. 우리는 의학적 대화와 활동이 일어날 것이라는 것과 우리가 테이블 위에 눕거나 숨을 깊이 들

이쉬도록 요청받을지도 모른다는 것을 안다. 우리는 의사가 우리에게 무엇을 요청할지, 어떤 질문이 주어질지, 그리고 그녀의 태도가 어떠할지 대비할 수 있다. 이는 물론, 우리가 무엇에든 그리고 모든 것에 준비되도록, 이러한 상황에 들어가기 전에 우리 머릿속으로 가능한 모든 사건들을 자주 목록화한다는 것을 말하려는 게 아니다. 사실, 우리는 일어날 모든 일을 상상하지 않고, 그렇게 하려는 시도도 하지 않으며, 그렇게 할 수도 없을 것이다. 그러나 우리는 무슨 일이 발생할지에 관한 적어도 몇 가지 생각은 정말 품어본다. 즉, 우리는 무슨 일이 생길지 상상한다. 그리고 역할과 상황에 의해 제공되는 관점에 대한 이해를 통해 무슨 일이 발생할 것인지에 대한 우리의 생각을 얻게 된다.

구문 [14행~15행] We do not, in fact, imagine *everything* [that will take place], **nor** *do* we *attempt* to do so, **nor** *could we do* so.

• [ ] 부분은 everything을 수식한다. 부정문에 연결된 「nor+V+S」는 '…도 또한 그렇지 않다'의 뜻이다. 밑줄 친 두 개의 do so는 모두 imagine everything that will take place를 뜻한다.

어휘 **catalog** 목록을 작성하다 **reasonably** 상당히, 꽤 **take a deep breath** 숨을 깊이 들이쉬다 **manner** 태도; 방식 **take place** 일어나다, 발생하다 **entertain** (생각을) 품다; 즐겁게 해주다 **perspective** 관점; 원근법

1 글의 주제   ⑤

해설 기계적으로 생성된 말은 인간의 말에 비해 형식적으로 한계가 있을 수밖에 없지만 내용 면에서 사회 규범을 따르지 않으면 인간의 말과 마찬가지로 각종 부정적 결과를 낳는다는 내용의 글이므로 주제로 가장 적절한 것은 ⑤ '인간과 기계의 상호작용이 사회 규범을 따라야 하는 이유'이다.
① 기술 생성어가 두뇌에 미치는 영향
② 기계가 만들어낸 말을 사용하는 의사소통의 어려움
③ 인간 상호 작용에서 말과 듣기의 사회 규범
④ 인간 담화와 기계 제작 담화 간의 차이

해석 말하기는 본질적으로 사회적이다. 사람에서 나오든 기계에서 나오든, 말은 한 인간의 본질과 그가 생각하고 느끼는 것을 표현하고 인식하기 위해 고안된 강력하고 다양한 인지적 장치를 활성화시킨다. 사람들은 각각의 사회적 판단과 말의 생성과 이해의 각 측면을 전담하는 별개의 두뇌 부분을 가지고 있지만, 인간의 말과 기술로 생성된 말에 대해서는 별개의 두뇌 부분을 가지고 있지 않다. 음성 인터페이스가 이상한 발음, 감정적 무지, 그리고 만성적 불일치를 포함하는 기계와 관련된 모든 한계를 보일 때조차도, 그것은 말하기와 듣기에 의해 활성화되는 사회적 기대로부터 면제를 받지 못한다. 기술이 품질과는 관계없이 사회 규범에 순응하는 데 실패할 때, 사용자들은 혼란과 좌절과 인지적 피로를 경험하며, 시스템의 능력과 효용과 향유 가능성에 의문을 제기한다. 사회적으로 서툰 인터페이스는 사회적으로 서툰 개인과 같은 운명을 겪는다. 그들은 무능하고 비난받으며 회피당한다.

구문 [1행~5행] **Whether** it comes from a person **or** a machine, // speech activates a powerful and varied cognitive apparatus that is designed **to** **express** and **recognize** who a person is and what she or he is thinking and feeling.
• 부사절로 쓰인 「whether A or B」 구문은 'A이든 B이든'의 뜻이다. 두 밑줄 부분은 express와 recognize의 공통 목적어이다.

[16행~18행] ~ users experience confusion, frustration, and cognitive exhaustion and question the competence, utility, and enjoyability of the system.
• 동사 experience와 question이 병렬구조를 이룬다.

어휘 intrinsically 본질적으로   activate 활성화시키다   varied 다양한   cognitive 인지적인   apparatus 장치, 기구   separate 별개의   be devoted to ~에 전념하다, 헌신하다   voice interface 음성 인터페이스   exhibit 전시하다, 보이다   ignorance 무지   chronic 만성적인   inconsistency 불일치, 모순 (↔ consistency 일관성, 한결같음)   exempt 면제하다   regardless of ~와 관계없이   conform to ~에 순응하다   norm 규범, 규준   exhaustion 피로; 소모, 고갈   competence 능력   utility 유용, 효용   enjoyability 향유 가능성, 즐길 수 있음   inept 서투른   ineffective 무능한; 효과 없는

2 밑줄 어법   ⑤

해설 ⑤ 목적격 관계대명사가 생략된 관계사절(we should ~ about)의 수식을 받는 주어 one thing에 대한 동사가 필요하므로 being을 is로 고쳐야 한다.
① 앞에 있는 명사 the idea와 동격을 이루며 명사절을 이끄는 접속사 that은 어법상 적절하다.
② 주어인 명사 Studies를 수식하면서 의미상 수동(수행했던 연구)의 관계를 이루므로 과거분사 conducted는 어법상 적절하다.

③ 선행사가 생략된 관계부사로 '~하는 때, ~하는 경우'의 의미를 가지면서 전치사 like의 목적어 역할을 하는 절을 이끄는 관계부사 when은 어법상 적절하다.
④ '그들 자신, 스스로'의 의미를 가지며 주어 they와 가리키는 대상이 같고, 문맥상 스스로를 설득시킨다는 의미가 되어야 하므로 재귀대명사 themselves는 어법상 적절하다.

해석 사람들은 정기적으로 일종의 역행적 사고를 하고, 실제로 그 사고를 믿는다. 심리학 연구에서 가장 유명한 예시 중 하나는 인지 부조화이다. 이것은 사람들이 상반되는 두 가지 생각을 동시에 진실이라고 여기기 싫어한다는 생각이다. 반세기가 넘는 이전에 했던 연구는 사람들이 자신들의 생각과 상반되는 행동을 하도록 유도될 때, (그 행동에) 맞추기 위해 단순히 자신의 생각을 바꾼다는 것을 밝힌다. 이것은 어떤 사람이 새로운 차를 사는데 결국 너무 많은 돈을 소비하게 될 때와 같은 것이다. 자신들의 애당초의 계획과 실제로 행한 것 사이의 충돌에 관해 나쁘게 느끼는 대신, 그들은 그 차가 더 많은 돈을 들일 가치가 있다고 그들 스스로를 납득시키는 것을 더 좋아한다. 이는 우리의 생각과 행동 간에 일관성을 유지하려는 우리의 자연적 욕구의 결과이다. 우리는 모두 올바르고 싶어 하고, 우리 모두가 옳을 수 있어야 하는 한 가지는 우리 자신이다. 역행적 사고는 우리가 바로 그렇게 하게 해 준다.

구문 [5행~8행] *Studies* (conducted more than half a century ago) **find** that when people are induced into *behaviour* [that is inconsistent with their beliefs], they simply change their beliefs to match (the behaviour).
• ( ) 부분은 주어 Studies를 수식하는 분사구이고 동사는 find이다. [ ]는 주격 관계대명사가 이끄는 관계사절로 앞의 behaviour를 수식한다.

[15행~16행] We all want to be right, and *one thing* [(that) we should all be able to be right about] is ourselves.
• [ ] 부분은 목적격 관계대명사 that이 생략된 관계사절로 선행사 one thing을 수식한다.

어휘 regularly 정기적으로; 규칙적으로   hold 여기다; 생각[간주]하다; 소유[보유]하다   inconsistent 상반[모순]되는; 일관되지[일치하지] 않는   conduct 하다; 지휘하다; 안내하다   induce 유도하다, 설득하다; 유발[초래]하다   end up v-ing 결국 v하게 되다   clash 충돌, 부딪침   convince 설득[납득]시키다; 설득하다   maintain 유지하다; 주장하다

3 빈칸 추론   ②

해설 대학에는 고등학교와 비할 수 없을 정도로 다양하고 생소한 분야의 학문이 존재하는데, 만약 그러한 분야에 대해 알지 못하고 알려는 노력도 하지 않는다면 자신에게 적합할 수 있었던 학문을 접할 기회를 상실하게 되므로 생소한 분야의 학문을 탐색하라는 내용의 글이다. 따라서 빈칸에는 ② '생소한 분야와 학과에 대해 배워라'가 가장 적절하다.
① 전공을 가능한 한 즐길만한 것으로 만들어라
③ 사교 능력을 향상시키기 위해 스터디 그룹에 참여하라
④ 많은 학교 행사와 활동에 참여하라
⑤ 공부를 단순한 덩어리들로 쪼개라

해석 고등학교에서 대학으로 이동할 때 여러분이 가질 수 있는 가장 중요한 목표 중 하나는 여러분의 대학에 있는 학교 강좌들을 폭넓게 맛보는 것이다. 가장 명문인 사립 고등학교들조차도 대부분의 대학에서 발견되는 범위의 학과를 가지고 있지 않다. 여러분의 고등학교에는 아마 교사진에 사회학자나 인류학자가 없었을 것이다. 그러나 단지 그들의 분야를 접하지 못함으로써 그것들에 대해 여러분이 무지한 것은 여러분에게 대가를 치르게 할 수 있다. 여러분은 행복하고 성공적인 인류학 전공

자가 되는 것이 전적으로 가능하지만 그것이 무엇을 의미하는지 알지 못하기 때문에 여러분은 그것을 탐구하려고 애쓰지 않는 것이다. 그러므로, 대학에 가면, 반드시 생소한 분야와 학과에 대해 배우라. 여러분은 거기에 있었던 것을 결코 알지 못했던 학문적 안식처를 발견하게 될지도 모른다.

구문 [1행~3행] **One of the most important goals** [(which[that]) you can have in **the transition from** high school **to** college] **is** to sample widely from the academic offerings at your college.

• 주어는 One ~ to college이고 동사는 is이다. [ ] 부분은 앞에 목적격 관계대명사 which[that]가 생략되어 the most important goals를 수식한다. 「the transition from A to B」는 'A에서 B로의 이동[변천]'의 뜻이다.

[13행~14행] You might find *an academic home* [(which[that]) (you never knew) was there].

• [ ] 부분은 앞에 관계대명사 which[that]가 생략되어 an academic home을 수식한다. you never knew는 삽입구이다.

어휘 **transition** 이동, 과도기 **sample** 맛보다, 시식하다 **academic** 학교의, 학구적인 **offering** (학교에서 개설한) 강좌 **elite** 엘리트, 정예 **sociologist** 사회학자 **anthropologist** 인류학자 **faculty** (학부의) 교수진 **discipline** 분야, 학과 **exposure** 접하기, 노출 **cost** 대가를 치르게 하다; (비용이) 들다 **bother** ~하도록 애를 쓰다; 성가시게 하다 **make it a point to-v** 반드시 v하다; v하는 것을 중시하다

[선택지] **unfamiliar** 생소한, 낯선 **chunk** 덩어리

4 무관 문장 ③

해설 이 글의 전반적인 내용은 우리 조상들이 생존하기 위하여 발효를 이용한 것으로서, 식량이 나지 않는 계절도 발효 식량으로 견뎌낼 수 있었다는 것인데, ③번 문장은 인간이 생존 문제를 해결하고 나자 주변 세계를 탐색하여 물질의 본질을 이해하고자 하였다는 내용이므로 글의 전체 흐름과 관계가 없다.

해석 왜 우리 조상들이 발효 과정을 활용하는 데에 처음으로 관심을 갖게 되었는지를 이해하기란 어렵지 않다. 그것은 생존의 문제였다. ① 계절에 따른 식사에 대한 현재 우리의 대단한 관심이 성공적으로 해낸 것이 하나 있다면, 그것은 우리 조상들이 이미 알고 있었던 것을 우리에게 상기시켜준 것이다. ② 즉, 한 철에서 다음 철까지 살아남으려면 준비할 필요가 있다는 것이다. ③ 우리의 조상들이 단순한 생존을 넘어 발전하게 되자, 그들은 삶과 주위 세계에 대해 질문하기 시작했는데, 질문의 가장 근본적인 것은 물질의 본질을 이해하는 것이었다. ④ 여러분은 여러분을 보호해 줄 장소, 여러분을 따뜻하게 해 줄 옷, 야생 사냥감이 사라지고 암소 젖이 마르고, 과일나무가 생산을 마쳤을 때조차 여러분을 강하게 해 줄 음식이 필요하다. ⑤ 이것은 미생물을 활용하여 우유를 치즈로, 포도를 포도주로, 멸치를 생선 소스로 만드는 것을 알게 된 사람들에 의해 우리에게 전해진 우리 인간의 유산이다.

구문 [3행~6행] If there is *one thing* [(that[which]) our current love affair with seasonal eating has done successfully], // it is to remind us of **what our ancestors always knew**.

• [ ] 부분은 one thing을 수식하는 관계사절로 our current love affair 앞에 목적격 관계대명사인 that[which]이 생략되어 있다. what our ancestors always knew는 선행사를 포함한 관계대명사로서 of의 목적어 역할을 하는 명사절을 이끌고 있다.

어휘 **ancestor** 조상 **current** 현재의; 흐름; 전류 **love affair** 대단한 관심[열정] **seasonal** 계절에 따른 **eating** 식사 **make it** 살아남다; 시간 맞춰 가다; 성공하다 **fundamental** 근본[본질]적인; 핵심적인 **matter** 물질; 문제, 일; 중요하다 **shelter** 보호하다, 숙소[피난처]를 정해주다 **game** 사냥감 **heritage** 유산 **pass down** (후대에) ~을 전하다 **microbe** 미생물

5 요약문 완성 ②

해설 정보가 폭발적으로 증가하는 오늘날의 사회에서 사람들은 조직체들이 인터넷 상에서 제공한 정보를 처리하기 위해 주변 사람들과 대화하고 조언을 구하는 등 자신의 사회적 관계망을 적극적으로 이용하여 그 정보를 이해하려 애쓴다는 내용의 글이다. 따라서 오늘날 세상에 정보가 더 풍요로워(abundant)지면서, 사람들은 정보를 해석하기(interpret) 위하여 조직체들로부터 벗어나 사회적 관계망으로 향하고 있음을 알 수 있다.

해석 덜 계층적이고 경계가 덜 분명한 네트워크화된 환경에서는, 전문 지식이 과거보다 더 많은 논란이 되고 (상호) 관계가 덜 안정적이어서, 누구를, 그리고 어떤 정보원을 신뢰할 것인가에 관한 불확실성이 더 크다. 정보와 정보원의 폭발적 증가는 사람들로 하여금 자신의 관계망에 더 의존하게 하는 길로 몰아가는 역설적인 영향을 가져왔다. 인터넷에서 조직체들이 제공하는 풍부한 정보는 사람들로 하여금 사실과 조언을 얻기 위해 친구와 동료들에게 덜 의존하도록 유도할 것으로 보일 수도 있을 것이다. 그러나 삶에 쏟아져 들어오는 점점 더 많은 양의 정보가 사람들로 하여금 그것을 이해하기 위해 사회적 관계망에 의존하도록 유도한다는 것이 밝혀지고 있다. 결과적으로 사람들은, 선택을 하는 데 도움이 될 정보를 모을 때, 의견을 교환하고 선택을 저울질하기 위해 직접적 대화, 전화 통화 및 이메일을 이용하면서, 인터넷 검색과 사회적 관계망의 구성원들과의 토론 사이를 왔다 갔다 하면서 순환하게 된다.

↓

오늘날 세상에 정보가 점점 더 (A) 풍요로워지면서, 사람들은 정보를 (B) 해석하기 위하여 조직체들로부터 벗어나 사회적 관계망으로 향하고 있다.

구문 [4행~5행] ~ there is more uncertainty **about whom** and what information sources to trust.

• whom 이하는 전치사 about의 목적어이며, 원래 whom to trust and what information sources to trust에서 간략히 변형된 것이다.

[5행~8행] **The explosion** of information and information sources **has had** the paradoxical impact of pushing people on the path of greater reliance on their networks.

• 주어는 The explosion이고 동사는 has had이다. 두 밑줄 부분은 동격 관계이다.

어휘 **hierarchical** 계급[계층]에 따른 **bounded** 경계가 있는; 한계가 있는 **in dispute** 논쟁 중인 **stable** 안정적인 **explosion** 폭발; 폭발적 증가 **reliance** 의존, 의지 **abundance** 풍부 **prompt** (행위를) 유도하다; 즉각적인; 신속한 **in-person** 몸소, 직접의 [선택지] **biased** 편향된, 선입견이 있는

1 빈칸 추론 ②

해설 일반화가 글쓰기에서 개관을 시작하는 출발점이지만, 확실한 뒷받침하는 증거 없이는 결정적 근거로서의 역할을 할 수 없다고 했으므로 빈칸에는 ② '여러분의 신뢰성에 손상을 입힐 가능성이 있다'가 적절하다.
① 어떤 상황에서는 받아들여질 수 있다
③ 구체적인 생각을 밝히는 데 중요하다
④ 부적절한 권위에 호소하는 것을 시도하는 것이다
⑤ 결국 여러분 주장의 전제를 부인하게 될 것이다

해석 일반화는 고정관념과 비슷하다. 고정관념에서는 하나의 작은 진실의 알맹이가 존재하지만, 그 진실이 전체 이야기를 알려주지는 않는다. 결론에 도달하기 위해 그 하나의 작은 진실에 의지하는 것은 진실 전체를 왜곡한다. 글쓰기에서 폭넓은 일반화에만 의지하는 것은 여러분의 신뢰성에 손상을 입힐 가능성이 있다. 이상하게도, 사실상 일반화는 여러분의 기본적인 메시지의 개관을 시작하는 데 필수적인 출발점이다. '사업이 호전되고 있다는 징후가 있다'를 예로 들어보자. 이 진술의 과제는 (아마도 판매나 생산 자료를 뒷받침하기 위해 판매 대행자와 구매자로부터의 전문적인 의견을 포함해서) 최근 매출액과 같은 수치 자료, 소비자 구매 경향 조사, 그리고 여러분의 회사의 상품이나 서비스에 관심이 더해지거나 되살아나고 있다는 사실에 기반을 둔 증거로 이루어진 보충 사실을 추가하는 것이 될 것이다. 그래서 일반화는 사고의 최초 근거로서의 역할을 할 수 있지만, 그것은 확실한 뒷받침하는 증거 없이는 결코 결정적인 근거로서의 역할을 처음 근거만큼 할 수 없다.

구문 [9행~14행] The challenge for this statement will be **to add** supporting
facts (**consisting of** numerical data, ~, surveys of consumer buying trends,
and factual proof of additional or resurgent interest in your company's
products or services (~)).
• 부정사 to add가 보어 역할을 한다. consisting of 이하는 현재분사구로 supporting facts를 수식하며, 목적어로 세 개의 어구 numerical data ~, surveys of consumer buying trends, factual proof ~가 and로 연결되어 병렬구조를 이룬다.

[16행~19행] So although generalizations can serve as initial *foundations* of thought, // they can never serve as conclusive **ones** as well without hard, supporting evidence.
• 주절의 ones는 앞에 나온 절의 foundations를 가리키는 대명사이다.

어휘 generalization 일반화 stereotype 고정관념 kernel 알맹이, 요점 distort 왜곡하다 broad 폭넓은 oddly enough 이상하게도 indication 징후, 기미 supporting 보충하는, 지지하는 consist of ~로 이루어지다 numerical 수치의, 숫자상의 figure 수치, 숫자 consumer 소비자 trend 동향, 추세 factual 사실에 기반을 둔 resurgent 되살아나는, 다시 유행하는 representative 대리인, 대행자 initial 처음의, 최초의 foundation 근거 conclusive 결정적인 hard 확실한, 엄연한 evidence 증거
[선택지] undermine 손상을 입히다 credibility 신뢰성 specific 상세한, 명확한 inappropriate 부적당한 authority 권위, 권한 premise 전제

2 글의 순서 ⑤

해설 주어진 글의 첫 문장은 상업화로 인해 사회 구조가 변화한다는 의미이며, 두 번째 문장은 전통 사회의 농부들의 쌀에 대한 인식을 설명하고 있다. (C)는 이러한

전통 사회에 대한 추가 설명과 함께 이와 대조되는 내용의 상업화에 대한 설명이 도입되고 있고 (B)는 이러한 상업화된 사회에서 농부들의 쌀에 대한 인식 변화가 설명되었다. 그리고 마지막의 (A)에서 (B)의 농부들이 결과적으로 어떤 태도를 취하게 되는지를 이어서 설명하고 있다.

해석 증가하는 상업화는 변화하는 사회 구조의 주요 원인이다. 전통적인 농부들을 보라. 그들은 쌀이 신으로부터의 선물이며 그야말로 생명 유지라고 여긴다.
(C) 이러한 농경 지역사회들은 쌀 재배 주기에 맞추어 사회와 종교적 축제를 구성한다. 그러나 상업화는 이러한 전통문화를 조금씩 무너뜨린다.
(B) 농부들이 자신들이 먹기 위해서가 아니라 수익을 위해 쌀을 재배하기 시작하면, 그들은 시간이나 돈, 그리고 쌀과 같은 자원을 전통적인 종교적 신념을 위해 사용하는 것을 별로 내켜 하지 않게 된다.
(A) 결국, 그들은 식량 생산을 아무런 종교적 의미가 없는, 단순히 돈을 버는 수단으로 보는 산업화된 나라의 다수의 농부들과 같은 태도를 취한다. 성공적인 쌀 재배는 비료, 농약 또는 농기계나 관개에 돈을 쓴 결과에 불과하게 된다.

구문 [5행~7행] Eventually, they adopt **the same** attitude **as** *many farmers in industrialized nations* [who see producing food simply as a means to make money].
• 「the same A as B」는 'B와 같은 A'의 뜻이다. [ ] 부분은 관계사절로 many farmers ~ nations를 수식한다.

어휘 commercialization 상업화 see A as B A를 B로 여기다 adopt 채택하다 means 수단, 방법 make money 돈을 벌다 nothing more than ~에 불과한 fertilizer 비료 pesticide 농약, 살충제 machinery 기계류 profit 이익, 이윤 be inclined to-v v하고 싶어 하다 annual cycle 연간 주기 break down 허물어뜨리다, 부수다 bit by bit 조금씩, 점점

3 문장 넣기

해설 비디오 게임에서 장려되는 기술과 능력이 다른 목적에 유용한 예를 나열하고 있는데, 주어진 문장도 그러한 예에 속한다. ③ 뒤의 문장은 주어진 문장에 언급된 시각적 인식이 개발되게 된 이유에 해당하므로 주어진 문장이 들어갈 위치는 ③이 적절하다.

해석 비디오 게임에서 장려되는 어떤 기술과 능력은 여러 가지 다른 목적에 유용하다. 예를 들어, 최근 연구에 의하면 그것들은 수술을 할 때 외과 의사가 자신의 손을 사용하는 기술을 상당히 향상시킬 수 있다고 한다. 또한 비디오 게임을 하는 것은 실험 집단 사람들의 단기 기억을 증가시켜준다고 나타났다. 무엇보다도, 비디오 게임은 시각적 인식을 개발하는 데 우수하다. 이것에 대한 이유는 대부분의 게임이 게임을 하는 사람들로 하여금 바뀌는 사건들을 재빨리 탐지하고 (거기에) 반응하기 위해 그들의 주의를 스크린 전반에 펼쳐놓을 것을 요구하기 때문이다. 사실 비디오 게임을 하는 것은 공간 주의력에 필요한 신경 통로를 개발하는 데 중요한 이전의 비활성 유전자를 촉발시킬지도 모른다. 요즘 연구에 의하면 비디오 게임을 하는 것은 심지어 집중 기간을 줄이기보다는 늘려줄 수 있다고 한다.

구문 [12행~15행] In fact, playing video games may trigger previously *inactive genes* [that are important for developing *neural pathways* (necessary for spatial attention)].
• [ ] 부분은 inactive genes를 수식하며, ( ) 부분은 neural pathways를 수식한다.

[16행~17행] ~ playing video games could even increase attention spans

rather than reduce them.
• 「A rather than B」는 'B라기보다는 오히려 A'라는 뜻이다.

어휘 **awareness** 인식   **significantly** 상당히   **short-term memory** 단기 기억
detect 감지하다, 발견하다   **trigger** 촉발하다   **inactive** 활동하지 않는, 활발하지 않은
spatial 공간의   **span** (어떤 일이 지속되는) 기간

4~5 장문   4 ① 5 ④

해설 4. 오늘날 정보 저장 매체는 값이 극도로 저렴해져서 회사 등이 개인들에 대한 막대한 양의 정보를 보유하는 것이 가능해졌고 이러한 정보는 어떤 형태로든 반드시 활용될 것이라는 내용의 글이므로, 제목으로 가장 적절한 것은 ① '어디에나 존재하는 개인 정보의 시대'이다.
② 당신의 디지털 발자국을 웹상에 남기지 마라
③ 미래의 매체 저장에 대한 전망
④ 대량 생산에서 주문 제작으로의 전환
⑤ 디지털 테크놀로지에 의해 일어난 정보의 불평등
5. 정보를 저장하는 비용이 저렴해지고 있어서 무한해 보이는 양의 정보를 저장하는 데 거대 기업의 자원이 필요 없다고 했다. 저장 가격의 붕괴는 새로운 방식으로 무제한적인 자료를 저장할 수 있게 할 것임을 알 수 있으므로 ④는 unlimited 등이 되어야 한다.

해석 오늘날 디지털 기술은 당신의 인구통계학적 개요부터 당신의 운전 기록과 모든 온라인상에서의 활동의 완벽한 목록에 이르기까지 당신에 관한 모든 종류의 정보를 수집하고 저장하고 분석하고 유통시키는 것을 가능하게 했다. 이러한 소위 데이터 마이닝(거의 모든 상상 가능한 주제에 대한 막대한 양의 정보를 수집하는 것을 향하는 추세에 대한 2010년대의 유행어)은 기술이 자료 수집과 저장을 거의 (a) 비용이 들지 않게 만들었기 때문에 존재한다. 오늘날의 디지털 데이터 저장의 용량을 이해하는 가장 쉬운 방법은 1테라바이트 디스크 드라이브가 평균적인 연구 도서관 한 곳에 (b) 수용되어 있는 것보다 더 많은 정보를 담고 있다는 점(을 보는 것)이다. 그러한 드라이브는 큰 바지 주머니나 작은 핸드백에 깔끔하게 (c) 맞아서 소비자들이 쉽게 이용할 수 있고, 비용은 부담 없이 100달러 미만이며, 가격은 매년 더 낮게 떨어지고 있다. 그 결과는 오늘날 한 회사나 한 개인이 다른 개인들에 대한 무한해 보이는 양의 개인 정보를 저장하기 위해 거대 기업의 자원을 가질 필요가 없는 것으로 나타난다. 이러한 저장 가격의 붕괴는 거의 (d) 제한적인(→ 무제한적인) 자료가 이전에는 결코 가능하지 않았던 방식으로 저장되고 처리될 수 있게 해준다.
디지털 데이터 저장이 실질적으로 공짜이기 때문에, 가능한 모든 것이 '영구적으로' 수집되고 저장될 것이다. 사실 어떤 데이터를 삭제할지 알아내려 애쓰는 것보다는 큰 데이터 세트를 유지하는 것이 빠른 속도로 더 저렴해지고 있다. 그리고 일단 데이터가 이용 가능해지면, 누군가가 그것에 대한 사용처를 찾아낼 것이라는 것을 확신해도 좋다. 결과적으로 (e) 막대한 디지털 서류 일체는 바로 당신이 방문하는 웹사이트와 당신이 클릭하는 링크까지, 모든 개인에 대하여 개발되고 있다.

구문 [1행~5행] Today, digital technology has made **it** possible / **to collect**, store, analyze, and distribute *all kinds of information about you*, / **ranging from** your demographic profile to your driving record to a complete list of all your online activities.
• it은 가목적어이고 to collect 이하가 진목적어이다. 「range from A to B」는 '범위가 A부터 B까지이다'의 뜻이며, ranging from 이하는 all kinds of information about you에 대해 부가적인 설명을 하는 분사구문이다.

[12행~15행] Such drives are readily available to consumers, **fit neatly in a large pants pocket or a small purse**, |and| cost comfortably less than $100 ~.

(우단)
• 동사 are와 cost가 병렬구조를 이루고 있으며, fit ~ a small purse는 수동 의미의 분사구문이다.

어휘 **range from A to B** (범위가) A부터 B까지이다   **demographic** 인구 (통계)학의
profile 개요   **so-called** 소위   **house** 수용하다   **massive** 거대한, 막대한
[선택지] **ubiquitous** 어디에나 존재하는

1 글의 요지   ③

해설 이 글은 인간 두뇌의 크기나 신체와의 비율이 다른 동물들보다 커서 말을 할 수 있는 것 같지만, 이에 대한 반례를 제시하면서 그것이 오해일 수 있음을 나타내고 있다. 그러므로, 이 글의 요지는 ③ '두뇌의 크기나 비율이 언어 능력을 담보하지 않는다.'가 된다.

해석 인간 두뇌는 말을 하기 위해 어느 정도로 프로그램되어 있는가? 그 답은 불분명하다. 우리의 뇌는 다른 동물들의 뇌보다 크지만, 크기만이 특별히 중요한 건 아니다. 코끼리와 고래는 인간보다 큰 뇌를 가지고 있지만 그들은 말하지 않는다. 그러나 코끼리와 고래는 몸도 더 크기 때문에, 어떤 사람들은 중요한 것은 바로 두뇌 대 신체의 비율이라고 말해왔다. 언뜻 보기에, 이것은 특히 성인 인간의 뇌가 자신의 총 몸무게의 2%를 넘는 반면 다 자란 침팬지의 뇌는 1% 미만임을 알게 될 때, 유망한 접근법인 것처럼 보인다. 그러나 그러한 비율은 매우 오해의 소지가 있을 수 있다. 어떤 동물들은 신체를 대단히 무겁게 만드는 막대한 예비 에너지를 지니고 다니도록 설계되어 있다. 예를 들어 낙타는 단지 거대한 혹이 있다는 이유만으로 말보다 반드시 더 멍청한 것은 아니다.

구문 [7행~8행] ~ **it is** *the brain-body ratio* **which** matters.
• 「it is ... which[that] ~」 강조구문으로 '~한 것은 바로 …이다'의 뜻이다. 여기서는 the brain-body ratio를 강조하고 있으며, 사람을 강조하는 경우 that 대신 who를 쓰는 것이 가능하다.

[9행~11행] ~ *the brain* of an adult human / is more than 2 percent of his or her total weight, // while **that** of an adult chimp / is less than 1 percent.
• that은 the brain을 가리킨다.

어휘 to what extent 어느 정도까지   ratio 비율   at first sight 언뜻 보기에; 첫눈에   promising 유망한, 촉망하는; 조짐이 좋은   misleading 오해의 소지가 있는, 오도하는   reserve 비축(물), 예비(물); 예약하다; (판단 등을) 보류하다   hump (특히 등에 난) 혹

2 빈칸 추론   ④

해설 새 혹은 나비의 나는 몸짓을 흉내 내는 소녀의 그림에서, 소녀의 옆에 나비가 있는 '생각 풍선'이 달려 있으면 3~5세 아동들은 이 소녀가 새가 아닌 나비를 흉내 내고 있다는 것을 추론할 수 있다는 내용의 글이므로, 아동들이 흉내 내는 행위는 ④ '심적 표상'과 관련이 있다는 것을 이해한다는 것을 알 수 있다.
① 의사소통 기술
② 모방을 통한 학습
③ 배경 정보
⑤ 실전 경험

해석 한 연구에서 심리학자인 Davis, Woolley, 그리고 Bruell은 아이들에게 한 소녀와 새 한 마리 그리고 나비 한 마리에 관한 이야기를 설명하는 일련의 삽화들을 보여 주었다. 마지막 그림에는 근처에 새가 있는 소녀가 묘사되어 있었다. 소녀는 마치 날려는 것처럼 자신의 팔을 흔들고 있었고, 소녀 머리 위의 '생각 풍선'은 그녀가 나비에 대해 생각하고 있다는 것을 나타냈다. 아이들은 두 동물 중에 어떤 것을 소녀가 흉내 내고 있는지를 묻는 질문을 받았다. 소녀의 나는 행동은 새와 나비 둘 다와 일치했기에, 흉내 내는 것은 무엇인가에 대한 생각과 관련이 있다는 것을 이해하지 못했다면 아이들은 두 동물들 사이에서 당연히 무작위로 선택을 했을 것이다. 하지만 3살 된 어린이들조차도 이 과업에서 꽤 성공적이었고, 4살 그리고 5살 된 어린

이들은 완벽하게 수행했다. 이 연구는 어린이들이 3살이 될 때는 흉내 내는 행위는 심적 표상과 관련이 있다는 것을 이해하기 시작했다는 것을 보여 준다. 이런 이해력은 나이가 들면서 향상되고 약 5살 때 비교적 잘 확립되는 것 같다.

구문 [7행~8행] Children were asked / **which** of the two animals the girl was pretending to be.
• which 이하는 간접의문문으로서, 「의문사(which of the two animals)+주어(the girl)+동사(was pretending)」의 어순을 따른다.

[11행~12행] ~ they **should have chosen** randomly between the two animals.
• 여기서 「should have p.p.」는 과거의 일에 대한 추측, 가능성을 나타내어 '당연히 ~했을 것이다'라는 의미로 쓰였다.

어휘 present 보여 주다, 제시하다   sequence 연속물, 연속   illustrate 설명하다, 삽화를 넣다   depict 묘사하다   indicate 나타내다, 보여 주다   pretend 흉내를 내다   consistent 한결같은, 일관된   randomly 임의로   relatively 비교적, 상대적으로   established 확립된

3 무관 문장   ④

해설 이 글은 곤충이 어떤 살충제에 노출되어 살아남게 되면 그 살충제에 대한 내성이 후손에게 유전되고, 또한 다른 살충제도 효과가 없게 될지 모른다는 내용을 담고 있다. 그러므로 살충제가 이로운 곤충의 개체수를 줄였다는 ④의 내용은 글의 흐름과 관계가 없다.

해석 왜 곤충은 특정한 살충제에 저항력을 갖게 되는가? 어떤 식물이나 곤충 개체군에서든지 유독성 물질에 노출되어도 살아남는 그런 드문 개체가 늘 있게 마련이다. ① 예를 들어 만약 살충제가 어떤 특정한 효소를 차단함으로써 작용한다면, 이 한 개체가 그 효소의 활성 부위 주변에 약간 다른 원자 배열을 가지고 있어, 이것이 독소가 접근하는 것을 막을지 모른다. ② 그래서, 그렇다면 그 후손들 역시 그런 보호를 누리게 되고, 몇 년 안에 저항력 있는 곤충의 상당한 개체수가 그것들을 모두 죽이려는 농부들의 노력을 좌절시킬 것이다. ③ 저항 유전자가 충분히 우세하다면, 그것은 곤충의 전체 종으로 퍼질 것이다. ④ 더군다나 살충제는 화학 약품에 심각하게 노출되게 하기 때문에 벌과 다른 꽃가루 매개자들과 같은 이로운 곤충들의 수를 줄여왔다. ⑤ 더 걱정스러운 것은 저항력 있는 유전자가 이 특정한 살충제를 차단할 뿐 아니라 다른 살충제 역시 차단할지 모른다는 것이다.

구문 [16행~18행] More worrying is **that** the resistant gene **not only** blocks this particular pesticide **but** may block other pesticides **as well**.
• that은 문장의 보어 역할을 하는 명사절을 이끄는 접속사이며, 명사절 안에 'A 뿐만 아니라 B도'라는 의미의 「not only A but B as well」 구문이 쓰였다.

어휘 resistant 저항력 있는, 저항하는   pesticide 살충제, 농약   exposure 노출, 폭로   toxic 유독성의 *cf.* toxin 독소   agent 물질; 대리인   block 차단하다, 방해하다   arrangement 배열, 배치   atom 원자   that being so 그래서, 그런 까닭에   descendant 후손, 자손   defeat 좌절시키다; 패배시키다   kill off 모두 죽이다   dominant 우세한, 지배적인   pollinator 꽃가루 매개자   acute 극심한; (질병이) 급성의; 예리한

8

4 글의 순서 ④

해설 주어진 문장이 동물에게 공감을 느끼는 사람이 사람에게 공감을 느낄 가능성이 더 크다는 것이 일반화된 특성이라고 말하고 있으므로, 그다음으로는 이러한 경향(This inclination)이 이해가 되는 이유를 언급한 (C)가 나오는 것이 적절하다. 그다음에는 앞서 말한 내용과 대조되는, 공감의 부재의 속성을 언급한 (A)가 나와야 하고, (A)의 마지막 문장 '공감이 더 특정적일 가능성 또한 있다'를 구체적인 예를 들어 설명하는 (B)가 마지막으로 나와야 한다.

해석 동물에게 공감을 느끼는 사람은 사람에게 공감을 느낄 가능성이 더 크다는 점에서 공감은 매우 일반화된 특성일 수 있다.
(C) 이러한 경향은 우리가 공감의 기저를 이루는 과정들(생명체가 연관되어 있다든지, 고통의 신호가 감지되고 정확하게 확인될 수 있다든지, 타인의 고통을 줄이는 것은 값진 특성이라든지 하는) 중 많은 것들이 사람과 동물 모두에게 해당된다고 추정한다면 이해가 된다.
(A) 그러나 유감스럽게도 공감의 '부재' 역시 어떤 사람들의 일반적인 특성일 수 있는데, 인간이든 동물이든 고통을 당하는 피해자에 대해 걱정이나 염려를 거의 나타내지 않는 것이다. 공감이 더 특정적일 가능성 또한 있다.
(B) 어떤 사람들은 다른 사람들의 고통에 매우 공감하지만 동물의 고통에는 무감각하거나 무관심할 수 있다. 어떤 사람이 동물에게는 큰 애정과 공감을 갖고 있지만 다른 사람들의 관심사와 행복에는 거의 신경을 쓰지 않는 경우에는 반대의 상황 역시 일어날 수 있다.

구문 [11행~14행] The opposite may also occur in *cases* [**where** a person has great affection and empathy for animals / but cares little for the concerns and welfare of other people].

• [ ] 부분이 cases를 수식하고 있다. where는 관계부사로 선행사가 cases인데 구체적인 장소뿐만 아니라 추상적인 공간을 뜻하는 situation, point 등도 관계부사 where의 수식을 받을 수 있다. [ ] 부분에서 주어는 a person이고 동사 has와 cares는 but으로 연결된 병렬구조를 이루고 있다.

어휘 empathy 공감, 감정 이입 *cf.* empathic 감정 이입의[에 입각한] generalize 일반화하다; 개괄적으로 말하다 victim 피해자, 희생자 distress 괴로움, 고통 insensible 무감각한 unconcerned 무관심한, 개의치 않는 affection 애착, 애정 welfare 안녕, 행복 inclination 경향; 성향; 경사(도) make sense 이해가 되다, 의미가 통하다; 타당하다 assume 추정하다; (책임을) 떠맡다 underlie 기저를 이루다, 밑에 있다 cue 신호 perceive 지각하다, 감지하다 identify 확인하다, 식별하다 relieve (고통을) 줄이다, 완화하다 trait 특성 applicable 해당되는, 들어맞는

5 문장 넣기 ④

해설 주어진 문장의 By doing this에서 this는 존 스노우의 연구 활동을 가리킨다고 볼 수 있는데, 그것은 ④번 바로 앞 두 문장의 내용이며, 여기서 나타난 그의 연구 활동은 '가정과 업체(예컨대 맥주 공장)의 물 공급 조사'로 정리할 수 있다. 이 내용 다음에 주어진 문장이 위치해야 한다. 또한 ④번 다음의 문장에서 this pump라는 표현이 나오는데, ④번 앞부분에서는 펌프가 단 한 번도 언급되지 않았다. 주어진 문장에 나온 the same pump를 ④번 다음 문장인 this pump가 지칭하고 있다.

해석 존 스노우는 1854년에 콜레라와 더러운 물 사이의 연관성을 발전시킨 의사였다. 그 시점에서 세균 이론이 발달되어 있지 않았기 때문에 그는 더러운 물이 콜레라를 일으켰음을 증명할 수 없었다. 대신에 그는 가장 최근의 발병에서 모든 콜레라의 사례를 세밀히 나타냈고 콜레라가 어떠한 사망의 원인도 되지 않은 가정과 업체의 물 공급에 대해 조사했다. 예를 들어 그는 지역 맥주 공장의 전 직원이 맥주나 맥주 공장 자체의 우물에서 나온 물을 마셨고, 그들 중 누구도 콜레라 발병에 의해 영

향받지 않았음을 발견했다. 이렇게 하여 그는 콜레라로 죽었던 모든 사람들이 Broad 가에 있는 같은 펌프에서 나온 물을 마셔왔음을 증명할 수 있었다. 그는 다른 누구라도 이 펌프에서 마시지 못하게 하기 위해 이 펌프에서 손잡이가 제거되어야 한다고 주장했다. 손잡이가 제거된 후, 콜레라 발병은 진정되었고, 따라서 그 특정 우물의 물로 그것이 유발됐다는 스노우의 이론을 증명하게 되었다.

구문 [14행~16행] He **insisted** that the handle **be removed** from this pump to prevent anybody else from drinking from it.

• 동사 insist가 주장의 의미를 가지므로 다음에 나오는 that절은 「that+S'+(should+)동사원형」 형태로 쓰였다. 「prevent O from v-ing」는 'O가 v하지 못하게 하다'의 뜻이다.

[16행~19행] After the removal of the handle, the cholera outbreak subsided, **thus proving** Snow's theory that it had been caused by the water in that particular well.

• thus proving 이하는 분사구문이다. that ~ well은 Snow's theory에 대한 동격절이다.

어휘 germ 세균 map out ~을 세밀히 나타내다 outbreak (전쟁·질병의) 발생, 발발 investigate 조사하다 well 우물 subside 가라앉다, 진정되다

1 글의 제목 ③

해설 이 글은 미국 대사관 앞에서 벌어진 한 시위가 갑자기 험악한 대규모의 시위로 변했지만, 한 젊은이의 재치 넘치는 유머로 시위 군중뿐만 아니라 시위를 진압하는 경찰의 긴장감도 줄어들게 되었다는 내용이다. 그러므로 제목으로 가장 적절한 것은 ③ '사람들을 진정시키고 통합하는 유머의 힘'이다.
① 외부 세력을 거부하는 한 용감한 행동
② 집회와 결사의 자유를 보장하라
④ 영국과 미국 간의 참을 수 없는 긴장감
⑤ 농담은 시위를 진압하기 위해 경찰이 사용하는 무기

해석 1970년대 어느 날, 런던에 있는 미국 대사관 밖에서 중간 규모의 시위가 갑자기 수많은 사람들의 대규모 폭동이 되었고, 그 사람들은 대사관 앞의 작은 광장으로 잔뜩 들어갔다. 말을 탄 경찰들이 점점 더 적대적으로 되는 군중들을 저지하고 있었다. 분위기가 험악해지기 시작했고, 사람들은 당황하기 시작했다. 갑자기, 앞줄 근처에 있던 한 어린 학생이 친구의 어깨 위로 올라가서 벌어지고 있는 일에 대한 재치 있는 언급과 의견으로 군중들을 즐겁게 해주기 시작했다. 그는 마치 혼자 재담을 하는 코미디언 같았다. 경찰을 포함해서, 위험 지대에 있는 모든 사람들이 그의 공연에 매료되었다. 긴장감, 분노, 그리고 두려움이 줄어들었고 상대적으로 편안한 상태가 군중을 사로잡았다. 그 젊은이는 (자신의) 최고의 무기인 유머를 이용해서, 일어날 수도 있는 심각한 부상으로부터 자신의 동료들을 구하기 위해 30분 넘게 계속했다.

구문 [1행~5행] ~, a medium-sized demonstration outside the American Embassy in London suddenly grew into *a massed uprising* (of *many thousands of people*), // **who** crammed into the small square in front of the Embassy.
• ( ) 부분은 전명구로서 앞의 a massed uprising을 수식하고, 계속적 용법의 관계대명사절인 who 이하는 many thousands of people을 보충 설명한다.
[15행~17행] The young man continued for over half an hour, **using** a superb weapon, humor, to save his fellows from probable serious injury.
• using 이하는 부대상황을 나타내는 분사구문으로 as he used a superb ~ injury와 같은 의미이며, 밑줄 친 a superb weapon과 humor는 서로 동격 관계이다.

어휘 demonstration 시위, 데모; 설명 embassy 대사관 uprising 폭동, 반란 hold A at bay A를 저지하다 increasingly 점점 더 hostile 적대적인, 반대하는 panic 당황하다, 공황 상태에 빠지다; 극심한 공포 entertain 즐겁게 해주다 witty 재치[기지] 있는 comment 언급, 논평; 지적 observation 의견, 논평; 관찰 stand-up (일어서서) 혼자 재담을 하는; 서 있는 fascinated 매료[매혹]된 tension 긴장감; 팽팽함 state 상태; 국가, 나라 relative 상대적인, 비교상의 possess 사로잡다; 소유[보유]하다 superb 최고[최상]의 weapon 무기 fellow 동료, 동년배; 친구 probable 일어날 가능성이 있는 injury 부상; 상처, 피해
[선택지] reject 거부[거절]하다 guarantee 보장[약속]하다; 품질 보증서 assembly 집회, 의회, 입법 기관 association 결사, 협회; 관련, 연계; 연상 calm down 진정시키다; 진정하다 unite 통합[결합]하다; 연합하다 unbearable 참을[견딜] 수 없는 suppress 진압하다; 참다, 억누르다 protest 시위; 항의[반대](하다)

2 밑줄 어휘 ④

해설 동물의 생물학적 특징이 그 동물의 행동과 관련이 있는 경우가 많지만 연관 관계가 거의 없는 것처럼 보이는 경우도 많은데, 긴 다리로 돌아다니기에 불편한 거미집을 짓는 ghost spider는 후자의 예가 되며, 이러한 동물들은 그들의 신체적 형태에서 예상될 수 있는 것과 ④ '유사한(similar)' 방식이 아니라 '다른, 정반대의(contrary)' 방식으로 행동하는 것이다.

해석 어떤 동물이 어떤 유형의 행동을 하도록 선천적으로 프로그램되어 있다면, 생물학적인 단서가 있을 ① 가능성이 있다. 물고기가 지느러미와 강력한 꼬리가 있는, 유선형이고 매끈한 몸을 가지고 있는 것은 우연이 아니다. 물고기의 몸은 물을 빠르게 헤치며 움직이는 데 구조적으로 ② 알맞다. 마찬가지로, 여러분이 죽은 새나 모기를 발견한다면, 그 날개를 보고서 비행이 그것들의 보편적인 ③ 이동 방식이었음을 추측할 것이다. 하지만, 우리는 지나치게 낙관적이어서는 안 된다. 생물학적인 단서는 필수적이지는 않다. 생물학적인 단서들이 발견되는 정도는 동물마다 다르고 행동마다 다르다. 예를 들어, 새들이 둥지를 짓는 것을 새들의 몸으로부터 추측하는 것은 불가능하고, 때로 동물들은 신체적 형태에서 예상될 수도 있는 것과 상당히 ④ 유사한(→ 다른) 방식으로 행동한다. 즉 ghost spider는 굉장히 긴 다리를 가지고 있지만, 그것들은 무척 짧은 실로 거미집을 엮는다. 관찰하는 인간에게는 그것들이 실을 내면서 거미집을 돌아다닐 때 다리가 큰 ⑤ 방해가 되는 것처럼 보인다.

구문 [3행~4행] It is no accident / **that** fish have *bodies* // [which are streamlined and smooth], ~.
It은 가주어이고 that ~ 부분이 진주어이며, [ ] 부분은 bodies를 수식한다.
[6행~8행] Similarly, if you found a dead bird or mosquito, // you could <u>guess</u> by looking at its wings **that** flying was ~.
　　　　　　　　　　　　　　　　　부사구　　　　　　V
• 「if+S′+과거동사, S+could+동사원형」 형태의 가정법 과거 표현으로, '…한다면 ~할 수 있을 것이다'의 뜻이다. that 이하는 guess의 목적어이다.
[10행] *The extent* [to which **they** are found] varies ~.
• 주어는 The extent이고 동사는 varies이며, [ ] 부분은 The extent를 수식한다. 여기서 they는 앞의 biological clues를 지칭한다.
[11행~13행] For example, it is impossible to <u>guess</u> <u>from their bodies</u> <u>that birds make nests</u>, and, ~.
　　　　　　　　　　　　　　　　　V′　　　부사구　　　　O′
• 앞서 나온 문장과 마찬가지로 동사인 guess와 목적어인 that ~ 사이에 부사구가 위치한 형태이다.

어휘 innately 선천적으로, 타고나서 biological 생물체의, 생물학의 clue 단서 accident 우연; 사고 streamlined 유선형의 fin 지느러미 structurally 구조상, 구조적으로 adapted for ~에 적당한, 알맞은 mosquito 모기 mode 방식, 유형 transport 이동, 수송 over-optimistic 지나치게 낙관적인 extent 정도, 규모 vary 가지각색이다, 다르다 tremendously 굉장히, 엄청나게 weave (직물 등을) 짜다, (거미가 집을) 엮다 web 거미집 strand 한 가닥의 실 hindrance 방해 spin (거미가) 실을 내다, 거미집을 짓다

3 빈칸 추론 ⑤

해설 보고서나 논문을 읽는 사람은 이전의 연구 결과는 이미 알고 있는 상태에서 새로운 연구 결과를 알고 싶어 읽는 것이므로, 논문의 순서를 이전의 연구 결과로 시작하는 것은 ⑤ '불필요하게 상기시키는 것'일 것이다.
① 창의적 표현 수단
② 안전 예방책
③ 강력한 동기 요인
④ 상세한 요약

해석 보고서, 논문 또는 다른 전문적인 문서를 위한 최고의 순서는 무엇인가? 물론 그것은 논리적이어야 한다. 하지만 그것은 그 논문이 연관성과 순서를 갖고 있어야 한다는 것과 이 표제 하에 다양한 순서가 가능하다는 것을 의미할 뿐이다. 너무나 많은 글 쓰는 사람들이 '논리적'이라는 용어를 연대기적인 것을 의미한다고 해석하고 보고서와 논문을 이전 작업에 대한 주의 깊은 재검토로 시작하는 것이 습관이 되었다. 보통 이것은 전술적으로 취약하다. 보고서와 논문을 읽는 대부분의 독자들은 그 주제에 그들이 관심이 있고 그 주제에 관해 뭔가 알기 때문에 그 문서를 읽고 있다. 그래서 그들에게 이전 작업의 연구 결과는 불필요하게 상기시키는 것이다. 그들에게 흥미로운 것은 새로운 정보, 즉 새로운 연구 결과와 결론이다. 그래서 그러한 정보로 시작하는 것이 보통 가장 좋다. 작업이나 절차에 관한 긴 연대기적인 설명을 하는 것은 보통 논문의 핵심적인 내용이 연대기적 순서일 때에만 적절하다.

구문 [15행~18행] **To give** a long chronological account of work or procedures **is** normally appropriate only when the essential point of the paper is the chronological sequence.

• 주어는 To give ~ procedures이고 동사는 is이다.

어휘 technical 전문적인, 기술적인　sequence 순서, 차례　heading 표제, 제목　interpret 해석하다　chronological 연대순의, 발생[시간] 순서대로 된　habitual 습관적인　tactically 전술적으로　finding 연구 결과　account 설명　procedure 절차, 진행　[선택지] outlet (감정·생각 등의) 발산[표현]수단　precaution 예방책　motivator 동기를 부여하는 사람, 동기 요인　reminder 상기시키는 것

4 무관 문장　③

해설 하천이 공기에 노출된 표면으로 산소를 공급받는데, 오염 물질이 폐기된 하천은 산소가 박테리아에 의한 부패 과정에서 소모되어 산소 부족을 겪게 된다는 내용의 글이다. ③번 문장은 정책 입안자들이 환경 문제와 경제 발전에 균형을 맞춰야 한다는 내용이므로 하천 오염과 산소의 관계를 논한 글의 전체 흐름과 맞지 않다.

해석 일반적으로 하천은 공기에 노출되어 있는 넓은 표면과 지속적인 물의 이동 때문에 녹색 식물이 없을 때조차도 도처에서 거의 균일하게 풍부한 산소 공급량을 함유하고 있다. 이것은 호흡을 쉽게 하는 데 도움이 된다. ① 이러한 이유 때문에 흐르는 물에 사는 동물들은 감소된 산소 함유량에 민감하다. ② 그러므로 하천의 생물 군집들은 산소의 공급을 감소시키는 어떠한 종류의 유기성 오염에도 특히 민감하다. ③ 정책 입안자들은 민감한 환경에 대한 우려 사항과 세계적 경쟁에 분투하는 경제 발전의 우려 사항 간에 균형을 맞추기 위해 계속해서 노력해야 한다. ④ 하수에서 나오는 유기물이나 제지 공장에서 나오는 폐기물이 하천에 대량으로 버려질 때, 물속에 있는 산소는 박테리아에 의한 부패 과정에서 소모되거나 모두 사용된다. ⑤ 이러한 종류의 하천 오염은 인구 밀도가 높고 산업화된 지역에서 가장 긴요한 문제들 중 하나이다.

구문 [3행~4행] ~ **because of** _the large surface_ (exposed to air) and constant motion of water.

• because of의 목적어 역할을 하는 두 개의 명사구가 and로 연결되어 병렬구조를 이루고 있다. exposed to air는 수동의 의미로 the large surface를 수식한다.

[12행~14행] **When** _organic matter_ (from sewage) or _waste_ (from a paper mill)
　　　　　　　　S′
is dumped in large quantities into streams, ~
　　V′

• When절에서 주어는 두 개의 명사구가 or로 연결된 병렬구조이며, 동사는 is dumped이다.

어휘 contain 함유하다, 포함하다　abundant 풍부한　uniform 획일적인, 균일한　throughout 도처에　sensitive 민감한　oxygen content 산소 함유량　community

군집　organic 유기의　policy maker 정책 입안자　sewage 하수　paper mill 제지 공장　dump (쓰레기를) 버리다, 처분하다　consume 소모하다, 소비하다; 먹다　decay 부패; 부패하다　use A up A를 다 쓰다　populate 거주하다

5 요약문 완성　①

해설 토머스 제퍼슨은 대표나 장관의 대의 민주주의가 아니라 시민(citizens)의 직접 참여로 이루어지는 민주주의가 국가의 활력을 유지시켜줄 것이라 보았고, 그 때문에 시민의(citizens') 직접 참여가 가능하도록 중앙집권적 정부가 아니라 분권화된 작은 지역(local) 정부를 지향했다.

해석 여러분이 서로의 흥미나 관심거리에 대해 여러분의 이웃과 이야기를 나눌 수 없다면 여러분은 민주주의 체제를 가질 수 없다. 민주주의에 대해 지속적 관심이 있었던 토머스 제퍼슨은 이와 유사한 결론에 이르렀다. 그는 기업에서든 정치적 지도자들에게서든 혹은 배타적인 정치 기관에서든 집중된 권력의 위험성을 이해하는 데 있어서 선견지명이 있었다. 시민의 직접적인 관여는 미국 혁명을 가능하게 만들었고 새로운 공화국에 활력과 미래에 대한 희망을 주었던 것이었다. 그러한 관여가 없다면 그 공화국은 없어질 것이다. 마침내, 그는 국가가 '구'로 세분되어야 할 필요성을 인식했는데, '구'는 그곳에 사는 모든 사람들이 정치적인 과정에 직접 참여할 수 있을 정도로 작은 정치 단위였다. 수도에 있는 각 구의 대표들은 이런 방식으로 조직된 시민들에게 빠르게 반응해야 할 것이다. 그런 다음 지역적으로 운영되는 활기찬 민주주의는 공화국의 민주적인 삶을 위한 활발한 기본적 단위를 제공할 것이다. 그런 유형의 관여가 있으면, 공화국은 생존하고 번영할 것이다.

↓

토머스 제퍼슨은 시의 업무에 대한 (B) 시민의 직접적인 참여를 강조하는 (A) 지역 정부의 형태를 찬성하는 주장을 했다.

구문 [6행~7행] ~ **whether** in corporations **or** in political leaders or exclusionary political institutions.

• 「whether A or B」 구문은 'A이든 B이든'을 뜻한다.

[7행~10행] Direct involvement of citizens was **what** had made the American Revolution possible and given the new republic vitality and hope for the future.

• what 이하는 was의 보어이다. had 다음의 과거분사 made와 given이 and로 연결되어 병렬구조를 이루고 있다.

어휘 mutual 서로의, 상호적인　enduring 지속적인　concentrated 집중된　corporation 기업　exclusionary 배타적인　institution 기관　involvement 관여, 참여　vitality 활력, 생기　eventually 마침내, 결국　subdivide 세분하다, 작게 나누다　representative 대표　responsive 빠르게 반응하는　vibrant 활기찬, 생기가 넘치는; (색채가) 강렬한　prosper 번영하다

1 빈칸 추론 ①

해설 우리가 보는 것이 기존에 믿고 있는 것에 영향을 받아서 오류가 생길 수 있다는 것이 글의 요지로 눈속임용 마술 트럼프 카드로 우리가 잘못 보는 것을 예로 들었다. 그러므로 빈칸에는 ① '정확한 인식을 방해했다'가 적절하다.
② 피실험자들의 자신감을 감소시켰다
③ 수행에 긍정적이고 부정적인 영향 둘 다 주었다
④ 능률적이고 효과적인 인식을 증진시켰다
⑤ 그들의 다양한 감각의 지원을 받지 못했다

해석 플라톤이 생각했을지도 모르는 것이 무엇인지에 상관없이, 우리의 정신이 '영원한 진리'에 직접 도달하는 방법은 없다. 우리의 감각, 특히 시각, 청각, 그리고 촉각은 실재로 가는 우리의 유일한 문이다. 그러나 그것들이 본질적이기는 하지만, 우리의 감각은 또한 우리를 잘못 인도할 수 있다. 시각이 몇 가지 좋은 예를 제공한다. '보는 것이 믿는 것'이지만, 우리가 보는 것이 항상 신뢰할 만한 믿음을 만들어 내는 것은 아니다. 우리가 보고 있다고 생각하는 것이 우리가 이미 믿고 있는 것에 의해 영향을 받기 때문에 오류가 생길 수 있다. 우리는 종종 우리가 보고자 하는 것을 '보고' 우리가 기대하지 않는 것은 보지 못한다. 1949년의 한 유명한 실험에서 심리학자 Jerome Bruner와 Leo Postman은 일단의 피실험자들에게 마술용 트럼프 카드의 그림을 재빨리 힐끗 보여 주었다. 상당히 자주 그 피실험자들은, 예를 들어 검은색 하트 3을 정상적인 스페이드 3(하트를 스페이드로 오인하는 것)이나 정상적인 하트 3(검은색을 빨간색으로 오인하는 것)이라고 말했다. 마술 트럼프 카드에 대한 예상이 정확한 인식을 방해했다.

구문 [4행~5행] **Essential as they are**, however, our senses can also mislead us.
• 「보어(형용사)+as+주어+동사」의 어순으로 된 Essential as they are는 양보구문으로 쓰였다. Although they are essential로 바꾸어 쓸 수 있다.

어휘 **regardless of** ~에 상관없이   **access** 접근하다, 도달하다   **eternal** 영원한   **mislead** 오도하다, 잘못 인도하다   **reliable** 신뢰할 만한   **anticipate** 기대하다; 예상하다   **glimpse** 잠깐[언뜻] 봄   **trick** 마술, 재주   **subject** 피실험자   **misperceive** 오인하다, 오해하다
[선택지] **interfere with** ~을 방해하다   **perception** 인식   **confidence** 자신감   **efficient** 능률적인   **recognition** 인식

2 글의 순서 ②

해설 주어진 글에서 도덕적 진보를 깨닫게 할 수 있는 유추가 있다고 한 후, 현미경 발명 이전 상황의 부정확한 판단을 설명한다. 그 뒤에는 연결사 however를 사용하여 현미경 발명 이후를 보여준 (B)가 와야 한다. 그 다음에는 연결사 Similarly를 사용하여 현미경에 비유될 수 있는 도덕적 도구가 없는 상황에서도 마찬가지임을 설명한 (A)가 나와야 한다. (C)는 (A)에 대한 구체적인 예에 해당하므로 마지막에 와야 한다.

해석 아래의 유추는 우리로 하여금 도덕적 진보가 가능하다는 것을 깨닫게 한다. 현미경의 발명 이전에는 사람들은 미세한 생명체를 보기 위한 도구가 전혀 없었기에 결과적으로 질병의 원인에 관하여 부정확한 판단을 했다.
(B) 그러나 현미경의 발명으로 과학자들은 이전에는 알아차리지 못했던 존재를 인지할 수 있었고 결과적으로 개선된 판단을 내릴 수 있었는데, 그 중에 많은 것들을 오늘날에도 우리가 여전히 인정한다.

(A) 마찬가지로 도덕의 영역에서도 사람들이 어떤 것의 옳고 그름을 깨닫는 데 필요한 도구가 없을 때에는 그들에게 그러한 도구가 있다면 그러할 것보다 덜 정확한 판단을 한다.
(C) 그러니까 우리는, 예를 들자면, 어떻게 19세기 미국의 일부 사람들의 제한된 시각이 그들로 하여금 인종 차별이 용인될 수 있다는 결론에 이르게 했는지, 그리고 오늘날의 우리의 더 넓은 시각이 우리로 하여금 그 이전의 판단이 얼마나 끔찍하게 잘못된 것이었는지를 어떻게 깨달을 수 있게 하는지 알 수 있다.

구문 [8행~9행] ~ they make *judgments* [that are less accurate than they **would be** (accurate) if they **had** such tools].
• [ ] 부분은 judgments를 수식하며, they would be에서 be 다음에 accurate가 생략된 것으로 볼 수 있다. [ ] 절 속에서 가정법 과거 표현인 「S+would+동사원형, if+S′+과거동사」가 사용되었다.

[11행~14행] ~ **scientists were** able to perceive *entities* [(which[that]) they'd previously been unable to (perceive)] and, as a result, **were** able to make *improved judgments* — many of **which** we still accept today.
• 주어는 scientists이고 동사는 두 were가 and로 연결되어 병렬구조를 이루고 있다. [ ] 부분은 앞에 목적격 관계대명사 which[that]가 생략되어 entities를 수식하며, been unable to 다음에 perceive가 생략된 것으로 볼 수 있다. many of which에서 관계대명사 which는 improved judgments를 지칭한다.

어휘 **progress** 발전(하다), 진보(하다)   **microscope** 현미경   **microscopic** 미세한   **consequently** 결과적으로   **inaccurate** 부정확한 (↔ accurate 정확한)   **regarding** ~에 관하여   **sphere** 영역   **perceive** 인지하다; 알아차리다, 깨닫다   **entity** 존재, 실재   **perspective** 시각, 관점; 원근법; 전망   **racism** 인종 차별   **acceptable** 용인될 수 있는   **terribly** 끔찍하게, 지독하게   **mistaken** 잘못된

3 문장 넣기 ④

해설 겨울잠쥐의 신체 기능이 둔화되는 예를 모두 언급한 다음에, 동면을 위해 그렇게 된다고 이유를 언급하는 주어진 문장이 오는 것이 적절하다.

해석 어떤 동물들은 에너지를 보존하고 음식에 대한 필요를 줄이기 위해 동면한다. 동면에 들어가기 전에 동물은 보통 지방 비축량을 많아지게 하려고 먹이를 먹는다. 동물이 동면을 할 때 신체 기능은 상당히 둔화된다. 예를 들어, 몸길이가 약 10센티가 되는 겨울잠쥐의 심장 박동 수는 몇 분마다 박동하도록 느려진다. 또한, 호흡은 느려지고 체온은 주위에 있는 땅의 온도보다 몇도 높은 정도로 떨어진다. 이 모든 변화가 이 작은 크기의 동물이 먹이 없이 오랜 기간 생존하도록 하고 에너지원이 되는 식량의 필요성을 줄인다. 하지만, 모든 동면하는 동물이 겨울 내내 잠을 잔다고 생각하는 것은 오해이다. 사실, 많은 동물들이 겨울 중 짧은 기간 동안 동면하며, 그들은 온화한 겨울 날씨 사이에나 하루에 서너 번 정도로 자주 깨어나기도 한다.

구문 [15행~18행] In fact, many animals hibernate for short spurts during the winter, and they may **wake** for an interval of mild weather or as often as three or four times a day.
• 밑줄 친 부분은 동사 wake를 보충 설명하는 시간의 부사구로 or로 연결되어 병렬구조를 이루고 있다.

어휘 **conserve** 보존하다   **heartbeat** 심장 박동   **spurt** 짧은 시간, 한순간   **interval** 사이, 간격   **mild** (날씨가) 온화한

4~5 장문 4 ② 5 ③

해설 4. 과학자는 가설을 세우고 그 가설을 여러 번 검증해야 하는데, 설령 가설이 그러한 검증을 통과한다 해도 그것이 진리라는 증거는 아니며 진리의 근사치로서 인정받는 기간이 연장될 뿐 가설 검증은 끝없는 과정임을 나타낸 글이다. 그러므로 제목으로 가장 적절한 것은 ② '과학은 결과물이 아닌 과정'이다.

① 완벽한 가설을 만드는 방법
③ 과학이 미래에 대한 통찰을 제공한다
④ 오직 검증을 통해서만 진리는 밝혀진다
⑤ 현실은 더 이상 과학과 보조를 맞출 수 없다

5. 뒤에서 가설은 검증 결과가 양립할 수 있는 새로운 가설로 수정되거나 폐기된다고 했으므로 검증 결과가 예측과 일치하지 않으면 가설은 틀렸음이 입증된다는 것을 알 수 있다. 그러므로 ③은 disagree 등이 되어야 한다.

해석 과학자들은 많은 사람들이 믿는 것처럼 사실을 발견하고 수집하는 데 주로 관심을 갖는 것은 아니다. 오히려 연구자들은 자연 세계에 대한 중대한 질문을 던지고 나서 그러한 질문들에 대한 (a) 진실한 답변이 무엇이 될지에 대한 창의적 통찰인 가설을 제안함으로써 그것에 답변하려 노력한다. 과학적 방법을 다른 앎의 방식과 진정으로 구별 짓는 것은 그것이 실험에 의한 혹은 추가적인 관찰의 수집에 의한 각각의 가설의 철저한 검증에 (b) 의존한다는 것이다. 검증의 명백한 의향은 가설이 틀린지 맞는지를 결정하는 것이다. 검증 결과가 예측과 (c) 일치하면(→ 일치하지 않으면), 평가되는 가설은 틀렸음이 입증되며, 이는 그것이 현실의 타당한 설명이 될 수 없음을 의미한다. 그러면 그것은 검증 결과와 양립할 수 있는 새로운 가설로 (d) 수정되거나 완전히 폐기되어 다른, 여전히 검증되어야 하는 가설들로 교체된다. 그러나 예측된 검증 결과와 실험상의 검증 결과 간의 일치가 그 가설이 참이라는 증거는 아니라는 점을 명심하라. 오히려 그것은 그 가설이 당분간만 계속하여 현실에 대한 타당한 견해가 됨을 의미할 뿐이다. 그것은 다음 검증에서 살아남지 못할지도 모른다. 가설이 여러 차례 반증을 (e) 피한다면, 과학자들은 그것을 현실에 가까운 근사치로 간주한다.

구문 [6행~10행] **What** really **separates** the scientific method **from** other ways of knowing / **is its** reliance on the rigorous testing of each hypothesis by experimentation [or] by the gathering of additional observations; ~.

• What ~ knowing이 주어이고 동사는 is이다. 주어 부분에서 「separate A from B (A를 B와 구별하다)」 표현이 사용되었다. its는 scientific method를 가리킨다. 두 밑줄 친 부분은 or로 연결되어 병렬구조를 이룬다.

[14행~17행] Then it is **either** modified into a new hypothesis [that is compatible with the test findings] **or** discarded altogether and replaced by other, still-to-be-tested hypotheses.

• 「either A or B」는 'A나 B 둘 중 하나'의 뜻이다. A 자리에는 modified가, B 자리에는 discarded와 replaced가 위치하여 병렬구조를 이룬다. [ ] 부분은 a new hypothesis를 수식한다.

어휘 **hypothesis** 가설 **insight** 통찰 **rigorous** 철저한, 엄격한 **experimentation** 실험 **explicit** 명백한 **intent** 의도, 의향 **disprove** 틀렸음을 입증하다 **legitimate** 정당한, 타당한 **compatible** 양립할 수 있는 **discard** 폐기하다, 버리다 **valid** 유효한, 타당한 **version** 생각, 견해; -판[형태] **approximation** 근사치

1 필자 주장 ④

해설 이 글은 기업의 채용 관행을 설명하는 것으로, 많은 대기업들이 특정 대학을 방문하여 취업 설명회 면접을 시행한다. 이러한 취업 설명회 면접이 학생 자신이 다니는 대학에서 열리지 않더라도 이에 구애받지 않고 적극적으로 지원하는 구직 활동을 해야 한다는 내용이므로, 필자의 주장으로 가장 적절한 것은 ④ '출신 대학에 구애받지 않고 적극적인 구직 활동을 해야 한다.'이다.

해석 많은 대기업들이 덜 인정받는 대학에서 학생들과의 공개 면접을 시행하지 않는다는 것은 불운한 사실이다. 당신이 이러한 대학 중 하나에 다니는 학생이라면, 이러한 소위 '취업 설명회 면접'이 당신이 닿을 수 있는 범위 바깥에 있지 않다는 점을 명심해라. 이것은 고용주들이 작은 학교 출신 학생들을 원치 않기 때문이 아니라, 단지 전통적으로 그들이 다른 대학에 방문해왔고 (설명회) 장소를 바꾸려면 마땅한 이유가 있어야 하기 때문이다. 그러므로 당신이 당신의 대학에 방문하지 않은 회사에 관심이 있으면, 본사나 그 회사의 채용 센터에 지원서를 보내라. 당신은 그러고 나서 근처 대학이나 회사의 평가 센터에서 열리는 취업 설명회 면접에 참석할 수도 있다. 취업 설명회는 모든 최종 학년 학부생들과 모든 회사들을 던져 넣은 거대한 용광로와 같다. 모두가 환영받는다.

구문 [1행~3행] **It** is an unfortunate fact **that** many large companies do not conduct open interviews with students at the less well-established universities.

• It은 가주어이고 that 이하가 진주어이다.

[14행~16행] The milk-round is like *a giant melting pot* [**into which** all final-year undergraduates and all companies are thrown].

• [ ] 부분은 '전치사+관계대명사' 형태인 into which가 이끄는 관계사절로 a giant melting pot을 수식하며, into which는 의미상 and into the melting pot으로 볼 수 있다.

어휘 **well-established** 확고부동한, 정착된 **out of one's reach** 손이 닿지 않는, 힘이 미치지 않는 **venue** (회담 등의) 장소 **application form** 지원서 **head office** 본사 **recruitment** 신규 모집, 채용 **melting pot** 용광로 **undergraduate** 학부생, 대학생

2 밑줄 함의 ②

해설 '룰렛의 휠은 그것의 최근의 결과를 기억하지 않는다.'는 말은 '검은색과 빨간색이 나올 확률은 여전히 47.4 대 47.4로 동일하며 개별 사건의 발생 확률이 과거 사건들의 이력에 아무런 영향을 받지 않는다'는 뜻이므로 ② '각각의 휠 회전은 독립적 사건이다.'라는 의미로 볼 수 있다.
① 운은 종종 어떤 숫자에 다른 숫자보다 더 큰 호의를 보인다.
③ 미래를 아는 것은 현재를 올바르게 분석하는 것이다.
④ 룰렛 휠은 무작위로 숫자를 선택하지 않는다.
⑤ 승리 가능성은 손실을 볼 때마다 증가한다.

해석 Laura는 사람들이 룰렛을 하는 모습을 보며 카지노에 있다. 룰렛 휠의 38개의 슬롯은 18개의 검은 숫자들, 18개의 빨간 숫자들과 2개의 녹색 숫자를 포함하고 있다. 따라서 어떤 한 번의 회전에서도 빨간색이나 검은색의 확률은 50대 50보다 약간 낮다(정확히 47.4이다). Laura는 비록 베팅은 하고 있지 않지만, 게임 결과의 패턴을 매우 주의 깊게 따라가고 있다. 공은 연속 7번 빨간색에 내려앉았다. Laura는 검은색이 나올 때가 한참 지났다고 결론을 내리고 게임에 뛰어들어, 검은색에 과도하게 베팅한다. Laura의 추론에 동의하는가? 대단히 많은 사람들이 Laura가 베팅

을 잘했다고 믿는 경향이 있다. 그러나 그들은 틀렸다. 사람들은 확률의 법칙이 공정한 결과를 산출해야 하며 무작위적인 과정은 자기 수정적일 것이 틀림없다고 믿는다. 이것은 장기적으로는 나쁜 가정이 아니다. 그러나 그 법칙들은 개별적, 독립적 사건에는 적용되지 않는다. 통계학자들이 말하듯이 "룰렛의 휠은 그것의 최근의 결과를 기억하지 않는다."

구문 [12행~15행] People **believe** that the laws of probability should yield fair results [and] that a random process must be self-correcting.

• 두 밑줄 친 부분이 and로 연결되어 병렬구조를 이루며 believe의 목적어로 쓰였다.

어휘 **slot** (가느다란) 구멍, 슬롯 **hence** 따라서 **spin** 회전 **probability** 확률 **slightly** 약간 **in a row** 연속으로 **overdue** 기한이 지난 **reasoning** 추론 **yield** 산출하다 **random** 무작위의 **self-correcting** 자기 수정적인 **in the long run** 장기적으로 **apply to** ~에 적용되다

3 빈칸 추론 ③

해설 부족량과 잉여량을 교환하는 상호 이익에 대해 설명하면서 Oaxaca 인디언이 자기가 후원하는 축제 때 다른 사람의 도움을 받고 나중에 그들에게 동등하게 그 도움을 상환해주는 예를 들었다. 그러므로 빈칸에는 ③ '상호 보험 제도'가 가장 적절하다.
① 기생적 관계
② 전통적인 법적 관행
④ 복잡한 사회 계급
⑤ 효과적인 의사소통

해석 균형 잡힌 상호 이익의 주요 경제적 동기 부여는 잉여 재화와 용역을 공급이 부족한 그것들(재화와 용역)과 교환하는 것이다. 부족량과 잉여량은 기술의 다른 수준, 환경의 차이, 또는 다른 생산 능력의 결과일 수 있다. 그러나 원인이 무엇이든, 균형 잡힌 상호 이익은 교환하는 양쪽으로 하여금 자신들의 소비를 최대화하는 것을 가능하게 한다. 멕시코의 Oaxaca 인디언들은 재화와 용역 둘 다의 교환에서 균형 잡힌 상호 이익의 좋은 예가 된다. 사회 관습에 따라서, 남자는 주요 성인(聖人)의 날을 축하하는 적어도 한 가지 축제에 후원할 것으로 기대된다. 그런 행사는 공들인 음식, 음료, 그리고 오락을 포함하는데, 거의 항상 한 남자가 혼자서 제공할 수 있는 능력을 넘어선다. 그 결과 그 남자는 자기의 친척, 친구 그리고 이웃의 도움을 구하고, 그것에 의해서 (그는) 자기의 미래 잉여량을 저당 잡힌다. 도와주는 사람들은 자기가 비슷한 축제를 후원할 때 동등한 양으로 상환받기를 기대한다. 사실상 Oaxaca 인디언들은 일종의 상호 보험 제도를 만들어냈다.

구문 [12행~14행] *Such an event*, **involving** elaborate food, beverages, and entertainment, is almost always beyond *the capacity of a man* (to provide by himself).

• 분사 involving은 앞에 나온 Such an event의 내용을 설명한다. ( ) 부분은 to부정사의 형용사적 용법으로 the capacity of a man을 수식한다.

어휘 **motivation** 동기 부여 **surplus** 잉여의, 과잉의; 잉여, 과잉 **shortfall** 부족량 **variation** 변화, 차이 **maximize** 최대[극대]화하다; 최대한으로 활용하다 **consumption** 소비 **exemplify** 예증하다, 좋은 예가 되다 **sponsor** 후원하다 **elaborate** 공들인, 정교한 **beverage** 음료 **consequently** 따라서, 그 결과로서 **thereby** 그것에 의해서 **equivalent** 동등한, 같은 **in effect** 사실상, 실제로는

4 글의 순서

③

해설 소비주의가 관광업에 영향을 끼쳤다는 글 다음에는 그 결과로 초래된 소비 중심 관광의 부정적 측면을 구체적으로 나열한 (B)가 나와야 연결이 자연스럽다. 그다음에는 '그러나 (However)'로 연결되며 이런 부정적 측면이 관광객들에게는 중요한 경험으로 여겨짐과 동시에 문화 보존에 대해 수요를 창출하는 긍정적인 면을 진술한 (C)가 나와야 하고, 구체적으로 소비가 문화 보존에 어떻게 긍정적으로 기능하는지를 좀 더 구체적으로 진술한 (A)가 나와 뒷받침되어야 한다.

해석 현대의 소비자 중심주의 사회는 도시 생활방식, 높은 서비스 수준에 대한 기대, 그리고 모든 것이 판매 중이라는 이해와 함께 관광업에 중대한 영향을 끼쳤다. (B) 그리고, 그 결과로 초래된 소비 중심 관광은 유해하며, 교통 체증, 혼잡함, 명소와 박물관과 식당에서의 긴 줄과 같은 환경적, 사회적 문제를 발생시킨다고들 흔히들 믿는다.
(C) 그러나 이러한 것들은 흔히 관광객에게 받아들여지며 그들의 경험의 중요한 일부로 여겨진다. 더욱이, 높은 관광 소비는 문화 보존과 보호에 대한 높은 수요를 창출한다.
(A) 그것은 지역의 전통과 진정성에 새로운 활력을 주고, 문화적 인식을 증진시키고, 가치와 권력에 대한 새로운 체계를 만든다. 문화의 어떤 요소들이 판매용이고 관광객 소비용인지, 어떤 요소들은 아닌지, 그리고 어떤 요소들이 보존될 필요가 있는지를 반드시 알아야 할 뿐이다.

구문 [5행~7행] It revitalizes local traditions and authenticity, promotes cultural awareness, and creates new systems of values and power.
● 밑줄 친 세 개의 동사 revitalizes, promotes, creates가 콤마와 and로 연결되어 병렬구조를 이루고 있다.

[7행~9행] One must only know **which** elements of culture are for sale and tourist consumption, **which** (elements of culture) are not (for sale and tourist consumption), and **which** (elements of culture) need to be preserved.
● know의 목적어로 which가 이끄는 세 부분이 and로 연결되어 병렬구조를 이룬다. 두 번째 부분과 세 번째 부분에는 반복을 피하기 위해 첫 번째 부분의 어구가 생략되어 있다.

어휘 -oriented ~지향의   revitalize 새로운 활력을 주다   authenticity 진짜임, 진정성   awareness 인지, 인식   consumption 소비   preserve 보존하다, 유지하다   *cf.* preservation 보존   generate 발생시키다   overcrowding 초만원, 과밀   attraction 명소   conservation 보호, 보존

5 문장 넣기

⑤

해설 주어진 문장은 우유를 마시는 것이 더 오래 살게 한다는 것을 의미하지는 않는다는 내용이므로 우유를 먹는 사람이 더 오래 살아서 암 발병률이 더 높아지는 것이라는 내용 다음에 오는 게 자연스럽다. 그리고 주어진 문장 다음에는 우유를 먹는 사람들이 더 좋은 의료 서비스에 접근하고 더 건강하게 먹을 가능성이 있다는 내용이 오는 것이 적절하므로 ⑤가 답이다.

해석 상관관계가 인과관계와 동일한 것인지 아닌지를 결정하는 데 있어서의 어려움은 매우 많은 오해를 초래한다. 어떻게 A가 B를 일으키는지를 설명하는 특정한 체계가 확인될 때까지는 어떠한 상관관계도 우연한 것이라고 가정하거나 A와 B가 둘다 어떤 제3의 요인과 별개로 관련되어 있다고 가정하는 것이 최선이다. 이것의 두드러진 한 예가 우유를 마시는 것과 암 발병률 간의 상관관계인데 몇몇 집단은 우유를 마시는 것이 암의 원인이 된다고 주장하기 위해 이것을 이용한다. 더 그럴듯한 설명은 암 진단과 우유 소비 모두가 상승된 연령과 양(+)의 상관관계가 있다는 것이다. 즉, 평균적으로 우유를 마시는 사람들은 우유를 마시지 않는 사람들보다 더 오래 살고, 그리고 사람들이 나이가 들수록 암이 생길 가능성이 좀 더 많아진다는 것이다. 그러나 이것이 실제로 우유를 마시는 것이 사람들을 더 오래 살게 한다는 것을 의미하지는 않는다. 우유를 마시는 사람들이 그렇지 않은 사람들에 비해 질이 높은 의료 서비스에 더 잘 접근하거나 더 건강에 좋게 먹을 가능성이 있다는 것이다.

구문 [5행~8행] Until a specific mechanism (**demonstrating** how A causes B is identified), // it's best **to assume** that any correlation is accidental, or that both A and B relate independently to some third factor.
● demonstrating이 이끄는 현재분사구가 a specific mechanism을 수식하며, how A causes B는 분사의 목적어절이다. it은 가주어이고 to assume 이하가 진주어이다. 진주어 to assume의 목적어는 두 개의 that절로 이루어져 있다.

어휘 determine 결정하다   correlation 상관관계   misunderstanding 오해   mechanism 체계   demonstrate 설명하다, 논증하다   assume 가정하다, 추정하다   accidental 우연한, 우발적인   highlight 강조하다, 두드러지게 하다   cancer 암   diagnose 진단   positive correlation 양(+)의 상관관계   access 접근, 이용

1 글의 주제   ⑤

해설 소멸 위기에 처한 지역 언어를 재활성화시키기 위해 교육과 그 언어를 읽고 쓰는 능력이 필수적인데 절반 이상의 지역 언어들이 문자를 갖고 있지 않으므로 문자가 개발되어야 하고 교육 자료와 참고 자료 역시 필요하다고 말하고 있다. 그러므로 글의 주제로는 ⑤ '지역 언어를 위한 문자와 교육 자료의 필요성'이 적절하다.
① 지역 언어를 빠르고 효율적으로 배우는 방법
② 새로운 지역 언어를 배우는 데 있어 가장 필수적인 단계
③ 지역 언어에서의 읽고 쓰는 능력 개발을 위한 다양한 교육
④ 문화 정체성을 보존하기 위해 지역 언어를 지키는 것의 중요성

해석 대부분의 언어학자와 지역 공동체 구성원들은 지역 언어 교육과 (그 언어를) 읽고 쓰는 능력이 (언어의) 생명력을 유지하거나 소멸 위기에 처한 언어를 재활성화시키는 데 필수적이라는 것에 동의한다. 어떤 지역 공동체들은 이러한 생각을 거부하면서 자신들의 구어(口語)적 전통을 보존하고 그것들에 전적으로 의존하기를 원한다. 그러나 언어가 사용될 수 있는 범위를 제한하기 때문에 이러한 결정에는 대가가 따른다. 그럼에도 대부분의 사람들은 지역 언어에서 읽고 쓰는 능력이 필수적이라고 여긴다. 하지만 모든 언어의 절반 이상은 문자 형태를 가지고 있지 않기에 교육과 읽고 쓰기 과정에 그런 언어들을 사용하기 위해서는 문자 체계가 개발되어야 한다. 교과서, 사전과 활용 가능한 기술(記述) 문법책을 포함한 기본적인 교육 자료와 참고용 자료가 필요하다. 그러한 자료들은 더 널리 소통되는 언어들에서는 쉽게 이용 가능하지만, 대부분의 지역 언어에 있어서는 그렇지 않다. 게다가 읽고 쓰는 능력을 위해서는 읽기 자료 역시 필요하다.

구문 [1행~4행] Most linguists and local community members agree **that** *education and literacy* (in the local language) are necessary to maintain vitality, or to revitalize *a language* (threatened with endangerment).
• agree의 목적어로 that이 이끄는 명사절이 쓰였고 첫 번째 ( ) 부분은 전명구로 that절 내의 주어 education and literacy를 수식한다. 밑줄 친 두 부분은 부사적 용법(목적)으로 쓰인 to부정사구로 or로 연결되어 병렬구조를 이룬다. 두 번째 ( ) 부분은 과거분사구로 앞의 a language를 수식한다.

[4행~6행] *Some local communities* reject this notion, **wanting to preserve their oral traditions and to rely solely on them**.
• wanting 이하는 some local communities를 의미상 주어로 하는 능동 분사구문이다.

어휘 linguist 언어학자 literacy 글을 읽고 쓰는 능력(이 있음) vitality 생명력, 활력; 활기 revitalize 재활성화시키다, 새로운 활력을 주다 endangerment 멸종 위기의 상황 notion 생각, 개념 oral 구어의 solely 전적으로; 단독으로 domain 범위, 영역 pedagogical 교육(학)의 reference 참고, 참조 descriptive (실제 사용 현황을 보여주는) 기술적인; 서술하는
[선택지] identity 정체(성); 동일함, 일치

2 밑줄 어법   ③

해설 ③ the connections 이하는 "dormant ties"와 동격 관계인 명사구이다. we once had는 앞에 목적격 관계대명사 which[that]가 생략되어 the connections를 수식한다. ③과 같이 what을 쓰면 명사절이 되는데 이렇게 되면 이 명사절은 주어, 목적어, 보어, 동격절 중 어느 역할도 수행하지 않으므로 명사절을 이끄는 관계대명사 what은 적절하지 않다. 따라서 what을 which[that]로 바꿔 써야 하며,

which[that] we haven't maintained는 관계사절로서 the connections를 수식한다.
① making 이하는 분사구문이며, requests 이하는 making에 대한 목적어이므로 능동의 형태를 잘 사용했다.
② extremely는 형용사 valuable을 수식하므로 부사 형태를 잘 사용했다.
④ to ask 이하는 '목적'의 의미(~하기 위하여)를 가지며 문맥상 부합한다.
⑤ helping은 hearing과 병렬구조를 이루어 적절한 형태로 사용되었다.

해석 우리 중 많은 사람들은 가족과 가까운 친구들로 구성된 우리의 '측근' 너머의 누구에게라도 부탁하는 것을 불편하게 느끼는 경향이 있다. 그러나 그렇게 하면서 우리는 '약한 유대', 즉 우리의 지인들과 우리가 그렇게 잘 알지 못하는 사람들의 반응성을 대단히 과소평가하는 것이다. 약한 유대는 사회적 집단 간의 다리가 되기 때문에 극히 귀중하다. 새로운 정보, 문제에 대한 새로운 해결책과 다른 자원들이 이 다리들을 건너 이동한다. 우리는 또한 '휴면기 유대', 즉 예전에 가지고 유지하지 못한 관계의 반응성도 대단히 과소평가한다. 예를 들어 대부분의 사람들은 25년간 만나지 못한 고등학교 친구에게 일자리의 실마리를 부탁하려고 연락을 해볼 생각조차 못 할 것이다. 우리는 다시 연락하고자 하는 그러한 시도가 거부될 거라고, 혹은 우리의 예전의 급우는 우리가 오직 부탁하기 위해 연락을 하는 것에 대해 분노할 거라고 가정한다. 그러나 조직 연구자들에 따르면 당신의 과거의 대부분의 사람들은 사실 당신의 소식을 듣는 것을, 그리고 당신을 돕는 것을 환영할 것이다. 시간의 경과는 함께 공유했던 이해, 감정, 신뢰의 역사를 지우지 못한다.

구문 [11행~16행] For example, / most people wouldn't even consider reaching out to *a high school classmate* [(whom[that]) they haven't seen in twenty-five years] / to ask for a job lead; we assume // (that) *such attempts* (to reconnect) would be rejected, or that our former classmate would resent our reaching out / only to ask for a favor.
• [ ]는 앞에 목적격 관계대명사 whom[that]이 생략되어 a high school classmate를 수식한다. such attempts 앞에는 접속사 that이 생략되어 있다. 두 밑줄 친 부분은 or로 연결되어 병렬구조를 이루며 동사 assume에 대한 목적어 역할을 한다.

어휘 vastly 대단히 responsiveness 반응성, 민감; 응답 tie 유대, 관계; 동점; 묶다 acquaintance 지인, 아는 사람 novel 새로운 reach out 연락을 취하다 lead 실마리, 단서 former 예전의 ask for a favor 부탁하다 passage 경과, 추이; 통과

3 빈칸 추론   ①

해설 현대 경제에서 제품은 홀로 존재해선 소용이 없으며 이를 받쳐주는 수많은 서비스를 필요로 한다는 내용의 글이므로, 빈칸을 완성하면 현대 경제에서 상품과 서비스 사이의 구별 그 자체가 ① '실제로는 모호해지고 있다'가 된다.
② 이전의 어느 때보다 더 명백하다
③ 앎의 특정한 방식들의 분류이다
④ 경제적 개념에서의 핵심 구별이다
⑤ 적용하기보다는 설명하기가 더 쉽다

해석 현대 경제에서 제품과 서비스 사이의 구별은 그 자체가 실제로는 모호해지고 있다. 서비스 경제로의 이런 변화의 한 가지 측면은 제품의 '서비스화'라고 불려졌다. 그 개념은 현대 경제에서 제품은 홀로 존재할 수 없으며, 그 제품들을 유용한 것으로 만들기 위해서는 어느 정도의 서비스가 필요하다는 것이다. 자동차를 생각해 보자. 그것은 물론 실제 제품이다. 그러나 그것은 소유자가 그것을 지역 사회의 도로에서 운전할 수 있도록 거듭되는 검사에 맡기고, 가스와 석유로 그것을 채우고, 그리고 보험료, 등록비, 그리고 세금을 내는 경우에만 장기간에 걸쳐 유용할 뿐이다. 자동차

는 실제적인 제품이지만, 또한 그것에 수반되는 많은 서비스가 포함되어 있지 않으면 그것이 반드시 유용한 것은 아니다.

구문 [9행~12행] ~ if the owner <u>submits</u> it to continual checkups, / <u>fills</u> it with gas and oil, / <u>and</u> <u>pays</u> for insurance, registration, and taxes // **so that** he can operate it on community roads.

• if 절에서 동사 submits, fills, pays가 병렬구조를 이루고 있으며, pays for의 목적어 insurance, registration, taxes가 병렬구조를 이루고 있다. 접속사 so that은 '~하도록, ~하기 위하여'의 뜻이다.

어휘 **distinction** 구별, 구분 **shift** 전환, 변화 **on one's own** 혼자서, 혼자 힘으로 **degree** 정도 **over an extended period of time** 장기간에 걸쳐 **submit** 맡기다; 제출하다 **continual** 거듭되는 **checkup** 검사 **registration** 등록 **operate** (기계를) 움직이다, 운전하다 **not necessarily** 반드시 ~한 건 아니다 **accompany** 동반[수반]하다

[선택지] **obscure** 이해하기 힘든, 모호한 **apparent** 분명한, 명백한

---

4 무관 문장 ③

해설 숲이 생명력을 유지하는 방식이 효율적이고 단순하다는 것에 대해 설명하는 글이다. 즉 어떻게 태양 에너지와 물 등을 결합하고 낙엽과 죽은 나무가 다시 영양소로 나무의 영양이 되는지 설명하는 글이므로 추운 날씨에 맞는 나무를 선택할 때 고려해야 할 사항을 설명하는 내용인 ③은 전체 흐름과 관련이 없다.

해석 숲이 자신의 생명력을 유지하는 방식의 효율성과 아름다운 단순성은 항상 인상적이다. ① 나무는 그들이 자라고 무성해지게 해 주는 나무껍질, 큰 가지와 잎을 만들기 위해 태양으로부터 에너지를 받아들여, 이것을 그들이 토양으로부터 끌어올린 영양소와 물과 결합한다. ② 그 잎들은 가을에 져서 땅으로 떨어지지만 결국 박테리아에 의해 분해되고 다시 나무를 키우는 영양소로 전환된다. ③ 혹독한 기후에서 나무를 선택할 때 수종(樹種)의 원산지의 환경이 세심하게 고려되어야 하는데, 그렇지 않으면 많은 수가 겨울에 살아남을 수 없을 것이다. ④ 나뭇가지가 떨어지거나 나무 전체가 죽을 때에도 같은 과정이 일어나는데, 그것들은 영양소가 풍부한 흙을 생산하여 다음 세대에게 영양분을 제공한다. ⑤ 물과 햇빛이 적절하게 안정적으로 공급된다면 숲은 수천 년 동안 어떤 새로운 외부 자원의 필요 없이 스스로를 유지할 수 있다.

구문 [15행~17행] **Given** a fairly stable supply of water and sunshine, / *a forest* can maintain itself for thousands of years without the need for any new outside resources.

• Given ~ sunshine은 분사구문으로 의미상의 주어는 a forest이다. If it(a forest) is given a fairly stable supply of water and sunshine으로 바꾸어 쓸 수 있다.

어휘 **efficiency** 효율성, 능률 **simplicity** 단순성 **striking** 인상적인, 두드러진, 주목할 만한 **combine** 결합하다 **nutrient** 영양소 **bark** 나무껍질 **limb** 큰 가지 **thrive** 무성해지다; 번영[번창]하다 **decompose** 분해하다 **convert** 전환시키다 **species** 종 **stable** 안정적인 **resource** 자원

---

5 요약문 완성 ①

해설 우리는 과학에서 가설을 세우고 일단 그것이 사실임을 입증하려는 접근법을 취하는데, 이는 실험자의 인식과 주의 집중의 방향을 제한하는 부작용이 있다고 했다. 따라서 현재의(current) 이론에만 집중해서 가능성을 제한하지 말고 열린(open)

태도로 여러 가지 표현 양식을 사용하여 가설을 세워보는 것이 낫다는 것을 알 수 있다.

해석 과학에서 실제로 우리는 한 가지 가설을 버릴 수 있을 때까지 그것에 계속 머무른다. 그런 다음 더 좋은 것으로 나아간다. 그 가설을 버리기 위해 우리는 실제로 그것을 확증하기를 희망하는 실험을 수행한다(그러한 것이 인간의 본성이고 인간의 자아 욕구이다). 이러한 접근법의 문제는 기존의 가설이 우리의 인식과 우리가 찾는 증거의 종류를 결정한다는 것이다. 그러므로 전통적인 가설을 유지하고 있을 때에 우리가 결코 찾을 수 없었을 거슬리는 증거를 제공하려면 실수, 사고, 혹은 우연을 자주 필요로 한다. 그렇다면 우리가 이것에 대해 무엇을 해야 하는가? 단순한 해답은 표현 양식을 바꾸는 것이다. 최고의 가설을 단지 유지하는 것 대신, 우리는 대안을 만들어 내는 데 많은 시간을 써야 하는데, 그것은 최고의 것을 위해 그것들을 버리기 위해서가 아니라 우리가 사물을 더 폭넓게 바라보게 하기 위해서다.

↓

과학 가설에 관해서는, 가능성에 대한 (A) <u>열린</u> 태도가 (B) <u>현재의</u> 이론에만 집중하는 것보다 더 낫다.

구문 [8행~10행] Thus **it** often needs mistake, accident or chance / **to provide** *the intrusive evidence* [(which[that]) we could never have looked for / when (we are) holding the orthodox hypothesis].

• it은 가주어이고 to provide 이하가 진주어이다. [ ] 부분은 앞에 목적격 관계대명사 which[that]가 생략되어 the intrusive evidence를 수식하며, when 다음에는 we are가 생략되어 있다.

[14행~16행] ~ **not** in order to reject ***them*** in favor of ***the best one*** but to allow us to look at things more broadly.

• 「not A but B」 구문은 'A가 아니라 B다'의 뜻이며 A와 B 부분에 '~하기 위하여'의 뜻을 지니는 구문이 위치해 있다. them은 alternatives를 지칭하고 the best one은 the best hypothesis를 가리킨다.

어휘 **in practice** 실제로 **hypothesis** 가설 **carry out** 수행하다 **confirm** 확증하다, 확인하다 **perception** 인식 **generate** 만들어 내다 **alternative** 대안 **in favor of** ~에 찬성[지지]하여 **superior** (~보다) 나은; 우수한

1 빈칸 추론   ④

해설 빈칸 문장 이전의 내용으로 보아, 약 처방과 함께 환자 자신의 생활 습관을 고치는 것이 강조되는 것이므로, 이러한 상황에서 환자가 권유받는 것을 다른 말로 표현하면 ④ '건강을 유지하는 것에 대한 책임을 의사와 함께 나누다'가 될 것이다.
① 가능할 때마다 일상 활동을 계속하다
② 의사에게 그들의 증상을 충분히 설명하다
③ 그들이 원하는 것을 하고 건강에 관해 의사를 신뢰하다
⑤ 약으로부터 예상되는 부작용에 대해 의사와 이야기를 나누다

해석 흔히 의사들은 자신들이 진료하는 사람들이 스트레스로 가득 찬 생활 습관을 바꾸는 것보다는 약을 사서 증상을 없애는 것에 관심이 더 많다는 것을 알게 된다. 이러한 환자들 중에 어떤 이들은 자신이 병에 대해 책임이 있다기보다는 그 병의 피해자라고 여긴다. 일부 의사들은 문제 있는 생활 습관으로 여기는 것에 대한 증상의 완화를 위해 약을 처방하기를 반대한다. 심리적인 것을 지향하는 의사들은 우리의 신체적 그리고 심리적 안녕의 매우 중요한 결정적 요인으로서 선택과 책임의 역할을 강조한다. 진료를 통해서 이러한 의사들은 환자들에게, 운동 부족, 복용하는 물질, 그리고 다른 해로운 행동을 통해 그들이 자신의 신체에 무엇을 하고 있는지를 보라고 요구한다. 어떤 사람의 매우 높은 혈압을 낮추기 위해서 그들이 약물을 처방할 수 있으나 그들은 환자에게 약물은 딱 그 정도만 할 수 있으며 필요한 것은 생활 습관의 근본적인 변화라고 알려준다. 환자는 <u>건강을 유지하는 것에 대한 책임을 의사와 함께 나누도록</u> 권유받는다.

구문 [14행~18행] Although they may prescribe medication / to lower a person's extremely high blood pressure, / they **inform** the patient // **that** medications can do only so much / and that <u>what is needed</u> is a fundamental change in lifestyle.

S′ V′

• 'A에게 ~을 알려주다'라는 의미의 「inform A that절 ~」 구문으로 inform의 두 개의 목적어절이 and로 연결되어 병렬구조를 이루고 있다. 두 번째 that절에서 주어는 what is needed이고 동사는 is이다.

어휘 **pill** 알약   **symptom** 증상   **victim** 피해자   **complaint** 병, 통증; 불평   **physician** 의사   **resist** 반대[저항]하다   **prescribe** (약을) 처방하다; 규정하다   **relieve** 완화시키다   **oriented** 지향하는   **critical** 매우 중요한   **practice** 업무   **challenge** 도전하다, (도전이 될 일) 요구하다   **substance** 물질   **medication** 약물, 약   **extremely** 매우; 극단적으로   **fundamental** 근본적인
[선택지] **give an account of** ~을 설명하다   **side effect** (약의) 부작용

2 글의 순서   ②

해설 인간이 큰 뇌를 가지고 있다는 내용에 이어, 그런 큰 뇌를 선택하는 것이 자연스럽고 뇌력이 클수록 좋다고 생각한다는 (B)가 오는 게 자연스럽다. 그 뒤에는 이를 반박하는 내용으로 시작해 거대한 뇌가 드문 이유에 대한 의문을 던지는 (A)가 와야 한다. 마지막으로 (A)의 질문에 대한 이유를 설명하는 (C)가 오는 것이 적절하다.

해석 인간은 다른 동물과 비교해서 엄청나게 큰 뇌를 가지고 있다. 60킬로그램이 나가는 포유류의 뇌 크기는 평균 200세제곱센티미터이다. 최초의 남자와 여자는 600세제곱센티미터 정도의 뇌를 가지고 있었다. 현대의 호모 사피엔스 종의 일원들은 평균 1,200에서 1,400세제곱센티미터가 되는 뇌를 자랑한다.
(B) 우리에게, 진화가 더 큰 뇌를 선택해야 한다는 것은 자연스러운 선택처럼 보일

수도 있다. 우리는 우리의 높은 지능에 너무나 매료된 나머지 뇌력에 관한 한 클수록 틀림없이 더 좋다고 생각한다.
(A) 하지만 만약 그것이 사실이라면 고양잇과 동물들도 미적분학을 할 수 있는 고양잇과 동물을 배출해 냈을 것이며 개구리는 지금쯤이면 자신들의 우주 프로그램에 착수했을 것이다. 왜 동물계에서는 거대한 뇌가 아주 드문 것일까?
(C) 그것은 거대한 뇌는 몸을 지치게 하기 때문이다. 그것은 특히 거대한 머리뼈 안에 싸여 있을 때 지니고 다니기 쉽지 않다. 그것에 연료를 공급하는 것은 훨씬 더 어렵다. 호모 사피엔스에게 있어 뇌는 전체 몸무게의 2~3퍼센트 정도를 차지하지만, 몸이 쉬고 있을 때 신체 에너지의 25퍼센트를 소비한다.

구문 [13행~15행] We are **so** fascinated by our high intelligence **that** we assume that **when it comes to** cerebral power, more must be better.

• 「so ~ that ...」 구문으로 '너무 ~해서 …하다'는 뜻이다. when it comes to ~는 '~에 관한 한'이라는 의미이며 여기서 to는 전치사로 명사나 동명사 목적어를 갖는다.

[17행~18행] It's not easy *to carry around*, // especially **when** (it is) **wrapped** inside a massive skull.

• 주어인 It은 a jumbo brain을 가리키고, to부정사구 to carry around의 의미상 목적어이다(= To carry it around is not easy). 접속사 when과 과거분사 wrapped 사이에는 '주어+be동사'인 it(= a jumbo brain) is가 생략되었다.

어휘 **extraordinarily** 엄청나게   **mammal** 포유류   **sport** 자랑해 보이다, 뽐내다   **case** 사실, 실정   **launch** 착수하다, 시작하다   **carry around** ~을 지니고 다니다   **skull** 머리뼈, 두개골   **account for** (~의 비율을) 차지하다

3 문장 넣기   ⑤

해설 주어진 문장을 먼저 보면, 선진국과 개발도상국 둘 다 지속 가능한 개발이라는 개념을 받아들였으나 방식이 달랐다고 했다. '지속 가능한 개발'은 ③번 이후부터 등장하고 있으며, ⑤번 뒤의 문장에서 역접의 however로 연결하며 둘(선진국과 개발도상국)의 공유된 목적을 가진다고 설명하므로 ⑤번 자리에 주어진 문장을 넣어야 흐름이 어색하지 않다.

해석 경제적 성장은 거의 어디서나 가치 있는 목표로 여겨진다. 생태계의 보호와 문화의 보존 또한 중요하게 받아들여진다. 이 세 가지 대규모 시스템은 독립적이지 않아서 사람은 나머지 두 가지 목표를 무시하면서 한 가지에 집중할 수는 없다. 계속 확대되는 세계화와 산업화의 복잡한 연결망은 팽창하는 인구에 의해서 부분적으로 발생하였고, 이 세 가지 시스템을 더 많이 연결해 주고 있다. 1987년에 '지속 가능한 개발'이라는 용어가 World Commission on Environment and Development(환경과 개발에 관한 세계 위원회)에 의해서 일상적으로 사용되게 되었다. 그 위원회의 보고서인 '우리의 공통된 미래'에서 그 용어를 '미래 세대가 그들 자신의 욕구를 충족시킬 수 있는 능력을 손상하지 않으면서 현재의 욕구를 충족시키는' 형태의 개발로 정의했다. <u>선진국과 개발도상국은 둘 다 지속 가능한 개발이라는 개념을 적극적으로 받아들였으나, 흔히 방식은 달랐다.</u> 하지만, 공유된 목적은 인간과 생태계 둘 다의 장기적인 번영을 유지하고 향상하는 것이다.

구문 [4행~5행] Economic growth is almost universally considered **a worthwhile goal**.

• a worthwhile goal은 주어 Economic growth의 주격보어 역할을 하는 명사구이다.

[9행~11행] *The ever-expanding web of globalization and industrialization, (partly caused by the expanding human population), further **links** these three systems.*

• ( )는 분사구로서 주어 The ever-expanding ~ industrialization을 부연 설명하고 있으며 동사는 links이다.

어휘 embrace (적극적으로) 받아들이다 universally 어디서나 worthwhile 가치 있는 ecological 생태계의 conservation 보호 preservation 보존 sustainable (환경 파괴 없이) 지속 가능한 commission 위원회 term 용어 compromise 손상시키다; 타협하다 welfare 번영

어휘 unpleasant 불편한; 불친절한 tend to-v v하는 경향이 있다 *cf.* tendency 경향, 추세 cooperate 협력[협동]하다; 협조하다 *cf.* cooperation 협력; 협조 *cf.* cooperative 협력[협조]적인 self-interest 이기심 sophisticated 정교한; 세련된 emerge 나타나다; 드러나다 anthropologist 인류학자 colleague 동료 transmission 전달; 전송; 전염 startling 놀라운, 깜짝 놀라게 하는 conclusion 결론; 판단 selfishness 이기심 *cf.* unselfishness 이타심 major 주요한, 중대한; 전공의 *cf.* majority (대)다수; 과반수 element (구성) 요소, 성분; 원소 rely on ~을 필요로 하다, ~에 의지하다 stable 안정된; 차분한 equilibrium 균형, 평형; (마음의) 평정 mechanism 기제, 구조; 방법; 기계 장치 spiral 소용돌이; 나선형(의) probability 가능성; 확률

4~5 장문

4 ① 5 ④

해설 4. 이 글은 인간이 서로 협력하는 이유가 이기심 때문이라는 수백 년간의 통념에 반박해서 인간의 모방하려는 심리가 그 이유라는 최근의 연구에 관한 내용이므로, 제목으로 가장 적절한 것은 ① '무엇이 우리를 협력하도록 만드는가?'이다.

② 이기심은 어떻게 사회에 이득이 되는가?
③ 이기심이 협력보다 나은 때는 언제인가?
④ 왜 우리는 성공적인 사람들과 사랑에 빠지는가?
⑤ 다른 사람들을 모방하는 경향은 어디로부터 나오는가?

5. 사람들의 모방이 더 많은 식량, 더 나은 건강 등을 가져온다고 했으므로 긍정적인 소용돌이를 가져온다는 것을 알 수 있다. 그러므로 ④는 positive 등이 되어야 한다.

해석 수백 년 동안 연구자들과 일반 대중은 우리 인간이 협력하는 경향이 있는 유일한 이유는 이기심 때문이라는 다소 (a) 불편한 '진실'에 합의를 해왔다. 지금은 다행히도 훨씬 더 복잡하고, 정교하며, 긍정적인 그림이 최근 연구에서 나타나고 있다. 미시건 대학교의 인류학자 Joseph Henrich와 그의 동료 UCLA의 Robert Boyd는 인간들 사이에서 사회적 행동과 문화의 전달에 대한 연구를 했다. 그들은 놀라운 결론에 도달했는데, 협력은 (b) 이기심의 결과물이 아니고, 두 개의 주요한 '두뇌의 경향'의 결과라는 것이다. Henrich에 따르면 "우리가 알고 있는 인간의 심리에는 두 가지 요소가 있는데, 하나는 인간이 다수를 모방하는 경향이 있다는 것이고, 다른 하나는 가장 성공적인 사람을 모방하는 경향이 있다는 것이다. 우리가 보여줄 수 있는 것은 인간이 성공적인 사람들과 다수를 모방하는 것을 필요로 하기 때문에, 이 두 가지 문화적 기제가 제자리를 잡고 있어야만 (c) 존재하는 안정된 협력적 균형이 만들어진다는 것이다."
이러한 이중적인 모방은 성공의 (d) 부정적(→ 긍정적) 소용돌이를 가져온다. 협력은 더 많은 식량, 더 나은 건강, 더 많은 창의성, 그리고 더 많은 일반적인 에너지의 높은 가능성을 가져오고 그 결과 공동체 전체에 보다 강력한 경제적 (e) 성장을 가져오게 된다.

구문 [1행~3행] For centuries / researchers and the public have agreed on the rather unpleasant "truth" // that *the only reason* [(why) we humans tend to cooperate] is self-interest.

• 밑줄 친 the rather unpleasant "truth"와 that절은 동격 관계이며, [ ] 부분은 관계부사 why가 생략된 관계사절로 the only reason을 수식한다.

[17행~21행] What we are able to show is **that** because humans rely on
　　　　　　　　S　　　　　 V
copying the successful and the majority, this creates *a stable cooperative equilibrium* [which doesn't exist] if those two cultural mechanisms aren't in place."

• 선행사를 포함한 관계대명사 What이 이끄는 절이 문장의 주어 역할을 하고, 보어 자리에는 접속사 that이 이끄는 명사절이 쓰였다. [ ]는 주격 관계대명사 which가 이끄는 관계사절로 a stable cooperative equilibrium을 수식한다.

---

1 글의 요지   ④

해설 창의성은 규칙에 도전하는 것으로 향상시킬 수 있다는 주제문과 이를 뒷받침하는 여러 예가 제시된 글이므로 요지로 가장 적절한 것은 ④ '기존의 규칙에 대해 의심하고 도전하는 것이 창의력을 높인다.'이다.

해석 인생에는 규칙이 있고 오직 어리석은 자들만이 이러한 규칙을 따르기를 한사코 거부한다. 그러나 때때로 우리는 이러한 삶에 대한 '규칙적' 접근법을 지나칠 정도로 확장시켜서 더 이상 삶에 적용할 수 없는 패턴에 갇혀 우리의 창의적 샘물을 쥐어짜져 말라버린다. 그러므로 우리의 창의성을 향상시키는 한 가지 방법은 규칙에 도전하는 것이다. 'IQ'라는 영화에서 월터 매튜가 아인슈타인 역을 맡았다. 맥 라이언은 아인슈타인의 조카딸로 나왔다. 영화의 한 지점에서 아인슈타인은 조카딸에게 말했다. "모든 것에 질문하라!" 그것은 좋은 충고이다. 역사상 모든 진보는 규칙에 도전한 자로부터 나왔다. 콜럼버스는 항해 규칙에 도전했기에 아메리카를 발견했다. 마틴 루서는 교회의 규칙에 도전했기에 종교 개혁을 일으켰다. 아인슈타인은 뉴턴 물리학의 규칙에 도전했기에 상대성 이론을 발견했다. 때때로 창의성은 사람들이 항상 해왔던 것과 동일한 방식으로 우리가 일을 할 필요는 없다는 인식에서 발생한다.

구문 [2행~5행] However, sometimes we expand this "rule" approach to life to **such *a degree* that** we get locked into *patterns* [that are no longer applicable to life] and our creative juices get squeezed out.
- 「such ... that ~」은 '너무 …해서 ~하다'의 뜻이며 such 다음에는 명사가 나온다. that 다음의 두 절이 병렬구조를 이룬다. [ ] 부분은 앞의 patterns를 수식한다.

[17행~19행] Sometimes creativity arises out of the awareness that we do not have to do things in *the same way* [(that) they have always been done].
- 밑줄 친 that 이하는 the awareness에 대한 동격절이다. [ ]은 앞에 that이 생략된 관계부사절로서 the same way를 수식한다.

어휘 degree 정도 applicable 적용할 수 있는 squeeze 쥐어짜다 enhance 높이다, 향상시키다 niece 조카딸 navigation 항해, 운항 the theory of relativity 상대성 이론 arise 발생하다, 일어나다

2 빈칸 추론   ⑤

해설 어린이들의 거친 놀이로 인해 무엇이 가능하게 되는지를 찾아야 한다. 뒤에 이어지는 예를 보면 표정과 몸짓 언어를 경험하게 되고 또래 집단 내에서의 자신의 위치를 알게 해준다고 하였으므로 이를 종합하면 ⑤ '몇 가지 중요한 사회적 기술을 완성하게' 해 준다는 말이 적절하다.
① 넘치는 에너지를 발산하게
② 공격적 행동을 강화하고 증가하게
③ 폭력의 사용으로 갈등을 해결하게
④ 분노에 대처하는 법을 스스로 알게

해석 〈우리는 여기서 총을 가지고 노는 게 아닙니다〉라는 자신의 책에서, 아동 연구자인 Penny Holland는 어린아이들에게 장난으로 하는 싸움, 총 놀이 그리고 거친 신체 놀이는 동물적 공격성의 원시적 표현도 아니고 아무 생각 없이 어제 TV에서 본 것을 흉내 내는 것도 아니라고 주장한다. 오히려, 그런 행동은 정교하고 주로 무의식적인 학습 과정이 겉으로 드러난 징후이다. 심리학자들에 따르면, 이러한 형태의 놀이는 아이들로 하여금 실제적인 위해가 놀이의 일부는 아닌 상황에서 몇 가지 중요한 사회적 기술을 완성하게 해 준다. 예를 들어, 그것들(놀이)은 아이들이 얼굴 표정과 몸짓 언어를 읽는 매우 귀중한 경험을 하게 해 주며 또래 집단에서 자신들의 위치와 지위에 대해 알도록 해 준다. 게다가, 연구자들은 놀이와 실제를 구분하는 것을 어렵다고 생각할 수 있는 어른들과는 달리 대부분 아이들이 놀이로 하는 싸움의 몸짓 언어를 읽어 내는 일에 빠르게 능숙해진다는 사실을 여러 해 동안 알고 있었다.

구문 [2행~5행] ~ Penny Holland argues // **that** for younger children / play fighting, gun play and rough-and-tumble play are **neither** primitive displays of animal aggression **nor** mindless imitations of yesterday's TV.
- that절에서 주어는 play fighting, gun play, rough-and-tumble play가 병렬구조를 이루고 있으며 동사는 are이다. 「neither A nor B」는 'A도 B도 아니다'의 뜻이다.

[16행~18행] ~ who can find it *difficult* **to distinguish** between play and the real thing.
- it은 가목적어이고 to distinguish 이하가 진목적어이며 difficult는 보어이다.

어휘 primitive 원시적인 display 전시 aggression 공격성 mindless 아무 생각이 없는 imitation 모방 context 상황, 배경 invaluable 매우 귀중한 facial expression 표정 status 지위 peer 또래, 동년배 what is more 게다가 skilled 숙련된 distinguish 구별하다
[선택지] perfect 완성하다

3 무관 문장   ②

해설 고객이 경쟁사의 제품으로 바꾸는 것을 막기 위한 전환 장벽에 대한 내용인데 항공사가 여행 거리가 아닌 탑승권의 금액에 근거해 탑승 마일리지를 부여한다는 ②는 전체 흐름과 관계가 없다.

해석 '전환 장벽' 즉, 경쟁사의 제품으로 바꾸는 것에 대한 인위적으로 만들어낸 재정적 위약금은 경쟁사로 바꾸는 것에 대해 상당한 불이익을 부과함으로써 고객 상실을 방지할 수 있다. ① 이동 전화 업계에서의 전환 장벽은 조기 계약 해지와 관련된 위약금의 형태를 취한다. ② 유사하게 많은 항공사들은 이제 여행자들이 얼마나 멀리 여행했는가가 아니라 탑승권에 얼마나 돈을 지불했는가에 근거해서 탑승 마일리지를 부여한다. ③ 초기에 IBM은 모니터와 프린터 같은 모든 하드웨어 구성요소도 또한 IBM에 의해 제조된 것이어야 한다고 규정함으로써 대형 컴퓨터 시장에 대한 지배력을 유지할 수 있었다. ④ 그렇게 하면서 IBM은 어떻게든 자사의 고객을 자사의 제품에 묶어 두었는데, 그것은 전산 시스템의 어떤 부품이라도 타사의 제품으로 바꾸는 것을 불편하게 만들었다. ⑤ 전환 장벽을 만들어내는 또 다른 접근법은 더 장기적인 계약에 서명하게 하는 고객 장려책을 제공해서 그것으로 인해 더 오랜 기간 동안 경쟁업체를 봉쇄하는 것이다.

구문 [1행~4행] *Switching barriers*, **or** artificially created financial penalties for switching to a competitor's product, / can prevent the loss of customers / by imposing a significant penalty / for switching to a competitor.
- Switching barriers와 artificially created ~ a competitor's product는 동격 관계이다. or는 '즉', '바꿔 말하면'의 뜻이다.

[16행~19행] Another approach to creating switching barriers is to provide customer incentives to sign longer-term contracts, **thereby locking** out competitors for a longer period of time.
- thereby locking out ~ of time은 '그것에 의해서'라는 뜻의 thereby와 함께 쓰여, 앞에 나온 내용을 덧보태는 분사구문이다.

어휘 switch 바꾸다, 전환하다 barrier 장벽, 장애물 artificially 인위적으로 financial 재정상의 penalty 벌금, 위약금 competitor 경쟁자 impose (벌·의무를) 부과하다 significant 상당한, 아주 큰 take the form of ~의 형태를 취하다 associated with ~와 관련된 cancelation 해지, 취소 air miles 탑승 마일리지 mainframe computer (컴퓨터의) 본체 component 구성 요소, 부품 incentive 장려책, 유인책 lock out 봉쇄하다, 폐쇄하다

4 글의 순서 ⑤

해설 주어진 문장은 독자들이 자신들의 기억 속에 이미 저장되어 있는 그림을 생각해내서 이미지를 만들어 낸다는 것이고, 경험해보지 못한 것을 시각화하는 것은 사진 파일 보관소를 샅샅이 찾아보는 것이기 때문에 더 도전적이라는 (C)가 오는 것이 적절하다. (B)는 (C)에서 언급된 파일 찾기 작업을 부연 설명하는 내용으로 시작하므로 (C) 뒤에 오는 것이 적절하며, (A)는 (B)의 마지막에 독자가 끌어낼 만한 구체적인 경험이나 기억이 전혀 없다 해도 상상력이 흔히 시각화를 뒷받침할 수 있다는 내용에 대한 구체적인 예시에 해당하므로 마지막에 나오는 것이 적절하다.

해석 대개 독자들은 자신들의 기억 속에 이미 저장되어 있는 그림을 생각해냄으로써 마음속 이미지를 만들어 낸다. 다시 말해서 그들은 자신들이 보았거나 알고 있는 것과 연결하는데, 그것이 그들로 하여금 그 이미지를 만들어 내도록 도와주는 것이다. (C) 우리가 개인적으로 경험해 보지 못한 것을 시각화하는 것은 더 도전적이다. 이것은 모두 순식간에 일어나지만, 만약 우리가 그것의 속도를 늦추어 본다면 특정한 사진 한 장을 찾기 위해 사진 파일 보관소를 샅샅이 찾아보는 것과 그것이 유사하다는 것을 알 수 있다.
(B) 우리가 읽고 있는 문서를 뒷받침하기 위해 사용할 수 있는 이미지를 발견할 때까지 우리의 뇌는 우리의 파일을 철저히 찾아본다. 독자가 끌어낼 만한 구체적인 경험이나 기억이 전혀 없다 해도 상상력이 흔히 시각화를 뒷받침할 수 있다.
(A) 예를 들어 Hogwarts 마법 학교를 처음 소개받은 독자는 그것을 직접 경험해본 적이 없었지만, J.K. 롤링의 풍부한 묘사가 우리 모두로 하여금 우리의 상상력으로 그것을 '보도록' 도와주었다.

구문 [11행~12행] Our brains search through our files until we find *an image* [(which[that] we can use] to support *the text* [(which[that] we are reading].
• [ ]로 표시된 두 부분은 앞에 목적격 관계대명사 which[that]가 생략되어 각각 an image, the text를 수식하는 관계사절이다.

[16행~17행] **It** is more challenging **to visualize** *things* [(which[that] we have not personally experienced].
• It은 가주어이고 to visualize이하가 진주어다. [ ]로 표시된 부분은 앞에 목적격 관계대명사 which[that]가 생략된 관계사절로 things를 수식한다.

어휘 make a connection 연결하다 witchcraft 마법 wizardry 마술, 묘기 description 묘사, 서술 specific 특정한, 특유한 draw 끌어내다 visualize 생생하게 마음속에 그리다, 시각화하다 in an instant 순식간에 search through ~을 철저하게 조사하다

5 문장 넣기 ③

해설 주어진 문장은 Instead로 시작하므로 앞에 주어진 문장과 대비되는 내용이 있어야 함을 알 수 있다. ③ 앞부분까지는 세포, 원자 등의 요소가 통합되면 새로운 총체성을 드러낸다는 내용이 오며, 세포와 생명체를 같은 차원에서 설명할 수 없다는 예시를 보여준다. ③ 이후에는 주어진 문장에서 말한 두 세계(물질, 세포 단위와 통합된 생물체)에 대한 설명이 구체적으로 나열되고 있으므로 주어진 문장은 ③에 들

어가는 것이 적절하다.

해석 우리는 통합된 몸이 총체성을 지닌다는 것을 잊지 말아야 한다. 그것 (통합된 몸)을 분석한다면 세포, 원자, 전자로 축소될 수 있지만, 이러한 원자나 전자들 자체가 나타내는 현상들이 통합된 몸이 나타내는 것을 모방할 수 없다. 예를 들어, 날거나 헤엄칠 수 없는 세포의 차원에서 왜 새들이 날고 물고기들이 헤엄을 치는지 설명하는 것은 바보 같은 짓이다. 대신에 우리는 생물체 혹은 생물체의 생명이 무엇을 의미하는지 그리고 그 두 세계 사이에 차이가 있다는 것을 이해해야 한다. 구체적으로 말하면, 하나는 생물체 혹은 생물체의 생명을 구성하는 물질 혹은 세포의 세계이지만, 그것들은 더 낮은 수준에 존재하며 그것들(물질 혹은 세포들)을 통합한 생물체의 나머지 다른 하나의 세계와는 다른 세계에 존재한다. 물질을 다루는 물리학과 화학은 더 일찍 생물학과는 별개로 발전했다. 지금은 세포 연구가 여전히 생물학에 포함되어 있지만, 미래에는 세포학이 생물체와 물질 사이에 있는 어딘가의 영역을 다루는, 뚜렷이 구분되는 종합 학문적인 분야로 발전할 것이라고 상상할 수 있을 것이다.

구문 [5행~8행] If you analyze it, it can be reduced to cells and atoms and electrons, but the phenomena **that** these atoms or electrons express themselves cannot simulate **what the integrated body expresses**.
• that은 접속사로서 the phenomena와 동격을 이루는 절을 이끌며, what the integrated body expresses는 선행사를 포함한 관계대명사 what이 이끄는 관계사절로 동사 simulate의 목적어 역할을 한다.

[8행~10행] For instance, **it** is nonsense **to explain why** birds fly and fish swim in terms of cells which cannot fly or swim.
• it은 가주어이고 to explain 이하가 진주어이며, why 이하가 관계부사 why가 이끄는 관계사절로 to explain의 목적어 역할을 한다.

어휘 integrated 통합된 wholeness 총체성 atom 원자 electron 전자 simulate 모방하다 in terms of ~의 측면에서 constitute 구성하다 integration 통합 physics 물리학 chemistry 화학 cellular 세포의 distinct 뚜렷이 구별되는

1 글의 제목 ④

해설 에너지에는 일종의 인력이 있어서, 긍정적인 에너지는 긍정적인 것을 끌어오고, 부정적인 에너지는 부정적인 것을 끌어오므로 부정적인 사람들과 함께 시간을 보내기에 인생은 너무 짧다고 했다. 그러므로 제목으로 가장 적절한 것은 ④ '에너지는 전염성이 있다! 함께 하는 사람들을 현명하게 골라라!'이다.
① 당신에게는 자동 시동기가 있다. 그것을 사용해봐라!
② 태도를 바꾸고, 인생을 바꿔라!
③ 감정은 사람들 내에서 빠르게 퍼진다
⑤ 에너지는 만들어지거나 파괴될 수 없고, 흘러간다

해석 상황을 앞서서 주도하는 사람들은 반응적이거나 소극적인 유형의 사람들보다 그들의 시스템을 통과하여 흐르는 긍정적인 에너지가 더 많다는 것을 연구는 보여주었다. 그리고 당신의 전선을 통해 흐르는 에너지의 양과 당신이 당신과 함께 있는 사람들에게 미치는 영향 간에 직접적인 상관관계가 있다. 긍정적인 에너지는 물리학의 법칙을 거스르는 이상한 영향력을 갖고 있다. '긍정적인 에너지'에서 Judith Orloff는 "가장 심오한 변형은 활기 넘치는 수준에서만 일어날 수 있다고 생각합니다."라고 썼다. 이 정신과 의사는 "더 긍정적인 에너지를 방출할수록, 더 많은 것을 우리에게 끌어오게 됩니다. 부정적 성향도 마찬가지죠. 이렇게 작동하는 겁니다. '열정은 열정을 끌어당기고 분노는 분노를 끌어당긴다.' 우리는 전부 교묘한 에너지 전송 장치라고 설명할 수 있습니다."라는 것을 발견했다. (여기서의) 교훈은 실패자들이 우리가 심지어 알지도 못하는 새에 우리에게 영향을 미치므로 그들과 함께 시간을 보내기에 인생은 너무나 짧다는 것이다. 부정적인 유형의 사람들 위를 맴도는 저 어두운 구름들은 그들이 만지는 모든 것과 그들의 영향력의 자장 속에 들어서는 모든 사람들에게 영향을 준다. 조심하라. 그들은 다른 사람들에게서 그들이 심지어 알지도 못하는 상태에서 그들의 에너지를 강탈한다.

구문 [10행~12행] **The more** positive energy we give off, **the more** we'll magnetize to us.
• 「The 비교급 ..., the 비교급 ~」은 '…하면 할수록 더 ~하다'의 뜻이다.

어휘 reactive 반응을 하는 inactive 활동하지 않는, 소극적인 correlation 상관관계 wire 전선 in one's presence 면전에서 weird 이상한 profound 심오한 transformation 변형 psychiatrist 정신과 의사 give off 방출하다, 내뿜다 magnetize 끌다, 매료시키다 negativity 부정적 성향 passion 열정 rage 분노 subtle 미묘한, 교묘한 transmitter 전송기 hover 맴돌다 sphere 영역 rob A of B A에게서 B를 강탈하다

2 밑줄 어휘 ②

해설 첫 문장에 나와 있듯이 번역은 작품 속에 가능한 한 자신을 적게 투입할 것을 요구하는 창작 영역이다. 번역가가 원작의 창작 정신을 가장 충실하게 유지하려면 번역 작품에 자신의 기여를 가능한 한 최소로 해야 한다. 그러므로 ② maximal(최대한의)을 minimal(최소한의)로 고쳐야 한다.

해석 개인이 작품 속에 가능한 한 자신을 적게 투입할 것을 요구하는 창작 영역이 많이 있다. 소설이나 시를 다른 언어로 번역할 때 번역가는 불가피하게 창의적인데, 이것은 번역가가 번역 작업을 한 것에 대해 ① 인정받고 그의 이름이 작품에서 원작자의 이름 옆에 발표된다는 사실로 잘 드러난다. 그러나 이상적인 번역가는 원작의 창작 정신을 가장 충실하게 유지하는 사람이며, 그렇게 함으로써 번역 작품에 대한 자신의 기여를 가능한 한 ② 최대한(→ 최소한)으로 한다. 외국 영화를 자기 나라

말로 더빙하는 것은 번역가에게 외국 배우의 입이 움직이는 시간 안에 가장 쉽게 말해질 수 있는, ③ 원래의 대사의 번역을 만들어 낼 것을 요구한다. 또한 성우가 움직이는 이미지에 자신의 말을 ④ 맞출 것을 요구한다. 이것들은 의심할 여지 없이 창의적인 활동이지만, 개인의 영감과 독창성이 작품에 ⑤ 해로울 수도 있는 활동이기도 하다.

구문 [3행~7행] In translating a novel or poem into a different language, the translator is unavoidably creative; this is reflected by the fact **that** the translator receives recognition, and his or her name is published in the work next to **that** of the original author.
• 밑줄 친 that절은 the fact와 동격 관계이다. 동격절 내의 두 번째 that은 the name을 지칭한다.

어휘 domain 영역 translate 번역하다 translator 번역가 unavoidably 어쩔 수 없이, 불가피하게 reflect 반영하다 recognition (공로 등의) 인정, 인식 retain 유지 [보유]하다 contribution 기여 maximal 최대한의 voice-over actor (화면에 나타나지 않고 목소리만으로 연기하는) 성우 delivery 말, 진술; 배달 unquestionably 의심할 여지 없이 inspiration 영감 originality 독창성

3 빈칸 추론 ③

해설 의복 착용의 관습이 없던 곳에 의복이 전파되었을 때 단지 의복의 '착용'만이 전파되었고 의복의 '관리' 방법은 전파되지 않아서 사람들은 옷을 세탁하지 않았고, 비에 젖은 옷을 그대로 착용하여 폐렴 등의 질환을 앓게 되었으므로, 빈칸을 완성하면 의복의 확산은 ③ '건강과 청결의 측면에서 비참한 결과들을 초래했다'가 된다.
① 문화유산의 지역적 가치와 충돌하게 되었다
② 사회에 예기치 못한 긍정적인 변화를 초래했다
④ 사람들이 서로 사귈 수 있는 기회를 제공했다
⑤ 현대 문명의 발달에 영향을 주고 (그것을) 가속화시켰다

해석 과거에는 의복을 거의 혹은 전혀 입지 않았던 지역으로까지 서양 의복이 확산된 것은 때때로 건강과 청결의 측면에서 비참한 결과들을 초래했다. 그러한 많은 경우에 사람들은 의복이라는 복합적 요소 중 단 하나의 부분, 즉 의복의 착용만을 받아들였다. 그들은 의복의 관리에 대해서는 전혀 몰랐고 많은 경우에 그러한 관리를 위해 필요한 장비가 부족했다. 옷을 입지 않았을 때, 그들의 몸은 빗속에서 몸을 씻는 샤워를 했고, 벌거벗은 피부는 햇볕과 공기 중에서 빨리 말랐다. 그러나 그들이 의복을 얻었을 때, 소나기는 벌거벗은 몸만큼 빨리 마르지는 않는 젖은 옷을 의미했고, 따라서 폐렴이나 다른 폐 질환들이 때때로 생겨났다. 그들이 그것을 하는 법을 알았다 해도 옷을 세탁하기 위한 물이 보통 그들에게 거의 혹은 전혀 없었다. 갈아입을 새 옷이 없어서 사람들은 대개 그들이 갖고 있는 것을 그냥 그 옷이 닳아서 해질 때까지 입었다.

구문 [15행~17행] There were no *fresh clothes* (to change into) // **so** people usually simply wore **what they had** / until the clothes fell apart.
• ( ) 부분은 fresh clothes를 수식한다. 접속사 so는 '그래서'의 뜻이다. what they had는 wore의 목적어이다.

어휘 spread 확산, 전파 clothing 의류 take over 인수하다, 인계받다 equipment 장비, 용품 cleansing 깨끗이 함 bare 벌거벗은 lung 폐 result (~의 결과로) 발생하다; 결과 fall apart 다 허물어질 정도이다
[선택지] accelerate 가속화하다

4 무관 문장

④

해설 전체적 글의 내용은 자원의 한계를 다른 자원의 한계를 늘림으로 해결하려고 하다 보니 고무 밴드처럼 보기에는 당겨져 늘어나는 것처럼 보이지만 남아있는 자원에 더 큰 긴장을 가하게 되고 그러다 보니 실패하게 될 시점이 있다는 내용이다. 그러므로 지금이 바로 세계적인 운송 네트워크에 투자할 때라는 내용의 ④는 전체 흐름과 무관하다.

해석 한 가지 자원의 한계를 다른 자원의 한계를 늘림으로써 극복하는 경우가 너무도 많다. ① 전체적으로 보면 그 결과는 늘어났다가 그다음에 조금 더 늘어날 수 있는 고무 밴드에 비유될 수 있다. ② 자주, 지역적인 자원 부족에 대한 우리의 해결책은 그 부족한 자원을 그것이 더 풍부한 지역으로부터 수송해 오거나 추가 에너지와 다른 자원들을 이용하여 대용물을 제조하는 것이다. ③ 잡아당겨지면 더 길어 보이는 고무 밴드처럼 이 과정이 점점 더 풍부해진다는 인상을 주기는 하지만, 계속된 확장은 남아있는 자원에 더 큰 긴장을 가한다. ④ 자원 부족이 불가피해짐과 더불어 세계적인 운송 네트워크를 가동하고 유지하는 데 투자하는 데 (지금보다) 더 좋은 시기는 결코 없었다. ⑤ 현재로서는, 자원을 이리저리 이동시키고 산업 공정에 동력을 제공하는 우리의 능력이 막대하지만, 고무 밴드처럼, 더 이상의 팽창이 실패를 하게 될 시점이 있을 것이다.

구문 [14행~17행] At the present time, *our capacity* **for** moving resources around `and` **for** powering industrial processes is enormous, // but, like the rubber band, there will be *a point* [**where** further expansion will fail].

• our capacity를 for로 시작하는 두 개의 전치사구가 병렬구조를 이루고 보충하고 있다. [ ] 부분은 관계부사 where가 이끄는 절로 앞에 나온 명사 a point를 수식한다.

어휘 **stretch** 늘이다, 잡아당기다 **overall** 전체적으로 **liken** 비유하다, 견주다 **shortage** 부족, 결핍 **transport** 수송하다, 운반하다 **abundant** 풍부한 **alternative** 대안, 다른 방도 **additional** 추가의 **impression** 인상, 기분 **expansion** 팽창, 확장 **tension** 긴장 **inevitable** 불가피한 **operation** 운용, 가동 **enormous** 매우 큰

5 요약문 완성

①

해설 사람들은 땅에 누워있는 사람을 발견하는 것과 같은 잠재적 비상사태에서 스스로 판단(judgement)하고 반응하는 것이 아니라 주변의 다른 사람들이 어떤 반응을 보이는지 살펴보며 상황 판단을 다른 사람들에게 의존하는(turn to) 모습을 보인다.

해석 (각각 혼자 걷고 있던) 몇몇 행인들이 한 남자가 땅에 누워있는 것과 같은 잠재적인 비상사태에 대략 동시에 마주쳤다고 상상해보자. 그들은 무슨 일이 일어나고 있고 자신들이 무엇을 해야 하는지를 결정할 필요가 있다. 이 남자가 아픈가? 술 취했나? 그들이 그에게 질문을 하면 그가 화를 낼까? 그들이 사용할 수 있는 한 가지 정보원은 그 상황에서 다른 사람들이 반응하는 방식이다. 다른 사람들이 이것이 조정을 요하는 비상사태라고 생각하는 것 같은가? 그들이 이 사건에 대해 어떤 일도 하지 않는다면, 아마 그것은 전혀 비상사태가 아닐 것이다. 피해자에게는 불행하게도, 모든 행인들이 어떻게 반응해야 할지에 대한 신호를 찾아 서로만 바라보고, 아무도 어떠한 일도 하지 않는 결과가 나올지도 모른다! 행인들은 다른 행인들의 행동하지 않음에 근거를 두어 상황을 비상사태가 아닌 것으로 잘못 해석할지도 모른다.

비상사태일 수 있는 상황에 직면할 때, 사람들은 그들 자신의 (B) 판단을 이용하기보다는 상황을 해석하기 위해 다른 사람들에게 (A) 의지한다.

구문 [6행~7행] *One source of information* [(which[that]) they might use] / **is** how other people in the situation are responding: ~

• [ ] 부분은 앞에 목적격 관계대명사 which[that]가 생략되어 One source of information을 수식한다. how other people ~ are responding은 동사 is 다음에 제시된 보어이다.

[14행~15행] Bystanders may **misinterpret** the situation **as** a non-emergency based on the inaction of other bystanders.

• 「misinterpret A as B」는 'A를 B로 잘못 해석[이해]하다'의 뜻이다.

어휘 **bystander** 구경꾼, 행인 **come upon** ~을 우연히 발견하다 **emergency** 비상사태 **intervention** 중재, 조정 **cue** 신호 **misinterpret** 잘못 해석하다 **inaction** 활동하지 않음

1 빈칸 추론   ③

해설 자녀가 규칙을 잘 지키고 적절히 행동하게 지도하려면 부모가 피곤하거나 주의가 분산되어서, 혹은 자녀에게 미안한 마음에서나 공개 장소에서 자녀가 짜증을 부리는 상황을 모면하려고 규칙 적용에 예외를 두어서는 안 된다는 내용의 글이다. 따라서 당신의 자녀가 규율을 잘 따르기를 원한다면 당신은 ③ '한결같아야' 함을 알 수 있다.

① 융통성 있는 ② 소통하는 ④ 도전적인 ⑤ 관대한

해석 당신의 자녀가 규율을 잘 따르기를 원한다면 당신은 한결같아야 한다. 당신이 피곤하거나 주의가 분산돼 있으면, 혹은 당신이 때로 단지 그들에게 미안함을 느끼기 때문에 그들의 잘못된 행동을 간과할 것 같다는 점을 당신의 자녀가 알고 있으면, 그들은 매번 적절히 행동하는 방법을 알지 못할 것이다. 힘들겠지만, 이것이 당신이 진지하게 받아들여지고 당신의 자녀가 당신의 지침을 이해하는 것을 확실히 할 유일한 방법이다. 예를 들어 당신 아이가 장난감을 부술 때마다, 그러고 나서 그 아이가 집 여기저기를 도와줌으로써 새 장난감을 (살 돈을) 벌어야 한다고 해보자. 단지 그 특정한 날에 당신이 그 아이에게 정말로 미안함을 느꼈다는 이유로 그 아이가 장난감을 부수었던 한 번의 때에 무너지지 마라. 당신이 보통 당신 아이에게 일주일에 한 번 넘게 맥도널드에 가게 하지 않는다면, 단지 아이가 다른 사람들 앞에서 짜증을 내보인다고 해서 아이가 (맥도널드에) 가도록 내버려두지 마라. 사람들 앞에서 짜증을 겪는 것은 당황스럽겠지만, 그것은 아이에게 공공장소에서 짜증을 부리려고 기다리기만 하면 원하는 것을 항상 얻을 수 있다고 가르치는 것보단 낫다.

구문 [2행~5행] If your children know // **that** you're liable to overlook their bad behavior / if you're tired, distracted, [or] because you sometimes just feel sorry for them, ~

• that you're liable ~ sorry for them은 know에 대한 목적어 역할을 하는 명사절이며, 명사절 내에서 if절과 because절은 병렬구조를 이루고 있다.

[15행~19행] Though **it** may be embarrassing **to suffer** through a public tantrum, // **it**'s better than teaching your child **that** he/she can always get what he/she wants if he/she just waits to throw a tantrum in public.

• Though 절에서 it은 가주어이고 to suffer ~ tantrum이 진주어이다. 주절에서 it은 to suffer through a public tantrum을 지칭하며, teaching의 간접목적어로 your child가, 직접목적어로 that 이하의 명사절이 왔다.

어휘 **well-disciplined** 규율에 따르는 **liable to-v** v하기 쉬운, v할 것 같은 **overlook** 간과하다 **distracted** 주의가 산만한 **properly** 적절히 **guideline** 지침 **give in** 굴복하다 **normally** 보통

2 글의 순서   ③

해설 예술에 대한 반응이 기초로 하는 요인들이 많이 있음을 언급한 주어진 문장 뒤에는 그러한 요인들에 대해 구체적으로 예를 열거한 (B)가 이어져야 한다. 과거의 예술이 현대 관객의 흥미를 불러일으키지만 과거의 관객들과 똑같이 반응하지는 않는다는 (B)의 내용에 대하여, 그것으로 인해 과거 예술이 전적으로 이해될 수 없는 것은 아니며 지금 문화와 양립하여 감상되며 오늘날의 관객은 과거와 다르다는 내용인 (C)가 이어지는 것이 적절하다. 그 뒤에는 (C)에 언급된 오늘날의 관객을 them으로 받으면서 그들이 과거의 관객과 똑같이 반응할 수 없다는 내용의 (A)가 마지막으로 이어지는 것이 적절하다.

해석 예술에 대한 반응은 수많은 객관적, 주관적인 요인들을 기초로 한다.
(B) 이것들은 성별, 교육, 감정, 그 외의 더 많은 것들뿐만 아니라 지식, 취향, 가치, 전통을 포함한다. 오늘날 세상에 있는 대부분의 예술은 현대의 관객과는 본질적으로 달랐던 관객들을 위해 지난 수 세기 동안에 만들어졌다. 과거의 예술 작품은 계속해서 현대의 관객들의 흥미를 강하게 끌지만, 원래의 관객들과 똑같은 방식으로 예술에 반응하는 것은 불가능하다.
(C) 이것이 이전 세기의 예술이 완전히 이해되거나 평가받을 수 없다는 것을 암시하지는 않을 것이다. 오히려 그것은 예술이 현대 문화와 양립 가능한 조건으로 이해된다는 것을 강조한다. 오늘날의 관객들은 르네상스 시대의 관객뿐만 아니라 20세기 초의 관객들과도 매우 다르게 생각하고, 말하며, 행동한다.
(A) 그들이 1500년대나 심지어 1950년대의 사람과 똑같은 방식으로 예술에 반응하고, 예술을 경험하고 바라보는 것은 불가능할 것이다.

구문 [3행~5행] **It** would be impossible *for them* **to respond to, experience, and** **look at** art in **the same** way **as** someone from the 1500s or even the 1950s.

• It은 가주어, to respond 이하가 진주어이고 for them은 to부정사의 의미상 주어이다. art는 respond to, experience, look at의 공통 목적어이다. 「the same A as B」는 'B와 같은 A'의 뜻이다.

[17행~19행] Today's viewers think, speak, and behave very **differently / not only from** Renaissance (audiences) **but also** (from) early twentieth-century audiences.

• differently from은 '~와 다르게'의 뜻이다. 「not only A but also B」는 'A뿐만 아니라 B도'의 뜻이며, Renaissance 다음에는 audiences가, also 다음에는 from이 각각 생략된 것으로 볼 수 있다.

어휘 **objective** 객관적인 **subjective** 주관적인 **A as well as B** B뿐만 아니라 A도 **substantially** 상당히 **contemporary** 동시대의, 현대의 **intrigue** 강한 흥미를 불러일으키다 **spectator** 관중 **underline** 강조하다 **appreciate** 진가를 인정하다; 감상하다 **terms** 조건 **compatible with** ~와 양립할 수 있는

3 문장 넣기   ③

해설 이 글은 고객에 대한 공감의 필요성에 관한 것이다. 실제로 존재하는 고객에 대한 이해를 바탕으로 정보를 다루는 것이 조직의 의사 결정자들에게 의미가 있다는 내용이다. 주어진 문장은 어떠한 해결책의 제시가 시작되는 부분인데, '이런 문제들(these challenges)'은 ③ 앞에서 말한 전반적인 문제들을 가리키고 '다른 사람을 직관적으로 이해하는 것'은 ③ 뒤에 이어지는 '서비스를 제공하는 사람에 대한 공감'을 나타내므로, 주어진 문장은 ③에 들어가는 것이 적절하다.

해석 어느 조직에서나, 의사 결정자들은 자신들이 아무런 맥락 없는 간소화된 자료를 가지고 일하고 있다는 것을 흔히 깨닫는다. 그들은 종종 자신들이 직접 경험하지 않고 개략적으로 정보를 다룬다. 많은 경우에, 고객들로부터의 단절은 그들이 결코 권위자가 아니지만 그렇게 일컬어지는 사람들에게 어쩔 수 없이 의존하게 한다. 다른 사람을 직관적으로 이해하는 것은 이런 문제들을 극복하는 데 도움을 줄 수 있다. 여러분이 서비스를 제공하는 사람에 대한 공감은 추상적인 것을 더 근거 있고 직접적인 것으로 만들어 줄 수 있는데 그 정보가 이제는 여러분이 알고 있는 실존 인물과 연결되기 때문이다. 그것은 중요하지 않게 여겨진 요소들을 포함함으로써 우리가 받는 자료에 대한 맥락을 제공할 수 있다. 그리고 시간이 지남에 따라, 다른 사람과의 이러한 종류의 연결은 한 조직 내의 사람들이 새로운 기회를 발견하는 데 필요한 종류의 어떤 영역 내에서의 깊은 경험을 제공할 수 있다.

구문 [14행~17행] And this kind of connection to other people / can, over time, provide / *the kind of deep experience in a territory* [**that** people inside an organization need **to identify** new opportunities].

• [ ] 부분은 목적격 관계대명사 that이 이끄는 관계사절로 the kind of deep experience in a territory가 선행사이다. to identify는 부사적 용법의 to부정사구로 목적을 나타낸다.

어휘 intuitive 직관[직감]적인 **simplified** 간소화된, 단순한 **in the abstract** 개략[추상]적으로 **so-called** 흔히 ~라고 일컬어지는 **authority** 권위(자) **anything but** 결코 ~이 아닌 **grounded** 근거 있는, 기초를 둔 **immediate** 직접적인, 즉각적인 **incorporate** 포함하다; 설립하다

4~5 장문　　　　　　　4 ⑤　5 ④

해설 **4.** 위대한 새 발견은 일련의 작은 발견인데 특허권 때문에 서로의 발견을 비밀로 하게 되어 그것이 혁신을 늦추는 것을 염려한다는 내용이므로 글의 제목으로는 ⑤ '특허권이 진정 혁신을 장려하는가?'가 가장 적절하다.
① 당신의 특허 가치를 최대화하라
② 특허법이 어떻게 발명가들을 돕는가?
③ 창의적 아이디어를 장려하고 실패를 벌하지 말라
④ 과학으로 가는 길은 질문하는 데 있다
5. 일련의 작은 발견들이 귀중한 새 발견이며, 새로운 발견과 아이디어가 은폐되면 혁신이 늦춰질 것이라고 했으므로 비밀 엄수는 과학의 적임을 알 수 있다. 그러므로 ④는 enemy 등이 되어야 한다.

해석 특허 제도는 정부가 연구와 개발을 촉진시키기 위해 사용하는 주요 수단 중 하나이다. 어떤 아이디어에 특허를 받는 것은 그것의 창안자가 어떻게 새로운 제품이나 공정이나 물질이 작동하는지에 대한 모든 설명을 발표하는 대가로, 시장에서 자기 노동의 결실을 20년간 이용할 독점권을 준다. 대부분의 경제학자들은 특허제도가 없는 성공적인 혁신으로 이어졌을 발명은 훨씬 더 적었을 것이라고 주장한다. 그러나 특허권이 생명 공학과 유전학과 다른 분야에서 일어난 것처럼, 실제로는 새로운 제품과 공정을 산출하는 발명들의 결합과 재결합을 (a) 방해한다면 어쩌겠는가?
과학자들이 지적 권위를 공유하기 위해 사용하는 비공식적인 제도와 달리 특허 제도는 승자가 독차지하는 제도이다. 지원서를 처음으로 (b) 승인받은 사람은 누구든지 돈을 모두 갖는다. 그것은 (c) 은폐를 하도록 장려하게 하는데 과학자의 아이디어가 새어나가면 다른 누군가가 더 빠르게 특허를 제출할 수 있을 것이다. 하지만 비밀 엄수는 과학의 (d) 핵심(→ 적)이다. 모든 정말로 위대한 귀중한 새 발견은 일련의 작은 발견들이다. 과학자들의 각각의 팀은 다른 연구실의 최신 결과를 열심히 읽고, 약간의 작지만 뛰어난 그들 자신의 통찰력을 (e) 덧붙인다. 그러나 10억 달러 특허권의 성패가 걸려 있다면 교수들의 발견으로부터 오는 지적 재산권의 대다수를 소유하게 되는 대학들이 자기들의 학자들에게 새로운 발견과 아이디어를 비밀로 하라고 압박하는 강력한 동기를 갖는다. 그러므로 학구적인 학자들과 정책입안자들 사이에는 특허권이 그 자체로 혁신을 늦춘다는 염려가 커가고 있다.

구문 [1행~2행] The patent system is *one of the main instruments* [governments use] **to promote** research and development.

• [ ] 부분은 관계사절로 앞에 나온 명사구 one of the main instruments를 수식한다. to promote는 부사적 용법의 to부정사구로 목적을 나타낸다.

[15행~16행] **Whoever gets** *his or her application* **approved** first / **gets** all the money.

• Whoever ~ first가 주어이고 두 번째 gets가 동사이다. whoever는 '~한 사람이면 누구든지'의 뜻으로 주어가 되는 명사절을 이끌고 있다. 「get O p.p.」는 'O가 ~되게 하다'의 뜻이다.

[23행~27행] But if billion-dollar patents are at stake, // ***universities*** — [which end up owning much of the intellectual property that comes out of professors' discoveries] — have *a strong incentive* (**to pressure** their scholars to keep new findings and ideas under wraps).

• 주절의 주어는 universities이고 [ ]는 삽입된 관계사절로 universities를 수식한다. to pressure 이하는 형용사적 용법으로 앞에 나온 명사구 a strong incentive를 수식한다.

어휘 patent 특허, 특허권; 특허를 얻다 **instrument** 도구, 수단 **monopoly** 독점권, 전매권 **exploit** 개발하다, 이용하다 **discourage** 억제하다, 저지하다 **combine** 결합시키다 **yield** 산출하다, 생기게 하다 **biotechnology** 생명 공학 **genetics** 유전학 **discipline** (학문의) 분야 **informal** 비공식의 **credit** 권위, (이용 자료 따위의) 출처 명시 **winner take all** 승자가 독차지하는 제도 **application** 신청, 지원 **incentive** 장려책, 우대책; 자극, 유인 **concealment** 숨김, 은폐 **leak out** 누설되다, 유출되다 **file** 제출하다 **breakthrough** (귀중한) 새 발견 **at stake** 성패가 달려 있는, 위태로운 **keep A under wraps** A를 숨기다, 비밀로 하다

1 필자 주장　⑤

해설 영감이 찾아오기를 무작정 기다리며 글을 쓰고자 한다면 생산성 있게 글을 쓸 수 없고, 스스로에게 명확한 목표를 부여하고 일정을 잘 세워야 글을 잘 쓸 수 있다는 조언을 제시하는 글이므로 필자의 주장으로 가장 적절한 것은 ⑤이다.

해석 처음 시작할 때 당신의 글에 대해 질문을 받는다면, 당신은 아마 영감이 부족하다는 말로 변명을 할 것이다. 그러나 당신이 최종 단계까지 진출한 엄숙한 글쓰기 대회에 있다고 상상해보라. 당신이 써야 하는 것이면 무엇이든지 시작하기 전에 무언가에 의해 영감을 받기 위해 기다릴 것이라고 말할 것인가? 아마 당신은 기다리지 않을 것이며, 그럼에도 걸작을 생각해낼 것이다. 이것은 단지 당신이 반대의 상황(기다리는 상황)보다 뮤즈를 넘어서는 더 큰 힘을 가지고 있음을 보여줄 뿐이다. 당신이 영감이라는 핑계로 변명하는 이유는 그저 수중에 너무 많은 시간이 있는데 달성해야 할 목표는 갖고 잊지 않기 때문이다. 글을 쓸 일정을 짬으로써, 당신은 자기 자신에게 기간과 작업할 목표를 부여하는 것이다. 훌륭한 일정을 세우고 "이번 주에 3개의 기사를 쓸 거야."와 같은 계획을 그저 떠올리지 말라. 당신은 아마 금요일 저녁에 첫 번째 기사의 첫 단락을 아직도 완성하지 못한 스스로의 모습을 발견하게 될 것이다.

구문 [1행~3행] If you **were asked** about your writing when you first start, you'd most likely **excuse** yourself with a lack of inspiration.

• 「If+S′+동사의 과거형 ~, S+조동사 과거형+동사원형」의 형태로 가정법 과거 표현이 쓰였다.

[4행~6행] Tell me, will you wait to be inspired by something before you kick off with **whatever** it is [that you have to write]?

• 복합관계대명사 whatever가 이끄는 명사절이 전치사 with의 목적어 역할을 한다. [ ] 부분은 whatever를 선행사로 하는 관계사절이다.

어휘 **most likely** 아마, 필시 **excuse** 변명(하다); 용서하다; 핑곗거리 **inspiration** 영감(을 주는 사람[것]) **kick off with** ~로 시작하다 **come up with** ~을 생각해내다[찾아내다]; 제시[제안]하다 **masterpiece** 걸작, 명작 **muse** 뮤즈 ((작가·화가 등에게 영감을 주는 것)) **the other way round** 반대로, 거꾸로 **time-frame** 기간, 시간 **article** (신문·잡지 등의) 기사; (계약서의) 조항

2 밑줄 함의　②

해설 인간의 기억은 불완전하지만, 이는 투입되는 막대한 양의 정보 중에서 필요한 정보만을 취할 수 있도록 진화된 결과이다. 즉 우리가 '완벽한 기억과 정보 처리 능력을 맞바꿨음'은 ② '우리는 중요한 것을 확인하기 위해(정보 처리 능력을 위해) 정보를 주의 깊게 살펴 추려낸다(완벽한 기억을 포기한다)'는 것을 나타낸다.
① 우리는 결정을 하기 위해 과거 기억에 의존한다.
③ 우리는 다음에 무엇을 할지 예측하기 위해 과거의 경험을 조합한다.
④ 우리는 처리 기능 부전으로 인해 기억을 잊는다.
⑤ 우리는 감각을 통해 끊임없이 정보를 받아들인다.

해석 인간의 기억이 시간이 흐르며 왜곡돼도, 그러한 왜곡이 우리 조상들의 생존에 해롭다고 입증됐다면 우리의 기억과 우리 종 자체가 살아남지 못했을 것이다. 우리의 기억 체계는 결코 완벽하지 않지만, 대부분의 상황에서 그것이 바로 진화가 요구하는 것이다. 그것만으로도 충분히 괜찮다. 사실 큰 그림에서 보면 인간의 기억은 놀랍도록 효율적이며 정확하다. 우리 조상들이 피해야 하는 동물들과 추적하여 사냥해야 하는 동물들, 최고의 송어가 있는 시내가 어디에 있는지, 그리고 야영장으로 돌아오는 가장 안전한 길을 일반적으로 식별할 수 있게 해 주기에 충분했다. 현대적 측면에서 기억이 작동하는 방식을 이해하기의 시작점은 정신이 너무나 거대하여 도저히 전부를 처리할 수 없는 양의 자료(대략 초당 1,100만 비트)로 계속 폭격 당한다는 점이다. 그래서 우리는 완벽한 기억을 정보를 처리하는 능력과 맞바꾼다.

구문 [1행~4행] ~ **if** those distortions **had proved** detrimental to our ancestors' survival, our memory, and perhaps our species itself, **would not have survived**.

• 「if+S′+had p.p ~, S+would have p.p. ... (~했다면 …했을 것이다)」라는 가정법 과거완료 구문으로 과거 사실과 반대되는 내용을 가정한다.

[8행~11행] ~ sufficient to have **enabled** *our ancestors* **to generally recognize** *the creatures* [(which[that]) they should avoid] and *those* [(which[that]) they should hunt down], where the best trout streams are, and the safest way back to camp.

• 「enable O to-v (O가 v할 수 있게 하다)」 구문이 사용되었다. 밑줄 친 네 부분은 recognize의 목적어로 병렬구조를 이룬다. 두 [ ] 부분은 앞에 목적격 관계대명사 which[that]가 생략되어 각각 앞의 명사를 수식한다. those는 the creatures를 지칭한다.

어휘 **distort** 왜곡하다 **detrimental** 해로운 **far from** 전혀 ~이 아닌 **sufficient** 충분한 **hunt down** 추적하여 잡다 **trout** 송어 **stream** 시냇물 **bombard** (폭격을) 퍼붓다 **roughly** 대략
[선택지] **sort through** ~을 자세히 살펴 분류하다

3 빈칸 추론　③

해설 어린이들이 혁신적인 신조어를 만들 때 그 단어들은 의미가 있고 나름의 어휘 생성 규칙을 따르고 있기 때문에, 어린이들의 혁신적인 언어 사용은 ③ '결코 임의적이지 않다'고 할 수 있다.
① 가정 내에서 만들어진다
② 완벽하게 일관성이 있다
④ 정신적 행동과 밀접한 관계가 있다
⑤ 실제로 다른 몸짓이 수반된다

해석 어린이들은 원하는 의미를 표현할 새로운 방법들을 자주 고안해 낸다. 1995년 자신의 논문에서 언어학자인 Clark는 24개월 된 아이가 말한 "저기 rat-man이 와요."와 25개월 된 아이가 말한 "엄마가 막 이 spear-page를 고쳤어요."와 같은 예들을 언급했다. 'rat-man'은 심리학 실험실에서 쥐를 가지고 작업을 했던 그 아이 아빠의 동료 중 한 사람이었고, 'spear-page'는 그 아이 엄마가 테이프로 이어 붙인, 창을 들고 있는 어떤 정글 부족의 찢어진 사진이었다. Clark는 또한 28개월 된 아이가 말한 "너는 sworder이고 난 gunner야."라는 예를 들었다. 이러한 예들이 시사하듯, 어린이들의 혁신적인 언어 사용은 결코 임의적이지 않다. 그 예들은 단어들 또는 그 나름대로 의미가 있고 함께 합쳤을 때 모호하지 않은 의미를 갖는 성분들을 결합하는 것과 같은 새로운 어휘를 형성하는 규칙을 보여준다. 그러한 언어적 창의성은 아동에게 자신들의 제한적인 어휘가 언어적 창의성 없이 허락하는 것을 훨씬 뛰어넘는 의미들을 표현할 수 있게 해 준다.

구문 [12행~16행] They reflect **rules for forming new words, such as combining words** or *other components* [that are meaningful in their own right] and [that, when (they are) put together, have an unambiguous meaning].

• such as 다음의 combining words와 other components는 rules for forming new words의 두 가지 예이다. 두 [ ] 부분은 other components를 수식한다. 두 번째 [ ] 부분에서 when 다음에 'they(= the new words) are'가 생략되어 있다.

[16행~18행] Such linguistic creativity allows children to express *meanings* [that are well beyond what their limited vocabularies would *otherwise* allow].

• [ ] 부분은 meanings를 수식한다. what their ~ otherwise allow는 전치사 beyond의 목적어이며, otherwise가 함축하는 바는 '그러한 언어적 창의성이 없다면'이다.

어휘 **novel** 새로운 **cite** 인용하다 **fix** 고치다 **colleague** 동료 **laboratory** 실험실 **tribe** 부족 **innovative** 혁신적인 **component** 구성 요소 **in one's own right** 자기 능력으로, 남을 의지하지 않고 **put A together** A를 조립하다 **unambiguous** 모호하지 않은, 분명한 **otherwise** 그렇지 않으면

[선택지] **bound up with** ~와 밀접한 관계가 있다

4 글의 순서　　　　　　　　　⑤

해설 커피를 마시는 민족 집단 간의 다양한 동기에 대해 말한 제시문 다음에는 그러한 동기의 다양성을 논하고 멕시코의 예를 든 (C)가 위치해야 하며, 멕시코 고지대의 커피 마시는 동기가 제시된 (B)가 그다음에 나와야 한다. (A)의 such structure는 (B)에 나온 소비의 동기 구조를 뜻하고, 커피 외의 다른 식품을 소비하는 동기는 커피 이야기가 마무리된 뒤에 나와야 하므로 (A)가 마지막에 위치해야 한다.

해석 미국에 있는 여러 인종 집단들은 커피 소비에 관한 동기 부여에서 차이가 있다. 예를 들어 Philadelphia 지역에서는 감각적인 (맛/냄새) 동기가 유대인들 사이에서 특히 중요하고, 반면 이탈리아계 미국인들 사이에서는 사회적인 요인들이 더 중요한 것 같다.
(C) 비교 문화적으로 보면, 특정한 동기와 그 동기의 복잡성 둘 모두에 차이가 있다. 멕시코 고산지의 한 마을에서는 잠에서 깬 지 한 시간쯤 후에 약하지만 뜨거운 커피를 하루에 한 번씩 마신다.
(B) 그렇게 하는 동기는 꽤 단순하며 한결같은데, 아침에 따뜻하게 몸을 풀어 주려는 것이다. 이것의 요점은 우리가 더 많은 분석과 일반적인 설명을 시도하기에 앞서 소비의 동기 구조를 이해해야 한다는 것이다.
(A) 그러한 구조의 관점에서 커피는 다른 많은 식품들보다 더 복잡하다. 쌀, 생선, 또는 고추를 소비하는 동기는 하나의 문화권 내의 개인들 사이에서도, 그리고 여러 문화권에 걸쳐서도 변동이 덜하다.

구문 [8행~10행] The motivation for consuming rice, fish, or chili pepper / is less changeable, **both** among individuals within a culture **and** across cultures.

• 「both A and B(A와 B 둘 다)」의 A와 B자리에 전명구가 쓰인 구조이다.

어휘 **ethnic group** 인종 집단 **motivation** 동기 부여 **sensory** 감각의 **Jew** 유대인 **in terms of** ~의 측면에서 **changeable** 바뀔 수도 있는, 변덕이 심한 **uniform** 획일적인, 균일한 **analysis** 분석 **cross-culturally** 비교 문화적으로 **highland** 산악 지대

5 문장 넣기　　　　　　　　　②

해설 본문은 자유 시장 결정과 정부 통제의 혼합 비율에 관하여 다룬 글이다. 이어서 국가 경제 체제별, 시간별로 자유 시장 결정 비율에 대해 예를 들어 설명하고, 경제 체제 안에서 또 부문별로 달라진다고 흐름이 전환된다. 주어진 문장을 살펴보면 유럽의 '농업' 시장이 정부의 통제를 많이 받는다는 예시(For example)가 제시된다. 따라서 주어진 문장은 ②번에 위치하고 다음에 '유럽의 농업 시장의 정부 통제'에 관한 보충 설명이 나오는 흐름이 적절하다.

해석 자유 시장 결정과 정부 통제의 혼합 비율은 경제 체제에 따라, 그리고 시간의 흐름에 따라 다르다. 프랑스보다 미국에서 자유 시장 결정이 더 많다. 40년 전보다 오늘날 영국에는 자유 시장 결정이 더 많다. 또한, 그 혼합 비율은 어느 경제 체제 안에서도 부문별로 다르다. <u>예를 들어, 유럽의 농업 시장은 상당히 많은 정부 통제를 받는다.</u> 시장 결정하에서라면 현재보다 농장의 평균 규모는 훨씬 더 클 것이며 농산물 가격은 훨씬 더 낮을 것이다. 대조적으로 정보와 컴퓨터 기술 시장은 대체로 정부의 개입이 없다. 자유 시장과 가장 근접한 경제 체제 안에서도 정부가 해야 할 중요한 역할을 가지고 있다. 따라서 시장에 많이 의존하지만, 또한 경제 체제의 여러 면에서 상당히 많은 정부의 개입이 있는 혼합 체제에 대한 현실적인 대안은 전혀 없어 보인다.

구문 [6행~8행] There is more free-market determination in the UK today than there **was** (free-market determination in the UK) forty years ago.

• was와 forty 사이에 free-market determination in the UK가 생략되었다.

[14행~16행] Even *the economies* [(**which are**) closest to free markets] have a significant role for government.

• [ ] 부분에서 closest 앞에는 주격 관계대명사 which와 be동사 are이 함께 생략되었으며, the economies를 수식하고 있다.

어휘 **agricultural** 농업의 **a substantial amount of** 상당히 많은 양의 **proportion** 비율 **determination** 결정 **sector** 부문 **largely** 대체로 **intervention** 개입, 간섭 **significant** 중요한 **alternative** 대안 **reliance** 의존 **presence** 존재 **aspect** (측)면, 양상

1 글의 주제   ②

해설 셔틀콕이 라켓에 접촉하기 바로 직전에 중단되는 동영상을 보고 어디에 떨어질지 예측하는 실험에서 숙련된 선수들이 행동을 관찰하고 이해하는 뇌 영역이 더 활발했고 경험이 많을수록 예측을 더 잘한다는 결론을 내렸다. 또한 축구 선수들을 대상으로 한 유사한 연구에서도 같은 결과를 보였다. 그러므로 글의 주제로는 ② '숙련도에 근거한 경기 예측 능력의 차이'가 적절하다.
① 선수들의 지능이 경기 예측 능력에 미치는 영향
③ 최적의 수행을 위해 상대편을 관찰하고 분석하는 것의 중요성
④ 경기력 발전과 예측 능력에 영향을 미치는 요소들
⑤ 뇌 손상과 관계없이 발생하는 선수들의 경기 예측의 향상

해석 Brunel University London의 팀원들과 함께 연구하는 브루스 애버네시는 엘리트 배드민턴 선발 선수들이 예측 기술을 발휘할 때 그들의 뇌를 조사하기 위해 fMRI(기능 자기공명영상)를 사용했다. 그들은 다양한 기술 수준을 가진 선수들이, 셔틀콕을 치는 장면이 담긴 차단된 동영상이 상영되는 것을 시청하면서 (그 동영상들은 셔틀콕과 접촉이 이루어지기 바로 전에 중단되곤 했다) 친 셔틀콕이 코트의 어느 구역에 떨어질 것인지 예측하려고 애쓰는 동안 그들을 정밀 촬영했다. 숙련된 선수들은 다른 사람들의 행동을 관찰하고 이해하는 것과 관련된 뇌 영역에서 더 많은 뇌 활동을 보여주었다. 선수가 경험이 많을수록 이렇게 하는 것을 더 잘 해낸다. 몇 년 후에 Brunel 대학에서 동일한 연구팀이 축구 선수들을 데리고 유사한 연구를 했는데, 그 선수들은 상대 선수가 공을 가지고 자신들을 향해 달려오는 차단된 동영상을 시청했다. 일부 동영상에서, 선수들은 동영상이 중단되기 직전에 상대방을 속이는 동작을 시작하곤 했고 진단 장치 안에 있는 축구 선수는 그들이 왼쪽이나 오른쪽 중 어디로 갈지를 예측해야 하곤 했다. 동영상이 더 일찍 중단될수록, fMRI 정밀 촬영에서 세미프로 축구선수와 초보 축구선수 간의 신경 활동에서 차이가 더 컸다.

구문 [5행~9행] They scanned players of various skill levels // **as** they **watched** *occluded clips of shots* **being played** (the video clips would cut off just before contact was made with the shuttlecock) and tried to predict in which area of the court the shots would land.
• as가 이끄는 부사절 내에서 동사 watched와 tried가 and로 연결되었다. 「지각동사(watched)+목적어(occluded clips of shots)+v-ing(being played)」의 구문이 쓰여 '목적어가 v하고 있는 것을 시청하다'의 의미이다.

[12행~13행] **The more** experience an athlete has, **the better** they are at doing this.
• 「the 비교급 ~, the 비교급 ...」 구문으로 '~하면 할수록, 더 …하다'의 의미이다.

[13행~16행] A few years later, the same group at Brunel did a similar study with *footballers*, // **who** watched occluded clips **of** *an opponent* **running** towards them with the ball.
• 계속적 용법의 관계대명사 who가 이끄는 절은 footballers를 보충 설명한다. 관계사절 내에서 전치사 of의 목적어로 running이 이끄는 동명사구가 쓰였으며 an opponent는 동명사의 의미상 주어이다.

어휘 **resonance** 공명(共鳴); (소리의) 울림 **anticipation** 예측 **scan** 정밀 촬영하다 **clip** 동영상 **cut off** ~을 중단시키다[자르다]; (기계 등이) 저절로 멈추다 **land** 떨어지다, 땅에 닿다 **expert** 숙련된; 전문가 **associated with** ~와 관련된 **footballer** 축구선수 **opponent** (경기·논쟁·게임 등의) 상대 **feint** 상대방을 속이는 동작; 가장, 시늉 **neural** 신경의 **novice** 초보[초심]자
[선택지] **proficiency** 숙련도 **optimal** 최적[최선]의

2 밑줄 어법   ③

해설 ③ these는 바로 앞에서 언급된 '몇몇 정확한 조각들(some accurate fragments)'을 가리킨다. '몇몇 정확한 조각들이 다시 합쳐져야 한다'라는 수동의 의미를 나타내므로 to-v의 수동형(to be p.p.)을 사용하여 put back을 be put back으로 바꿔 써야 한다.
① 뒤에 완전한 절이 이어지므로 have long known의 목적어 역할을 하는 명사절을 이끄는 접속사 that이 올바르게 쓰였다.
② 단수명사 an event를 가리키므로 it이 올바르게 쓰였다.
④ '기억을 재구성하기 위해 필요로 되는 조각들'이라는 수동의 의미이므로, 과거분사 needed가 올바르게 쓰였다.
⑤ '자동적으로 일어난다'라는 의미로 동사 occurs를 수식하는 부사 automatically가 올바르게 쓰였다.

해석 기억은 사람들이 생각해온 것과 들어온 것의 합으로 알려져 있다. 오랫동안 인지 심리학자들은 기억이 적어도 중요한 부분에서 사건들의 재구성이라는 것을 알고 있었다. 우리가 어떤 것, 예를 들어 몇 년 전에 발생한 어떤 사건을 기억할 때, 우리는 우리의 마음속에서 그 사건에 대해 정확하게 기록된 버전을 재생하지 않는다. 우리는 시각, 소리, 느낌인 경험의 조각들을 부호화한다. 우리가 기억에 접근할 때, 우리는 몇몇 정확한 조각들을 회수할지도 모르지만, 이러한 조각들은 다시 합쳐야 하고, 이러한 조각들 사이의 틈은 기대, 상식, 그리고 논리를 사용하여 메꾸어진다. 때때로, 기억을 재구성하기 위해 필요로 되는 조각들이 없거나 부정확할 수도 있고, 그 기억은 실제 상황이 어떠했는지보다는 우리가 기대하는 것에 대한 반영이 된다. 이는 그 기억이 비록 거짓일지라도 마치 정확하고 진실된 기억인 것처럼 우리가 느끼게 하며, 이러한 과정은 우리가 인식하지 못한 채로 자동적으로 일어난다.

구문 [1행~2행] Memories are known to be the sum of **what** people have thought and **what** they **have been told**.
• 여기서 what은 선행사를 포함한 관계대명사로 '~것'이라는 뜻을 나타낸다. have been told는 현재완료 수동태(have been p.p.)로, 행동을 당하는 과거의 일이 현재까지 영향을 미쳐 현재와 관련이 있을 때 사용한다.

어휘 **sum** 합(계) **cognitive psychologist** 인지 심리학자 **significant** 중요한, 의미 있는 **reconstruction** 재구성 **faithfully** 정확하게; 충실하게, 성실하게 **encode** 부호[암호]화하다 **fragment** 조각, 파편 **access** 접근하다 **retrieve** 회수하다, 되찾다 **gap** 틈, 간격 **inaccurate** 부정확한 **recollection** 기억(력) **awareness** 인식

3 빈칸 추론   ①

해설 조직이 사업상 목표를 달성하기 위해 모든 데이터를 분석해야만 하는 것은 아니며, 어떤 데이터가 필요한지를 고려하고, 목표에 부합하는 데이터를 살펴봐야 한다는 내용이다. 빈칸 포함 문장의 앞 문장에서 몇몇 경우는 모든 것을 포함할 수 있다고 나오지만, 뒤에 '그러나'라는 뜻의 역접 연결사 though가 쓰여 다른 경우에는 가지고 있는 빅 데이터의 ① '부분 집합만을 이용하는 것'을 의미한다는 것이 가장 적절하다.
② 콘셉트를 파는 것
③ 규모를 이해하는 것
④ 틀린 분석을 지적하는 것
⑤ 신뢰할 만한 측정법을 만드는 것

해석 바로 그 본질상, 빅 데이터 분석 프로젝트는 대규모 데이터 세트를 수반한다. 그렇지만 그것이 한 회사의 모든 데이터 원본이나 관련 있는 데이터 원본 안의 모든 정보가 분석될 필요가 있다는 것을 의미하지는 않는다. 조직들은 유용한 분석적 통찰로 이끌 전략적인 데이터를 파악해야 한다. 예를 들어, 어떤 데이터의 조합이 핵심적인 고객 유지 요소를 정확히 찾아내는 데 도움이 되는가? 또는 어떤 데이터가 주식 시장의 거래에 있어 숨겨진 패턴을 알아내는 데 필요할까? 계획 단계에서 프로젝트의 사업상 목표에 집중하는 것은 조직이 필요로 하는 정확한 분석된 정보에 전념하는 데 도움이 될 수 있으며, 그런 다음 그 조직은 그러한 사업상의 목표에 부합하는 데 필요한 데이터를 살펴볼 수 있고 또 살펴봐야 한다. 몇몇 경우에는 이것이 정말로 모든 것을 포함하는 것을 의미할 것이다. 그러나 다른 경우에는, 가지고 있는 빅 데이터의 <u>부분 집합만을 이용하는 것</u>을 의미한다.

구문 [10행~14행] **Focusing on a project's business goals in the planning stages** / can help an organization *home in on the exact analytics that are required*, // **after which** it can — and should — look at the data needed to meet those business goals.

• Focusing ~ stages가 문장의 주어이다. after which 이하는 home ~ required를 선행사로 하는 계속적 용법의 관계사절이다.

어휘 nature 본질 analysis 분석 relevant 관련 있는 strategic 전략적인 analytical 분석적인 insight 통찰(력), 이해 combination 조합, 결합 retention 보유, 유지 uncover (비밀 등을) 알아내다 transaction 거래, 매매 home in on ~에 전념하다 on hand 구할 수 있는

[선택지] subset 부분 집합 reliable 신뢰할 만한

4 무관 문장　　　　　　　　　　　④

해설 이 글은 자율 주행 차량이 특히 도시에서 우리의 삶에 가져다줄 편의적 잠재성에 관한 내용이다. ④번 문장은 자율 주행 택시가 가능한 한 빨리 해결해야 할 문제점이 있다는 내용이므로 글의 흐름에 부합하지 않고, 특히 ⑤번 뒤 문장까지 계속 이어지는 편의성의 구체적 사례들 앞에 위치하여 글의 흐름을 끊고 있다.

해석 자율 주행 차량은 특히 도시 환경 내에서 우리가 자동차에 대해 생각하는 방식을 완전히 바꿀 가능성을 가지고 있다. ① 자율 주행 택시는 언젠가 모든 도시의 모든 도로에 주차될지도 모른다. ② 당신이 어딘가에 가고 싶을 때, 휴대전화를 사용하여 한 대를 호출할 수 있을 것이고 그러면 그것은 당신이 현관문 밖으로 걸어 나올 때까지 당신의 집 밖에 주차되어 대기하고 있을 것이다. ③ 일단 그것이 당신을 목적지로 데려다주고 나면, 다음 손님을 위해 떠난다. ④ 이와 같은 자율 주행 택시의 편의성에도 불구하고 가능한 한 빨리 해결되어야 할 많은 문제 또한 있다. ⑤ 자율 주행 차량은 당신이 차량을 소유하기 위해 지출할 것으로 예상하는 비용의 적은 비율로 학교에 아이들을 데리러 가고, 노인들을 가게에 데려다주고, 모든 평범한 일상 여정을 실행하는 것 모두에 이용될 수도 있다.

구문 [12행~16행] Self-driving vehicles may be used **to collect** children from school, **take** elderly people to shops, and **carry out** all the usual, everyday journeys, all at a small percentage of the cost of what you would expect to pay to own a car.

• 세 개의 부정사구 to collect, (to) take, (to) carry out이 and로 연결되어 병렬구조를 이루고 있다.

어휘 self-driving vehicle 자율 주행 차량; 무인 자동차 autonomous 자율적인 *cf.* autonomy 자율; 자치 carry out 수행하다

5 요약문 완성　　　　　　　　　　　⑤

해설 일반적인 인식이나 이론과 다르게 의견 일치는 강압적이어야만 가능한 것이고, 견해 차이는 당연히 존재하기 때문에 논쟁으로도 해소되지 않으며 이것이 부정적인 것은 아니라는 내용의 글이다. 이를 다른 말로 요약하면 '완전한 정치적 합의(agreement)가 바람직하고 실현 가능하다고 믿는 것이 매력적일지도 모르지만, 현실에서는 반대 의견과 토론이 바람직하며 불가피하다(inevitable)'가 된다.

해석 어떤 정책 과정이 사용되든, 그리고 그 정책 과정이 얼마나 민감하고 차이를 얼마나 존중하든, 정치적 견해가 억압될 수는 없다. 다시 말해서, 정치적 견해에는 끝이 없다(다양성이 있을 수밖에 없다). 적절한 제도나 지식이나 협의 방법이나 참여 구조가 의견 차이를 사라지게 만들 수 있다고 생각하는 것은 틀렸다. 모든 종류의 이론들은, 의견 차이가 사라지게 만들 수 있도록 의견 차이가 처리되거나 다뤄질 수 있는 방법들이 있다는 인식을 조장한다. 그런 이론들의 배경에 있는 전제는 의견 차이가 잘못된 것이고 의견 일치가 상황의 바람직한 상태라는 것이다. 사실, 의견 일치는 몇몇 형태의 교묘한 강압이 없이는 거의 일어나지 않고, 이견을 표현할 때에 두려움이 없는 것이 진정한 자유의 원천이다. 논쟁은 이견들이 자주 더 나은 쪽으로 전개되게 하지만, 긍정적으로 전개되는 논쟁이 반드시 의견 차이의 감소와 같은 것은 아니다. 의견 차이의 억압은 정치적 숙고에서 목표로 삼아져서는 절대 안 된다. 정치적 의견 차이가 상황의 정상적인 상태가 아니라는 어떤 제언에도 맞서는 방어가 요구된다.

↓

完전한 정치적 (A) 합의가 바람직하고 성취 가능하다고 믿는 것이 매력적일지도 모르지만, 현실에서는 반대 의견과 토론이 바람직하며 (B) 불가피하다.

구문 [6행~9행] Theories of all sorts promote <u>the view</u> **that** there are *ways* [**by which** disagreement can be processed or managed so as to make it disappear].

• that 이하는 the view와 동격을 이루는 절이며, 그 안에서 [ ]는 '전치사+관계대명사' 형태인 by which가 이끄는 절로 앞에 있는 ways를 수식한다.

[21행~24행] It may be tempting **to believe** that total political agreement is desirable and achievable, // but in reality dissent and debate are **both** <u>desirable</u> **and** <u>inevitable</u>.

• It은 가주어이고 to believe ~ achievable 부분이 진주어이며, 「both A and B (A와 B 둘 다)」의 A와 B 자리에 형용사가 쓰인 구조이다.

어휘 politics 정치적 견해 suppress 억압하다 institution 제도 consultation 협의 participatory 참여의, 참가하는 mechanism 구조, 방법 promote 조장하다 so as to ~하도록, ~하기 위해 assumption 전제 consensus 의견 일치 state 상태 subtle 교묘한 genuine 진정한 evolve 전개되다 equal (동일한 결과를) 가져오다 tempting 매력적인, 유혹하는 dissent 반대 (의견)

[선택지] inevitable 불가피한, 필연적인

1 빈칸 추론　　②

해설 앞에서는 상황을 있는 그대로 보는 것이 아니라 자세히 살피고, 질문하고 분석하는 작가의 눈으로 보는 것을 배우는 것이 모든 전문직 종사자에게 도움이 된다는 내용이고, 뒤에는 그 예시를 들고 있으므로 성공은 ② '예리한 관찰과 심도 있는 분석'에 달려 있음을 알 수 있다.

① 동향과 혁신에 반박하는 것
③ 자원 관리와 경제의 이해
④ 다양한 상황들과 인적 네트워크 형성 기회들
⑤ 문학적인 성과들과 교양 있는 교육

해석 훌륭한 작가들은 수동적이지 않고 즉각적인 반응을 단순히 기록만 하지는 않는다. 그들은 '자세히 살피고', '질문하고', '분석하고', '연관시키고', 그리고 '생각한다'. 작가의 눈으로 보는 것을 배우는 것은 생업으로 글을 쓰는 사람들뿐만 아니라 모든 전문직 종사자들에게 도움이 된다. 여러분이 선택하는 그 어떤 직업에서든, 성공은 예리한 관찰과 심도 있는 분석에 달려 있다. 노련한 의사는 신체검사에서 가벼운 증상을 찾아내거나 환자의 푸념에 대해 더 알아보고 다른 사람들은 못 보고 넘어갈 수도 있는 진단으로 이끄는 질문을 한다. 성공한 증권 중개인은 새로운 투자 기회를 찾아내기 위해 간과된 동향을 관찰하고 연구를 수행한다. 행인은 분주한 가게가 틀림없이 번창한다고 추측할 수도 있지만, 소매 분석가는 사람들이 어떤 상품을 구매하고 있는지, 그리고 그것을 어떻게 지불하고 있는지 관찰할 것이다. 만약 모든 쇼핑객이 할인 품목을 구매하면서 신용카드로 지불하고 있다면, 그 가게는 판매할 때 돈을 잃고 있을 수 있다.

구문 [3행~5행] Learning to see with a writer's eye / benefits **not just** *those* [who write for a living] **but** all professionals.

● those who write for a living과 all professionals가 '~뿐만 아니라 …도 (또한)'라는 의미의 「not just ~ but (also) …」로 연결되어 동사 benefits의 목적어로 쓰였다. [ ] 부분은 관계사절로 those를 수식한다.

[7행~9행] A skilled physician detects minor symptoms in a physical or follows up on a patient's complaint and asks *questions* [that lead to *a diagnosis* [(which[that]) others might miss]].

● 문장의 동사 detects와 asks가 and로 연결된 병렬구조이다. 첫 번째 [ ] 부분은 questions를 수식하는 관계사절이고, 그 안의 others might miss는 목적격 관계대명사 which[that]가 생략된 관계사절로 a diagnosis를 수식한다.

[12행~13행] A passerby might **assume** (that) a busy store must be successful ~.

● a busy store must be successful은 동사 assume의 목적어 역할을 하는 명사절이며, 앞에 접속사 that이 생략되었다.

어휘 passive 수동적인　analyze 분석하다 *cf.* analyst 분석가　benefit 도움이 되다; 이익　skilled 노련한　physician 의사　detect 찾아내다　physical 신체검사　follow up 더 알아보다　diagnosis 진단(법) stockbroker 증권 중개인　overlook 못 보고 넘어가다　passerby 행인　retail 소매(의)　merchandise 상품

[선택지] counter 반박하다　keen 예리한　observation 관찰　in-depth 심도 있는　diverse 다양한　networking 인적 네트워크 형성　literary 문학의　attainment 성과

2 글의 순서　　④

해설 야생 동물을 위한 접근법인 야생 동물 보호 지구 또는 공원을 만들어야 한다

는 내용 다음에, 이 접근법이 가진 문제점을 말해주는 (C)가 오는 것이 적절하다. 그 다음에는 또 다른 문제점이 also와 함께 제시되는 (A)가 오고, 마지막으로 앞서 나온 문제점들을 보완할 방법을 찾아야 한다는 내용인 (B)가 오는 것이 적절하다.

해석 인간과 야생 동물 간의 충돌에 대한 한 가지 접근법은 야생 동물에 미치는 인간의 영향이 최소화되는 보호 구역, 야생 동물 보호 지구, 또는 공원을 만드는 것이다. (C) 이 접근법이 의도는 아주 좋지만, 천연자원에 대한 사회의 수요가 너무 커서 공원에서 오직 환경의 작은 부분밖에 확보될 수 없기 때문에 그것은 인간과 야생 동물 간의 충돌을 해결하는 데에는 거의 도움이 되지 않는다. (A) 야생 동물이 우리의 경계선을 준수하지 않을지도 모르고 공원 안에 머물지 않을 것이라는 문제도 또한 있다. 사실상, 야생 동물 대다수는 공원 밖에, 사람들이 거주하는 같은 곳에 산다. 야생 동물 개체군들은 우리의 가장 빽빽하게 정착된 도시에서 번성한다. (B) 분명히, 만약 인간과 야생 동물 간의 충돌이 해결되려면 인간과 야생 동물이 둘 중 어느 쪽도 상대방에게 해로운 영향을 끼치지 않고 조화롭게 공존하는 방법을 찾아야 한다.

구문 [1행~3행] One approach to human-wildlife conflicts is to create *preserves, wildlife refuges, or parks* [**where** human impact on wildlife is minimized].

● 관계부사 where가 이끄는 절이 preserves, wildlife refuges, or parks를 수식하고 있다.

어휘 preserve (생물·삼림 등의) 보호 구역(= reserve); 보존하다　wildlife refuge 야생 동물 보호 구역　boundary 경계, 한계선　population 개체군; 인구　densely 조밀하게; 빽빽하게 *cf.* sparse 밀도가 낮은　settle 정착하다　resolve 해결하다; 결심하다　coexist 공존하다　adverse 해로운; 불리한; 부정적인 *cf.* adversity 고난; 역경　societal 사회의　fraction 부분; 소량; 분수　set aside 확보하다; 따로 떼어 두다

3 문장 넣기　　②

해설 이 글은 네거티브 섬 게임(negative sum game)에 대해 다루고 있다. 주어진 문장은 역접을 나타내는 However로 시작하며 지나친 경쟁으로 추가 비용이 생겨서 제로섬 게임이 네거티브 섬 게임이 될 수 있다고 말하고 있다. ② 앞에서 제로섬 게임에 관해 설명하고 있고, ② 뒤에서 '이것의 한 가지 예'로 영국의 대형 소매 은행을 이야기하며 결론적으로는 네거티브 섬 게임으로 판명되었다고 말하고 있으므로 가장 적절한 위치는 ②이다.

해석 충분히 발달한 시장에서는, 경쟁적 지위들에서의 중요한 변화와 시장의 성장을 가져오는 돌파구는 드물다. 이 때문에, 경쟁은 한 조직이 다른 조직들을 희생시켜야만 승리할 수 있는 제로섬 게임이 된다. 하지만, 경쟁의 정도가 특히 극심해지는 경우, 제로섬 게임은 시장의 모두가 추가적인 비용에 직면하므로, 급속하게 네거티브 섬 게임이 될 수 있다. 이것의 한 가지 예로, 영국의 주요 시내 중심가 은행 중 한 곳이 토요일 오전에 영업함으로써 경쟁 우위를 점하려고 했을 때, 그 은행은 전통적인 월요일부터 금요일까지의 은행 영업시간을 제약이라고 여기던 많은 새로운 고객을 끌어모았다. 하지만 고객의 감소에 직면한 경쟁 상대는 마찬가지로 토요일에 영업함으로써 대응했다. 이것의 최종 결과는 고객들은 이득을 얻었지만, 은행들은 비용은 증가했으나 고객의 총수는 그대로였기 때문에 손해를 보았다는 것이었다. 본질적으로, 이것은 네거티브 섬 게임으로 판명되었다.

구문 [1행~4행] However, where the degree of competition is particularly intense a zero sum game can quickly become a negative sum game, // **in that** everyone in the market is faced with additional costs.

• 콤마 뒤 in that은 '~하므로, ~라는 점에서'의 의미이며, that은 접속사이다.

어휘 intense 극심한　mature (충분히) 발달한; 성숙한　breakthrough 돌파구
competitive 경쟁적인 *cf.* competitive advantage 경쟁 우위　at the expense of
~의 희생으로　growth 성장　constraint 제약　net effect 최종 결과　in essence
본질적으로

어휘 replay 다시 보기; 재현　account for (비율을) 차지하다; 설명하다　visualization
심상; 시각화　alternative 대안적인　close off ~을 차단[고립]시키다; 폐쇄(시키다)
distraction 집중을 방해하는 것　external 외부의, 밖의　stimulus 자극(제)
interference 간섭, 참견; 개입　deactivate 정지시키다　bizarre 기이한, 특이한
be subject to ~의 지배를 받다[종속되다]　neuroscientist 신경 과학자　preformed
미리 형성된　enhance 향상시키다　neuronal 뉴런의, 신경 단위의　flexibility 유연성
burst forth 터져 나오다, 분출하다　extensively 널리, 광범위하게　novel 새로운; (장편)
소설　emerge 나오다; 드러나다; 생겨나다　spin (정보를) 제시하다, 자아내다
[선택지] intersect 교차하다, 만나다

4~5 장문 　　　　　　　　 4 ⑤ 5 ②

해설 **4.** 우리가 꿈을 꿀 때 뇌 작용의 어떤 원리로 인하여 멋지고 새로운 아이디어를 생각해내게 되는지를 열거하여 설명한 글이므로, 제목으로 가장 적절한 것은 ⑤ '꿈이 우리를 창조적 생각으로 인도하는 방법'이다.
① 꿈은 두뇌의 기능을 넘어선다
② 당신의 꿈을 이야기로 전환시키는 방법
③ 꿈은 당신이 깨어 있을 때 이루어진다
④ 꿈과 현실이 교차하는 마법의 방법들
5. 우리가 꿈을 꾸며 새로운 아이디어를 생각해내는 이유를 들고 있으므로 잠이 외부 자극의 간섭을 막아서 상상력이 번성하게 한다는 것을 알 수 있다. 그러므로 ②는 flourish 등이 되어야 한다.

해석 대부분의 꿈은 우리의 일상생활의 단순한 다시 보기가 아니며, 그것들은 꿈에서 단지 약 1~2%만 차지할 뿐이다. 나머지 시간에 우리의 다양한 생각과 심상은 새롭고 종종 창의적인 방식으로 결합된다. 꿈을 통해 두뇌의 무의식적 체계는 우리에게 깨어 있는 삶의 모든 주의 산만으로부터 차단되어 개념들을 연관 지을 수 있는 (a) 대안적 방식을 제공한다. 생각은 머릿속에서 자유롭게 춤출 수 있다. 아마 그것이 우리가 잠을 잘 때 멋진 새로운 아이디어에 대해 생각하는 이유일 것이다.
대체 꿈꾸는 뇌에 관한 어떤 점이 우리의 생각과 경험을 독특한 방식으로 결합시켜 주는 걸까? 한 가지 설명은 잠이 우리를 외부 자극으로부터 보호해주어서, 간섭을 막아주고 우리의 상상력이 (b) 쇠퇴하게(→ 번성하게) 한다는 것이다. 또 다른 가능성은 전두엽 피질이 대체로 정지되어서, 우리의 좀 더 추상적이고 심지어 이상한 생각들이 우리의 (c) 평상시의 판단적, 분석적 논리에 지배되지 않고 자유롭게 놀 수 있다는 것이다. 꿈이 그토록 창의적인 이유에 대한 좀 더 근본적인 세 번째 설명이 있을 수 있다. 몇몇 신경과학자들은 수면 동안 뇌가 우리의 기억과 학습된 개념 간의 연결고리를 (d) 느슨히 해주며 미리 형성된 시냅스를 풀어준다는 이론을 세웠다. 이것은 신경의 유연성을 향상시켜서 새로운 통로가 뇌 속에 형성되고 창의적인 아이디어가 터져 나오게 해준다고 여겨진다. 실제로 낮 동안 가장 광범위하게 합동 작업을 했던 뉴런들이 우리가 잘 때는 가장 조용해진다는 것이 몇몇 연구로 밝혀졌다. 우리의 시냅스를 풀어주는 것이 꿈꾸기로 향하는 문을 열어준다는 것이 이론이다. 그것은 우리의 생각들 간의 새로운 연결이 (e) 나올 기회를 만들어주고, 두뇌가 자신의 이야기를 자아내게 해준다.

구문 [11행~13행] *What* **is it** *about the dreaming brain* **that makes** our thoughts and experiences come together in unique ways?

• 「it is … that ~」 강조구문으로 '~한 것은 바로 …이다'의 뜻이다. 이 문장에서는 what … about the dreaming brain이 강조되고 있다. makes는 사역동사로, 「make O 동사원형 (O가 v하게 하다)」와 같이 쓴다.

[29행~32행] **It** creates *the opportunity* for novel connections between our thoughts (to emerge), / **allowing** the brain to spin its stories.

• It은 relaxing our synapses를 지칭한다. ( ) 부분은 the opportunity를 수식하며 밑줄 친 for novel connections between our thoughts는 to emerge의 의미상 주어이다. allowing 이하는 분사구문이며 「allow O to-v (O가 v하는 것을 허락하다[v 하게 해주다])」와 같이 쓴다.

---

1 글의 요지　　　　　　　　　　　　　②

해설 인간의 개입 없이 내버려두는 것은 자연 보호가 아니며, 인간이 적극적으로 개입하여 보호하고자 하는 자연에 침투하려는 '다른 자연'에 맞서는 것이 진정한 개념임을 말하는 글이므로 요지로 가장 적절한 것은 ②이다.

해석 인간의 개입이 없는 자연으로서, 황무지는 자연 보호를 필요로 하지 않는다. 적극적인 자연 보호 활동가가 황무지에 대해 극찬할 때, 자연 보호 활동가에게 황무지는 단순히 아무것도 안 하는 것을 의미하기 때문에, 그는 자기 자신의 발밑의 양탄자를 잡아당기고 있음을(자기 자신을 곤경에 빠뜨리고 있음을) 인식해야 한다. 자신의 정원에 황무지를 원하는 사람은 누구든지 자신의 정원사를 해고하는 셈이다. 여러 가지 면에서 자연 보호는 황무지의 반의어이다. 많은 경우 자연 보호는 어떤 지역에 속한 자연의 어떤 특정 상태를 (보통 일시적이며 인간의 영향을 받은) 보호하는 것, 그러나 다른 종류의, '다른 자연'의 위협으로부터의 보호를 요구한다. 인간이 그것을 '다른 자연'으로부터 보호하지 않으면 이러한 '다른 자연'은 문제되는 지역에서 발판을 마련할 것이다. 극단적인 경우에 자연 보호는 황무지의 침투와 지배에 맞서서 한 특정 지역에서 지배하는 자연을 보호하는 것을 의미한다.

구문 [8행~12행] In many cases, nature conservation requires the protection of a particular state of nature in an area (usually temporary and influenced by humans); but protection from the threat of a different, 'other nature'.
• the protection ~ by humans와 protection from ~ 'other nature'가 ;와 but으로 연결되어 병렬구조를 이룬다. usually temporary and influenced by humans는 앞의 the protection에 대한 설명이다.

[12행~14행] This 'other nature' would gain a foothold in *the area in question* if man did not protect it from the 'other nature'.
• 가정법 과거 문장으로 「if+S'+과거동사 ~, S+would+동사원형… (~한다면 …할 것이다)」의 형태와 의미를 가진다. protect 다음의 it은 the area in question을 지칭한다.

어휘 intervention 개입; 간섭　wilderness 황무지, 황야　conservation 보존, 보호　conservationist 환경 보호 활동가　pull the rug from under somebody's feet ~의 계획을 망치다　respect (측)면　opposite 반의어; 정반대의　temporary 일시적인　foothold 발판　dominate 지배하다　penetration 침투

2 빈칸 추론　　　　　　　　　　　　　⑤

해설 빠른 속도로 변화하는 사회적 생태계는 예측할 수 없으므로 학생들을 적응시키려면 다양한 사회 상황에 적절하게 행동할 수 있도록 융통성과 적응력을 교육하는 것이 중요하다는 것이 글의 요지이다. 따라서 이러한 교육을 통해, 학생들이 다양한 우발적 사건을 인지하고 ⑤ '자신들의 행동을 그에 맞춰 조정할 수 있도록' 준비시킬 수 있음을 알 수 있다.
① 분쟁 없이 협력에 참여할 수 있도록
② 가능한 모든 수단을 시도해 보상을 얻을 수 있도록
③ 자신들의 필요에 가장 잘 맞는 교실의 유형을 고를 수 있도록
④ 건전한 경쟁을 위해 이상적인 토대를 만들 수 있도록

해석 우리의 세상은 빠른 속도로 변화하고 있으며 (이에 대해) 걱정하고 있는 교육자로서 우리는 더 이상 우리의 학생들이 성숙한 개인으로서 맞닥뜨리게 될 사회적 생태계의 유형을 확신을 가지고 예측할 수 없다. 그러므로 우리가 적응 과정에서 유일하게 의지할 수 있는 것은 학생들이 융통성 없이 협동적이거나 경쟁적이거나 또는 개인주의적이게 되지 않고 융통성이 있도록, 즉 광범위한 사회 상황과 각각의 상황에 적절한 행동 유형을 인지하도록 준비시키는 것이다. 경쟁이 적응 전략인 상황이 있고, 협동이 적응성을 나타내는 다른 상황도 있으며, 또한 개인주의적인 접근법이 가장 성공적인 상황도 있다. 교실 안에 다양한 과업과 보상 체계를 포함함으로써 교사들은 학생들이 더 넓은 범위의 환경에서의 우발적 사건을 인지하고 자신들의 행동을 그에 맞춰 조정할 수 있도록 준비시킬 수 있다.

구문 [1행~4행] Our world is changing at a rapid rate, // and as concerned educators, we no longer can predict with confidence **the kind of social ecology** [that our students will encounter as mature individuals].
• the kind of social ecology는 predict의 목적어이며 [ ] 부분의 수식을 받는다.

[4행~8행] Our only adaptive recourse, therefore, is to prepare pupils **not** to be rigidly cooperative, competitive, or individualistic, **but** to be flexible — to recognize a broad range of social situations and the kinds of behaviors appropriate to each.
• 「not A but B」는 'A가 아니라 B이다'라는 뜻이며 두 개의 to부정사구 to be rigidly ~ or individualistic과 to be flexible ~ to each 부분이 A, B 자리에 위치했다.

어휘 concerned 걱정하는, 염려하는　ecology 생태계　encounter 맞닥뜨리다　adaptive 적응하는, 적응력이 있는　pupil 학생　rigidly 융통성 없이　cooperative 협동적인　individualistic 개인주의적인　flexible 융통성 있는
[선택지] engage in ~에 참여하다　foundation 토대. 기초　adjust 조정하다　accordingly 그에 맞춰, 부응해서

3 무관 문장　　　　　　　　　　　　　③

해설 많은 스포츠가 변화하는 소비자의 욕구를 충족시키기 위해 여러 측면을 수정해 왔다는 것에 관한 글이다. 크리켓 경기를 예로 들며 스포츠가 변화한 사례를 설명하였는데, 명성을 얻고자 하는 뛰어난 젊은 크리켓 선수들을 설명하는 ③은 전체 흐름과 관련이 없다.

해석 스포츠에서는 경기의 원래의 형태가 자연적으로 흥미를 돋우고 따라서 소비자의 욕구를 충족시킨다고 생각되어 왔다. 호주의 스포츠 단체에 대한 한 분석은 이것이 시대에 뒤떨어진 시각이라는 것을 보여 준다. ① 많은 스포츠가 경기를 더욱 흥미롭게 만들기 위해서 규칙을 변경했고, 전통적으로 4~5일에 걸쳐 시합이 이루어졌던 크리켓 경기의 경우에는 1일 경기가 제품군의 다양성에 중요한 부분이 되었다. ② 호주에서 여름 동안에 열리는 1일 국제 경기는 압축된 오락과 빠른 (경기) 결과에 대한 소비자의 욕구를 더 쉽게 만족시켰다. ③ 요즘에는, 매우 경쟁력 있고 명성을 갈망하는 많은 젊은 크리켓 선수들이 국제 무대에서 두각을 나타내고 있다. ④ 청소년 수준에서는 많은 스포츠가 더 많은 청소년의 경기에 참여하고자 하는 욕망을 충족시키기 위해 상당히 수정되었다. ⑤ 이러한 변화에는 청소년들이 실제 참여를 통해서 경기 기술을 발전시키고 재미있게 놀며 보통 스포츠가 열리는 상황에서 자신의 친구들과 함께 있기를 원한다는 인식이 내재되어 있다.

구문 [4행~7행] Many sports have modified rules **to make** their games more attractive, // and in the case of *cricket matches*, [**which** have traditionally been played for 4–5 days], ~
• to make their games more attractive는 목적을 나타내는 to 부정사구이며, 관계사 which가 이끄는 [ ]은 cricket matches를 선행사로 한다.

[15행~17행] At junior levels, many sports have been significantly modified to satisfy *the desire of many more young people* (to participate in the game).

• ( ) 부분은 the desire ~ people를 수식하는 형용사적 용법의 to 부정사구이다.

[18행~21행] *Inherent in this change* **has been the recognition that** juniors **wish to develop** game skills through actual participation, **to have** fun, and in general **to be** with their friends in a sport setting.

• Inherent in this change가 문장 앞으로 이동하면서 주어 the recognition ~ setting과 동사 has been이 도치되었다. that juniors wish ~ a sport setting은 the recognition과 동격 관계의 that절이고, 밑줄 친 세 개의 to 부정사구가 and로 연결되어 동사 wish의 목적어 역할을 한다.

――――――――――――――――――――――

어휘 **original** 원래의: 독창적인 **organisation** 단체 **outdated** 시대에 뒤떨어진 **modify** 변경[수정]하다 **readily** 쉽게 **compressed** 압축된: 간결한 **competitive** 경쟁력 있는 **distinguish oneself** 두각을 나타내다 **significantly** 상당히 **inherent** 내재하는 **recognition** 인식 **in general** 보통, 대체로

4 글의 순서 ⑤

해설 광고주들이 사용하는 효과적인 방법인 '광고 속에 자신들의 제품의 사소한 약점 언급'을 소개한 후 이에 대한 자세한 보충 설명(정직하다는 인식을 가져옴)을 That way 이후에서 제시하는 (C)가 오는 것이 알맞다. 그다음으로 광고뿐만 아니라 변호사들도 이러한 방법을 사용한다는 (B)가 나오고, 변호사들의 전략이 실험으로 증명되었다는 내용인 (A)가 마지막으로 나와야 적절하다.

――――――――――――――――――――――

해석 광고주들은 그들 자신의 이익에 반론을 제기하는 것처럼 보이는 특별히 효과적인 한 가지 방법을 생각해 냈다. 그들은 자신들의 제품을 홍보하는 광고에서 그 제품의 사소한 약점이나 결점을 언급한다.
(C) 그런 식으로, 그들은 그 제품의 강점에 관해 더 설득력이 있을 수 있는 정직하다는 인식을 만든다. 광고주들만 이 전략을 사용하는 것은 아니다.
(B) 변호사들은 상대측 변호사보다 먼저 자신들의 소송에서의 약점을 언급하여 '상대에게 선수를 치도록' 배우는데, 그렇게 함으로써 배심원들의 눈에 정직하다는 인식을 확립해낸다.
(A) 실험은 이 전략이 효과가 있음을 입증했다. 배심원들이 변호사가 자기 자신의 소송 사건에서의 약점을 먼저 제기하는 것을 들었을 때, 그들은 그에게 더 많은 정직성을 부여했고 그 인식된 정직성으로 인해 최종 평결에서 그의 전반적인 소송에 대해 더 우호적이었다.

――――――――――――――――――――――

구문 [7행~10행] ~, **jurors** assigned him more honesty // and were more favorable to his overall case in their final verdicts / because of that perceived honesty.

• 주어 jurors 다음에 두 개의 동사구 assigned ~ honesty와 were ~ honesty가 and로 연결되어 병렬구조를 이룬다.

[11행~14행] **Attorneys** are taught to "steal the opponent's thunder" / by mentioning a weakness in their case before the opposing lawyer does, / **thereby establishing** a perception of honesty in the eyes of jury members.

• thereby establishing 이하는 문장의 주어 Attorneys를 설명해주는 분사구문이다.

――――――――――――――――――――――

어휘 **hit on** ~을 생각해 내다 **ads** 광고(= **advertisements**) **drawback** 결점, 문제점 **tactic** 전략 **juror** 배심원 *cf.* **jury** 배심원단 **attorney** 변호사 **bring up** ~을 제기하다, 말 꺼내다 **favorable** 우호적인, 호의적인 **verdict** (배심원단의) 평결, 의견 **steal someone's thunder** ~에게 선수를 치다 **thereby** 그렇게 함으로써

5 문장 넣기 ⑤

해설 이 글의 경우 주어진 문장에 연결어 등의 단서가 없으므로 전체적인 흐름을 파악한다. 흐름상 주어진 문장의 'get some distance from the work(일에서 어느 정도 거리를 두다)'는 ⑤ 앞에 있는 'some idle time(약간의 한가한 시간)', 'taking a walk ~ a cup of coffee(캠퍼스 주변을 걷거나 커피 한 잔을 마시러 가는)'를 의미하므로, 주어진 문장은 ⑤에 들어가는 것이 가장 적절하다.

――――――――――――――――――――――

해석 성공적인 과학자들은 최대한의 창의성을 위해 자신들의 근무 시간을 구조화하는 법을 알아 왔다. 그들은 자신들이 하루 중 주어진 시간에 무엇을 가장 효과적으로 하는지를 바탕으로 한 프로젝트에서 다른 프로젝트로 이동한다. 독창적이고, 새롭고, 개념적인 작업인 문제를 발견하는 작업은 아침에 맨 처음에 할 때 가장 잘 된다. 많은 과학자들은 또한 글을 쓰는 일은 아침으로 계획하는데, 왜냐하면 이 일이 창의적인 개념화를 수반하기 때문이다. 과학자들은 늦은 아침과 점심 후에 구체적이고, 직접 해 보는 실험실 작업의 일정을 잡는 경향이 있다. 마지막으로, 많은 과학자들은 오후 늦게인 힘든 작업의 구체적인 단계 후에, 아마 캠퍼스 주변을 걷거나 커피 한 잔을 마시러 가는 약간의 한가한 시간을 잡는다고 이야기한다. 그들은 일에서 어느 정도 거리를 둘 때 소중한 통찰력이 자주 생겨난다는 것을 경험으로부터 배웠다. 그런 다음 과학자들은 글쓰기와 개념적인 작업으로 돌아감으로써 하루를 마감하는데, 종종 저녁을 먹은 후에 오랫동안 계속 일을 한다.

――――――――――――――――――――――

구문 [1행~3행] They've **learned** from experience / **that** valuable insights often emerge // when they get some distance from the work.

• that 이하는 동사 have learned의 목적어로, that은 접속사이다.

[13행~16행] Finally, many scientist **report** // **that** they schedule some idle time in the late afternoon, / after the concrete phase of hard work, / **perhaps taking a walk around campus** **or** **going for a cup of coffee**.

• that they schedule ~ the late afternoon은 동사 report의 목적어이며, that은 접속사이다. perhaps 이하는 분사구문이며 현재분사 taking a walk around campus와 going for a cup of coffee가 병렬구조를 이룬다.

――――――――――――――――――――――

어휘 **insight** 통찰력; 이해, 간파 **emerge** 생겨나다: 나타나다, 출현하다 **structure** 구조화하다, 조직하다; 구조(물); 건축물 **shift** 이동하다, 옮기다 **based on** ~을 바탕으로, ~에 근거하여 **conceptual** 개념적인, 개념의 *cf.* **conceptualization** 개념화 **first thing (in the morning)** (특히 아침에) 맨 처음에[먼저] **concrete** 구체적인; 콘크리트 **hands-on** 직접 해 보는, 실천하는 **laboratory** 실험실(의) **idle** 한가한; 게으른 **phase** 단계, 시기; 국면

1 글의 제목   ⑤

해설 이 글은 우리의 행동을 결정하는 요소는 본성과 양육뿐만이 아니라 자유 의지, 정황적 요인, 문화도 있다는 내용이므로, 제목으로 가장 적절한 것은 ⑤ '우리가 행동하는 방식으로 우리를 행동하게 만드는 것은 무엇인가?'이다.
① 우리의 자유 의지는 환상인가?
② 문화는 인간 행동에 어떤 영향을 미치는가?
③ 본성과 양육의 영향은 무엇인가?
④ 우리는 왜 우리가 선택한 방식으로 행동할 수 없는가?

해석 우리의 행동 중 어느 정도가 사실상 양육보다는 본성에 영향을 받는가? 더 나아가, 본성과 양육이 유일한 요소인가? 본성이 우리의 기질을 구성한다고 일반적으로 여겨지는 출생 전에 작동할 수 있는 생물학적 요소를 전부 포함하는 것은 아니다. 그렇다면 우리의 다른 모든 특징과 성향은 양육으로 설명되는가? 행동을 결정하는 데 있어 자유 의지와 정황적 요인은 원인이 되는 역할을 맡지 않는가? 문화가 불가피하게 행동에 영향을 미치지만, 시간이 흐르며 '일탈하는' 개인 결정자들이 문화에 영향을 미친다. 어떤 경우든 본성 대 양육은 쉬운 답을 내놓지 않는 저 근본적인 질문들 중 하나이다. '자유 의지'라는 어려운 문제에 관해서는, 우리가 상황을 고려하여 무엇을 할 것인지 결정하는 의식적 경험을 갖고 있기 때문에 자유 의지는 우리들 대부분이 믿고 있는 것이다. 이러한 의식적 경험은 환경적 요인이 우리가 하는 방식으로 결정하는 것을 대단히 그럴듯하게 만들어준다는 것을 안다고 해서 결코 제거되지 않는다는 점이 첨언될 수 있을 것이다.

구문 [3행~5행] Nature **does not cover** *all* the biological factors [that may be at work before birth] [that are generally considered to constitute our make-up].
● does not cover all은 '전부 포함하는 것은 아니다'라는 의미의 부분부정 구문이다. 두 개의 [ ]은 관계사절로 선행사 all the biological factors를 수식하고 있다.

[16행~19행] **It** might be added **that** this conscious experience is in no way removed by knowing **that** environmental factors make **it** *more than likely* **that** we decide in the way we do.
● It은 가주어이고 that 이하가 진주어이다. knowing 뒤에 that 이하는 knowing의 목적어 역할을 하는 명사절이며, 그 안의 it은 가목적어이고 more than likely는 보어이며, that we decide in the way we do가 진목적어이다.

어휘 nurture 양육   **at work** 작용하는   constitute 구성하다, 이루다   **make-up** 기질   trait 특징, 특질   account for 설명하다   contributory 원인이 되는   fundamental 근본적인, 기본적인   yield (결과를) 내다, 산출하다   **as to** ~에 관해서는   given ~을 고려하여   **in no way** 결코 ~ 않다
[선택지] illusion 환상, 망상; 착각

2 밑줄 어휘   ⑤

해설 이야기를 여러 번 다시 하는 과정에서 진위가 불분명한 세부 사항이 추가되어 반복되면 그 새로운 이야기가 기억 속에서 영구적인 버전으로 공고화되는데, 이때 애초에 그 이야기를 낳았던 실제 사건은 강화되는 것이 아니라 잊히는 것이므로 ⑤ strengthened를 forgotten으로 바꿔 써야 한다.

해석 당신이 여러 번 다시 말했던 이야기를 또 말하기 시작할 때, 당신이 기억에서 생각해내는 것은 이야기 그 자체에 대한 색인이다. 그 색인은 다양한 방식으로 꾸며질 수 있다. 시간이 흐르며, 심지어 꾸밈조차 ① 표준화된다. 한 노인이 수백 번 한 이야기에는 거의 변화가 없으며, 정말 존재하는 어떠한 변화도 그 기원과 관계없이 이야기 자체의 일부가 된다. 사람들은 발생했을지도 혹은 발생하지 않았을지도 모르는 세부 사항을 자신의 이야기에 첨가한다. 그들은 색인을 기억하고 세부 사항을 ② 재구성하고 있다. 어떤 시점에서 그들이 그것의(세부 사항의) 타당성을 정말로 확신하지 못한 채로 멋진 세부 사항을 첨가하면, 그 동일한 세부 사항을 곁들여 몇 번 더 이야기를 하는 것은 이야기 색인에서 그것의 ③ 영구적 장소를 보장해줄 것이다. 다시 말해서 우리가 되풀이하여 하는 이야기들은 그 이야기가 말하는 사건들에 대해 우리가 갖고 있는 기억과 일치한다. 이야기는 이야기하기의 과정 때문에, 이야기꾼이 덧붙인 윤색 때문에 시간이 흐르며 ④ 변화한다. 애초에 그 이야기를 낳았던 실제 사건들은 오래전에 ⑤ 강화되었(→ 망각되었)다.

구문 [5행~8행] An old man's story [**that** he has told hundreds of times] shows little variation, // and *any variation* [**that** does exist] becomes part of the story itself, regardless of its origin.
● 첫 번째 [ ]은 목적격 관계대명사 that이 이끄는 관계사절로 An old man's story를 수식하고, 두 번째 [ ]은 주격 관계대명사 that이 이끄는 관계사절로 any variation을 수식한다.

[13행~16행] In other words, *the stories* [(which[that]) we tell time and again] are identical to *the memory* [(which[that]) we have of *the events* [that the story relates]].
● 첫 번째 [ ]은 목적격 관계대명사 which[that]가 생략된 관계사절로 the stories를 수식한다. we have ~ relates 역시 which[that]가 생략된 관계사절로 the memory를 수식하고 그 안의 that the story relates는 the events를 수식한다.

어휘 retrieve 생각해내다, 되찾다   index 색인, 지표; 표시   standardize 표준화하다   variation 변화, 변형   validity 타당성; 유효성   ensure 보장[확보]하다   permanent 영구적인   time and again 되풀이하여   identical 일치하는; 동일한   relate 관련시키다   **in the first place** 애초에

3 빈칸 추론   ③

해설 아이들은 눈의 작은 근육을 움직이는 것이 힘들기 때문에, 성인이 초점의 왼쪽으로 두 글자, 오른쪽으로 여섯에서 여덟 글자를 보는 데 비해 아이들은 양쪽으로 한 글자씩 본다고 설명한다. 아이들이 눈 근육이 발달하기 시작할 때 빈칸의 내용을 할 수 있으며, 더 길고 생소한 단어를 처리할 수 있다는 것으로 보아 능숙한 어른의 경우처럼 되는 것, 즉 ③ '초점의 오른쪽에 있는 더 많은 글자를 받아들일' 수 있다는 내용이 가장 적절하다.
① 초점이 되는 측면을 뒤집을
② 양쪽 정보의 양을 조절할
④ 자신들이 보는 단어들의 가장 핵심적인 부분을 파악할
⑤ 자신들이 양쪽에서 보는 글자의 수를 균형을 맞출

해석 아이들이 직면하는 어려움 중 일부는 눈을 인쇄된 활자의 행을 가로질러 왼쪽에서 오른쪽으로 움직이도록 훈련하는 데 있다. 눈은 작은 근육 움직임으로 통제되는데, 아이들에게 작은 근육 움직임은 그 자체로 힘든 일이다. 눈이 인쇄된 활자의 행을 가로질러 움직일 때, 눈은 초점을 맞추기 위해 잠시 멈추면서 일련의 급격한 이동을 한다. 경험 많은 성인 독자는 보통 초점의 왼쪽으로 두 글자를 보고 (초점의) 오른쪽으로 여섯에서 여덟 글자를 본다. 하지만 경험이 없는 아이 독자는 초점의 왼쪽으로 한 글자를 보고 (초점의) 오른쪽으로 한 글자를 본다. 이런 신체적 현실은 읽기를 배우는 아이들이 다섯 글자 미만으로 이루어진 단어를 이해하기가 더 쉽다고 여기는 이유를 설명한다. 눈 근육이 발달하기 시작하면서, 아이들은 차츰 초점의 오른

쪽에 있는 더 많은 글자를 받아들일 수 있으며 더 길고, 생소한 단어를 처리할 수 있다.

구문 [11행~13행] This physical reality explains // **why** *children* (learning to read) find **it** easier **to decode** *words* (made up of fewer than five letters).

• 의문사 why가 이끄는 의문사절이 동사 explains의 목적어 역할을 하며, 의문사절에서 it은 가목적어이고 to decode 이하가 진목적어이다. 두 ( ) 부분은 각각 children과 words를 수식한다.

어휘 **face** 직면하다; 마주보다 **in and of oneself** 그것 자체로 **a series of** 일련의 **typically** 보통 **decode** 이해하다; 해독하다 **gradually** 차츰, 서서히 **handle** 처리하다, 다루다

[선택지] **grasp** 파악하다

4 무관 문장 ④

해설 전체적인 글의 내용은 통념과는 달리 사망률의 급격한 감소는 의학보다는 위생과 영양의 개선에 힘입은 바가 크다는 내용인데, ④번 문장은 의학이 우리의 삶을 근본적으로 바꾸었다는 내용이므로 글의 흐름과 맞지 않다.

해석 건강과 좋지 못한 건강의 분포는 역사학과 사회 과학적 관점에서 분석되어 왔다. ① 어떤 사람들은 자주 주장되는 것만큼 의학이 효과적인 것은 아니라고 주장해 왔다. ② 의학 분야 저자인 토머스 매큐언은 19세기 가장 치명적인 질병의 대부분이 항생제나 면역 프로그램이 도래하기 이전에 사라졌다는 것을 입증했다. ③ 그는 실질 임금 상승에서 연유한 위생 향상과 더 나은 영양 섭취와 같은 전반적인 생활 환경에 있어서의 사회적 진보가 지난 세기 동안 이룩된 사망률 감소의 대부분에 대한 원인이었다고 추론했다. ④ 이러한 결론에 따르면, 주요 의학적 돌파구에서 나온 대중 건강 증진은 우리가 사는 환경을 급격히 변화시킴으로써 인간적이라는 것이 무엇을 의미하는지를 근본적으로 바꾸어놓았다. ⑤ 그의 주장은 이의가 제기되고 있지만, 생활 환경의 향상으로 인한 영향과 비교할 때 사망률 감소에 대한 의학의 기여는 사소했다는 것에 대한 이의는 거의 없다.

구문 [8행~12행] He reasoned // **that social advances** in overall living conditions, such as *improved sanitation and better nutrition* (resulting from rising real wages), **have been** responsible for the majority of *the reduction in mortality* (achieved during the last century).

• 동사 reasoned의 목적어 역할을 하는 that절의 주어는 social advances이고 동사는 have been이다. ( ) 부분은 각각 improved sanitation and better nutrition, the reduction in mortality를 수식한다.

어휘 **distribution** 분포, 분배 **fatal** 치명적인(= **lethal**) **antibiotic** 항생제 **immunization** 면역 **reason** 추론하다 **advance** 진보, 발전; 전진하다, 나아가다 **overall** 전반적인 **nutrition** 영양 (처리 과정) **wage** 임금 **responsible for** ~에 원인[책임]이 있는 **mortality** 사망률 **breakthrough** 돌파구 **assertion** 주장 **dispute** 이의를 제기하다, 반박하다

5 요약문 완성 ②

해설 대부분 사람은 이야기되지 않고 있는 것에 대해서는 주의를 기울이거나 알아차리지 못하지만, 능동적인 청자는 말하는 사람의 어조나 몸짓에서 이야기되지 않고 있는 것을 알아차려서 더 깊은 수준의 응답을 할 수 있다고 했다. 따라서, 이를 요약하면 '표면적으로 (superficially) 듣는 이들과는 다르게, 쉽게 눈치채지 못하는 것들을 감지하는(detect) 이들은 말해지지 않은 것을 종종 들을 수 있다'가 된다.

해석 우리 대부분은 일반적으로, 꽤 표면적인 수준에서 (남의 말을) 듣고 (내 말이 남에게) 들리는 데 익숙하다. 우리는 이야기되지 않고 있는 것에 대해서는 많은 주의를 기울이거나 말속에서 미묘하게 부조화한 것을 알아차리지 못하며, 또한 사람의 말 뒤에 숨은 감정도 그것이 명백하거나 분명하지 않다면 듣지 못한다. 이사를 하여 새로운 도시에 살게 되어 신난다고 말하는 고객을 생각해 보라. 우리는 그 말을 듣고 그에 따라 반응을 하여, 그녀를 위해 우리가 얼마나 기쁜지, 그리고 그녀가 얼마나 멋진 경험을 하게 될지 그 고객에게 말한다. 능동적인 청자라면 말하는 사람이 대답하기 전에 깊이 숨을 들이쉬거나 어깨를 살짝 으쓱하는 것에 주목하면서 말 사이의 숨은 뜻을 들을지도 모른다. 그들은 (그녀의 말에서) 살짝 침울한 어조를 듣거나, 그녀의 눈에 나타난 표정에 주목할 수도 있을 터인데, 그것은 비록 이사가 신나는 일일지는 모르지만, 다른 감정도 작용하고 있다는 것, 즉 어쩌면 그녀는 그렇게 큰 걸음을 내딛는 것을 두려워하고 있거나 친구와 가족을 두고 떠나는 것에 대하여 조심스러울지도 모른다는 것을 나타낸다. 능동적인 청자는 그녀의 말을 듣고 그녀가 전하는 다른 정보에 주목하며, 그래서 더 깊은 수준에서 응답할 수 있다.

(A) 표면적으로 듣는 이들과는 다르게, 능동적인 청자는 말해지지 않은 것을 종종 (B) 감지할 수 있다.

구문 [1행~2행] Most of us **are** typically **used to listening** (on a fairly surface level) and (are used to) **being listened** to on a fairly surface level.

• 「be used to v-ing」는 'v 하는 데 익숙하다'의 뜻이다. 밑줄 친 부분은 반복되는 어구가 생략되고 and로 연결된 병렬구조이다.

[7행~9행] We hear the words and respond accordingly, **telling** the person **how** happy we are for her and **what** a great adventure she will have.

• telling the person ~ she will have 부분은 능동의 의미인 분사구문이며, 현재분사 telling의 직접 목적어로 의문사 how절과 what절이 and로 연결된 병렬구조이다.

어휘 **fairly** 꽤, 매우 **pick up on** ~을 알아차리다[이해하다] **subtle** 미묘한 **obvious** 명백한 **intake** (숨을) 들이쉼 **shrug** (어깨를) 으쓱하다 **indicate** 나타내다 **at play** 작용하고 있는 **cautious** 조심스러운, 신중한

[선택지] **superficially** 표면적으로 **detect** 감지하다, 알아내다 **disregard** 무시하다 **attentively** 유심히, 신경 써서 **perceive** 인지하다

1 빈칸 추론   ①

해설 백열전구를 더 많이 팔기 위해 기업 연합을 만들어 백열전구의 수명을 의도적으로 줄이고 이를 어기면 벌금까지 부과했다는 내용이므로, 이는 ① '계획적 파손 가능성'의 가장 유명한 사례라고 할 수 있다.
② 경쟁적 이점
③ 점진적인 개선
④ 안정화 실험
⑤ 실패한 기술

해석 아마도 계획적 파손 가능성의 가장 유명한 사례는 백열전구의 사례일 것이다. 백열전구가 발명된 지 150년이 넘은 오늘날, 현대의 일반적인 백열전구는 750시간 동안 지속된다. 그렇다면 110년 동안 멈추지 않고 환히 비춰 오고 있는 캘리포니아 주 리버모어의 백열전구는 왜 존재하는가? 그것은 1924년 제네바에서 모든 백열전구 제조업체가 모여, 백열전구의 수명을 줄이기 위해 그 당시 Phoebus라고 불리는 기업 연합을 만들었기 때문이다. 필라멘트를 요구되는 것보다 덜 안정적으로 만듦으로써, 백열전구는 더 빠르게 소진되곤 했고 기업 연합은 더 많이 팔 수 있었다. 그것(기업 연합)은 매우 엄중해서, 백열전구가 1,500시간 넘게 지속되면 제조업체는 벌금이 부과되었다. 1924년 이전에는 일반적인 백열전구는 약 2,500시간 지속됐다. 십 년 이내에 그것은 1,500시간이 되었고 그로부터 오늘날의 750시간으로 감소했다.

구문 [6행~9행] It's because in 1924 in Geneva, all the light bulb manufacturers got together and created *a cartel*, **at the time called Phoebus**, **to cut** the life of a light bulb.

• at the time called Phoebus는 a cartel을 부가적으로 수식하는 분사구이다. to cut ~ bulb는 목적을 나타내는 to부정사구이다.

[11행~13행] It was **so** serious **that** manufacturers were fined // **if** their light bulbs lasted more than 1,500 hours.

•「so ~ that ...」 구문은 '너무 ~해서 …하다'의 뜻이다. if their ~ 1,500 hours 부분은 조건의 의미를 나타내는 if절이다.

어휘 manufacturer 제조업체   cartel 기업 연합   fine 벌금(을 부과하다)
[선택지] breakability 파손 가능성, 깨지기 쉬움   gradual 점진적인, 단계적인
improvement 개선, 향상   stabilization 안정화

2 글의 순서   ③

해설 매우 긴 시간을 다루는 지질학을 설명하는 주어진 글 이후에는 '그럼에도 불구하고(Nevertheless)'로 시작하여 '지질 활동의 시간의 척도가 중요하다'는 내용의 (B)가 와야 한다. (B)에서 그 이유로 인간이 자연계에 끼친 영향을 측정하기 위함이 언급되었고, 이어서 (A)의 '지구 온난화 평가를 위한 수백만 년간 기후 변화 이해'와 (C) '농업으로 인한 표토(表土)의 부식에 대한 이해'는 유사한 맥락으로 모두 (B)에 대한 예시이므로 '예를 들어(For example)'로 시작하는 (C)가 먼저 오고, '마찬가지로(Likewise)'로 시작하는 (A)가 그 뒤에 와야 한다.

해석 극도로 긴 시간에 대한 관심은 지질학과 천문학을 다른 과학과 구별해준다. 지질학자들은 지구의 나이와 지구의 가장 오래된 암석들에 대해 수십억 년의 관점에서 생각하는데, 그런 숫자들은 국가 부채처럼 쉽게 이해되지 않는 것이다.
(B) 그럼에도 불구하고 지질 활동에 대한 시간의 척도는 환경 지질학자들에게 중요한데, 그것은 자연계에 끼친 인간의 영향을 측정하는 방법을 제공하기 때문이다.

(C) 예를 들어 우리는 농업으로 인한 표토(表土)의 부식이 매우 큰지 아닌지를 밝히기 위해서 단단한 암석으로부터의 자연적인 토양 생성의 속도를 알고 싶어 한다.
(A) 마찬가지로 기후가 지난 수백만 년 동안 어떻게 변해 왔는지 이해하는 것은 현재의 지구 온난화 경향을 제대로 평가하기 위해 필수적이다. 다행히 과거 환경 변화에 관한 단서들은 서로 다른 많은 종류의 암석들에 잘 보존되어 있다.

구문 [3행~5행] Geologists think in terms of billions of years for *the age of Earth and its oldest rocks* — **numbers** [**that**, (like the national debt), **are** not easily understood].

• numbers는 the age of Earth ~ rocks를 의미한다. [ ] 부분은 관계사절로 numbers를 수식하며, 여기서 관계대명사 that과 동사 are 사이에 전명구가 삽입된 구조이다.

[6행~8행] Likewise, <u>understanding **how** climate has changed over millions of years **is** vital</u> to properly assess current global warming trends.

• 밑줄 친 부분은 동명사구 주어이고, is가 동사이다. how climate ~ of years는 명사절로 understanding의 목적어 역할을 한다.

[15행~17행] For example, we would like to know the rate of natural soil formation from solid rock **to determine whether** topsoil erosion from agriculture is too great.

• to determine 이하는 목적을 나타내는 to 부정사구이다. whether 이하의 명사절이 determine의 목적어 역할을 하고 있으며, whether는 '~인지 아닌지'의 의미이다.

어휘 extremely 극도로   set A apart from B A를 B와 구별시키다   geology 지질학
cf. geologist 지질학자   astronomy 천문학   in terms of ~의 관점에서   debt 빚, 부채   vital 필수적인   assess 평가하다   scale 척도, 기준; 규모   natural world 자연계   topsoil 표토(表土) (퇴적한 토층(土層)의 가장 윗부분)   agriculture 농업

3 문장 넣기   ⑤

해설 주어진 문장은 ③ 뒤에서 언급된 '자신의 먹는 행동을 적절히 조정한다'는 것의 구체적 내용이다. 주어진 문장에 likewise(마찬가지로)가 있으므로 비슷한 내용의 다른 구체적인 내용이 앞에 와야 하는데, ⑤ 앞에서 소금이 부족해지면 소금에 대한 즉각적인 선호를 보인다는 구체적 내용이 나왔으므로, 주어진 문장은 ⑤에 들어가는 것이 가장 적절하다.

해석 인간은 음식에 대한 선호를 진화시켜 왔는가? 사람과 쥐 둘 다 '단' 음식에 대한 맛의 선호를 진화시켜 왔는데, 그 단 음식은 풍부한 열량의 원천을 제공한다. 탄자니아의 Hadza 수렵 채집인들 사이에서의 음식 선호에 관한 연구는 가장 높은 열량 값을 가지는 식품인 꿀이 가장 선호되는 식품인 것을 발견했다. 인간의 갓난아기 또한 단 액체에 대한 강한 선호를 보인다. 사람과 쥐 둘 다 '쓰'고 '신' 음식을 싫어하는데, 그 음식들은 독소를 함유하는 경향이 있다. 그들은 또한 자신의 먹는 행동을 물, 열량, 소금의 부족에 응하여 적절히 조정한다. 실험은 쥐가 소금 결핍을 처음 경험할 때 소금에 대한 즉각적인 선호를 나타내는 것을 보여주었다. 마찬가지로 그것들은 에너지와 체액이 고갈되면 단것과 물 섭취를 증가시킨다. 이것들은 음식 선택의 적응적 문제를 다루고 섭취 패턴을 신체적 욕구와 조화시키도록 고안된, 특정한 진화된 메커니즘처럼 보인다.

구문 [5행~8행] A study of food preferences among the Hadza hunter-gatherers of Tanzania found // that <u>honey</u> was the most highly preferred food item, / *the item* [that has the highest caloric value].

of penmanship must be protected.

- Although절은 비교 구문으로서 현재와 과거를 비교하고 있다. 과거 내용을 말하는 than ~ 부분에서 was 다음에는 widespread가 반복을 피하기 위해 생략되었다.

[23행~27행] In fact, **it seems highly unlikely that** handwritten communication will ever disappear completely, since there is always <u>the possibility</u> **of** <u>not having a computer available at a particular moment</u>.

- 「it seems likely that ~」은 '~할 가능성이 있다'는 뜻이므로, 「it seems highly unlikely that ~」은 '~일 가능성이 별로 없다'라는 뜻이 된다. 밑줄 친 the possibility와 of 뒷부분은 서로 동격 관계이다.

어휘 **constantly** 끊임없이 **hammer away** ~를 열심히 하다, ~을 거듭해서 하다 **penmanship** 서법, 습자 **outdated** 시대에 뒤떨어진, 구식의 **inefficient** 비효율적인, 쓸모없는 **at one time** 일찍이 **document** 문서 **widespread** 광범위한, 널리 퍼진 **maintain** 유지하다 **tragedy** 비극, 비극적인 이야기 **distinctive** 독특한, 특색 있는, 뚜렷이 구별되는 **alive and well** 남아서, 건재하여

[선택지] era 시대

• honey와 the item ~ caloric value가 동격 관계이고, [ ] 부분은 the item을 수식하는 관계사절이다.

[16행~19행] *These* appear to be specific evolved mechanisms, / **designed** to deal with the adaptive problem of food selection / and (to) coordinate consumption patterns with physical needs.

- designed 이하는 These를 의미상 주어로 하는 수동 분사구문이다. 밑줄 친 두 to부정사구가 and로 연결되어 병렬구조를 이룬다.

어휘 **intake** 섭취(량); 흡입(구) **fluid** 체액; 액체, 유동체 **deplete** 고갈시키다 **evolve** 진화하다; 발전하다 **preference** 선호(도), 기호 *cf.* **prefer** 선호하다, ~을 (더) 좋아하다 **calorie** 열량, 칼로리 **hunter-gatherer** 수렵 채집인 **newborn infant** 갓난아기, 신생아 **liquid** 액체; 액상의; 유동적인 **contain** 함유하다; 억누르다 **toxin** 독소 **adjust** 조정하다; 적응하다 **in response to A** A에 응하여[답하여] **deficit** 부족; 적자 *cf.* **deficiency** 결핍, 부족 **immediate** 즉각적인; 직접적인 **coordinate** 조화시키다; 조정하다 **consumption** 섭취; 소비

4~5 장문   4 ② 5 ④

해설 4. 첫 단락에서 디지털 시대에 이르러 손으로 거의 글씨를 쓰지 않게 됨에 따라 손 글씨 보존이 필요한가에 대한 문제 제기를 하였고 두 번째, 세 번째 단락에서는 손 글씨가 계속해서 보존이 되어야 하는 필요성들을 나열한 뒤 손 글씨가 미래에도 건재할 것이라는 내용으로 마무리하고 있으므로 제목으로는 ② '손 글씨가 디지털 시대에 살아남을 것인가?'가 적절하다.

① 디지털 텍스트의 이해와 생성
③ 손 글씨 종말의 원인과 결과
④ 무선 의사소통 대 손 글씨 메모
⑤ 손 글씨의 종말로 우리는 무엇을 잃고 있는가?

5. 손 글씨는 사람의 목소리나 웃음과 같이 독특하다고 했으므로, 손 글씨 의사소통을 보존함으로써 쓴 사람의 개성과 연결을 유지할 수 있음을 알 수 있다. 그러므로 ④는 preserving 등이 되어야 한다.

해석 오늘날 사람들은 끊임없이 키보드를 열심히 치거나 스마트폰으로 문자메시지를 보낸다. 그들은 더 이상 손으로 글을 쓰지 않는다. 이로 인해 손 글씨 쓰기가 시대에 뒤떨어지고 비효율적인 의사소통의 방식으로 되는가? 혹은 이것을 보존하려고 노력하는 것이 가치가 있는가? 일찍이, 명확하고 빠르게 글씨를 쓰는 것이 공적 문서부터 개인적인 편지에 이르기까지 모든 것에 필수적이었다. 하지만, 이메일과 문자메시지의 시대에서 대부분의 사람들은 쇼핑 목록이나 짧은 메모 이상으로 글씨를 쓸 필요가 (a) 거의 없다.

비록 손 글씨 의사소통이 이전에 그랬듯이 (b) 일반적이지 않을지라도, 많은 사람들은 계속해서 손 글씨 기술이 반드시 보호되어야 한다고 믿는다. 그들은 그것이 손 글씨로 된 문서를 읽고, 그럼으로써 과거와 직접적인 연결을 유지하는 데 필수적이라고 주장한다. 그들에게는 어떤 사람이 어느 날 할머니의 일기장을 발견해서 그것을 읽을 수 없다는 게 비극이다. 게다가 사람들은 한 사람의 손 글씨는 (c) 독특하고 사람의 목소리나 웃음과 같은 것이 될 수 있다는 데 주목한다. 손 글씨 의사소통을 (d) 끝냄(→ 보존함)으로써, 우리는 또한 쓴 사람의 개성과 연결을 유지할 수 있다고 그들은 주장한다.

흥미롭게도, 기술의 발전이 손으로 글씨 쓰는 것의 필요성을 완전히 없앤 것은 아니다. 사실, 손 글씨 의사소통이 완전히 (e) 없어지리라는 가능성은 별로 없어 보이는데 왜냐하면 특정한 순간에 사용 가능한 컴퓨터를 가지고 있지 않을 가능성이 항상 있기 때문이다. 디지털 시대에서조차, 손으로 쓰인 단어는 아주 몹시 건재하며, 이것은 바뀌지 않을 것으로 보인다.

구문 **[10행~12행]** **Although** handwritten communication is **less** widespread **than** it once was (widespread), // many people continue to believe that the art

1 필자 주장　　　　　　　　　　　　⑤

해설 훌륭한 교사는 '그들의 지혜가 현실에서 검증받는 자들', 그리고 '자신이 아는 것을 계속하여 변화하는 세상에 맞추는 사람'이라는 내용이므로 필자의 주장으로 가장 적절한 것은 ⑤ '교사는 자신의 지식을 세상에 맞게 변화시키려고 노력해야 한다.'이다.

해석 교사 측에서 가장 중요한 것 중 하나는 기꺼이 약간의 겸손을 보이는 것, 자신의 분투를 드러내는 것, 그리고 자신의 삶과 메시지를 일치하게 만드는 것이다. 그들은 완벽할 필요는 없지만, 자신의 삶을 자신의 이상과 방법을 위한 실험실로 사용하고 있다면 더 나은 교사가 될 것이다. 가장 훌륭한 교사들은 '상처 입은 치유자들', 즉 그들의 지혜가 현실에서 검증받는 자들이다. 좋은 교사들은 자신이 아는 것을 계속하여 변화하는 세상에 맞추면서 항상 스스로 배운다. 수년에 걸쳐 정적인 채로 남아 있는 개인 성장에 대한 연설이나 영적 설교를 다듬어온 사람들의 말을 듣는 것보다 더 나쁜 것은 없다. 종교적 혹은 학문적 수련, 학위, 책, 그리고 이전의 교직 직위가 고도로 훈련받은 교사 혹은 치료사임을 나타낼지도 모르는 증명서이기는 하지만, 이 사람이 지속적으로 자기 주위의 세상에서 자신의 지식을 검증하는 방식이 마찬가지로 중요하다.

구문 [1행~4행] One of the most important things on the part of the teacher is a willingness to show some humility, to reveal their struggles, and to attempt to make their life and their message congruent.
- 밑줄 친 세 부분이 and로 연결되어 병렬구조를 이룬다.

[16행~18행] ~ equally important **are *the ways*** [in which this person continually tests her knowledge in the world around her].
- 문장의 동사는 are, 주어는 the ways인 도치 문장이다. equally important는 주어를 설명하는 보어이다. [ ]은 the ways를 수식한다.

어휘 willingness 기꺼이 하는 마음　humility 겸손　struggle 분투, 투쟁　ideal 이상　superb 최고의, 훌륭한　wound 부상을 입히다　healer 치유자　adapt A to B A를 B에 맞추다, 조정하다　polish 다듬다, 닦다　sermon 설교　static 정적인, 정체된; 고정된　indicate 나타내다　therapist 치료사

2 밑줄 함의　　　　　　　　　　　　②

해설 놀이는 쓸모가 없어서 우리로 하여금 우리 존재를 '자유롭게' 표현하도록 해주기 때문에 중요한데, 놀이가 직업이 되면 그것이 더 이상 자기 존재의 표현을 위한 것이 아닌, 타인의 목적을 위해 사용되는 것이므로 '철제 우리'의 일부가 된다고 한다. 따라서 '철제 우리'의 의미로는 ② '자유가 완전히 사라지는 지루한 일상'이 적절하다.
① 철제 가면 뒤에 숨겨진 비밀스러운 정체
③ 생계를 위한 노동이 아닌 삶 자체를 위한 일
④ 인내심을 잃게 하는 짜증의 근원
⑤ 다른 사람들의 기준에 의해 측정된 세속적 성공

해석 놀이는 중요한 생존 과정을 다루지 않기 때문에, 즉 쓸모가 없기 때문에 종종 어린이를 위한 것이라고 치부되곤 한다. 그러나 이것은 엄청난 오해이다. 놀이는 쓸모가 없기 '때문에' 중요한데, 그것이 우리로 하여금 필요나 편리함 때문이 아니라 우리 존재를 자유롭게 표현하기 위해 행동하도록 해주기 때문이다. 그러나 놀이가 직업이 되어서 이것이 수반하는 모든 외적인 보상과 책임을 갖게 되면, 다시 문제가

시작된다. 일류의 관현악단에서 연주하는 음악가나 정예 팀과 수백만 달러의 계약을 맺고 뛰는 선수들은 자신의 존재를 표현하기 위해 (그것을) 한다고 더 이상 느끼지 않는다. 대신에, 그들은 자신들의 기술이 다른 사람들의 목적을 위해 다른 사람들에 의해 사용되고 있다고 느끼기 시작한다. 그렇게 되면, 의식의 자유로운 흐름을 허용하는 대신, 놀이조차도 철제 우리의 일부가 되어 버린다.

구문 [7행~9행] The problem, however, starts again // when play becomes a profession — with *all the external rewards and responsibilities* [that this entails].
- [ ] 부분은 목적격 관계대명사 that이 이끄는 관계사절로 앞의 명사구 all the ~ responsibilities를 수식한다.

[9행~12행] *Musicians* (playing for leading symphony orchestras), **or** *athletes* (playing for multimillion contracts with elite teams), no longer feel that they play to express their being.
- 밑줄 친 두 부분이 or로 연결된 Musicians ~ elite teams가 주어이며, 두 개의 ( ) 부분은 모두 현재분사구로 각각 Musicians와 athletes를 수식한다.

어휘 discount 치부하다, 무시하다　deal with ~을 다루다[처리하다]　useless 쓸모 없는　profound 엄청난, 대단한; 심오한　necessity 필요(성)　convenience 편리함, 편의　profession 직업, 전문적인 일　external 외적인, 외부의　entail 수반하다　allow for ~을 허용하다[가능하게 하다]　consciousness 의식
[선택지] identity 정체(성); 동일함, 일치　make a living 생계를 꾸리다　irritation 짜증(나게 하는 것); 자극(물)　patience 인내(심); 참을성　worldly 세속적인; 속세의

3 빈칸 추론　　　　　　　　　　　　③

해설 패션과 스타일의 근대사에 관한 글이다. 빈칸 문장 앞에서 이 시기의 패션은 수 세기 동안 변하지 않고, 부유하지 않으면 많은 품목을 소유하지 못한다고 했다. 또한, 후반부에서 however(그러나)로 흐름을 전환하기 전까지는 사회적 계급이 누가 무엇을 입는지를 결정했다고 했으므로, 이 기간에 스타일은 ③ '시간이 지나면서 고정되었을 뿐만 아니라 계급에 의해 엄격히 나뉘었다'는 것을 알 수 있다.
① 외부의 힘에 쉽게 영향을 받았다
② 가장 부유한 사람들의 선호에 대한 반영이었다
④ 사회적 위치보다는 스타일에서의 선호에 의해 결정되었다
⑤ 그 안에 내재하는 혁명적 힘 때문에 변하기 어려웠다

해석 근대기로 한창 접어들 때까지, 직물은 세계 제1의 공장 생산품이었다. 흔히 은, 금, 그리고 비단으로 짜인 그것들(직물)은 또한 빈부 모두에게 축적된 부를 나타내는 주요 형태이기도 했는데, 대부분의 가정은 자신들의 등에 재산을 걸치고 벽과 창문에 그것을 매달았다. 더 중요한 것은, 사람들이 이러한 직물 재산을 자신들의 부모로부터 물려받았다는 것이다. 패션은 수 세기 동안 비교적 변하지 않았으며, 가장 부유한 사람들 외에 모두는 다만 몇 안 되는 품목들만 소유했다. 이 기간에 스타일은 시간이 지나면서 고정되었을 뿐만 아니라 계급에 의해 엄격히 나뉘었다. 사치 금지법으로 강화된 경직된 사회 구조는 바로 누가 무엇을 입을 수 있는지를 결정했다. 그러나 17세기 중반에 동인도 회사는 단지 몇십 년 만에 영국의 산업, 무역, 패션, 그리고 사회적 계급의 세계를 다 뒤집어엎으면서 이 아주 오래된 현상을 파괴했다. 이 상업적 혁명에서 그 회사의 도구는 면화였다.

구문 [2행~6행] **Often woven with silver, gold, and silk,** / *they* were also the chief form of stored wealth for both rich and poor; // most families wore their estate on their backs and hung it on their walls and windows.

• Often woven ~ and silk는 앞에 being이 생략된 분사구문이며, 의미상의 주어는 they(= textiles)이다.

어휘 **era** 시대 **textile** 직물, 옷감 **primary** 제1의, 주요한 **weave** (실을) 짜다, 엮다 **estate** 재산; 소유지 **inherit** 물려받다, 상속받다 **all but** ~외에 모두 **inflexible** 경직된, 유연성이 없는 **reinforce** 강화하다 **age-old** 아주 오래된 **state of affairs** 현상, 상황 **turn A upside down** A를 다 뒤집어엎다 **decade** 10년
[선택지] **readily** 손쉽게 **rigidly** 엄격히 **revolutionary** 혁명적인 **inherent** 내재하는

4 글의 순서

해설 이 글은 식물은 제대로 된 분류가 이뤄지지 않고 있다는 점을 지적하고 있다. 주어진 문장에서 문제를 제기하며 다른 식품부에는 상세한 항목 분류가 있다는 점을 언급한다. 이에 대한 구체적인 예로 (B)가 이어지고, (B)의 고기류와 대조되는 농산물의 경우가 (C)에 이어지며, (C)의 건강상의 문제에 대한 예가 (A)에서 이어지는 것이 적절하다.

해석 분명히, 식물은 제대로 분류될 만큼 중요하다고 여겨지지 않는다. 심지어 일반 슈퍼마켓에서조차 다른 식품 (판매)부에는 더 상세한 품목들이 있다는 것을 알 수 있다.
(B) 고기 (판매)부는 가금류, 생선, 그리고 붉은 육류로 분류된다. 불편하고 명확하지 않기 때문에 아무도 치즈와 고기를 함께 한 종류의 '샌드위치 식품'으로 분류하려고 하지 않는다.
(C) 하지만, 이런 종류의 혼동과 실수가 농산물 파트에서는 계속해서 발생한다. 이러한 실수 중의 일부는 그 정도가 상당히 심각해서 그것들이 건강상의 문제를 일으킬 수도 있다.
(A) 예를 들어, 전분 뿌리 식물들을 토마토와 함께 진열하게 되면 고객들이 부적절한 식품 결합 선택을 하게 만드는데, 이는 장에서 발효가 일어나게 하고 가스를 만들어낼 수 있다.

구문 [5행~8행] For example, **placing** starch roots in the same category with tomatoes **could prompt** customers to make *improper food-combination choices*, // **which can create fermentation and gas in our intestines.**
• 동명사 placing으로 시작하는 placing ~ tomatoes가 문장의 주어이며, 동사는 could prompt이다. 관계대명사 which가 이끄는 계속적 용법의 관계사절이 improper ~ choices를 보충 설명한다.

어휘 **classify** 분류[구분]하다 *cf.* **classification** 분류, 구분; 유형, 범주 **detailed** 상세한, 세부적인 **starch** 전분, 녹말가루 **root** 뿌리; 근원, 기원 **prompt** 유도[촉발]하다; 즉각적인, 신속한 **improper** 부적절한; 부당한, 부도덕한 **fermentation** 발효 (작용) **poultry** 가금류 **confusion** 혼동; 혼란(스러운 상황) **produce** 농산물; 생산하다

5 문장 넣기

해설 이 글은 우리 인간이 사회적 유대를 형성하려는 욕구를 갖고 있기도 하지만 낯선 사람들에 대한 선천적인 두려움도 갖고 있어서 비교적 규모가 작은 사회 집단을 형성하게 된 것이라는 내용이다. 주어진 문장의 This inherent conflict(이 타고난 충돌)를 통해 이 문장 앞에 선천적으로 충돌하는 두 가지 요소(사회적 접촉에 대한 욕구와 낯선 사람들에 대한 두려움)가 나와야 하고 이러한 충돌의 해법(비교적 규모가 작은 사회 집단을 형성하는 것)이 ④ 다음에 나오고 있으므로 주어진 문장은 ④에 들어가는 것이 가장 적절하다.

해석 인간의 사회생활은 부모의 돌봄과 모자 간 유대의 발전에서 시작된다. 엄마와 유아, 그리고 나중의 아빠와 유아 사이의 행동은 성인의 긴밀한 유대, 우정, 그리고 사랑을 위한 주춧돌이 되는데, 이것들 모두는 사회 조직의 중심에 있다. 안타깝게도 인간을 포함해서 모든 포유동물들은 (같은 종의) 다른 동물들에 대해 모순된 감정을 보여준다. 우리가 사회적 접촉을 하도록 강력하게 유전적으로 정해진 만큼 우리는 또한 '낯선 사람 공포증', 즉 낯선 사람들을 두려워하도록 유전적으로 정해져 있다. 이 두려움은 삶의 첫해의 후반기에 시작되고, 비록 그것이 문화로 경감될 수는 있긴 하지만 인간의 사회적 관계에서 절대 완전히 없어지지는 않는다. 이 타고난 충돌이 우리가 비교적 규모가 작은 사회 집단으로 발전해 가도록 몰고 간 것일지도 모른다. 즉, 우리는 사회적 유대를 필요로 했지만 두려움을 자아내는 낯선 사람들과의 접촉은 되도록 적게 해야 했던 것이다. 따라서, 완벽한 해결책은 친숙한 사람들로 구성된, 고정되고 비교적 규모가 작은 집단이다. 물론, 현대의 도시 생활은 이 점에 있어서는 심각한 문제를 제기한다.

구문 [6행~10행] *The behavior* (between mother and infant, and later between father and infant), **is** the foundation stone for *adult bonding, friendliness, and love*, // **all of which are at the heart of social organization.**
• between ~ infant는 전명구로서 주어 The behavior를 수식하고 동사는 is이다. all of which ~ organization은 '대명사+전치사+관계대명사'가 이끄는 계속적 용법의 관계사절로 adult bonding, friendliness, and love를 부연 설명하고 있다.

[12행~14행] As powerfully wired as we are for social contact, // **so too are we** wired for "xenophobia": the fear of strangers.
• so가 절의 맨 앞에 와서 「so+V+S」 어순으로 도치가 일어났다. '~도 역시 그렇다[그렇지 않다]' 뜻의 so[neither, nor] 다음에는 '주어-동사'가 도치된다.

어휘 **inherent** 타고난, 내재하는 **conflict** 충돌, 갈등; 상충하다, 모순되다 **propel** 몰고 가다; 나아가게 하다 **evolution** 발전; 진화 **relatively** 비교적, 상대적으로 **bond** 유대(감); 유대감을 형성하다; 채권 *cf.* **bonding** 긴밀한 유대, 유대(감 형성) **minimize** 되도록 적게 하다; 최소화하다 **arouse** 자아내다, 불러일으키다; 자극하다 **originate with** ~에서 시작되다[일어나다] **foundation stone** 주춧돌, 초석 **friendliness** 우정, 친절; 친목 **mammal** 포유동물 **demonstrate** 보여주다; 증명하다; 시위하다 **people** (특정한 환경에 사는) 동물, 생물; 사람들 **wired** 유전적으로 정해진, 타고난 **modifiable** 경감[조절]될 수 있는 **absent** 없는, 부재의; 결석[결근]한 **fixed** 고정된; 일정한 **urban** 도시의; 도시에 사는 **pose** (위협·문제 등을) 제기하다; 포즈[자세]를 취하다 **in this regard** 이 점에 있어서는

1 글의 주제   ③

해설 이 글은 관광이 이제 대중화되어, 소비되는 방식이 문화나 개인마다 어떻게 다양한 양태로 나타나는지를 나열한 것이다. 그러므로, 주제로 가장 적절한 것은 ③ '관광이 소비재로서 기능하는 방식'이다.
① 관광에서 낭비를 줄여야 할 필요성
② 관광이 지역 주민에게 미치는 부정적인 영향
④ 해외 관광에 의해 지역 정체성이 약화되는 이유
⑤ 경제적 성공으로 인한 관광의 빠른 성장

해석 소비가 중요한 것은 정체성 창조의 영역에서만이 아니다. 예를 들어 특정 상품이나 서비스가 개별 소비자의 사회적 세상에 문화적으로 들어오는 방식은 그것들이 소비되는 방식 혹은 이유를 결정할지도 모르며, 관광도 예외는 아니다. 한때는 부유층의 전유물로 여겨졌으나, 그것은 '민주화'되었고, 용인되며 아마 기대되는 현대 사회생활의 요소가 되었다. 게다가 관광은 여러 다른 소비자들의 개인적인 문화적 맥락과 관련하여 그들에게 다른 의미를 가진다. 예를 들어 어떤 사람들에게 그것은 영적 원기 회복을 나타낼 것이며, 다른 사람들에게는 꿈이나 공상의 달성을 나타낼 것이다. 마찬가지로 관광은 다른 관광객들과 함께 (임시적인) 사회적 세상을 공유하는 수단으로서 소비될지도 모른다. 그것은 공유된 경험에 대한 기대에서 목적의식에 충만하여 소비될지도 모른다.

구문 [1행~2행] It is *not only in the realm of identity creation* **that** consumption is *of significance.*
• 「It is ... that ~」 강조구문은 '~한 것은 바로 …이다'의 뜻으로, It is와 that사이에 강조될 어구가 위치한다. 「of+추상명사」는 형용사적 의미를 가지므로 of significance는 significant와 같은 의미이다.

[6행~7행] **Once** (it was) considered the preserve of the wealthy people, it has become 'democratized', ~
• Once 다음에 'it(= tourism) was'가 생략되어 있다.

어휘 **realm** 영역 **embed** 끼워 넣다 **preserve** 전유물 **democratize** 민주화하다 **contemporary** 동시대의, 현대의 **in relation to** ~에 관하여 **refreshment** 원기 회복 **fulfillment** 이행, 완수, 달성 **temporary** 일시적인, 임시의 **purposefully** 목적을 갖고

2 밑줄 어법   ⑤

해설 ⑤ the very people 다음에 'they(politicians) claim to be acting in their(people's) interests'라는 절이 붙어서 the very people을 수식하는데, 접속사가 없으므로 their라는 소유격 대명사를 소유격 관계대명사 whose로 바꾸고, '전치사+관계대명사'를 절의 맨 앞으로 위치시킨 형태가 되어야 한다. 따라서 which를 whose로 바꾸는 것이 적절하다.
① 주어 Our insatiable appetite for seafood가 단수이므로 단수동사 has는 적절하다.
② lacking ~ of our time은 앞의 a scientific community를 수식하는데, lack이 '~이 부족하다, 결핍되다'라는 뜻이므로 현재분사 lacking은 알맞다.
③ 접속사 that이 is의 보어 역할을 하는 명사절을 이끈다.
④ International Commission for the Conservation of Atlantic Tuna (ICCAT)라는 단수 명사구를 지칭하므로 단수 소유격 its는 적절하다.

해석 우리의 해산물에 대한 만족할 줄 모르는 식욕은 산업적 어업 기술의 잔혹한 효율성과 결부되어 많은 문제를 초래했다. 그러나 무엇보다도, 그것은 정부의 허약함, 산업적 탐욕과 우리 시대의 가장 큰 생태적 비극 중 하나를 초래한 경보를 울릴 용기가 결여된 과학계의 합작이었다. 의사 결정자들은 일상적으로 경고 신호를 무시했다. 그 이유는 그들이 '어업 로비'를 뒤엎기를 두려워했기 때문이다. 결과적으로 그들은 절망적이게도 비현실적인 할당량을 설정했고, 산업적 어업 회사들의 요구를 들어주기 위해 특별한 노력을 기울였다. 예를 들어 2008년 11월에 부적절한 이름을 가진 '대서양 참치 보존을 위한 국제 위원회(ICCAT)'는 바로 자기 기관의 과학자들이 충고한 것보다 거의 50퍼센트 더 높은 참다랑어 어획량 할당을 정했다. 일자리, 생계와 소비자 이익에 대한 우려를 표명하며 정치인들은 어류군 집단을 붕괴 직전까지 몰고 갔으며, 자신들의 실패로 그들은 자기들이 사람들의 이익을 위해 활동하고 있다고 주장하는 바로 그 사람들을 위협하고 있다.

구문 [1행~3행] *Our insatiable appetite for seafood*, **coupled with the brutal efficiency of our industrial fishing technologies,** has wreaked havoc.
• coupled with ~ technologies는 Our insatiable appetite for seafood를 의미상 주어로 하며 수동의 의미를 가지는 분사구문이다.

[12행~17행] For example, in November 2008, the inappropriately named International Commission for the Conservation of Atlantic Tuna (ICCAT) set *a catch quota for bluefin tuna* [that is nearly 50 per cent higher than its own scientists advise].
• [ ]은 주격 관계대명사가 이끄는 관계사절로 a catch quota for bluefin tuna를 수식한다.

어휘 **appetite** 식욕 **coupled with** ~와 결부된 **brutal** 잔혹한; 인정사정없는 **greed** 탐욕 **ecological** 생태계[학]의 **routinely** 일상적으로 **quota** 할당량, 몫 **go out of one's way to-v** ~하려고 않던 노력까지 다하다 **commission** 위원회 **catch quota** 어획량 할당 **bluefin tuna** 참다랑어 **cite** 표명하다; 인용하다 **livelihood** 생계 **to the brink of ~** ~ 직전까지 **collapse** 붕괴(하다) **act in one's interest** ~의 이익을 위해 행동하다

3 빈칸 추론   ②

해설 편지, 수필, 연설, 문서 등 어떤 종류의 글쓰기라도 초안이 최고의 작품이 되지 않으며, 모든 사람이 쓰고 수정하는 과정을 반복해야 한다는 것이 글의 요지이므로, 마지막 빈칸에 들어갈 말로 가장 적절한 것은 ② '양질은 다시 쓰기와 함께 온다.'이다.
① 작가들은 요리사들과 비슷하다
③ 글쓰기는 특별한 재능을 요구한다
④ 실수는 배움의 비결이다
⑤ 편집하면서 개인의 특색이 손실된다

해석 내가 만났던 많은 사람들은 자신들이 항상 실수를 저지른다는 것을 알게 되어서 편지나 어떤 것도 절대 쓰지 않는다고 말한다. 의사소통은 당신이 제대로 할 기회를 단 한 번밖에 갖지 못하는 요리와 다르다. 요리에서는 따라야 하는 요리법이 있어서 그것에서 벗어나면 음식은 잘못 만들어진다. 내가 만난 사람들에게 이 말을 하고서야 그들이 비로소 알게 된 것은 처음에 또는 두 번째에 또는 세 번째에 제대로 하는 사람은 아무도 없다는 것이다. 모든 사람은 쓰고 수정하고 그런 다음 다시 쓰고 다시 수정하고, 그 과정을 마침내 더할 나위 없이 좋아질 때까지 계속하는 것이 필요하다. 편지, 연설문 또는 어떤 계획된 서신이든, 그것을 쓰는 비결은 전체를 적어도 일곱 번은 수정할 때까지 그것에 몰두하는 것이다. (편지, 수필, 연설, 문서)

거의 어떤 것이든 그것의 초안은 결코 최고의 작품이 되지 않을 것이다. 어떤 경우에 사적인 편지는 예외일 수 있지만, 심지어 그것조차 종종 발송하기 전에 다시 쓸 필요가 있다. 양질은 다시 쓰기와 함께 온다.

구문 [1행~3행] *Many people* [(whom[that]) I've met] say (that) **they never write letters or anything at all** // because they've learned that they always make mistakes.

• [ ] 부분은 주어 Many people을 수식하는 관계사절이며, 앞에 목적격 관계대명사 whom[that]이 생략되었다. they never ~ at all 부분은 동사 say의 목적어 역할을 하는 명사절로 접속사 that이 생략되었다.

[3행~4행] Communication is not like *cooking*, // **where** you only get one chance to get it right.

• 관계부사 where 이하는 동명사 cooking을 보충 설명하는 계속적 용법의 관계사절이다.

어휘 recipe 요리법 stray 벗어나다, 빗나가다 revise 수정하다 keep up ~을 계속하다 work at ~에 몰두하다 draft 초안 exception 예외
[선택지] edit 편집하다

4 무관 문장 ③

해설 사람들은 선천적으로 귀엽고 아기 같은 생김새의 봉제 장난감 곰에 마음이 끌리고, 이에 따라 장난감 곰이 더 아기 같은 모습으로 발전하게 되었다는 내용이다. 시간이 지나면서 나이가 든 소비자들에게 호감을 사기 위해 기존의 곰에 성숙성을 더하였다는 내용의 ③은 전체 흐름과 관련이 없다.

해석 봉제 장난감 곰이라는 개념은 아주 명백하게 유전학적으로 물려받은 특성이 아니기 때문에 우리는 문화적 특성을 보고 있는 것이라고 자신할 수 있다. 하지만, 그것은 다른, 진정으로 생물학적인 특성, 즉 우리를 아기(높은 이마와 작은 얼굴)에게 이끄는 신호 때문에 유도되고 있는 것처럼 보이는 문화적 특성이다. ① 귀엽고 아기 같은 생김새는 선천적으로 사람의 마음을 끌어, 대부분의 인간 속에 있는 보살피려는 반응을 불러일으킨다. ② 처음에는 아무리 사소했을지는 모르지만, 더 아기 같은 모습을 지닌 봉제 장난감 곰들은 그렇기 때문에 소비자들에게 더욱 인기 있었다. ③ 하지만, 시간이 지나면서 봉제 장난감 곰 제조사들은 기존의 곰에 성숙성을 더하면서 더 나이가 든 소비자들로 그들의 타깃을 확장함에 따라 봉제 장난감 곰의 역할에 변화가 생겨났다. ④ 봉제 장난감 곰 제조사들은 어느 곰이 최고로 잘 팔리고 있는지를 분명히 알아챘으며 그래서 자기들의 이익을 최대화하기 위해서 이런 것들을 더 많이 그리고 인기가 덜한 모델을 더 적게 만들었다. ⑤ 이렇게 해서 소비자에 의해 고조된 선택 압력으로 제조사들은 더 아기 같은 곰을 점진적으로 발전시키게 되었다.

구문 [8행~11행] *Teddy bears* [**that** had a more baby-like appearance] — **however** slight this may have been initially — were thus more popular with customers.

• [ ] 부분은 주격 관계대명사 that이 이끄는 관계사절로 Teddy bears를 수식하고, however는 복합관계부사로 「however+형용사/부사」 형태로 쓰여 '아무리 ~하더라도'를 의미한다.

어휘 concept 개념 obviously 명백하게 inherited 물려받은; 유전의 *cf.* inherently 선천적으로 trait 특성 genuinely 진정으로 biological 생물학적인 cue 신호; 단서 forehead 이마 appealing 사람의 마음을 끄는, 매력적인 nurture 보살피다 initially 처음에 expand 확장시키다 maturity 성숙함 manufacturer 제조사 build up 고조시키다 evolution 점진적인 발전

5 요약문 완성 ②

해설 두 실험의 결과는 인구 밀도가 높을수록 남을 배려하는 관대함이 줄어든다는 것이므로 생활 환경이 더 조밀할(packed)수록, 거주자들이 덜 관대한(generous) 것을 알 수 있다.

해석 큰 규모의 심리학자들과 건축가들은 매사추세츠와 펜실베이니아에 있는 세 기관에서 8,000명의 대학생들을 대상으로 두 가지 실험을 했다. 실험에 참가한 학생들 중의 일부는 인구 밀도가 높은 고층 건물에 살았으며, 일부는 인구 밀도가 중간 정도인 아파트 단지에 살았고, 다른 학생들은 인구 밀도가 낮은 교외 주택에 살았다. 이때 연구자들은 건물 안의 곳곳에 우표가 붙고 주소가 적힌 편지 봉투 여러 장을 흩뜨려서, 누군가 편지를 우편함에 넣으려다 흘렸다는 느낌을 만들어냈다. 그 연구자들이 4시간 후에 돌아갔을 때, 그들은 인구 밀도가 낮은 주택에는 편지의 100퍼센트가 우편함에 넣어졌고, 인구 밀도가 중간 정도의 단지에서는 87퍼센트가 우편함에 넣어졌고, 인구 밀도가 높은 고층 건물에서는 단지 63퍼센트만이 우편함에 넣어졌다는 것을 발견했다. 인구 밀도가 위와 비슷하게 차이가 나는 또 다른 아파트 단지에 연구자들은 주민들에게 사용한 우유 팩을 예술 프로젝트를 위해 기부해 달라고 부탁하는 박스를 설치했다. 단지의 주민들이 사용한 우유 팩의 수를 계산했을 때, 연구자들은 이번에도 인구 밀도가 높은 단지의 주민들이 덜 협조적이라는 것을 발견했다. 인구 밀도가 낮거나 중간인 단지의 주민들은 자신들이 사용한 우유 팩의 55퍼센트를 기부한 반면 인구 밀도가 높은 단지의 주민들은 겨우 37퍼센트를 내놓았다.

┌───┐
│ 두 개의 실험에 따르면, 생활 환경이 더 (A) 조밀할수록, 그곳의 거주자들은 덜 │
│ (B) 관대하다고 가정할 수 있다. │
└───┘

구문 [4행~6행] Some of the students lived in high-density towers, **some** (lived) in medium-density apartment blocks, and **others** (lived) in lower-density halls of residence.

• 굵게 표시한 some과 others 다음에는 동사 lived가 생략되었다.

[6행~9행] The researchers began by scattering a series of stamped addressed envelopes inside the buildings, / **creating** the sense **that** the letters had been lost on the way to the mailbox.

• creating 이하는 분사구문으로 앞에 나온 내용을 보충하고 있다. the sense와 that the letters ~ to the mailbox는 서로 동격 관계이다.

어휘 high-density 고밀도의 tower 고층 건물 medium 중간(의) residence 거주 scatter 흐트러뜨리다 stamped 우표를 붙인 address (편지 봉투에) 주소를 쓰다 donate 기증하다 carton 상자, 갑[통] dweller 거주자, 주민 contribute 기부하다, 기증하다

1 빈칸 추론　　④

해설　빈칸 문장은 However로 시작하므로, 활기찬 활동과 정신 건강 간의 관련성이 단지 유전적 성향이라는 바로 앞 내용과 반대되는 내용이 빈칸에 와야 한다. 또한, 빈칸 뒤에 규칙적인 운동을 하지 않으면 8년 후에 우울 증상이 증가한다는 연구 결과가 제시되고 있으므로 빈칸에 들어갈 내용으로 가장 적절한 것은 ④ '미래의 심리적 문제의 위험성을 감소시킨다'이다.
① 사교적 오락 활동을 대체하는 것에 실패한다
② 사람의 유전자 건강과 일치한다
③ 체중 감소와 근력 증가에 기여한다
⑤ 건강한 사람이 아니라면 우울증을 초래할 수 있다

해석　대부분의 규칙적으로 운동하는 사람들이 말하는, 자신들의 신체 활동 지속의 주된 이유는 그것이 매일 그들이 기분이 나아지도록 돕는다는 것이다. 활기찬 활동과 정신 건강 간의 관련성은 단지 유전적 성향의 작용이라고 주장할 수도 있다. 그러나 규칙적인 운동이 직접적으로 미래의 심리적 문제의 위험성을 감소시킨다는 증거가 있다. 거의 2,000명의 성인에 관한한 연구에서 오락 삼아 하는 운동을 거의 혹은 아예 안 하는 것은 8년 후에 우울 증상이 증가하는 전조가 되었다. 초기 평가에서 우울증 증상이 많았던 남성들은 규칙적으로 운동하는 것을 시작하지 않은 한 대개 계속해서 그런 기분을 느꼈다. 원래는 증상을 거의 보이지 않았던, 주로 앉아서 지내는 여성들도 또한 8년의 추적 검사에서 증가된 우울증의 징후를 보여주었다.

구문　[1행~3행] The primary reason (**given by most regular exercisers**) for continuing their fitness activities / is that they help them feel better on a day-to-day basis.
• given by most regular exercisers는 분사구이며, The primary ~ activities가 문장의 주어이다.

[10행~12행] Men [**who** had many depressive symptoms during the initial assessment] usually remained feeling that way unless they began to regularly exercise.
• [ ] 부분은 who가 이끄는 관계사절로 Men을 수식한다.

어휘　**on a day-to-day basis** 매일　**vigorous** 활기찬　**genetic** 유전적인　**predictive** 전조가 되는, 예언하는　**symptom** 증상, 징후　**initial** 최초의, 초기의　**assessment** 평가　**manifest** 보이다, 나타내다　**follow-up** 추적 검사, 후속 조치
[선택지] **substitute** 대체물　**correspond to** ~와 일치하다

2 글의 순서　　⑤

해설　산악 지역이 낮은 평지보다 더 다양한 종의 분포를 이루고 있는 이유가 (C)에 나와 있으므로, 주어진 문장 바로 다음에 (C)가 와야 하고, 이것에 대한 예시가 시작되는 부분이 For example로 시작하는 (B)이며, (B)와 비슷한 구체적인 예가 (A)에 나와 있으므로, (B) 다음에 (A)가 와야 한다.

해석　사이에 낮은 계곡을 가지고 있는 산악 지역들은 에워싸고 있는 평평한 지역보다 더 많은 종의 풍부함을 가지는 경향이 있다는 것은 의심할 여지가 없다. (C) 이것은 부분적으로 더 다양한 환경이 있고, 각각의 환경은 그 자체의 특징적인 종의 집단을 가지고 있기 때문이다. 우선, 산에는 다양한 기후대가 있는데, 평평한 저지대에는 오직 한 가지 기후만 있다. (B) 예를 들어, 애리조나주의 Santa Catalina 산맥에는, 많은 다양한 식물종이 똑같

은 산이지만 별개의 고도에 존재하는데, 각각의 종은 그 자체의 기후 최적 조건에 있다.
(A) 고도에 따른 종 구성의 비슷한 다양성은 오리건주의 Siskiyou 산맥과 사실상 거의 모든 높은 산에서 발견되는데, 그것은 단지 그곳에 광범위한 기후가 있기 때문이다.

구문　[1행~3행] There is no doubt / that *mountainous areas* (**with low valleys among them**) / tend to have higher species richness / than *surrounding areas* (**of flat land**).
• with low valleys among them과 of flat land는 전명구로 각각 mountainous areas와 surrounding areas를 수식한다.

어휘　**mountainous** 산악의; 산이 많은　**valley** 계곡, 골짜기　**richness** 풍부[풍성]함, 풍요로움　**diversity** 다양성　**composition** 구성; 구성 요소　**a wide range of** 광범위한　**occur** 존재하다, 발견되다; 일어나다, 발생하다　**distinct** 별개의; 뚜렷한, 분명한　**altitude** 고도, 해발 (= **elevation**)　**climate zone** 기후대 *cf.* **climate** 기후 *cf.* **climatic** 기후의　**characteristic** 특징적인, 독특한　**lowland** 저지대의

3 문장 넣기　　③

해설　이 글은 늑대 무리의 크기가 이용 가능한 먹이 자원에 의해 조절된다는 통념과는 달리 사회적인 요인에 의해 조절된다는 내용이다. 주어진 문장은 hunting such large animals(그러한 큰 동물들)가 있으므로 늑대의 먹이가 되는 덩치가 큰 동물들이 나온 이후에 나와야 한다. 또한, ③ 이후부터는 역접의 연결사 However가 나오면서 늑대의 무리가 먹이와 관련된 요인이 아닌 사회적 요인에 의해 조절된다는 다른 견해가 나와 흐름이 바뀌므로 주어진 문장은 ③에 들어가는 것이 가장 적절하다.

해석　수많은 동물들의 사회생활은 연합하고 협동하는 행동으로 강력하게 형성된다. 늑대를 생각해 보라. 오랫동안 연구자들은 무리의 크기가 이용 가능한 먹이 자원에 의해 조절된다고 생각했다. 늑대는 전형적으로 엘크와 무스 같은 동물을 먹고 사는데, 그것들 모두 한 마리의 늑대보다 더 크다. 그러한 큰 동물들을 성공적으로 사냥하는 데는 일반적으로 한 마리가 넘는 늑대가 필요해서, 늑대 먹이의 크기 때문에 늑대 무리가 진화했다고 가정하는 것은 타당하다. 그러나 데이비드 미치의 장기간의 연구는 늑대 무리의 크기가 먹이와 관련된 요인이 아닌 사회적인 요인에 의해 조절된다는 것을 보여 준다. 미치는 조직화된 무리 내에서 함께 살아갈 수 있는 늑대의 숫자는 각각의 늑대가 경쟁을 견딜 수 있는 개체의 숫자에 비교하여, 각각의 늑대가 친밀하게 유대감을 형성할 수 있는 늑대의 숫자에 의해 통제된다는 것을 발견했다. 너무 많은 늑대가 있으면 무리와 무리의 행동 강령이 무너져 내린다.

구문　[2행~4행] ~, so **it** makes sense **to suppose that wolf packs evolved because of the size of wolves' food.**
• 여기에서 it은 가주어, to suppose ~ food가 진주어이며, that ~ food는 to suppose의 목적어 역할을 하는 명사절이다.

[13행~18행] Mech discovered // **that** the number of *wolves* [**who** can live together in a coordinated pack] is governed / by the number of *wolves* [**with whom** individuals can closely bond] balanced against the number of *individuals* [**from whom** an individual can tolerate competition].
• that이 이끄는 명사절이 동사 discovered의 목적어 역할을 한다. who ~ pack은 주격 관계대명사가 이끄는 절로 앞에 있는 wolves를 수식한다. 동물이 선행사라 하더라도 이를 글쓴이가 의인화해서 which 대신 who를 쓰기도 한다. with whom ~ bond와 from whom ~ competition은 모두 '전치사+관계대명사'가 이끄는 관계사

절로 각각 wolves와 individuals를 수식한다.

어휘 **take** 필요하다; 이용하다 **make sense** 타당하다, 이치에 맞다; 의미가 통하다 **suppose** 가정하다; 추측하다 **pack** 무리, 떼; 묶음 **evolve** 진화하다 **numerous** 수많은 **cooperative** 협력하는; 협조하는 **regulate** 조절하다; 규제하다 **available** 이용 가능한 **resource** 자원; 재료 **typically** 전형적으로; 보통 **feed on** ~을 먹고 살다 **long-term** 장기간에 걸친 **factor** 요인, 요소 **coordinate** 조직화하다, 조정하다 **govern** 통제[좌우]하다; 통치하다 **bond** 유대감을 형성하다; 접착하다 **tolerate** 견디다, 참다; 용인하다 **conduct** 행동(하다); 수행(하다); 지휘하다; 전도하다

4~5 장문　　　　　　　　4 ② 5 ⑤

해설 **4.** 첫 번째 단락에서는 허구 속 인물들이 현실에서 만나는 사람들보다 더 흥미롭다고 하였고, 두 번째 단락에서는 허구 이야기인 소설이 현실에서는 얻지 못하는 사적인 정보나 다른 사람의 생각도 알려준다고 하였다. 세 번째 단락에서는 역시 허구 이야기에 속하는 연극, 뮤지컬, 텔레비전과 영화가 소설과 마찬가지로 다른 사람의 생각을 알려주는 기법을 사용하여, 처음 접한 아이들에게는 이것이 매우 짜릿한 경험임에 틀림없다고 하였다. 이를 종합하면 사람들이 허구의 이야기에 끌리는 이유들을 설명한 것이라고 볼 수 있으므로 정답은 ② '우리는 왜 허구 이야기에 그렇게 끌리는가?'가 적절하다.
① 허구는 실제보다 더 사실적일 수 있다
③ 소설을 읽는 것은 자기 발전을 위한 도구이다
④ 독서를 통해 인간의 본성을 이해하기
⑤ 우리의 두뇌는 허구와 현실을 구분할 수 없다
5. 다른 사람의 생각이 표현되는 기법이 처음에는 뜻밖의 발견이었을 것이라고 했으므로, 요즘에는 흔한 것임을 알 수 있다. 그러므로 ⑤는 common 등이 되어야 한다.

해석 상상력에는 어떤 강력한 특징들이 있다. (a) 허구 속 인물들은 친구나 가족보다 더 재치 있고 더 명석한 경향이 있고, 그들의 모험은 보통 훨씬 더 흥미롭다. 나 역시 주변 사람들의 삶과 얽혀 있지만 이것은 전체 인류에 비하면 작은 한 부분일 뿐이고, 아마도 가장 흥미로운 부분은 아닐 것이다. 내가 사는 실제 세계에는 연쇄 살인범을 추적하는 감정적으로 상처 입은 경찰도, 마음씨 착한 가게 좀도둑도, 재치 있는 뱀파이어도 없다. 하지만 나는 상상의 세계에서 그러한 사람들을 모두 만날 수 있다.
상상력의 기술은 현실에서 얻는 것이 (b) 불가능한 민감하고 사적인 정보를 제공한다. 소설 한 권은 (주인공의) 출생에서 죽음까지 전개되면서 (소설을 읽지 않는다면) 우리가 (c) 관찰할 수 없을 상황에서 사람이 어떻게 행동하는지를 보여준다. 현실에서는 남이 무슨 생각을 하는지 알 수 없지만 소설에서는 작가가 알려준다. 그러한 초자연적인 친밀감은 글에만 (d) 국한되지 않는다.
같은 목적으로 창작되는 다른 예술적 매체에서도 그러한 관습이 있다. 연극에서 등장인물은 관객을 향해 돌아서서 그 사람이 무슨 생각을 하는지를 표현하는 극적인 독백을 시작한다. 뮤지컬에서는 노래로 생각을 밝힌다. 텔레비전과 영화에서는 보이스오버가 사용된다. 이것은 요즘에는 (e) 흔하지 않은(→ 흔한) 것이지만, 처음 이런 기법이 발명되었을 때는 뜻밖의 발견이었음에 틀림이 없을 것이다. 나는 어린 아이들이 처음으로 이것을 접했을 때, 즉 다른 사람의 생각이 큰 소리로 표현되는 것을 들었을 때 무슨 생각을 할까 궁금하다. 아마 짜릿한 경험임에 틀림이 없다.

구문 [7행~10행] My real world doesn't **include** *an emotionally wounded cop* (**tracking** down a serial killer), *a shoplifter with a heart of gold,* or *a wisecracking vampire.*
● 밑줄 친 세 부분은 동사 include의 목적어로 병렬구조를 이루고 있다. ( ) 부분은 분사구로 앞에 나온 an emotionally wounded cop을 수식한다.

[14행~16행] A novel can span birth to death and **can show** you **how** the person behaves in *situations* [that you could never otherwise observe].

● how the person ~ otherwise observes는 동사 can show의 직접목적어이고, [ ] 부분은 관계사절로 앞에 나온 명사 situations를 수식한다.

[26행~30행] This is common now, but it **must have been** a revelation when the technique was first invented, // and I wonder **what** young children think when they come across this for the first time, when they hear someone else's thoughts expressed aloud.

● 「must have been」은 '~했음에 틀림이 없다'는 뜻으로 과거 사실에 대한 확신을 표현한다. what young children ~ expressed aloud는 동사 wonder의 목적어이고, 두 개의 부사절 when they come ~ the first time과 when they hear ~ expressed aloud는 서로 동격 관계이다.

어휘 **compelling** 강력한, 흥미를 돋우는 **feature** 특징, 특색 **slice** 부분, 몫 **humanity** 인류 **cop** 경찰 **track down** 추적하다 **shoplifter** 가게 좀도둑 **wisecracking** 재치가 있는 **vampire** 흡혈귀 **sensitive** 민감한 **span** (시간적으로) ~에 걸치다 **otherwise** 그렇지 않고는 **psychic** 마음의, 심적인 **convention** 관습, 관례 **artistic** 예술적 **medium** 매체, 매개물 **revelation** 뜻밖의 새 사실, 폭로된 것 **come across** 우연히 마주치다, 발견하다 **thrilling** 감격적인, 짜릿하게 하는

1 글의 요지   ②

해설 역사를 가르칠 때 교사들이 나무와 숲보다는 잔가지를 가르치려는 충동이 있다고 하면서 잔가지를 가르치면 대부분의 학생이 그것들을 자신들의 삶과 관련시킬 수 없고 거의 다 잊어버린다는 문제점을 서술하고 있다. 그러므로 글의 요지로 가장 적절한 것은 ②이다.

해석 취사선택하지 않고서는 세계사를 다루기를 바랄 수 없다는 사실을 세계사 교사들은 이미 파악하고 있다. 그렇지 않으면, 아마도 그들은 말레이시아의 역사에 13분을, 싱가포르의 역사에 7분을, 그리고 태국의 역사에 28분을 바쳐야 하는데, 그것은 불가능하다! 하지만 미국 역사에서, 교사들은 훨씬 더 적은 수의 나무들과 겨우 몇 안 되는 숲보다는 4,444개의 잔가지를 가르치고자 하는 충동을 여전히 느낀다. 때때로 그들은 주 전체의 '표준화된' 잔가지를 묻는 시험에 의해 그렇게 하고자 하는 충동을 느낀다. 유감스럽게도, 교사들이 더 많은 것을 다루면 다룰수록, 아이들은 더 적은 것을 기억한다. 역사를 관련이 없는 '사실들'로 분해하게 되면, 학생들은 거의 틀림없이 이러한 많은 용어를 그들 자신의 삶과 관련시킬 수 없을 것이다. 1학년 과정을 가르치는 것을 전문으로 하는 교수로서, 나는 보통 하던 대로 미국 역사를 배운 대부분의 학생이 대학에 들어올 무렵에는 1차 세계대전이 2차 세계 대전보다 먼저 일어났다는 것을 제외하고는 다 잊어버렸다고 장담할 수 있다.

구문 [11행~13행] **Fragmenting** history into unconnected "facts" practically **guarantees** // that students will not be able to relate many of these terms to their own lives.

• 밑줄 친 동명사구가 문장의 주어이며, 동사는 guarantees이다. that절은 guarantees의 목적어 역할을 한다.

어휘 **grasp** 이해하다, 납득하다   **cover** 다루다   **devote** 쏟다, 바치다   **compulsion** 충동   **statewide** 주 전체의   **fragment** 분해하다   **unconnected** 관련이 없는   **practically** 거의, 사실상   **guarantee** 보장하다, 장담하다, 확인하다   **relate A to B** A와 B를 관련시키다   **specialize in** ~을 전문으로 하다   **precede** 앞서 일어나다

2 빈칸 추론   ②

해설 빈칸 문장을 보면, 당신이 먹을 것을 키우는 데 썼어야 하는 시간과 공간, 에너지를 빈칸에 들어갈 '무엇'에 써버렸다는 내용이며 이것이 밭을 계획할 때 지켜야 할 원칙이라고 했다. 빈칸 앞을 보면 밭에서 썩어가는 양배추와 수 미터씩이나 자란 깍지콩은 먹지 않으면 공간 낭비라고 했다. 즉 그 작물들을 재배만 해 두고 먹지 않은 것이므로 정답은 ② '실제로 섭취되지 않는 것은 무엇이든'이다.
① 대지를 임대한 모든 사람은
③ 바람직한 음식에 초점을 둔 사람은 누구나
④ 현재 대지에서 기르는 모든 것은
⑤ 계절에 맞지 않게 심어진 것은 무엇이든

해석 (작물을) 가꿀 공간에 대한 대기자 명단이 길어지고 있는 가운데 많은 대지의 크기는 줄어들고 있지만, 과일과 채소를 기르고자 하는 욕구는 그 어느 때보다 더 강하다. 그럼 (무엇인가를) 키울 넓은 공간이나 적어도 표준 크기의 대지가 없다면 무엇을 할 것인가? 땅을 어떻게 사용할 것인가는 최종 산물에 근거해야 한다. 질문은 "내가 무엇을 기르고 싶은가?"가 아니라 "내가 무엇을 먹고 싶은가?"가 되어야 한다. 늦겨울이나 초봄에 몇 군데 밭을 가보면 반쯤 썩어가고 있는 양배추와 겨울의 일반적인 잔해들을 볼 것이다. 늦봄과 여름에 돌아보면 수 미터 높이로 자란 깍지콩을 종종 볼 것이다. 먹지 않으면, 이것들은 공간 낭비이다. 따라서 밭을 계획하는 데 첫

번째 원칙은 이것이다. 실제로 섭취되지 않는 것은 무엇이든 당신의 배 속에 자리 잡을 다른 것을 기르는 데 들였어야 할 시간, 공간, 에너지를 써 버린 것이다.

구문 [14행~17행] ~ *anything* [**that** is not actually consumed] has taken *time, space, and energy* [**that should have been** spent on growing *something else* [**that** finds a home in your stomach]].
    S   V   O

• 세 개의 that은 모두 주격 관계대명사로 각각의 선행사를 수식하는 절을 이끌고 있다. 「should have p.p.」는 '~했어야 하는데 (하지 않았다)'라는 뜻으로 '과거에 대한 후회·비난'을 나타낸다.

어휘 **waiting list** 대기자 명단   **plot** (특정 용도의) 대지; (소설 등의) 구성, 줄거리; 음모   **rot** 썩다, 부식하다; 썩히다   **debris** 잔해; 쓰레기   **runner bean** 깍지콩
[선택지] **consume** (연료·에너지·시간을) 소모하다; 먹다, 마시다   **desirable** 바람직한, 호감 가는

3 무관 문장   ①

해설 본문은 집단 순응 사고가 초래하는 참사에 관하여 다루고 있는데, ①번 문장에서 집단 순응 사고의 장점에 대하여 언급하고 있고, ②번 문장부터 마지막까지 다시 집단 순응 사고로 인한 참사의 예시가 이어지고 있다. 따라서 ①번 문장이 글 전체의 흐름과 무관하다.

해석 '좋은 팀 플레이어(조직 내에서 협력하여 조직의 성공에 기여하는 사람)'인 것은 단점을 가질 수 있는데 이는 집단의 의견 일치가 때로는 잘못 인도되거나 위험할 수 있기 때문이다. 반대가 실수를 하는 것으로부터 집단을 구할 수 있으나, 때때로 '집단 순응 사고'라 불리는, 개별적인 의혹에도 불구하고 생각을 같이해야 한다는 압박감이 참사를 초래할 수 있다. ① 그러나 특정 그룹에서 다른 사람들에게 동의하려는 자연적 성향은 효과적이고 빠른 의사 결정 과정을 보장할 수 있다. ② 예를 들어, 2003년 우주 왕복선 컬럼비아호 참사에 앞선 고위급 회의들에서 집단 순응 사고가 작용했다. ③ NASA에서 열린 그 회의들의 기록에 의하면, 엔지니어가 아니면서 우주 왕복선 담당자 회의들을 주재한 임원은 발포 단열재의 잔해가 우주선에 손상을 입힐 수 없을 것이라고 처음부터 믿었다고 한다. ④ 한 엔지니어가 우려를 나타냈을 때 그녀는 그 문제를 일축했고 논의를 중단시켰다. ⑤ 참석한 나머지 사람들은 회의를 주재한 그 사람의 방침에 신속히 따랐다. 며칠 뒤, 발포 단열재 잔해에 의해 가해진 손상이 컬럼비아호가 지구의 대기권으로 재진입하던 중 산산조각이 나게 했다.

구문 [11행~15행] Transcripts of those meetings at NASA **show that** *the official* [who ran shuttle management meetings], a nonengineer, **believed** from the beginning **that** foam insulation debris could not damage the spacecraft.

• 첫 번째 that 이하는 동사 show의 목적어 역할을 하는 명사절이며, 이 안에서 관계사절인 who ~ meetings가 명사절의 주어 the official을 수식하고 있다. 또한 두 번째 that 이하는 believed의 목적어 역할을 하는 명사절이다.

[18행~20행] A few days later, *damage* (**caused** by foam insulation debris) / **caused** / *Columbia* to break ~.

• ( ) 부분은 과거분사구로 수동의 의미로 명사 damage를 수식한다. 두 번째 caused는 문장의 동사이다.

어휘 **downside** 결점   **consensus** 의견 일치   **dissent** 반대   **conform** (생각[행동]을) 같이하다; 순응하다   **groupthink** 집단 (순응) 사고   **disaster** 참사, 재난   **predisposition** 성향   **assure** 보장하다   **precede** 앞서다   **transcript** (구술된 내용을) 글로 옮긴 기록   **shuttle** 우주 왕복선   **dismiss** 일축[묵살]하다   **cut off** ~을 중단시키다; 자르다   **present** 참석한; 현재의   **fall into line** 동의하다   **reentry** 재진입

4 글의 순서 ④

해설 한 카우보이가 잃어버린 소를 찾아 말을 타고 가고 있는 상황이 제시된 주어진 글 다음에 잃어버린 소 대신에(Instead) 뼈들과 그 옆에 돌로 만든 창끝을 발견해서 목장으로 가져갔다는 (C)가 이어진다. 그다음 그것들(they)이 목장(There)에 보관되었다가 자연사 박물관으로 옮겨져 오래전 멸종된 들소의 뼈라는 사실이 밝혀졌다는 (A)가 이어지고, 이보다 더 영향력이 큰 사실(the more far-reaching implications), 즉 돌로 된 창끝을 통해 빙하시대에 사냥이 행해졌음을 알게 되었다는 (B)가 이어져야 한다.

해석 1908년에 George McJunkin이라는 이름의 카우보이가 뉴멕시코의 소도시인 Folsom 근처에서 잃어버린 소를 찾으며 말을 타고 가고 있었다.
(C) 대신에, 그는 뼈들을 우연히 발견했는데, 그것들 옆에는 돌로 만든 창끝이 있었다. 그 뼈들은 소의 뼈라고 하기에는 너무나도 컸다. 호기심을 느낀 McJunkin은 그것들을 목장 주택으로 가져갔다.
(A) 그것들은 거기에 보관되었다가 1925년이 되어서야, 콜로라도 자연사 박물관의 Jesse Figgins의 책상 위에 놓이게 되었다. Figgins는 그 뼈들이 빙하 시대 말에 평지를 돌아다녔던 오래전에 멸종된 형태의 들소의 뼈라는 것을 쉽게 알아봤다.
(B) 하지만 더 지대한 영향을 미친 것은 바로 McJunkin이 그 뼈들 옆에서 발견했던 돌 창끝들이었다. 이 창끝들이 들소를 죽이기 위해 사용된 사람이 만든 무기였다면, 그것은 인간이 빙하 시대 동안 아메리카 대륙에서 사냥을 했다는 (그리고 살았다는) 것을 의미했다.

구문 [4행~6행] There they stayed until *1925*, // **when** they landed on the desk of Jesse Figgins of the Colorado Museum of Natural History.
• when ~ History는 관계부사 when이 이끄는 절로서 선행사 1925를 보충 설명한다.

[9행~11행] But **it was** *the stone spearpoints* [(which[that]) McJunkin had found beside the bones] **that** had the more far-reaching implications.
• 「it was ... that ~」 강조구문으로 '~한 것은 바로 …이었다'의 뜻이다. [ ]은 목적격 관계대명사 which[that]가 생략된 관계사절로 the stone spearpoints를 수식한다.

[17행~18행] ~; **intrigued**, McJunkin took them back to the ranch house.
• intrigued 이하는 수동 분사구문으로 because McJunkin was intrigued로 바꿔 쓸 수 있다.

어휘 identify 알아보다, 확인하다; 발견하다 **extinct** 멸종된; 더 이상 존재하지 않는, 사라진 **roam** 돌아다니다, 배회[방랑]하다 **plain** 평지, 평원; 분명한; 간결한; 솔직한 **Ice Age** 빙하 시대 **spearpoint** 창끝; 선두에 서는 사람, 선봉 **implication** 영향, 결과; 암시 **manmade** 사람이 만든 **weapon** 무기 **come across** 우연히 발견하다; 이해되다; (특정한) 인상을 주다 **intrigued** 호기심을 느낀, 흥미 있는 **ranch** 목장, 목축장

5 문장 넣기 ④

해설 시인이 황홀경의 직관에 의해 글을 쓴다고 남들이 알아주는 것을 선호했다는 말 다음에 직관과 관련 없이 수학 문제처럼 논리적으로 쓴 글에 대한 언급이 나왔으므로 주어진 문장은 그 사이인 ④에 들어가는 것이 가장 적절하다.

해석 1845년에 에드거 앨런 포는 The Raven을 완성했다. 일 년 후, 포는 The Philosophy of Composition이란 평론을 출간했는데, 그것은 어떻게 이 시가 창작되었는지의 과정을 설명했다. 우리는 낭만주의 시대의 시인으로서 포가 전체 시가 순식간에 나타나게 해 준 영감의 번쩍임에 관해 이야기했을 거라고 예상했을지도 모른다. 포가 설명했듯이, "대부분의 작가들, 특히 시인들은 자신들이 일종의 광란, 즉

황홀경의 직관을 통해 작문을 한다고 남들이 알아주는 것을 더 선호한다." 하지만 포는 항상 자신의 분석력을 자랑스럽게 여겼다. 그 결과, 포는 반대되는 관점에서 The Raven의 창작을 보여주기로 선택했다. "그 작품에 있어서 어떠한 한 지점도 우연이나 직관에 의거하지 않았다는 것, 즉 그 작업은 수학 문제의 정확성과 엄격한 결과로 그 완성까지 한 단계, 한 단계 진행되었다는 것을 분명히 하는 것이 내가 의도한 바이다." 그는 그 시의 길이와 주제에서부터 단어 하나와 심상 하나에 이르기까지 논리에 의해 모든 결정이 이끌어내어졌음을 강조했다.

구문 [9행~12행] As Poe put it, "Most writers — poets especially — prefer **having it understood that** they compose through a type of intense frenzy — an ecstatic intuition."
• 「have+O+p.p.」는 'O가 ~되다, ~당하다'의 의미이다. 여기서 it은 가목적어이며 that ~ intuition이 진목적어이다.

어휘 origination 시작, 개시; 시작, 창작 **light** 빛; 가벼운; 관점, 견지 **inspiration** 영감; 영감을 주는 사람[것] **ecstatic** 황홀해 하는, 열광하는 **intuition** 직관력; 직감, 직관 **pride oneself on** ~을 자랑하다 **analytical** 분석적인 **render** 만들다; 주다; 표현하다 **manifest** 나타내다; 분명해지다; 분명한 **attributable** ~가 원인인, ~에 기인하는 **proceed** (하던 일을 계속) 진행하다; 나아가다 **rigid** 엄격한, 융통성 없는

1 글의 제목 ③

해설 과학은 그것이 존재하는 문화의 배경 안에서 작용한다고 하면서, 동일한 증상을 각 문화마다 다른 병으로 진단할 것이라는 예를 들고 있다. 마지막에 결론적으로 생체 의학이 그것이 속한 문화의 배경 안에서 작용한다고 했으므로 글의 제목으로는 ③ '과학적 정보의 핵심은 문화적 맥락이다'가 적절하다.
① 과학은 문화적 편견을 뛰어넘을 수 없다
② 과학적 지식과 문화적 다양성
④ 과학은 문화적 차이를 해석하는 도구이다
⑤ 과학의 추구가 문화의 한계를 극복한다

해석 과학은 그것이 객관적 과정을 설명하는 물리 법칙에 근거를 두고 있다고 믿지만, 과학 역사학자 토마스 쿤은 과학적 사실은 오히려 문화적 관행이나 이론적 체계 내에 깊숙이 뿌리박혀 있다고 지적했다. 과학은 그것이 존재하는 문화의 맥락 안에서 작용하며, 완전한 절대적 객관성이 만연하는 진공(외부와 단절된 상태)에서 존재하지 않는다. 예를 들어, 생체 의학에서 의사는 항상 자신의 문화 맥락 안에서의 추정에 근거하여 진단을 내린다. 미국에서는 상당히 건강한 사람이 비대해진 비장을 갖고 있다면 단핵증을 의심받을 것이다. 남아메리카에서는 이 똑같은 사람이 샤가스병을 가진 것으로 의심받을 것이다. 에티오피아에서는 유잉종양으로 의심받을 것이다. 이 모든 진단은 옳을 것이다. 미국 의사가 사하라 사막 이남 아프리카에 있게 되거나 사우디아라비아 의사가 네브래스카에 있게 되면, 그들 각자는 자신들의 환자에 대해 적절한 진단을 내리는 데 어려움을 겪을 것이다. 생체 의학은 그것이 일부가 되는 문화의 배경 안에서 작용하기 때문에, 이 의사들은 물 밖의 물고기처럼 되어 현지 국가의 문화적 관습에 대해 충분히 인식하지 못할 것이다.

구문 [5행~7행] Science operates within the context of *the culture* [(which[that]) it exists in]; it does not exist in *a vacuum* [where pure absolute objectivity prevails].
• 첫 번째 [ ]는 목적격 관계대명사 which[that]가 생략된 관계사절로 the culture를 수식하며, 두 번째 [ ]는 관계부사 where가 이끄는 절로 a vacuum을 수식한다.

[14행~17행] **If** an American physician **were put** in sub-Sahara Africa, [or] a Saudi physician (were put) in Nebraska, each **would have** trouble making proper diagnoses of their patients.
• 「If+S′+과거동사 ～, S+조동사 과거형+동사원형....」의 가정법 과거 구문이 쓰였고, or 다음에 반복되는 were put은 생략되었다.

어휘 **embed** 깊숙이 뿌리박다; 파견하다　**practice** 관행; 실행　**paradigm** 사고[이론]의 틀; 모범　**vacuum** 진공 (상태)　**prevail** 만연하다; 우세하다　**biomedicine** 생체 의학　**diagnosis** 진단　**assumption** 추정; 가정　**reasonably** 상당히, 꽤; 합리적으로　**enlarged** 비대해진　**suspect** 의심하다; 용의자　**cognizant** 인식하고 있는, 알고 있는　[선택지] **transcend** 뛰어넘다, 초월하다　**bias** 편견; 성향

2 밑줄 어휘 ⑤

해설 넘치는 정보와 데이터의 시대에 살고 있는 우리는 생활 전반을 수량화하여 기록하게 되었는데, 이는 일상생활의 활동이 주는 기쁨을 달성해야 하는 과업으로 전환시키므로 우리의 의욕을 떨어뜨린다. 따라서 마지막 문장에서 너무 많은 데이터는 그에 대해 무슨 일이라도 하려는 우리의 욕구를 충족시키는 것이 아니라 꺾어버린다고 표현해야 하므로 ⑤의 fulfills를 defeats 등으로 고쳐야 한다.

해석 너무 많은 정보는 행동 변화를 방해할 수 있다는 것을 보여주는 연구가 증가하고 있다. 앱이 지출과 인터넷 사용과 다른 행동들은 말할 것도 없이 수면, 심박동수, 칼로리, 운동, 걸음, 계단과 호흡을 추적 관찰하면서 우리는 개인의 ① 수량화 시대에 살고 있다. 우리는 우리가 모든 것 중에서 얼마나 많은 일을 하고 있고, 해 왔으며, 해야 하는지를 즉시 알 수 있다. 이것이 알아두기에 좋은 정보이긴 하지만, 너무 많은 데이터는 운동, 수면, 식단과 저금 같은 심지어 건강한 활동에서 우리가 얻는 기쁨을 실제로 ② 줄일 수 있다. 데이터가 ③ 축적됨에 따라, 그리고 우리가 그것을 측정하고 추적하고 생각하기 위해 노력해야 하게 됨에 따라, 활동 그 자체가 '생활 방식'에서 '④ 일'로 옮겨갈 수 있다. 결과적으로 이러한 건강한 활동에 참여하고자 하는 우리의 동기는 떨어진다. 따라서 데이터가 우리에게 무엇을 '해야' 하는지 이해하는 데 도움을 줄지라도, 너무 많은 데이터는 그에 대해 무슨 일이라도 하려는 우리의 욕구를 ⑤ 충족시킨다(→ 꺾는다).

구문 [2행~6행] **With** *apps* **monitoring** sleep, heart rate, calories, exercise, steps, stairs, and breathing — not to mention spending and Internet use and other behaviors — / we live in *an age* (of personal quantification).
• 「with+O+v-ing」 분사구문이 쓰였으며, 'O가 v한 채로, O가 v하면서'의 의미이다. of personal quantification은 an age를 수식한다.

어휘 **monitor** 추적 관찰하다; 감시하다　**not to mention** ～은 말할 것도 없고　**quantification** 수량화, 정량화　**savings** 저금, 예금　**accumulate** 축적되다, 쌓이다　**engage in** ～에 참여하다

3 빈칸 추론 ⑤

해설 빈칸 문장을 먼저 읽고 지문에서 무엇을 파악해야 하는지 판단한 후 단서를 찾아 읽어 내려간다. 빈칸 문장으로 보아 실제로 냄새의 인식을 바꾸는 것이 무엇인지 찾아야 한다. 같은 냄새에 대해서 사람들의 반응이 다른 것은 처음에 들었던 냄새에 대한 정보 때문이며, 이것을 마지막에 'prejudice(선입견)'라고 표현해 놓았으므로, 빈칸에 들어갈 말로 가장 적절한 것은 ⑤ '예상'이다.
① 욕망 ② 관심사 ③ 행동 ④ 경험

해석 Monell Chemical Senses Center의 심리학자인 파멜라 달튼은 예상이 실제로 냄새의 인식을 바꾼다는 것을 증명했다. 참가자들은 세 그룹으로 나누어졌고, 그들은 실험실에 앉아, 유쾌하지도, 불쾌하지도 않은 냄새에 20분간 노출되었다. 달튼은 한 그룹에게는 그 냄새에 대해서 아무 말도 하지 않았고, 반면에 두 번째와 세 번째 그룹에게는 각각 그 냄새가 해로울 수도 있는 산업용 화학물질과 증류하여 얻은 순수 자연 추출물이라고 말했다. 그 결과는 아무 말도 듣지 않거나 긍정적인 정보를 들은 실험 대상자들은 시간이 지남에 따라 냄새가 약해진다고 느꼈다는 것이다. 대조적으로, 부정적인 정보를 들은 실험 대상자들은 시간이 지남에 따라 냄새가 강해진다고 느꼈다. 다시 말해서, 좋다고 생각되는 냄새는 의식에서 빠르게 사라지고, 반면에 해롭다고 생각되는 냄새는 계속 우리의 주의를 끌고 강하게 남아 있다. 이 실험은 선입견이 감각을 왜곡시키는 데 상당히 효과적이라는 것을 보여준다.

구문 [10행~12행] The result was // that *the subjects* [who were either told nothing or (told) positive information] felt the odor to be weaker **as** time passed.
• [ ] 부분이 the subjects를 수식하고 있으며, the odor는 felt의 목적어, to be weaker는 보어이다. 부사절 as time passed에 쓰인 접속사 as는 '～함에 따라'의 의미이다.

[14행~17행] In other words, / an odor [**that** is thought to be good] / disappears from consciousness fast, // **while** an odor (thought to be harmful) / keeps our attention and remains strong.

• [ ] 부분은 that이 이끄는 관계사절로 주어인 an odor을 수식한다. 접속사 while 이 포함된 절 내에서 ( )는 분사구로서 an odor을 수식한다.

어휘 **psychologist** 심리학자 **perception** 인식; 지각, 자각; 통찰력 **participant** 참가자; 참가하는 **lab** 실험실, 연구실 (= **laboratory**) **expose** 노출시키다; 드러내다; 폭로하다 **odor** 냄새, 향기 **pleasant** 유쾌한; 친절한 (↔ **unpleasant** 불쾌한; 불친절한) **industrial** 산업(용)의; 공업(상)의 **chemical** 화학물질; 화학의, 화학적인 **pure** 순수한, 깨끗한 **extract** 추출물; 추출(하다) **respectively** 각각, 각자 **subject** 실험[연구] 대상자, 피실험자; 주제 **consciousness** 의식, 자각 **prejudice** 선입견; 선입견을 갖게 하다 **distort** 왜곡시키다

4 무관 문장   ④

해설 글 전체의 내용은 논문의 제목에 색인 목록에 들어갈 단어를 포함하라는 것인데, ④는 논문의 길이에 대한 내용이므로 글 전체의 흐름과 무관하다.

해석 과학 논문의 제목은 장래의 독자가 그 논문을 읽을 때 계속해 나가야 할지 아닐지를 결정할 수 있는 첫 번째 근거를 제공해 주기 때문에 신중하게 선택해야 한다. ① 따라서 그것은 논문의 성격에 관해 가능한 한 많은 정보를 제공해야 하지만, 길이 제한을 넘어서서는 안 된다. ② 실제로 그것은 색인 작성자가 의지할 주된 출처가 될 것이다. ③ 그러므로 가능하다면, 색인 단어, 즉 논문이 주제 색인의 목록에 포함되어야 할 단어를 제목에 넣는 것이 바람직하다. ④ 그 결과, 학술지 논문은 보통 2~20페이지의 길이가 되는데, 그것은 저자들로 하여금 제한된 공간에 독자들이 필요로 하는 정보를 압축하게 만든다. ⑤ 예를 들어, 적은 수의 화합물이 어떤 방식으로 연구가 되었고, 그래서 그 논문이 그 화합물의 이름으로 된 색인 목록에 들어가야 한다면, 그 이름을 제목에 넣도록 하라.

구문 [1행~4행] The title of a scientific article / should be chosen with care // because it provides the first basis [**on which** a prospective reader can decide / whether or not to go further in reading the article].

• '전치사+관계대명사' 형태인 on which가 이끄는 [ ] 부분은 the first basis를 수식한다.

[8행~11행] Therefore, **it** is desirable, / if possible, / **to get index words into the title,** / i.e ., words [**under which** the paper should be listed in the subject index].

• 여기에서 it은 가주어, to 이하가 진주어이다. under which 이하는 '전치사+관계대명사'가 이끄는 관계사절로서 words를 수식한다.

어휘 **article** 논문; (신문, 잡지의) 기사 **basis** 근거; 기초, 기반 **prospective** 장래의, 곧 있을 **exceed** 넘다, 초과하다 **limitation** 제한, 한계 **in practice** 실제로, 실제는 **chief** 주된 **indexer** 색인 작성자 *cf.* **index** 색인; 색인에 넣다; 지표, 지수; 가리키다 **rely on** ~에 의지[의존]하다; ~을 믿다 **desirable** 바람직한; 호감 가는 **i.e.** 즉 ((라틴어 id est 의 약자)) **journal** (특정 분야를 다루는) 학술지, 신문, 잡지, 저널; 일기 **compress** 압축하다, 꾹 누르다 **chemical compound** 화합물

5 요약문 완성   ②

해설 새로운 것과 신기한 소비 경험에 의해서 자극과 흥분이 추구되지만, 그 소비 품목이 일단 매일의 일상에 포함되면 자극과 흥분은 사라지고, 그것들을 획득하고 이용하는 즐거움은 감소한다는 것이 글의 요지이다. 따라서 새로운 제품의 소비를

증가시킬(increases)수록 만족은 감소한다(declines)는 것을 알 수 있다.

해석 사회에서 어떤 사람들은 왜 늘 더 많은 것을 원하는가? 한 가지 분명한 해답은 안락의 지루함이다. 풍요로운 경제에서 물질적 편안함은 쉽게 성취된다. 가난한 사회에서는 매우 하기 어려운, 간단한 욕구를 충족하는 즐거움이 없어진다. 매일이 잔칫날이다. 긴장은 단지 새로운 것과 신기한 것에 의해서만 생긴다. 그러지 않으면 지루한 세상에서 새롭고 신기한 소비 경험을 통해서 자극과 흥분이 추구된다. 새로운 소비성 품목의 신기함은, 일단 매일의 일상에 포함되면 차츰 사라지고, 그것들을 획득하고 이용하는 즐거움은 감소한다. 새로운 컴퓨터 게임을 하는 것은 흥분을 유발하고 긴장을 만들어내는데, 그 게임을 하는 것을 배우고 그것을 잘해 나가는 것은 긴장 감소라는 즐거움을 가져온다. 그 경험이 반복되면서 흥분의 수준이 감소하고, 즐거움도 또한 그러하다.

> 한 개인이 새롭고 신기한 제품의 소비를 (A) 증가시킬수록, 그 소비 경험에서 나오는 개인의 만족이나 행복은 결국 (B) 감소한다.

구문 [9행~12행] **Once** (it is) **incorporated** into daily routines, // the novelty of new consumer items wears off and the pleasure of acquiring and making use of them diminishes.

• Once ~ routines는 접속사가 포함된 분사구문으로, '일단 ~하면'이라는 뜻의 접속사 once 다음에 it(= the novelty of new consumer items) is가 생략되어 있다고 보면 이해가 쉽다.

[15행~16행] As the experience is repeated, the level of arousal *diminishes*, and **so does pleasure.**

• '~도 또한 그렇다'라는 뜻의 「so+대동사+주어」 구문으로 여기서 대동사 does는 diminishes를 대신한다.

어휘 **obvious** 분명한 **boredom** 지루함 **comfort** 안락, 편안함 **satisfy** 충족시키다, 만족시키다 **want** 욕구, 욕망 **remove** 제거하다, 없애다 **feast** 축제, 잔치 **tension** 긴장(감) **arouse** 야기하다, 자극하다 **novel** 신기한, 새로운 **stimulation** 자극 **arousal** 흥분, 각성 **consumption** 소비 **incorporate** 포함하다, 통합하다 **novelty** 신기함, 새로움 **wear off** 차츰 사라지다 **diminish** 감소하다, 줄어들다 **spark** 유발하다, 갑자기 불러일으키다 **reduction** 감소

[선택지] **equalize** 동등하게 하다 **reinforce** 강화하다 **postpone** 연기하다, 미루다

1 빈칸 추론   ②

해설 빈칸 문장으로 보아 인간이 어떠한 경향이 있는지를 찾아야 한다. 무작위로 배치되어 있는 별을 통해서 북두칠성을 바라보고, 부분적인 일을 통해서 전체를 일반화시키는 예시가 이어서 나오므로 정답은 ② '부분적이거나 무작위적인 증거로부터 전체적인 패턴을 보는'이 가장 적절하다.

① 옛것을 더 자세히 연구함으로써 새로운 것을 이해하는

③ 쉽게 이해될 수 있는 간단한 답을 선호하는

④ 기존에 있던 믿음을 뒷받침하지 않으면 중요한 증거를 무시하는

⑤ 함께 발생한 두 사건이 틀림없이 관련이 있다고 가정하는

해석 인간은 부분적이거나 무작위적인 증거로부터 전체적인 패턴을 보는 경향이 있다. 비록 우리가 실제로 보는 것은 단지 일곱 개의 빛의 점일 뿐이지만, 우리는 모두 밤하늘의 별들 속에서 북두칠성을 본 적이 있다. 인간은 시각적인 인식뿐만 아니라 다른 정보를 가지고서도 역시 의미를 추론한다. 이용 가능한 증거에 의해서 그런 결론이 보장되지 않을 때조차도, 몇 가지 사실로부터 결론을 도출함으로써 논리에서의 오류가 저질러진다. 소매업자들은 몇 가지 눈에 아주 잘 띄는 물건에 낮은 가격을 표시할 때 이러한 사실을 알고 있는데, 이는 그 가게에서는 전체적인 가격이 낮다는 추론을 하도록 한다. 어떤 사람이 동네 구멍가게에서 산 복권이 당첨되면, 그곳이 복권을 구입하는 행운의 장소가 되는 것이다.

구문 [3행~4행] ~, even though *the only thing* [(that) we have really seen] are
                         C   V
seven points of light.
S

• 보어인 the only thing이 강조되어 나가고 주어와 동사가 도치되었다. 주어 seven points of light가 복수명사이므로 복수동사 are가 쓰였다. [ ] 부분은 목적격 관계대명사 that이 생략된 관계사절로 선행사 the only thing을 수식한다.

[5행~6행] Humans infer meanings **not only** with visual perceptions **but** (with) other information as well.

• 「not only A but (also) B」 구문으로 'A뿐만 아니라 B도'의 의미이다.

[9행~11행] Retailers know this // when they announce low prices / on a few very visible items, / **leading** to the inference / that overall prices are lower at that store.

• 밑줄 친 the inference와 that ~ store는 동격 관계이다. leading이 이끄는 분사구는 앞 절 내용에 대한 '결과'를 나타내는 것으로 which leads ~로 바꿔 쓸 수 있다.

어휘 be predisposed to-v v하는 경향이 있다 **Big Dipper** 북두칠성 **infer** 추론[추측]하다; 암시하다 **perception** 인식; 지각, 자각; 통찰력 **commit** 저지르다, 범하다; 약속하다; 헌신하다 **warrant** 보장하다, 보증하다; 보증(서) **evidence** 증거, 흔적; 증거가 되다; 증언하다 **retailer** 소매업자, 소매상; 소매업 **lottery** 복권 **purchase** 구입(하다), 구매(하다)

[선택지] **comprehend** 이해하다; 포함하다 **partial** 부분적인; 불공평한 **assume** 가정[추정]하다

2 글의 순서   ⑤

해설 고대 영어에서 중세 영어로의 이행의 시발점이 된 것이 노르만 정복이었다는 주어진 글 뒤에 정복민인 노르만인들(They)이 자신의 언어를 버리고 프랑스어를 적극적으로 사용하게 되었다는 (C)가 이어지고, 이러한 프랑스어가 영국의 상류층의 언어가 되었다는 (B)가 이어진다. 다음으로 반면(On the other hand) 하위층들은 계

속해서 영어를 사용해서 우리가 중세 영어라고 부르는 것은 바로 고대 영어와 프랑스어가 혼합된 것이라는 내용을 담은 (A)가 이어져야 한다.

해석 고대 영어에서 중세 영어로의 이행을 시작한 사건은 1066년 노르만의 정복이었는데, 그때에는 정복자 윌리엄이 프랑스 북부의 노르망디로부터 영국을 침략해서 정복한 노르만인들이 영국을 지배하기 시작했다.
(C) 그들(노르만인들) 자신은 약 200년 전 프랑스 북부에 정착했던 바이킹의 후손들이었다. 하지만 그들은 자신들의 언어를 완전히 버렸고 노르망디에서 단 하나의 노르만어도 살아남지 못할 정도까지 온 마음을 다해 프랑스어를 받아들였다.
(B) 프랑스어는 300년 이상 동안 영국의 왕과 귀족의 언어가 되었다. 그것(프랑스어)이 궁정, 행정, 그리고 문화의 구어였던 반면, 라틴어는 대개 문어로 특히 교회와 공식 기록에서 사용되었다.
(A) 반면, 소작농들과 하위 계층들(인구의 절대다수인 어림잡아 95%)은 계속해서 영어를 사용했는데, 그것은 노르만인들에 의해 하위 계층의 저속한 언어로 간주되었다. 이렇게 고대 영어와 프랑스어가 혼합된 것이 바로 중세 영어라 여겨지는 것이다.

구문 [6행~9행] On the other hand, the peasantry and lower classes (the vast majority of the population, an estimated 95%) continued to speak *English*, //
which <u>was considered</u> **(by the Normans)** a low-class, vulgar tongue.
               V

• 계속적 용법의 관계대명사 which가 이끄는 절이 English를 보충 설명한다. which가 이끄는 관계대명사절은 원래 SVOC 문형의 수동태로, O가 주어로 나가서 관계대명사가 되고 C인 a low-class, vulgar tongue이 그 자리에 그대로 남은 형태이다.

어휘 **transition** 이행; 변천; 과도 **conquest** 정복 *cf.* **conqueror** 정복자 *cf.* **conquer** 정복하다; 이기다 **invade** 침략[침입]하다; (사생활 등을) 침해하다 **rule** 지배하다, 통치하다; 규칙 **peasantry** 소작농 (계층) **estimated** 어림의, 추측[예상]의 **tongue** 언어; 혀 **mixture** 혼합물 **refer to A as B** A를 B라고 여기다[간주하다] **nobility** 귀족 (계층); 고귀함 **verbal language** 구어 **court** 궁정; 법원; (테니스 등의) 경기장 **administration** 행정 (업무), 관리; 집행; 투약 **descend from** ~의 후손[자손]이다; ~로부터 내려오다 **abandon** 버리다; 포기하다 **wholeheartedly** 온 마음을 다해 **adopt** 받아들이다; 입양하다 **to the extent that** ~한 정도까지

3 문장 넣기   ③

해설 이 글은 예술이 창의적인 통찰력의 강력한 원천으로 작용한다는 것을 갈릴레오의 사례를 예로 들어 설명하고 있는 내용이다. 주어진 문장의 Instead를 통해 지그재그 패턴을 인식할 수 있었던 것과 대조되는 내용이 주어진 문장 앞에 나와야 함을 알 수 있으며, ② 이후 문장의 망원경의 충분하지 못한 확대력이 그 내용이 될 수 있다. ③ 이후에 나온 the dark and light regions(그 어둡고 밝은 지역들)가 주어진 문장의 the light and dark areas of the moon(달의 밝은 지역과 어두운 지역)을 가리키는 것이므로 주어진 문장은 ③에 들어가는 것이 가장 적절하다.

해석 단지 특정 종류의 독창적인 사람이 예술에 대한 노출을 추구하는 것은 아니다. 예술은 또한 결과적으로 창의적인 통찰력의 강력한 원천으로서의 역할을 한다. 갈릴레오가 달 표면에 산이 있다는 정말 놀라운 발견을 했을 때, 사실 그의 망원경은 그 발견을 뒷받침해 줄 만큼 충분한 확대 능력을 갖추고 있지 않았다. 대신, 그는 달의 밝은 지역과 어두운 지역을 구분 짓는 지그재그 패턴을 알아보았다. 다른 천문학자들도 유사한 망원경을 통해 관찰을 하고 있었지만, 갈릴레오만이 그 어둡고 밝은 지역들이 암시하는 바를 제대로 인식할 수 있었다. 그는 물리학과 천문학에서 필요로 하는 깊이 있는 경험뿐 아니라 회화와 소묘에 폭넓은 경험도 또한 지니고 있었다. 빛과 그림자를 묘사하는 데 집중하는 'chiaroscuro'라 일컬어지는 기법에서의 예

술적 훈련 덕분에, 갈릴레오는 다른 이들은 발견하지 못한 (달 표면의) 산을 발견할 수 있었다.

구문 [14행~17행] Thanks to artistic training in *a technique* (called chiaroscuro), **which focuses on representations of light and shade**, Galileo was able to detect *mountains* [which others were not able to detect].

• ( )는 a technique를 수식하고, which focuses ~ and shade는 계속적 용법의 관계대명사로 a technique called chiaroscuro를 보충 설명한다. [ ]는 목적격 관계대명사 which가 이끄는 관계사절로 앞의 mountains를 수식한다.

어휘 **recognize** 알아보다, 인식하다 **separate** 구분 짓다; 구분[분리]된 **original** 독창적인; 최초의; 원래의 **seek** 추구하다; 찾다 **exposure** 노출; 폭로 **serve as** ~의 역할을 하다 **in turn** 결과적으로; 차례로 **insight** 통찰력; 이해 **astonishing** 정말 놀라운, 믿기 힘든 **telescope** 망원경 **magnify** 확대하다; 과장하다 **astronomer** 천문학자 *cf.* **astronomy** 천문학 **appreciate** (제대로) 인식하다; 이해하다; 감사하다; 감상하다 **implication** 암시, 함축 **region** 지역, 지방; 분야 **physics** 물리학 **representation** 묘사, 표현; 대표, 대리 **detect** 발견하다, 감지하다

4~5 장문　　　　4 ⑤　5 ⑤

해설 **4.** 자제력이 높은 사람들은 남다른 의지력을 갖고 있는 것이 아니라 자신의 행동을 자동적으로 이행해줄 좋은 습관을 형성한 사람들이라는 내용의 글이므로 제목으로 가장 적절한 것은 ⑤ '자제력은 의지력이라기보다는 전략이다'이다.
① 자제력의 심리적 이점
② 우리는 언제, 그리고 왜 자제력에 실패하는가?
③ 좋은 습관을 만들고 의지력을 쌓기
④ 의지력에 대한 통념은 당신을 어떻게 제지하는가
5. (e)가 있는 문장의 주어 They는 자제력이 낮게 측정된 사람들이다. 이전 내용에 의하면 '자제력이 높은 사람들'은 외부 환경을 통제함으로써 자제력을 높일 수 있었다. 따라서 '자제력이 낮은 사람들'이 확립하기 위해 노력하지 않고 있는 것은 내부의 힘이 아니라 외부 환경에 대한 힘임을 추론할 수 있다. 따라서 (e)의 internal을 external로 바꿔 써야 한다.

해석 높은 수준의 자제력을 가진 학생들은 건강, 부(富), 행복을 달성하는 데 특히 유능하다. 그들의 삶은 여러 영역에서 성공으로 특징지어진다. 우리는 이러한 개인들이 (a) 예상되는 방식으로, 즉 의지력을 적극적으로 발휘함으로써 이러한 감탄스러운 결과를 이룬 것이 아님을 발견했다. 그들의 성공은 원치 않는 행동을 억제하는 어떤 초인적인 능력에 기인한 것이 아니다. '자제력' 척도에서 고득점을 내는 사람들은 효과적인 전략을 가지고 있다. 그들은 통제력을 전혀 사용하지 않는다. 대신에 그들은 자신의 행동을 자동화해줄 습관들을 형성한다. 습관이 그들의 목표를 달성하는 것을 쉽게 만들어준다.
높은 '자제력'을 가진 사람들이 어떻게 성공하는지에 대한 또 다른 중요한 이야기가 있다. 그것은 (b) 상황과 관계있다. 높은 '자제력'을 가진 사람들의 재능은 이로운 습관을 형성하는 방법을 단지 알기만 하는 것을 넘어서는 것 같다. 한 온라인 설문조사에서, '자제력' 척도에서 높은 점수를 받은 사람들은 '나는 내 장기적 목표를 달성하기 위해 나를 잘 붙잡아주는 친구를 선택한다' 혹은 '일하거나 공부할 때, 나는 일부러 주의를 산만하게 하는 것이 없는 장소를 찾아나선다' 그리고 '나는 비도덕적으로 행동하도록 유혹받을지 모르는 상황을 (c) 회피한다'와 같은 진술에도 동의했다. 이러한 사람들은 행동을 쉽게 혹은 어렵게 만드는 상황의 힘을 이해하고 있었다. 그들은 자신의 환경을 통제하면, 자신의 행동 또한 통제하리라는 것을 인식하고 있었다. 일단 누군가가 이 점을 이해하면, 이로운 습관을 형성하기가 더 쉬워진다. '자제력' 시험에서 (d) 낮은 점수를 받은 학생들은 이 진술들에 그만큼 강하게 동의하지 않았다. 그들은 올바른 (e) 내부의(→ 외부의) 힘, 즉 바라는 행동을 추동하고 바라지 않는 행동에는 마찰을 가하는 힘을 확립하여 자신의 삶을 더 쉽게 만들기 위해 노력하지 않고 있었다. 높은 '자제력'을 가진 사람들은 단지 올바른 것을 말하지 않는다.

그들은 그것을 실천한다.

구문 [11행~12행] Habits **make it** *easy* **to accomplish their goals**.

• it은 가목적어이고 to accomplish 이하가 진목적어이다. easy는 목적어를 설명하는 보어로 「make+it+형용사+to-v」는 'v하는 것을 (형용사)하게 만들다'의 뜻이다.

[27행~28행] **Once** someone understands this, // **it** gets easier **to form beneficial habits**.

• 접속사 Once는 '일단 ~하면'의 뜻이다. it은 가주어이고 to form 이하가 진주어이다.

어휘 **front** (활동의) 영역; 앞면 **exert** 행사하다, 가하다 **inhibit** 억제하다 **scale** (판단의) 척도 **automate** 자동화하다 **have to do with** ~와 관계가 있다 **keep A on track** A가 계속해서 나아가도록 확실히 하다 **deliberately** 일부러, 고의로 **distraction** 주의 산만 **circumstance** 상황 **friction** 마찰

1 필자 주장　③

해설 이 글은 부모의 책무에 대한 글로서, 부모는 자녀가 결정한 것에 대해 가능한 모든 영향을 알게 하고 자녀가 그에 대해 독립적으로 사고할 수 있도록 지도하여, 결과적으로 자녀가 꿈을 키워나갈 수 있게 해주어야 한다는 내용이다. 그러므로, 필자의 주장으로 가장 적절한 것은 ③이다.

해석 부모는 단호해야 하지만 제안을 잘 받아들여야 한다. 즉 권위가 있어야 하지만 독재자가 되어서는 안 된다. 그들은 또한 자녀들에게 너무 많은 자유와 독립을 주는 것도 경계해야 하는데, 왜냐하면 아이들은 자신의 결정에 대한 가능한 모든 영향을 알지 못하기 때문이다. 따라서 아이들이 자신의 결정에 대한 가능한 결과를 이해하도록 돕는 것은 부모에게 달려 있다. 부모의 의무는 자신의 자녀에게 사고의 독립을 주는 것, 즉 아이가 상황에 대해서, 무슨 일이 발생할 수 있는지, 무슨 일이 발생하지 않을지, 선택지가 있다면 무엇이 가장 효과가 좋을지 등에 대하여 생각하게 하는 것이다. 당신의 자녀가 불가능한 것을 생각하게 하고, 그들이 꿈꾸고 희망하고 열망하게 하라! 그들이 당신의 신념에 도전하게 하라. 왜냐하면 그로부터 새로운 답과 새로운 신념이 생겨날 것이기 때문이다!

구문 [12행~13행] Let *them* **challenge** your beliefs // — because from those will arise new answers and new beliefs!
　　　　　　　　　　　　　　　　　　　V　　　　S
• 「let O 동사원형」의 형태로서 'O가 v하게 하다'의 뜻이다. because절에서 동사는 will arise이고 주어는 new answers and new beliefs인 도치구문이 나타났는데, 「장소부사구(from those)+동사+주어」의 어순을 따랐다.

어휘 authoritative 권위 있는　dictator 독재자　wary 경계하는, 조심하는　be up to ~에게 달려 있다　work out (일이) 잘 풀리다　aspire 열망하다

2 밑줄 함의　③

해설 소화관 미생물은 자기들이 원하는 것을 우리가 먹도록 하기 위해 독소를 생산해 기분이 나빠지게 만들거나 화학적 보상 물질을 방출해 기분이 좋게도 만든다. 이를 미생물이 우리를 꼭두각시처럼 조종한다고 다시 한번 언급하므로 밑줄 친 당근과 채찍 접근법은 ③ '소화관 미생물은 자기들의 목적을 위해 우리 신체를 여러 방식으로 통제한다.'를 의미한다.
① 소화관 미생물은 우리 건강을 위해 두 종류의 화학물질을 만들어낸다.
② 소화관 미생물은 우리 몸에서 자기들이 필요로 하는 것을 선택해서 흡수한다.
④ 소화관 미생물은 자기가 원하는 것을 얻기 위해 우리 신체가 좋은 건강을 유지하도록 돕는다.
⑤ 소화관 미생물은 인간의 신체에 이롭고 해로운 영향을 모두 줄 수 있다.

해석 서로 다른 박테리아 종에게는 서로 다른 영양소가 필요하다. 어떤 것들은 당분을 선호하고, 다른 것들은 지방을 주식으로 한다. 그러나 그것들은 먹이를 얻기 위해서, 그리고 생태계 내에서 발판을 유지하기 위해서, 서로 싸우기만 하는 것은 아니다. 소화관 미생물은 흔히 여러분이 원하는 것과는 다른 것들을 원하며, 자기들의 목표를 추구하는 데 거리낌이 없다. 소화관 미생물은 여러분의 미주 신경의 신경 신호를 바꿈으로써 여러분의 행동과 기분에 영향을 주는 능력을 가지고 있다. 그것들은 자기들이 원하는 것을 여러분이 먹지 않을 때 여러분을 기분 나쁘게 만들기 위해 미각 수용기를 변화시키고 독소를 생산하거나, 아니면 여러분이 (그것들이 원하는 것을) 할 때 여러분이 기분 좋아지도록 화학적 보상 물질을 방출한다. 따라서 여러분 소화관 내의 박테리아는 실제로는 여러분을 조종하고 있다. 이것을 이해하는 것이

중요한데, 왜냐하면 그것이 바로 여러분의 식단을 바꾸는 것을 매우 힘들게 만드는 것이기 때문이다. 몸속의 미생물은 여러분을 큰 꼭두각시처럼 이용하여 자기들이 갈망하는 것을 여러분이 주도록 강요하고자 한다. 그것은 당근과 채찍 접근법이다.

구문 [8행~11행] They change taste receptors and produce toxins **to make** *you* **feel** bad when you don't eat *the things* [(which[that]) they want], or release chemical rewards **to make** *you* **feel** good when you *do*.
• to make 이하는 「사역동사(make)+목적어(you)+원형부정사(feel)」의 구조이다. [ ] 부분은 목적격 관계대명사 which[that]가 생략되어 the things를 수식하는 관계사절이다. 밑줄 친 do는 eat the things they want를 대신하는 대동사이다.

[13행~16행] It's important to understand this, because it's what makes **it** so hard **to change your diet**: // *the bugs* inside you are playing you like a big marionette, / **trying** to force you to give them what they crave.
• 밑줄 친 It은 가주어, to understand this가 진주어이고, 굵게 표시된 it은 가목적어, to change your diet가 진목적어이다. trying 이하는 부대상황을 나타내는 분사구문으로 의미상의 주어는 the bugs이다.

어휘 bacterial 박테리아[세균성]의　nutrient 영양소, 영양분　live off ~을 주식으로 하다　retain 유지[보유]하다　gut 소화관; 위장　be shy about ~을 꺼리다[두려워하다]　go after ~을 추구하다　alter 바꾸다, 변경하다　neural 신경의　taste receptor 미각 수용기　toxin 독소　release 방출하다; 발표하다　manipulate 조종하다, 조작하다　crave 갈망[열망]하다　approach 접근(법); 접근하다
[선택지] absorb 흡수하다　stay in good shape 좋은 건강을 유지하다

3 빈칸 추론　⑤

해설 빈칸 문장으로 보아 'they(그것들)'가 무엇을 말하는지, 또 그것들을 '가입자들끼리의 암호'라고 말한다면 '무엇을 하는 것'인지 찾아야 한다. 첫 문장을 통해서 오늘날의 문자 메시지와 이집트 문자의 유사성이 rebus라는 개념이며, 이것은 새로운 것이 아니라 예전부터 계속 이어져 오는 전통적인 것이므로, 비밀 단체에 속한 사람들만의 암호라고 하는 것은 앞에 언급된 전통적으로 이어져 내려왔다는 것을 모르고 하는 말이라는 것을 알 수 있다. 따라서 답은 ⑤ '언어의 역사를 무시하는 것'이다.
① 그 기원을 밝히는 것
② 재치의 핵심을 왜곡하는 것
③ 전통에 경의를 표하는 것
④ 그것들을 진부한 표현이라고 생각하는 것

해석 문자 메시지와 이집트 문자 사이에는 닮은 점이 있는데, 바로 'rebus'라는 개념이다. 원래의 정의에 의하면, rebus는 그림이 나타내는 물체라기보다는 단어의 소리를 나타내도록 사용된, 전적으로 그림으로 구성된 메시지이다. 그것들은 라틴어에 알려져 있고, 유럽의 예술과 문학에도 등장한다. 레오나르도 다빈치는 rebus 수수께끼를 만들어 냈다. 벤 존슨은 자신의 한 희곡에서 그 수수께끼들을 조롱했다. 그래서 사실 영어로 'see you later'를 'c u l8r'로 쓰는 그런 종류의 문자 메시지에 새로울 것이 전혀 없다. 그것들은 유럽의 언어 전통의 일부이며, 유사한 특징들은 기록된 모든 언어에서 찾아볼 수 있을 것이다. 개별적인 문자 메시지를 보내는 사람들은 그러한 전통을 의식하지 못한 채 몇몇 현대의 약어들을 고안했을지도 모르지만, 그들은 자기들에 앞서서 수 세대의 사람들이 했던 것을 하고 있을 뿐이다. 그리고 분명히 우리가 문자 메시지에서 그러한 형태들을 만날 때 놀랄 이유는 없는데, 우리 모두는 전에 그것들을 본 적이 있기 때문이다. 그것들이 '비밀 의식을 통해 단체에 가입한 가입자들끼리의 암호'의 일부라고 말한다면 언어의 역사를 무시하는 것이다.

구문 [2행~5행] A rebus is *a message* [**which**, (in its original definition), consists entirely of *pictures* [**that** are used to represent the sounds of words, / rather than *the objects* [(**which[that]**) they refer to]]].

• which, in its 이하는 주격 관계대명사가 이끄는 관계사절로 a message를 수식한다. that are used ~ they refer to 부분은 주격 관계대명사가 이끄는 관계사절로 pictures를 수식한다. 세 번째 [ ] 부분은 목적격 관계대명사 which[that]가 생략된 절로 the objects를 수식하고, 여기에서 밑줄 친 they는 pictures를 지칭한다.

어휘 similarity 닮은 점; 유사성 notion 개념, 관념, 생각 entirely 전적으로, 완전히 literature 문학 (작품) ridicule 조롱하다, 비웃다 novel 새로운; (장편) 소설 linguistic 언어(학)의 devise 고안[발명]하다 abbreviation 약어; 생략 generation 세대, 대(代); 발생 be taken aback 놀라다 encounter (우연히) 만나다; 만남 suggest 말하다; 제안하다; 암시하다

[선택지] reveal 밝히다, 드러내다 origin 기원, 근원 distort 왜곡하다; 비틀다 pay respect to A A에 경의를 표하다 cliché 진부한 표현 ignore 무시하다

4 글의 순서 ②

해설 대구 개체 수 감소에 대해 캐나다 정부가 바다표범을 사냥한다는 방안을 내놓았다는 주어진 문장 다음에는 바다표범을 잡는 것이 대구의 개체 수 회복에 도움이 될 것이라는 정부 측의 기대가 기술된 (B)가 나와야 한다. (B) 마지막의 정부 측이 놓친 생태계의 역학 관계로 인한 영향에 대한 구체적인 예가 for example이라는 연결어와 함께 (A)에서 제시된다. (C)는 (A)의 내용을 재확인하며 생태계의 개체 수 통제의 어려움을 결론으로 제시하며 글을 마무리 짓는다.

해석 대서양 대구 개체수가 남획으로 인해 붕괴됐을 때, 캐나다 정부는 북대서양 하프 바다표범이 대구를 먹는다고 알려져 있었기 때문에 바다표범을 죽이는 사냥 원정을 제안했다.
(B) 대구의 주된 포식자인 바다표범을 없애는 것이 대구 개체수가 회복되게 해 줄 것이라고 추정되었다. 정부가 깨닫지 못한 것은 대구와 바다표범의 관계가 생태계에서의 많은 다른 덜 두드러진 종들에 의해 영향을 받는다는 것이었다.
(A) 예를 들어 바다표범은 대구뿐만 아니라 다른 150종을 먹는데, 그중 많은 것이 또한 대구를 먹는다! 그래서 바다표범의 개체수를 줄이는 것이 실제로 더 많은 대구를 낳게 할지 더 적은 대구를 낳게 할지를 미리 알 방도가 전혀 없었다.
(C) 여덟 종만 포함되어 있는 먹이 그물에서 바다표범을 대구와 연결시켜줄 1천만 개가 넘는 별개의 인과관계의 연결고리가 있을 수 있다. 그토록 복잡하고 역동적인 사회에서 우리가 어떻게 효과적인 통제 관리를 행사할 수 있겠는가?

구문 [5행~6행] The seals, for example, **not only** fed on cod **but also** (fed) on *150 other species*, **many of which** also fed on cod!

• 「not only A but also B」는 'A뿐만 아니라 B도'의 의미이다. but also 다음에 fed가 생략된 것으로 볼 수 있다. many of which는 fed의 주어이며 여기서 which는 150 other species를 지칭한다.

[10행~12행] **It** was assumed // **that eliminating the seals**, a principal cod predator, would allow the cod populations to rebound.

• It은 가주어이고 that 이하는 진주어이다. eliminating the seals는 that절 내의 동명사 주어이다.

어휘 cod 대구 collapse 붕괴되다 overfishing 남획 expedition 원정 feed on ~을 먹고살다 in advance 미리 eliminate 제거하다 principal 주요한 rebound 원래대로 되돌아가다 prominent 두드러진 distinct 별개의 cause and effect 인과관계 exercise 행사하다, 발휘하다 dynamic 역동적인

5 문장 넣기 ③

해설 트라우마 이후에 사람들은 세계관을 재구축하고 미래에 더 잘 대처할 수 있다는 주어진 문장은 ③번 바로 앞 문장에 나온 '성장'의 긍정적 내용을 서술한 것으로 볼 수 있다. 또한 ③번 뒤의 문장에서는 사람들이 전에 없던 기회를 '또한' 부여받을 수 있다 하는데, 이는 '성장'의 두 번째 긍정적 내용을 추가 서술한 것으로 볼 수 있으므로 주어진 문장은 두 문장의 사이인 ③번에 위치해야 한다.

해석 사람들은 인생을 살아갈 때 자신이 누구인지, 세상은 어떻게 돌아가는지에 대한 여러 가지 믿음을 쌓아나간다. 이러한 여러 가지 믿음은 "심장병은 나보다 나이가 더 많은 사람들에게만 영향을 미친다."와 같은 구체적인 믿음을 포함한다. 물론 문제는 실제 세상에서의 사건이 그러한 믿음에 도전을 가할 수 있다는 것이다. 도전이 충분히 크면, 사람들은 어쩔 수 없이 그들의 믿음을 단념하고 새로운 믿음을 개발해야 할지도 모른다. 성장이 일어나는 것은 바로 이러한 상황에서이다. 트라우마 다음에 사람들은 현재 그들에게 느껴지는 세상의 모습대로 세상에 대해 더욱 면밀하게 지도를 그리는 방식으로 그들의 가정을 다시 세울지도 모르며, 이는 차례로 미래의 대처를 용이하게 할지도 모른다. 사람들은 또한 전에 못 보던 기회(예를 들면 새로운 경력, 새로운 관계)를 부여받을지도 모른다. 이런 식으로, 그리고 다른 방식으로, 사람들이 트라우마와 관련된 상실과 고통과 나란히, 혹은 그 때문에 어떤 성장을 경험하는 것이 가능하다. 성장(예를 들어 사회적 지지의 개선)은 사실 트라우마를 처리하려는 사람들의 시도에서 생겨나는 것일지도 모른다.

구문 [12행~13행] **It is** in this context **that** growth can occur.

• '~한 것은 바로 …이다'라는 의미의 「It is ... that ~」 강조구문이 쓰여 in this context를 강조하고 있다.

[15행~18행] In these ways, and others, **it** is possible *for individuals* **to experience** some growth alongside of, and because of, *the loss and pain* (associated with the trauma).

• others는 other ways로 바꿔 볼 수 있다. it은 가주어, to experience 이하가 진주어이며 for individuals는 to experience의 의미상 주어이다. ( ) 부분은 수동의 의미로 the loss and pain을 수식하며, the loss and pain은 alongside of와 because of의 공통 목적어이다.

어휘 subsequent 그다음의, 차후의 trauma 정신적 외상 rebuild 다시 세우다 facilitate 용이하게 하다 cope 대처하다 heart trouble 심장병 alongside 옆에, 나란히

1 글의 주제 ②

해설 노화에 대해 두려움을 갖고 어떻게든 피하려는 움직임이 있지만, 건강한 노화를 위해 태도가 가장 중요하며 긍정적인 태도를 갖는 것의 이점에 대해 설명한 글이므로 주제로 가장 적절한 것은 ② '노화에 대해 긍정적인 태도를 갖는 것의 중요성'이다.
① 노화의 생물학적 원인과 노화 관련 질병
③ 노화 과정을 늦추는 데 도움이 되는 효과적인 전략들
④ 노인들 간의 노화에 대한 지식과 태도
⑤ 노화에 대한 태도와 삶의 만족 간의 관계

해석 느린 노화는 노화를 노쇠, 악화, 쇠퇴와 관련된 경험이라기보다는 긍정적인 성장 경험으로 재정의할 것을 추구한다. 안티 에이징 운동은 일반적으로 '늙어감'을 무슨 수를 써서라도 피해야 할 것으로 자리매김하고자 한다. 그것은 사람들의 두려움을 먹고 살고 일반적으로 진짜 해법을 제공하지도 않는다. 이것은 비현실적이며 불필요하다. 우리는 노화를 두려워하는 것이 아니라 늦추고 싶어 한다. 건강한 노화에서 태도가 가장 중요한 단 하나의 요소이다. 긍정적인 태도는 건강한 행동을 북돋우고 우리에게 우리 삶의 통제권을 준다. 그것은 실패할지도 모르는 다른 많은 것들을 보상하는 것 이상을 할 수 있다. 노화는 개인으로서의 우리 자신뿐만 아니라 우리 사회를 위해서도 가치 있는 경험으로 다시 자리 매겨질 필요가 있다. 노화 과정을 '사랑하는 것', 노화를 긍정적인 경험으로 재설정하고 기쁨과 회복과 성장과 더불어 나이들 수 있도록 주도권을 쥐는 것이 가능하다.

구문 [12행~14행] Ageing needs to be re-positioned as an experience of value, **not only** for ourselves as individuals, **but** for our society.
• 「not only A but (also) B (A뿐만 아니라 B도)」 구문인데 A와 B에 해당하는 부분에 for로 시작되는 전치사구가 위치했다.

어휘 ageing 노화 degeneration 악화 decline 쇠퇴 position 배치하다 at all costs 어떤 희생을 치르더라도 feed on ~을 먹고 살다 compensate for ~을 보상하다 of value 가치 있는

2 밑줄 어법 ③

해설 ③ 요구·주장·제안 등을 나타내는 동사(require, insist, recommend, suggest 등)에 이어지는 that절이 '~해야 한다'는 당위성을 나타낼 때에는 「(should)+동사원형」을 쓴다. 따라서 is의 원형 be가 와야 한다.
① '(미래에) 생각하기를 잊어버렸다'는 문맥이므로 forget to-v가 적절. *cf.* forget v-ing: (과거에) ~한 것을 잊어버리다
② a set of rules를 수식하는 분사로, 규칙들이 방법에 관한 모든 면을 '기술하므로' 현재분사인 describing이 적절하다.
④ '피하는 데 매우 신경을 쓰다'의 의미로 전치사 to의 목적어인 following과 and로 연결된 동명사구 병렬구조로 보는 것이 적절하다.
⑤ 주어가 a leading cause이므로 단수동사가 적절하다.

해석 사람들이 규칙에 너무 치중한 나머지 생각할 것을 잊어버린 전형적인 예는 1980년대에 석면 제거 프로젝트에서 일어난 일이다. 정부가 건물에서 석면을 포함한 물질을 제거하는 방법에 관한 모든 면을 기술한 수백 페이지 두께의 일련의 규칙들을 발표하였다. 근로자들이 마스크를 착용해야 하고, 공기 중에 떠 있는 (석면) 먼지의 양을 줄이기 위해 석면이 젖어 있어야 한다고 요구하는 것들과 같은 대부분의 규칙은 사람들이 석면 섬유를 들이마시는 것을 방지하기 위해 고안되었다. 사람들은 이 규칙을 따르고 석면 섬유를 들이마시는 것을 피하고자 너무 신경을 써서 (석면을 젖은 채로 유지하는 데 필요한) 물과 (조명과 장비를 위해 필요한) 전기가 합쳐지면 무슨 일이 일어나는지 잊었다. 이렇게 하여, 이 현장에서 일어난 부상의 주된 요인은 감전이었다. 규칙이 너무 철저해서 사람들은 상식을 무시하고 그저 규칙을 따르면 된다고 생각했다.

구문 [1행~3행] The classic example of *people* (focusing **so** much on rules **that** they forget to think) is **what happened in asbestos removal projects in the 1980s**.
• '너무 ~해서 …하다'의 의미의 「so ~ that ....」 구문이 쓰였다. ( ) 부분은 분사구로 people을 수식한다. 관계대명사 what이 이끄는 명사절은 보어의 역할을 한다.

어휘 classic 일류의; 전형적인, 대표적인; (스타일이) 고전적인 issue 발행하다; 발표하다; 쟁점, 주제; 발행(물) airborne 비행 중인, 하늘에 떠 있는; 공기로 운반되는 fiber 섬유; 섬유질, 섬유 조직 leading 주된, 주요한; 선두적인 thorough 빈틈없는, 철두철미한 common sense 상식

3 빈칸 추론 ②

해설 빈칸 문장으로 보아 훈련 적응력을 촉진시키기 위해 시스템에 '무엇을' 해야 하는지 파악해야 한다. 훈련 적응력을 계속해서 증진시키기 위해서는 운동의 다양성을 늘려야 하고 속도, 빠르기, 그리고 민첩성을 향상시키기 위해 전문화된 훈련을 또한 포함하는 것과 같이 끊임없이 시스템을 다양화해야 한다는 내용이므로, 빈칸에 가장 적절한 것은 ② '과부하가 걸리게 하다'이다.
① 단순화하다 ③ 분배하다 ④ 약화시키다 ⑤ 표준화하다

해석 고급의 저항력 훈련 프로그램을 설계할 때 난이도를 높이고 긍정적인 적응을 연장시키기 위해 변경될 수 있는 많은 변수들이 있다. 가장 중요한 변수들 중의 하나는 다양성이다. 대부분의 고급 훈련 프로그램은 다양한 훈련 기간 동안 여러 가지 방식의 프로그램을 포함한다. 그 근거는 훈련 적응력을 촉진시키는 것을 계속하기 위해 끊임없이 시스템에 과부하가 걸리게 해야 한다는 것이다. 똑같은 훈련 방법(예를 들어, 운동 순서, 운동 유형, 운동량, 강도 등)을 사용하면서 오랜 기간 동안 훈련해 온 사람들은 그만큼 적응력을 경험하지 못한다. 몸이 프로그램에 너무 익숙해지지 않도록 계속해서 그것을 변경해야 한다. 그래서 고급의 훈련 결과에 이르기 위해 운동의 다양성을 증가시켜야 한다. 그것은 하나의 프로그램 안에서 더 많은 무게를 추가하거나 반복하는 횟수를 바꾸는 것처럼 언제나 간단한 것은 아니다. 고급 수준에 이른 경쟁심이 강한 개인은 자신들의 특정한 운동과 관련이 있는 훈련 목표를 성취하는 것에 도움이 되도록 속도, 빠르기, 그리고 민첩성을 향상시키기 위해 전문화된 훈련도 또한 추가할지도 모른다.

구문 [9행~12행] *Individuals* [who have been training for long periods of time using identical training methods] ~ **do not experience** as much adaptation.
• [ ] 부분은 주격관계대명사 who가 이끄는 관계사절로 주어인 Individuals를 수식하며, 동사는 do not experience이다. 관계사절 내에서 using identical training methods는 부대 상황을 나타내는 분사구문이다.

어휘 advanced 고급의; 선진의 resistance training 저항력 훈련 variable 변수; 변화를 줄 수 있는 *cf.* variety 다양성; 품종 *cf.* various 다양한, 여러 가지의 alter 변경하다, 바꾸다; 고치다 enhance 높이다, 향상시키다 prolong 연장하다, 길어지게 하다 adaptation 적응; 각색 incorporate 포함하다; 설립[창립]하다 promote 촉진하다; 홍

보하다; 승진하다 **identical** 똑같은, 동일한 **workload** 운동량; 작업량 **intensity** 강도, 세기, 격렬함 **be accustomed to A** A에 익숙해지다 **attain** 이르다; 성취[달성]하다 (= **accomplish**) **outcome** 결과 **repetition** 반복, 되풀이 **add in** ~을 추가[포함] 하다 **specialize** 전문적으로 다루다; 전공하다

[선택지] **simplify** 단순화하다 **overload** 과부하가 걸리게 하다; 과적[과중]하다 **distribute** 분배하다; 분포시키다 **undermine** 약화시키다 **standardize** 표준화하다

4 무관 문장 ④

해설 이 글은 전기의 특징과 전기를 읽는 것이 학생들에게 어떤 도움을 줄 수 있는 지에 대한 내용이다. ④는 전기 작가가 인물에 대해 어떻게 쓸 것인지에 대한 태도 와 관련된 내용이므로, 글 전체의 흐름과 관계가 없다.

해석 전기는 3인칭 시점의 서사구조로 쓰인 한 사람의 삶에 대한 이야기를 해준다. 전기는 사람들이 역사적인 시기에 기회들에 어떻게 반응했고, (기회들을) 만들었고, 구성했는지와 그들이 살았던 문화적 환경을 배우기 위해 연구될 수 있다. ① 전기는 비허구적인 정보를 제공하고 어떤 사람의 업적이 매우 중요해서 기록이 되는 이유 를 전달해 준다. ② 전기를 읽는 것은 학생들이 연속성과 변화의 역동적인 과정의 측 면에서 역사상의 인물과 사건에 대해 어떻게 느껴야 하는지에 대해 심사숙고하도록 도움을 줄 수 있다. ③ 더구나, 역사 속의 인물들은 학생들이 특정한 성격과 현실을 경험하면서 과거와 가까워지게 하는 전기에 의해 인간화된다. ④ 전기 작가는 만약 자신의 대상(전기의 주인공)을 불완전한 인간으로 나타내는 것을 망설인다면, 자신 의 대상에 대한 완전한 그림을 제시하는 것이 불가능하다는 것을 필연적으로 발견 하게 된다. ⑤ 이것을 통해, 전기는 학생들에게 역사의 보다 풍부한 맥락을 제공하 며, 그 시기의 사건들뿐만 아니라 사람들과도 연결되기 때문에 더 많은 참여의 기회 를 제공해준다.

구문 [2행~5행] Biographies can be studied to learn / about how people reacted to, shaped, and constructed opportunities / during historical periods / and (about) *the cultural contexts* [**in which** they lived].

• [ ] 부분은 '전치사+관계대명사' 형태의 in which가 이끄는 절로 선행사 the cultural contexts를 수식한다.

[8행~10행] Reading biographies / can **help** *students* **reflect** / about how they should feel about historical people and events / in terms of a dynamic process of continuity and change.

• 「help+O+C(원형부정사) (O가 ~하도록 돕다)」 구문이 쓰였다.

[14행~16행] A biographer inevitably finds **it** impossible / **to give a complete picture of his subject** // if he hesitates to present his subject / as an imperfect human being.

• 밑줄 친 it은 가목적어, to give a complete picture of his subject가 진목적어 이다.

어휘 **biography** 전기 *cf.* **biographer** 전기 작가 **account** 이야기, 설명(하다); 이유, 근거; 계좌 **third person** ((문법)) 3인칭 (시점); 제삼자 **narrative structure** 서사구조 **construct** 구성하다; 건설하다 **context** 환경, 배경; 문맥 **nonfiction** 비허구적인; 실화 **document** 기록하다; 문서 **reflect** 심사숙고하다; 반사[반영]하다 **in terms of** ~의 측 면[관점]에서 **dynamic** 역동적인; 활발한 **continuity** 연속성, 지속성 **humanize** 인간 화하다 **inevitably** 필연적으로 **hesitate** 망설이다, 주저하다 **engagement** 참여; 약 혼; 약속

5 요약문 완성 ①

해설 광고 디자인에서 작은 변화도 심적 시뮬레이션을 용이하게 해서 구매 의도를 늘린다는 것이 글의 요지이다. 따라서 광고 디자인의 미묘한 변화는 소비자의 정신 적 시뮬레이션을 도와주는데(assist), 그것은 물품을 구매하려는 의도의 상승 (elevation)으로 이어질 수 있음을 알 수 있다.

해석 광고 디자인에서 객체 지향 방법론의 아주 미묘한 조작조차도 구매 행동에 영 향을 줄 수 있다. 광고주들은 제품에 대한 시각적 묘사를 통해 심적 시뮬레이션을 가 능하게 해서 구매 의도를 늘릴 수 있다. 그들은 단지 제품(가령, 포크가 있는 케이크) 을 오른쪽으로 향하게 해서 이 일을 할 수 있다. 이것이 더 적은 비율의 왼손잡이들 에게는 적합하지 않을 수도 있지만, 더 많은 비율의 오른손잡이들은 제품과의 더 나 은 정신적인 상호작용을 하게 될 것이다. 이러한 결과는 또한 소매 환경에서의 선반 진열 디자인에도 유효하다. 예를 들어, 커피숍 창문에 놓인 머그잔의 진열 디자인의 아주 작은 변화는 소비자들이 그 커피잔을 들고 커피를 마시는 것을 상상해서 구매 에 영향을 줄 수 있을 것이다. 심적 시뮬레이션을 가능하게 하는 도구(가령, 광고된 수프를 먹기 위한 숟가락)를 포함하는 것 또한 구매 의도를 늘릴 것이다. 시각적 묘 사의 이러한 결과들은 광고 디자인뿐만 아니라 제품 포장 디자인과 진열 디자인에 도 영향을 미친다.

↓

> 광고 디자인에서의 미묘한 변화는 소비자의 정신적 시뮬레이션을 (A) 도와주는 데, 그것은 물품을 구매하려는 의도의 (B) 상승으로 이어질 수 있다.

구문 [10행~14행] For example, **_a very slight change_** (in display design of mugs in the window of a coffee shop) **could affect** purchases / **with** *consumers* **imagining** picking up that coffee mug and drinking from it.

• ( ) 부분은 전명구로 주어 a very slight change를 수식하고, 동사는 could affect 이다. with 이하는 「with+O+v-ing」 구조의 분사구문으로 부대 상황을 나타낸다.

어휘 **subtle** 미묘한, 교묘한 **manipulation** 조작 **facilitate** 가능하게[용이하게] 하다 **depiction** 묘사 **orient** 방향을 특정한 곳에 향하게 하다; 동쪽으로 향하게 하다 **suit** 적합하다 **hold** 유효하다, 적용되다 **retail** 소매(의); 소매를 하는 **instrument** 도구 **consequence** 결과

[선택지] **alleviate** 경감하다, 완화하다 **elevation** 상승, 들어올리기; 높이 **impede** 방해 하다 **abatement** 감소; 폐지

1 빈칸 추론　　　　　　　　　　②

해설 이 글은 가장 이성적인 결정조차도 감정적 요소를 가지며 감정적인 결정도 매우 이성적이라는 것을 통해 모든 의견 결정에는 이성적인 것과 감정적인 것이 동시에 작용한다는 내용이다. 빈칸에는 우리가 하는 중요한 결정들의 속성이 very few (거의 없는)라는 부정의 표현과 함께 설명되어 이러한 결정들의 속성과 반대되는 내용이 들어가야 하므로, 가장 적절한 것은 ② '전적으로 이성에 근거하거나 전적으로 감정에 근거하는'이다.

① 이성보다 감정에 더 높은 가치를 두는
③ 시간 소모적이거나 에너지 집약적이 되는
④ 다른 무엇보다도 환경을 고려하는
⑤ 우리가 경험한 것에 감정적으로 연결하는

해석 우리 대부분은 우리의 의견이 감정에 대한 호소에 의해 강하게 영향을 받을 수 있음을 인정하기를 무안해한다. 우리는 마치 이성이 옳을 가능성이 더 많고 감정은 이에 비례하여 옳지 못할 가능성이 더 많은 경향이 있는 것처럼, 우리의 이성에 자부심을 갖고 감정에 대해서는 조금은 부끄러워하는 경향이 있다. 이성에 관한 일이라면, 우리는 통제하고 있다고 느낀다. 감정이 지배하는 곳에서는 마치 우리의 감정이 스스로의 생명이 있고 심지어 다소 우리에게 이질적인 것처럼 통제할 수 없다고 느낀다. 이것은 문화적인 편견이다. 이성의 기능보다 못하지 않은 우리의 감정은 우리의 일부이며, 감정에 의해서 움직여지는 것에 관해선, 수치스러운 것은커녕 이상하거나 유감스러울 것이 전혀 없다. 사실, 우리가 하는 중요한 결정들 중에 전적으로 이성에 근거하거나 전적으로 감정에 근거하는 것은 거의 없다. 심지어 가장 이성적인 결정조차도 일반적으로 중요한 감정적인 요소를 가지며, 감정적으로 자극받은 많은 결정도 꽤 이성적이다.

구문 [4행~6행] ~, **as if** rationality **were** more likely to be right and the emotions commensurately (were more likely to be) **apt** to be wrong.

• 「as if+S'+과거동사」는 '마치 ~하는 것처럼'이라는 뜻의 가정법 과거 구문이다. apt 앞에는 were more likely to be가 생략되어 있다.

[10행~13행] Our emotions, **no less than our faculty of reason**, are part of us, and there is *nothing* (abnormal or regrettable), **let alone shameful**, about being moved by emotion.

• no less ~ of reason과 let alone shameful이 문장 중간에 삽입된 형태이고, ( ) 부분은 nothing을 뒤에서 수식한다.

어휘 **embarrassed** 무안한, 난처한; 당황스러운 **admit** 인정[시인]하다 **appeal** 호소; 매력; 간청 **tend to-v** v하는 경향이 있다 (= be apt to-v) **take pride in** ~에 자부심[자신감]을 갖다 **rationality** 이성, 합리성 *cf.* **rational** 이성적인, 합리적인 **ashamed** 부끄러운, 창피한 **where A be concerned** A에 관한 일이라면 **dominate** 지배[군림]하다 **alien** 이질적인; 외국[외계]의 **prejudice** 편견, 선입관; 편견을 갖게 하다 **no less than** ~에 못지않게; ~와 마찬가지로 **faculty** 기능, 능력 **abnormal** 이상한, 비정상적인 **regrettable** 유감스러운 **let alone** ~커녕 **component** (구성) 요소, 부품

[선택지] **purely** 전적으로, 순전히 **time-consuming** 시간 소모적인, (많은) 시간이 걸리는 **energy-intensive** 에너지 집약적인, 많은 에너지를 소비하는 **take A into account** A를 고려하다 **first and foremost** 다른 무엇보다도 더; 맨 처음에

2 글의 순서　　　　　　　　　　③

해설 역사 연구에서 공통된 학문적 특성에 대한 언급 다음에는 그 특성에 대한 설명에 해당하는 (B)가 와야 자연스럽다. 그다음에는 (B)에서 서술한 증거 유형에 대해 그 범위가 확대되고 있다는 내용과 증거가 반드시 필요하다는 내용의 (C)가 오고, (C)의 마지막 문장과 인과관계를 이루는 문장으로 시작하는 (A)가 와야 적절하다.

해석 역사학자들의 과거에 대한 접근법은 아주 다양하지만, 몇 가지 공통된 학문적인 특징이 그것들을 묶어 준다.
(B) 역사학자들이 연구할 수 있는 것에는 제한이 있는데, 그들은 증거를 남겼고 그에 대한 증거가 존속되어 온 과거 시기의 일부만을 연구할 수 있는 것이다. 증거의 주요한 유형은 기록물 형태였는데, 예컨대 정부 공문서, 개인 서류, 신문, 출판물이 오랫동안 가장 많이 참고된 형태의 자료였다.
(C) 최근 그 범위는 넓어졌는데, 많은 역사학자들이 이제는 인공물, 건물, 시각적 증거물, 구두 증언과 글로 쓰이지 않은 많은 다른 자료를 기꺼이 사용하고 있다. 그러나 증거의 유형과 무관하게 중요한 점은 증거가 없으면 역사학자들은 제대로 기능할 수 없다는 것이다.
(A) 그러므로 모든 역사 연구는 연구되는 시기로부터의 증거를 발견하고, 그것을 분석하고 해석함으로써 추진된다. 역사학자들은 어떤 일이 일어났는지 기술하고, 그 일이 어떻게, 왜 일어났는지 설명하고, 과거의 사건을 더 넓은 맥락과 시간의 흐름과 연결 짓는 것을 목표로 한다.

구문 [9행~11행] There are limits to what historians can study: they can study only **parts of the past** [that left evidence behind] **and** [for **which** evidence has survived].

• [ ] 부분은 둘 다 parts of the past를 수식하는 관계사절이다. 두 번째 [ ]에서 관계대명사 which는 parts of the past를 받기 때문에 풀어쓰면 evidence for parts of the past has survived의 의미이다.

어휘 **enormously** 대단히, 엄청나게 **disciplinary** 학문의, 학과의 **analysis** 분석 **interpretation** 해석 **passage** (시간의) 흐름, 경과 **leave A behind** A를 뒤에 남기다, A를 놓아둔 채 잊고 오다 **dominant** 지배적인, 우세한 **documentary** 기록의, 문서로 이루어진; 기록물 **consult** 참고하다; 상의하다 **broaden** 넓어지다 **artefact** 인공물 **regardless of** ~에 상관없이 **function** 역할을 다하다

3 문장 넣기　　　　　　　　　　①

해설 후속 우편물을 보내는 것이 필요하다는 주제문 뒤에 그런 우편물의 운영 방식이 소개되고 있다. 첫 번째 방식인 ①번 앞부분은 단순히 참여를 독려하는 편지 발송에 관한 내용이지만, ①번 이후로는 후속 편지와 조사 설문지의 새로운 사본을 보내는 것이 왜 필요한지에 대한 설명이 이어지므로 두 번째 방식에 해당하는 주어진 문장은 ①번에 위치해야 한다. ③번 뒤는 주제문을 뒷받침하는 것이므로 우편물의 운영 방식에 대한 내용인 주어진 문장이 들어가기에 적합하지 않다.

해석 우편 송부 설문조사에 대한 응답에서의 가변성으로 인해 후속 우편물을 보내는 것이 종종 필요하다. 그러한 우편물은 몇 가지 방식으로 운영될 수 있다. 가장 간단한 방법으로, 비응답자들은 단지 참여하라는 추가적인 장려 편지를 발송 받는다. 그러나 더 나은 방법은 후속 편지와 함께 조사 설문지의 새로운 사본을 보내는 것이다. 잠재적 응답자들이 2주 혹은 3주 후에도 그들의 설문지를 회송하지 않으면, 아마 설문지를 잃어버렸거나 제자리에 두지 않았을 것이다. 후속 편지를 받는 것은 그들이 원래의 설문지를 찾아보게 격려할지도 모르지만, 그들이 설문지를 쉽게 찾지

못하면, 편지는 아무 소용도 없을 것이다. 방법론적 문헌은 후속 우편물이 우편 조사에서 회수율을 증가시키기 위한 효과적인 방법을 제공함을 강력하게 암시한다. 일반적으로 잠재적인 응답자가 답변을 더 오래 미루면 미룰수록, 그가 조금이라도 답변할 가능성은 더 낮아진다. 그러면 적절히 타이밍을 맞춘 후속 우편물이 응답할 추가적인 자극을 제공한다.

구문 [11행~12행] Receiving a follow-up letter might **encourage** them **to look for** the original questionnaire, ~

• 「encourage O to-v」는 'O가 v하도록 장려하다'의 뜻이다.

[17행~18행] In general, **the longer** a potential respondent delays replying, **the less** likely he or she is **to do so** at all.

• 「the 비교급…, the 비교급~」은 '…하면 할수록 더 ~하다'의 뜻이다. to do so는 to reply로 바꾸어 볼 수 있다.

어휘 questionnaire 설문지　follow-up 후속의, 뒤따르는　mailing 우편물　administer 운영하다, 주다　nonrespondent 미응답자　misplace 제자리에 두지 않다　good for nothing 아무짝에도 쓸모없는　methodological 방법론의　literature 문헌　time 시간을 맞추다　stimulus 자극 ((복수형 stimuli))

4~5 장문　　　　　4 ⑤　5 ③

해설 4. 자연과의 단절로 정서적으로 고통을 받고 있는 현대인들이 자연 속을 산책하며 치유 받을 수 있다는 에코 테라피를 소개한 글이므로 제목으로 가장 적절한 것은 ⑤ '어머니 자연은 벽이 없는 병원'이다.
① 우울증을 어떻게 떨쳐버릴 수 있을까?
② 자연은 적도 친구도 아니다!
③ 정서적 고통의 주요 원인들
④ 자연과 접하게 되는 방법들
5. 인간이 자연과 분리되면 고통받을지도 모른다고 했으므로, 자연으로부터 단절되는 소외는 정서적, 신체적 고통을 일으킬지도 모를 것이다. 그러므로 ③은 distress 등이 되어야 한다.

해석　공원을 산책하거나 아름다운 석양을 본 후 기분이 더 나아지는가? 그렇다면 당신은 모르는 새에 당신 자신만의 형태의 '에코 테라피'(인간을 자연과 환경과 다시 이어줌으로써 정서적 건강을 (a) 향상시키기 위해 고안된 치료의 한 유형)를 사용하고 있는 것일지도 모른다. 에코 심리학 분야는 미국에서 1990년대에 처음 인기를 얻게 되었는데, 인간은 자연 세계의 (b) 필수적인 일부이며 그것에서 분리되어서는 안 된다고 주장한다. 그들이 도시화나 현대 삶의 다른 측면에 의해 자연으로부터 단절된다면 그들의 정서적 건강은 고통받을지도 모른다. 뿐만 아니라 이러한 소외는 정서적 그리고 신체적 (c) 위안(→ 고통)을 일으킬지도 모른다.
이러한 움직임에서 에코 테라피가 발전하여 인간이 자연과 맺는 관계를 강화시켜주기 위한 전략을 제안한다. 이것은 범위가 복잡한 것에서 단순한 것까지 이른다. 예를 들어 황무지에서 홀로 살아남는 법을 배우는 것은 자신감을 높일 수 있지만 심지어 한 번의 간단한 야외 산책도 효과적일 수 있다. 어떤 치료는 동물을 포함한다. 돌고래와 함께 수영하는 것, 당신의 반려동물과 함께 노는 것, 혹은 열대 어류 어항을 보는 것은 모두 (d) 이롭다. 심지어 야외 장면 그림을 보는 것도 도움이 될 수 있다.
그 결과 한 영국 정신 건강 자선단체는 지금 에코 테라피가 네덜란드와 노르웨이에서 이미 그런 것처럼 정신 건강 관련 환자들을 위해 더 (e) 쉽게 이용 가능하게 만들어져야 한다고 제안하고 있다. 그래서 당신이 약간 우울함을 느낀다면, 당신은 항우울제나 비용이 많이 드는 치료를 필요로 하지 않을지도 모른다. 우선 자전거를 타거나 해변가를 산책하는 것을 시도해보라. 이러한 활동들은 당신의 신체 건강에 확실히 좋을 것이고 정신도 튼튼하게 해줄지도 모른다.

구문 [14행~16행] Out of this movement **grew ecotherapy**, / **offering** strategies to strengthen people's relationship with nature.

• 동사는 grew이고 주어는 ecotherapy인 도치구문이다. offering 이하는 부대 상황을 나타내는 분사구문이다.

[24행~27행] ~ one UK mental-health charity is now **proposing** that ecotherapy (should) **be** made more readily available for mental-health patients, // **as** it already is in Holland and Norway.

• '제안'을 나타내는 동사(proposing) 뒤의 that절은 「that+S'+(should) 동사원형」의 형태로 쓴다. 접속사 as는 '~처럼, ~대로'의 뜻이다.

어휘 integral 필수적인, 없어서는 안 될　urbanization 도시화　strengthen 강화하다　range from A to B 범위가 A부터 B까지이다　sophisticated 세련된　wilderness 황야, 황무지　readily 쉽게　anti-depressant 항우울제　costly 많은 비용이 드는

1 글의 요지 ③

해설 가치와 그것을 지지하는 신념이 우리가 세상을 보는 렌즈라고 했고 또 그것이 보여주는 것은 삶이 어떠해야 하는가(당위)에 관한 것이라고 설명한다. 그 예로 미국인이 성공에 관해 갖고 있는 가치가 성공을 이루지 못하게 하는 실제적인 현실을 보지 못하게 하고 성공하려면 어떠해야 한다는 당위적 결론만을 내게 한다고 했으므로 글의 요지는 ③이다.

해석 가치와 그것들을 지지하는 신념은 우리가 세상을 보는 렌즈이다. 이 렌즈들이 제공하는 시야는 흔히 삶이 무엇인가가 아니라 삶이 어떠해야 하는가에 관한 것이다. 예를 들어, 미국인들은 개인주의를 아주 높게 가치 평가하여 거의 모든 사람이 성공이라는 목표를 추구함에 있어 자유롭고 평등하다고 보는 경향이 있다. 이 가치는 사람들이 성공을 이루지 못하게 하는 상황의 중요성을 그들(미국인들)이 보지 못하게 한다. 가족의 빈곤, 부모의 낮은 교육, 그리고 장래성이 없는 직업의 끔찍한 결과는 시야에서 사라지는 경향이 있다. 대신에, 미국인들은 성공하지 못한 사람들을 기회를 활용하지 못하거나, 어느 정도 타고난 게으름이나 우둔한 머리를 지닌 것으로 여긴다. 그리고 그들은 자신들이 옳다고 '아는데', 왜냐하면 대중매체가 엄청나게 불리한 조건에도 불구하고 성공한 사람들에 대한 매력적인 이야기를 그들의 눈앞에 제시하기 때문이다.

구문 [1행~2행] Values and their supporting beliefs are *lenses* [**through which** we see the world].

• [ ] 부분은 '전치사+관계대명사'가 이끄는 관계사절로 lenses를 수식한다.

[10행~12행] Instead, Americans **see** the unsuccessful **as** not taking advantage of opportunities, or **as** having some inherent laziness or dull minds.

• 「see+O+as ~」는 'O를 ~로 보다'라는 의미의 동사구로 두 개의 밑줄 친 전명구가 or가 병렬 연결되었다.

[12행~15행] And they "know" they are right, // because the mass media **dangle** (before their eyes) enticing stories of *individuals* [who have succeeded despite the greatest of handicaps].

• 부사절의 동사 dangle과 목적어 enticing stories of individuals 사이에 전명구인 before their eyes가 삽입되었다. [ ] 부분은 관계사절로 individuals를 수식한다.

어휘 significance 중요성 dead-end 장래성[발전성]이 없는; 막다른 drop from sight 시야에서 사라지다 inherent 타고난; 내재하는 dull 우둔한; 흐릿한 enticing 매력적인; 마음을 홀리는 handicap 불리한 조건; 장애

2 빈칸 추론 ④

해설 빈칸에는 두뇌가 the little room 즉, 작은 방으로 표현되어 그것이 '어떠하다'라고 생각하는 것은 실수라고 설명되어야 하므로, 두뇌의 속성과 반대되는 내용이 들어가야 한다. 이 글은 작은 다락방처럼 인간의 두뇌도 무언가를 채워 넣을 수 있으나 빈 공간이 없어지면 더 이상 받아들일 수 없어서 이전에 알았던 것을 잊어버릴 수밖에 없다는 내용이다. 그러므로 두뇌의 속성과 반대되는 내용으로 빈칸에 들어가기에 가장 적절한 것은 ④ '신축성 있는 벽을 가지고 있어서 어떤 범위까지도 늘어날 수 있다'이다.

① 모든 세부적인 것들로 엉망이 될 것이다
② 그 어떠한 허락 없이는 접근할 수 없다
③ 당신이 필요로 하는 모든 것에 맞게 조정될 수 없다
⑤ 온갖 형태의 쉽게 잊혀질 것들로 가득 차 있다

해석 당신의 두뇌는 원래 텅 빈 작은 다락방과 같아서 당신은 당신이 선택하는 그러한 가구로 그곳을 채워야 한다. 만약 뇌가 받아들이는 모든 것을 계속 보유하고 있다면, 뇌는 너무 많은 기억을 가지고 있어서 곧 빈 공간이 없어질 것이고 더 이상 받아들일 수 없게 될 것이다. 바보는 마주치는 온갖 종류의 가구를 모두 받아들여서, 자신에게 유용할 수도 있는 지식은 밀려서 빠져나가거나 기껏해야 다른 많은 것들로 뒤죽박죽이 되어서 그는 그것이 있는 곳을 찾아내는 데 어려움을 겪는다. 그 작은 방이 신축성 있는 벽을 가지고 있어서 어떤 범위까지도 늘어날 수 있다고 생각하는 것은 실수이다. 매번 지식을 더할 때마다, 당신은 전에 알았던 어떤 것을 잊어버리는 때가 온다는 것을 믿어라.

구문 [2행~5행] If the brain **held on to** *everything* [that it received], // it **would have so** many memories **that** it <u>would</u> soon <u>run</u> out of room, [and] could accept no more.

• 현재나 미래에 있을 법하지 않은 것을 가정하는 것으로서, 「If+S′+동사의 과거형, S+조동사 과거형+동사원형」 구조의 가정법 과거 구문이 쓰였다. [ ] 부분은 목적격 관계대명사 that이 이끄는 관계사절로 everything을 수식한다. '너무 ~해서 …하다'의 의미의 「so ~ that …」절이 쓰였고, that절 안에서 would run과 could accept가 and로 연결되어 병렬구조를 이룬다.

[5행~9행] A fool takes in *all the furnishings of every sort* [that he comes across], // **so that** *the knowledge* [which might be useful to him] gets crowded out, [or] at best is mixed up with a lot of other things, **so that** he has difficulty laying his hands on it.

• 두 개의 [ ] 부분은 관계사절로 각각 all the furnishings of every sort와 the knowledge를 수식한다. 「~(,) so (that)」은 결과를 나타내는 접속사로 '그래서, ~하여'의 의미이다. 종속절 내에서 gets와 is가 or로 연결되어 병렬구조를 이룬다.

어휘 originally 원래 attic 다락(방) stock 채우다, 갖추다; 재고품 hold on to A A를 계속 보유하다; 고수하다 run out of ~이 없어지다; ~을 바닥내다 take in 받아들이다; 포함하다; 섭취하다 furnishing 가구; 비품 sort 종류, 유형; 분류 come across (우연히) 마주치다[발견하다] crowd out 밀어내다, 내쫓다 at (the) best 기껏해야, 잘해야 be mixed up 뒤죽박죽이 되다 lay one's hand on ~이 있는 곳을 찾아내다; ~을 붙잡다 depend upon[on] ~을 믿다[신뢰하다]

[선택지] mess up 엉망으로 만들다 accessible 접근 가능한 permission 허락, 허가 adjust 조정[조절]하다; 적응하다 elastic 신축성이 있는; 탄력 있는 extent 범위, 정도, 규모

3 무관 문장 ③

해설 글 전체의 내용은 아이스크림의 조직상의 특징을 결정하는 설탕의 역할에 대한 것인데, ③은 아이스크림의 저장 온도가 맛에 끼치는 영향에 대한 것이므로 글 전체의 흐름과 관계가 없다.

해석 아이스크림에서 설탕의 분명한 역할은 그 제품을 달게 만드는 것이다. 하지만 설탕은 또한 냉동 아이스크림의 조직상의 특징을 결정하는 역할도 하는데, 그 이유는 설탕이 혼합물의 결빙 온도를 떨어지게 하기 때문이다. ① 사실, 1쿼트의 아이스크림 혼합물에 들어 있는 한 컵의 설탕은 어는점을 약 화씨 2도 정도 내려가게 할 것이다. ② 이것은 만약 얼음 결정이 형성되려면, 그 아이스크림은 일반적인 물의 결빙 온도 밑으로 냉각되어야 한다는 것을 의미한다. ③ 아이스크림 맛은 매우 낮은 온도에 그것을 저장함으로써 향상될 수 있는데, 그것은 아이스크림이 입 안에서 녹는 동안 차가운 것에 대한 뛰어난 감각을 만들어내기 때문이다. ④ 아이스크림 안에 설탕의 함유량이 더 많으면 많을수록, 어는점은 더 낮아진다. ⑤ 이렇게 지연된 결빙 온

도는 아이스크림 안에 있는 결정의 크기를 매우 작게 유지시키는 데 도움을 주는데, 그 이유는 얼음 결정 집합체가 천천히 형성되므로, 그것들을 분쇄하는 것을 돕기 위해서 결빙 과정 동안 상당한 양의 휘젓기를 할 수 있기 때문이다.

구문 [9행~12행] The flavor of ice cream can be enhanced / by *storing it at an extremely low temperature*, / **which creates an outstanding cold sensation** / **while the ice cream melts in your mouth**.

● 여기에서 which는 an extremely low temperature 혹은 storing ~ low temperature를 의미하며, which가 이끄는 절이 이를 보충 설명한다.

[12행~14행] **The greater** the content of sugar in an ice cream, **the lower** the freezing point.

●「the+비교급 ~, the+비교급 ....」 구문으로 '~하면 할수록 더욱더 ···하다'로 해석된다.

[14행~18행] This delayed freezing temperature / helps to keep *the size of crystals in the ice cream* **very small** // because a reasonable amount of stirring can be done / during the freezing process / **to help break up any ice crystal aggregates** / as they slowly form.

● 형용사구 very small은 목적어인 the size of crystals in the ice cream의 보어의 역할을 한다. to help break up any ice crystal aggregates는 목적을 나타내는 to부정사구이다.

어휘 obvious 분명한, 명백한　sweeten 달게 하다　textural 조직[구조]상의　characteristic 특징: 독특한　freezing 결빙의: 영하의 *cf.* freezing point 어는점　mixture 혼합(물)　quart ((액량의 단위)) 쿼트　approximately 약, 거의　chill 냉각시키다: 냉기　crystal 결정(체): ((광물)) 수정　flavor 맛, 풍미: 맛을 내다　enhance 향상시키다　store 저장하다: 가게, 상점　outstanding 뛰어난　sensation 감각: 기분: 돌풍　melt 녹다. 녹이다　content 함유량: 내용(물): 만족하는　reasonable 상당한: 합리적인　stir 휘젓다. 섞다: 휘젓기

4 글의 순서　　　　　　　　　　　　　　　⑤

해설 이제까지의 디지털 테크놀로지는 시작에 불과하다는 주어진 문장 다음에는 이를 뒷받침하는 내용으로서 엄청난 속도로 앱과 기기가 개발되고 있는 현재의 상황을 보여주는 (C)가 나와야 한다. (B)의 This modern digital world는 (C)의 내용을 지칭한다. 우리의 여러 가지 잡무를 도와주는 (A)의 It은 (B) 마지막에 언급된 'an app as our personal assistant'를 지칭하므로 (B) 다음에 (A)가 나오게 된다.

해석 우리 중 인터넷과 모바일 컴퓨팅의 발명을 경험하며 살아온 사람들에게. 디지털 테크놀로지는 마침내 성숙한 단계에 도달한 것처럼 느껴진다. 그러나 대부분의 기술 전문가들이 당신에게 말할 것처럼, 우리는 가까스로 수박 겉핥기식으로만 했을 뿐이다.
(C) 매일 수만 개의 새로운 앱들이 개발되며, 더 똑똑하고 더 강력한 장치들이 우리 주머니 속에 있는 것을 대체하여 여전히 디지털화되어야 하는 우리 생활의 틈새를 메꾸도록 디자인된다.
(B) 이러한 현대의 디지털 세상은 우리를 즐겁게, 놀라게, 그리고 기쁘게 할 많은 것들을 제공하며, 우리가 5년 전만 하더라도 가능하리라 생각지 못한 것들을 할 수 있게 해준다. 예를 들어 오늘날 우리는 우리의 개인 조수로 앱을 '고용할' 선택지를 가진다.
(A) 그것은 우리를 위해 생일 인사를 보내고, 친구가 곤란한 소식을 게시할 때 우리의 주의를 환기시키며, 비가 올 것 같을 때 내일 옷을 적절히 입으라고 우리에게 상기시킬 수 있다.

구문 [6행~9행] It can send birthday greetings for us, nudge us when a friend posts troublesome news, `and` even **remind** *us* **to dress** appropriately

tomorrow when it looks like it might rain.

● 밑줄 친 세 부분이 and로 연결되어 병렬구조를 이룬다.「remind O to-v」는 'O에게 v할 것을 상기시키다'의 뜻이다.

[10행~12행] This modern digital world offers *much* (to amuse, amaze, `and` delight us), / **enabling** *us* **to do** things [(that[which]) we didn't think possible just five years ago].

● ( ) 부분은 much를 수식하며, 여기서 us는 amuse, amaze, delight의 공통 목적어이다. enabling 이하는 분사구문이며「enable O to-v (O가 v할 수 있게 하다)」 구문이 사용되었다. [ ]은 앞에 목적격 관계대명사 that[which]이 생략되어 things를 수식한다.

어휘 live through (살면서) ~을 겪다　mobile computing 모바일 컴퓨팅 ((이동 장소에서 네트워크에 연결하여 컴퓨터를 이용하기))　mature 성숙한　phase 단계, 국면　barely 가까스로　scratch the surface 수박 겉핥기식으로 하다　post 게시하다　troublesome 까다로운, 곤란한　appropriately 적절히　digitize 디지털화하다

5 문장 넣기　　　　　　　　　　　　　　　④

해설 주어진 문장에서 은화의 부재(this absence of silver coins)가 언급되므로 은화 없이 오직 금화만이 발견되었다는 문장 뒤에 위치해야 하므로 ④번이 정답이다.

해석 인도의 국산품은 영속성이 있는 금화와 은화로 구매되었는데, 각각의 금화와 은화는 로마 황제의 이미지로 연대가 추정되었다. 이러한 동전들의 은닉물이 인도 남부에서 여전히 발견되고 있으며, 우리에게 2천 년 전의 무역 패턴을 엿보게 한다. 그것들은 아우구스투스 황제와 티베리우스 황제(기원전 27년부터 기원후 37년까지) 치세의 금화와 은화를 포함하는데, 이는 대량의 상품의 활발한 무역을 암시한다. 티베리우스 황제의 죽음 이후에 인도 동전 은닉물의 구성은 변하게 된다. 칼리굴라 황제, 클라우디우스 황제와 네로 황제(기원후 37년~68년)의 두상을 담고 있는 상당수의 금화가 은화 없이 발견된다. 역사가 E. H. 워밍턴에 따르면, 이러한 은화의 부재는 그 시기 동안 주로 사치품의 교역을 암시한다. 기원후 180년 마르쿠스 아우렐리우스 황제 사후에 어떠한 종류의 로마 동전도 발견되지 않는다. 로마와 한나라의 권능이 기원후 200년경 마침내 무너졌을 때, 동방과의 무역은 거의 완전히 정지했다.

구문 [4행~6행] Local goods in India were purchased with durable gold and silver coins, / *each* **dated by the image of a Roman emperor**.

● dated 이하는 수동의 의미를 가지는 분사구문이며 의미상 주어는 each이다. each는 each gold and silver coin을 나타낸다.

[6행~8행] Caches of these coins **are** still **being discovered** in south India, / **offering us a glimpse of trade patterns two thousand years ago**.

●「be being v-ing」는 'v되고 있다'의 뜻이다. offering 이하는 분사구문이다.

[13행~15행] Significant numbers of ***only gold***, but not silver, ***coins*** (bearing the heads of Caligula, Claudius, and Nero (AD 37-68)) **are found**.

● 주어는 only gold coins이고 동사는 are found이며 ( )은 only gold coins를 수식한다.

어휘 absence 부재, 없음　durable 영속적인　date 연대를 추정하다　glimpse 언뜻 봄　reign 통치 기간, 치세　vigorous 활발한, 격렬한　composition 구성　significant 상당한　bear 갖다, 품다　authority 권위, 권능　collapse 무너지다, 붕괴하다　come to a standstill 멈추다, 정지하다

1 글의 제목   ⑤

해설 이 글은 독일과 네덜란드 국경 지대의 사람들이 서로 의사소통이 가능하다는 것을 소재로, 언어가 달라도 뜻이 통하는 이런 현상은 '방언'으로 설명될 수 있다는 내용이다. 그러므로, 제목으로 가장 잘 표현한 것은 ⑤ '국경 지역 방언이 언어의 공동의 장을 찾다'이다.
① 네덜란드어는 독일어와 왜 그토록 가까운가
② 세계화가 더 이루어질수록 언어는 더 적어진다
③ 언어 표준화는 현대적 추세
④ 하나 되는 사회, 갈라지는 언어

해석 네덜란드어 글과 독일어 글을 보거나, 이 두 언어로 텔레비전이나 라디오에서 얘기되는 것을 들을 때, 우리는 그것들이 분명히 두 개의 별개의 언어라는 것을 알 수 있다. 평범한 독일어 사용자라면 네덜란드어를 이해할 수 없을 것이며 그 반대의 경우도 마찬가지이다. 게다가, 네덜란드와 독일의 국경에서 네덜란드 측에 있는 시골 지역 사회에 살고 있는 사람들은 자신들이 네덜란드어를 하고 있다고 말할 것이다. 국경의 독일 측에서 몇 마일 떨어진 곳에 있는 시골 지역 사회의 거주민들은 자신들이 독일어를 하고 있다고 말할 것이다. 그러나 그들이 말하는 언어는 매우 비슷하며 상호 이해가 가능하다. 그것들은 각각의 언어로 쓰인 글보다 그것들끼리 더 비슷하다. 이 상황을 설명하는 한 가지 방법은 이 국경 지역 사회의 거주민들이 독일어와 네덜란드어의 '이종' 혹은 '방언'을 사용하고 있다고 하는 것이다. 이 '방언들'은 글이나 공식적인 구어 용법에서 사용되는 언어의 '표준적' 형태와는 다르다.

구문 [1행~3행] If we look at written Dutch and written German, or listen to these two languages // **as** (they are) spoken on television or radio, ~
• as 뒤에 'they(= these two languages) are'가 생략되어 있으며, 여기서 접속사 as는 '~할 때'의 의미이다.

어휘 vice versa 반대로, 반대의 경우도 마찬가지 rural 시골의 border 국경 (지역) inhabitant 주민 mutually 서로, 상호간에 intelligible 이해할 수 있는 respective 각각의, 각자의 variety 이종, 변종 dialect 방언, 사투리 employ 이용하다, 쓰다; 고용하다
[선택지] globalize 세계화하다[되다] converge 모여들다, 집중되다 diverge 갈라지다, 나뉘다; 일탈하다

2 밑줄 어휘   ⑤

해설 행동에 문제가 있거나 인기가 없는 아이들은 자신의 감정이 표정에 드러나지 않도록 억제할 가능성이 적고 진짜 감정을 드러내는 경향이 크다는 내용이다. 즉 감정을 숨겨야 하는 때가 있다는 것을 아는 아이들은 사회적으로 '유능하다'는 문맥이 적절하므로 ⑤ incompetent를 competent로 바꿔야 한다.

해석 대부분의 아이들은 자신이 느끼지 않은 감정을 얼굴 표정으로 지어내는 능력을 개발하지만, 모든 아이들이 이것을 똑같이 잘하거나 그렇게 하는 것이 좋은 것이라고 생각하지 않는다. 예를 들어, 일부 아이들은 미소로 화를 ① 억누르지 않는다. 이런 아이들이 더 일반적으로 행동 문제가 있는 아이들인 경향이 있다. 심리학자들은 인기가 없는 아이들이 인기 있는 아이들에 비해 게임에서 졌을 때 얼굴을 찡그릴 가능성이 더 크고 게임에서 이겼을 때 자신들의 미소를 ② 억누를 가능성이 더 적다는 것을 관찰했다. 그들은 아마도 자신의 '진짜' 감정을 드러낼 것이고 다른 사람들의 감정을 생각해서 그것을 자제할 가능성이 ③ 더 적다. 크게 씩 웃으면서 승리를 기념한다면 다른 사람의 ④ 호감을 사지 못할 것이다. 사회적으로 ⑤ 무능한(→ 유

능한) 아이들은 감정을 숨기거나 감추는 것이 친구로서 해야 하는 것이 되는 때가 있다는 것을 안다.

구문 [14행~16행] Socially competent children understand that there are *times* [**when** hiding or disguising emotions is **what** friends do].
• [ ]는 관계부사 when이 이끄는 절로서 선행사 times를 수식한다. 관계부사절의 주어는 hiding or disguising emotions, 동사는 is이며, what friends do는 관계사 what이 이끄는 명사절로 동사 is의 보어 역할을 한다.

어휘 manufacture 제조하다; 제조(품) suppress (감정을) 억누르다; (반란 등을) 진압하다 frown 얼굴을 찌푸리다[찡그리다]; 찡그림 (= grimace) contain (감정을) 억누르다; ~이 들어 있다 vent (감정·분통을) 터뜨리다; 통풍구, 환기구 for the sake of A A 때문에, A를 위해서 (= for A's sake) grin (소리 없이) 활짝 웃다; 활짝 웃음 endear A to B A를 B에게 사랑받게 하다 incompetent 무능한, 기술이 부족한 (↔ competent 유능한) disguise 변장시키다; 위장하다, 숨기다; 변장 (도구)

3 빈칸 추론   ①

해설 빈칸 문장으로 보아 당신이 '무엇'한다면, 더욱 창의적이게 될 것인지 파악해야 한다. 이 글은 문제 해결을 위해 창의적인 접근이 필요한데, 자유가 창의력을 방해하고 그런 자유를 전략적으로 제한하는 것이 창의성을 오히려 촉진시킨다는 내용이다. 빈칸에는 더욱 창의적이게 되기 위한 조건이 들어가야 하므로 가장 적절한 것은 ① '당신의 정신이 자유롭게 배회하도록 허락되지 않는다'이다.
② 당신 자신을 계속해서 새로운 경험들에 노출시킨다
③ 당신의 정신이 당신 주변에 있는 것들의 반응과 관련이 있다
④ 당신 자신이 가장 쉬운 해법에 속아 넘어가도록 허락하지 않는다
⑤ 당신이 모든 것에 이의를 제기하거나 호기심을 갖기 시작한다

해석 많은 영역에서, 아직 해결되지 않은 문제들, 아직 제기되지 않은 문제들, 그리고 명백한 해결책이 없는 문제들이 있다. 이러한 '제대로 구조화되지 않은' 문제들은 창의적인 접근이 필요하다. 역설적이게도 사람들이 문제를 해결할 수 있는 자유가 주어질 때, 그들은 과거에 가장 효과가 좋았던 것에 초점을 맞추어 전혀 창의적이지 않게 되는 경향이 있다. 이것은 인간의 인식의 근본적인 특성 때문인데, 그것은 미래를 상상하기 위해서 과거로부터 우리가 이미 알고 있던 것을 만들어내는 것이다. 그러한 자유는 창의력을 방해할 수 있으며, 반면에 제약의 전략적인 사용은 창의성을 촉진시킬 수 있다. 제약을 사용함으로써, 의지할 수 있는 반응은 제외되고, 새롭고 놀라운 반응이 촉진된다. 만약 당신의 정신이 자유롭게 배회하도록 허락되지 않는다면 당신은 더욱 창의적이게 될 것이다.

구문 [5행~7행] Paradoxically, when people are given *free rein* (to solve a problem), // they tend to be wholly uncreative, / **focusing on** what's worked best in the past.
• ( ) 부분은 to-v의 형용사적 용법으로 free rein을 수식한다. focusing on 이하는 분사구문이며, as they focus on what's worked best in the past의 의미이다.

[8행~9행] ~: **to imagine** the future we generate **what we already know from the past**.
• to imagine은 '목적'을 나타내는 to-v의 부사적 용법으로 '상상하기 위해서'로 해석하며, 관계사 what이 이끄는 명사절이 동사 generate의 목적어 역할을 한다.

어휘 domain 영역, 분야; 범위 resolve 해결하다; 결심하다; 분해하다 pose a question 문제를 제기하다 obvious 명백한, 분명한 require 필요[요구]하다, 필요로

하다 **approach** 접근(법); 접근하다 **paradoxically** 역설적이게도, 역설적으로 **give A a free rein** A에게 자유를 주다 **tend to-v** v하는 경향이 있다 **wholly** 전혀, 아주, 완전히 **be due to A** A 때문이다 **fundamental** 근본[본질]적인; 핵심적인 **cognition** 인식, 인지 **generate** 만들어내다, 발생시키다 **hinder** 방해[저해]하다, 못하게 하다 **strategic** 전략적인 **constraint** 제약(이 되는 것); 제한, 통제 **promote** 촉진[고취]하다 **reliable** 의지할 수 있는; 확실한 **response** 반응, 대응, 부응 **novel** 새로운; 소설 **encourage** 촉진시키다; 용기를 주다

[선택지] **roam** 배회[방랑]하다, 돌아다니다 **expose** 노출시키다, 드러내다; 폭로하다 **refer to A** A와 관련이 있다; A를 나타내다 **fall for** ~에 속아 넘어가다

4 무관 문장 ④

해설 글 전체의 내용은 랩 음악이 정교한 음반 장비 없이 녹음되고, 독립적인 음반 회사에 의해 보급되며, 랩을 내보내는 라디오 방송국도 없이 번성했다는 내용의 글이다. 그러므로 라디오 광고가 강력한 힘을 가지고 있다는 ④는 글의 전체 흐름과 관계가 없다.

해석 랩 음악은 음악 시설의 접근 없이 번성했다. 대부분의 랩은 다른 음악 장르의 음향 스튜디오와 정교한 음반 장비와는 대조적으로, 값싸고 널리 이용할 수 있는 장비를 사용하는 아티스트들에 의해 그들 자신의 집에서 행해졌다. ① 랩 음악은 주로 집에서 제작한 카세트 그리고 지역이 소유한 독립적인 음반 회사에 의해 보급된다. ② 십 년 동안, 주요 음반 회사들은 랩을 반대했고, 심지어 1990년대 중반에는 '빌보드' 랩 싱글 음반 순위표에 오른 음악의 단지 일부만이 주요 음반 회사에 의해 제작되었다. ③ 랩 음악 청취자들은 라디오 광고주들이 마음을 움직이려는 우선 사항이 아니기 때문에 (일반적으로 음악 작품의 성공을 만들어 내거나 방해하는) 라디오 산업은 랩을 무시하였다. ④ 사실상, 매주, 90%가 넘는 미국인들이 라디오를 청취하기 때문에 라디오 광고는 당신의 사업을 위한 여전히 강력하고 효과적인 도구이다. ⑤ 예를 들어, 뉴욕에는 전 시간 클래식 음악 라디오 방송국이 두 개나 있지만, 단 하나의 랩 방송국도 없다.

구문 [2행~4행] Most rap is performed by *artists* in their own homes, (using inexpensive, widely accessible equipment), ~.

● 형용사구 using inexpensive, widely accessible equipment가 문장 중간에 삽입되어 artists를 수식한다.

[11행~14행] *The radio industry* [(which usually makes or breaks the success of any piece of music)] ignored rap because its audience is not a *priority* for radio advertisers (**to reach**).

● [ ]는 The radio industry를 수식하는 관계대명사절이다. to reach는 형용사적 용법의 to부정사구로 앞에 나온 a priority를 수식한다. for radio advertisers는 to reach의 의미상 주어이다.

어휘 **flourish** 번성[번창]하다 **access** 접근; 접촉 기회 *cf.* **accessible** 이용할 수 있는, 접근하기 쉬운 **establishment** 시설, 기관 **equipment** 장비, 용품 **sophisticated** 정교한, 복잡한; 세련된 **genre** 장르, 유형 **resist** 반대[저항]하다; 참다, 견디다 **portion** 일부, 부분; 나누다 **label** 음반 회사; 라벨, 상표 **audience** 청취[시청]자; 청중, 관객 **priority** 우선 (사항); 우선권 **reach** (사람의 마음을) 움직이다; 이르다[닿다] **classical** ((음악)) 클래식의; 고전적인

5 요약문 완성 ④

해설 성공한 작가들에 대한 연구 결과 그들은 걱정, 불안, 낙담과 같은 정신적 부담을 겪는데 그러한 기분 장애가 수년간의 문학 작품 집필을 계속할 수 있게 돕는 요인임이 드러났다. 그러므로 성공한 작가들이 우울증(depression)을 겪는 한 가지 이

유는 끈기(perseverance)가 창의적 작업의 중요한 요소이기 때문임을 알 수 있다.

해석 1980년대 초에 아이오와 대학의 신경 과학자 낸시 안드리아센은 아이오와 작가 워크숍 소속의 수십 명의 성공한 작가들에게 그들의 정신사에 대한 인터뷰를 했다. 안드리아센은 그 작가들 중 80%가 극도로 걱정하고 불안한 상태임을 발견했다. 왜 심한 정신적 부담이 창의성과 그토록 밀접하게 관련되어 있는가? 그녀의 설명은 간단하다. 좋은 소설을 쓰는 것은 쉽지 않다. 그 과정은 예술가가 실수를 고치고 오류를 교정하면서 종종 수년간의 주의 깊은 집중을 요한다. 결과적으로, 과정을 계속하는 능력이 극도로 중요하다. "성공한 작가들은 계속하여 얻어맞지만 쓰러지지 않으려 하는 프로 권투 선수와 같습니다." 안드리아센은 말한다. "그들은 괜찮아질 때까지 계속할 것입니다. 그리고 그것이 기분 장애가 도움이 되는 점인 것 같습니다." 비슷한 주제가 존스 홉킨스 (대학)의 정신 의학 교수인 케이 레드필드 제이미슨이 수행한 영국의 소설가와 시인에 대한 전기적 연구에서 나타났다. 그녀의 자료에 따르면, 성공한 작가들은 심한 낙담과 실의의 감정으로 고통받을 가능성이 일반적 인구 집단의 사람들보다 8배 높았다.

> 성공한 작가들이 (A) 우울증을 겪는 경향이 있는 한 가지 이유는 창의적 작업의 중요한 요소가 (B) 끈기이기 때문이다.

구문 [18행~21행] According to her data, successful writers were **eight times as likely as** *people* (in the general population) to suffer from feelings of severe despondency and dejection.

● 「배수사+as 원급 as ~」의 구조로 '~보다 몇 배 …한'의 의미로 쓰였다. ( )은 people을 수식하는 전명구이다.

어휘 **neuroscientist** 신경 과학자 **exceedingly** 극도로, 몹시, 대단히 **burden** 부담; 책임 **straightforward** 간단한; 확실한 **stick with** ~을 계속하다 **prizefighter** 프로 권투 선수 **biographical** 전기의 **despondency** 낙심; 실망 **dejection** 실의, 의기소침

[선택지] **publicity** 널리 알려져 있음; 홍보 **novelty** 새로움; 신기함 **perseverance** 끈기, 인내, 참을성

1 빈칸 추론   ③

해설 빈칸 문장으로 보아 '무엇을 한다'면 중요한 발전을 하지 못할 것인지 찾아야 한다. 악기와 우리의 영혼 사이에 좋은 연결을 맺을 수 있는 방법으로 밴드와 함께 연주하고 실제 음악가들과 상호 작용하는 것이 가장 중요하다고 했으므로 실제 음악가들과 함께하지 않는 것과 같은 내용이 나와야 한다. 따라서 빈칸에 들어가기에 가장 적절한 것은 ③ '자신의 방에서 계속 연주를 한다'이다.
① 경연대회에 참가한다
② 인생에서 자신의 위치를 안다
④ 전문가의 공연을 관람한다
⑤ 온 마음을 다해 음악을 사랑한다

해석 당신이 악기와 당신의 영혼 사이에 좋은 연결을 맺을 수 없다면 악기는 쓸모가 없다. 우리가 우리 악기로 연주하는 곡은 우리의 영혼, 경험 그리고 감정으로부터 나온다. 이것을 개선하기 위해 공들이는 많은 방법이 있다. 대부분의 음악 기관에서, 사람들은 귀 훈련 수업에 참석하고 있다. 학생들은 자신들의 악기가 아니라, 자신들의 목소리와 뇌를 사용해서 적힌 음표를 처음 보고 연주하는 법을 배운다. 이것은 당신과 당신의 악기 사이의 강한 유대를 창조하는 매우 편리한 방법이지만, 유일한 방법은 아니다. 가장 좋은 방법이 무엇인가를 추측해 보라. 밴드와 함께 연주하고 실제 음악가들과 상호 작용하는 것이 핵심이다. 당신이 아무리 많은 연습을 하더라도 혹은 아무리 많은 귀 훈련 수업을 수강하고 있더라도, 자신의 방에서 계속 연주를 한다면 당신은 결코 어떤 중요한 발전도 하지 못할 것이다.

구문 [2행~4행] The music [that we play on our musical instruments] comes from our souls, our experience and our feelings.
• [ ] 부분은 관계대명사절로 선행사 The music을 수식한다. 밑줄 친 세 개의 명사구가 콤마(,)와 and로 연결되어 병렬구조를 이루고 있다.

[8행~10행] This is *a very convenient way* (**to create** *a strong bond* (between you and your instrument)), but not the only **one** (way to create a strong bond between you and your instrument).
• 첫 번째 ( )는 to부정사의 형용사적 용법으로 a very convenient way를 수식하며, 그 안의 전명구 between you and your instrument는 a strong bond를 수식한다. one 뒤에는 반복되는 way to create ~ your instrument가 생략되었다.

어휘 (musical) instrument 악기   work on (개선하기 위해) 공들이다   institute 기관, 협회; 도입하다; (절차를) 시작하다   attend 참석하다; 다니다   bond 유대, 끈; 채권   interact with ~와 상호 작용[교류]하다   session 수업 (시간); 학기   progress 발전, 진보; 전진, 진행
[선택지] take part in ~에 참가[참여]하다   professional 전문가; 직업의, 전문적인

2 글의 순서   ⑤

해설 태양이 에너지와 입자를 지구에 보내지만 우리는 보호 자기장으로 인해 이를 알아차리지 못하는 평소의 상황이 나온 주어진 글 뒤에는 태양이 보내는 에너지와 입자가 폭증하는 특수한 시기를 But으로 시작하여 소개하는 (C)가 나온다. 이러한 폭증한 에너지와 입자가 지구의 산소와 질소를 특히 극지방에서 활발히 이온화한다는 (B)가 그다음에 나오고 (A)의 There는 (B)에서 언급된 극지방을 가리키므로 마지막에 위치해야 한다.

해석 태양은 우리에게 열과 빛 이상의 것을 보내는데, 즉 그것은 많은 다른 에너지와 작은 입자들을 우리 쪽으로 보낸다. 지구 둘레의 보호 자기장은 대부분의 에너지와 입자로부터 우리를 지켜주며, 우리는 심지어 그것들을 알아차리지도 못한다.
(C) 그러나 태양이 항상 같은 양의 에너지를 보내주는 것은 아니다. 코로나 질량 방출이라 불리는 일종의 태양 폭풍 기간 동안 태양은 고속으로 우주를 이동할 수 있는 대전된 기체의 거대한 거품을 뱉어낸다.
(B) 그것이 지구를 향해 올 때 에너지와 작은 입자 중 일부는 대기의 산소와 질소 기체를 이온화한다. 이는 보통 자기장선이 집중되고 대기가 두꺼워지는 행성의 극지방 주변에서 일어난다.
(A) 그곳에서 입자들은 대기의 기체들과 상호 작용하여 오로라라 불리는 하늘의 아름다운 빛의 향연을 발생시킨다. 산소는 녹색과 적색 빛을 방출한다. 질소는 파란색과 보라색으로 빛난다.

구문 [15행~16행] But the sun **doesn't** send the same amount of energy **all the time.**
• 「not ~ all the time」은 '항상 ~한 것은 아니다'라는 뜻의 부분부정 표현이다.

어휘 particle 입자   magnetic field 자기장   shield 보호하다   give off 내뿜다, 방출하다   ionize 이온화하다   pole 극   electrify 전기를 통하게 하다, 대전시키다

3 문장 넣기   ②

해설 ②번 이전 문장은 인간에게는 '내 것이 더 낫다'고 생각하는 경향이 있지만 사람들은 이것이 모든 사람에게 보편적인 인식임을 알고 균형을 잡는다는 내용이다. 반면 ②번 다음 문장은 '그것은 그들의 특정 상황에 유일한 특별하고도 더 높은 진리이다'라고 하여 이전에 제시된 보편성과 반대되는 진술을 보이고 있다. 따라서 '내 것이 더 낫다'라는 생각을 보편적으로 인식하지 못하는 사람들이 있음을 제시한 주어진 문장은 ②에 위치해야 연결이 자연스럽다.

해석 대부분의 경우 대부분의 사람들에게 "내 것이 더 낫다"는 경향은 다른 사람들도 자신의 것에 대해 같은 방식으로 느끼고, 이와 같이 생각하는 것은 인간으로서 불가피한 일부라는 것을 이해함으로써 균형을 이루게 된다. 다시 말해, 대부분의 사람들은 우리 모두가 우리 자신이 아닌 모든 것과는 다른 특별한 방식으로 자기 자신을 보며, 우리가 우리 자신과 연관 짓는 것은 무엇이나 우리 마음속에서 우리의 일부가 된다는 것을 깨닫는다. 그러나 어떤 사람들에게는 "내 것이 더 낫다"가 모든 사람이 자신의 것에 대하여 가지고 있는 태도는 아니다. 오히려 그것은 그들의 특별한 상황에 유일한, 특별하고도 더 높은 진리이다. 그들은 자신에게만 유일한 정답이 있다고 믿고 모든 다른 사람들에게 그들과 같아질 것을 강요하고 싶어 한다. 다행히도 이와 같이 생각하는 대부분의 사람들은 지배하고자 하는 경향을 조절할 수 있다. 문제는 몇몇 사람들이 각각의 사람에게 특별한 관점이 있다는 점을 이해조차 할 수 없다는 것이다.

구문 [3행~6행] ~ the "mine-is-better" tendency is balanced by the understanding **that** other people feel the same way about their things, and **that** it's an unavoidable part of being human **to think like this**.
• 두 개의 that이 이끄는 절은 모두 the understanding에 대한 동격절이며, and로 연결되어 병렬구조를 이루고 있다. 두 번째 동격절에서 it은 가주어, to think like this가 진주어이다.

[9행~10행] ~ **whatever** we associate with ourselves / **becomes** part of us in our minds.
• whatever가 이끄는 절이 주어이며 becomes가 동사이다. whatever는 '~한 것이면 무엇이든지'의 뜻이다.

어휘 **tendency** 경향, 추세; 성향 **unavoidable** 불가피한 **associate with** ~와 연관 짓다; ~와 어울리다 **dominate** 지배하다 **viewpoint** 관점, 시각; 방향

4~5 장문　　　　　4 ⑤　5 ③

해설　**4.** 똑똑한 개인의 성취가 인간의 업적의 비결이라는 생각이 잘못 짚은 것이며 집단 지성이 진짜 비결이라고 했다. 그러므로 답은 ⑤ '인간의 성취는 집단 지성의 열매'이다.

① 두뇌가 뛰어난 사람들이 놀라운 일을 성취한다

② 똑똑한 사람들이 단체 성취를 가치 있게 여긴다

③ 어떻게 집단 지성을 최대화할 수 있는가?

④ 개인의 성취 대 집단 책임

5. 인간 업적의 비결은 개인의 지성이 아니며, 인적 정보망 형성을 통한 지적 능력의 결합이 비결이라고 했으므로 고립된 사람들의 결과는 기술의 붕괴임을 알 수 있다. 그러므로 ③은 collapse 등이 되어야 한다.

해석　두뇌가 뛰어난 개인들은, 그들이 인류학자이든 심리학자이든 경제학자이든 간에, 두뇌가 뛰어난 것이 인간의 업적의 비결이라고 추정한다. 그들은 정부를 운영하기 위해 가장 똑똑한 사람에게 투표하고, 경제 계획을 고안하기 위해서는 가장 영리한 전문가에게 요청하고, 가장 예리한 과학자가 발견을 할 것이라고 (a) 믿는다. 그들은 모두 잘못 짚고 있다. 인간 업적의 비결은 (b) 개인의 지성이 전혀 아니다. 인간의 업적은 전적으로 인적 정보망 형성 현상이다. 인간 사회가 생활수준, 기술적 기교와 종의 지식 기반을 끌어올리는 방법을 발견한 것은 노동의 분배를 통해 지적 능력을 결합함으로써 된 것이다. 우리는 모든 종류의 현상에서 이것을 볼 수 있다. 태즈메이니아 원주민처럼 고립되게 된 사람들에서의 기술의 (c) 발전(→ 붕괴), 그리스, 이탈리아, 네덜란드와 남동아시아에서의 무역 도시 국가의 번영과 무역의 창의적 결과가 그것이다. 인간의 업적은 집단적 지성에 뿌리를 두고 있는데 인간의 신경망에서 중요점은 사람들 자신이다. 각각이 한 가지 일을 하고 그것에 통달한 다음, 결과를 (d) 교환을 통해 결합함으로써 사람들은 그들이 이해조차 하지 못한 것들을 할 수 있게 된다. 경제학자 Leonard Read가 그의 에세이, "나, 연필"에서 지적했듯이 하나의 개인은 연필 하나조차 어떻게 만들어지는지 알지 못한다. 사회에서 그 지식은 많은 수천의 흑연을 캐내는 광부, 목재 벌채업자, 디자이너와 공장 근로자들 사이에 (e) 나누어져 있다.

구문　[10행~14행] **It is** *by combining brainpower through the division of labor* **that** *human society happened upon a way to raise the living standards, technological virtuosity and knowledge base of the species.*

● '…한 것은 바로 ~이다'라는 의미의 「It is ~ that ...」 강조구문으로 by combining brainpower through the division of labor을 강조하고 있다.

어휘 **anthropologist** 인류학자 **assume** 추정하다 **brilliance** 두뇌의 뛰어남 **devise** 고안하다 **credit A with B** A에게 B가 있다고 믿다 **bark up the wrong tree** 잘못 짚다, 잘못 알다 **phenomenon** 현상 **division** 분배 **happen upon** 우연히 발견하다 **virtuosity** 기교, 묘기 **collective** 집단적인 **node** 중요점, 접속점 **neural** 신경의 **graphite** 흑연 **lumberjack** 벌채 노동자

1 필자 주장   ②

해설 광고는 가능한 한 최고의 제품을 구매하려는 소비자의 목적에 관심이 없으며 자사의 제품을 판매하는 것을 최우선의 목표로 두기 때문에 소비자가 광고에만 의존하여 구매한다면 자신의 이익에 맞는 최고의 제품을 구매하지 못할 수 있다는 내용의 글이므로 이 글이 주장하는 바로 가장 적절한 것은 ②이다.

해석 광고는 설득의 한 형태이다. 이것은 처음부터 당신의 목표와 관심사가 자주 광고주의 목표와 관심사와 매우 다르다는 것을 의미한다. 당신의 목표가 당신이 구매할 형편이 되는 최고의 식기세척기를 사는 것이라고 해 보자. 이것이 가전제품 회사의 광고 카피라이터의 주된 관심사가 아니라는 것을 여러분에게 처음으로 알려 주는 사람이 나일 필요는 없다. 자신이 아름답게 공들여 제작한 광고 속의 세척기를 구입함으로써 당신이 더 현명한 구매의 기회를 놓쳤다는 것을 그가 알게 되자마자 실패의 고통을 하나라도 겪을 가능성은 없을 것 같다. 만일 당신의 최고의 관심사를 염두에 두고 쓰인 것을 정말 읽고 싶다면, 당신은 'Consumer Reports' 한 부를 집어들지, 당신이 지난주에 본 그 식기세척기 광고를 찾기 위해 'Good Housekeeping'을 훑어보지 않는다. 그 광고를 정말 읽어볼 때, 그 광고가 경쟁사에 대해 하는 그 어떤 비교도 반드시 '공정하고 균형 잡힌' 것은 아니라는 것을 당연하게 여기게 된다.

구문 [7행~10행] He's unlikely to suffer a single pang of failure **upon finding out** that, (by buying the washer in his beautifully-crafted ad), you've passed up a wiser purchase.
• 「upon v-ing」는 '~하자마자'의 뜻이다. 밑줄 친 that절은 finding out의 목적어이고, that절 내에 전명구(by buying ~ ad)가 삽입되었다.

[14행~16행] When you do read the ad, you take **it** for granted **that** *any comparisons* [(which[that]) it makes to the competition] are **not necessarily** "fair and balanced."
• it은 가목적어이며 that 이하가 진목적어이다. [ ]은 앞에 목적격 관계대명사 which[that]가 생략된 관계사절로 any comparisons를 수식한다. not necessarily는 부분부정 표현으로 '반드시 ~한 건 아니다'의 뜻이다.

어휘 persuasion 설득   from square one 다시 처음부터   break it to ~에게 말하다   home appliance 가정용 전자기기   craft 공들여 만들다   pass up (기회를) 놓치다   flip through ~을 훑어보다[획획 넘기다]   take it for granted that ~을 당연한 것으로 여기다

2 밑줄 함의   ①

해설 운동을 할 때 기력이 다하고 한계에 도달했다고 생각될 때가 있지만, 이것은 두뇌가 생명 유지 자원을 통제해서 실제 한계치보다 훨씬 이른 지점에 브레이크를 건 것이므로, 우리는 이 지점을 뛰어넘어서도 계속 운동할 수 있다. 이것을 '당신이 두 번째 바람을 경험하게 된다'라고 비유적으로 표현한 것이므로 밑줄 부분이 의미하는 바는 ① '당신은 계속할 수 있는 새로운 에너지와 힘을 찾게 될 것이다'이다.
② 당신은 패배의 수치를 피하도록 강요받는다는 느낌을 더 많이 받을 것이다
③ 당신은 육체적 한계를 극복하여 뇌를 통제할 것이다
④ 당신은 진짜 동기와 내재적 욕구로 움직여질 것이다
⑤ 당신은 치열한 경쟁으로부터 휴식을 취하는 것을 허락받을 것이다

해석 우리는 운동 훈련을 하는 동안 생리학적 에너지가 다 떨어져서 속도가 늦어지고 멈춘다고, 즉 우리의 최대 에너지 소비의 한도를 정하는 것은 우리의 근육의 강도 혹은 우리의 혈중 산소라고 대개 생각한다. 그러나 개인들이 자신의 육체적 한계에 도달했다고 느낄 때 실제로 훨씬 더 오랫동안 계속할 능력이 있다고 연구에서 밝혀졌다. 무언가를 정지시키는 것은 당신의 몸이 아니라 당신의 정신이다. 두뇌는 신체의 생명 유지 자원에 구두쇠 같은 통제를 가한다. 그것은 안팎의 환경을 감시하고, 당신이 너무 피로하고 지치게 될 위험이 있다고 느낄 때 당신의 노력에 브레이크를 걸며 당신이 위험할 정도로 기력이 소진될 실제 지점이 전혀 아닌 곳에서 스위치를 누른다. 그러나 경쟁의 압박 같은 특이한 필요가 당신이 이러한 시기상조의 장벽을 넘어서게 할 때 놀라운 일이 일어난다. 두뇌의 권력은 약해지고, 당신이 두 번째 바람을 경험하게 한다.

구문 [1행~4행] We often think // (that) we slow down and stop during athletic training / because we run out of physiological energy — / that **it is** *the strength of our muscles or the oxygen in our blood* **that** caps our maximum expenditure.
• 두 밑줄 친 부분은 think의 목적어 역할을 하며 서로 동격 관계이다. 두 번째 that절에서 「it is ~ that ... (…한 것은 바로 ~이다)」 강조구문이 쓰여 the strength ~ our blood가 강조되고 있다.

[10행~14행] ~, and when it feels there's a risk **of** your **getting** too fatigued and run-down, // it puts the brakes on your efforts, / **throwing** the switch far from *the actual point* [**at which** you would become dangerously exhausted].
• a risk of your getting에서 전치사 of의 목적어는 동명사 getting이며 your는 동명사의 의미상 주어이다. throwing 이하는 분사구문이며, [ ]는 '전치사+관계대명사'로 시작되는 관계사절로서 the actual point를 수식한다.

어휘 run out of ~이 다 떨어지다   physiological 생리학적인   cap 한도를 정하다   expenditure (에너지 등의) 소비; 지출   shut A down A를 중지시키다   miserly 구두쇠인; 아주 적은   life-sustaining 생명을 유지하는   within and without 안팎에   fatigued 피로한   run-down 지친   premature 시기상조의; 너무 이른   barrier 장벽; 장애물

3 빈칸 추론   ③

해설 빈칸 문장으로 보아 '무엇이' 아이들로 하여금 선의의 거짓말을 하게 만들었는지 찾아야 한다. 아이들에게 어른들의 잘 그린 한 장의 그림과 형편없는 한 장의 그림을 보여주고, 그림을 그린 어른들이 자신의 형편없는 그림 실력에 대해 슬프게 행동했을 때 아이들이 서둘러 그림이 나쁘지 않다는 선의의 거짓말을 했다는 내용이다. 이를 통해 아이들이 선의의 거짓말을 하는 것은 슬퍼하는 사람들의 마음을 위로하려는 공감 능력이 있다는 것을 보여주므로, 빈칸에 들어가기에 가장 적절한 것은 ③ '공감하는 유대감'이다.
① 갈등을 모면하려는 전략
② 화가들에게 감명을 주기 위한 시도
④ 빠른 관심을 얻고자 하는 욕망
⑤ 스스로를 기쁘게 하려는 의도

해석 하버드 대학의 심리학자인 Felix Warneken은 어른들이 초등학교 연령의 아이들에게 자신들이 그린 두 장의 그림을 보여주도록 했는데, 한 장은 상당히 잘 그린 그림이었고, 한 장은 형편없는 그림이었다. 어른들이 그림에 대해 특별한 자부심을 보이지 않으면, 아이들은 그것이 좋은지 형편없는지 말하는 데 정직했다. 어른들이 (자신이) 형편없는 화가인 것에 대해 슬프게 행동하면, 대부분의 아이들은 그림이 너무 끔찍하지는 않다고 서둘러 그녀를 안심시키곤 했다. 다시 말해, 그들은 선의의 거짓말을 한 것이다. 아이들이 나이가 많을수록, 형편없는 그림이 좋다고 말할 가능

성이 더욱 높았다. 이 형편없는 화가들에게 진실을 말하는 것에 그 어떠한 부정적인 결과도 없었지만, 아이들은 단지 이 낯선 사람들이 그들 자신에 대해 더 기분 좋게 느끼기를 원했던 것뿐이었다. 다시 말해, 아이들로 하여금 선의의 거짓말을 하게 만드는 것은 공감하는 유대감이라고 Warneken은 말한다. 사실상, 아이들은 정직 대 친절이라는 두 개의 상충하는 규범을 해결하려고 노력하며, 그의 연구에 따르면, 일곱 살 정도가 되면 그들은 일관적으로 친절의 편에 서기 시작한다.

구문 [3행~5행] If the adults didn't show any particular pride in the picture, // the kids were truthful in saying **whether it was good or bad.**

• whether는 명사절을 이끄는 접속사로, '~인지 아닌지'를 의미하며, 이 명사절은 saying의 목적어 역할을 한다.

[8행~10행] ~ ; **the older** they were, **the more** likely the kids were to say a bad drawing was good.

• 「the+비교급 ~, the+비교급 ...」 구문으로, '~하면 할수록 더욱더 …하다'의 의미이다.

어휘 **truthful** 정직한, 솔직한; 정확한 **grown-up** 어른, 성인; 성숙한 **rush** 서두르다; 분주함; 돌진(하다) **reassure** 안심시키다, 위로하다 **awful** 끔찍한, 형편없는 **white lie** 선의의 거짓말 **consequence** 결과; 중요성 **drive** 만들다, 몰아가다 **resolve** 해결하다; 결심(하다); 분해하다 **conflicting** 상충[상반]되는, 모순되는 *cf.* **conflict** 상충하다, 모순되다; 갈등, 충돌 **norm** 규범; 표준; 기준 **honesty** 정직(성), 솔직함 **consistently** 일관적으로, 한결같이

[선택지] **strategy** 전략, 계획 **attempt** 시도(하다) **impress** 감명을 주다; 깊은 인상을 주다 **empathic** 공감할 수 있는; 감정 이입의 **desire** 욕망, 욕구; 바라다 **intention** 의도, 목적

4 글의 순서　　　　　　　　　　③

해설 전자기력은 중력처럼 그것들이 멀리 떨어져 있을수록 힘이 더 약해진다는 말 다음에는 중력과 다른 점을 언급한 (B)가 먼저 나와야 한다. (B)의 두 번째 문장의 내용을 가리키는 This로 시작하는 (C)가 그다음으로 나와야 한다. 동등한 양으로 밀고 당겨서 결과적으로 전혀 전자기력을 받거나 작용하지 않는다는 (C)의 내용을 가리키는 This balance로 시작하는 (A)가 마지막으로 나와야 가장 적절하다.

해석 전자기력은 전하를 띠는 어떤 두 물체 사이에 작용한다. 더 많은 전하가 있을수록 힘도 더 강해진다. 그리고 중력처럼, 그 힘은 물체들 사이의 분리에 달려 있다. 그것들이 멀리 떨어져 있을수록 힘은 더 약해진다.
(B) 그러나 중력과 달리 전자기는 인력이 있을 수도 있고 척력이 있을 수도 있는데, 그것은 물체들을 서로 당길 수 있고 떠밀어버릴 수 있다. 하나는 양이고 다른 하나는 음인 반대의 전하들은 끌어당긴다. 둘 다 양이거나 둘 다 음인 같은 전하들은 밀어낸다.
(C) 이것은 같은 양의 양전하와 음전하를 가진 합성된 물체는 동등한 양으로 밀고 당겨서 결과적으로 전혀 전자기력을 받거나 작용하지 않는다는 것을 의미한다.
(A) 전하 중성의 결과인 이런 균형은 중력에서는 절대 일어날 수가 없다. 음의 질량이 존재하지 않아서, 질량이 중성인 물체의 가능성은 전혀 없다. 당신이 전자기력을 중화할 수 있듯이 중력을 중화할 수는 없다. 바로 이 때문에 그것이 우리의 경험에 항시 존재한다.

구문 [7행~8행] **There being no negative mass,** / there is no possibility of a mass-neutral object.

• There ~ mass는 분사구문으로 문맥상 이유를 나타내며 Because there is no negative mass로 바꾸어 쓸 수 있다.

어휘 **electromagnetic** 전자기의 *cf.* **electromagnetism** 전자기 **gravity** 중력, 만유

인력, 지구의 중력 **neutrality** 중성; 중립 **neutral** 중성의; 중립의 **attractive** 인력이 있는; 매력 있는 **opposite** 정반대인 **positive** 양의, 양전기의; 긍정적인 **negative** 음의, 음전기의; 부정적인 **repel** 밀어내다, 물리치다 **consequently** 결과적으로, 그 결과 **exert** 작용하다, 행사하다

5 문장 넣기　　　　　　　　　　⑤

해설 언론의 이미지의 위대함과 권위를 결정하는 것은 대중이 아닌 엘리트의 몫이라는 주제의 글이다. 주어진 문장의 '사진의 위대함의 평가에 동의하게 된 대중의 그러한 관찰'은 ⑤번 직전까지 계속해서 언급된 '언론 관련 엘리트들이 계속하여 이미지에 권위를 실어주는 모습'을 지칭한다고 볼 수 있다. 그리고 그러한 대중의 동의에 따라 엘리트들이 위대함의 의제를 설정하고 이미지 판단의 규준을 확립한다는 말이 마지막에 위치하는 것이 자연스럽다. 그러므로 주어진 문장이 들어갈 적절한 곳은 ⑤이다.

해석 대중은 포토저널리즘의 '큰 사진'을 고르는 데 있어 표현적인 혹은 심지어 승인하는 거의 어떤 역할도 맡지 않는다('올해의 사진'을 선정하기 위한 몇몇 대회는 예외). 편집자들은 그날의 뉴스 이미지를 전시하고 더 광범위한 보도와 논평의 가치가 있는 것들을 선정하기 전에 대중에게 여론 조사를 하지 않는다. 퓰리처상 역시 엘리트 기자들에 의해 투표로 결정된다. 사진작가들과 기자들(시상 위원회를 통해), 편집자들(선정을 통해), 그리고 정치와 편집 엘리트들(주석과 해설을 통해)은 이미지에 위대함과 따라서 명성을 부과한다. 역사학자들과 교과서 회사들은 토론용으로, 혹은 단지 삽화용으로 그러한 이미지를 재사용하거나 '인용'함으로써 그것들이 '위대함'을 재차 확인한다. 확실히 그러한 관찰을 반복적으로 보고 흡수한 후에 대중의 구성원들은, 그 사진들이 그들의 신념이나 행동에 영향을 미치는 데에 결코 흔들리지 않는다 해도, 이러한 평결에 동의할 것 같다. 따라서 엘리트들이 주로 위대함의 의제를 설정하고 이미지가 위대하다고 판단되는 규준을 확립한다.

구문 [3행~5행] ~ even if they may be **less than** susceptible **to** *the pictures'* **affecting** their beliefs or actions.

• less than은 '결코 ~이 아닌(not at all)'의 뜻이다. 전치사 to의 목적어는 동명사 affecting이고 the pictures'는 affecting의 의미상 주어이다.

[7행~9행] ~ (*the exception* **being** some contests to name "photo of the year").

• being은 분사이며 the exception은 분사의 의미상 주어이다.

[19행~21행] Elites, thus, largely set the agenda of greatness and establish *the criteria* [for which images are judged great].

• 동사 set과 establish가 and로 연결되어 병렬구조를 이루고 있다. [ ]은 the criteria를 수식한다.

어휘 **absorb** 흡수하다 **less than** 결코 ~이 아닌 **approve** 승인하다 **exception** 예외 **name** 선정하다, 지명하다 **editor** 편집자 **poll** 설문 조사하다 **extensive** 광범위한 **coverage** 보도 **comment** 논평, 언급 **vote upon** ~에 대해 투표로 결정하다 **committee** 위원회 **editorial** 편집의 **notation** 주석, 메모 **commentary** 해설, 논평 **impose** 부과하다 **quote** 인용하다 **illustration** 삽화 **reaffirm** 재차 확인하다 **agenda** 의제, 안건 **criterion** 규준

1 글의 주제 ①

해설 어린이가 예술 활동을 할 때 어른의 관점에서 어린이에게 충고를 하면 어린이는 열등감을 느끼고 자신감을 상실할 수밖에 없으며 섣부른 충고보다는 마음껏 창작할 자유를 누리도록 해주는 게 훨씬 낫다는 내용의 글이므로 주제로 가장 적절한 것은 ① '어린이에게 더 큰 창조적 자율성을 부여할 필요성'이다.
② 미술 교육이 정말로 중요한 과목인 이유들
③ 학습자의 창의성을 증진시키기 위한 예술 활동의 중요성
④ 어린이의 독립심을 조성하기 위한 미술 교육
⑤ 어린이들의 인성을 개발하기 위한 도구로서의 예술 교육

해석 4살 된 Sally가 점토 코끼리를 만들고 있는데 코끼리 코로 당근을 사용한다고 가정해보자. Sally의 엄마는 당근이 가마에서 타거나, 먼저 썩어버릴 거라고 설명한다. Sally는 마지못해 동의하는데 매우 실망한 표정이다. 그녀의 엄마가 자신이 무슨 일을 했는지 깨달았을 때는 너무 늦었다. Sally는 완성품보다는 즉각적인 결과에 더 관심이 있었는데, 이를 그녀는 대단히 만족스럽게 성취했었다. 고군분투하는 화가나 조각가에게 도움의 손길을 내미는 것은 얼마나 유혹적인가! 이러한 종류의 행동은 어린이가 자신의 표현이 우리의 것보다 열등하다고 느끼게 하며 아이의 자신감은 약화된다. 우리가 가진 성인의 가치를 어린이의 창의성에 부과하지 않는 것이 중요하다. 이것은 우리가 어린이에게 선택할 수 있는 다양한 과정을 보여줄 수 없다는 뜻은 아니다. 그러나 어린이는 혼자서 그것을 마음껏 개발할 수 있어야 한다.

구문 [5행~8행] Sally is **not** interested in the finished product **so much as** *the immediate effect*, **which** she has achieved *to her immense satisfaction*.
• 「not A so much as B」는 'A라기보다는 B'의 뜻이다. which는 the immediate effect를 지칭한다. 「to one's 감정 명사」는 '(…가) ~하게도'의 뜻이다.

어휘 **clay** 점토, 찰흙　**trunk** (코끼리의) 코　**rot** 썩다　**reluctantly** 마지못해서　**immense** 거대한　**tempting** 유혹적인　**struggle** 고군분투하다　**sculptor** 조각가　**version** (독자적인) 작품 해석, 표현　**inferior to** ~보다 열등한　**undermine** (자신감을) 약화시키다　**impose A on B** A를 B에 부과하다
[선택지] **autonomy** 자율성; 자치권

2 밑줄 어법 ②

해설 ② 주어 Scientific research에 상응하는 동사이므로 단수형인 has로 바꿔 써야 한다. aimed at ~ between fungi and plants는 Scientific research를 수식하는 과거분사구이다.
① and로 연결된 분사구문에 「keep+O+C (O를 C인 상태로 두다)」의 구문이 쓰였으므로 목적격보어 자리에 형용사 alive를 적절히 사용했다.
③ 앞의 the unique atmospheric conditions를 수식하는 관계사절인데 뒤에 완전한 절 trees can grow and thrive가 이어지므로 관계부사 where를 알맞게 사용했다.
④ 비교 대상이 isolated trees와 trees living together in forests이므로 복수형인 those가 알맞다.
⑤ to-v의 완료형인 「to have p.p.」는 문장의 동사보다 더 이전의 일을 표현할 때 쓰는데, 고립된 식물이 소통 능력을 상실한 것이 동사 seem보다 더 이전의 상황이므로 to have lost는 알맞다.

해석 나무에 관한 가장 놀라운 점은 나무들이 얼마나 사교적인지이다. 숲의 나무는 서로를 돌보며, 때로는 심지어 베어 넘어뜨려진 나무 그루터기에 당분과 다른 양분들을 먹여서 그것에 수 세기 동안 영양분을 공급하기까지 해서 그것을 계속 살려 둔다. 다른 나무들과 연결된 상태로 있게 해주는 나무의 가장 중요한 수단은 초목을 친밀한 연결망 속에서 연결시켜주는 흙 곰팡이의 '우드 와이드 웹'이다. 곰팡이와 식물 간의 이러한 파트너 관계의 놀라운 능력을 이해하는 것을 목표로 한 과학 연구는 단지 이제 막 시작되었을 뿐이다. 나무들이 먹을 것을 공유하고 소통하는 이유는 그들이 서로를 필요로 하기 때문이다. 나무들이 자라고 번성할 수 있는 독특한 대기 환경을 만드는 데에는 숲 하나가 필요하다. 그래서 고립된 나무들이 숲속에서 함께 사는 나무들보다 훨씬 더 짧은 생을 사는 것은 놀랍지 않다. 아마 모든 것 중 가장 슬픈 식물은 우리가 우리의 농업 체계 속에 노예로 만들어 버린 식물들일 것이다. 그것들은 오래 전에 소통 능력을 상실한 것 같고, 따라서 귀머거리이자 벙어리가 되었다.

구문 [5행~8행] *A tree's most important means* (of staying connected to other trees) **is** *a "wood wide web"* of soil fungi [that connects vegetation / in an intimate network].
• 밑줄 친 A tree's ~ other trees가 주어이고 동사는 is이다. [ ]는 a "wood wide web" of soil fungi를 수식하는 관계사절이다.

[14행~16행] So **it**'s not surprising **that** isolated trees have far shorter lives / than *those* (living together in forests).
• it은 가주어이고 that 이하가 진주어이다. ( )는 those를 수식하는 현재분사구이다.

어휘 **go so far as to-v** 심지어 v하기까지 하다　**nourish** 영양분을 공급하다　**fell** (나무를) 베어 넘어뜨리다　**means** 수단, 방법　**fungus** 균류, 곰팡이류 ((복수형 **fungi**))　**vegetation** 초목　**atmospheric** 대기의, 공기의　**conditions** 환경, 상황　**thrive** 번성하다　**enslave** 노예로 만들다　**render** (어떤 상태로) 만들다

3 빈칸 추론 ④

해설 빈칸 문장으로 보아 '무엇이' 상상력을 증가시키는 중요한 도구인지 찾아야 한다. 문제를 제시하는 틀을 바꿈으로써 상상력을 향상시켜 가능한 해법의 범위를 급격하게 넓힐 수 있다는 내용이므로 빈칸에 들어가기에 가장 적절한 것은 ④ '문제의 틀을 다시 만드는 능력을 익히는 것'이다.
① 당신의 정신이 자유롭게 흐르도록 내버려 두는 것
② 새로운 것들을 기꺼이 배우려 하는 것
③ 고정관념과 편견을 없애는 것
⑤ 당신의 주안점을 바꿈으로써 관심사를 넓혀가는 것

해석 "5 더하기 5의 합은 무엇일까?" "어떤 두 개의 숫자가 합쳐서 10이 될까?" 첫 번째 문제는 단 하나의 정답만을 가지고 있고, 두 번째 문제는 음수와 분수를 포함해서 무한히 많은 해법을 가지고 있다. 단순한 덧셈에 의존하는 이러한 두 문제는 단지 그것들이 틀에 넣어지는 방식에서만 다르다. 사실상, 모든 문제는 답이 나오는 틀이다. 그리고 당신이 보다시피, 그 틀을 바꿈으로써, 가능한 해법의 범위를 극적으로 바꿀 수 있다. 알베르트 아인슈타인의 말을 인용하자면, "만약 내가 한 문제를 해결할 한 시간이 있고 내 인생이 그 해법에 달려 있다면, 나는 처음 55분을 묻기에 적절한 문제를 결정하는 데 보낼 것입니다. 왜냐하면 일단 내가 적절한 문제를 알면, 5분 이내로 그 문제를 해결할 수 있으니까요."라고 했다. 어마어마한 다수의 해법을 열어주기 때문에 문제의 틀을 다시 만드는 능력을 익히는 것이 당신의 상상력을 증가시키는 중요한 도구이다.

구문 [5행~6행] *These two problems*, (**which rely on simple addition**), differ only in *the way* [(**that**) they are framed].
• which ~ addition은 삽입된 관계대명사절로 앞의 These two problems를 보충

설명한다. the way (that)은 how로 바꿔 쓸 수 있으며 이때의 how는 관계부사이다.

[6행~7행] In fact, all questions are *the frame* [**into which** the answers fall].
- '전치사+관계대명사' 형태인 into which가 이끄는 절이 명사 the frame를 수식하고 있다.

어휘 **add up to A** 합계[총] A가 되다 **infinite** 무한한, 무한정의; 무한한 것 **negative number** (수학) 음수(陰數) **fraction** 분수; 부분, 일부 **differ** 다르다; 의견이 맞지 않다 **frame** 틀에 넣다; 틀 *cf.* **reframe** ~(의 틀)을 다시 만들다, 재구성하다 **dramatically** 극적으로; 희곡[연극]적으로 **quote** 인용하다, 전달하다, 옮기다 **proper** 적절한, 제대로 된 **an array of** 다수의 **vast** 어마어마한, 방대한
[선택지] **be willing to-v** 기꺼이 v하다 **stereotype** 고정관념, 정형화된 생각[이미지] **prejudice** 편견, 선입견; 편견을 갖게 하다 **expand** 넓히다; 팽창시키다 **shift** 바꾸다; 옮기다, 이동하다

4 무관 문장 ④

해설 민족지학자들에게 관찰 기법이 믿을 수 있는 증거를 제공하긴 하지만 어떤 일들이 '왜' 일어나는지 그리고 행위자들이 그 일들에 있다고 생각하는 의미까지 제공하기에는 한계가 있으므로 직접적인 관찰 이외의 방법도 결합되어야 한다는 내용의 글이다. 그러므로 관찰상의 편견을 피하기 위해 설문지를 신중하게 설계해야 한다는 ④는 전체 글의 흐름과 관계가 없다.

해석 관찰은 민족지학자들에게 특정한 시간에 특정한 환경 안에서 일어나는, 보여진 행동이라는 믿을 수 있는 증거를 제공할 수 있다. ① 예를 들어, 사람들이 말하는 주장을 독립적으로 입증하기 위해 사람들의 행위를 이용하길 원할 때, 누구도 우리와 말을 할 수 있지 (또는 하려 하지) 않을 때 무슨 일이 발생하고 있는지 묘사하고 이해하길 원할 때 그리고 특히 사물과 환경에 관하여 더 높은 수준의 행동 패턴을 더 잘 포착하길 원할 때 관찰기법은 도움이 된다. ② 체계적이고 관찰 기반의 데이터는 무엇이 실제로 일어나고 있는지 알아내는 것과 다른 사람들에게 우리의 주장이 옳음을 증명하는 것 둘 다에 도움을 줄 수 있다. ③ 하지만 관찰은 '왜' 일들이 일어나는지, 그리고 행위자들이 그 일들에 있다고 생각하는 의미에 관해 단서와 부분적인 답을 제공할 뿐이다. ④ 그러한 관찰상의 편견을 피하기 위해 우리는 연구의 설문지를 신중하게 설계해야 한다. ⑤ 이것이 대다수 민족지학자들이 흥미 있어 하는 문제를 다루기 위해, 직접적인 관찰이 다른 이해 방법들과 결합되어야 하는 이유이다.

구문 [3행~9행] Observational skills help, for instance, // **when** we want to use people's actions to independently verify their spoken claims; (to) describe and (to) make sense of what is happening when no one can — or will — talk with us; and (to) better capture higher-level patterns of behavior especially regarding objects and environments.
- when이 이끄는 부사절 안에 동사 want의 목적어로 to use, (to) describe, (to) make sense of, (to) better capture가 세미콜론(;)과 and로 연결되어 병렬구조를 이루고 있다.

[11행~13행] But observation only gives clues and partial answers **as to** why things happen and *the meanings* [(which[that]) actors attribute to them].
- 밑줄 친 두 부분이 as to(~에 관해)의 목적어 역할을 한다. [ ] 부분은 목적격 관계대명사 which[that]이 생략된 관계사절로 앞의 the meanings를 수식한다.

어휘 **observation** 관찰(력); (관찰에 따른) 의견 *cf.* **observational** 관찰[관측](상)의 **solid** 믿을 수 있는, 확실한; 고체(의); 단단한 **demonstrate** (증거, 실례를 통해) 보여주다; 시위하다 **specific** 특정한; 구체적인; 명확한 **independently** 독립적으로 **claim** 주장; 권리; 요구하다 **make sense of** ~을 이해하다 **capture** 포착[포획]하다; 사로잡다; 기록하다 **regarding** ~에 관하여 **systematic** 체계적인 **justify** 옳음을 보여주다; 정당화시

키다 **clue** 단서, 실마리 **attribute A to B** B에 A(의 성질 등)가 있다고 생각하다; A를 B의 탓[덕]으로 보다 **bias** 편견, 선입견; 편견을 갖게 하다 **questionnaire** 설문지 **combine** 결합하다 **method** 방법 **address** (문제를) 다루다; 연설(하다); 주소

5 요약문 완성 ④

해설 첫 번째 연구에서 참가자들은 5명의 수락을 얻기 위해 20명이 필요하다고 추산했지만, 실제 결과는 10명이 필요했고, 또 다른 연구에서는 휴대전화를 빌리기 위해 10명이 필요하다고 예측했지만, 실제 결과는 3번의 수락을 위해 6.2명이 필요했다. 즉 부탁을 받는 사람들은 부탁하는 사람이 예상한 것보다 부탁을 잘 들어준다는 내용이므로 요약하면 부탁을 하는 사람들은 부탁을 받아들일(accept) 가능성을 과소평가(underestimate)하는 경향이 있다는 말이 된다. 그러므로 ④가 정답으로 가장 적절하다.

해석 경영 대학원 교수 Frank Flynn과 이전 박사 과정 학생인 Vanessa Lake에 의해 수행된 한 연구에서 참가자들은 5명의 사람들에게 짧은 설문지를 작성시키기 위해 얼마나 많은 수의 낯선 사람에게 접근해야 할지를 추산하도록 요청받았다. 평균 추산 인원은 약 20명 정도였다. 참가자들이 실제로 사람들에게 그 짧은 설문지를 작성하게 하도록 노력했을 때, 5명에게 그 요청을 응하게 하는 데는 평균적으로 단지 약 10명에게만 접근해야 할 필요가 있었다. 낯선 사람들로부터의 약간의 작은 도움을 요청하는 것은 명백히 매우 불편했으므로 그 연구 참가자 5명 중 약 1명은 그 임무를 완수하지 못했다. 이런 탈락자 비율은 모든 사람이 참가하기로 동의만 하면 거의 모든 사람이 완수하는 실험에서의 일반적인 비율보다 훨씬 더 높다. 또 다른 연구에서, 사람들은 짧은 통화를 위해 낯선 사람의 휴대전화를 빌리려고 10명의 낯선 사람에게 접근해야 할 것이라고 추정했지만, 3번의 수락이라는 목표에 도달하기 위해 접근한 실제 숫자는 6.2명이었다.

↓

> 연구에 따르면, 부탁할 생각을 하는 사람들은 그들의 요청을 받는 사람이 실제로 (B) 받아들일 것이라는 가능성을 (A) 과소평가하는 경향이 있다.

구문 [1행~5행] In *one study* (conducted by business school professor Frank Flynn and a former doctoral student, Vanessa Lake), / participants were asked **to estimate** how many strangers they would need to approach in order to get 5 people to fill out a short questionnaire.
- ( )는 one study를 수식하는 분사구이다. 밑줄 친 부분은 to estimate의 목적어 역할을 하는 간접의문문이며, 「의문사(how many strangers)+주어(they)+동사(would need to ~)」의 어순으로 쓰였다.

[10행~12행] **Asking for some small help from strangers** was apparently **so** uncomfortable **that** about one in five of the study participants did not complete the task.
- Asking for ~ strangers는 동명사구로 문장의 주어 역할을 한다. '너무 ~해서 …하다'의 뜻인 「so ~ that ...」 구문이 사용되었다.

어휘 **conduct** 수행[실시]하다 **business school** 경영 대학원 **doctoral student** 박사 과정 학생 **estimate** 추산[추정]하다; 추산(치), 추정 **comply** 응하다, 승낙하다 **task** 임무, 과업 **dropout** 탈락자; 낙오자 **acceptance** 수락; 동의, 승인 **likelihood** 가능성 **recipient** 받는 사람, 수취인; 받아들이는

1 빈칸 추론   ②

해설 빈칸 문장으로 보아 약하거나 인기 없는 입장을 지닌 특히 똑똑한 개인들이 '어떻게' 우리가 그 입장에 동조하게 만들 수 있는지를 찾아야 한다. 정보를 검열하는 것의 효과는 오히려 그 검열된 정보를 대중들이 더욱 신뢰하게 된다는 것이며, 이에 대한 걱정스러운 점은 약하거나 인기가 없는 비주류 집단의 구성원들이 자신들의 견해를 오히려 검열을 당하게 만들어서 그 견해의 가치를 더욱 높이는 것이라는 내용의 글이므로 빈칸에 들어갈 가장 적절한 것은 ② '자신들의 메시지가 제한되도록 만들어'이다.

① 자신들의 약점에 대한 공감을 불러일으켜
③ 자신들의 견해를 가능한 한 자주 제시해
④ 자신들의 주장에 충분한 증거를 제시해
⑤ 검열을 제거하기 위해 여론을 형성해

해석 정보를 검열하는 효과에 관해 아주 흥미로운 것은 그것이 당연한 것처럼 보이지만, 청중이 전보다 그 정보를 더 많이 갖기를 원한다는 것이 아니다. 오히려, 그들이 그 정보를 받지 못했음에도 불구하고 그들은 그것을 더욱 신뢰하게 된다는 것이다. 예를 들어, North Carolina 대학의 학생들이 캠퍼스에서 남녀 공용 기숙사를 반대하는 연설이 금지되었다는 것을 알게 되었을 때 그들은 남녀 공용 기숙사라는 아이디어에 더 반대하게 되었다. 그래서 그 연설을 전혀 듣지 않았어도 그들은 그 주장에 보다 더 공감하게 되었다. 이것은 약하거나 인기 없는 입장을 지닌 특히 똑똑한 개인들이 자신들의 메시지가 제한되도록 만들어서 우리가 그 입장에 동조하게 만들 수 있다는 걱정스런 가능성을 제기한다. 아이러니하게도 예를 들면 비주류 정치 집단의 구성원 같은 사람들에게 가장 효과적인 전략은 그들의 인기 없는 견해를 공표하는 것이 아니라 그런 견해가 공식적으로 검열되고 나서 그 검열을 공표하는 것이다.

구문 [11행~14행] This raises the worrisome possibility that *especially clever individuals* (holding a weak or unpopular position) can get us to agree with that position by arranging to have their message restricted.

• the worrisome possibility와 that ~ restricted는 동격 관계이다. ( )는 분사구로 especially clever individuals를 수식한다.

[16행~18행] ~ the most effective strategy may **not** be to publicize their unpopular views, **but** (be) to get those views officially censored and then to publicize the censorship.

• 「not A but B (A가 아니라 B)」 구문이 쓰였다.

어휘 intriguing 아주 흥미로운   censor 검열하다, (검열하여) 삭제하다; 검열관 *cf.* censorship 검열   oppose 반대하다; 겨루다   ban 금(지)하다   sympathetic 공감하는, 동조하는; 동정적인 *cf.* sympathy 공감; 동정, 연민   worrisome 걱정스러운, 걱정스럽게 만드는   strategy 전략, 계획   publicize 공표하다; 광고[선전]하다
[선택지] provoke 불러일으키다; 유발하다   restrict 제한[한정]하다; 방해하다   set forth 제시[발표]하다   evidence 증거, 흔적

2 글의 순서   ③

해설 주어진 첫 문장에서 한 개인이 미국에 살고 있는 3억이 넘는 사람 중에 일부를 넘어서는 (많은) 사람들과 상호 작용하는 것이 불가능하다는 말을 하고 있으므로, 그럼에도 불구하고 동료 시민으로 유대감을 느낀다는 Nonetheless로 시작하는 (B)가 먼저 나와야 한다. (B)의 마지막 문장이 학생들의 유대감을 언급하고 있으므로 그

내용을 보충 설명하는 (C)가 나와야 적절하다. (C)에서 상상 속의 공동체를 언급하고 있으므로 그 공동체를 설명하는 내용인 (A)가 나와야 적절하다.

해석 많은 사회적 생활이 대부분의 집단 구성원들을 알지 못하거나 그들과 상호 작용하지 않는 2차적인 집단에 소속하는 것을 포함한다. 한 개인이 미국에 살고 있는 3억이 넘는 사람 중의 작은 일부를 넘어서는 사람들과 상호작용하는 것은 불가능하다.

(B) 그렇지만 대부분의 미국인들은 그들의 동료 시민들에 대해 강한 유대감을 느낀다. 마찬가지로 여러분의 학교에 있는 학생들에 대해 생각해보라. 그들은 그들이 2차적인 그룹에 속해 있다는 것을 알지만, 그들 중의 많은 사람들이 아마도 그 집단에 아주 충실할 것이다.

(C) 그러나 여러분은 여러분의 학교에서 얼마나 많은 사람들을 만났는가? 아마도 전체의 아주 일부만을 만났을 것이다. 거리에도 불구하고 친근하다는 역설을 이해하는 한 가지 방법은 여러분의 학교나 미국을 '상상 속의 공동체'로 여기는 것이다.

(A) 그것은 여러분이 그 집단의 대부분의 구성원을 만날 수 없을 것이고, 그들이 반드시 어떨 것이라고 생각할 수밖에 없기 때문에 형성된다. 그럼에도 불구하고 그것은 사람들이 그것의 존재와 중요성을 강하게 믿기 때문에 공동체이다.

구문 [1행~3행] Much social life involves **belonging** to secondary groups without knowing 〔or〕 interacting with **most group members**.

• belonging 이하는 involves의 목적어 역할을 하고 있고, most group members는 전치사 without의 목적어 역할을 하는 동명사 knowing과 interacting의 공통 목적어이다.

어휘 secondary 제2의, 부차적인   fraction 아주 조금   speculate 사색하다, 숙고하다   fiercely 지독히   loyal 충실한   paradox 역설   intimacy 친밀함

3 문장 넣기   ⑤

해설 ⑤번의 앞 문장은 신뢰를 깨고 단기적인 이익을 얻는 사람들이 제시된다. But으로 시작되는 주어진 문장은 ⑤번 앞 문장과 역접의 내용으로서, 그들은 장기적으로 얻을 수 있는 이익의 가능성을 줄이게 된다는 내용이다. 그러므로 주어진 문장은 ⑤번에 들어가야 한다.

해석 대부분의 사람들은 진실성의 대용물로 평판을 사용한다. 그러나 그러한 전략에는 문제가 있다. 일반적인 믿음과는 반대로, 진실성은 안정적인 특성이 아니다. 과거에 공정하고 정직했던 사람이 미래에도 반드시 공정하고 정직한 것은 아닐 것이다. 왜 그런지 이해하기 위해 우리는 인간이 '선'과 '악'의 충동과 씨름한다는 개념을 버릴 필요가 있다. 심각한 정신 병리학의 경우를 제외하면, 그들의 두뇌는 그런 식으로 작동하지 않으며, 오히려 그들은 두 가지 유형의 이득(단기적 이득과 장기적 이득)에 집중한다. 그리고 일반적으로 어떤 특정 순간에 진실성을 좌우하는 것은 그것들 간의 균형이다. 예를 들어 지키지 않을 혹은 지킬 수 없을 일을 약속함으로써 신뢰를 깨는 사람들은 즉각적인 보상을 거둘지도 모른다. 그러나 그들은 미래에 동일한 동업자(그리고 아마 다른 사람들)와의 교류와 협동으로부터 더 큰 이익을 쌓을 가능성을 줄이는 것이다. 그들에게 어떤 결과가 더 나은지는 상황과 관련 당사자들에 달려 있다.

구문 [13행~15행] And **it's** *the trade-off between them* **that** typically dictates integrity at any given moment.

• 「it is ~ that ... (…한 것은 바로 ~이다)」 강조구문이 쓰여 the trade-off between them이 강조되고 있다.

[18행~19행] Which outcome is better for them **depends** on the situation and the parties involved.

• Which outcome is better for them은 간접의문문 형태인 주어이며 depends가 동사이다.

어휘 likelihood 가능성 accumulate 축적하다 reputation 명성, 평판 integrity 진실성 strategy 전략 contrary to ~와 반대로 trait 특성 not necessarily 반드시 ~한 건 아닌 wrestle 몸싸움을 벌이다 impulse 충동 psychopathology 정신 병리학 trade-off 균형 dictate 좌우하다 deliver (약속을) 지키다 reap 수확하다, 거두다 party involved 당사자

4~5 장문   4 ④   5 ⑤

해설 4. 어떤 상황의 한 측면에만 집중하는 것이 착각의 원인이 될 수 있다고 하면서 실제로는 그 상황이나 문제가 집중했을 때 보이는 것만큼 크게 변화나 영향을 줄 수 없다는 내용이다. 그러므로 제목으로는 ④ '삶의 어떤 것도 당신이 생각하는 것만큼 중요하지 않다'가 가장 적절하다.
① 사람이 아니라 문제를 공략하라
② 당신이 이미 성취한 것에 만족하라
③ 인생에서 돈보다 중요한 것
⑤ 도전 없이는 누구라도 같은 상태에 머물러 있다
5. 마케팅 담당자들은 상품이 삶의 질에 주는 차이를 크게 과장한다고 했으므로, 사람들은 새로운 스마트폰이 생산성을 크게 증가시킬 것이라고 생각할 것이다. 그러므로 ⑤는 increase 등이 되어야 한다.

해석 복권에 당첨되는 것은 행복한 사건이지만, 그 흥분 상태는 지속되지 않는다. 평균적으로 높은 수입을 가진 사람은 낮은 수입을 가진 사람보다 더 기분이 좋지만, 그 차이는 대부분의 사람들이 예상하는 것의 약 3분의 1 정도의 (a) 크기이다. 여러분이 부유하고 가난한 사람에 대해 생각할 때, 여러분의 생각은 자연스럽게 수입에 집중한다. 그러나 행복은 수입에 달려 있기보다는 다른 요인에 더 많이 달려 있다. 이는 '초점 집중 착각'에 대한 완벽한 예시인데, 이는 어떠한 물건이나 상황의 한 측면에 집중하는 사람들의 성향에 대해 주어진 명칭이다. 이 예시에서, 복권에 당첨되는 것은 사람들이 돈에 대해서만 생각하도록 이끌고 분명 (액수가) 많을수록 (b) 좋다. 복권 당첨자들이 여전히 건강, 인간관계, 지루함 등의 문제를 처리해야 함에도 불구하고, 초점 집중 착각은 이러한 면을 (c) 못 보게 한다.
마케팅 담당자들은 초점 집중 착각을 (d) 이용한다. 보통, 그들은 그 상품이 소비자의 삶의 질에 주는 차이를 크게 과장한다. 마케팅 담당자들은 사람들이 새로운 스마트폰이 그들의 생산성을 크게 (e) 감소시킨다(→ 증가시킨다)고 생각하거나 새로운 차가 높은 수준의 자유를 보장해 줌으로써 그들의 삶의 질에 큰 영향을 미칠 것이라 생각하도록 만드는 데 능숙하다. 좋건 나쁘건, 이러한 구매는 소비자의 삶에 변화를 가져오지만, 그 차이는 예상한 것보다 작을 것이다.

구문 [17행~19행] Usually, they greatly exaggerate *the difference* [that the good will make to the quality of a consumer's life].

• [ ] 부분은 목적격 관계대명사 that이 이끄는 관계사절로 선행사 the difference를 수식한다.

어휘 on average 평균적으로 exploit 이용하다, 활용하다; 착취하다 skilled 숙련된, 노련한 productivity 생산성 in turn 결국, 결과적으로 for better or worse 좋건 나쁘건

1 글의 요지 ②

해설 이 글은 철학과 과학은 언뜻 별개의 영역으로 보이지만 철학은 과학의 방향을 결정하고 과학은 철학적 탐구에서 자라나는 등 그 두 학문이 서로 영향을 주고받으며 많은 영역을 공유한다는 내용이다. 그러므로, 요지로 가장 적절한 것은 ②이다.

해석 철학과 과학 간의 강력한 구분선을 보려 하는 것은 유혹적이다. 결국 과학은 정확하며, 증명된 구체적 사실로 정의되는 반면 철학은 사실을 넘어서 아마 결코 증명될 수 없는 추측의 영역으로 들어서니 말이다. 그래도 중첩되는 상당한 영역이 있다. 과학은 차갑고 딱딱한 사실에 의존할지 모르지만, 그것의 방향은 어떤 다른 학문 영역보다도 철학에 의하여 더 많이 결정되어 왔다. 과학적 기법 그 자체는 의미와 진리와 지식의 본질에 대한 철학적 탐구에서 자라났고, 이러한 탐구는 오늘날 철학 분야에서 계속된다. 동시에 윤리 철학은 우리가 과학자들에게 수행할 것을 허용하는 실험 유형을 결정한다. 결국, 하나는 관찰 가능한 자료에 관심이 있고 나머지 하나는 의미와 가치에 관심을 가질 수 있겠지만, 과학도 철학도 진공 속에서 존재하지는 않는다.

구문 [6행~8행] ~ its directions have been determined by philosophy **more than** by **any other area** of study.

• 「비교급 than any other ...」는 '다른 어떤 ...보다 더 ~한'의 뜻으로, 최상급을 의미한다.

[13행~16행] In the end, **one** may be concerned with observable data and **the other** (may be concerned) with meanings and values, // but **neither** science **nor** philosophy **exists** in a vacuum.

• one은 science를 지칭하고 the other는 philosophy를 지칭한다고 볼 수 있다. the other 다음에는 may be concerned가 생략되어 있다. 「neither A nor B (A도 B도 아니다)」 구문이 사용되었는데 동사는 B에 수일치 시키므로, philosophy에 맞추어 단수동사 exists가 쓰였다.

어휘 tempting 유혹하는 concrete 구체적인 speculation 추측 considerable 상당한 overlap 공통부분, 겹침 inquiry into ~에 대한 연구 be concerned with ~에 관심이 있다 observable 관찰할 수 있는 in a vacuum 외부와 단절된 상태에서 *cf.* vacuum 진공

2 빈칸 추론 ③

해설 돌고래의 휘파람은 특히 다른 구성원들로부터 고립된 상황에서 잘 들린다고 하였고, 고립된 동물들은 자신의 이름을 알려서 정체와 위치를 드러내며 집단이 재결합하면 휘파람 소리를 내지 않는다고 했으므로 빈칸에 들어갈 말은 ③ '집단 응집력의 유지'임을 유추할 수 있다.
① 당면한 위험에 대한 경고
② 집단의 영역 방어
④ 공격적 행동의 특징
⑤ 소외감을 다루는 전략

해석 각각의 돌고래는 특징적 휘파람이라 불리는 자신만의 발성을 가지고 있고, 그것은 이 동물의 상대적으로 긴 생애 전체에 비교적 변함없이 남아 있을 것이다. 연구에 의하면 돌고래들은 적어도 8개의 다른 특징적 휘파람을 기억할 수 있음이 드러났으며, 재생 실험에 의하면 그들이 개체 간에 신뢰성 있게 차등을 두기 위하여 그것들을 사용할 수 있다고 한다. 휘파람 소리는 다양한 행동 맥락에서 사용되지만,

Vincent Janik과 Peter Slater는 포획된 동물을 연구하던 중 동물 하나가 자신의 무리의 다른 구성원들로부터 고립된 상황에서 휘파람 소리가 특히 흔하게 들린다는 것을 보여주었다. 이 동물들은 특징적 휘파람 소리를 낼 때 자신들의 '이름'을 효과적으로 부르고, 그렇게 함으로써 자신들의 정체를 널리 알리고 위치를 누설한다고 추정된다. 일단 고립된 동물이 재결합하면 특징적 휘파람 방송은 멈춘다. 그러므로 휘파람의 적어도 한 가지 기능은 집단 응집력의 유지이다.

구문 [4행~7행] Research has revealed that dolphins can remember at least eight different signature-whistles and playback experiments suggest that **they** can use **them** to reliably discriminate between individuals.

• 접속사 and가 앞뒤로 두 개의 절을 연결한다. 두 번째 절에서 they는 dolphins를, them은 at least eight different signature-whistles를 지칭한다.

[12행~15행] **It** is supposed **that** these animals effectively call out their "name" // **when** they emit their signature-whistle and thereby broadcast their identity and give away their location.

• It은 가주어이고 that 이하가 진주어이다. when이 이끄는 절에서 동사 emit, broadcast, give away가 and로 연결되어 병렬구조를 이룬다.

어휘 vocalization 발성 be referred to as A A로 지칭[언급]되다 signature 특징 playback 재생 reliably 믿을 수 있게 captive 사로잡힌 isolate 고립시키다 call out 외치다 emit 방출하다 thereby 그렇게 함으로써 give away 누설하다 reunite 재결합하다

3 무관 문장 ④

해설 과거에는 질병을 신의 섭리 탓으로 돌렸기 때문에 대규모 질병이 발생하면 신을 달래기 위해 종교적 행진을 했고, 그것이 여러 사람을 모이게 해 더 큰 전염을 초래했다는 내용의 글이다. 따라서 질병이 퍼진 시기에 많은 사람이 집과 가족을 버리고 도망을 쳤다는 내용의 ④는 글의 흐름과 무관하다.

해석 질병의 대규모 발생에 대한 인간 개체군의 전략과 대응은 현저하게 유사한 모습을 보여 왔다. ① 질병은 매우 흔히 신의 섭리 탓으로 돌려졌기 때문에, 많은 사회가 신을 달래기 위해 만들어진 의식, 제물 바치기, 그리고 행진을 발전시켰다. ② 기독교 공동체에서 전염병의 출현에 대한 가장 흔한 대응 중 하나는, 성직자들과 평신도들이 신의 자비를 빌며 자신들의 교회에서 성자의 그림을 떼어 그것을 들고 그 지역사회의 거리 사이를 다니는 종교적 행진을 준비하는 것이었다. ③ 예를 들어, 1466년에 파리에서 전염병이 발생한 동안에, 성인(聖人) Crepin과 Crepinien의 유해를 들고 거리에서 줄지어 행진하는 것을 보기 위해 수천 명이 모습을 나타냈다. ④ 그럼에도 불구하고, 질병이 널리 퍼진 시기에 파리의 많은 사람들은 그 과정에서 집과 가족을 버리고 정말 도망을 쳤다. ⑤ 역설적이게도, 공공 집회를 위해 대규모의 사람들을 함께 모이게 하는 것은 실제로는 전염병의 확산을 가능하게 했으며 실은 여러 경우에서 전염병을 악화시켰을 수도 있다.

구문 [6행~12행] In Christian communities one of *the most common responses* (to the appearance of epidemic disease) was the organization of *religious processions* [**during which** clergy and laypeople removed the images of saints from their churches and carried them through the streets of the community, / **praying for divine mercy**].

• ( ) 부분은 전명구로 the most common responses를 수식한다. '전치사+관계대명사' 형태의 during which가 이끄는 관계사절은 선행사 religious processions를 수식한다. [ ] 내에 두 개의 밑줄 친 동사구는 병렬구조를 이루고 있다. praying ~ mercy는 동시동작을 나타내는 분사구문으로 의미상 주어는 clergy and laypeople

이다.

[12행~15행] During an epidemic in Paris in 1466, for example, thousands turned out to **watch** *the remains of Saints Crepin and Crepinien* **being paraded** through the streets.

• 지각동사 watch가 「watch O v-ing(being paraded) (O가 v하고 있는 것을 보다)」 형태로 사용되었다.

어휘 **strategy** 전략 **massive** 대규모의 **outbreak** (질병 등의) 발생: 발발 **remarkably** 현저하게, 매우 **attribute A to B** A를 B의 탓으로 돌리다 **sacrifice** 제물 바치기; 희생물 **procession** 행진, 행렬 **epidemic** 전염[유행]성의; 전염병 **organization** 준비: 조직 **religious** 종교의; 독실한 **clergy** 성직자들 **laypeople** 평 신도; 비전문가 **saint** 성자(같은 사람) **divine** 신의; 신성한 **mercy** 자비 **turn out** 모 습을 나타내다; ~인 것으로 밝혀지다 **remains** 유해; 유적; 남은 것 **parade** 줄지어 행진 하게 하다 **flee** 도망치다; 달아나다 **abandon** 버리고 떠나다; 포기하다 **bring together** 함께 모으다, 집합시키다 **public gathering** 공공 집회 **facilitate** 가능하게[용이하게] 하다 **contagious** 전염성의 **worsen** 악화시키다

4 글의 순서 　　　　　　　　　　④

해설 물에 젖었을 때 손과 발에 생기는 주름에 대한 내용이다. 우선 주어진 글에서 이에 대한 일반적 통념이 나오고 역접 연결어로 시작되는 (C)에서 이 통념에 대한 과학자들의 의문이 이어지는 것이 자연스럽다. 그 뒤에는 그 의문에 대한 답변을 탐 구하는 논문을 소개하는 (A)가 이어져야 하고 그 연구의 좀 더 구체적인 내용을 서 술한 (B)가 와야 한다.

해석 지나치게 오랫동안 빗속에 있어 봤거나 몇 시간 동안 욕조에서 몸을 흠뻑 적 셔본 사람은 누구라도 그들의 손과 발이 주름지게 될 수 있다는 사실을 알고 있다. 일반적 통념은 그것이 단지 피부가 물을 흡수한 것에 지나지 않는다고 말한다. (C) 그러나 많은 의문이 과학자들을 혼란스럽게 했다. 왜 '젖은 주름'은 손과 발에만 나 타나는가? 그리고 왜 가장 두드러진 주름은 손가락과 발가락 끝에 나타날까? (A) 이 제 '두뇌, 행동 그리고 진화'라는 학술지에 실린 한 논문이 젖은 주름이 도움이 된다 는 증거를 제공한다. 타이어의 접지면과 유사하게, 그것들은 정지 마찰력을 향상시 킨다. 그 연구에서, 한 진화 신경 생리학자와 그의 공동 저자들이 물로 인해 주름진 28개의 손가락을 조사했다. (B) 그들은 손가락들이 모두 나무의 가지처럼 갈라지는 주름 패턴을 지녔음을 발견했다. 이 가지 형태의 패턴은 물이 손끝에서 빠지게 하고, 더 많은 피부 접촉을 돕고 (물건을) 더 잘 쥐게 해준다.

구문 [1행~3행] *Anyone* [who has ever stayed out in the rain too long or soaked for hours in a tub] **knows** their hands and feet can become wrinkled.

• 주어는 Anyone이고 동사는 knows이다. [ ]는 관계사절로 Anyone을 수식하며, 이 절에서 has stayed와 (has) soaked가 or로 연결되어 병렬구조를 이룬다.

어휘 **soak** 푹 담그다; 흠뻑 적시다 **tub** 통, 욕조 **absorb** 흡수하다; 빨아들이다 **serve a purpose** 도움이 되다 **evolutionary neurobiologist** 진화 신경 생리학자 **drain away** (물이) 빠지다 **grip** 움켜쥠, 꽉 붙잡음; 꽉 잡다 **prominent** 중요한; 눈에 띄는, 두드 러진 **digit** 숫자; 손[발]가락

5 문장 넣기 　　　　　　　　　　⑤

해설 글의 내용은 기분이 의사소통에 미치는 영향을 탐구하는 실험에 대한 것이다. 주어진 문장의 주어가 Negative affect이고, 중간에 연결어 thus가 있으므로, 부정 적인 감정에 대한 실험을 끝낸 다음에 주어진 문장이 들어가는 것이 적절하다. 즉 부 정적인 감정에 해당하는 '슬픈 기분'을 느끼는 실험 참여자들은 남을 속이는 사람들

을 더 정확히 가려냈다는 문장 다음인 ⑤에 들어가는 것이 적절하다.

해석 기분이 의사소통에 미치는 영향을 탐구하기 위해, 연구원들은 행복하거나 슬 픈 기분을 느끼는 실험 참여자들에게 일부러 꾸민 도난 사건 이후에 심문을 받아 유 죄이거나, 유죄가 아닌 사람들의 녹화 진술을 받아들이거나 거부하도록 요청했다. 비디오 영상 속의 사람들은 남이 보지 않을 때 영화표를 훔치거나 그것을 빈방에 그 대로 두고는 영화표를 가져간 것을 부인하도록 지시를 받았다. 그러므로 절도 혐의 를 부인할 때 사람들 일부는 거짓말을 하고 일부는 진실을 말하고 있었던 셈이었다. 긍정적인 기분을 느끼는 실험 참여자들은 그러한 부인을 진실한 것으로 받아들일 가 능성이 더 높았다. 슬픈 기분을 느끼는 실험 참여자들은 유죄 판정을 훨씬 더 많이 내렸고, 남을 속이는 (유죄의) 사람들을 정확히 가려내는 것을 훨씬 더 잘했다. 그러 므로 부정적인 감정은 관찰 면접에서 진실과 거짓의 정확한 구별 능력을 향상시켰 다. 또한 신호 감지 분석 결과도 슬픈 감정의 심사위원들은 중립적이거나 행복한 기 분의 심사위원들보다 속임을 더 정확히 감지한다는 (유죄인 사람들을 유죄라고 알 아본다는) 사실을 확증하였으며 이는 예상된 기분이 유도해 낸 처리 과정상의 차이 와 일치한다.

구문 [3행~7행] To explore the effects of mood on communication, researchers **asked** *either happy or sad participants* **to accept or reject** the videotaped statements of *targets* [who were questioned after a staged theft, and were either guilty, or not guilty].

• 「ask O to-v」 구문의 형태에서 either happy or sad participants는 목적어로, to accept or reject 이하는 목적격보어로 쓰였다. [ ] 부분은 관계사절로 targets를 수 식한다.

어휘 **affect** 감정, 정서 **distinction** 구별, 구분 **participant** (실험) 참여자 **reject** 거부하다, 부인하다 **target** 대상자, 목표 **instruct** 지시[명령]하다 **deny** 부인한다, 부정 하다 **detect** 감지하다, 알아내다 **confirm** 확인하다, 입증하다 **consistent with** ~와 일치하는 **induce** 유도하다, 유발하다

1 글의 제목　　③

해설 우리가 꿈에서 기존에 갖고 있던 신념이나 자기 필요에 맞는 것만을 수용하면서 편향적으로 그것을 해석한다고 하고 있다. 이런 편향된 해석이 꿈의 내용보다 우리 자신에 대해 더 많은 것을 말해준다고 했으므로 글의 제목으로는 ③ '우리의 꿈 해석은 우리의 자아에 의해 영향받는다'가 적절하다.
① 꿈은 정신과 자아 사이의 교량이다
② 꿈과 공상의 인지 패턴
④ 꿈 해석은 우리에게 가치 있는 통찰력을 제공한다
⑤ 꿈 해석 방법 즉, 꿈은 무엇을 의미하는가?

해석 우리들 모두는 어떤 우리 꿈들은 일상의 문제와 관련이 있는 것 같고, 어떤 것은 모호하고 일관성이 없으며, 그리고 어떤 것은 우리가 걱정하거나 우울할 때 꾸게 되는 불안 꿈이라는 것을 경험으로부터 알고 있다. 그러나 우리의 잠자고 있는 뇌 속의 영상의 근원이 무엇이든 간에, 우리는 우리 자신의 꿈 또는 누군가의 꿈을 해석하는 데 신중할 필요가 있다. 사람들에 대한 최근의 연구는 개개인들이 자신들의 기존의 신념이나 필요에 맞는 것들은 수용하고 그렇지 않은 것들은 거부하면서 꿈 해석에서 편향되고 이기적이라는 것을 보여 주었다. 예를 들어, 그들은 신이 그들에게 1년간 휴가를 내어 구호 캠프에서 일하라고 명령하는 꿈보다 신이 그들에게 1년간 휴가를 내어 세계를 여행하라고 명령하는 꿈을 더 중요시할 것이다. 우리의 편향된 해석은 우리의 실제 꿈이 말해주는 것보다 우리 자신에 대해 더 많은 것을 우리에게 말해 줄지도 모른다.

구문 [7행~11행] A recent study of people showed that individuals are biased and self-serving in their dream interpretations, / **accepting** those [that fit in with their preexisting beliefs or needs] and **rejecting** those [that do not].
• 밑줄 친 두 개의 분사구문이 and로 연결되어 병렬구조를 이루고, 두 개의 [ ] 부분은 관계사절로 각각 바로 앞에 있는 선행사 those를 수식한다.
[11행~14행] For example, they will give **more** weight to *a dream* [in which God commands them to take a year off to travel the world] **than** *one* [in which God commands them to take a year off to work in a relief camp].
• 「비교급+than」 구문이 쓰여 a dream ~ the world와 one ~ a relief camp를 비교하는데, 이때 one은 a dream을 지칭한다. 두 개의 [ ] 부분은 '전치사+관계대명사' 형태의 in which가 이끄는 관계사절로 각각 앞에 있는 a dream과 one을 수식한다.
[14행~16행] Our biased interpretations may tell us more about ourselves **than do** our actual dreams.
• than 이후에 주어(our actual dreams)와 동사(do)가 도치되었고, 이때 do는 tell us about ourselves를 대신하는 대동사이다.

어휘 vague 모호한　incoherent 일관성 없는, 비논리적인　interpret 해석[설명]하다　biased 편향된, 선입견 있는　self-serving 이기적인　preexisting 기존의　give weight to ~을 중요시하다　command 명령하다, 지시하다　relief camp 구호 캠프　interpretation 해석, 설명
[선택지] ego 자아; 자부심　cognitive 인지[인식]의　daydream 공상, 몽상　insight 통찰력; 이해

2 밑줄 어휘　　④

해설 친구가 우리 인간에게 가장 소중한 이유는 우리의 표현 욕구를 조바심 내지 않고 기꺼이 받아들여 주기 때문이므로 ④는 앞의 without appearance of와 결합

해서 '조바심을 보이지 않고'가 되어야 하므로 impatience로 고쳐야 한다.

해석 대체로 예술은 공감에 대한 보편적인 인간 욕구의 결과로 존재한다. 인간은 자신을 자신의 동료로부터 ① 분리하는 벽을 허물기 위해 끊임없이 애쓰고 있다. 우리가 그것을 자기중심주의라고 부르든, 단순히 인간성이라고 부르든, 우리 모두는 타인이 우리의 감정을 ② 이해하게 하려는, 예를 들어 우리가 어떻게 고통받고, 우리가 어떻게 즐기는가를 그들에게 보여주려는 소망을 알고 있다. 우리는 충분히 자주 우리의 의견으로 동료들을 난타하지만, 이것은 우리가 우리의 감정을 쏟아내는 집요함에 비하면 ③ 아무것도 아니다. 친구는 세상의 소유물 중 가장 소중한 존재인데, 대체로 그(친구)는 우리가 마음속으로 느낀 것에 대한 끊임없는 이야기를 ④ 인내심(→ 조바심)을 보이지 않고 기꺼이 받아들이기 때문이다. 우리는 모두 우리 자신을 ⑤ 표현하도록 촉구하는 끊임없는 욕구와 그리고 우리의 생각, 경험, 그러나 무엇보다도 감정을 다른 사람들이 공유하도록 만드는 지속적인 노력 쪽으로 우리를 이끄는 내적 필요성을 대체로 자각하고 있다. 나에게는 우리가 이 본능적인 욕구를 충분히 멀리 거슬러 올라가면 예술의 발단에 도달할 것으로 보인다.

구문 [4행~7행] Whether we call it egotism or simply humanity, // we all know the wish to **make** *others* **appreciate** our feelings; to show them how we suffer, how we enjoy.
• the wish와 to make ~ we enjoy는 동격 관계이고, 이때 make는 '~하게 하다'라는 의미의 사역동사로 「make O 원형부정사」의 형태로 쓰였다.
[15행~17행] ~; of *the inner necessity* [which moves us to continual endeavors to make others share our thoughts, our experiences, but most of all our emotions].
• [ ] 부분은 주격 관계대명사 which가 이끄는 관계사절로 the inner necessity를 수식하고, continual endeavors와 to make ~ our emotions는 동격 관계이다.

어휘 broadly speaking 대체로, 대략으로　as a consequence of ~의 결과로, ~ 때문에　universal 보편적인; 일반적인　endeavor 애쓰다, 노력(하다)　fellow 동료, 친구; 녀석 *cf.* fellowman 동료, 같은 인간　egotism 자기중심(주의)　humanity 인간성; 인류　appreciate 이해하다; 감상하다; 감사하다　in comparison to A A에 비하면, A와 비교할 때　insistence 집요(함); 고집; 주장　earthly 세상의; 세속적인　be willing to-v 기꺼이 v하다　patience 인내(심), 참을성(↔ impatience 조바심, 성급함)　sensation 느낌, 감각　more or less 대체로, 상당히　conscious of ~을 자각[의식]하는　impulse 욕구, 충동　urge 촉구[권고]하다; 충고하다　necessity 필요(성); 필수품　trace A back A를 거슬러 올라가다　instinctive 본능[직감]적인

3 빈칸 추론　　④

해설 전 세계 유아들은 매우 다른 환경에서 성장하지만 심리적 발달 단계는 세계 어디서나 보편적 양상을 보이고 정신 질환의 발병률도 전 세계적으로 비슷하다는 내용의 글이므로, 어린이들 간의 심리적 차이는 ④ '유사함의 긴 목록에 비하면 사소하다'고 할 수 있다.
① 그들을 사회로부터 고립되게 한다
② 많고 다양한 정서적 반응을 유발한다
③ 그들에게 동년배와 관계를 형성할 기회를 준다
⑤ 자극이 더 다양하고 복잡할 때 감소된다

해석 오늘 전 세계에서 태어날 수천 명의 아기들은 그들의 첫 두 해에 매우 다른 환경을 경험할 것이다. 어떤 아기들은 할머니나 누나들의 돌봄을 받을 것이다. 어떤 아기들은 어린이집에 다닐 것이다. 어떤 아기들은 엄마와 집에 있을 것이다. 어떤 아기

들은 많은 장난감을 가질 것이다. 어떤 아기들은 하나도 못 가질 것이다. 어떤 아기들은 낡은 누더기에 감싸여 어둡고 조용한 오두막에서 첫해를 보낼 것이다. 어떤 아기들은 장난감, 그림책, TV 이미지로 가득한 밝은 조명의 방에서 기어 다닐 것이다. 그러나 이러한 차이에도 불구하고, 심각한 두뇌 손상이나 유전적 결함을 가진 적은 비율을 제외하면, 대부분은 2살이 되기 전에 말하고, 3살 생일쯤에는 자의식이 생기고, 7살 때쯤에는 가족의 어떤 책임을 맡을 수 있게 될 것이다. 이 어린이들 간의 심리적 차이는 유사함의 긴 목록에 비하면 사소하다. 어린이들이 다른 환경에서 양육되고 있음에도 손상이 덜한 불안 장애뿐 아니라 조현병과 우울증 같은 심각한 정신질환의 발병률은 전 세계적으로 놀라울 정도로 비슷하다.

구문 [10행~14행] But **despite** these differences, **excluding** the small proportion with serious brain damage or a genetic defect, / **most** will speak before they are two years old, become self-conscious by the third birthday, and be able to assume some family responsibilities by age seven.

• despite는 '~에도 불구하고'라는 뜻의 전치사이고, excluding ~ a genetic defect는 분사구문이다. 주어는 most이고 동사는 will 다음의 동사원형 speak, become, be가 ,와 and로 연결되어 병렬구조를 이룬다.

[16행~21행] **The prevalence** of serious mental disorders like schizophrenia and depression, **as well as** the less impairing anxiety disorders, **is** surprisingly similar around the world, // even though children **are being reared** in different environments.

• The prevalence가 주어이고 동사는 is이다. 「A as well as B」는 'B뿐만 아니라 A도'의 뜻이다. be being p.p.는 수동과 진행의 의미를 나타내는 시제로 '~되고 있다'의 뜻이다.

어휘 infant 유아 attend 다니다 day care center 어린이집 hut 오두막 rag 누더기 crawl 기다 proportion 비율 genetic 유전의 defect 결함 self-conscious 자의식이 강한 assume (책임을) 맡다 prevalence 발병률 depression 우울증 impair 손상시키다 rear 양육하다

4 무관 문장 ③

해설 인간과 동물 모두 유사하게, 얼굴 표정을 통한 감정 표현은 그 상황이 구체적이고 다른 많은 요인과 관계됨을 설명한 글로서, ③번 문장은 얼굴 표정에 관련된 상황이나 관련이 있는 요인에 대한 내용이 아니라, 전반적으로 인간과 동물 간에 유사성이 있다는 진술이므로 글의 흐름에 맞지 않다.

해석 인간에 있어서와 마찬가지로 동물에 있어서 얼굴 표정을 통한 감정 표현이 다소 일정하긴 하지만, 그러한 감정들이 촉발되고 표현되는 상황은 매우 상황 구체적이며 사회화, 개인적 관계, 그리고 다른 요소들과 관계된다. ① 예를 들어, 우리는 우리와 친한 사람들의 얼굴 표정을 더 잘 읽을 수 있다. ② 게다가 우리 인간들은 잘못된 얼굴 표정을 사용하여 우리의 감정에 가면을 씌울 수 있고, 싸움 놀이를 하는 동안 한 동물이 다른 동물을 무표정으로 놀라게 할 때 볼 수 있는 것처럼 많은 동물들도 이것을 할 수 있다. ③ 연대감과 같이 인간에게만 독특한 몇몇 핵심 특질이 있지만, 우리가 인간이 아닌 영장류와 공유하는 많은 중요한 유사성이 있다. ④ 마지막으로, 인간과 마찬가지로, 인간이 아닌 동물들, 특히 영장류들은 다른 동물들의 얼굴 표정을 흉내 낼 수 있다. ⑤ 예를 들어 오랑우탄은 다른 오랑우탄들과 놀 때 놀이 미소에 거의 즉시 그들 자신의 미소로 반응할 것이다.

구문 [3행~6행] ~ the context [in which those emotions are triggered and expressed] / is very context specific, **and** relates to socialization, individual relationships, and other factors.

• [ ] 부분은 주어 the context를 수식하고 있으며, 동사는 is와 relates가 and로 연결되어 병렬구조를 이루고 있다.

어휘 via ~을 통하여, 경유하여 **more or less** 다소 **invariable** 변치 않는, 일정한 **trigger** 촉발하다 **socialization** 사회화 **intimate** 친밀한 **trait** 특질 **kinship** 친족, 유대감 **primate** 영장류 **mimic** 흉내를 내다

5 요약문 완성 ①

해설 언어적 묘사를 통해 범죄 수사 화가가 그린 여성의 얼굴 그림에서 여성 자신이 묘사한 얼굴의 그림보다 낯선 사람에 의해 묘사된 여성의 얼굴 그림이 더 아름다웠다는 내용이므로 여성들이 자기 자신에 대해서는 비평가(critics)인 반면, 다른 사람들은 그들을 매력적(attractive)이라고 생각한다는 것을 알 수 있다.

해석 Dove의 Real Beauty Campaign은 거의 10년 전에 시작되었고, 그것은 강력한 메시지를 (사람들에게) 다양한 방법으로 납득시켜 오고 있다. 2013년 4월 15일, Dove는 'Dove Real Beauty Sketches'라는 제목의 3분짜리 영상을 게시했다. 그 영상은 순식간에 인기를 모았고, 수백만 회가 시청되었다. 즉, (사람들 사이에서) 널리 회자되는 급속히 확산되는 성공적인 캠페인이었다. 영상에서, 소그룹 여성들은 자신들이 볼 수 없는 사람에게 자기 얼굴을 묘사하도록 지시를 받는다. 그 사람은 그곳에서 여성들의 언어 묘사에 기초하여 그들을 그리는 범죄 과학 수사 화가이다. 커튼이 화가와 여성들을 분리시키고, 그들은 서로를 절대 볼 수 없다. 이 모든 것을 하기 전에, 각 (참가) 여성들은 낯선 사람과 어울리도록 요청받고, 그 낯선 사람은 추후에 따로 범죄 과학 수사 화가에게 그 여성을 묘사한다. 마지막에, 여성들은 두 개의 그림을 보게 되는데, 하나는 자기 자신의 묘사에 바탕을 둔 것이고 다른 하나는 낯선 사람의 묘사에 바탕을 둔 것이다. 매우 놀랍고도 기쁘게도, (참가) 여성들은 낯선 사람의 묘사에 바탕을 둔 그림들이 훨씬 더 아름다운 여성을 묘사함을 깨닫는다.

↓

우리가 우리 자신을 어떻게 보는지와 다른 사람들이 우리를 어떻게 보는지를 비교하는 Dove의 캠페인에서, 참가자들의 묘사는 여성들이 명백히 자기 자신에 대해서는 (A) 비평가들인 반면, 다른 사람들은 그들이 (B) 매력적이라고 생각한다는 것을 보여 주었다.

구문 [3행~4행] On April 15, 2013, Dove launched *a 3-minute video* (entitled "Dove Real Beauty Sketches.")

• ( ) 부분은 분사구로 앞의 a 3-minute video를 수식한다.

[13행~15행] Before all this, each woman is asked to socialize with *a stranger*, // **who** later separately describes the woman to the forensic artist.

• who는 계속적 용법의 관계대명사로 who가 이끄는 절이 a stranger를 보충 설명한다.

어휘 sell 납득시키다; 팔다 **launch** 개시[시작]하다 **entitle** 제목을 붙이다; 자격[권리]을 주다 **instant** 순식간, 순간; 즉시 **viral** (입소문으로) 급속히 확산되는; 바이러스성의 **verbal** 언어(말)의 **separate** 분리하다; 분리된 *cf.* **separately** 따로, 개별로; 단독으로 **socialize** 어울리다, 사귀다, 교제하다 **depict** 묘사하다, 그리다

[선택지] **critic** 비평가, 평론가 **plain** 아름답지 않은; 간결한; 분명한; 솔직한 **supporter** 지원[지지]자; 부양자 **appealing** 매력적인, 마음을 끄는

1 빈칸 추론   ⑤

해설 건물이 특이해 보이게 하기 위해 통상적인 건축 규칙을 깨거나 중력을 초월한 듯 보이는 건물을 건축하는 방법이 제시되었으므로, 구조 공학자들에게 가해지는 요구가 ⑤ '트릭이 성사된 방법을 숨기면서 역설적인 형태가 작용하게 만들어야' 하는 것임을 추론할 수 있다.
① 다양한 각도에서 쉽게 인식되도록 건물을 디자인해야
② 건물의 실용성과 아름다움 간의 긴장을 조정해야
③ 명성과 지위 둘 다를 가져다주는 어떤 것을 성취해야
④ 기술적 진화와 건축적 미학을 둘 다 이해해야

해석 지구의 인구 중 절반이 넘는 사람들이 현재 도시에서 살며, 그 비율은 예견 가능한 미래에 계속하여 증가할 것 같다. 도시에 건물을 짓는 것이 점점 더 중요해지고 있고, 도시의 형태와 도시의 건축은 많은 토론의 중점이다. 몇몇 건축가들은 명백히 기이하고 도시의 랜드마크가 될 것으로 의도된 건물들을 창조함으로써, 도시의 형체 없고 특색 없을 가능성이 있는 속성으로 인지하는 것에 대응하기로 결심했다. 건물이 특이해 보이게 만드는 가장 단순한 방법들 중 하나는 구조물의 통상적인 규칙을 깨거나 적어도 마치 중력이 중요하지 않은 것처럼 보이게 만드는 것이다. 그러한 건물들은 구조 공학자들에게 까다로운 요구를 가하여, 그들은 트릭이 성사된 방법을 숨기면서 역설적인 형태가 작용하게 만들어야 한다.

구문 [3행~4행] Building in cities is becoming **more and more** important, ~
• 「비교급 and 비교급」 구문은 '점점 더 ~한'의 뜻이다.

[6행~9행] Some architects have decided to respond to **what they perceive to be the potentially formless and anonymous nature of the city** / by creating *buildings* [that are obviously strange ⃞and⃞ are intended to become urban landmarks].
• respond to의 목적어로 선행사를 포함한 관계대명사 what이 이끄는 명사절이 쓰였다.
• [ ]는 buildings를 수식하는 관계사절이며, 관계사절 내에서 are와 are intended가 and로 연결되어 병렬구조를 이룬다.

[10행~12행] One of the simplest ways of making a building look unusual **is to** break the normal rules of structure / — or at least **make** it **seem as if** gravity is of no consequence.
• 밑줄 친 One of ~ unusual이 주어이고 동사는 is이다. make는 사역동사로 「make O 동사원형 (O가 ~하게 하다)」 구문이 사용되었다. 접속사 as if는 '마치 ~인 것처럼'의 뜻이다.

어휘 **proportion** 비율 **foreseeable** 예견할 수 있는 **perceive** 인지하다 **formless** 형체 없는 **anonymous** 특색 없는; 무명의 **landmark** 랜드마크, 주요 지형지물 **of no consequence** 전혀 중요하지 않은 **structural engineer** 구조 공학자
[선택지] **paradoxical** 역설적인 **pull off** (힘든 것을) 해내다, 성사시키다

2 글의 순서   ②

해설 화석 연료 이용 설비에 대한 막대한 투자를 내용으로 한 주어진 문장 다음에 그러한 투자(such investment)가 나오는 (B)가 위치해야 한다. 설비 교체의 속도에 한계가 있을 것이라는 (B)의 마지막 내용과 그 한계에 대한 구체적인 예를 서술하고 있는 (A)가 잘 연결된다. (B)의 완벽한 대체 기술은 (A)에서 '매주 일주일에 한 번 계속 건설되는'으로 구체적으로 서술되고 있다. (C)의 '저 석탄 발전소들(those coal plants)은 (A)에 등장한 coal-fired plants와 잘 연결되며 (A)의 예에 이어지는 또 다른 예들의 첨가이다.

해석 세계는 땅에서 화석 연료를 추출하여 그것을 태우는 설비, 즉 광산, 유정, 발전소, 배와 항공기 수십만 대. 차량 십억 대에 막대한 투자를 했다.
(B) 그러한 투자가 장악할 수 있는 정치적 로비의 힘은 차치하고라도, 단지 규모 확대만을 필요로 하는 이용 가능한 완벽한 대체 기술이 있더라도 그토록 많은 설비가 얼마나 빨리 교체될 수 있을지는 한계가 있을 것이다.
(A) 세계가 매주 일주일에 한 번 계속 건설되는 가장 큰 원자력 발전소들 중 하나를 내놓을 능력을 갖고 있다면, 석탄을 때는 발전소의 현재의 비축물을 교체하는 데 20년이 걸릴 것이다. (현재 세계는 일 년에 약 서너 개의 원자력 발전소를 건설하고 있으며, 거의 그만큼 빨리 낡은 발전소를 폐기하고 있다.)
(C) 2013년에 태양 전지판이 설치되던 속도로 저 석탄 발전소들을 전지판으로 교체하는 것은 약 150년이 걸릴 것이다. 그것은 전부 휘발유와 석유, 자동차, 용광로와 배를 대체하는 일에 착수하기 전의 일이다.

구문 [6행~9행] If the world had *the capacity* (to deliver one of *the largest nuclear power plants* (ever built) once a week, week in and week out), **it would take 20 years to replace** the current stock of coal-fired plants ~
• 가정법 과거 문장으로 「If+S'+과거동사 ~, S+would+동사원형....」은 '~한다면 ...할 것이다'의 의미를 가진다. to deliver ~ week out은 the capacity를 수식하고, 그 안의 ever built는 the largest nuclear power plants를 수식한다. 「it takes 시간 to-v」는 'v하는데 (시간)이 걸리다'의 뜻이다.

[12행~16행] **Leaving aside *the political lobbying power* [that such investment can command]**, / there would be a limit **to** how quickly that much kit **could be replaced** // even if there **were** *perfect substitute technologies to hand* [that simply needed scaling up].
• Leaving ~ command는 양보의 의미를 가지는 분사구문이며, [ ]는 the political lobbying power를 수식한다. 밑줄 친 부분은 전치사 to의 목적어 역할을 하는 간접의문문이며, 가정법 과거 구문이 쓰였다. 두 번째 [ ]는 perfect substitute technologies to hand를 수식한다.

어휘 **extract** 추출하다 **mine** 광산 **oil well** 유정 **power station** 발전소 **aircraft** 항공기 **capacity** 능력 **nuclear power plant** 원자력 발전소 **week in and week out** 매주 계속 **stock** 비축물, 재고 **retire** 물러나게 하다 **leave aside** ~을 차치하다. 제쳐놓다 **command** 장악하다 **kit** 장비, 세트 **substitute** 대체물 **to hand** 이용 가능한 **scale up** (규모를) 확대하다 **solar panel** 태양 전지판 **install** 설치하다 **furnace** 용광로

3 문장 넣기   ⑤

해설 야생 동물 통제 방식에 대한 내용이다. 주어진 문장은 하나의 대안으로서 동물이 탐지될 때만 작동시키는 소음 발생 장치에 관한 이야기이므로, 그렇지 않은 경우에 작동되는 장치에 대한 언급, 즉 사람이 직접 작동시키는 장치에 대한 언급이 끝난 다음에 오는 것이 적절하다. 따라서 ③ 이후에 나와야 하는데. ④ 뒤의 This는 ③ 뒤에서 언급된 장치를 말하므로, 주어진 문장이 들어갈 곳은 ⑤가 된다.

해석 동물은 공포를 유발하는 자극에 더 많이 노출되면 될수록, 그 공포에 더 금방 익숙해지게 된다. 이런 이유로 폭죽은 드물게 사용되어야 하고 프로판가스 대포는 시간당 두어 번만 발사되도록 설치해야 한다. 이상적으로는 프로판가스 대포나 다른 청각적 자극들은 오직 야생 동물이 그것에 가까이 있을 때에만 발사되어야 한다. 이

것을 이루는 한 방법은 오직 동물이 근처에 있을 때에만 발사하는 사람에 의해 원격으로 조정되는 소음 발생 장치를 갖는 것이다. 그러나 이것은 너무 노동 집약적이라, 대부분의 야생 동물 통제 문제에 있어서는 실용적이지 않다. 하나의 대안은 동물이 탐지될 때마다 소음 발생 장치를 활성화시키는 동작 탐지기, 청각 탐지기, 혹은 적외선 탐지기에 소음 발생 장치에 연결시키는 것이다. 예를 들어 Belant 등은 사슴이 시간차로 발사되는 가스 폭발 장치보다 동작에 의해 작동하는 가스 폭발 장치에 덜 빠른 속도로 익숙해졌다는 것을 발견했다.

구문 [5행~6행] **The more** animals **are exposed** to a fear-provoking stimulus, **the sooner** they will become habituated to it.

• 「the+비교급 ~, the+비교급 ....」 구문으로 '~할수록, 더 ...하다'의 뜻이다. 앞의 The more는 형용사 many의 비교급으로서 animals를 수식하는 것이 아니라, 동사 are exposed를 수식하는 부사 much의 비교급으로 쓰인 것이다.

어휘 alternative 대안 detector 탐지기 *cf.* detect 발견하다 auditory 청각의 infrared 적외선의 fear-provoking 공포를 도발하는 stimulus 자극(제) habituate 익숙하게 하다 sparingly 드물게 propane 프로판(가스) cannon 대포 remotely 멀리 떨어져서 labor-intensive 노동 집약적인 et al. (특히 이름들 뒤에 써서) 외, 그리고 다른 사람 activate 작동시키다 exploder 폭발 장치 timed 일정 시간 후 작동하도록 장치한; 시한의; 정기의 interval 간격, 사이

4~5 장문   4 ② 5 ⑤

해설 **4.** 과업이 어디에서 만들어졌는가에 따라 그것을 수행하는 데 더 많은 창의력을 발휘하는 실험 결과를 설명하고 있으므로 ② '거리는 더 창의적인 사고를 이끈다'가 제목으로 가장 적절하다.
① 반복된 연구가 사람들을 창의적으로 만든다
③ 창의적 아이디어를 떠올리는 몇 가지 방법들
④ 무엇이 가장 효율적인 교통수단인가?
⑤ 해외여행은 여러분을 더 창의적으로 만든다
5. 더 멀리 떨어진 그리스에서 이루어진 과업이라고 들은 피실험자들이 더 많은 교통수단의 가능성을 찾아냈다고 했으므로, 그들이 지역 운송 선택권에 덜 제한받아서 주변을 돌아다니는 것에만 주목하지 않고 더 나아가 생각했음을 알 수 있다. 그러므로 ⑤는 restricted 등이 되어야 한다.

해석 사회 심리학자들이 창의성이 상황과 정황에 따라 (a) 변할 수도 있다는 것을 인식하게 되면서 흥미로운 질문이 생겼다. 어떤 상황이 우리를 창의적으로 만드는가? 최근의 한 실험에서 인디애나 대학의 심리학자인 Lile Jia는 창의성에 영향을 미칠 수 있는 한 요인에 대해 조사했다. 그는 수십 명의 학생들을 무작위로 두 그룹으로 (b) 나누었고, 두 그룹 모두는 가능한 한 많은 교통수단의 명칭을 대라는 요청을 받았다. (이것은 창의력 발생 과업이라고 불린다.) 한 그룹의 학생들은 그 과업이 해외의 그리스에서 공부하는 인디애나 대학 학생들에 의해 개발되었다고 들었고, 반면에 다른 그룹은 그 과업이 인디애나주에서 공부하는 인디애나 대학 학생들에 의해 개발되었다는 이야기를 들었다.
언뜻 보기에는 그런 차이점이 피실험자들의 수행 능력에 영향을 미치지 (c) 않을 듯했다. 그 과업이 어디에서 개발되었는지가 왜 중요하다는 것인가? 그럼에도 불구하고, Jia는 두 그룹 사이의 (d) 현저한 차이점을 발견했다. 학생들이 그 과업이 그리스에서 가져온 것이라고 들었을 때, 그들은 상당히 더 많은 교통수단의 가능성을 찾아냈다. 그들은 단순히 버스, 기차, 비행기를 목록에 포함했을 뿐만 아니라 말, 스쿠터, 자전거, 심지어 우주선까지 언급했다. 문제의 원천이 훨씬 멀리 떨어져 있기 때문에, 피실험자들은 그들의 지역 운송 선택권에 덜 (e) 붐비는(→ 제한받는) 것을 느꼈다. 그들은 인디애나 주변을 돌아다니는 것에만 주목하지 않고, 전 세계와 심지어는 먼 우주를 돌아다니는 것을 생각했다.

구문 [7행~10행] He randomly divided a few dozen students into *two groups*, // **both of which** were asked to name as many different modes of transportation as possible.

• '명사+전치사+관계대명사' 형태인 both of which가 이끄는 계속적 용법의 관계사절이 two groups를 보충 설명한다.

어휘 randomly 무작위로, 임의로 generation 세대; 산출, 발생 at first glance 처음에는, 언뜻 보기에는 striking 눈에 띄는, 두드러진, 인상적인 significantly 상당히, 의미가 있게

1 필자 주장 ②

해설 논쟁에 감정적 요소가 개입되는 것은 불가피하며, 감정이 개입되었다고 그 주장이나 결론 전체를 잘못되었다고 선언하는 것은 잘못된 것이라는 내용의 글이므로 주장하는 바로 가장 적절한 것은 ②이다.

해석 논쟁에 대한 어떠한 좋은 이론도 감정적 호소와 반응이 인지적 고려 사항들과 균형을 이뤄야 한다는 것을 인정해야 한다. 그러나 반면에, 인생에서 대부분의 주요한 개인적 결정에서, 타인들의 것뿐만 아니라 자기 자신의 감정과 기분에 대한 세심함도 지극히 중요하다. 그러한 호소를 완전히 무시하는 어떠한 논쟁 이론도, 많은 중요한 일상적 상황에 적용할 수 없는 매우 제한된 이론임에 틀림없다. 특히 매우 흔한 상식적인 추론, 예를 들어 정책이나 후보자 선택에 관한 논쟁의 여지가 많은 정치적 논쟁에서, 본능과 감정적 반응은 항상 비판적 숙고의 영향을 받으며 중요한 자리를 차지하고 있다. 심지어 부분적으로라도 감정에 대한 호소로부터 생기는 어떠한 결론이라도 잘못된 것임이 틀림없다고 선언하는 것은 효과적이지 않고 심지어 잘못 판단한 접근법이다.

구문 [6행~9행] *Any theory of argument* [that ignores such appeals altogether] must be a very limited theory, / (being) **inapplicable** to many, significant everyday situations.

• [ ] 부분은 Any theory of argument를 수식한다. inapplicable 이하는 앞에 being이 생략된 분사구문이다.

[14행~16행] To declare that *any conclusion* (resulting even partly from an appeal to emotion) must be false / is an ineffective and even misguided approach.

• 밑줄 친 부분이 주어이며 동사는 is이다. ( ) 부분은 현재분사구로 any conclusion을 수식한다.

어휘 appeal 호소　cognitive 인지의　consideration 고려 사항; 사려, 숙고　sensitivity (남의 기분을 헤아리는데) 세심함; 민감, 예민함　inapplicable 적용할 수 없는　common-sense 상식적인　reasoning 추론　controversial 논란의 여지가 있는　concerning ~에 관한　candidate 후보자　subject to ~의 영향을 받는　declare 선언하다　misguided 잘못 이해한[판단한]

2 밑줄 함의 ⑤

해설 농구 선수들이 경기 시간을 얻기 위해 평소 팀원 간에 경쟁하는 모습은 90퍼센트의 침팬지로, 팀으로서 뭉쳐야 할 때 개인적 경쟁의식을 제쳐두고 화합하는 모습이 10퍼센트의 벌로 비유되었다. 따라서 '90퍼센트의 침팬지이고 10퍼센트의 벌이다'라는 말은 ⑤ '주로 이기적이지만 협동적인 생물이다'를 의미한다.
① 선천적으로 사회적이지만 때때로 혼자임을 즐긴다
② 근본적으로 탐욕스럽지만 우리 가족에게는 자애롭다
③ 추론에 능하지만 자주 판단의 오류를 범한다
④ 천성적으로 공격적이지만 타인에게 친절하고자 노력한다

해석 우리 아버지께서는 농구 감독이셨기에 어렸을 때 나는 매일 연습에 아버지와 함께 갔다. 나이가 듦에 따라 나는 새벽부터 저녁까지 체육관이나 운동장에 있었다. 이러한 시간과 에너지 투자는 결국 오하이오주 남부 대학의 농구 장학금으로 이어졌다. 농구 선수로서 나는 팀 스포츠의 역설, 즉 개인의 경쟁과 집단의 경쟁 간의 긴장에 관해 매우 일찍이 배웠다. 연습하는 동안 선수들은 침팬지들이 더 큰 몫의 먹이를 가지려고 맹렬히 싸우는 것과 꼭 마찬가지로 경기 시간을 얻기 위해 동료 팀원들과 경쟁했다. 그러나 경기 일이 돌아오면, 팀원들은 모든 개인적 경쟁의식은 제쳐둘 것을 요구받았고 벌집을 위해 일하는 벌처럼 되었다. 우리는 대립하는 적을 이긴다는 더 높은 목적을 위해 화합하는 단체로서 하나가 되었다. 이것은 이루기 어렵지만, 인간들은 적절한 상황에서 이것을 해낼 능력을 갖추고 있다. 우리는 천성적으로 '호모 듀플렉스(이중의 인간)'이기에 이것을 해낼 수 있다. 조나단 하이트가 말했듯이 우리는 90퍼센트의 침팬지이고 10퍼센트의 벌이다.

구문 [8행~11행] During practice, / athletes competed with fellow teammates for playing time, // **just as** chimps fight fiercely / to have a bigger share of food.

• just as는 '~한 것과 꼭 마찬가지로'의 뜻이다.

어휘 accompany 함께 가다, 동행하다　from dawn to dusk 새벽부터 저녁까지　paradox 역설　collective 집단의, 단체의　fiercely 맹렬하게, 사납게　roll around (다시) 돌아오다　put A aside A를 제쳐두다　rivalry 경쟁(의식)　for the sake of ~을 위하여　hive 벌집　cohesive 화합[결합]하는　foe 적　equipment 능력; 장비　pull A off A를 해내다　duplex 이중의, 두 부분으로 된
[선택지] inherently 선천적으로　benevolent 자애로운　aggressive 공격적인　cooperative 협동적인

3 빈칸 추론 ③

해설 본문 내용과 빈칸 문장으로 보아, 창의성을 발휘하는 사람들이 나타날 때 '어떤 상황인지'를 찾아야 한다. 본문에서 창의성은 전에는 연결된 적이 없는 것들 사이에 관계를 만드는 것이고, 보이지 않는 것을 보는 것, 어떤 것을 다르게 보고 다른 사람들이 놓친 것을 발견하는 것, 세상이 전에 보았던 것과는 다르게 보는 것 등으로 설명하고 있다. 그러므로 빈칸에는 ③ '사고의 틀이 달라진다'가 가장 적절하다.
① 두뇌가 작동한다
② 분석이 시작된다
④ 인내심이 득이 된다
⑤ 열정이 물러간다

해석 창의성은 '점들을 연결하는 것'으로 전에는 결코 연결된 적이 없는 것들 사이에 관련을 만드는 것에 관한 것이다. 그것은 어떤 시나리오 안에서든지 존재하는 가능성과 모든 상황 안에서의 기회를 인지할 수 있는 능력이다. 형세를 바꾸는 것은 평범한 것에서도 보이지 않는 것을 보는 것으로 시작한다. 평범한 대리석 평판에서, 미켈란젤로는 자신의 최고 작품을 조각했다. 독일의 철학자인 아르투어 쇼펜하우어는 "재능은 아무도 맞힐 수 없는 과녁을 맞힌다. 천재적인 재능은 다른 아무도 볼 수 없는 과녁을 맞힌다."라고 말했었다. 창의적인 해결 방법과 획기적인 진전은 어떤 것을 다르게 보고 다른 사람들이 놓친 것을 발견하는 것에서 나온다. 참신한 생각, 과정, 그리고 방법론에 대한 특허는 누군가가 어떤 것을, 세상이 전에 그것을 보았던 것과는 다르게 보는 것의 실체적인 결과물이다. 어떻게 점들을 연결하고, 다양한 관점을 적용하여 관련되지 않은 생각들 사이에 다리를 건설하는지를 아는 사람들이 나타날 때, 사고의 틀이 달라진다.

구문 [3행~5행] It is the ability **to recognize** *the possibilities* [that exist within any scenario] and the opportunities in every situation.

• It은 가주어이고 to recognize 이하가 진주어이다. [ ] 부분은 the possibilities를 수식하는 관계사절이다.

어휘 dot 점　ordinary 평범한　marble 대리석　carve 조각하다　target 과녁, 표적

breakthrough 획기적인 진전 novel 참신한 methodology 방법론 come along 나타나다 multiple 다양한, 다수의 perspective 관점
[선택지] analysis 분석 paradigm 사고의 틀, 이론의 체계 persistence 끈질김, 지구력 enthusiasm 열의, 의욕 retreat 물러서다, 하락하다

4 글의 순서   ②

해설 주어진 글은 실직한 사진사들이 일반 사진과 차이를 나타내도록 자신을 특화시킬 방법이 필요하다고 했으므로, 그들이 찾은 방법을 가리키는 '그 대응(the response)'이 언급된 (B)가 맨 먼저 나와야 한다. pictorialism 운동은 사진 원판과 인화 과정상의 다른 재료에 직접 작업하는 것이라는 (B)의 마지막 내용 다음으로는 작업한 것을 활용하는 내용인 미술관에서 회화 작품 옆에 자신들의 작품을 전시했다는 (A)가 이어지고 마지막으로 pictorialism 운동의 결과를 언급한 (C)가 나오는 것이 적절하다.

해석 1890년에 Kodak은 모두가 구입할 수 있는 값싼 소비자용 카메라를 소개했다. 이것은 인물 사진을 찍는 사진관을 폐업하게 했고, 새로이 실직한 사진사들은 자신들이 하는 일과 이러한 새로운 인기 있는 사진술의 차이를 나타내는 방법이 필요했다.
(B) pictorialism 운동이 그 대응이었는데, 사진사들은 회화의 예술적 과정을 모방하는 것을 시도했다. 사진사들은 복제할 수 있는 사진이 아니라, 사진 원판과 인화 과정상의 다른 재료에 곧바로 작업했다.
(A) 그들은 미술관에서 회화 작품 옆에 자신들의 작품을 전시했다. 예술계의 여러 구성 요소들이 형성되기 시작했는데, '사진 클럽'이라고 불리는 조합 단체, Camera Work라고 불리는 잡지, 전시회와 (전시장의) 개장 같은 것이 그것이다.
(C) 하지만 예술 사진술은 여전히 무시되었다. 시장도, 구매자도, 수집가도 없었고, 미술관은 자신들의 소장품에 사진을 추가하는 데 관심이 없었다. 결국, 제1차 세계 대전의 발발과 함께 pictorialism은 자취를 감추었다.

구문 [1행~2행] In 1890, Kodak introduced *a cheap consumer camera* [**that** everyone could afford].
• [ ] 부분은 목적격 관계대명사 that이 이끄는 관계사절로 선행사 a cheap consumer camera를 수식한다.
[10행~12행] The movement of *pictorialism* was the response, / **with** *photographers* **attempting** to imitate the artistic processes of painting; ~.
• 「with O v-ing」 구조의 분사구문이 사용되어 부대 상황을 나타낸다.

어휘 portrait 인물 사진, 초상화 out of business 폐업한, 망한 unemployed 실직한 element 구성 요소, 성분 collegial 조합의; 대학의 process (인화) 과정 reproducible 복제[모사]할 수 있는 marginalize 무시하다; 하찮은 존재로 만들다 eventually 결국에는 die out 자취를 감추다 outbreak (전쟁 등의) 발발; 돌발

5 문장 넣기   ③

해설 주어진 문장의 내용은 집단이 더 적절한 프로그램을 위해 그 프로그램을 폐기하기보다는 단순히 파일을 변환하거나 문서를 재작성할지도 모른다는 것으로서, 프로그램에 문제가 있다는 내용 다음에 나와야 한다는 것을 추론할 수가 있다. 그러므로 사무실 환경에서, 특정한 컴퓨터 응용 프로그램이 구식이 되거나 지원되지 않게 될 것이라는 내용이 ③ 이전에 나오고 있으므로 주어진 문장은 그다음인 ③에 들어가야 가장 적절하다. 또한 그런 처리 방식의 문제는 문서 처리가 아니라 프로그램 자체라는 내용이 ③ 다음에 나오고 있으므로 연결이 자연스럽다.

해석 문제 정의는 어느 분야에서든 사회적 상황에 의해 영향을 받는다. 개인은 집단의 태도로 인해 문제를 재정의하거나 현재 문제의 진행 사항에 대해 평가할 수 없게 될 수 있다. 예를 들어 사무실 환경에서, 개인은 문서 처리를 위한 어떤 특정한 컴퓨터 응용 프로그램이 친근할지도 모른다. 하지만, 그 프로그램은 결국에는 구식이 되거나 지원되지 않게 될 것이다. 처음에, 그 집단은 더 적절한 프로그램을 위해 그 프로그램을 폐기하기보다는 단순히 파일을 변환하거나 문서를 재작성하는 과정을 거칠지도 모른다. 여기서 문제는 문서 처리가 아니라 문서 처리 프로그램 그 자체가 되었다. 그 문제를 발견하는 것이 특히 어렵지는 않지만, 집단의 방식이 매우 견고해서 프로그램을 바꾸는 것은 받아들일 수 없는 선택지가 된다. 다시 말해, 집단의 태도가 개인의 선택 과정에 침투할 수 있다.

구문 [1행~4행] Initially, the group may simply go through the process of converting files or rewriting documents, **rather than** abandoning the program for *one* [that is more appropriate].
• 「A rather than B」는 'B라기보다는 A'의 뜻인데, 밑줄 친 A와 B 자리에 동명사구가 위치했다. [ ] 부분은 one을 수식하는 관계사절이다.

어휘 convert 전환하다, 바꾸다 definition 정의 evaluate 평가하다 current 현재의 computer application 컴퓨터 응용 프로그램 outdated 구식의 pervasive 침투하는; 만연한

1 글의 주제   ①

해설 모든 사람들이 같은 음식을 먹었을 때 맛을 똑같이 인지하는 것은 아닌데, 이러한 맛 인지의 차이에 영향을 미치는 요인들로는 음식의 온도, 심리적 고정관념과 과거 경험 등이 있다는 내용의 글이므로, 글의 주제로 가장 적절한 것은 이들을 포괄하여 표현한 ① '맛의 인지에 영향을 미치는 다양한 요인들'이다.
② 미뢰가 온도에 영향을 받는 이유들
③ 식품에 인공 색소를 사용하는 것을 그만두어야 할 필요성
④ 기후가 저장 식품 발달에 미치는 영향
⑤ 온도와 맛 선호 간의 관계

해석 모든 사람들이 애플파이의 맛을 같은 방식으로 인지하는 것은 아니다. 개인들 간에 기본적 맛에 대한 민감성에 상당한 유전적 차이가 존재한다. 맛보기 능력은 또한 여러 외적 영향에 따라 개인 내에서도 다양할 수 있다. 맛에 영향을 미치는 그러한 한 가지 요소는 음식이나 음료의 온도이다. 미뢰는 약 30℃의 온도에서 가장 잘 작동한다. 음식이나 음료의 온도가 20℃ 미만이나 30℃ 초과가 되면, 그것들의 맛을 정확히 구별하는 것은 더 어려워진다. 예를 들어, 매우 뜨거운 커피는 쓴맛이 덜한 반면, 약간 녹은 아이스크림은 더 단맛이 난다. 외양이나 비슷한 음식에 대한 경험에 기반을 둔 선입견과 같은 심리적 요인들 또한 사람의 맛 인지에 영향을 미친다. 예를 들어, 체리 맛 음식은 빨간색일 것으로 기대되지만 그것이 노란색이면 그것을 체리로 식별하기가 어려워진다. 또한 음식과 관련된 불쾌한 경험이 미래에 그 음식에 대해 인지되는 맛에 영향을 줄 수 있다.

구문 [12행~15행] **Psychological factors**, such as *preconceived ideas* (based on appearance `or` on previous experiences with a similar food), / also **affect** a person's perception of taste.

• 주어는 Psychological factors이고 동사는 affect이다. ( ) 부분은 preconceived ideas를 수식하며, on으로 시작하는 두 전치사구는 or로 연결되어 병렬구조를 이룬다.
[15행~17행] For instance, *cherry-flavored foods* are expected to be red, // but if they are *colored yellow*, **they** become difficult to identify as cherry.

• 굵게 표시된 they는 cherry-flavored foods colored yellow를 지칭한다.

어휘 **genetic** 유전의   **variation** 차이   **sensitivity** 민감   **vary** 다르다, 다양하다   **beverage** 음료   **operate** 작동되다   **preconceive** 미리 생각하다   **perception** 인식, 인지   **identify** 확인하다, 식별하다

2 밑줄 어법   ④

해설 ④ until이 이끄는 절에서 understand의 목적어 역할을 할 명사절이 필요하다. 뒤에 이어지는 you're not as worthless as you think는 「S+V+C」 구조의 완전한 문장이므로 문장에서 주어, 목적어, 보어의 역할을 대신해 명사절을 이끄는 관계대명사 what을 완전한 명사절을 이끄는 접속사 that으로 바꿔 써야 한다.
① 명사구 the mistaken belief가 목적어이므로 전치사 because of를 적절히 사용했다.
② 복수명사 thoughts를 가리키는 ones를 적절히 사용했다.
③ 동명사 주어 Making ~ possess는 단수 취급하므로 단수동사 is를 적절히 사용했다.
⑤ 완전한 문장 they will return the favor 뒤에 결과를 나타내는 분사구문을 적절히 사용했다.

해석 낮은 자존감은 당신이 성공을 얻을 자격이 없는 것처럼 느껴지게 만들 수 있다. 일이 잘 돌아가고 있을지라도 당신은 단지 자신이 목표를 달성할 자격이 없다는 잘못된 믿음으로 인해 자신을 고의로 방해할 것이다. 자존감을 쌓는 것은 자기 인식과 자기 점검으로 시작된다. 당신 내면의 비평가를 감시하고 나쁜 생각들을 긍정적인 생각들로 교체하기 시작하면 당신은 당신의 자기 비판적인 목소리를 죽이는 과정에 있게 될 것이다. 당신이 갖고 있다고 믿는 긍정적인 자질의 목록을 만드는 것은 자존감을 향상시키는 또 다른 유용한 기법이다. 핵심은 정직하고 어떤 판단도 없이 목록을 작성하는 것이다. 일단 그것이 준비되면 당신이 자신의 생각만큼 가치 없지 않다는 것을 이해할 때까지 그것을 매일 매일 다시 읽어라. 또 다른 유용한 방법은 다른 사람들에게 더 친절해지는 것이다. 다른 사람들을 잘 대하면 그들은 호의를 돌려줄 것이고, 따라서 당신이 자신에 대해 더 나은 기분을 느끼게 할 것이다.

구문 [2행~4행] Even if things are going well, // you'll sabotage yourself / just because of the mistaken belief (that) you don't deserve to achieve your goal.

• you don't ~ your goal은 앞에 that이 생략되어 있으며 the mistaken belief와 동격 관계이다.
[8행~10행] Making a list of *your positive attributes* [(which[that]) you believe you possess] **is** *another useful technique* (to improve your self-esteem).

• 동명사구 Making ~ possess가 주어이며 동사는 is이다. [ ]는 앞에 목적격 관계대명사 which[that]가 생략되어 your positive attributes를 수식한다. ( )는 to부정사의 형용사적 용법으로 another useful technique을 수식한다.

어휘 **self-esteem** 자존감   **deserve** ~할 자격[가치]이 있다   **sabotage** 고의로 방해[파괴]하다   **self-monitoring** 자기 점검   **attribute** 자질, 속성   **favor** 호의

3 빈칸 추론   ⑤

해설 빈칸 문장으로 보아 교실이 어떤 배열로 되어 있지 않으면 교사가 사람들 앞에서 질책을 하게 되는지를 알아야 하는데, 근접성을 이용하는 장점을 설명하는 구체적 내용 중에 단호한 주의와 경고는 사적이며 신중하게 이루어져야 한다고 했으므로 ⑤ '교사가 개개의 학생에게 접근할 수 있게 하는'이 빈칸에 가장 적절하다.
① 다양한 형태의 그룹 활동을 용이하게 하는
② 어린이들에게 독립적으로 일하도록 장려하는
③ 어린이의 내적 호기심을 이용하는
④ 어린이들 사이에 긍정적인 상호 작용을 촉진하는

해석 교사와 자신의 학생 간의 거리와 인지된 또는 실제의 장벽은 의사소통에 상당한 영향을 미칠 수 있다. 책상이란 '장애물' 뒤에 안전하게 자리 잡고 있는 교사는 자동적으로 효율적인 개인 간의 접촉을 방해하고 교실에서 특정 영역에 대한 느낌을 주는 경계를 만든다. 그에 반해 근접성을 이용하는 것은 강력한 행동 조절 도구가 될 수 있다. 단호한 주의와 경고는 사적이며 신중하게 이루어질 때가 가장 좋다(그것은 학생에게 있어서 부끄러움이나 위협을 줄이며 구경꾼 효과를 최소화하는데, 이 둘 모두는 저항이나 반격을 부채질할 수 있다). 학생의 눈높이로 낮추는 것(그리고 위협적으로 학생 위에서 내려다보지 않는 것)은 배려의 모범을 보이고 학생들로 하여금 마찬가지로 공손한 방식으로 반응하도록 이끈다. 그러나 교실이 교사가 개개의 학생에게 접근할 수 있게 하는 그런 방식으로 배열되어 있지 않다면 이것은 문제가 있을 것이며 교사는 많은 사람들 앞에서 질책을 하는 것에 의지해야 할지도 모른다.

구문 [3행~7행] *Teachers* [who stay securely ensconced behind the 'barricade' of their desk] automatically **create** *a boundary* [that blocks effective interpersonal contact and gives a territorial feel to the room].

• 주어는 Teachers이고 동사는 create이다. 두 개의 [ ] 부분은 관계사절로 각각 Teachers, a boundary를 수식한다. 두 번째 [ ]에서 동사 blocks와 gives가 and로 연결되어 병렬구조를 이루고 있다.

어휘 **perceived** 인지된 **barrier** 장벽 **securely** 안전하게 **barricade** 장애물 **boundary** 경계 **interpersonal** 개인 간의 **territorial** 특정 영역의, 영토의 **firm** 단호한, 확고한 **reminder** 주의, 조언; 상기시키는 것 **privately** 개인적으로, 은밀히 **discreetly** 신중하게, 사려 깊게 **spectator** 구경하는 사람, 관중 **fuel** 자극하다, 부채질 하다 **counter-attack** 반격 **tower over** ~ 위에 우뚝 서다 **model** 모범[모형]을 만들다 **consideration** 배려 **equally** 마찬가지로, 똑같이 **respectful** 공손한 **resort to** ~에 의지하다, ~에 기대다 **public** 많은 사람들이 있는, 공개적인

[선택지] **access** 접근하다

4 무관 문장

④

해설 이 글은 문화가 다르면 같은 환경에 대해서 다른 방식의 반응을 보인다는 내용이다. 이에 대한 예로 태평양 피지 제도의 멜라네시아 문화가 언급되고 있는데, ④는 환경 자체가 긍정적인 면과 부정적인 면이 존재한다는 내용이므로 글 전체의 흐름과 관계가 없다.

해석 문화는 인간이 환경에 반응하는 방식에 영향을 주는 주된 요소이며, 매우 다양한 문화가 있기 때문에, 심지어 똑같은 환경에 대해서도 매우 다양한 문화적 반응이 있다. ① 예를 들어, 태평양의 피지 제도에서는 두 개의 뚜렷이 구별되는 문화가 확인될 수 있는데, 각각은 환경과 다른 관계를 맺고 있다. ② 한편으로는 옛 멜라네시아 문화가 있는데, 그 부족민들은 작은 범위의 자급용 작물을 재배하기 위해 환경을 이용하고, 그들이 필요한 것은 매우 한정되어 있다. ③ 대조적으로, 주로 인도인 이주민들인 신 멜라네시아인들이 있는데, 그들은 환경에 대해 훨씬 더 서구화된 관점을 가지고 있으며, 수출을 위해 사탕수수 같은 환금 작물을 재배한다. ④ 따라서, 모든 환경은 긍정적인 측면과 부정적인 측면을 모두 가지고 있으며, 가장 위험하고 예측 불가능한 환경이 가장 바람직한 것일 수 있다. ⑤ 비슷한 차이가 말레이시아의 중국인과 말레이인 사이에, 케냐의 아프리카인과 유럽인 사이에, 멕시코의 인디오족과 라틴 아메리카인 사이에서, 세계 전역에서 발견될 수 있다.

구문 [1행~4행] Culture is *the primary factor* (**affecting** *the way* [**in which** man responds to the environment]), // and since there is a wide variety of cultures, / there is a wide variety of cultural responses, / even to the same environment.

• ( )는 affecting이 이끄는 현재분사구로 the primary factor를 수식한다. [ ]는 '전치사+관계대명사' 형태인 in which가 이끄는 관계사절로 the way를 수식한다.

[8행~10행] ~ there is *the old Melanesian culture*, **whose** members utilize the environment to grow a small range of subsistence crops and **whose** wants are very limited.

• whose가 이끄는 두 개의 계속적 용법의 관계대명사절이 and로 병렬 연결되어, the old Melanesian culture를 보충 설명한다.

어휘 **primary** 주된, 뚜렷한; 초기의 **a wide variety of** 매우 다양한 **distinct** 뚜렷이 구별되는; 독특한; 명백한 **utilize** 이용[활용]하다 **contrast** 차이, 대조 **immigrant** 이주민, 이민자 **cash crop** 환금 작물 ((시장에 내다 팔기 위하여 재배하는 농작물)) **sugar cane** 사탕수수 **export** 수출(하다); 수출품 **desirable** 바람직한, 호감 가는

5 요약문 완성

④

해설 실험에서 자신의 나이 든 모습의 아바타를 본 참가자들은 자신의 미래의 모습을 시각화(visualizing)해본 것이 자극이 되어서, 돈을 어떻게 쓸지를 선택할 때 은퇴 자금에 투자를 하는 장기적인(long-term) 선택을 내렸다.

해석 심리학자 Ersner-Hershfield는 사람들이 미래를 위해 만족감을 지연시키는 경향을 어떻게 증가시킬 수 있을지 알아보려는 시도로 실험을 수행했다. 실험이 시작되기 전에 그는 참가자들의 사진을 찍었고 그들의 디지털 아바타를 만들기 위해 소프트웨어를 사용했다. 참가자들 중 절반은 현재의 자신으로 아바타를 얻은 반면 나머지 절반의 아바타는 주름과 흰 머리가 있는 나이 든 모습이었다. 피실험자들은 그러고 나서 자신의 아바타로서 가상 환경을 탐험했고, 최후에는 현재의 자신 혹은 미래의 자신을 비추는 거울에 도달했다. 가상 현실을 경험한 후, 참가자들은 4개의 선택, 즉 특별한 사람에게 선물 사주기, 혹은 은퇴 자금에 투자하기, 혹은 재미있는 이벤트 계획하기, 혹은 돈을 당좌 예금 계좌에 예금하기가 주어졌을 때 1,000달러를 어떻게 할당할 것인지를 질문받았다. 자신의 나이 든 버전이 가상의 거울에 비친 것을 봤던 사람들은 이것이 그 미래의 자신이 훨씬 덜 낯선 존재로 보이게 만들어서, 다른 참가자들보다 거의 두 배의 돈을 은퇴 자금에 투입했다.

↓

실험에 따르면, 우리의 미래의 자신을 (A) 시각화하는 것은 자신을 미래와 더 잘 연관 짓는 것에 도움이 되며, (B) 장기적인 재정적 목표를 세우는 데 대한 관심을 증가시킨다.

구문 [8행~11행] The subjects then explored virtual environments as their avatars, / eventually **coming** to *a mirror* (reflecting **either** their current **or** future self).

• coming 이하는 분사구문이다. ( )는 현재분사구로 a mirror를 수식한다. ( )에는 「either A or B (A나 B 둘 중 하나)」 구문이 쓰였다.

[16행~20행] *Those* [that **had seen** *an aged version of themselves* **reflected** in the virtual mirror], // **which made** *that future self* **seem** much less like a stranger, / **put** nearly double the amount of money into the retirement fund / than the other participants.

• 주어는 Those이고 동사는 put이며 [ ]는 Those를 수식하는 관계사절이다. [ ]에서 지각동사 see가 「see+O+p.p. (O가 ~된 것을 보다)」의 형태로 쓰였다. which는 앞 문장의 내용을 지칭하며 which 다음에는 사역동사 make가 「make+O+동사원형 (O가 v하게 하다)'의 형태로 쓰였다.

어휘 **inclination** 경향, 성향 **gratification** 만족감 **virtual** 가상의 **allocate** 할당하다 **deposit** 예금하다 **checking account** 당좌 예금 계좌

[선택지] **modify** 수정[변경]하다

1 빈칸 추론   ③

해설 빈칸 뒷부분에 등장하는 Peter of London의 예시를 통해 성(姓)은 명백한 신원을 밝히는 특징이 되어야 함을 알 수 있다. 따라서 빈칸에 들어갈 성(姓)의 기능은 ③ '한 사람이나 한 가족을 다른 모든 이들로부터 구별하는 것'이다.
① 계층과 신분의 중요성을 강조하는 것
② 그 사람의 가장 흥미로운 특징을 강조하는 것
④ 다양한 공동체 구성원 간의 유대감을 형성하는 것
⑤ 개인의 출생지와 배경을 밝히는 것

해석 장소에 근거한 이름에 관한 한 가지 호기심을 끄는 사실은 그것들이 너무나 흔히 잘 알려지지 않은 것이며 대부분 사람들이 들어본 적이 거의 없는 장소로부터 유래한다는 것이다. 왜 London보다 그렇게 훨씬 더 많은 Middleton들이 있고 Bristol들보다도 훨씬 더 많은 Worthington들이 있어야 하는가? 중세 영국의 주요 도시인 London, York, Norwich, Glasgow는 그곳에서 수천 명의 사람이 그곳을 고향이라 일컬음에도 성(姓)으로서는 비교적 흔하지 않다. 이 외견상의 역설을 이해하기 위해서는 성의 기능이 한 사람이나 한 가족을 다른 모든 이들로부터 구별하는 것이라는 점을 명심해야 한다. 어떤 사람이 자신을 Peter of London이라고 부른다면 그는 그런 수천 명의 Peter들 중 단지 한 사람이 될 것이고 그를 찾는 사람은 누구나 어쩔 줄 모르게 될 것이다. 그러므로 일반적으로 한 사람이 시골 지역으로 이사한 경우에만 Peter of London라는 이름을 얻을 것인데, 그곳에서는 London이 명백한 신원을 밝히는 특징이 될 것이다.

구문 [14행~17행] So as a rule a person **would earn** the name Peter of London only **if** he **moved** to a rural location, // **where** London would be a clear identifying feature.

• 「S+would+동사원형 ~, if+S′+동사의 과거형 ....(만약 ~라면 , …할 텐데)」의 가정법 과거 구문이다. where는 a rural location을 보충 설명하는 관계부사절을 이끌며, and there로 대신할 수 있다.

어휘 obscure 잘 알려져 있지 않은; 이해하기 힘든; 모호한 **medieval** 중세의 **relatively** 비교적 **surname** 성(姓) (= family name) **paradox** 역설; 모순된 일 **be at a loss** 어쩔 줄 모르다 **as a rule** 대체로, 일반적으로
[선택지] bond 유대, 끈; 접착하다

2 글의 순서   ②

해설 조직이 직원과 고객의 의견을 어떻게 평가하는지에 대한 예를 들겠다는 주어진 글 다음에는 구체적으로 한 조직의 관리자가 한 직원의 지속적인 요청을 받고 판단해야 하는 상황이 나와 있는 (B)가 이어지고, 그다음에는 이러한 지속적인 요청(frequent requests)이 관리자의 인식에 선입견을 갖게 하는지에 대한 연구자들의 답이 나오는 (A)가 이어져야 한다. 또한, 이러한 답을 (B)에서 언급한 연구자들(they)이 어떻게 입증하는지 구체적인 내용이 나오는 (C)가 마지막에 위치해야 한다.

해석 조직 안에서의 (일) 처리의 능숙함과 관련된 흥미로운 하나의 질문은 조직이 그들의 직원과 고객의 의견을 어떻게 평가하는지에 관련된 것이다. 다음의 예를 살펴보자.
(B) 한 관리자가 한 직원으로부터 회사 정책이 바뀌어야 한다는 요청을 끊임없이 받는다. 그러한 요청으로, 그 관리자는 조직 안에서의 다른 사람들이 문제가 되고 있는 이 사안에 대해 어떻게 느끼는지를 판단해야 한다.
(A) 강경하게 의견을 밝히는 직원의 잦은 요구는 조직 안에서의 나머지 사람들이 그 정책에 대해 어떻게 느끼는지에 대한 관리자의 인식에 편견을 갖게 할 것인가? Weaver, Garcia, Schwartz, 그리고 Miller의 연구가 그 답은 그렇다는 것을 시사한다.
(C) 여섯 차례의 연속된 실험에서, 그들은 인지된 친숙함이 특히 강경하게 의견을 밝히는 한 구성원에게서 나오는 결과라고 할지라도, 사람들은 친숙한 의견이 일반적인 의견이라고 추론하는 경향이 있다는 것을 입증했다.

구문 [1행~3행] An interesting question (**related to processing fluency in organizations**) concerns **how** organizations gauge their employees' and customers' opinions.

• related가 이끄는 과거분사구가 수동의 의미로 An interesting question을 수식한다. concerns의 목적어로 「의문사(how)+주어(organizations)+동사(gauge)」 어순의 간접의문문이 쓰였다.

[14행~16행] In a series of six experiments, they demonstrated **that** people have a tendency to infer that a familiar opinion is a prevalent one, ~.

• that people ~ a prevalent one은 접속사 that이 이끄는 명사절로 동사 demonstrated의 목적어 역할을 한다. 밑줄 친 a tendency와 to infer ~ a prevalent one은 동격 관계이다.

어휘 processing 처리, 과정 fluency (일의) 능숙함; (언어의) 유창함 concern 관련된 것이다; 걱정(스럽게 만들다) gauge 평가[판단]하다; 측정하다 vocal (의견을) 강경하게 밝히는 bias 편견을 갖게 하다; 편견; 성향 policy 정책, 방책 consistently 끊임없이, 일관되게 issue (논쟁의) 사안, 문제; 발행[발급](하다) demonstrate 입증하다; 시위하다 tendency 경향, 기질; 동향, 추세 infer 추론하다; 암시하다 perceive 인지하다, 감지하다

3 문장 넣기   ③

해설 주어진 문장에는 however가 있는데, 토양이 단단해지고 잡초가 우거진다는 내용이므로, 앞에는 비옥한 토양에서 농작물을 생산하는 내용이 올 것이다. 또한 뒤에는 척박해진 토양을 다시 비옥하게 하려는 노력에 대한 내용이 오는 것이 적절하므로 정답은 ③이다.

해석 농업이 일단 시작되면 빨리 확산되는 이유 중 하나는 처음 몇 번의 농작물이 이후의 농작물보다 더 많이 생산되고 더 쉽게 자라며, 따라서 농부들이 경작되지 않은 땅으로 옮겨가는 데 언제나 열성적이기 때문이다. 숲을 태워 없애면, 비옥한 토양이 남는다. 땅에 작은 구멍을 파고, 씨앗을 심고, 그것이 자라기를 기다리기만 하면 된다. 그러나 몇 년 후에, 토양은 단단해져서 갈아야 하며, 잡초가 급증해 있다. 이제 그 비옥함을 다시 증가시키고자 그 땅을 쉬게 하면, 좋은 모판을 만들기 위해 억센 풀뿌리를 제거할 필요가 있다. 그리고 그것을 위해서는 쟁기와 쟁기를 끌 소가 필요하다. 그러나 소는 먹이를 먹어야 하므로, 경작할 수 있는 땅뿐만 아니라 목초지도 필요하다. 이동 농업이 숲에 사는 많은 종족에게 오늘날까지 인기가 많은 것은 놀라운 일이 아니다.

구문 [3행~5행] One of the reasons [**that** farming spreads quickly / once it has begun] is **that** the first few crops are both more productive and more easily grown than later crops, ~.

• 첫 번째 that은 선행사인 the reasons를 수식하는 절을 이끄는 관계부사이고, 두 번째 that은 문장의 보어 역할을 하는 명사절을 이끄는 접속사이다.

어휘 **compact** 단단하게 하다; 소형의[간편한]; (공간이) 작은 **break up** 완전히 부수다
[깨지다]; 끝이 나다 **productive** 대량으로 생산하는; 생산적인 **uncultivated** (땅이) 경작
되지 않은; 미개한 *cf.* **cultivable** (땅이) 경작할 수 있는 *cf.* **cultivate** (땅을) 경작하다; 재배
하다; (말·행동 방식 등을) 함양하다 **fertile** (토양이) 비옥한; 다산(多産)의 (= **fruitful**)
cf. **fertility** 비옥함; 생식력 **seedbed** 모판 ((씨를 뿌려 모를 키우기 위해 다듬은 곳))
plough 쟁기; 쟁기로 갈다 **pasture** 초원, 목초지 (= **meadow**) **shifting** 이동하는;
이동; 교환, 교대 **agriculture** 농업 **tribal** 부족의, 종족의

4~5 장문 4 ⑤ 5 ④

해설 **4.** 영화를 볼 때 어두운 영화관 환경은 감정을 고양시키고, 강화된 자극은 관
객에게 신체적 반응을 일으킨다는 내용의 글이므로 제목으로 가장 적절한 것은
⑤ '영화를 볼 때 우리에게 무슨 일이 생기는가?'이다.
① 영화를 볼 때 할 질문들
② 정신 속의 영화들 즉, 우리의 스크린 중독
③ 영화 보기는 단지 예술을 위해서가 아니다
④ 영화는 왜 그토록 흥미롭고 매력적인가?
5. 영화의 강력한 시각적, 청각적 자극이 눈과 귀와 정신을 에워싼다고 했으므로 감
각을 가득 채운다는 것을 알 수 있다. 그러므로 ④는 flood 등이 되어야 한다.

해석 관객들은 의심 없이 자연스럽게 영화를 받아들이고 그것의 관습적인 것들에
안심하는 경향이 있다. 그들은 대부분의 신만함이 제거된 편안하고 어둡게 만든 극
장에 앉아, 종종 오직 유일한 광원인 스크린에 나타난 깜박이는 이미지에 (a) 최적의
주의를 기울인다. 어두운 환경은 낮춰진 방어 반응과 높아진 감정적 반응을 (b) 생산
하는 경향이 있다. 심리학자 Gordon Globus와 Roy Shulman은 영화관에서 어둠
이 관객들에게 미치는 영향에 대해 연구했고 다음과 같은 결론을 내렸다. "어둠, 부
동 상태, 산만함의 상대적 결여, 그리고 객관적인 현실 지향의 대인관계 일로부터의
고립은 자아가 현실과 비현실 간의 (c) 차이를 분간하지 못하게 한다. 게다가 감정적
각성의 상승이 있으며 더 원시적인 방어 또한 환기된다."
영화는 또한 관객을 생리학적으로 사로잡는데, 그것은 감각을 (d) 막는(→ 가득 채우
는) 시각적, 청각적 자극들로 관객을 감싸기 때문이다. 영화는 작곡, 색채, 소리와 리
듬을 통해 자신의 말을 한다. 시각적 사진과 사운드트랙은 단번에 눈과 귀와 정신을
에워싼다. 로마 대학 심리학 연구소에서 수행된 연구는 영화의 움직임이 근육의 반
사 작용, 운동 충동, 상승된 맥박수, 그리고 다른 신진대사 행동과 같은 관객의 운동
감각 반응을 (e) 유발한다고 밝혔다. 영화관 주인들은 실험 연구의 혜택 없이도 이를
알았는데, 그들이 공포 영화를 틀어줄 때, 흥분한 관객의 증가된 땀으로 인해 에어컨
의 양을 늘려 달라는 요청을 종종 받기 때문이다.

구문 **[29행~33행]** Movie theater owners have known this without the benefit
of experimental research, // **for** (when they show horror pictures,) **they are**
often **asked** to increase the amount of air conditioning due to the increased
perspiration of the excited viewers.

● 접속사 for는 '이유'의 뜻을 나타내고 있다. when they show horror pictures는 삽
입절이고 접속사 for 다음의 주어는 they, 동사는 are asked이다.

어휘 **suspicion** 의심, 의혹 **feel at ease** 안심하다 **convention** 관습 **distraction**
주의를 산만하게 하는 것 **optimal** 최적의 **flicker** 깜박거리다 **immobility** 부동성, 부동
상태 **-oriented** ~ 지향의 **interpersonal** 대인관계에 관련된 **arousal** 각성, 환기
primitive 원시적인 **invoke** 환기시키다 **engage** 사로잡다 **statement** 진술
composition 작곡 **all at once** 갑자기 **provoke** 유발하다 **reflex** 반사 작용 **motor**
운동의 **impulse** 충동 **pulse rate** 맥박수 **metabolic** 신진대사의 **perspiration** 땀
[선택지] compelling 흥미로운; 강제적인

1 글의 요지   ④

해설 이 글은 법을 따르는 것이 항상 올바른 일이 아니라는 말 뒤에 부당한 법을 따르기를 거부했던 역사적 인물의 예를 들고 있다. 따라서 글의 요지로 가장 적절한 것은 ④이다.

해석 소크라테스는 "dura lex, sed lex"라고 말했는데, 이는 법은 가혹하지만 그래도 법이라는 의미이다. 하지만, 법을 따르는 것이 항상 올바른 일은 아니다. 역사상, 부당한 법을 따르기를 거부했던 많은 사람들이 있었다. 두 명의 주목할 만한 예는 마하트마 간디와 마틴 루터 킹이다. 이 두 사람 모두 자기 시대의 법은 정당하지 않다고 믿었다. 마하트마 간디는 영국의 인도 통치에 반대했다. 그는 인도인들이 자기 자신들의 국가를 통치해야 한다고 믿었다. 마틴 루터 킹은 미국에서 흑인들을 차별 대우하는 법에 반대했다. 이 두 사람 모두 자신들이 옳지 않다고 느끼는 시스템을 바꾸기 원했기 때문에 법을 어겼다. 결과적으로, 그들은 인권 역사에 큰 변화를 가져왔다.

구문 [1행~2행] Socrates said, "dura lex, sed lex," // **which** means (that) the law is harsh, but it is the law.

• which는 "dura lex, sed lex"를 선행사로 하는 계속적 용법의 관계대명사로 which가 이끄는 절이 선행사를 보충 설명한다. 동사 means의 목적어절을 이끄는 접속사 that이 생략된 형태이다.

[12행~13행] ~ because they wanted to change *the system* [(which[that]) (they felt) was wrong].

• [ ] 부분은 the system을 수식하는 관계사절로 주격 관계대명사 which[that]가 생략된 형태이다. 여기서 they felt는 삽입절로 주격 관계대명사는 바로 뒤에 삽입절이 나올 때 흔히 생략된다.

어휘 harsh 가혹한, 혹독한; 거친   obey 따르다, 순종[복종]하다   refuse 거부[거절]하다 unjust 부당한, 불공평한 (→ fair 공정한, 공평한)   remarkable 주목할 만한, 놀랄 만한 rule 통치(하다), 지배(하다); 규칙   discriminate against ~을 차별 대우하다   human rights (기본적) 인권

2 빈칸 추론   ②

해설 빈칸 뒤에 이어지는 내용에서, 일련의 생각들을 평가하는 방법으로 다른 일련의 생각들을 대비하여 검증해보는 것을 제시했으므로 빈칸에는 ② '대립 관계의 토론'이 들어가는 것이 적합하다. 이어지는 구체적인 예시로 주어진, 정치, 철학, 과학, 법률 분야에서의 내용도 모두 이를 뒷받침한다.

① 부단한 연습
③ 자발적 참여
④ 전통적 지식
⑤ 비판적 사고

해석 현대 서구 사상의 기원은 기원전 6세기와 5세기의 고대 그리스의 황금기로 거슬러 올라갈 수 있는데, 그 시대에 그리스 사상가들은 현대 서양의 정치, 철학, 과학 및 법률의 기반을 다졌다. 그들의 새로운 접근법은 대립 관계의 토론을 통하여 합리적인 탐구를 추구하는 것이었다. 일련의 생각들을 평가하는 가장 좋은 방법은 그것을 다른 일련의 생각들에 대비하여 검증해 보는 것이라고 그들은 믿었다. 정치 영역에서 그 결과는 민주주의였는데, 민주주의와 대립하는 정책의 지지자들은 수사법상의 우위를 얻기 위해 경쟁했다. 철학에서 이것은 세계의 본질에 대한 이성적 논쟁과

대화로 이어졌으며, 과학에서는 이것이 자연 현상을 설명하려 애쓰는 대립하는 이론들의 구축을 촉진시켰다. 법률 분야에서는 그 결과가 검사와 피고 측 변호사이다. 이러한 접근법은 현대 서양의 생활방식을 뒷받침하는데, 여기에서 정치, 상업, 과학, 그리고 법률이 모두 질서 있는 경쟁 속에 기인하고 있다.

구문 [7행~9행] *The best way* (to evaluate *one set of ideas*), (they believed,) / **was** by testing **it** against another set of ideas.

• to evaluate one set of ideas가 주어 The best way를 수식하며 they believed는 삽입구문이고, 동사는 was이다. it은 앞의 one set of ideas를 지칭한다.

어휘 trace back to A ~의 기원이 A까지 거슬러 올라가다   inquiry 연구, 탐구; 조사; 질문, 문의   sphere 구(球); 영역   rhetorical 수사적인; 미사여구식의; 수사학의 supremacy 패권, 우위   commerce 무역; 상업   orderly 정돈된, 정연한; 질서 있는 [선택지] adversarial 대립 관계의

3 무관 문장   ④

해설 어떤 것을 과도하게 경험해서 생겨난 기존의 굳어진 생각을 깨뜨려야 할 필요성을 언급한 글이다. ③은 어린이의 호기심을 비유로 들어 의문을 품는 태도로 문제를 이해하고 해결하라는 내용으로 적절하지만, ④는 호기심 있는 어린이 성격의 속성을 언급하므로 흐름과 무관하다.

해석 경험은 특별히 유용한 도구가 될 수 있지만, 어떤 것을 과도하게 경험하는 것은 개인의 정신적 짐을 만들어낼 수 있다. ① 정신적 짐이 널리 퍼져 있을 때는 과도하게 친숙해져 있는 방향 외에 어떤 창의적인 방향을 고려하기가 어려울 수 있으며, 다른 사람들도 또한 제품이 무엇인지에 대한 선입견을 품고 있을 때 그들이 대안 경로를 탐색하도록 설득하는 것이 힘들 수 있다. ② 시장을 혁신하는 것이 타당해 보이는 것은 바로 익숙해진 장벽이 없이 상황을 다르게 생각해 볼 수 있을 때뿐이다. ③ 어린아이가 끊임없이 어떤 것에 대해 질문하는 것과 비슷한 '이유에 대해 의문을 품는 태도'를 가지고 문제에 직면하지 않는다면, 이해하고 해결하는 것이 거의 불가능하다. ④ 호기심 많은 아이들은 그들 주위에서 무슨 일이 일어나고 있는지 인식하고 대개 그들 자신을 우주의 중심으로 여기지 않는데, 이것은 그들이 덜 이기적이고 덜 응석을 부린다는 것을 의미한다. ⑤ 되풀이되는 탐구와 조사를 통해 정신적 짐이 분해될 수 있는 경우에는, 즐겁고 실용적인 제안이 등장해서 널리 받아들여질 수 있게 될 것이다.

구문 [3행~7행] When mental baggage is prevalent **it** can be difficult **to consider** any creative direction other than that of the overfamiliar, // and **it** can be arduous **to persuade** others to explore an alternative path when they also have a preconceived notion of **what the product is.**

• 두 개의 it은 모두 가주어이고, to consider와 to persuade가 이끄는 두 개의 to부정사구가 각각 진주어를 이끈다. what the product is는 전치사 of의 목적어로 쓰인 간접의문문이다.

[8행~10행] **It is** *only when things can be thought of differently, without accustomed barriers,* **that it** is plausible **to innovate markets.**

• 「it is ~ that ...」 강조구문이 쓰여 only when이 이끄는 절을 강조한다. that이 이끄는 절 내에서 밑줄 친 it은 가주어, to innovate markets가 진주어이다.

[10행~13행] If the problem is not confronted with a *'why attitude'*, (which is) similar to *a small child* (constantly asking questions about something), // **it** is almost impossible **to understand and solve.**

• similar to ~ something은 which is가 생략된 관계사절로 a 'why attitude'를 보충 설명한다. constantly asking ~ something은 분사구로 앞에 있는 a small child를 수식한다. it은 가주어, to understand and solve가 진주어이다.

어휘 **overexposure to** ~을 과도하게 경험하는 것 **baggage** 짐; 수화물 **prevalent** 널리 퍼진, 유행하는 **alternative** 대안[대체]의 **preconceived notion** 선입견 **accustomed** 익숙해진 **barrier** 장벽 **plausible** 타당한, 그럴듯한 **innovate** 혁신 하다 **be confronted with** ~에 직면하다 **selfish** 이기적인 **spoiled** 응석을 부리는, 버릇이 없는 **enquiry** 탐구 **probe** (철저히) 조사하다 **practical** 실용적인; 실제적인

4 글의 순서 ②

해설 (B)는 주어진 글에서 말한 '살아 있는 것을 분류하는 방법'의 구체적인 예시로 시작하고 있으므로 맨 앞에 와야 한다. (A)는 (B) 후반부에 언급된 동식물 연구가들의 노력에 대한 결과이며, (C)의 첫 단어인 It은 (A)의 Such classification(그러한 분류)을 가리키므로 (C)는 마지막에 나오는 것이 적절하다.

해석 아마도 '살아 있는 세포'와 '종' 같은 구분들 사이의 유일한 차이점은 유기체를 종으로 분류하는 것이 더 의식적인 노력을 요구한다는 것인데, 왜냐하면 살아 있는 것을 분류하는 방법은 사실상 무한하기 때문이다.
(B) 사람들은 유기체를 형태나 색깔이나 맛으로, 그리고 알을 낳을 수 있는 능력 등으로 분류할 수 있을 것이다. 동식물 연구가들은 생물의 무한한 다양성을 구조화하는 최고의 시스템을 만들기 위해 수 세기 동안 일했다.
(A) 마침내 그들 중 대다수는 그러한 시스템이 생물의 계보, 곧 그것의 진화 역사에서의 유기체의 위치를 반영해야 한다는 데에 동의했다. 그러한 분류는 살아 있는 것에 대해 우리가 아는 것을 구조화할 뿐만 아니라 두 유기체가 생물 계보의 같은 가지에 속하는지를 우리에게 말해준다.
(C) 그것(그러한 분류)은 유인원을 예를 들어 쥐, 파리 또는 박테리아보다 인간과 더 가깝게 두는데, 단순히 인간과 유인원의 공동 조상이 인간과 쥐, 파리 또는 박테리아의 공동 조상보다 더 최근에 살았기 때문이다. 하지만 이 계보 주변에서 생물을 구조화한다는 것은 난제를 제시한다. 그것은 생명체의 역사 그 자체를 재구성하는 것을 필요로 한다.

구문 [16행~19행] It places apes closer to humans than, say, mice, flies, or bacteria, // simply because *the common ancestor* of humans and apes lived more recently than **that** of humans and mice, flies, or bacteria.
• that은 앞에 나온 명사 the common ancestor를 지칭한다.

어휘 **category** 범주, 부문, 구분 **organism** 유기체; 미생물 **classify** 분류하다; 등급을 매기다 *cf.* **classification** 분류(법); 유형, 범주 **practically** 사실상, 거의; 현실적으로 **infinite** 한계가 없는, 무한한 (= **boundless**) **evolutionary** 진화의; 점진적인 **naturalist** 동식물 연구가 **ape** 유인원 **reconstruct** 재건하다; 복원하다

5 문장 넣기 ⑤

해설 주어진 문장이 역접의 의미를 나타내는 But을 포함하여 대학에서 동일한 스포츠의 코치를 맡은 사람은 대단히 높은 연봉을 받을 수 있다는 내용이므로 이 문장 앞에는 '동일한 스포츠를 가르치지만 연봉이 낮은 사람'에 대한 진술이 있어야 하는데 그 내용이 ⑤ 앞 문장에 제시되어 있다. 그리고 ⑤ 뒤 문장은 캠퍼스 코치들보다 한 단계 더 높은 수준의 연봉을 받는 분야도 있다는 내용이므로 주어진 문장은 ⑤에 들어가야 가장 적절하다.

해석 스포츠 분야의 직업 진출 과정은 종종 피라미드 모양에 비유된다. 넓은 밑 부분에는 유소년팀이나 고등학교 운동팀의 많은 일자리가 있는 반면 좁은 끝부분에는 프로 조직의 거의 몇 안 되는 사람들이 대단히 탐내는 일자리가 있다. 따라서 전체적으로 많은 스포츠 일자리가 있지만 위로 올라가려 함에 따라 경쟁은 점점 힘들어진다. 다양한 위치의 급여는 이 피라미드 모형과 일치한다. 예를 들어 고등학교 미식축구와 농구 코치는 종종 그들의 방과 후 업무로 약간의 추가적인 돈을 받는 교사들이다. 그러나 큰 대학에서 동일한 스포츠들의 코치들은 대학 총장의 급여와 맞먹는, 백만 달러가 넘는 연봉을 버는 전국적인 유명 인사가 될 수 있다. 한 단계 더 높은 곳이 NFL(미국 프로 미식축구 협회)과 NBA(미국 프로 농구 협회)인데, 거기에서 수석 코치는 종종 최고의 연봉을 받는 캠퍼스의 코치들보다 몇 배 더 많은 돈을 받는다.

구문 [6행~9행] *At the wide base* **are** many jobs with youth or high school athletic teams, // **while** *at the narrow tip* **are** the few, highly-coveted jobs with professional organizations.
• 주절과 while절 둘 다 「장소부사구+동사+주어」 어순의 도치구문이 사용되었다. 각각 동사는 are, 밑줄 친 부분이 주어이다.
[16행~17행] *One level higher up* **are** the National Football League and the National Basketball Association, ~
• 보어가 강조를 위해 문두에 위치하여 동사 are와 주어 the National ~ Association이 도치되었다.

어휘 **celebrity** 유명 인사 **advancement** 전진, 진출 **athletic** 운동 경기의 **tip** 끝부분 **correspond to** ~에 일치하다 **head coach** 수석 코치 **counterpart** 상대방

1 글의 제목

②

해설　이 글은 미기후가 작은 영역의 기후이며, 이것이 인공적인 원인과 자연적인 원인(물과 토양 등)으로 발생한다는 내용의 글이므로, 이를 반영한 제목은 ② '미기후의 정의와 원인들'이 가장 적절하다.
① 미기후 만들기와 활용하기
③ 미기후는 어떤 이익을 가져오는가?
④ 미기후 형성과 그것의 의의
⑤ 미기후는 농경의 양날의 검이다.

해석　당신은 초원을 통과해 숲을 향해 걷고 있는데, 이 숲에 발을 들여놓자마자 갑자기 온도가 시원하고 공기는 축축하다. 당신은 미기후에 들어선 것이다! 기후는 장기간에 걸친 한 장소에서의 날씨를 묘사한다. 'Micro-'는 '작다'를 의미하므로 미기후는 주변의 기후와는 다른 작고 제한된 영역의 기후이다. 미기후가 만들어질 수 있는 몇 가지 방법들이 있다. 땅의 형태는 지역의 날씨에 영향을 미칠 수 있다. 그것은 자연적인 것일 수도 있고 혹은 인간에 의해 변형된 것일 수도 있다. 집, 바위와 자동차는 모두 작은 영역의 기후를 변화시킬 수 있다. 호수, 시냇물과 심지어 바다조차 그것들과 가장 가까운 지역의 기후를 변화시킬 수 있다. 이것은 물이 땅보다 더욱 느리게 열을 얻고 상실하기 때문이다. 흙 또한 기후를 형성할 수 있다. 정글의 풍요로운 토양과 같이 많은 물을 보유하고 있는 흙은 공기를 축축하고 습하게 만든다. 사막의 모래와 같은 건조한 흙은 같은 방식으로 물을 보유하지 않는다.

구문　[13행~14행] This is because water *gains and loses heat* more slowly than land **does.**
• 대동사 does는 gains and loses heat를 대신한다.

[15행~16행] *Soils* [that hold lots of water], (like the rich soils in the jungle), **make** the air wet and humid.
• 주어는 Soils이고 동사는 make이다. [ ]은 Soils를 수식하는 관계사절이다. ( )는 삽입구이다.

어휘　grassy plain 초원　all of a sudden 갑자기　damp 축축한　microclimate 미기후(微氣候)　restrict 제한하다　humid 습한

2 밑줄 어휘

③

해설　정반대의 것을 인식하여 '어떤' 것에 대한 개념을 바꾸는 것이 아니라 더욱 잘 인지하고 형성할 수 있으므로 ③ transform(바꾸다)을 formulate(형성하다) 등으로 바꿔 써야 한다.

해석　인간 두뇌의 한 가지 특징은 '유도', 즉 긍정적인 어떤 것이 ① 대비되는 부정적인 이미지를 우리의 정신에 만들어 내는 방식으로 알려져 있다. 이것은 우리의 시각 체계에서 가장 명백하다. 우리가 어떤 색깔, 예를 들어 빨간색이나 검은색을 볼 때 그것은 우리 주변에 있는 반대색에 대한 우리의 인식을 ② 강화하는 경향이 있는데, 이 경우에는 녹색이나 흰색이다. 빨간 물체를 볼 때 우리는 흔히 녹색 후광이 그것의 주변에 형성되고 있는 것을 볼 수 있다. 일반적으로 정신은 대조되는 것들에 의해 작동한다. 우리는 어떤 것에 대한 개념을 그것의 정반대인 것을 인식함으로써 ③ 바꿀(→ 형성할) 수 있다. 두뇌는 지속적으로 이런 대조되는 것들을 떠올리고 있다. 이것이 의미하는 것은 우리가 어떤 것을 보거나 상상할 때마다 우리의 정신은 정반대인 것을 보거나 상상하지 않을 수 없다는 것이다. 우리의 문화로 인해 우리가 특정한 생각을 하거나 특정한 욕망을 품는 것을 ④ 금지당한다면 그 금기는 즉각적으

로 우리에게 금지된 바로 그것을 연상시킨다. 모든 부정은 그에 상응하는 긍정을 촉발한다. 우리는 정신 속에서 대조적인 것들 사이의 이런 동요를 제어할 수 없다. 이것은 우리가 가지지 않은 바로 그것에 관하여 생각하고 나서 ⑤ 바라도록 만든다.

구문　[7행~8행] As we look at the red object, // we often can **see** *a green halo forming* around it.
• 지각동사 see가 「see O v-ing (O가 v하고 있는 것을 보다)」 형태로 사용되었다.

[14행~17행] If we are forbidden by our culture to think a particular thought or entertain a particular desire, that taboo instantly brings to mind *the very thing* [(which[that]) we are prohibited from].
• 밑줄 친 두 부분은 접속사 or로 연결되어 병렬구조를 이룬다. [ ]은 앞에 목적격 관계대명사 which[that]가 생략되어 the very thing을 수식한다.

어휘　induction 유도, 귀납법　contrast 대조(를 이루다)　intensify 강화하다　perception 인식, 지각　cannot help but v v하지 않을 수 없다　entertain (생각을) 품다　taboo 금기　bring to mind 연상시키다　spark 촉발시키다, 유발하다　corresponding 상응하는　predispose ~하게 만들다, ~하는 성향을 갖게 하다

3 빈칸 추론

③

해설　문을 닫는 법을 배워야 한다고 하고 모든 가능성을 다 시도해보기보다는 무엇을 하지 말아야 할지 목록을 만들어 그것을 참고하라고 했다. 그러므로 대부분의 문은 ③ '들어갈 가치가 없다'는 것을 알 수 있다.
① 실제로 닫혀 있지 않다
② 들어가기 어렵다
④ 기회로 이어진다
⑤ 당신의 면전에서 닫힌다

해석　우리는 가능한 한 많은 일을 벌이고, 아무것도 제외시키지 않으며, 모든 것에 열린 마음을 가져야 하는 생각에 사로잡혀 있다. 그러나 이것은 성공에 방해가 된다. 우리는 문을 닫는 법을 배워야만 한다. 사업 전략이란 다른 무엇보다도 더 무엇에 관여하지 말아야 하는가에 대한 서술이다. 기업 전략과 비슷한 인생 전략을 채택하라. 여러분의 인생에서 추구하지 말아야 할 것을 적어두라. 다시 말해서, 어떤 가능성들을 무시해 버리도록 신중히 결정을 내리고, 선택 사항이 나타나면 여러분의 추구하지 말아야 할 것 목록과 대조하여 시험해 보라. 그것은 여러분이 어려움을 겪지 않게 해줄 뿐만 아니라 많은 생각할 시간을 줄여 줄 것이다. 새로운 문이 소리 내며 열릴 때마다 결정을 내려야 하는 대신에 한 번 열심히 생각해보고 그다음에는 단순히 여러분의 목록을 참고하라. 비록 손잡이가 매우 손쉽게 돌아갈 것 같다 해도, 대부분의 문은 들어갈 가치가 없다.

구문　[1행~3행] We **are obsessed with** having as many irons as possible in the fire, ruling nothing out, and being open to everything.
• be obsessed with의 목적어로 동명사 having, ruling, being이 콤마(,)와 and로 연결되어 병렬구조를 이루고 있다.

어휘　be obsessed with ~에 사로잡히다　have many irons in the fire 많은 일을 벌이다　rule out ~을 제외시키다, 배제하다　get in the way of ~의 방해가 되다　strategy 전략, 작전　first and foremost 다른 무엇보다도 더　engage in ~에 관여[참여]하다; ~에 종사하다　adopt 채택하다, 채용하다　corporate 기업의, 회사의　deliberate 고의의, 의도적인; 신중한, 찬찬한　disregard 무시하다, 경시하다; 무시, 묵살　consult 상담하다, 의논하다; 참고하다, 고려하다　make up A's mind 결심하다　crack

open 소리 내며 열리다

4 무관 문장 ④

해설 무의식적으로 남의 행동을 따라 하게 되는 사례와 그 이유를 설명한 글이다. 즉, 뇌의 한 작은 부분에 위치한 거울 뉴런이 운동 뉴런 바로 옆에 있어서 다른 사람의 행동을 복사한다는 것이다. 그런데, ④는 거울 뉴런에 관한 대부분의 증거가 부정확하다는 내용으로, 거울 뉴런의 발현 현상을 열거한 ③, ⑤ 사이에서 글의 흐름을 방해하며, ⑤의 도입부 And it's why ~와도 연결되지 않으므로 글의 흐름과 맞지 않는 문장이다.

해석 텔레비전에서 누군가가 골프 치는 것을 보다가 자신도 모르는 사이에 그가 휘두르는 방향으로 움직이는 자신을 발견한 적이 있는가? ① 분명히, 당신의 의식하는 뇌는 당신이 감자 칩을 먹으면서 소파에 앉아 있다는 것을 알지만, 거울 뉴런이 있는 부분인 당신의 뇌의 다른 작은 부분에서는 당신이 저 골프장 그린에 나가 있다고 생각한다. ② 그다음에, 거울 뉴런은 뇌에서 흔히 운동 뉴런 바로 옆에 있기 때문에, 복사된 느낌은 복사된 행동을 낳아서, 자신도 모르게 당신은 갑자기 골프채를 휘두르고 있는 것처럼 움직이고 있는 것이다. ③ 이것이 미소가 전염되고 아기들이 부모가 짓는 우스꽝스러운 얼굴을 자동으로 흉내 내는 이유이다. ④ 사람의 뇌에서 단일 신경을 연구하는 것은 보통 가능하지 않으므로 사람의 거울 뉴런에 관한 대부분의 증거는 부정확하다. ⑤ 그리고 이것이 브리즈번에서 누군가가 팔꿈치에 얼굴을 찍히는 것을 보고 시드니에 있는 럭비 팬들이 고통스러워하며 즉시 자신의 얼굴 쪽으로 손을 뻗게 하는 이유이다.

구문 [16행~19행] And it's (the reason) **why** watching someone get elbowed in the face in Brisbane immediately **caused** *rugby fans in Sydney* **to reach** toward their own faces in agony.

• why 앞에는 the reason이 생략된 것으로 볼 수 있어서 '~한 이유'라는 뜻이 된다. cause는 to부정사를 목적격보어로 사용하여 「cause O to-v (O가 v하도록 야기하다)」의 구문으로 쓰인다.

어휘 **involuntarily** 모르는 사이에; 본의 아니게 **neuron** 뉴런, 신경 세포 **reside** 거주하다 **motor** 모터, 전동기; 운동의, 운동 신경의 **contagious** 전염되는, 전염성의 **mimic** 흉내 내다, 모방하다 **elbow** 팔꿈치; (팔꿈치로) 밀치다 **agony** 심한 고통, 고뇌

5 요약문 완성 ①

해설 어떤 사회가 최상의 기술을 도입하고자 해도, 이 기술이 최상으로 수행되는 것은 물적 기반과 관행에서 비롯되는 제조, 마케팅, 구매, 사용과 관련된 많은 제약을 극복한 후에야 비로소 가능하다는 내용의 글이다. 따라서 기술은 결코 오로지 기술적(technical) 특성에만 기반을 두어 채택되지 않고 그 결정을 둘러싼 다양한 다른 제약(restrictions)에 의해 결정된다는 것을 알 수 있다.

해석 '최상'의 가장 좁은 엄밀한 의미에서, 어떤 장치가 문제시되는 일을 최상으로 수행할 것인지 결정하는 것으로 기술 선택이 결코 이루어지지 않는다는 점은 꽤 분명하다. '최상으로' 선택된 것은 특정 기술적 업무를 가능한 한 잘 수행하는 것의 제약 외에도 온갖 종류의 제약과 관련되어 있다. 이것은 기술이 해결하도록 도입된 문제가 결코 기술적인 문제가 아님을 다른 방식으로 말하는 것이다. 기술이 널리 채택되기 위해서는 대량으로 제조되고, 마케팅되고, 구매되고, 성공적으로 사용되어야 한다. 따라서 추가적인 제약은 그 장치가 제조되고, 구매되고, 사용될 상황에서 나온다. 이러한 것들 중 많은 것이 물질적 기반 시설과 기존 관행과 관련이 있는데, 이는 물론 나라마다 다르며 다양한 관련된 측면을 지니고 있다.

↓

> 기술은 결코 오로지 (A) 기술적 특성에만 기반을 두어 채택되지 않는다. 그 채택은 또한 그 결정을 둘러싼 다양한 다른 (B) 제약에 의해 결정된다.

구문 [1행~3행] **It** is quite clear **that** technology choices are never made [by determining, (in a narrowly technical sense of 'best'), which device best performs the task in question].

• It은 가주어이고 that 이하가 진주어이다. which ~ in question 부분은 determining의 목적어이며 ( )에는 전치사구가 삽입되어 있다.

[3행~6행] The 'best' chosen (device) is relative to all sorts of *constraints* **other than those** of performing a certain technical task as well as possible.

• The 'best' chosen 다음에는 의미상 device가 생략되어 있다. other than은 '~ 외에'의 뜻이며, those는 the constraints를 지칭한다.

어휘 **technical** 엄밀한 **relative to** ~와 관련된 **constraint** 제약, 제한(= restriction) **other than** ~ 외에 **derive from** ~로부터 나오다 **have to do with** ~와 관계가 있다 **infrastructure** 사회 기반 시설 **vary** 다르다, 다양하다

1 빈칸 추론 ⑤

해설 우선 빈칸 바로 앞의 they는 inclinations를 가리킨다. 빈칸 문장 뒤에서 예시가 시작되고 있으므로 예시를 통해 inclinations가 어떠하다는 것인지 추론한다. 예시에서는 다이어트에 대한 욕구와 먹고 싶은 욕구가 등장하는데, 때에 따라 특정 욕구가 커졌다 줄어들었다 하는 것을 설명하고 있다. 즉 ⑤ '때에 따라 그 강도가 달라지기' 때문에 헷갈린다는 것을 알 수 있다.
① 우리가 세운 목표로 구성되기
② 시간이 흐름에 따라 힘이 강해지기
③ 우리의 진정한 목표와 충돌하기
④ 우리가 결정을 내리는 것을 방해하기

해석 우리는 그 순간 가장 강렬히 하고 싶은 것에 근거하여 결정을 내린다. 이것은 간단한 사실이다. 여러분이 가장 강렬히 하고 싶어 했던 것과 일치하지 않았던, 여러분이 내렸던 선택을 생각해 보라. 하지만 이것이 때때로 헷갈리기도 하는데, 그 이유는 우리가 아주 다양한 기호에 공격을 받고 그것들이 때에 따라 그 강도가 달라지기 때문이다. 예를 들어, 푸짐한 한 끼 식사를 끝마친 후에는, 다이어트를 하기로 마음먹기 쉽다. 그렇지만, 몇 시간이 지난 후에는 다시 배가 고파지며 음식에 대한 욕구가 커진다. 파이를 먹고자 하는 욕구가 체중을 줄이고자 하는 욕구를 능가하면, 우리는 다이어트보다 파이를 택하게 된다. 모든 조건이 같다면, 우리는 과도한 체중을 줄이고 싶어 할지도 모른다. 우리는 정말로 날씬해지기를 원하지만, 그 목표는 음식을 먹는 즐거움과 충돌한다. 문제는 모든 것들이 동일하게 유지되지 않는다는 것이다.

구문 [2행~4행] ~ try to think of *a choice* [**(that)** you have made] [**that** was not in accord with your strongest inclination].
• 두 개의 [ ]이 모두 a choice를 수식하고 있다.

어휘 **inclination** 기질, 성향; 기호(嗜好), 좋아하는 것 **in accord with** ~와 조화되는, 일치하는 **assault** 공격하다; 폭행하다; 폭행(죄), 공격 **surpass** 능가하다, 뛰어넘다 **all things being equal** 모든 조건이 같다면[그대로라면] **shed** (원하지 않는 것을) 없애다[버리다]; (피·눈물 등을) 흘리다; (털 등을) 갈다 **excess** 초과[량], 과잉; 초과한 **be in conflict with** ~와 충돌하다, 싸우다 **culinary** 요리(음식)의
[선택지] **hinder A from v-ing** A가 v하는 것을 방해하다 *cf.* **hinder** 방해하다, 못하게 하다 **intensity** 강렬(함); 세기, 강도

2 글의 순서 ②

해설 주어진 글이 애덤 스미스가 보편적인 공교육의 설립을 권장했다는 내용이므로, This suggestion으로 시작하는 (B)가 먼저 나와야 한다. 그다음에 스미스가 의무적인 교육을 주장한 것은 아니라는 내용에 이어지는 연결어인 Instead가 있는 (A)가 나와야 한다. (C)의 Such incentives(그러한 보상)가 (A)의 내용을 가리키고 있으므로 마지막으로 (C)가 나와야 적절하다.

해석 애덤 스미스는 사회의 가난한 사람들조차 읽기, 쓰기, 그리고 연산의 필수 기술을 습득할 수 있도록 주로 정부가 비용을 대는 보편적인 공교육의 설립을 권장했다.
(B) 이러한 제안은 영국 지배층 사이에 널리 퍼진 지식에 반하는 것이었는데, 그들은 그것이 복종하려는 의욕을 꺾을 것이라고 두려워했다. 하지만 스미스가 교육을 의무적인 것으로 만들자고 주창한 것은 아니다.
(A) 대신에 그는 교육을 더 접근하기 쉽고 더 실용적으로 만들려는 계획을 내놓았다.

그는 부모들이 자녀를 교육시키도록 권장하는 지원을 제공할 것을 제안했다.
(C) 그러한 보상은 필요했는데, 왜냐하면 스미스가 알고 있었듯 분업으로 뒷받침되는 제조업의 확산은 아이들이 소득을 창출하는 일에 고용되는 것을 가능케 함으로써, 부모가 심지어 매우 어린 자녀들까지도 일자리로 내몰게 했기 때문이다.

구문 [12행~16행] ~ because, as Smith knew, *the spread of manufacture* (supported by the division of labor), by **making it** possible *for children* to be **employed at income-generating tasks**, **led** many parents to send even very young children out to work.
• because 이하 절에서 주어는 the spread of manufacture이고 동사는 led이다. ( )는 수동의 의미로 주어를 수식한다. 동명사 making 다음에 나오는 it은 가목적어이고 to be employed ~ tasks가 진목적어이다. 밑줄 친 possible은 making의 목적격보어이고 for children은 to부정사의 의미상 주어이다.

어휘 **schooling** (학교) 교육 **accessible** 접근하기 쉬운; 다가가기 쉬운, 편한 **prevailing** 우세한, 지배적인; 일반적인, 널리 유행하는 **dominant** 우세한, 지배적인 **compulsory** 강제적인, 의무적인, 필수의 **incentive** 장려책, 보상물; 자극 **division of labor** 분업

3 문장 넣기 ③

해설 ③ 다음 문장에서 this movement가 나오는데, ③ 이전에는 어떤 운동이 구체적으로 기술되어 있지 않다. 주어진 문장에 있는 The Slow Food movement가 이 this movement에 대응된다고 볼 수 있기 때문에 주어진 문장은 ③에 위치해야 한다.

해석 먹거리 정치는 새로운 현상이 아니다. 파리의 빵 생산을 둘러싼 전투는 케이크를 먹는 것에 대한 마리 앙투아네트의 유감스러운 발언의 원인이 되었으며, 먹거리 가격이나 세금의 증가는 식민지 시대의 미국을 포함하여 수많은 나라에서 폭동을 유발했다. 하지만 21세기 유럽에서 먹거리 정치는 부족이나 정의가 아니라 정체성을 겨냥한다. 슬로우 푸드 운동의 주된 관심은 장인의 식품 생산을 책임지는 다양하고 지역적인 전통을 보호하고 사람들에게 지역의 식자재를 먹도록 권장하는 것이다. 특정한 맛이 상실될 위협과 그것을 만들어내는 지역 문화가 이 운동에 생기를 불어넣는다. 그들은 지역 전통에 기반을 둔 더 진정한 생활 양식을 찾는 데 있어 미적이고 상징적인 내용을 활용하며, 그다음 그것은 흔히 사용하는 구호가 되어 그것을 통해 정치 동원이 일어난다. 그래서 슬로우 푸드 운동은 식품 장인을 진보에 방해가 되는 보수주의자로서가 아니라 지역 유산의 보존에 책임이 있는 중요한 사람으로 이해한다.

구문 [10행~12행] But in Europe in the twenty-first century, food politics is directed **not** at scarcity or justice **but** at identity.
• 「not A but B」는 'A가 아니라 B이다'의 뜻이고, 밑줄 친 두 부분이 각각 A, B에 해당한다.

[18행~21행] Thus, the Slow Food movement understands the food artisan, **not** as *a conservative* (standing in the way of progress) **but** as *someone* (charged with the preservation of local heritage).
• 역시 「not A but B」 구문이 쓰였다. A, B 자리에는 as로 시작되는 전명구가 위치했다. 첫 번째 ( )은 a conservative를, 두 번째 ( )은 someone을 각각 수식하는 분사구이다.

어휘 **prime** 주요한 **ingredient** 요리 재료 **occasion** 원인, 이유; 때 **remark** 발언

말(하다); 주목(하다) **provoke** 유발하다 **revolt** 폭동; 반란(을 일으키다) **colonial** 식민지 시대의 **scarcity** 부족 **animate** 생기를 불어넣다 **aesthetic** 미적인 **authentic** 진짜의 **be anchored in** ~에 단단히 기반을 두다 **idiom** 관용구, 숙어 **mobilization** 동원 **conservative** 보수주의자 **stand in the way of** ~을 방해하다 **charged with** ~에 책임이 있는 **heritage** 유산

4~5 장문   4 ① 5 ③

해설 **4.** 서커스 공연을 창조한 사람들(단원들)이 자신들의 공연에 대해 다른 사람들의 객관적인 평가보다 더 높게 평가했다는 예를 들어 창조자들이 자신의 아이디어를 판단하는 데 있어 객관적이지 못하고 자만하는 경향이 있다는 것을 보여주는 내용이므로, 제목으로 가장 적절한 것은 ① '우리는 자신을 모른다'이다.
② 칭찬의 말이 기적을 낳는다
③ 보다 현실적일수록, 보다 예술적이다
④ 낮은 자존감이 창의성을 억누른다
⑤ 서커스로부터 배울 수 있는 삶의 교훈
5. 창조자들은 관리자들보다 평가가 현실적이지 않았으며 우리는 스스로를 평가할 때 자만하는 경향이 있다고 했으므로 창조자가 자신들의 공연을 두 단계 더 높게 평가했음을 알 수 있다. 그러므로 ③은 high 등이 되어야 한다.

해석 창조자들이 그들 자신의 아이디어를 판단하는 데 있어 객관적일 수 있을까? 내 예전 제자 중 하나인 Justin Berg는 현재 수년간 이 문제에 관해 조사해 온 스탠퍼드의 성공한 젊은 교수이다. 그는 참신한 아이디어의 성공을 예측하는 기법인 창의성 예측을 전문 분야로 다룬다. 한 연구에서, 그는 서로 다른 그룹의 사람들에게 서커스 공연 영상을 보여주고 각각의 공연이 얼마나 잘 될지(성공할지) 예측해 볼 것을 요청했다. 'Cirque du Soleil (태양의 서커스)'와 다른 (서커스) 조직의 서커스 단원들은 자신들의 영상이 얼마나 인기 있을지에 관한 예측을 제출했다. 서커스 관리자들도 그 영상을 봤고 자신들의 예측을 기록했다.
그들의 예측의 (a) 정확성을 시험하기 위해, Berg는 그런 다음 일반 대중들이 얼마나 많이 그 영상을 좋아하고, 공유하고, 자금을 지원했는지 추적하여 각 공연의 실제 성공을 측정해 보았다. 그는 13,000명이 넘는 사람들에게 그 영상을 (b) 평가하도록 했고, 그들은 또한 영상을 페이스북, 트위터, 구글 플러스 그리고 이메일을 통해 공유할 기회도 가졌으며, 그 공연자들에게 기부할 수 있는 10센트의 배당금을 받았다. 창조자들은 자신들의 공연이 평가에 참여한 관객들에게 어떻게 받아들여질지 판단하는 데 있어 형편없음이 입증되었다. 평균적으로 자신들의 공연 영상을 다른 아홉 팀의 서커스 단원들의 공연과 비교해서 평가할 때, 그들은 자신들의 공연을 두 단계나 더 (c) 낮게(→ 높게) 평가했다. 관리자들은 보다 현실적이어서 공연과 어느 정도 (객관적) 거리를 두어, 보다 (d) 중립적인 입장을 취했다. 사회과학자들은 우리가 자신을 (e) 평가할 때 자만하는 경향이 있음을 오랫동안 알아 왔다.

구문 **[2행~4행]** One of my former students, Justin Berg, is now *a successful young professor at Stanford* [who has spent years investigating this question].
• 밑줄 친 두 부분은 동격 관계이며, [ ] 부분은 관계대명사 who가 이끄는 관계사절로 앞의 a successful young professor at Stanford를 수식한다.

[14행~17행] To test the accuracy of their forecasts, / Berg then measured the actual success of each performance / **by tracking** how much general audience members liked, shared, and funded the videos.
• 「by v-ing」는 'V함으로써'의 의미이다. 밑줄 친 부분은 「의문사+주어+동사」 어순의 간접의문문으로 tracking의 목적어로 쓰였다.

[24행~26행] On average, / **when ranking** their videos against the performances of nine other circus artists, / they put their own work two slots too low.
• when ranking ~ circus artists는 접속사를 생략하지 않은 분사구문으로, 의미를 명확하게 하기 위해 분사구문 앞에 접속사를 두기도 한다.

어휘 **objective** 객관적인; 목표 **former** 예전의, 과거의 **investigate** 조사하다, 연구하다 **specialize in** ~을 전문으로 하다 **forecast** 예측(하다), 예보(하다) **predict** 예측하다, 예견하다 *cf.* **prediction** 예측, 예견 **novel** 참신한, 새로운; (장편) 소설 **make a projection** 예측하다 **submit** 제출하다; 복종하다 **register** 기록하다; 등록하다 **accuracy** 정확성 **measure** 측정하다; 판단[평가]하다 **track** 추적하다, 뒤쫓다 **general** 일반적인, 보편적인 **fund** 자금을 대다; 자금 **rate** 평가하다, 등급[순위]을 매기다 **donate** 기부하다, 기증하다 **on average** 평균적으로 **rank** (순위를) 평가하다; 차지하다 **slot** 단계; 자리; 구멍 **realistic** 현실적인; 사실적인 **distance** 거리 **neutral** 중립적인; 중간[중성]의 **evaluate** 평가하다
[선택지] **blind to A** A를 모르는[못 보는]; A를 깨닫지 못하는 **work wonders** 기적을 낳다 **self-esteem** 자존감; 자부심 **suppress** 억누르다; 진압하다

1 필자 주장   ④

해설 프루스트로부터 인용한 말에서 습관에 대한 필자의 주장이 잘 드러나 있다. 습관을 우리가 거의 전 우주를 보지 못하게 하고 스스로를 아는 것을 방해하는 커튼이라고 보고, 이것을 열고, 꿰뚫어야 익숙하게 지나쳤던 것들을 보고 의미를 찾고 경이로움을 발견할 수 있다고 했으므로 필자의 주장으로는 ④가 가장 적절하다.

해석 습관을 대수롭지 않게 여기는 우리의 성향은 습관 자체의 한 측면으로 설명될 수 있는데, 그것은 익숙함과 반복이 우리의 감각을 둔하게 만드는 방식이다. 마르셀 프루스트는 습관을 '우리로부터 거의 전 우주를 감추고 우리가 우리 자신을 아는 것을 방해하는' '두꺼운 커튼'이라고 묘사한다. 이것뿐만이 아니다. 습관은 '우리가 여러 번 목격했던 것들로부터 그것들에 참 의미를 부여해 주는 심오한 인상과 생각의 근원을 차단한다.' 프루스트는 예술가는 우리 세상의 가장 익숙한 특징들이 눈에 보이고 유의미해지고 경이감의 원인이 될 수 있도록 이 습관의 커튼을 걷거나 찢어서 열어야 한다는 것을 깨달았다. 그러나 이것은 또한 철학자들의 과제이기도 하다. 비록 플라톤이나 아리스토텔레스를 인용해 철학은 경이에서 시작한다고 종종 이야기되지만 경이로워하는 마음의 상태는 오로지 습관이라는 두꺼운 커튼을 우선 꿰뚫어야만 도달할 수 있다.

구문 [1행~3행] *Our tendency* (to overlook habit) can be explained by one aspect of habit itself: *the way* [**in which** familiarity and repetition dull our senses].

• ( ) 부분은 Our tendency를 수식하는 to부정사구이다. [ ] 부분은 '전치사+관계대명사' 형태의 in which가 이끄는 관계사절로 the way를 수식한다.

[6행~9행] Not only this: habit '**cuts off** (from *things* [**which** we have witnessed a number of times]) *the root of profound impression and thought* [**which** gives them their real meaning].'

• the root ~ real meaning은 동사 cuts off의 목적어이고, 동사와 목적어 사이에 ( )가 삽입되었다. 첫 번째 [ ]는 목적격 관계대명사 which가 이끄는 관계사절로 things를 수식한다. 두 번째 [ ]는 주격 관계대명사 which가 이끄는 관계사절로 the root ~ thought를 수식한다.

어휘 **tendency** 성향, 경향 **overlook** 간과[무시]하다 **aspect** (측)면; 양상 **familiarity** 익숙[친숙]함 **repetition** 반복, 되풀이 **dull** 둔하게[무디게] 하다; 둔한; 따분한 **conceal** 감추다, 숨기다 **witness** 목격하다; 목격자 **profound** 심오한; 엄청난 **tear open** 찢어서 열다, 찢다 **feature** 특징, 특성 **quote** 인용하다

2 밑줄 함의   ⑤

해설 진화론적으로 봤을 때 예컨대 90%의 이득과 10%의 손실이 예상되는 상황에서 그 10%의 손실이 죽음인 경우가 많았기 때문에 살아남기 위해 사람들이 손실을 회피하게 되었다는 내용의 글이다. 따라서 한 번의 실수로 유전자 풀 바깥으로 밀려난다는 밑줄 친 부분이 의미하는 바는 ⑤ '내기에서 지면, 죽음을 피할 수 없다.'이다.
① 당신의 유전자가 당신이 언제 죽을지를 결정한다.
② 큰 수익은 큰 위험을 감수하지 않고서는 나오지 않는다.
③ 인생의 모든 것은 당신의 선택에 기반해 발생한다.
④ 손실에 대한 두려움이 당신의 행동 패턴을 바꾼다.

해석 생각해보라. 당신은 동전 던지기에서 내기를 해볼 것을 제안받는다. 앞면이 나오면 150달러를 얻는다. 뒷면이면 100달러를 잃는다. 이것에 대해서 어떻게 생각하

는가? 예상되는 값은 확실히 플러스지만(내기를 100번 반복하면 거의 확실히 이익을 얻을 것이다), 대부분의 사람들은 내기를 거절한다. "100달러를 잃는 동등한 확률을 상쇄하기 위해 필요한 최소 이득은 무엇인가?"라는 질문을 받으면, 대부분의 사람들은 200달러, 즉 손실의 두 배로 대답한다. 이는 사람들이 일반적으로 내기를 하기 위해 적어도 200퍼센트의 예상되는 수익을 보기를 원한다는 것을 의미한다. 이것은 우리의 진화론적 과거로부터 온 사고방식이다. 당신이 아프리카의 사바나를 가로질러 걷고 있을 때 덤불이 바스락거리고 그것이 맛있는 식사일 가능성 90%와 그것이 굶주린 사자일 가능성 10%가 있다면, 당신은 살피지 않는 편이 더 낫다. 당신은 당신의 유전자가 유전자 풀 바깥으로 밀려나기 전에 한번 잘못하기만 하면 된다. 현대 세계에서도 마찬가지로, 심각한 결과가 정말 가능한 일인 경우에, 그것은 효과적인 전략일 수 있다.

구문 [6행~8행] When (they are) asked, "What is *the smallest gain* [that you need to balance an equal chance to lose $100]?," // most people answer $200 — **twice as much as** the loss.

• When과 asked 사이에 they(most people) are가 생략되어 있다. [ ]는 목적격 관계대명사절로 the smallest gain을 수식한다. 「배수사 as much as ...」는 '…보다 몇 배 더 많다'의 뜻이다.

[11행~14행] If a bush rustles as you walk across the African savannah and there's a 90% chance (that) it's a delicious meal and a 10% chance that it's a hungry lion, // you're better off not investigating.

• If 다음에 이어지는 두 밑줄 친 절이 and로 연결되어 병렬구조를 이룬다. it's a delicious meal과 that it's a hungry lion은 각각 앞의 명사구 a 90% chance와 a 10% chance에 대한 동격절이다. it's a delicious meal 앞에는 동격을 나타내는 접속사 that이 생략되어 있다.

어휘 **value** 값; 가치 **positive** 플러스의, 양의; 확신하는; 긍정적인 **balance** 상쇄하다; 균형을 잡다 **not less than** 적어도 **return** 수익 **mentality** 사고방식 **evolutionary** 진화의 **rustle** 바스락거리다 **be better off** ~하는 편이 더 낫다

3 빈칸 추론   ③

해설 빈칸 문장의 they는 small companies를 가리키는데, 그것들은 지리적인 규모의 경제를 이용할 수 있다고 하였고, 이어지는 예시는 예술 지구에 예술 관련 직종이 서로 가까이에 있어 서로 도움이 된다는 것이므로 ③ '비슷한 기업들을 모음'으로써 지리적인 규모의 경제를 이용한다는 내용이 가장 적절하다.
① 지역 서비스를 다각화함
② 예술 사업에 보조금을 지급함
④ 다른 지역으로 확장함
⑤ 지역적 특성을 강조함

해석 외적 규모의 경제는 대기업이 단순히 그들의 규모 때문에 정부 혹은 다른 외부 원천으로부터 특혜적 대우를 받는 결과를 야기한다. 예를 들어, 대부분의 주는 대기업이 주민들에게 일자리를 제공해줄 것이므로 대기업을 끌어들이기 위해 세금을 낮춰줄 것이다. 대기업들은 또한 대학들과의 합동 연구로 혜택을 얻으며, 그들 자신의 연구 비용을 낮출 수 있다. 소기업들은 그저 외적 규모의 경제를 이용할 영향력을 가지고 있지 않으며, 따라서 경쟁하는 것이 힘들거나 적어도 비용이 더 많이 든다는 것을 깨닫게 될 것이다. 그러나 그것들은 작은 지역에서 비슷한 기업들을 모음으로써 지리적인 규모의 경제를 이용할 수 있다. 예를 들어, 시내 예술 지구의 화가 작업 구역, 화랑, 그리고 식당은 서로 가까이 있음으로써 혜택을 얻는다.

구문 [8행~11행] Small companies just don't have *the leverage* (to take advantage of external economies of scale), and thus may find **it** *difficult or at least more expensive* **to compete**.

• to take advantage of ~ scale은 앞의 명사 the leverage를 수식한다. find 다음의 it은 가목적어이고 difficult or at least more expensive는 형용사 보어, to compete 가 진목적어이다.

어휘 **economies of scale** 규모의 경제 **preferential** 특혜를 주는 **geographic** 지리적인 **loft** 로프트 ((예전의 공장 등을 개조한 아파트)) **district** 지역, 지구

[선택지] **diversify** 다각화하다 **subsidize** 보조금을 주다 **cluster** 무리를 이루다, 모이다

4 글의 순서 ①

해설 주어진 문장은 포식자가 세부 사항에 집중하여 먹이를 찾는 것에 이점이 있다는 내용이다. (A)에는 그 예를 제시한 후, 세부에 집중하는 것에는 단점도 있다는 진술이 이어진다. (C)에는 세부에 집중하는 것의 단점에 대한 예를 제시하고, 보호색이 생존에 약간의 유리한 우위를 일관되게 제공해준다는 진술을 제시한다. (B)는 그 우위에 대한 구체적인 설명에 해당한다.

해석 자연환경의 혼돈과 혼란의 한복판에서 포식자들은 그들의 탐색을 특정 세부 사항에만 한정하고 다른 모든 것은 무시한다. 이는 굉장한 이점이 있다. (A) 소수의 것만을 찾아보는 데 특화되면, 심지어 훌륭하게 잘 숨어 있는 먹이조차 분명해 보일 수 있다. 그러나 한 가지에 과도하게 집중하는 것에는 또한 대가가 있는데, 대안을 눈치채지 못할지도 모르기 때문이다. (C) 예를 들어, 새가 작은 가지처럼 생긴 애벌레를 열심히 찾을 때, 그것은 나무껍질처럼 생긴 근처의 나방은 놓친다. 보호색의 이점은 그것이 생존에 대한 절대적인 보장을 제공해서가 아니라, 연속적으로 위협을 마주하며 살아가는 투쟁 속에서 항상 약간의 유리함을 산출한다는 것이다. (B) 최소한, 교묘한 보호색 때문에 포식자의 접근과 뒤이은 공격 사이에 약간의 지연이 있을 때조차 먹잇감 동물이 달아나는 것에 도움을 줄 수 있다. 그리고 최고의 경우에는 먹이는 완전히 무시될 것이다.

구문 [10행~12행] At a minimum, even *a minor delay* (between the approach of a predator and its subsequent attack) **can help** *a prey animal* **escape**.

• 주어는 a minor delay이며 동사는 can help이다. ( ) 부분은 전명구로 주어를 수식한다. 동사 help는 「help O (to) 동사원형」 형태로 'O가 v하는 것을 돕다'의 의미이다.

[16행~19행] The benefit of concealing coloration is **not** that it provides an absolute guarantee of survival, **but** that it consistently yields a small edge in *the struggle* (to live through each successive threatening encounter).

• 「not A but B」는 'A가 아니라 B다'의 뜻인데, A와 B 자리에 각각 that절이 위치하여 병렬구조를 이루고 있다. ( ) 부분은 the struggle을 수식하는 형용사적 용법의 to부정사구이다.

어휘 **amid** ~의 한복판에서 **predator** 포식자 **expertly** 훌륭하게, 전문적으로 **blind to** ~을 눈치채지 못하는, 깨닫지 못하는 **alternative** 대안 **subsequent** 그다음의, 차후의 **intently** 열심히 **caterpillar** 애벌레 **twig** 작은 가지 **moth** 나방 **bark** 나무껍질 **concealing coloration** 보호색 **guarantee** 보장 **consistently** 항상, 일관되게 **yield** 산출하다, 내다; 양보하다; 굴복하다; 넘겨주다 **edge** 가장자리; (칼 등의) 날; 우위, 유리함 **successive** 연속적인

5 문장 넣기 ③

해설 주어진 문장에 particularly architects라는 말이 나온 것으로 보아 주어 it은 건축가를 포함하는 집단이 되어야 한다. 또한 However로 시작하는 것을 근거로 주어진 문장에 반대되는 내용 다음에 주어진 문장이 들어가야 함을 알 수 있다. 그러므로 건설 분야에서 이러한 전파 집단(건축가, 컨설턴트, 디자이너, 엔지니어)은 매우 작고, 비교적 보수적이며, 여러 집단으로 나누어 있다는 내용 다음인 ③에 주어진 문장이 들어가야 가장 적절하다. ③ 뒤 문장의 such high levels of technical sophistication(그렇게 높은 수준의 정교함)은 주어진 문장의 innovation and forward thinking(혁신과 진보적인 사고)을 나타낸다.

해석 완전히 발달한 산업의 모든 분야와 마찬가지로, 건설 분야는 유행을 혁신하고 추적하는 비교적 소수의 주도적인 생각을 하는 사람들과 혁신과 새로운 아이디어를 받아들이고 전파하는 더 큰 집단의 기술 전문가들로 특징지어진다. 이 전파하는 집단은 건축가, 컨설턴트, 디자이너, 엔지니어로 이루어져 있다. 건설 분야에서 이러한 전파 집단은 매우 작고, 비교적 보수적이며, 여러 집단으로 나누어 있다. 그러나 그 집단, 특히 건축가들은, 혁신과 진보적인 사고 때문에 매체의 막대한 주목을 받는다. 하지만 대부분의 건설 공사에 있어서, 그렇게 높은 수준의 기술적인 정교함은 불필요하며 비용이 많이 들기 때문에 지지받지 못한다. 대부분 건물은 기능적인 목적을 위해 지어지는 것이지, 기술의 한계를 진보시키거나 탐구하기 위해 지어지지 않는다. 흥미롭거나 기교가 뛰어난 전면을 가진 실용적인 건물은 대부분의 용도에 매우 충분하다.

구문 [4행~8행] Like all sectors in mature industries, the construction sector is characterized by *a relatively few leading thinkers* [**who** innovate and monitor trends] and *a larger group of technical experts* [**who** receive and disseminate innovation and new ideas].

• 밑줄 친 두 개의 명사구는 and로 연결되어 병렬구조를 이룬다. 또한 두 개의 [ ] 부분은 모두 주격 관계대명사 who가 이끄는 관계사절로 각각 바로 앞에 있는 선행사 a relatively few leading thinkers와 a larger group of technical experts를 수식한다.

[17행~19행] A practical building (with *a facade* [that is interesting or artful]) is more than sufficient for most purposes.

• ( ) 부분은 주어인 A practical building을 수식하는 전명구이고, 그 안의 [ ] 부분은 관계사절로 a facade를 수식한다.

어휘 **publicity** 주목, 관심; 홍보 **architect** 건축가 **sector** 분야, 부문 **mature** 완전히 발달한; 성숙한 **conservative** 보수적인 **sophistication** 정교함, 세련 **functional** 기능적인 **artful** 기교가 뛰어난 **sufficient** 충분한

1 글의 주제　　　　　　　　　　　①

해설 연구 결과 입원 환자들은 자신의 환경에 대한 통제권을 갖기를 원했고, 이것이 환자의 무력감 해소와 회복 촉진에 기여한다는 결론이 나왔으므로 글의 주제로 가장 적절한 것은 ① '환자들에게 자율권을 주는 것의 중요성'이다.
② 환자와 돌보는 사람 간의 관계
③ 병원에서 청결이 중요한 이유
④ 환자의 회복에 환경이 미치는 영향
⑤ 환자들이 환경을 통제하는 것의 위험성

해석 영국에서의 몇몇 주요 연구는 환자들이 자신을 보살펴주는 환경에 대하여 무엇을 중요하다고 여기는지 그리고 간호사들과 다른 건강 관리 직원들이 어떻게 그 환경을 개선시킬 수 있는지를 알아내려 시도했다. 환자들은 자신들의 개인적 환경을 더 많이 통제하고 싶다고 일관적으로 말했다. 예를 들어 Douglas와 Douglas의 연구에서, 병원 입원 환자들은 자신의 활동에 대해 통제감을 원한다고 보고했다. 인터뷰한 환자들은 병동 구역을 자유롭게 여기저기 다니고, 커튼을 여닫고, 조명과 온도를 조절하고, 건물의 외부 지역에 접근하고 싶다고 설명했다. 이러한 연구 결과는 Lawson과 Phiri의 이전 연구에 의해 뒷받침되는데, 이는 또한 환자의 개인적 통제를 증가시키는 것의 필요성과 그들이 그들의 돌봄의 측면에 책임을 지도록 도와주는 것이 어떻게 무력감을 감소시키고 회복을 도울 수 있는지에 대해 보고했다.

구문 [1행~4행] Several major studies in the UK have attempted to discover / **what** patients find important about their care environment |and| **how** nurses and other healthcare staff can improve that environment.
• what과 how가 이끄는 절이 병렬구조를 이루며 discover의 목적어 역할을 하고 있다.

[9행~12행] ~ they wanted to **be able to** move freely about the ward area, open and close curtains, control lights and temperature, |and| access external areas of the building.
• be able to 다음에 연결되는 동사원형 move, open and close, control, access가 콤마와 and로 연결되어 병렬구조를 이루고 있다.

[15행~17행] ~ how **helping them to take responsibility for aspects of their care** / can reduce helplessness |and| aid recovery.
• helping them ~ their care가 주어이고, 동사 can reduce와 aid가 and로 연결된 병렬구조이다.

어휘 **consistently** 일관되게　**remark** 말하다　**inpatient** 입원 환자　**ward** 병동
finding (연구) 결과　**helplessness** 무력감
[선택지] **empower** 권한을 주다, 자율권을 주다　**caregiver** (환자나 아이들을) 돌보는 사람

2 밑줄 어법　　　　　　　　　　　⑤

해설 ⑤ '웹 페이지의 내용을 이해하지 못하는 컴퓨터'라는 의미로 '이해하지 (못하다)'라는 일반동사 understand를 대신하는 것이므로 aren't는 don't로 바꾸어야 한다.
① 사용자들이 친구들에게 '연결되어 있다'라는 수동의 의미이므로, 과거분사 connected는 올바르다
② 주어가 셀 수 없는 명사 the only information이므로 단수동사 is는 올바르다.
③ '다른 사람들이 검색할 수 있도록' 또는 '다른 사람들이 검색하는 것을 가능하게 하기 위하여'라는 목적을 나타내는 to-v의 부사적 용법으로 사용되었다.

④ '전치사+관계대명사' 형태로 관계사절 내에서 관계대명사가 전치사의 목적어인 경우 전치사를 관계대명사 앞에 둘 수 있다. which[that] they are interested in으로 바꾸어 쓸 수도 있다.

해석 소셜 네트워킹 시스템이 사용자들로 하여금 친구들과 계속 연결되도록 하는 반면에, 소셜 북마킹은 북마크를 공유하는 방법이다. 즉, 이것은 여러분이 사용하는 웹페이지를 친구들의 네트워크 또는 전 세계와 함께 공유하는 방법이다. 파일 공유와는 달리, 소셜 북마킹에는 불법적인 것이 없는데, 이는 공유되고 다운로드되는 유일한 정보는 실제 콘텐츠가 아니라 웹 주소이기 때문이다. 주어진 주제에 대한 인기 있는 사이트를 다른 사람들이 검색할 수 있도록 사용자가 자신들이 좋아하는 사이트를 북마킹해서 주제 태그로 그 사이트에 대해 색인을 달음으로써 소셜 북마킹은 작동한다. 여러 면에서, 이것은 사용자가 관심 있어 하는 웹사이트를 찾기 위해 전통적인 검색 엔진을 이용하는 것보다 더 효과적이다. 이는 웹 페이지의 내용을 이해하지 못하는 컴퓨터가 아니라 그 내용을 이해하는 사람에 의해서 검색 태그가 지정되기 때문이다. 이러한 효과 때문에, 소셜 북마킹 시스템은 점점 더 인기를 얻고 있다.

구문 [1행~3행] **Whereas** social networking systems **allow** *users* **to stay** connected to their friends, // social bookmarking is a way of sharing bookmarks.
• whereas는 부사절 접속사로서 '반면에'라는 의미로 두 개의 절을 역접으로 연결한다. 「allow O to-v (O가 v하는 것을 허락하다[v하게 해주다])」 구문이 사용되었다.

어휘 **bookmark** 북마크; 북마크하다　**filesharing** 파일 공유　**index** 색인을 달다
enable 가능하게 하다　**conventional** 전통적인　**assign** 지정하다, 부여하다

3 빈칸 추론　　　　　　　　　　　③

해설 변호사들은 낮은 보수로 의뢰를 받았을 때는 일을 거절했으나 무보수로 의뢰받았을 때는 수락했는데, 이는 시장 거래가 아니라 자선 행위가 되었기 때문이다. 이는 공짜로 해 달라고 부탁하는 것보다 돈을 지불하는 것이 ③ '그들로부터 노력을 덜 이끌어 낼' 경우를 보여준다.
① 그들이 체면을 덜 잃게 할
② 더 나은 결과를 가져올
④ 더 본질적인 관심을 유도할
⑤ 그들의 동기를 더욱 활용할

해석 행동 경제학자인 댄 애리얼리는 특히 선한 행위의 경우에는 사람들에게 일을 해 달라고 돈을 지불하는 것이 그들에게 공짜로 어떤 일을 해달라고 부탁하는 것보다 그들로부터 노력을 덜 이끌어 낼지도 모른다는 것을 증명하는 일련의 실험들을 했다. 그는 자신의 연구 결과를 예증하는 실생활의 일화를 이야기해준다. 미국 은퇴자 협회(AARP)가 여러 명의 변호사들에게 시간당 30달러라는 할인된 가격으로 어려운 은퇴자들에게 법률 서비스를 기꺼이 제공해줄 의향이 있는지 문의했다. 변호사들은 거절했다. 그러고 나서 미국 은퇴자 협회는 그들이 도움이 필요한 은퇴자들에게 무료로 법률적 조언을 제공해줄 수 있는지 문의했다. 변호사들은 동의했다. 그들이 시장 거래가 아니라 자선 활동에 참여하도록 부탁받고 있음이 일단 명백해지자, 변호사들은 자선을 베푸는 자세로 반응했다.

구문 [12행~14행] Once **it** was clear **(that) they were being asked to engage in a charitable activity as opposed to a market transaction**, // the lawyers responded charitably.
• it은 가주어이고, 접속사 that이 생략된 절 they ~ a market transaction이 진주어

이다.

어휘 behavioral economist 행동 경제학자　demonstrate 보여주다, 입증하다　anecdote 일화　illustrate 예증하다　needy 어려운, 궁핍한　retiree 은퇴자　charitable 자선의 *cf.* charitably 자비롭게, 너그럽게, 관대하게　transaction 거래
[선택지] lose face 체면을 잃다　elicit (행동·반응 등을) 이끌어 내다, 유도해 내다　induce 설득하다, 유도하다　intrinsic 고유한, 본질적인　utilize 이용하다, 활용하다

4 무관 문장　　　　　　　　　　　　③

해설　단말기를 로그인한 상태에서 다른 사람이 시스템에 접근하는 위험을 이야기하는 글로, 바이러스로 인한 손상에 관한 ③은 글의 흐름과 관계가 없다.

해석　사용자가 단말기를 시스템에 로그인된 상태로 놔둬서 그 단말기가 주인이 없는 상태로 있게 되면 시스템의 보안에 위험이 실제로 있다. 이 단말기는 승인되지 않은 사람에 의해 사용될 수 있게 공개된 상태로 남겨진다. ① 그런 상황에서는 승인되지 않은 사람이 승인된 사용자의 인증 혹은 비밀번호를 알거나 추측해야 할 필요 없이, 마치 그 승인된 사용자가 존재하는 것처럼, 그 단말기를 사용하여 시스템에 접근할 수 있다. ② 이러한 이유로, 사용자들은 비밀번호로 보호받는 스크린 세이버를 사용하지 않은 채 단말기를 로그인된 상태로 남겨두지 말 것을 유념해야 한다. ③ 바이러스와 다른 악의적인 소프트웨어가 개인 삭제 파일에서 드라이브 파티션을 사용할 수 없게 하는 문제에 이르기까지 당신의 데이터에 다수의 문제를 야기할 수 있다. ④ 어떤 시스템은 키보드나 마우스가 미작동이 되면 승인된 사용자가 비밀번호를 입력하지 않는 한 자동으로 단말기를 잠그는 프로세스를 갖추고 있을지도 모른다. ⑤ 그런 프로세스가 존재한다면, 기업 방침은 명백히 그것의 사용을 요구해야 한다.

구문　[13행~17행] Some systems may themselves have *a process* [whereby inactivity of the keyboard or mouse will automatically lock down the terminal] // **unless** the authorized user enters a password.

● [　]은 앞의 a process를 수식하는 관계부사절이다. unless는 '만약 ~ 않는다면, ~이 아닌 한'의 뜻이다.

어휘　terminal 종점의; 단말기　unattended 주인이 옆에 없는; 주의하지 않은　unauthorized 승인되지 않은　malicious 악의적인　a wide array of 다수의　range from A to B 범위가 A부터 B까지이다　whereby (그것에 의하여) ~하는　inactivity 무활동, 정지　explicitly 명백히

5 요약문 완성　　　　　　　　　　　　④

해설　현대의 예술 작품은 원래 환경에서 분리되어(disconnected) 박물관과 미술관 같은 공식적이고 엄숙한 장소에 전시되고 있으며, 예술품과 감상자 간에는 의무적으로 거리가 있어 감상자와 작품의 상호 작용(interaction)은 더욱 어려워지게 된다.

해석　많은 관람객들이 예술을 보고 반응할 때 경험하는 불안은 매우 타당한 이유가 있다. 예술 작품은 보통 박물관과 미술관 안의 그것이 최종적으로 놓일 장소에서 그것의 원래 환경과 분리되어 전시된다. 이러한 수동적인 전시는 그 작품의 창작, 의미, 그리고 가치를 결정했던 역사와 과정의 대부분을 숨긴다. 기관(미술관과 박물관)에 의해 정당하게 지켜지고 있는 관객과 예술품 간의 의무적인 거리는 예술품에 대한 신비감을 더욱 강화한다. 꼬리표, 설명, 그리고 다른 자료가 유용한 보조물이 되기는 한다. 그러나 그 정보가 비판적 탐구를 위한 시작점이 아니라 결론적 진술로 제시되기 때문에 많은 관객들에게 대답 없는 질문을 남긴다. 그 예술품은 어떻게 만들어졌을까? 그것은 왜 값이 그렇게 비싼가? 그것은 왜 박물관에 있나?

┌───┐
│ 그 예술의 창작과 (A) 분리된 환경에 예술을 전시하는 것은 감상자에게 그것과 │
│ 개인적으로 (B) 상호 작용할 여지를 거의 남겨두지 않는다. │
└───┘

구문　[1행~2행] *The anxiety* [(which[that]) many spectators experience // when (they are) looking at and responding to **art**] / **is** well justified.

● 주어는 The anxiety이고 동사는 is이며, [　] 부분은 앞에 목적격 관계대명사 which[that]가 생략되어 The anxiety를 수식한다. when 다음에는 'they(many spectators) are'가 생략되어 있고, art는 looking at과 responding to의 공통 목적어이다.

[7행~9행] *The mandatory distance* (between viewers and art), / **rightfully observed by institutions**, further **heightens** the mystery of art.

● (　) 부분은 주어 The mandatory distance를 수식하며 동사는 heightens이다. rightfully ~ institutions는 수동의 의미로 쓰인 분사구문이다.

어휘　spectator 관람객　justified 타당한 이유가 있는　disconnected 분리된　conceal 숨기다　rightfully 정당하게, 마땅히　observe 지키다, 준수하다　aid 보조물　inquiry 탐구

1 빈칸 추론　③

해설 빈칸 바로 뒤에 예시가 이어지므로 이를 통해 추론한다. 실험 대상인 아이들이 누군가 자신을 보고 있다는 것을 알아차리면 다르게 행동할지도 모르기 때문에 심리학자는 실험 대상인 아이들에게 자신이 발각되지 않게 할 것이라고 했다. 그러므로 빈칸에는 ③ '자신이 관찰되고 있다는 것을 알지 못하는'이 적절하다.
① 완전히 무작위로 선택되는
② 실험실 환경에 편안함을 느끼는
④ 연구 대상 집단을 대표하는
⑤ 실험 참여에 관심이 없는

해석 행동을 연구하는 한 가지 전략은 사건들이 삶에서 자연스럽게 발생할 때 그 사건들을 관찰하고 기록하는 것이다. 자연주의적 관찰이라고 불리는 이 방법을 이용하는 연구자들은 실험 대상자들을 실험실로 데리고 와서 어떤 식으로도 그들의 행동을 조작하지 않는다. 그들은 실험 대상자 집단을 고르지도, 서로 다른 실험 조건을 만들지도 않는다. 자연주의적 관찰은 곰의 동면 습관이나 암탉의 모성 행동과 같은 동물의 행동을 연구하는 데 흔히 이용된다. 그러나 실험 대상자가 자신이 관찰되고 있다는 것을 알지 못하는 것이 중요하다. 예를 들어, 다양한 인종의 아이들이 어떻게 함께 노는가를 연구하려고 자연주의적 관찰을 이용하는 심리학자는 아이들 무리가 학교 운동장이나 공원에서 놀고 있는 것을 관찰은 하겠지만, (아이들에게) 발각되지 않기 위해 멀리 떨어져 있을 것이다. 낯선 어른이 보고 있다는 것을 아이들이 알아차리면, 그들은 알아차리지 못했을 때와 다르게 행동할지도 모른다.

구문 [5행~7행] **Nor do they choose** groups of subjects or create different experimental conditions.
• nor가 앞 문장의 내용을 받아 문두에 오는 경우, 「nor+(조)동사+주어」의 어순으로 쓰인다. '~도 역시 그렇지 않다'란 뜻이다.

[10행~11행] **It is important**, however, **that** the subject (**should**) **be** unaware that he is being observed.
• 「It is+형용사+that+주어+(should+)동사원형」 구문이 쓰였다. 당연·필요 등을 나타내는 형용사(necessary, essential, important, vital 등)에 계속되는 that절에는 「(should+)동사원형」을 쓴다.

[11행~15행] For example, *a psychologist* (using naturalistic observation / **to study how** children of various races play together) would **watch** *groups of children* **playing** in the school yards or parks, // but he would remain at a distance **so as not to be** detected.
• ( )는 분사구로서 주어 a psychologist를 수식한다. 여기서 to study는 부사적 용법의 to부정사구로 목적을 나타내며, how가 이끄는 의문사절이 study의 목적어 역할을 한다. watch는 목적격보어로 원형부사 또는 현재분사를 취할 수 있다. 「so as to-v (v하기 위하여)」의 부정형이 쓰였다.

어휘 observe 보다; 관찰하다; (법을) 준수하다 *cf.* observation 관찰, 관측; 감시; 주시 naturalistic 자연주의적인　manipulate 교묘하게 조종하다; (사물을 능숙하게) 다루다 experimental 실험의; 시험적인　maternal 어머니의, 모성의　otherwise (만약) 그렇지 않으면[않았다면]; (~와는) 다르게
[선택지] be unaware that ~을 알지[눈치채지] 못하다　representative 대표(자); 외판원; 대표하는; (美) 하원 의원　indifferent 무관심한; 썩 좋지는 않은

2 글의 순서　⑤

해설 연극이 실제로는 일어나지 않을 것임을 충분히 이해한다는 말 다음에는 그러나 작품에 몰두하기 위해 불신을 자발적으로 중지시킨다는 내용인 (C)가 오는 것이 자연스럽다. 그다음에는 배우가 연기를 잘하는지에 따라 자발적 불신이 중지되거나 중지되지 않는다는 내용을 다룬 (B)와 (A) 중 연결어 But이 있는 (A)가 마지막으로 오는 것이 문맥상 자연스럽다.

해석 연극 작품을 관람할 때 여러분은 '불신의 자발적 중지'라고 불리는 것에 관여한다. 즉 여러분의 의식적인 마음은, 묘사되고 있는 사건들은 극작가가 쓴 것이고 실제로는 결코 일어나지 않았을 수도 있다는 것을 충분히 이해하고 있다.
(C) 하지만 여러분은 작품에 끌어들여져서 여러분이 가진 모든 감정으로 이야기를 경험하도록 무대에서의 연기에 대한 여러분의 불신을 기꺼이 중지시킨다.
(B) 배우들이 그들의 일을 성공적으로 하고 있으면 여러분은 여러분 앞에서 일어나는 것이 실제이고 여러분이 보고 있는 사건과 상호 작용이 오로지 바로 지금 처음으로 일어나고 있는 중이라고 잠시 실제로 믿을 수 있다.
(A) 하지만 반면에 배우들이 자기만족에 빠져 연기가 지루해지면 여러분은 불신을 완전히 중지시키지 못할 것이고 단지 암기한 대사를 암송하고 있는 배우를 보고 있다는 불편한 인식을 갖게 될 것이다.

구문 [3행~6행] That is, your conscious mind fully understands **that** *the events* (being portrayed) **were written** by a playwright and **may** never **have** truly **taken** place at all.
• that 이하 절에서 주어는 the events이고 동사는 were written과 may have taken이다. ( )는 수동 진행형의 분사로 앞에 나온 명사 the events를 수식하고 있다. 즉, the events being portrayed는 '묘사되고 있는 사건들'이라는 의미이다.

어휘 theatrical 연극의　production 생산; 작품　engage in ~에 관여하다, 참여하다 willing 자발적인　suspension 정지, 중지 *cf.* suspend 매달다; 중지하다　disbelief 불신　conscious 의식하고 있는; 의식적인　portray 묘사하다; 연기하다　playwright 극작가　complacent 자기만족적인, 현실에 안주하는　awareness 인식　recite 암송하다; 나열하다　interaction 상호 작용; 대화　onstage 무대 위의[에서]

3 문장 넣기　④

해설 영업사원들이 밀려 들어와 무엇을 어렵게 할 수 있는지를 파악해야 한다. ④ 앞에서 스트레스가 많은 사건을 겪었을 때 재정에 관한 결정을 내리는 것을 연기하라고 했고, ④ 이후에 주어진 문장에 대한 구체적인 예가 제시되고 있으므로 주어진 문장은 ④에 들어가는 것이 적절하다.

해석 여러분이 재정 계획을 일찍 시작할수록, 개인 환경이 바뀔 때 여러분의 계획을 조정할 준비를 더 잘할 것이다. 직위가 바뀌는 것, 새로운 주로 이사하는 것, 결혼하는 것, 자녀를 갖는 것, 심각한 자동차 사고를 당하는 것, 은퇴하는 것과 그 외의 스트레스가 많은 사건들이 여러분의 재정적 목표와 계획의 재평가를 요구하는 '재정적 타격'이다. 그러나 여러분이 가장 취약한 이런 때에 중요한 재정적 결정을 성급하게 내리지 않는 것이 중요하다. 그 사건으로부터 회복하고 여러분의 모든 선택을 주의 깊게 평가하기 위한 시간을 가졌을 때까지 어떤 행동이든 연기하라. 이러한 상황에서 일부 재정 관련 영업사원들이 여러분과 접촉하기 위해서 밀려들 것이기 때문에 이것은 어려울 수 있다. 예를 들어, 자녀를 가지게 되면, 보험 설계사, 재정 설계사, 증권 중개인이 여러분에게 보험에 가입하고 대학 학자금 펀드에 투자를 시작하도록 적극적으로 권한다는 것을 알게 될 것이다. 비록 이것들이 타당한 목표이기

는 하지만, 압박감에 어떠한 돈이 많이 드는 결정도 하지 말라.

구문 [3행~5행] **The sooner** you begin financial planning, / **the better prepared** you'll be to adapt your plans when personal circumstances change.

• 「the+비교급 ~, the+비교급 …」 구문으로 '~하면 할수록 더욱더 …하다'라는 뜻이다. the better prepared는 you'll be의 보어 역할을 하고, 따라서 you'll be better prepared를 의미한다.

어휘 **financial** 재정의 **adapt** 조정하다, 적응시키다 **relocate** 이사하다, 이전하다 **reevaluation** 재평가 **vulnerable** 상처 입기 쉬운, 취약한 **evaluate** 평가하다 **insurance agent** 보험 설계사, 보험 대리점 **stockbroker** 증권 중개인 **invest** 투자하다 **valid** (논리적으로) 타당한 **objective** 목표, 목적

어휘 **hand** 건네주다; 도움 **subject** 피실험자; 주제; 주어 **recruit** 모집하다; 구성하다 **identify A as B** A를 B로 파악하다[증명하다] **terribly** 대단히; 극심하게, 지독히 **read** 적혀 있다, 읽히다 **accordingly** 그에 따라, (상황에) 부응해서 **assignment** 과제, 임무; 배정 **elegant** 정밀한; 고상한, 우아한 **demonstrate** 보여주다, 입증[실증]하다 **beautifully** 아주 잘, 훌륭하게; 아름답게 **clue** 단서, 실마리
[선택지] **make it a rule to-v** v하는 것을 규칙[습관]으로 하다

4~5 장문   4 ② 5 ⑤

해설 **4.** 신문에 적힌 지시 사항에 주의를 기울여서 정답을 빨리 알아내는 사람들과 주의를 기울이지 않아서 시간도 오래 걸리고 정답도 찾지 못한 사람들의 실험을 통해 운이 좋은 사람들과 불운한 사람들이 실제로 세상을 달리 바라보는지에 대해 알아보는 내용이다. 그러므로 제목으로 가장 적절한 것은 ② '당신은 주의를 기울이고 있는가?'이다.
① 사람은 스스로 믿는 대로 된다
③ 성공은 단지 운의 문제이다
④ 규칙적으로 신문을 읽어라
⑤ 타인을 따라 하지 말고, 그저 자신을 믿어라
5. 운이 좋은 사람들은 답을 담은 메시지를 보고 몇 초 만에 답을 찾아냈다고 했으므로 환경 속의 정보를 무시하면 문제 해결에 필요한 단서를 놓칠 것임을 알 수 있다. 그러므로 ⑤는 ignoring 등이 되어야 한다.

해석 영국 하트포드셔 대학의 리처드 와이즈먼은 자신의 실험실에서 피실험자들에게 신문을 건네고 신문 안에 있는 모든 사진들을 세어보게 했다. 와이즈먼은 자신을 매우 운이 좋거나 대단히 불운하다고 (a) 파악하는 사람들을 모집하여 이 실험의 피실험자들을 꾸렸다. 그는 자신의 삶이 행운으로 가득 차 있는 사람들이 불운한 사람들과 실제로 세상을 (b) 달리 바라보는지 알기를 원했다. 무슨 일이 벌어졌을 것 같은가?
이 실험에서 불운한 사람들은 신문 속의 모든 사진들을 세는 데 몇 분을 보냈고 대부분은 오답을 냈다. 반면에 운이 좋은 사람들은 불과 몇 초 만에 답을 찾아냈고, 모두 정답이었다. 왜 그랬을까?
와이즈먼은 이 실험을 위해 특별한 신문을 고안했다. 각 신문의 첫 장에 '세는 것을 중단하시오. 이 신문에는 43장의 사진이 있습니다.'라고 적혀 있는 2인치 크기의 메시지가 있었다. 두 집단 모두 요구대로 사진을 찾았지만, 운이 좋은 사람들은 또한 이 메시지를 읽고 (c) 그에 따라 응답했다. 반면에 불운한 사람들은 그것(사진을 세는 것)이 (d) 특정한 과제였기 때문에 단지 사진을 세는 데만 몰두했고 그들이 필요로 하는 답을 담은 메시지를 보지 못했다. 이 정밀한 실험은 환경 속에 있는 정보를 (e) 인식(→ 무시)함으로써 문제 해결의 열쇠인 중요한 단서들을 놓친다는 것을 아주 잘 보여준다.

구문 [7행~10행] He wanted to see // **whether** *those people* [whose lives are filled with good fortune] actually *see* the world differently than **do** *those* [who are unlucky].

• 명사절을 이끄는 접속사 whether가 이끄는 절이 to see의 목적어 역할을 한다. 첫 번째 [ ]은 소유격 관계대명사 whose가 이끄는 관계사절로 those people을, 두 번째 [ ]는 주격 관계대명사 who가 이끄는 관계사절로 those를 수식한다. than 다음에는 「동사+주어」의 어순으로 도치가 일어났다. as나 than 뒤의 주어가 길고 동사가 짧으면 종종 도치된다. 여기서 do는 see를 대신하는 대동사이다.

1 글의 요지　　③

해설　우리의 두뇌는 불완전성을 견디지 못하는 특성이 있어서, 일을 자주 미루는 버릇이 있는 사람들은 일단 일을 그저 시작하면 끝을 내려 하는 두뇌의 약점을 이용할 수 있다는 내용이므로 글의 요지로 가장 적절한 것은 ③이다.

해석　불완전성은 우리 두뇌가 불안정함을 나타낸다. 이것의 기본적 실례는 열린 원 실험이다. 종이 한 장에 원을 그리되 원이 완전히 닫히지 않도록 작은 틈을 남겨두어라. 이제 그것을 2~3분 동안 응시하고 무슨 일이 일어나는지 주목하라. 당신의 두뇌는 원을 닫고 싶어 한다. 어떤 사람들에게는 그것을 닫으려는 충동이 너무 강해서 그들은 결국 연필을 집어 들고 그것을 닫힌 모습으로 그린다. 미루는 것으로 인해 당신이 속을 끓이는 것을 멈추게 하는 데 마찬가지의 역학이 적용될 수 있다. 요령은 당신 앞에 있는 어떤 과제라도 단지 시작하는 것이다. 그냥 어느 곳에서나 시작하란 말이다. 심리학자들은 이것을 Zeigarnik 효과라고 부르는데, 누군가가 압도적인 목표에 직면하여 결과적으로 미루고 있을 때, 어느 지점에서라도 시작하는 것이 시작된 것을 끝마치는 동기 부여를 개시한다는 연구 결과를 처음으로 기록한 러시아 심리학자의 이름을 따서 명명된 것이다. 당신이 과제를 시작할 때, 비록 가장 작고 가장 단순한 부분부터 시작한다 하더라도, 당신은 원을 그리기 시작한다. 그러고 나서 다른 부분으로 이동하고 (원의 더 많은 부분을 그리고), 또 다른 부분으로 이동하는 (원을 더 그리는) 등등을 행하라.

구문　[6행~8행] For some people the urge to close it is **so** strong **that** they'll eventually pick up the pencil and draw it closed.

• 「so ~ that ...」은 '너무 ~해서 …하다'의 뜻이며 that절에서 동사원형 pick up과 draw가 병렬구조를 이룬다.

[10행~11행] The trick is simply to start **whatever project is front of you** ~

• whatever ~ you는 to start의 목적어 역할을 하며 whatever는 '~한 어떤[모든] 것'의 뜻이다.

어휘　instability 불안정　illustration 실례　such that ~하는 정도로　all the way 내내, 완전히　stare at ~을 응시하다　urge 충동　dynamic 역학　stop A from v-ing A가 v하지 못하게 하다　procrastination 지연, 연기　document 기록하다　finding 연구 결과　overwhelming 압도적인　launch 시작하다, 착수하다　motivation 동기 부여　and so forth 기타 등등

2 빈칸 추론　　①

해설　도덕과 법의 차이에 대한 글로, 지문 전체에서 법의 영역 밖에 있는 도덕적 관습들에 대한 예시와 함께 법은 극단적인 것이지만 도덕은 일상적인 영역이라는 내용을 제시하고 있다. 빈칸 문장의 앞부분에서 기부가 도덕적으로는 옳지만 그렇게 해야 한다는 법은 없다는 내용이 나오므로, 빈칸 문장은 평범한 상황과 사소한 문제라면 자신의 몫 이상을 갖는 것이 ① '도덕적 문제이지 법적인 문제는 아니다'가 가장 적절하다.
② 모든 사회에서 윤리학에 의해 다뤄진다
③ 도덕적으로는 장려되지만, 법적으로는 막아진다
④ 법이 머지않아 다뤄야 하는 문제이다
⑤ 영국에서 더 흔히 있는 문제이다

해석　도덕과 법이 항상 똑같은 영역을 다루는 것은 아니다. 성스러운 것과 세속적인 것 사이에 어느 정도 구분이 있는 사회에서는 사회의 화합을 유지하기에 법 단독으로는 충분치 않을 것이며, 도덕적 규범이 필수적이다. 일반적으로 도덕적이거나 비도덕적이라고 간주되는 어떤 행동들은 법의 범위 밖에 있다. 보통 법은 사람이 하지 말아야 할 것들의 더욱 극단적인 예들에 관계가 있고, 반면에 도덕은 일상적인 잘못된 행동들과 사람이 해야 할 일을 강조한다. 예를 들어 자선 단체에 기부하는 것은 도덕적으로 옳다고 여겨지지만 (영국에서) 그렇게 해야 한다는 법은 없다. 그러니까 이러한 경우에 도덕은 공익을 존중하지만, 법은 기껏해야 기부를 권장한다. 따라서 평범한 상황과 사소한 문제에서는 자신의 몫 이상을 갖는 것이 <u>도덕적 문제이지 법적인 문제는 아니다</u>.

구문　[7행~10행] In general, the law is concerned with **the more extreme examples of what one should not do**, // while morality **emphasizes** everyday misdeeds and what one should do.

• the more ~ not do는 명사구로서 전치사 with의 목적어 역할을 한다. 여기서 what ~ do는 what이 이끄는 선행사가 포함된 관계절이며, of의 목적어로 쓰였다. 두 밑줄 친 부분은 and로 연결되어 병렬구조를 이루며 emphasizes의 목적어로 쓰였다.

어휘　ground 영역, 분야　sacred 성스러운　insufficient 불충분한, 부족한　prescription 규범, 규정　immoral 비도덕적인　scope 범위, 영역　misdeed 잘못된 행동　charity 자선 (단체)　have regard for ~을 존중하다　common good 공익　at most 기껏해야　trivial 사소한
[선택지] ethics 윤리학　discourage 말리다, 막다

3 무관 문장　　②

해설　이 글의 전반적인 내용은 미국 음악이 세계 각처의 음악과 서로 얽혀 있다는 것을 여러 구체적인 예를 제시하여 설명하고 있는데, ②번 문장은 재즈와 블루스, 재즈와 록 사이의 구별이 분명하지 않은 이유를 설명한 것이므로 글의 흐름과 관계가 없다.

해석　미국 음악은 세계 각처에서 온 음악과 서로 얽혀 있어서, '미국 음악'이 무엇인가에 대해 확고한 선을 긋는 것은 가능하지도 않고 바람직하지도 않다. ① 재즈는 분명히 미국적인 것이라는 말이 있어 왔지만, 그것은 세계의 전역에서 온 음악에 영향을 받았다. ② 많은 예술가들은 그들 자신의 독특한 사운드를 만들어내기 위해 장르를 섞기 때문에 그런 문제에 대해서 재즈와 블루스, 또는 재즈와 록 사이의 구별은 분명하지 않다. ③ 전쟁과 박해를 피하려고 했든지 출세를 할 의도였든지 간에 미국으로 이주해 온 음악가들은 자신들의 고국과 문화의 영향을 함께 가지고 와서 미국 음악과 문화에도 역시 깊은 영향을 끼쳤다. ④ 에런 코플런드와 같은 작곡자들은 뚜렷하게 미국적인 음악을 만들려고 노력했으나, 그의 작품은 파리에서 나디아 불랑제와 함께 한 연구, 멕시코에서 작곡가 카를로스 차베스와 함께 작업하기 위한 여행 및 아프리카와 유럽으로의 여행, 그리고 재즈와 기타 음악 형식에 대한 관심에 의해 영향을 받았다. ⑤ 미국 음악은 창조된 것이 아니며 세계의 다른 지역으로부터 고립되어 존재하는 것도 아니다.

구문　[8행~13행] Musicians [who relocated to the United States, **whether** <u>escaping from war and persecution</u> **or** <u>attempting to advance their careers</u>], have also had a profound impact on American music and culture, / **bringing** with them the influences of their home countries and cultures.

• [ ] 부분은 주어 Musicians를 수식한다. 여기서 부사절로 쓰인 「whether A or B」 구문은 'A이든 B이든'의 뜻이다. bringing 이하는 동시 상황을 나타내는 분사구문이다.

어휘 **be intertwined with** ~와 얽혀 있다, 밀접한 관계가 있다 **desirable** 바람직한 **distinctly** 뚜렷하게 **fuzzy** 분명하지 않은 **relocate** 이주하다 **persecution** 박해 **advance one's career** 출세하다 **have an impact on** ~에 영향을 주다 **profound** 깊은, 심오한 **composer** 작곡가 **in isolation** 별개로; 홀로, 고립되어

4 글의 순서 ②

해설 주어진 문장은 두려움과 죄책감의 정서를 기반으로 캠페인이 제작되는 현실을 소개하고 있다. 그다음에 과연 이러한 캠페인이 효과가 있는지 의문을 제기하는 (B)가 나와야 한다. 그다음에는 그 의문을 뒷받침하는 내용으로서, 두려움으로 인해 바뀌고자 하는 욕망은 쉽사리 사라지는 경향이 있다는 (A)가 나와야 하고, 마지막으로 두려움이 또한 사람들로 하여금 오히려 현안에서 회피하게 하는 단점도 있다고 진술하는 (C)가 나와야 한다.

해석 많은 건강 교육 캠페인은 사람들이 두려움이나 죄책감을 통해 행동을 바꾸도록 고무하기 위해 노력해왔다. 크리스마스 때의 음주 운전 반대 캠페인은 도로 사고 희생자들의 가족에게 가해지는 파괴적인 영향을 묘사한다. 흡연 예방 포스터는 부모들이 그들의 자녀들에게 담배 피우는 방법을 가르치지 말 것을 촉구한다.
(B) 점점 이러한 직설적인 캠페인은 다른 데서도 과도한 음주, 흡연, 약물 사용의 결과에 대한 의식을 높이기 위해 사용된다. 그러한 캠페인이 흡연자들에게 충격을 주어 그들의 행동을 바꾸게 하는 데 효과적인지는 논쟁이 계속되는 주제이다.
(A) 비록 두려움으로 인해 부정적인 태도와 심지어는 바뀌려는 욕망이 고무될 수도 있지만, 그러한 느낌은 시간이 흐르면서 그리고 결정을 내려야 하는 진짜 상황에 직면했을 때 사라지는 경향이 있다.
(C) 몹시 두려운 상태로 인해 사람들이 그 메시지를 부인하고 회피하게 될 수도 있다. 보호 동기 이론에 의하면 두려움은 위협이 심각해 보이고 추천되는 충고를 따르지 않으면 일어날 것 같다고 여겨지는 경우에만 효과가 있음을 암시한다.

구문 [13행~15행] **Whether** such campaigns are effective at **shocking** *people* **into changing** their behavior / **is** the topic of ongoing debate.
• Whether가 주어절을 이끌며 동사는 is이다. 「shock O into v-ing」는 'O에게 충격을 주어 v하는 상태가 되게 하다'의 뜻이다.

[18행~20행] ~ fear only works if the threat **is seen as** serious 〔and〕 likely to occur if the person does not follow the recommended advice.
• 「be seen as」는 '~로 여겨지다'의 뜻이다. as 뒤에 형용사 serious와 likely가 병렬구조로 연결되어 있다.

어휘 **depict** 묘사하다 **devastating** 파괴적인 **urge** 촉구하다 **hard-hitting** 직설적인 **ongoing** 계속되는

5 문장 넣기 ⑤

해설 주어진 문장은 이전에 많이 연구가 되지 않은 주제와 관련된 문헌 자료를 찾는 것의 어려움에 관한 내용으로서 However가 이끌고 있다. ⑤ 이전까지는 문헌 자료가 풍부한 주제를 연구할 때 자료의 취사선택에 어려움이 있다는 내용이고, ⑤ 뒤는 자료가 부족하여 중심적 자료가 아닌 주변적 자료라도 사용해야 할지를 고려해야 하는 상황이 제시되므로 주어진 문장은 ⑤에 위치해야 한다.

해석 여러분이 문헌 조사를 시작할 때쯤이면, 여러분은 아마도 연구의 주요 주제와 또한 핵심 연구 목적을 이미 결정했을 것이다. 그러므로 필수적인 과업은 어느 정도 미리 결정되어 있다. 여러분은 이전에 상당히 많은 연구가 수행된 연구 주제를 선택했을지도 모른다. 그런 경우라면, 검토할 저작물이나 연구물을 찾는 것은 어렵지 않을 것이다. 사실, 주된 어려움은 여러분이 포함하고자 하는 것과 제외하고자 하는 것

을 고르는 데 있을 수 있다. 하지만, 여러분이 만약 거의 쓰이지 않은 상당히 드문 주제를 선택했다면, 검토할 충분한 자료를 찾는 것이 힘들 수도 있다. 여러분은 선택된 주제의 주변에 존재하는 것일 뿐인 자료에 대한 논의를 포함시키는 것을 고려해야 할지도 모른다.

구문 [1행~3행] However, if you have selected *a fairly uncommon subject* [**on which** little has been written], // then **it** may be difficult **to find sufficient material to review**.
• on which가 이끄는 [ ] 부분은 a fairly uncommon subject를 수식한다. it은 가주어이고 to find 이하는 진주어이다.

[8행~10행] You **may have selected** *a research topic or theme* [**around which** a great deal of research has been previously conducted].
• 「may have p.p.」는 '~했을지도 모른다'의 뜻이다. [ ] 부분은 '전치사+관계대명사' 형태인 around which가 이끄는 관계사절로 a research topic or theme을 수식한다.

어휘 **literature** 문학; (특정 분야의) 문헌, 인쇄물 **objective** 목적, 목표; 객관적인 **to some extent** 어느 정도, 얼마간 **predetermine** 미리 결정하다 **previously** 이전에, 미리 **conduct** 수행하다 **exclude** 제외하다, 배제하다

1 글의 제목   ②

해설 이 글은 네덜란드어에서 일본어로 바뀔 때 그 변화를 아기들이 알아차렸다는 내용이므로 글의 제목으로는 ② '아기들은 언어를 구별할 수 있다'가 가장 적절하다.
① 보편 문법에 대한 증거
③ 유창하게 거꾸로 말하는 방법
④ 언어 습득의 비밀
⑤ 무엇이 언어를 언어로 만드는가?

해석 프랑스의 인지 학자 프랑크 라무스는 불어를 말하는 가정에서 자라는 유아들이 스피커를 통해서 듣는 다른 언어를 구별할 수 있다는 것을 발견했다. 라무스는 아기들이 고무젖꼭지를 빠는 속도를 그들의 관심 수준의 증거로 사용했다. 그는 아기들이 네덜란드어로 말해지는 문장을 들은 뒤에, 스피커의 소리가 일본어로 바뀔 때 언어의 변화가 일어났다는 것을 알아차리는 것을 발견했다. 하지만 아주 놀라운 발견은 아기들이 녹음이 거꾸로 재생될 때는 이런 구별을 하지 못했다는 것이다. 다시 말해서, 아기들은 거꾸로 재생되는 문장에는 없는 어떤 언어적인 특성을 이해했고, 그에 따라 두 언어의 차이를 판단하였다.

구문 [1행~4행] French cognitive scientist Franck Ramus **discovered** // **that** *human infants* (raised in French-speaking households) / could distinguish *other languages* [(which[that]) they heard over a loudspeaker].
• that 이하는 동사 discovered의 목적어 역할을 하는 명사절이다. ( ) 부분은 과거분사 raised가 이끄는 형용사구로 human infants를 수식하고 있다. [ ] 부분은 목적격 관계대명사 which[that]가 생략된 관계사절로 other languages를 수식하고 있다.

어휘 cognitive 인식의, 인지의 infant 유아 distinguish 구별하다; 차이를 보이다 loudspeaker 스피커, 확성기 rate 속도; 비율; 요금 suck 빨다 pacifier 고무젖꼭지 evidence 증거(= proof) Dutch 네덜란드어; 네덜란드인 recognize 알다; 인정하다 startling 아주 놀라운, 깜짝 놀랄 만한 distinction 구별, 구분; 차이 cf. make a distinction 구별[구분]하다; 차별하다 backward 거꾸로(의), 뒤로 property 특성; 재산 lack 없다[부족하다]; 부족, 결핍 accordingly 그에 따라
[선택지] universal 보편적인; 일반적인 tell A apart A를 구별하다, 분간하다 fluently 유창하게 acquisition 습득, 획득

2 밑줄 어휘   ⑤

해설 생각에서의 결함이 의학적 실수의 주요 원인이며 그 예로 항생제의 남용 사례를 제시하고 있다. 바이러스성 감염에는 항생제가 소용이 없다고 했으므로, 항생제는 바이러스성 감염을 극복하도록 도움을 주는 데 '효과가 없다'는 문맥이 적절하다. 따라서 ⑤ effective를 ineffective로 바꿔야 한다.

해석 의학적 실수 중 대다수는 기술적이거나 실행 상의 결함이라기보다 생각에서의 결함이다. 체크리스트와 구조화된 의사 결정 모델의 충분한 사용으로 의료 행위는 대개 ① 높은 정확성을 갖고 실행된다. 하지만 의사가 발현 증상을 놓치거나 대립 가설을 배제하지 않는다면(다른 질병일 가능성이 없다는 것을 밝히지 않는다면), 그 치료는 환자의 실제 필요를 ② 충족시키지 않을 것이며 결과는 바라던 것이 아닐 것이다. 이것의 전형적인 예는 항생제의 ③ 남용이다. 항생제는 박테리아성 감염을 치료하는 데 효과적일 수 있지만, 바이러스성 감염에는 소용이 없다. 축농증의 원인이 바이러스성인지 박테리아성인지를 결정하는 데 도움이 되는 검사가 분명 있다. 하지만 그 검사가 비용이 많이 들고 결과를 얻는 데 시간이 걸리기 때문에 많은 의사들이 그러한 검사를 ④ 건너뛰고 박테리아성 감염이라고 가정하고 항생제를 처방하곤 했다. 항생제는 바이러스성 감염을 이겨내도록 도움을 주는 데 ⑤ 효과가 있을 (→ 효과가 없을) 뿐만 아니라, 한때는 유용한 약물이었던 것에 대해 내성이 생긴 박테리아 종류의 수가 증가하게 되는 의도치 않은 결과를 가져온다.

구문 [12행~14행] There are certainly tests to help determine **whether** the source of a sinus infection is viral **or** bacterial.
• 「whether A or B」 구문은 'A이든 B이든'을 뜻한다.

[14행~17행] However, because the tests are costly |and| take time to produce results, // many physicians **used to skip** those tests, **(to)** assume a bacterial infection, |and| **(to)** prescribe antibiotics.
• are costly와 take ~ results가 and로 연결되어 부사절의 주어 the tests의 술어 역할을 한다. 「used to-v」는 'v하곤 했다'의 의미이며, 세 개의 부정사 to skip, (to) assume, (to) prescribe가 콤마(,)와 and로 연결되어 병렬구조를 이루고 있다.

어휘 flaw 결함 ample 충분한 procedure 조치 precision 정확성 physician 의사 presenting symptom 발현 증상 rule out ~을 배제하다 alternate hypothesis 대립 가설 antibiotic 항생제 bacterial 박테리아의 infection 감염(병) assume 가정하다, 추정하다 resistant 내성이 있는 medication 약물

3 빈칸 추론   ⑤

해설 이전보다 더 나은 과제를 수행한 학생에게 쉽게 칭찬을 해서는 안 되는데 그것은 학생에 대한 교사의 기대 수준이 낮다는 메시지를 전달할 수 있기 때문이다. 따라서 칭찬은 학생의 ⑤ '향상을 요하는 것이 수반되어야' 한다는 것을 알 수 있다.
① 사람들이 있는 데서 직접 이루어져야
② 구체적이기보다는 일반적이어야
③ 가능한 한 즉시 표현되어야
④ 그 사람의 행동이나 행위에 집중되어야

해석 평소에 과제를 다 끝내지 못하는 학생이 있다고 가정해 보자. 그는 과제를 아주 잘 한 것은 아니라도 시간에 맞춰 제출하는 데 성공한다. 어쨌든 그 학생이 뭔가 제출했다는 사실은 과거의 수행에 비하면 향상된 것이어서 그 학생을 칭찬하고 싶은 마음이 들 것이다. 하지만 평범한 과제를 칭찬하는 것이 보내는 메시지를 생각해 보라. "잘했다"라고 말을 하지만 그 말은 사실 "너 같은 학생으로서는 잘했다"라는 의미가 된다. 그 학생은 아마 자기 과제가 정말 그토록 대단하다고 여길 만큼 그렇게 순진무구하지는 않을 것이다. 수준에 미치지 못하는 과제를 칭찬해서 여러분은 이 학생에 대한 기대 수준이 낮다는 메시지를 전한다. 여러분의 칭찬이 효과를 보기 원한다면, 당신의 칭찬은 향상을 요하는 것이 수반되어야 한다. "시간에 맞춰 과제를 끝마친 것도 잘했고 첫 단락이 흥미롭다고 생각하지만 더 짜임새 있게 할 수도 있었다고 생각한다. 어떻게 하면 될지 이야기해 보자."라고 말하는 편이 더 낫다.

구문 [8행~10행] The student is probably not **so** *naive* **as to think** that his project is really all that great.
• 「so ~ as to-v」는 '너무 ~하여 v하다', '~할 정도로 v하다'의 의미이다.

[10행~12행] By praising substandard work, you send the message that you have lower expectations for this student.
• that 이하는 the message에 대한 동격절이다.

어휘 manage to-v 가까스로 v하다 submit 제출하다 tempting 유혹적인 substandard 수준 이하의 compliment 칭찬 take effect 효과를 보다

organize 조직하다

[선택지] in person 직접, 몸소

4 무관 문장　　　　　　　　　　　　　　④

해설　전체적인 글의 내용은 노화 속도의 통제가 가능해지고 수명을 연장시킬 수 있게 될 것이라는 내용이다. ④는 의료비 지출 증가의 원인에 대한 내용이므로 전체 글의 흐름과 맞지 않다.

해석　노화는 죽음이 그러하듯 보편적이다. 하지만 당신이 얼마나 빨리 늙는가 하는 것은 보편적이지 않다. 그리고 당신 자신의 개인 수명 또한 그렇지 않다. ① 당신이 늙는 속도와 이 세상에서 보내는 시간 둘 다 당신이 꿈꿔왔던 것, 그리고 과학자들이 최근까지 상상했던 것보다 더 많이 통제 가능하다. ② 노화와 관련 질병에 대한 폭발적으로 증가하는 연구는 이제 일부 놀라운 전망을 만들어 내고 있다. ③ 최근의 발견은 과학자들과 우리에게 매우 놀라운 일인데, 그 이유는 과학자들이 훨씬 더 가까운 거리에서 삶과 죽음의 궁극적인 생물학적 미스터리를 목격하면서 이전에 한 번도 탐구해 본 적이 없는 영역으로 들어서기 때문이다. ④ 노령 인구가 국가 보건비 지출에서의 연간 증가의 주된 요인인 것은 아닌데, 이 증가는 주로 늘어난 소득과 값비싼 신(新)의료 기술 때문이다. ⑤ 이러한 새로운 연구는 인류 역사에서 처음으로 우리의 수명을 연장시키고 노화에 대한 두려움을 극복할 방법을 약속한다.

구문　[1행] Aging is universal, **as is death**.

• as is death를 풀어 쓰면 as death is universal이다. as가 '~다시피, ~듯이'라는 뜻의 접속사로 쓰일 때, as가 이끄는 절에서는 주절과 동일한 술어 부분을 생략하고 주어와 동사를 도치시킬 수 있다.

어휘　lifespan 수명　prospect (어떤 일이 있을) 가능성; 예상; 전망　**astonishing** 정말 놀라운, 믿기 힘든　**territory** 지역, 영토; 영역

5 요약문 완성　　　　　　　　　　　　　②

해설　물건이 얼마나 주변에 흔하고 쉽게 접할 수 있는(accessible)지가 사람들이 그 물건에 대해 가지는 수요를 증가시키는 경향이 있는데, 이는 우리의 식품 취향에도 영향을 끼쳐서 사람들은 그 식품의 유익함(wholesomeness)에 개의치 않고 흔히 접할 수 있는 식품을 소비하게 될 것이라는 내용이다.

해석　우리가 상품을 전혀 찾을 수 없다면, 우리는 그것을 사용할 수 없다. 그리고 상품이 어디에서나 쉽게 닿을 수 있는 범위 내에 있다면, 우리는 그것을 훨씬 더 사용할 가능성이 높아질 뿐만 아니라 우리가 이미 그것을 사용하고 있다면 그것을 더 자주 사용하는 경향이 생기게 된다. 공급은 수요를 충족시키기만 하는 것은 아니다. 공급은 수요를 자극한다. 그것이 자극하는 수요는 '충동적 수요'일지 모르지만, 그것은 판매 (그리고 소비)를 의미한다. 그것은 공급이 수요를 결정한다고 말하는 것은 아니다. 사람들이 널리 이용 가능한 상품을 소비할 필요는 없다. 누구도 우리를 묶어 놓고 간식을 우리의 목구멍으로 밀어 넣지 않는다. 그러나 제품이 기본적인 생물학적 필요를 채워주거나 다른 식으로 유혹적일 때 우리는 그것이 우리에게 좋다고 믿든 그렇지 않든 그것을 움켜쥐도록 유도될 수 있다. 우리가 우리의 현대의 살인자들에게 굴복하느냐 아니냐가 우리가 소비하는 품목들에 엄청난 정도로 달려 있기 때문에 이러한 영향은 우리의 건강에 너무나 중요하다.

> 어떤 소비재가 (A) 접근하기 쉬울수록 우리는 그것을 더 많이 사용한다는 사실은 우리가 음식의 (B) 유익함을 고려하지 않고 음식을 섭취하도록 만든다.

구문　[2행~4행] ~ **not only** are we more likely to use **it** at all, **but also** if we are already using **it** we tend to use **it** more often.

• 「not only A but also B」는 'A뿐만 아니라 B도'의 뜻이다. 부정어(not) 혹은 only가 문두에 위치하게 되면 '동사+주어' 어순으로 도치가 일어난다. 세 개의 it은 전부 앞 부분의 (the) product를 지칭한다.

[14행~16행] This effect matters so much to our health // because **whether or not we succumb to our modern killers** / **depends** to such a great extent on *the items* [(which[that]) we consume].

• because 절에서 whether ~ killers 부분이 주어이며 동사는 depends이다. [ ] 부분은 앞에 목적격 관계대명사 which[that]가 생략된 관계사절로 the items를 수식한다.

어휘　reach (닿을 수 있는) 거리, 범위　stimulate 자극하다　impulsive 충동적인　strap 끈으로 묶다　shove 아무렇게나 넣다　tempting 유혹하는　give in to ~에 굴복하다　extent 정도

[선택지] wholesomeness 유익함, 건전함

1 빈칸 추론 ④

해설 실험 결과, 두뇌에 인지적으로 부담을 주는 일을 하자 다이어트 중인 학생들이 두 배나 초콜릿케이크를 선택했다. 즉 인지적 부담이 ④ '신중한 선택을 방해하기'에 충분했던 것이다.
① 더 나은 배움으로 이어지기
② 의지력을 상승시키기
③ 더 많은 인내심을 낳기
⑤ 설탕 먹은 것을 상쇄하기

해석 스탠포드 대학교수인 바바 시브의 연구는 우리의 의지력이 어떻게 작용하는지를 바로 설명한다. 그는 다이어트를 하고 있는 165명의 대학 재학생을 2개의 집단으로 나누고 그들에게 두 자리 숫자나 일곱 자리 숫자 중 하나를 암기하라고 요구했다. 두 과제 모두 보통 사람들의 인지 능력 안에 있는 것이었고, 그들은 필요한 만큼 시간을 쓸 수 있었다. 그들이 준비되었을 때 학생들은 그들이 숫자를 읊을 두 번째 방으로 갔다. 이동 중에 그들은 연구에 참여한 것에 대해 간식을 받았다. 초콜릿케이크와 한 그릇의 과일샐러드, 즉 죄의식을 동반한 즐거움과 건강에 좋은 간식이라는 두 가지 선택이 있었다. 여기 의외의 결말이 있었다. 일곱 자리 숫자를 암기하라고 요청을 받은 학생은 거의 두 배로 케이크를 선택하는 경향이 있었다. 이런 작은 인지적 부담은 신중한 선택을 방해하기에 충분했다. 그 결과의 의미는 경이로웠다. 즉, 의지력이라는 것은 쉽게 피곤해지고 휴식을 필요로 하는 근육과 같다.

구문 [12행~14행] Here's the kicker: students who had been given the seven-digit number were nearly **twice as likely to choose cake** (as those who had been given a two-digit number).
• 「배수사＋as＋형용사＋as」 구문으로 twice as likely to choose cake 다음에는 as those who had been given a two-digit number가 생략된 것으로 보면 이해하기가 쉽다.

어휘 **willpower** 의지력, 정신력 **undergraduate** 대학 재학생, 대학생 **digit** 한 자리 숫자 **cognitive** 인식[인지]의 **recite** 읊다, 암송하다 **guilty** 죄의식의 **kicker** 의외의 결말 **load** 짐, 부담 **implication** 영향, 결과; 함축, 암시 **staggering** 경이적인, 어마어마한
[선택지] **endurance** 인내력, 참을성 **prudent** 신중한 **offset** 상쇄하다

2 글의 순서 ②

해설 주어진 문장은 우리가 일반적으로 정의를 법과 절차에 의해 보장받는 기회의 평등이 보장되는 것으로 생각하는 내용이다. 그 뒤에는 역접의 연결사 But을 사용하여 주어진 문장 즉, 우리가 일반적으로 정의에 대해 생각하는 것(this way of thinking about justice)에 대한 한계점을 제시하는 (B)가 와야 한다. 그다음에는 연결사 Thus를 사용하여 (B)에 대한 결과로 재화 분배의 결과가 불평등하게 나타날 수 있다는 (A)가 나와야 한다. (C)는 (B)에서 설명한 재화 분배의 불평등한 결과에 대해 연결사 But을 사용하여 사회적 약자에게 기회의 평등이 돌아가지 않는 문제점을 언급하므로 마지막에 와야 한다.

해석 우리의 전통은 우리가 정의를 모든 개인이 자신이 원하는 것이면 무엇이나 추구할 동등한 기회의 문제로 생각하도록 부추긴다. 동등한 기회는 공정한 법과 정치적 절차, 즉 모든 사람에게 같은 방식으로 적용되는 법과 절차에 의하여 보장된다. (B) 그러나 정의에 대한 이러한 사고방식은 본질적으로, 개인이 꿈을 추구할 동등한 기회를 가진다면 사회에서의 재화의 분배가 결국 어떤 모습이 될지에 대한 비전을 제시해주지 못한다. (A) 따라서 모든 사람이 보수가 좋은 일자리를 얻을 동등한 기회가 있는 어떤 공정한 사회에서 다른 직업의 사람들에게 주어지는 임금에서 큰 차이가 있을 수 있다. (C) 그러나 현재 고통스럽게 명백해지고 있는 것처럼 흥미로운 직업에서의 빈자리보다 더 많은 자격 있는 지원자들이 존재한다면, 정의를 확실히 하는 데 평등한 기회가 충분한 것일까? 출발선에 한참 못 미치는 곳에 남겨졌기 때문에 공정한 경주의 기회를 얻을 수 없는 곳에 있는 사회적 약자들은 어떻게 되는가?

구문 [1행~3행] Our traditions encourage us to think of justice as an issue of *equal opportunities* for every individual (**to pursue whatever** he or she desires).
• ( ) 부분은 equal opportunities를 수식하며 밑줄 친 for every individual은 to pursue의 의미상 주어이다. 'whatever ~'는 '~한 것이면 무엇이든지'의 뜻이다.

[12행~14행] ~ what the distribution of goods in a society **would end up** looking like **if** individuals **had** an equal chance to pursue their dreams.
• 가정법 과거 문장으로 「if+S'+과거동사 ~, S+would+동사원형 ... (~한다면 …할 것이다)」의 형태와 의미를 가진다.

어휘 **guarantee** 보장하다 **so long as** ~하는 동안은, ~하는 한은, ~하기만 하면 **in itself** 그 자체로, 본질적으로 **distribution** 분배 **end up v-ing** 결국 v하게 되다 **apparent** 명백한 **qualified** 자격(증)이 있는 **applicant** 지원자 **opening** 빈자리 **sufficient** 충분한 **what of** ~은 어떻게 되는가 **socially disadvantaged** 사회적으로 취약한 **beyond reach** 손닿지 않는

3 문장 넣기 ④

해설 주어진 문장에 'this gap(이러한 차이)'과 '이름은 그런 똑같은 식별 기능을 갖지 못한다'라고 제시되었다. 그러므로, 주어진 문장 앞에는 'this gap'이라 할 만한 내용이 나와야 하고, 주어진 문장 이후로는 이름이 똑같은 식별 기능을 하지 못하는 것에 대한 보충 설명이 나와야 한다. ④ 앞에서 외국어 이름을 번역해서 소개하지 않으면 독자들에게 그 이름이 다르게 기능하리란 것이 'this gap'에 해당하며, ④ 뒤부터는 어느 축구 선수의 이름이 사람에 따라 달리 인식되는, 즉 이름이 똑같은 식별 기능을 하지 못하는 예시가 제시되고 있으므로 주어진 문장은 ④에 위치해야 한다.

해석 번역가는 흔히 외국어로 된 이름을 바꾸지 않은 채로 남겨두는데, 이렇게 번역되지 않은 것은 번역본의 독자에게 생경함을 만드는 영향을 미칠 수 있다. 이는 때로 독자가 등장인물들과 동질감을 갖기 어렵게 만든다. 더욱이 읽기가 너무 어려운 원래의 이름은 독서의 순전한 즐거움을 망칠 수 있다. 잘 알려진 사람의 이름이 번역되지 않은 채 남아있는 경우, 번역본의 독자가 그 이름이 지칭하고 있는 사람을 잘 모른다면 그 이름은 다르게 기능할 것이다. 이러한 차이를 메우는 데 맥락이 이용될 수 있지만, 그 이름은 똑같은 식별 기능을 갖지 못한다. 노르웨이 작가 Kjersti Wold의 작품으로서 네덜란드어 번역물인 Juist en Tweemeter에서는 등장인물 Ole Gunnar Solskjaer가 축구 선수라는 사실이 맥락을 통해 번역본의 독자에게 명확해진다. 그런데도 번역은 다른 감정적 영향을 주는 경향이 있는데, 이는 네덜란드어를 말하는 어린이 중 Solskjaer라는 이름과 국민 영웅의 이름을 관련지어 생각하는 어린이들은 거의 없을 것이기 때문이다.

구문 [6행~7행] This sometimes makes **it difficult** *for the reader* **to identify with the characters**.
• it은 가목적어이고 to identify 이하가 진목적어이며, for the reader는 to부정사의 의미상 주어이다. 형용사 difficult는 목적어에 대한 보어이다.

[15행~17행] ~, the context makes **it** clear to the reader of the translation **that the character Ole Gunnar Solskjaer is a football player**.

• it은 가목적어이고 that 이하가 진목적어이다.

어휘 identify 확인하다, 식별하다 **partially** 부분적으로 **bridge** 다리를 놓다, (틈을) 메우다 **translator** 번역가 *cf.* translation 번역[본] **identify with** ~와 동일시하다[동질감을 갖다] **spoil** 망치다 **mere** 단순한, 순전한 **refer to** ~을 언급하다

어휘 psychologist 심리학자 **reasonable** 합리적인, 이성적인 **theory** 이론; 학설 **perceive** 인식[인지]하다 **manipulative** 속임수의; 조작하는 **conduct** 수행(하다); 행동(하다) **experiment** 실험; 실험하다 *cf.* experimenter 실험자 **subject** 실험 대상자; 주제; 대상 **yield to** ~에 따르다[응하다] **deed** 행동, 행위 **seemingly** 겉으로 보기에는, 외견상으로 **unrelated** 관련[관계]이 없는 **encounter** 만남; 맞닥뜨리다 **patron** 손님; 후원자; 홍보대사 **dime** 10센트 동전 **unwitting** 의식하지 못하는; 모르는 **a stack of** 한 더미의

[선택지] incident 사건, 일 **valid** 타당한; 정당한; 유효한 **willingness** 기꺼이 하는 마음

4~5 장문   4 ① 5 ④

해설 **4.** 이 글은 기분이 좋은 상태에서 남을 기꺼이 도와주려 한다는 것을 밝혀낸 실험에 대한 내용이므로 글의 제목으로는 ① '기분이 도움을 주는 것에 영향을 끼치는가?'가 가장 적절하다.
② 인생에서의 사건의 역할
③ 인정받는 느낌은 어떤 것인가?
④ 실험은 믿을 수 있을 만큼 충분히 타당한가?
⑤ 돈이 있는 곳에 기꺼이 하는 마음이 있다
5. 실험자들이 10센트 동전을 이용하여 앞선 도서관에서 알아낸 것을 똑같이 하려고 했으므로, ④는 replicate 등이 되어야 한다.

해석 일부 심리학자는 만약 당신이 기분이 좋고, 어떤 사람이 무엇인가를 해 달라고 부탁하면, 당신은 그 부탁하는 사람이 진짜 도움이 필요하다고 생각하는 경향이 있다고 믿는다. 호의를 베푸는 것이 (a) 합리적인 것처럼 보인다. 반대로, 그 이론은 만약 당신이 화가 났을 때는 당신은 부탁을 하는 사람이 속이는 것이라고 인식한다고 말한다. 산드라 밀베리 박사와 마가렛 클라크 박사는 실험 대상자들이 행복하면 행복할수록, 그들은 다른 사람이 바라는 것에 (b) 따를 가능성이 높다는 것을 밝혀낸 실험을 수행했다.

다른 연구에서, 앨리스 아이센과 폴 레빈은 우리가 다른 사람에게 선행을 더 기꺼이 베풀려고 하는지를 알아보기 위해서 우리를 좀 더 행복하게 만들었다. 앨리스와 폴은 도서관을 선정했다. 그들 중의 한 명이 도서관을 방문한 사람들 중 일부에게 쿠키를 무작위로 나누어 주었다. 나중에, 겉으로 보기에는 (c) 관련이 없는 것 같은 만남에서, 다른 연구가는 그 손님들에게 어떤 일을 도와달라고 부탁을 했다. 당신이 짐작했듯이, 쿠키를 받은 손님들이 더 기꺼이 도와주려 하였다.

그 후 실험자들은 공중전화 부스에 10센트 동전을 남겨 둠으로써 그들이 알아낸 것을 (d) 버리려고(→ 똑같이 하려고) 했다. 전화 사용자들 중 일부는 뜻하지 않게 약간의 (e) 이익을 얻게 되었지만, 다른 사람들은 아무것도 발견하지 못했다. 10센트 동전을 발견하든 아무것도 발견하지 못하든 간에 그 이후 즉시, 실험 대상자들은 서류 더미를 떨어뜨리는 사람을 보게 되었다. 10센트 동전을 발견한 사람들 중 상당히 많은 사람들이 서류를 줍는 것을 도와준 것으로 밝혀졌다. 만약 당신이 어떤 사람의 하루를 약간 더 밝게 만들 수 있다면, 여러분의 관대함이 여러분에게 그것에 대해서 보상을 해 줄 것이다.

구문 [6행~9행] Dr. Sandra Milbery and Margaret Clark / conducted *an experiment* [that found (that) **the happier** the subjects, / **the more** likely they were to yield to the wishes of another].

• [ ] 부분은 앞의 an experiment를 수식하며, found와 the happier 사이에 접속사 that이 생략되었다. 'the happier ~ the more ...'는 「the 비교급 ~, the 비교급 ...」 구문으로 '~하면 할수록, 더 …하다'의 의미이다.

[25행~26행] **It turns out** // **that** significantly more of *those* [who found the dime] / helped pick up the notes.

• 여기에서 It은 비인칭 주어로 「it turns out that ~」은 '~로 밝혀지다, ~임이 드러나다'의 뜻이다. [ ] 부분은 주격 관계대명사 who가 이끄는 관계사절로 those를 수식한다.

----

1 필자 주장　　　　　　　　　　⑤

해설 기억을 집중적으로 행하면 기억력이 향상될 수 있으며, 경험을 정기적으로 기록해보는 것이 기억력 향상의 첫걸음이 될 수 있다는 내용이다. 그러므로 필자의 주장으로 가장 적절한 것은 ⑤이다.

해석 기억은 빛과 같다. 집중되지 않으면 그것은 분산되고 흩어진다. 그러나 집중된 기억은 강력한 레이저 빔과 흡사하여, 당신의 기억에 대해 당신의 정신 속에서 무심코 만들었을지도 모르는 장벽과 제약을 가로질러 갈 수 있다. 내가 오랫동안 "난 항상 이름을 잊어버려" 혹은 저 보편적인 인기 어구인 "여보, 내 자동차 키 봤어요?"와 같은 부정적인 어구로 내 기억을 방해했기 때문에 안다. 그러한 집중된 기억으로 가는 당신의 여정에서의 첫걸음은 종잇조각이나 컴퓨터 스크린에서 시작된다. 기억하는 방법을 학습하는 최고의 방법은 규칙적으로 당신의 경험을 적어보는 것이다. 하루의 끝 무렵에 앉아서 당신의 경험들에 대해 조금이라도 적어볼 때, 당신은 정신적으로 그날을 재건하고 있다. 당신이 이 일을 처음 할 때, 그날의 일부는 놀랍도록 또렷할 것이다.

구문 [2행~5행] But a focused memory, ~ , can cut through *the barriers and limitations* [(which[that]) you **may have** inadvertently **created** in your mind about your memory].

• [ ]은 앞에 목적격 관계대명사 which[that]가 생략되어 the barriers and limitations를 수식한다. 「may have p.p.」는 '~했을지도 모른다'의 뜻이다.

[8행~10행] **The first step** in your journey to that focused memory **begins either** on a piece of paper **or** on your computer screen.

• 주어는 The first step이고 동사는 begins이다. 「either A or B」는 'A나 B 둘 중 하나'의 뜻이다.

어휘 diffuse 분산시키다　scatter 뿌리다　beam 빛줄기　cut through ~을 가로질러 가다　barrier 장벽　limitation 제한　inadvertently 무심코　sabotage (고의로) 방해하다　universal 보편적인　on a regular basis 정기적[규칙적]으로　reconstruct 재건하다　startlingly 놀랄 만큼

2 밑줄 함의　　　　　　　　　　⑤

해설 의사소통이나 이동 등과 관련하여 현대인의 능력에 비해 고대의 신들이 더 무능하다는 것이 글의 요지이다. 창조주 Chukwu가 무능해서 인간의 죽음이 영구적인 것이 되었다는 나이지리아 신화가 이를 뒷받침하는 사례로 제시되었으므로 밑줄 친 부분이 의미하는 것은 ⑤ '고대 신의 무능 때문에, 우리 인간은 반드시 죽는다.'이다.
① 고대의 신들은 조화롭게 사는 것에 형편없었다.
② 개와 양 모두 이보 신화에서 사라진다.
③ 그 메시지는 인간에 의해 왜곡되었을 것이다.
④ 의사소통 능력은 점점 더 중요해지고 있다.

해석 수천 년 동안 신성하다고 여겨졌던 특정한 능력들은 오늘날 너무나 평범해져서 현대를 살아가는 사람들은 그것들에 대해 거의 생각하지 않는다. 보통 사람은 이제 고대 그리스, 힌두, 또는 아프리카의 신보다 훨씬 더 쉽게 거리를 가로질러서 이동하고 의사소통한다. 예를 들어, 나이지리아의 이보족은 창조주 Chukwu가 처음에 사람들을 불멸의 존재로 만들고 싶어 했다고 믿는다. Chukwu는 누군가 사망하면, 시신 위에 재를 뿌려야 하고, 그러면 그 시신은 다시 살아날 것이라고 인간에게 말하기 위해 개를 보냈다. 불행히도, 개는 지쳐서 가는 도중에 꾸물거렸다. 그러자 참

을성이 없는 Chukwu는 이 중요한 메시지를 서둘러 처리하라고 말하면서 양을 보냈다. 아, 숨을 가쁘게 내쉬며 목적지에 도착했을 때, 양은 지시사항을 혼동해서, 사람들에게 시신을 묻으라고 말했고, 이렇게 하여 죽음을 영구적인 것으로 만들었다. Chukwu가 SNS 계정을 가지고 있었다면 좋았을 텐데!

구문 [1행~3행] *Certain abilities* [that were considered divine for many millennia] have today become **so** commonplace **that** people (living in modern times) hardly think about them.

• [ ]는 Certain abilities를 수식하는 관계사절이다. '너무 ~해서 …하다'라는 뜻의 「so ~ that ...」 구문이 사용되었다. ( )는 people을 수식하는 현재분사구이다.

어휘 divine 신성한　millennium 천년 ((복수형 millennia))　commonplace 평범한, 흔한　initially 처음에　immortal 불멸의, 죽지 않는 (↔ mortal 언젠가는 반드시 죽는)　sprinkle 뿌리다　corpse 시체　linger 꾸물거리다　make haste 서두르다　destination 목적지　permanent 영구적인 (↔ temporary 일시적인)
[선택지] ancient 고대의　distort 왜곡하다　significant 중요한; 의미 있는　incompetence 무능

3 빈칸 추론　　　　　　　　　　③

해설 학생에 대한 개인 지도 교사의 이해가 어떠해야 하는지를 찾아야 한다. 이어지는 내용을 보면 어떤 학생도 받아들이고 함께 하도록 열려있어야 한다고 하였으며, 이것이 어렵지만 아무런 예견 없이 개인 지도에 착수하려고 노력하도록 권고된다고 하였다. 그러므로 정답은 ③ '백지상태여야 한다'가 적절하다.
① 현실과 맞지 않는다
② 관찰로 이루어질 수 있다
④ 잘못된 해석에 근거한다
⑤ 자신의 아이디어여야 한다

해석 각각의 아이는 독특하다. 그들은 다른 배경, 다른 강점, 그리고 다른 약점을 가지고 있다. 어떤 아이들은 개인 교습을 받는 것에 대해 신이 날 수도 있는 한편, 다른 아이들은 못 미더워할 수도 있다. 학생에 대한 개인 지도 교사의 이해는 백지상태여야 한다. 개인 지도 교사는 그들에게 배정된 어떤 학생도 받아들이고 함께 하도록 열려있어야 한다. 이는 매우 어려울 수 있는데 우리의 기대는 우리의 가치 체계, (가정) 교육, 과거 경험에 의해 결정되며 다른 사람들의 것과 상당히 다를 수 있기 때문이다. 이러한 기대는 개인 교습을 받는 학생들의 행동과 같은 다른 사람들의 행동과 충돌할 때 좌절감의 주요 원천이 될 수 있다. 그러므로 아무런 기대 없이 개인 지도에 다가가려 노력하도록 권고된다. 물론 이것은 미래의 학생과 그들의 성격, 학업 능력이나 향상, 그들의 동기 부여와 당신을 향한 태도에 대해 당신이 가질 수 있는 기대를 포기하는 것을 포함한다.

구문 [14행~17행] This, of course, includes giving up *expectations* [(which[that]) you may have of your future students and their personalities, their academic skills or progress, and their motivation and attitude toward you].

• [ ] 부분은 앞에 목적격 관계대명사 which[that]이 생략되어 앞의 expectations를 수식한다.

어휘 tutor 개인 지도 교사; 개인 교습을 하다 *cf.* tutee 개인 교습을 받는 학생　suspicious 의심하는, 못 미더워하는　assign 맡기다, 배정하다; (사람을) 배치하다　upbringing 양육, (가정) 교육　vastly 대단히, 엄청나게　motivation 자극; 동기 부여
[선택지] at odds with ~와 다투어, 불화하여; ~와 조화하지 못하는

4 글의 순서 ②

해설 죽음의 두려움이 종교적 믿음으로 증가된다는 언급 뒤에 에피쿠로스가 이 두려움에 대해 어떻게 설명하려 했는가의 내용인 (B)가 오고, 그것을 설명하기 위해 우주가 원자로 이루어졌다는 추론을 한다는 내용의 (A), 마지막으로 이런 원자가 죽으면 소멸되어 아무런 고통도 느낄 수 없으므로 죽음에 대한 두려움은 어리석다는 내용의 (C)가 오면서 결론을 이끌고 있다.

해석 고요한 마음의 평안을 향유하는 것에 대한 방해 중 하나는 에피쿠로스에 따르자면 죽음에 대한 두려움이며, 이러한 두려움은 우리가 사후에 심한 처벌을 받을 것이라는 종교적 믿음으로 증가된다.
(B) 그러나 대안으로 불멸의 상태를 제안하여 이 두려움에 반박하는 대신에, 에피쿠로스는 죽음 자체의 성질에 대해 설명하려고 했다. 그는 우리가 죽을 때 우리의 의식(우리의 영혼)이 죽음의 순간에 존재하는 것을 멈추기 때문에 우리는 죽음에 대한 인식이 없다고 제시함으로써 시작한다.
(A) 이를 설명하기 위해, 에피쿠로스는 온 우주가 원자 아니면 텅 빈 공간으로 구성되어 있다는 가정에서 시작한다. 에피쿠로스는 그리고 나서 영혼이 몸과 함께 역동적으로 작동하기 때문에 영혼은 텅 빈 공간일 수 없고, 따라서 원자로 이루어져 있음이 틀림없다고 추론한다.
(C) 그는 영혼의 이러한 원자들이 몸 전체에 분포되어 있지만, 매우 부서지기 쉬워서 우리가 죽을 때에 소멸되며, 그래서 우리는 더 이상 정신적으로나 육체적으로나 어떤 것도 느낄 수 없게 되는 것으로 묘사한다. 당신이 죽을 때 아무것도 느낄 수 없다면, 당신이 아직 살아있는 동안 죽음에 대한 두려움이 당신에게 고통을 유발하게 하는 것은 어리석은 일이다.

구문 [17행~20행] He **describes** these atoms of the soul **as** being distributed around the body, [but] **as** being **so** fragile **that** they dissipate when we die, and so we are no longer capable of sensing anything, mentally or physically.
• 「describe A as B」는 'A를 B로 묘사하다'의 뜻이다. as being ~ the body와 as being so fragile 이하는 but으로 연결되어 병렬구조를 이루며, 여기서 「so ~ that …(너무 ~해서 …하다)」 구문이 쓰였다.

어휘 tranquil 고요한, 평온한   severely 심하게, 엄격하게   afterlife 사후 세계   operate 작동하다; 수술하다   dynamically 역동적으로   counter 반대; 반박하다   immortality 불멸   cease 중단되다, 끝나다   fragile 부서지기 쉬운, 연약한   dissipate 소멸되다; 흩뜨리다

5 문장 넣기 ②

해설 ② 앞부분은 이주를 한 후 새로운 식품 문화에 노출될 수 있다는 내용이며 주어진 문장은 비록 원래 갖고 있던 음식 풍습이 영양적으로 뛰어나도, 새로운 환경이 식습관 변화를 유도할 수 있다는 내용이다. ② 뒷부분에는 이주를 한 후에 영양적으로는 열등하지만 값은 싼 탄산음료나 사탕을 선택할 수도 있다는, 주어진 문장에 대한 예가 제시되어 있으므로 주어진 문장은 ②에 위치해야 한다.

해석 사람들이 이 나라에서 저 나라로 혹은 이 지역에서 저 지역으로 이동할 때, 그들의 경제적 지위가 변할지도 모른다. 그들은 새로운 식품과 새로운 음식 풍습에 노출될 것이다. 그들의 원래 음식 풍습이 영양적으로 충분했을지도 모르지만, 그들의 새로운 환경은 그들로 하여금 그들의 식습관을 바꾸도록 유도할지도 모른다. 예를 들어 우유가 이사 전에 그들 식단에서 주식이었는데 새로운 환경에서는 대단히 비싸다면, 탄산음료, 커피, 혹은 차와 같은 더 저렴하고 영양적으로 열등한 음료를 위해 우유는 포기될지도 모른다. 사탕이 그들의 이전 환경에서는 사치였을지도 모르지만 그들의 새로운 환경에서는 비싸지 않고 널리 퍼져 있을지도 모른다. 결과적으로 한 가정이 탄산음료나 사탕의 소비를 증가시키고 영양이 더 풍부한 식품의 구매는 제한할지도 모른다. 식품의 영양가를 잘 모르는 사람은 쇼핑을 할 때 그러한 실수들을 쉽게 저지를 수 있다.

구문 [1행~3행] Although their original food customs **may have been** nutritionally adequate, // their new environment may lead them to alter their eating habits.
• 「may have p.p.」는 '~했을지도 모른다'의 의미이다.

어휘 nutritionally 영양적으로 cf. nutritious 영양분이 풍부한   alter 바꾸다   expose 노출시키다   prior to ~에 앞서   inferior 열등한   beverage 음료

1 글의 주제 ③

해설 소셜 네트워크 사용자의 보호를 위해 조직에서 소셜 네트워크 사용을 기술적으로 제한하는 전략을 취하고 있지만, 이러한 전략이 여러 이유로 인해 반드시 효과적인 것만은 아니라는 내용의 글이다. 그러므로 ③ '사용자 보호를 위한 소셜 네트워킹 사이트 통제의 부정적인 면'이 주제로 가장 적절하다.
① 공공장소에서의 소셜 미디어의 잠재적 긍정적인 효과
② 특정 상황에서 소셜 미디어를 금지하거나 제한하는 몇 가지 이유
④ 직장과 가정의 경계를 모호하게 하는 소셜 네트워킹
⑤ 특정 상황에서 소셜 네트워킹에 대한 접근을 제한할 필요성

해석 폭로나 사생활의 위협 또는 침해로부터 소셜 네트워크 사용자들을 보호하기 위해 기술이 사용될 수 있는 방법은 여러 가지가 있다. 더 철저한 기술적 해결책에는 소셜 미디어/소셜 네트워킹을 작동하지 않게 하거나 사용을 금지하는 것이 포함된다. 예를 들어, 일부 학교와 직장은 소셜 네트워킹 사이트에 대한 명백한 제한을 두거나, 어떤 경우에는 완전한 금지를 시행하고, 학생 및 직원들이 이러한 사이트에 접근하지 못하도록 그것들(소셜 네트워크)을 정보 통신 기술 차원에서 사용할 수 없게 만든다. 이런 해결책이 가진 문제는 이런 사이트를 이용하는 이점 또한 없어진다는 것이다. 게다가, 이렇게 하면 학교에 있는 동안이나 근무 시간 동안에는 이러한 사이트의 사용을 막을 수는 있지만, 수업이나 일하는 시간 후에 이루어지는 일들에는 아무런 영향을 주지 못한다. 온라인 환경에서 발생하는 맥락의 붕괴는 학교 시간이나 근무 시간 외에 발생한 온라인 정보 교환이 사람들의 학교생활이나 직장 생활에 영향을 줄 정도로 사람들의 직장 생활과 사생활 간 경계를 모호하게 한다. 그러므로 이러한 전략을 사용하는 것이 잠재적 위험을 전반적으로 최소화하는 데 반드시 효과적이지는 않다.

구문 [1행~3행] There are *a number of ways* [in which technology can be used to **protect** social network users **from** disclosure or privacy threats or violations].

• [ ] 부분은 '전치사+관계대명사' 형태의 in which가 이끄는 관계사절로 a number of ways를 수식한다. 「protect A from B」는 'A를 B로부터 보호하다'의 의미이다.

[13행~17행] *The context collapse* [that occurs in an online environment] **blurs** *the line* (**between** people's professional **and** personal lives) **such that** *online information exchanges* [that occur outside of school or work hours] impact people's lives at school or work.

• 첫 번째 [ ] 부분은 주어 The context collapse를 수식하는 관계사절로 동사는 blurs이다 ( ) 부분은 「between A and B」가 쓰인 전명구로 the line을 수식하고 밑줄 친 두 명사구가 A, B에 해당한다. such that은 '~할 정도로'의 의미이다. 두 번째 [ ] 부분은 선행사 online information exchanges를 수식하는 관계사절이다.

어휘 **disclosure** 폭로; 밝혀진 사실   **violation** 침해, 위반   **disable** 사용하지 못하게 만들다; 무력하게 하다   **ban** 금지(하다)   **explicit** 명백한; 솔직한   **restriction** 제한   **after hours** 수업[근무] 시간 후에   **context collapse** 맥락의 붕괴 ((소셜 미디어상에서 어떤 게시물이나 정보를 불특정 다수가 봄으로써, 인간관계나 규범의 경계가 허물어지는 현상))   **blur** 모호하게[흐리게] 하다   **overall** 전반적으로, 전체에 걸친

[선택지] **restrict** 제한하다; 금지하다   **downside** 부정적인[불리한] 면

2 밑줄 어법 ④

해설 ④ 원급 표현 「as+원급+as ~」 구문인데 앞의 동사구 could be bought를 수식하는 부사가 와야 하므로 easily로 바꿔야 한다.

① privatized and decontextualized의 목적어로서 명사절이 와야 할 자리고 뒤에 주어 없이 동사가 이어지는 불완전한 구조의 절이 왔으므로 선행사를 포함한 관계대명사 what이 적절히 쓰였다.
② 뒤의 주어 music을 받는 소유격 대명사 its가 이어지는 명사구 simplest level과 함께 쓰인 형태로 적절히 쓰였다. 대명사는 앞에서 나온 명사의 중복을 피하기 위해 뒤에서 쓰이는 것이 원칙이지만 주절에 선행하는 부사구, 부사절에서는 주절의 명사를 대명사가 미리 받을 수 있다.
③ 앞의 to enhance와 병렬구조를 이루는 원형부정사가 등위접속사 or 뒤에 적절하게 쓰였다. 병렬구조에서 접속사 뒤에 오는 to부정사의 to는 생략할 수 있다.
⑤ 구동사 called for의 목적어구를 이끄는 동명사가 적절히 쓰였다.

해석 축음기의 도입으로 인해 많은 변화가 일어났다. 녹음된 음악은 흔히 사교 행사였던 것을 사유화하고 탈맥락화했는데, 교회 음악이나 뱃노래를 이제는 아침에 옷을 입으면서 들을 수 있었고, 한편 베토벤의 음악은 '벽지'로 변형되었다. 가장 간단한 수준으로 음악은 '들렸지만' 연주자는 더 이상 '보이지' 않았다. 온갖 종류의 소리는 그래서 일종의 청각 배경으로서 일상생활 속에 통합될 수 있었지만, 관심이 집중된 대상으로서보다는 분위기를 향상시키거나 어떤 환경을 꾸미기 위한 경우가 더 많았다. 1913년에 클로드 드뷔시는 '사람이 한 잔의 맥주를 살 수 있는 것'만큼 쉽게 음반을 구매할 수 있다고 고민했다. 그리고 비꼬는 기미가 전혀 없이 '그라모폰'의 창간호(1923년)에서는 면도하면서 녹음된 음악을 들어 보라고 요구했다.

구문 [2행~3행] Recorded music privated [and] decontextualized **what had often been a soicial event** ~

• what had often been a soicial event는 privated와 docontextualized의 공통 목적어이다.

어휘 **phonograph** 축음기   **privatize** 사유화하다   **transform** 변형시키다   **integrate** 통합하다   **aural** 청각의   **enhance** 향상시키다   **hint** 기미, 기색   **irony** 비꼬기   **issue** (정기 간행물의) 호   **call for** ~을 요구하다

3 빈칸 추론 ③

해설 말하는 이의 눈이 커지는 것, 손동작, 몸의 흔들림 등을 듣는 사람이 주목하여 들어오는 정보를 분류하고 우선순위를 정한다고 했다. 그러므로 빈칸에는 ③ '이해할 동기를 증가시킴'이 들어가야 적절하다.
① 언어적 의미에 주목함
② 효과적인 의사소통 기술을 정의함
④ 의사소통에서 듣는 이의 중요한 역할을 함
⑤ 인간의 언어 능력의 기원을 이해함

해석 인쇄술의 발명 전에, 인간은 생각과 정보를 전달하는 별개의 수단을 갖고 있었다. 그것은 말하기라고 불렸다. 그것은 수백만 년에 걸쳐 서서히 발전했고, 단순히 단어들이 뇌에서 뇌로 전달되는 것보다 훨씬 더 많은 일들이 일어난다. 거기에는 억양, 어조, 강조, 열정이 있는데, 이것들을 각각은 듣는 이의 주의를 끌게 된다. 또한 듣는 이는 듣고 있는 것뿐만 아니라 바라보고 있다. 잠재의식적으로 듣는 이는 말하는 이의 눈이 커지는 것, 손의 동작, 몸의 흔들림, 다른 듣는 이의 반응에 주목한다. 말하는 이가 바르게 이것을 사용하면, 이 모든 것은 그것을 받아들이는 뇌가 들어오는 정보를 분류하고 우선순위를 정하는 방식에 긍정적으로 영향을 준다. 이해할 동기를 증가시킴으로써, 듣는 이의 지적 세계에 미치는 말하는 이의 지속적인 영향력은 인쇄물상의 같은 단어들보다 훨씬 더 클지도 모른다.

구문 [4행~5행] ~ and there is a lot **more** happening **than** just *the words* passing from brain to brain.

• 「more ~ than ...」의 비교 구문으로 happening과 passing이 비교되고 있다. the words는 동명사 passing의 의미상의 주어이다.

어휘 **printing** 인쇄술, 인쇄 **evolve** 서서히 발전하다, 진화하다 **tone** 어조, 말씨 **emphasis** 강세, 강조 **passion** 열정 **grab the attention of** ~의 관심을 끌다 **subconsciously** 잠재의식적으로 **note** 주목하다 **sway** 흔들리다 **correctly** 바르게, 정확하게 **employ** 쓰다, 사용하다 **prioritize** 우선순위를 정하다

4 무관 문장 ④

해설 인간관계에서 상대방에게 자신이 바라는 모습을 투사하지 말고 스스로가 변하려고 노력해야 한다는 내용의 글인데, ④는 사회가 기대한다고 생각하는 관계의 투사에 대한 내용이므로 글의 전체 흐름과 관련이 없다.

해석 "그가 자신이 생각하고 있는 것을 내게 말해 주면 좋을 텐데." 또는 "그녀가 그렇게 많이 비난하지 않으면 좋을 텐데."라고 말하고 있는 자신을 발견하면, 멈추고 자신에게 현실적이 되라고 일깨워라. ① 그런 관계에서 몇 가지 변화를 가져오고 싶으면, 이런 '좋을 텐데'를 치우고 사람들을 있는 그대로 받아들여야 한다. ② 일단 자신을 바꾸기 시작하면, 아마 상대방도 바꾸기 시작할 것이다. ③ 그런 다음에 여러분이 서로에게 맞추고 잘 지낼 수 있는지를 알 수 있게 될 것이다. ④ 당신이 다른 사람들과 갖는 관계는 사회가 기대한다고 당신이 느끼는 관계의 투사이다. ⑤ 변하려고 노력한 후에도 여전히 그 관계가 조금도 더 좋아지지 않음을 발견한다면, 그리고 상대방이 다르기를 여전히 계속 소망한다면, 그러면 그 관계를 끝내는 것이 더 좋을지 모른다.

구문 [8행~9행] Then you will be able to find out / **if** you can accommodate to each other and get on].

• 접속사 if는 '~인지'의 뜻으로서 find out의 목적어가 되는 명사절을 이끈다. if절에서 can 다음의 accommodate to each other와 get on이 and로 연결되어 병렬구조를 이룬다.

[11행~15행] **If** (after you have tried to change) you still find the relationship is no better, and you still keep wishing the other person were different, // then **it** might be better **to end the relationship**.

• 접속사 If가 이끄는 절은 you still find ~ no better와 you still keep ~ different가 and로 연결되어 병렬구조를 이룬다. ( )는 If절 속에 삽입된 절이다. then 다음의 it은 가주어이고 to end 이하가 진주어이다.

어휘 **if only** ~이면 좋을 텐데 **criticize** 비난하다, 비판하다 **bring about** ~을 초래하다, 야기하다 **accommodate to** ~에 적응하다 **projection** 투사, 투영

5 요약문 완성 ③

해설 스탠포드 대학에서 진행된 연구 결과를 통해 너무 많은 기술이 부정적인 면, 즉 주의 집중과 기억이 달라져서(altered) 이로 인해 학습이 어려워졌음(difficult)을 알 수 있다.

해석 우리는 학교 내 기술 시대에 공식적으로 접어들었다. 우리가 21세기로 좀 더 나아감에 따라 새로운 주제를 학생들에게 도입하고 있는 방식에 대해 면밀히 들여다볼 필요가 있다. 우리는 학생들을 장차 사회의 생산적인 구성원으로서 준비시키고 있는 것일지를 확실히 할 필요가 있다. 기술은 학생들의 학습을 동기 부여하는 멋진 방법이지만, 스탠포드 대학에서 진행된 한 연구에 의하면 너무 많은 기술을 도입하

는 것은 부정적인 면이 있음이 밝혀졌다. 학생들의 주의 지속 기간이 줄어들고 있는 것이다. 그들은 교실에서 좀 더 오랜 시간 집중하기가 어렵다는 것을 종종 깨닫는다. 그 연구는 학생들이 이전에는 학교에서 배운 정보를 저장하는 데 사용하던 뇌의 기억 부분을 다 써버리고 있다는 것도 밝혔다. 기술은 즉각적이라서 학생들에게 학습 또한 즉각적일 수 있다는 생각이 들게 하였다. 물론 이는 사실이 아닌데, 우리가 알고 있듯이 학습은 연습과 반복이 필요하기 때문이다.

> 연구에 따르면 학습은 학생들에게 점점 (A) 어려워지고 있으며, 기술 사용 증가로 인해 학생들의 주의 집중과 기억이 (B) 달라졌다.

구문 [6행~9행] Although technology is *a fantastic way* (to motivate students' learning), // *a study* was conducted at Stanford University [that revealed the negative side to introducing too much technology].

• ( ) 부분은 a fantastic way를 수식하는 형용사적 용법의 to부정사구이다. [ ] 부분은 주격 관계대명사 that이 이끄는 관계사절로 주어인 a study를 수식한다.

어휘 **era** 시대 **take a close look at** ~을 주의 깊게[세심히] 보다 **span** (어떤 일이 지속되는) 기간[시간] **prolonged** 오래 계속되는, 장기적인 **use up** ~을 다 쓰다
[선택지] **alter** 변하다, 달라지다; 바꾸다

1 빈칸 추론   ④

해설 전체 사회에서 어떤 변화가 발전이었는지 평가하는 것은 개인의 변화를 평가할 때와 유사한 어려움과 추가적인 어려움이 있다는 내용이고 For instance(예를 들어) 뒤의 내용은 그 어려움에 대한 구체적인 예에 해당한다. 변화를 평가한다는 것을 포괄적으로 기술하여 빈칸을 완성하면 ④ '변화가 개선이었는지 아니었는지' 말하는 것은 때때로 어렵다는 말이 된다.
① 자유가 평등보다 더 가치 있는지
② 개인이 사회보다 더 중요하다고
③ 폭력뿐만 아니라 행동하지 않는 것도 용서받지 못할 일이라고
⑤ 자주성이 건강한 인류 발전을 위해 필수적이라고

해석 변화가 개선이었는지 아니었는지 말하는 것은 때때로 어렵다. 가벼운 실패 후에 억지로 심사숙고하고 다시 시작해야 하는 사람에 대해 생각해 보자. 실패가 있은 직후의 동안에, 그 사람은 덜 만족스러워도 더 큰 자주성을 가지고 행동한다. 그 사람의 상태에 있어서의 변화를 평가하기 위해, 우리는 많은 사람들이 그것들이 그렇지 않다고 주장할지라도 만족함의 값과 자주성을 지니게 됨의 값을 같은 단위로 잴 수 있는 것으로 다루어야 한다. 전체 사회에서의 변화를 평가하는 것은 유사한 종류의 어려운 비교뿐만 아니라 분배 관심사에 근거한 전반적인 여러 가지 추가적 비교를 포함한다. 예를 들어, 만약 한 사회가 시간이 흐르면서 더 부유해지고 덜 평등해진다면 어떠하겠는가? 마지막으로, 비록 우리가 모든 상황이 효과적으로 비교될 수 있다고 생각하더라도, 우리는 폭력이나 다른 재앙의 정당화에는 의문을 품을지도 모른다. 단지 폭력적인 전쟁이 제도적 개선을 위한 장을 마련했다고 해서 우리가 왜 그것(폭력적인 전쟁)을 받아들여야 하겠는가?

구문 [6행~9행] To evaluate the change in the individual's state, / we must treat *the values of being content and being autonomous* as commensurable, // though many will believe that **they are not** (commensurable).
• they are not에서 they는 the values of being content and being autonomous를 가리키며, not 뒤에는 commensurable이 생략되어 있다.

어휘 start over 다시 시작하다   setback 실패; 역행; 차질   autonomy 자치권, 자율성 *cf.* autonomous 자주적인, 자치의   distributive 분배의, 배분적인   state of affairs 상황, 정세   catastrophe 재앙   reconcile 화해시키다; (어쩔 수 없는 불쾌한 상황을 체념하고) 받아들이다   institutional 제도의, 기관의
[선택지] equality 평등, 균등   inexcusable 용서[용납]할 수 없는

2 글의 순서   ②

해설 주어진 글은 머리가 두 개인 못에 대해 상상해보자는 것이다. 그러므로 이에 대한 사람들의 반응을 서술한 (B)가 이어지는 것이 자연스럽다. 이어서 그러한 반응에 대해 글쓴이의 주장(그러한 반사적 반응을 극복해야 하며 형태에 따라 기능, 즉 유용한 용도를 발견해야 한다)인 (A)가 나오는 것이 알맞으며, (C)는 (A)에 언급된 유용한 용도의 구체적인 예로, 앞서 서술된 글쓴이의 주장을 뒷받침하므로 맨 마지막에 위치한다.

해석 머리가 두 개인 못을 발견했다고 상상해보자. 하나는 못 윗부분에 있고 하나는 옆에 있다.
(B) 즉시 그것은 우리의 관심을 끈다. 분명히 그것은 결함이 있는 게 틀림없다. 구조적 고착 때문에, 우리의 생각은 그 이상한 점을 바로잡아 못이 그냥 다시 하나의 머리를 가지도록 복원하고 싶어 한다.

(A) 이것이 우리가 극복해야 하는 반사적 반응이다. '기능은 형태를 따른다'는 것을 기억하는가? 못은 그렇게 되어야 한다. 우리가 두 개의 머리를 가진 못의 유용한 용도를 발견하도록 스스로를 몰아붙이면 우리는 정말로 혁신적인 어떤 아이디어들을 우연히 발견할지도 모른다.
(C) 예를 들어 두 번째 못 머리가 여러분이 망치질할 때 못을 제자리에 있게 붙들도록 해서 엄지손가락을 내려치지 않게 한다고 가정해보자. '기능은 형태를 따른다'는 우리가 이상한 형태를 받아들이고 그것들의 유용한 용도를 상상함으로써 고착을 깨도록 돕는다.

구문 [9행~11행] Because of structural fixedness, our minds want **to correct** the oddity **and** **(to) restore** the nail **back to** having just one head.
• want 뒤에서 to correct와 (to) restore가 병렬로 이어져 want의 목적어 역할을 하고 있다. 「restore A back to B」는 'A를 B로 돌려놓다'는 의미로, to가 전치사이므로 뒤에 동명사 having이 쓰였다.

어휘 spike 못, 뾰족한 것   reflex (습관적인) 반응, 행동양식   run across ~을 우연히 발견하다   innovative 혁신적인   grab 붙잡다; 관심을 끌다   defective 결함이 있는   fixedness 고착, 고정   oddity 이상함, 특이함   restore 되찾다, 복원하다   in place 제자리에 (있는)   hammer 망치; 망치로 치다   smash 힘껏 치다, 박살내다   configuration 형태; 배열, 배치

3 문장 넣기   ⑤

해설 ⑤를 기점으로, 이전 내용은 안전을 위해 자유에 제한을 가하는 법에 찬성하는 사람들의 내용이고, 이후 문장은 모든 사람이 자유와 안전의 거래에 대해 동일한 평가를 하는 것은 아니라는 내용으로서 흐름이 전환되고 있다. 주어진 문장은 자유와 안전 사이에서 추구하는 균형이 사람마다 다르다는 내용이고 마지막 문장의 This variation은 곧 주어진 문장에서 언급된 '사람마다 다르다'를 뜻하므로 주어진 문장이 들어가기에 적절한 곳은 ⑤이다.

해석 비록 자유에 대한 주장이 강력하기는 해도, 이 목표는 무제한 추구될 수 없다. 거의 모든 사람들은 개인적 자유의 행사가 다른 이들을 위험에 처하게 하거나 큰 외적 대가를 가할 때 어떤 제한이 필요하다고 인정한다. 자유에 대해 더 미묘하지만 더 널리 퍼진 제한은 그것이 안전에 대한 개인의 열망과 충돌할 때 생겨난다. 현대 생활의 복잡성과 불확실성에 직면하여, 많은 사람들이 더 큰 안전에 대한 약속의 대가로, 그들 자신과 다른 이들의 자유를 제한하는 계획에 기꺼이 찬성표를 던진다. 예를 들면, 수많은 법들이 소비자들에게 위험하다고 판단된 제품을 살 자유를 주지 않는다. 하지만 모든 사람이 그 거래에 대해 동일한 평가를 내리지는 않는다. 합리적인 사람들이라면 자유와 안전 사이에 완벽한 균형을 추구하겠지만, 이 균형은 사람마다 다른데, 자유로부터 이익을 얻고 불안의 대가를 부담하는 그들의 능력에 좌우된다. 이러한 차이가 이 문제에서 합의에 도달하기가 왜 그토록 어려운지에 대한 주된 이유이다.

구문 [11행~15행] In the face of the complexities and uncertainties of modern life, / many people willingly vote for *programs* [that restrict **freedom** — their own and **that** of others —] in exchange for the promise of greater security.
• [ ] 부분은 앞의 programs를 수식하며, 그 안의 두 번째 that은 대명사로 앞의 freedom을 지칭한다.

어휘 rational 이성적인, 합리적인   security 안전 (↔ insecurity 불안(정))   case for (토론 등에서 한 쪽을 지지하는) 주장, 논거   without limit 무제한으로, 한없이   restriction

제한, 구속 **endanger** 위험에 처하게 하다 **impose** 부과하다, 지우다 **external** 외적인 **subtle** 미묘한 **pervasive** 널리 퍼지는, 만연하는 **arise** 생겨나다 **conflict with** ~와 상충하다 **complexity** 복잡성 **in exchange for** ~을 대가로 **deny** 인정하지 않다, 부인하다; 거부하다 **tradeoff** 거래, 교환 (협정) **variation** 차이, 변화

4~5 장문　　　　4 ③　5 ④

해설　4. 의식이 일체감을 주고, 행사 분위기를 강조하고 통제감을 준다는 내용으로 보아 ③ '의식의 의미와 기능'에 대한 내용임을 알 수 있다.
① 의식의 기원과 형태
② 우리는 어떻게 의식을 거행하는가?
④ 결혼 의식과 그것의 상징
⑤ 의식 변경에 무슨 문제가 있는가?
5. 의식이 사람들에게 통제감을 준다고 하며, 장례식을 예로 들어 슬퍼하는 사람을 위로하는 장례식의 기능을 설명했다. 그러므로 ④는 evident 등이 되어야 한다.

해석　겉보기에 의식은 생각 없이 공허한 단어들이 말해지는 시간 낭비 같아 보일 수도 있다. 그러나 그것은 (a) 더 깊은 의미를 가지고 있다. 우리는 소속감을 만들어 내기 위해 이 의식을 사용한다. 야구 경기 전에 국가가 불리는 동안 군중과 선수들은 하나의 단위로 연주를 하는 것이다. 마찬가지로 교회의 신도들은 찬송가를 부르거나 기도를 암송할 때 하나가 된다. 의식은 행사에 참여한 사람들을 (b) 하나로 묶는 데 도움이 된다.
의식은 또한 행사의 분위기를 (c) 강화하는 데 사용된다. 결혼 서약을 반복하는 부부는 영구히 함께 살겠다는 결혼할 의사를 공개적이고 엄숙하게 진술하는 것이다. 그들의 결정은 즉석에서 "아파트를 함께 쓰자"고 하는 말보다 훨씬 더 의의가 있는 것 같다. 이와 비슷하게, 대통령이 미국의 헌법을 받들겠다고 사람들 앞에서 서약할 때 나라 전체는 그 일의 중요성과 헌법에 대한 그의 헌신을 깨닫는다.
마지막으로, 기본적인 수준에서 의식은 사람들에게 통제감을 준다. 이러한 기능은 특히 장례식에서 (d) 모호한(→ 명백한)다. 우리는 사랑하는 사람의 죽음을 막을 수 없지만, 슬퍼하는 사람이 상실과 죽음과 비극을 극복하는 것을 도와주기 위해 의식을 준비할 수가 있다. 이러한 의식은 우리가 자연의 힘에 전적으로 좌우되는 것은 아니라고 느끼게 만들며 마음속 감정의 혼란을 (e) 진정시켜주는 결과를 낳는다.

구문　[14행~16행] Their decision seems much more significant **than an offhand "Let's share an apartment" would be** (significant).
● 접속사 than 이하 절의 주어 an offhand "Let's share an apartment"에서 형용사 offhand가 "Let's share an apartment"를 수식하고 있고, 동사는 would be이다. would be 다음에는 significant가 생략되어 있다.

어휘　**on the surface** 겉보기에는 **unthinkingly** 생각 없이 **ritual** 의식, 의례 **a sense of belonging** 소속 의식, 일체감 **the National Anthem** 국가 **congregation** 회중; 신도들; 집회 **hymn** 찬송가, 성가 **recite** (시·산문 등을) 암송하다 **unify** 하나로 하다, 통합하다 **reinforce** 강화[보강]하다 **solemn** 엄숙한 **intention** 의도, 목적; ((복수형)) 결혼할 의사 **permanently** 영구히, 불변으로 **offhand** 즉석에서, 사전 준비 없이 **swear** 맹세하다, 선서하다 **uphold** (법·원칙 등을) 유지하다, 지지하다 **constitution** 헌법; 체질; 구성, 구조 **commitment** 공약, 서약 **vague** 모호한, 애매한 **funeral** 장례식 **grieve** 비탄에 젖게 하다, 슬프게 하다 **cope with** ~에 대처하다, 극복하다 **tragedy** 비극 **at the mercy of** ~에 휘둘리는, ~의 처분대로 **chaos** 혼돈; 혼란

1 글의 요지　①

해설 이 글은 자신이 가지고 있는 부정적인 감정을 무시하는 것은 방향을 모른 채 운전하는 것과 같아서 그러한 감정이 일어나면 감정을 이해하여 다스리라고 하고 있다. 그러므로 이 글의 요지는 ①이다.

해석 여러분은 직장에 가기 전에 가족과 좋지 않은 상호 작용이 있을 수가 있다. 그 날이 흘러가면서 여러분은 여러분의 부정적인 감정을 아침의 사건에서 생겨난 오래 가는 부정적인 영향이라기보다는 여러분이 애쓰고 있는 프로젝트에 대한 좌절로서 해석할 수 있다. 많은 사람들이 부정적인 감정을 이해하려고 시도하기보다는 부정적인 감정을 극복하려고 한다. 그러나 이것은 놓친 기회이다. 감정은 여러분 자극 시스템의 상태에 대한 귀중한 정보를 제공한다. 그것들을 무시하는 것은 오직 방향을 묻기를 거부하면서 길을 잃은 상태로 운전하는 것과 같다. 여러분의 감정의 출처를 이해하기 위해서 여러분을 괴롭히는 일들에 대해 생각할 필요가 있다. 여러분의 감정에 대해 생각하지 않고 감정을 다룰 수는 없다. 일단 여러분의 감정이 어디에서 왔는가를 더 잘 이해할 수 있다면, 여러분은 그것을 다룰 수 있는 훨씬 더 좋은 능력을 가지게 될 것이다.

구문 [2행~5행] As the day wears on, you may interpret your negative feelings as frustration for *the project* [(which[that]) you're working on] **rather than** lingering negative effects from the events of the morning.

• [ ]은 목적격 관계대명사가 which[that]가 생략된 관계사절로 선행사 the project 를 수식한다. 「A rather than B」는 'B라기보다는 오히려 A'라는 의미이다.

[11행~12행] You need to think about *things* [that bother you] **in order to understand** the source of your feelings.

• [ ] 부분은 주격 관계대명사 that이 이끄는 관계사절로 things를 수식한다. in order to understand 이하는 '목적'을 나타낸다.

어휘 **wear on** 시간이 흘러가다; 마모되다 **interpret** 해석[이해]하다 **frustration** 좌절(감) **work on** ~에 애쓰다[공들이다] **lingering** (쉽게 사라지지 않고) 오래 가는[끄는] **power through** (난관 등을) 극복하다; (어려움에도 불구하고) 끝까지 해내다 **motivational system** 자극 시스템 **bother** 괴롭히다, 귀찮게 하다 **comprehend** (충분히) 이해하다 **deal with** ~을 다루다[처리하다]

2 빈칸 추론　①

해설 아이에게 선택권을 줌으로써 행복을 보장하기보다는 아이의 시야를 넓혀 주는 것을 선택하는 사례를 통해 가끔은 긍정적인 방식으로 권위를 사용하는 것이 바람직하다는 내용의 글이다. 이 경우 시야를 넓히는 일을 아이가 좋아하지 않을 수도 있으므로, 아이의 행복을 보장하는 것과 아이의 시야를 넓혀 주는 두 가지 목표는 서로 일치하지 않는다. 따라서 빈칸에 들어갈 말로 가장 적절한 것은 ① '항상 일치하는 것은 아니다'이다.
② 공정한 환경에서 번성한다
③ 서로에게 긍정적으로 영향을 미친다
④ 동시에 달성되어야만 한다
⑤ 단 한 번의 시도로 달성될 수 없다

해석 자녀의 시야를 넓혀 주거나 착한 행동에 대해 보상해 주기 위해 긍정적인 방식으로 당신의 권위를 사용하는 것을 나타낼 때 나는 '긍정적인 훈육'이라는 어구를 사용하는 것을 좋아한다. 당신이 가족 휴가를 계획하는 것을 상상해 보자. 당신과 당신의 배우자는 멕시코로 여행가길 원하지만, 아이들은 디즈니월드를 선호한다. 하지만, 당신의 아이들 중 누구도 멕시코에 가본 적은 없다. 이 상황에서 아이들은 선택권이 없다. 잘 운영되는 가족은 민주주의 국가가 아니다. 아이가 멕시코에 가본 적이 없다면, 그 아이에게 멕시코에 가고 싶은지 묻는 것은 먹어본 적도 없는 카레 치킨을 좋아하냐고 묻는 것과 다를 바 없다. 아이의 대답은 경험에 기반을 둔 것이 아니다. 아이에게 "우리는 멕시코에 갈 거고 너도 함께 갈 거야."라고 말하라. 그 아이가 그것을 좋아하지 않을 수도 있으므로 그 아이가 그것을 좋아할 것이라고 약속하지 마라. 당신의 일은 아이의 행복을 보장하는 것이 아니라 아이의 시야를 넓혀 주는 것이다. 그러한 두 가지 목표는 항상 일치하는 것은 아니다.

구문 [1행~3행] I like to use the phrase *positive discipline* to refer to using your authority in positive ways, **either** to broaden your child's horizons **or** to reward good behavior.

• 「either A or B」는 'A나 B 둘 중 하나'라는 뜻이고, 이때 A와 B는 병렬구조를 이룬다. 여기서는 to부정사구가 각각 A, B에 위치했다.

어휘 **discipline** 규율, 훈육, 훈련 **authority** 지휘권; 권위; 당국; 권위자 **spouse** 배우자 **democracy** 민주주의; 민주주의 국가
[선택지] **coincide** 일치하다; 동시에 일어나다 **thrive** 번성하다; 잘 자라다 **simultaneously** 동시에; 일제히

3 무관 문장　④

해설 셰익스피어, 존 던, 바흐 등 예술가들의 가치에 대한 재평가를 이야기하고 있으므로 존 던의 작품 주제를 언급하고 있는 ④는 글 전체의 흐름과 관계가 없다.

해석 내 예전 동료는 무엇보다 셰익스피어는 여성에 대한 이해가 아주 부족했기 때문에 셰익스피어를 가르치는 것은 이제 더는 중요치 않다고 생각한다고 말했다. ① 이것은 진지하게 받아들여 보면, 전체 (고전) 주요 작품 목록에서 누구의 자리도 아주 확고하지는 않으며 끊임없이 바뀐다는 것을 의미한다. ② 존 던의 위치는 19세기에 전혀 중요하지 않았고 The Oxford Book of English Verse에는 그의 시가 단 한 편밖에 없었다. ③ 그리고 지금은 물론, 허버트 그리어슨과 T. S. 엘리엇에 의해 되살아나서 그는 17세기 시에 있어 가장 위대한 인물 중 하나이다. ④ 또 다른 중요한 던의 시의 주제는 그가 오랜 시간 숙고하고 그것에 대해 종종 이론화했던 진정한 종교에 관한 생각이었다. ⑤ 심지어 거장 바흐도 멘델스존에 의해 재발견되기까지 200년간 비교적 인기가 없었는데, 이는 음악에서도 우리가 과거를 끊임없이 재평가하고 있다는 것을 증명한다.

구문 [1행~4행] A former colleague of mine said that she thought // (that) **it** was now no longer important **to teach Shakespeare** // because among other things he had a very feeble grasp of women.

• it was now 이하는 동사 thought의 목적어 역할을 하는 명사절이며, 앞에 접속사 that이 생략되었다. 여기서 it은 가주어이고 to teach Shakespeare가 진주어이다.

어휘 **feeble** 아주 약한; 허약한 **grasp** 움켜잡다; 파악하다; 이해, 파악 **of no consequence at all** 전혀 중요하지 않은 **figure** 인물; 숫자 **theorize** 이론을 세우다 **relatively** 비교적, 상대적으로 **reassess** 재평가하다

4 글의 순서　③

해설 주어진 글은 우리의 성격 특성을 반영하여 신체의 변화가 일어난다는 내용이므로, 이어서 우리의 습관을 반영해 얼굴의 주름이 생기거나 자신만의 굳어진 방식으로 몸도 유연하지 않게 된다는 내용의 (B)가 오는 것이 자연스럽다. (B)의 유연성 예시에 대한 부연 설명으로 반대의 경우(정신적으로 유연하면 몸도 유연해진다)도 가능하다는 설명이 등장하는 (C)가 이어지고, (C)에서 언급된 '반대의 경우'의 예시를 보여주는 (A)가 와야 한다.

- -

해석 여러분의 몸은 여러분이 거주하는 매개체가 아니라, 여러분의 육체가 아닌 것의 창작물이며 그로 인해 여러분의 성격 특성을 반영한다.
(B) 얼굴의 주름(감정선)은 사람들의 무의식적 반응, 즉 습관적으로 똑같은 일을 하고 반복적으로 똑같은 선택을 하는 것의 외적인 징후일 수 있다. 유연하지 않은 몸은 자신의 방식에 굳어진 것의 신체적 표현일 수 있다.
(C) 많은 사람이 나이가 들면서 정신적으로 덜 유연해지고, 따라서 매우 많은 노인이 뻣뻣함과 신체적 유연성의 상실을 겪는다. 그것은 또한 반대로도 발생할 수 있는데, 우리가 정신적으로 더 유연해지면 우리 몸의 유연성이 향상될 수 있다. 나는 이것이 가능하다는 것을 보여 주는 살아 있는 증거이다.
(A) 나는 더 젊었을 때 사고방식이 꽤 완고했고 신체적으로도 또한 유연하지 않았다. 놀랄 것도 없이 나는 스트레칭 운동을 싫어했다. 우리가 나이를 먹으면서 일어날 것이라고 예상되는 것과 반대로 내 몸의 유연성은 상당히 증가했고, 나는 이제 스트레칭 운동을 즐긴다.

- -

구문 [6행~8행] Contrary to **what is expected to occur as we age**, my physical flexibility has increased considerably, ~.
- what is ~ we age는 선행사가 포함된 관계사절로 전치사 to의 목적어 역할을 한다.

[15행~17행] Many people become less mentally flexible as they get older, / hence *the stiffness and loss of physical flexibility* (experienced by so many older adults).
- ( )는 과거분사구로 the stiffness and loss of physical flexibility를 수식한다.

[20행] I'm living proof **that** this is possible.
- that은 접속사로서 living proof와 동격을 이루는 절을 이끈다.

- -

어휘 **vehicle** 매개체; 운송 수단 　**inhabit** 거주하다[살다] 　**rigid** 완고한; 엄격한 **inflexible** 유연하지 않은 (↔ **flexible** 유연한) 　**considerably** 상당히 　**set in one's way** 자신의 방식에 굳어진 　**hence** 따라서, 이런 이유로 　**stiffness** 뻣뻣함; 완고함

5 문장 넣기　⑤

해설 주어진 문장에서 '이곳에서(Here)' 경제력을 과시하기 위해 사치품에 돈을 쓰는 것이 표준이었고 기대되었다고 했으므로, 주어진 문장은 '이곳'이 지칭하는 것 뒤에 나와야 한다. ⑤ 앞에서 세련된 식습관을 가진 유럽은 왕족에 의해 지배되었다고 하고, 뒤에서는 그와 반대되는 미국의 정치 제도를 설명했다. 따라서 주어진 문장은 유럽에 대한 내용 다음인 ⑤에 위치해야 한다.

- -

해석 유럽 문화에서는 식습관의 경향은 항상 음식 준비와 소비에서 세련됨을 향했다. 유럽 문화와는 대조적으로, 초기의 미국 식습관의 발전은 세련됨과 확대보다는 오히려 식사 준비 방법의 간소화를 더 향해 왔다. 18, 19세기 유럽의 식습관은 요리사들에 의해 발전된 요리 기술에서의 세련됨에 의해 생겨났다. 대조적으로, 18, 19세기의 미국의 식습관은 준비에서의 간소함과 대량 생산에서의 효율성에 의해 생겨났다. 이것은 그 땅의 정치 제도를 반영한 것이었다. 초기 유럽에서는 정치 제도가 봉건적이었고 왕족에 의해 지배되었다. 이곳에서는 경제력을 공공연히 과시하기 위해 사치품에 돈을 쓰는 것이 표준이었고 기대되었다. 미국의 민주적 정치 제도는 국가 지도자들에 의한 과도한 음식 소비의 사치를 장려하지 않았는데, 그것이 권력의 집중을 상징하기 때문이었다.

- -

구문 [1행~2행] Here **spending** money on luxury goods **to publicly display economic power was** a norm ｜and｜ expected.
- 문장의 주어는 동명사구 spending ~ power이고 동사는 was이다. to publicly ~ power는 부사적 용법의 to부정사구로 목적(~하기 위해서)을 나타낸다. 명사 a norm과 과거분사 expected는 주격보어로 and로 연결되어 병렬구조를 이룬다.

- -

어휘 **luxury goods** 사치품 　**display** 과시하다: 전시하다 　**norm** 표준 　**sophistication** 세련(됨) 　**consumption** 소비 　**simplification** 단순화 　**expansion** 확대 　**efficiency** 효율성 　**mass production** 대량 생산 　**reflection** 반영 　**democratic** 민주주의의 **excessive** 지나친, 과도한

1 글의 제목 ⑤

해설 헐리웃 영화에 미국 중산층이 가지고 있는 계층별 왜곡된 이미지가 반영되어 있다는 내용의 글이다. 이러한 중산층이 미국 사회에서 지배적이므로 제목으로 가장 적절한 것은 ⑤ '중산층 헐리웃 주인공은 널리 퍼진 편향의 반영'이다.
① 십대들 대 어른들은 헐리웃의 주제
② 헐리웃 영화의 경제적 관점
③ 해외 미국 문화에 대한 헐리웃의 기여
④ 헐리웃 영화에서의 소수 민족에 대한 왜곡된 묘사

해석 가난한 학생들은 헐리웃 영화에서 좀처럼 주인공으로 받아들여지지 않는 (어른들이 항상 그들을 '구해야' 한다) 반면 중산층 학생들은 그들이 나오는 영화에서 거의 항상 주인공이다 (그들은 항상 영화 속 어른들보다 더 영리하다). 나는 이러한 이중 잣대가 미국 문화의 중산층 편향을 반영한다고 생각한다. 중산층의 관점이 영화 속에서 항상 지배적이며 주인공적인 관점이다. 이러한 이중 잣대에 대하여 단순히 헐리웃을 비난하는 것이 편리하겠지만, 진실은 가난한 십대와 중산층 십대에 대한 이러한 왜곡된 이미지가 미국인들이 전체적으로 다양한 사회 계층에 갖고 있는 왜곡된 이미지의 반영이라는 것이다. 이러한 묘사는 중산층이 가지고 있는 환상 (즉 가난한 학생들은 곤경에 처해 있고 중산층 학생들은 현명하다는 환상)이지만, 미국 사회에서 중산층의 관점은 지배적이기 때문에 그것은 중산층을 넘어나가는 환상인 것이다.

구문 [9행~10행] While **it** would be convenient / **to simply blame Hollywood for this double standard**, ~
• While 절에서 it은 가주어이고 to simply blame ~ standard가 진주어이다.

[10행~13행] ~, the truth is **that** *these distorted images* (of poor and middle-class teens) / are a reflection of *the distorted image* [that Americans as a whole have of various social classes].
• is 다음의 that절은 문장의 보어이며, ( ) 부분은 전명구로서 앞의 these distorted images를 수식하고, [ ] 부분은 목적격 관계대명사 that이 이끄는 관계사절로 앞의 the distorted image를 수식한다.

어휘 middle-class 중산층의　　feature 특색; 이목구비; 특집(기사); 특별히 포함하다　bias 편향　perspective 관점　predominant 두드러진, 우세한　distort 왜곡시키다　as a whole 전체로서　representation 묘사, 표현　fantasy 공상, 환상　extend 뻗다　dominant 지배적인, 우세한
[선택지] versus (소송·스포츠 경기 등에서) ~대(對)　portrait 초상화; (상세한) 묘사　ethnic minority 소수 민족　widespread 광범위한, 널리 퍼진

2 밑줄 어휘 ⑤

해설 기계적으로 생각하는 사람들은 자신의 의견을 확고하게 믿고 엄격한 입장을 취하는 경향이 있다고 했다. 따라서 눈에 띄는 불편함을 드러내는 상황은 '일관성'이 없는 상황 즉, 익숙하지 않은 상황인 것이 흐름상 자연스러우므로 ⑤ familiar(익숙한)를 unfamiliar(익숙하지 않은)로 고쳐야 한다.

해석 기계적으로 생각하는 사람은 자기의 의견에 상당한 자부심을 가지며, 그것을 '옳다'고 믿는다. 그는 사람이란 여러 상황, 즉 사실상 거의 모든 상황에 대해 '입장을 갖는 것'이 적절하고 필요하다고 믿는다. 어떤 주제에 대해 전면적으로 일반화된 말을 할 때마다, 그는 비슷한 주제에 대해서도 엄격한 입장을 취하겠다고 맹세한다.

그는 무엇보다도 꼭 ① '일관되어야'만 한다. 기계적으로 생각하는 사람을 면밀하게 연구해보면 아마도 ② 호기심인 것처럼 보이는 것의 두드러진 결핍 상태를 알아차릴 것이다. 그는 거의 질문을 하지 않고, 자신의 세계에 대한 ③ 새로운 정보도 좀처럼 구하지 않는다. 그는 좀처럼 다른 사람에게서 무언가를 배웠다고 ④ 인정하지 않을 것이다. 그는 책을 읽는 적이 거의 없으며, 분명히 논픽션 자료도 읽지 않는다. 그가 남자라면 스포츠면을 읽을지도 모르는데, 그것이 그가 사는 사회의 남자에게 용인될 수 있는 행동이기 때문이며, 혹은 여자라면 그녀는 신문의 여성란을 읽을지도 모른다. 기계적으로 생각하는 사람은 ⑤ 익숙한(→ 익숙하지 않은) 상황에서 눈에 띄는 불편함을 드러낼지도 모르며, 그가 굳게 품고 있는 의견을 수정하도록 하는 사실에 직면할 때는 당황할지도 모른다.

구문 [2행~4행] **It** is proper and necessary, (he believes), *for a person* **to "take a stand"** on things — on just about everything, in fact.
• It은 가주어이고, to take a stand 이하가 진주어이며, for a person은 to부정사의 의미상 주어이다.

어휘 mechanical 기계적인; 기계로 작동되는　considerable 상당한, 많은　voice (말로) 나타내다　sweeping 전면적인　adopt (특정한 방식을) 쓰다[취하다]　rigid 엄격한, 융통성 없는　consistent 한결같은, 일관된　singular 두드러진　reveal 드러내다　be confronted with ~에 직면하다[마주치다]　revise 변경[수정]하다

3 빈칸 추론 ②

해설 석탄, 석유, 천연가스 등 방사능과 관계없어 보이는 연료들도 실제로 가공 과정에서 방사능을 배출한다는 내용의 글이다. 따라서 모든 에너지 자원들이 ② '환경에 방사능을 배출할' 수 있다는 것을 알 수 있다.
① 추출 과정에서 많은 것을 잃을
③ 우리가 아는 것 이상으로 환경을 오염시킬
④ 방사능의 위험을 제거하는 데 사용될
⑤ 방사성 폐기물 관리를 도와줄

해석 모든 에너지 자원들이 환경에 방사능을 배출할 수 있다는 것에 주목하는 것은 흥미롭다. 예를 들어 우라늄이 환경에서 작용하는 방식 때문에, 우라늄의 많은 양이 석탄 속에서 발견될 수 있다. 결과적으로, 석탄을 태우는 것은 우라늄을 환경에 배출할 수 있고 석탄재의 처리 또한 환경에 방사능을 배출할 수 있다. 연료유의 대다수도 또한 소량의 우라늄을 포함하고 있어서, 석유를 추출하는 것, 그것을 연료유 형태로 만들기 위해 정제시키는 것, 그리고 나서 그것을 연소시키는 것 역시 방사능을 배출한다. 석탄과 연료유 발전소를 합치면 전 세계에 있는 핵 발전소가 배출하는 것보다 더 많은 방사능을 실제 환경으로 배출한다는 것이 드러난다. 천연가스도 약간의 방사능을 포함하고 있으나 석유나 석탄만큼은 아니다. 그래서 천연가스 발전소도 분명 약간의 방사능을 배출하지만, 그 양은 원자로에 의해 배출되는 것보다는 적다.

구문 [7행~10행] The majority of fuel oil also contains small amounts of uranium, // so extracting petroleum, refining it to form fuel oil, [and] then burning it / **releases** radioactivity as well.
• so 뒤의 주어는 extracting ~ burning it이고 동사는 releases이다. 주어가 콤마(,)와 and로 연결된 세 개의 동명사구이나 전체적으로 하나의 개념으로 보아 단수 취급하므로 동사는 단수형인 releases로 쓰였다.

어휘 coal 석탄　disposal 처리, 처분　ash 재; 화산재　extract 발췌; 추출물; 추출하다

4 무관 문장 ③

해설 학생들의 지식을 유연하게 만들기 위해 하나의 맥락에서 학습한 과학 지식을 관련된 다른 맥락들에도 적용하여 해결책을 찾는 능력을 갖추는 것이 필요하다는 내용이므로 전공 분야에 대해 더 많이 알아야 이미 아는 것을 그 분야의 문제로 옮기는 게 쉬워진다는 내용의 ③은 글의 전체 흐름과 관련이 없다.

해석 자연 과학에서는 대개 몇 안 되는 개념들이 광범위한 맥락에 걸쳐 있는 문제들을 해결하는 데 적용될 수 있는 것이 사실이다. ① 지식의 전이에 관한 연구 문헌은 사람들이 하나의 맥락에서 지식을 획득할 때, 해결하거나 분석하는 데 적용될 수 있는 주요한 개념에 의해 연결되어 있지만, 본래의 맥락과 외면적으로 다르게 보이는 관련 맥락 속의 상황에는 이 지식을 좀처럼 적용할 수 없다는 것을 보여 준다. ② 이것이 함축하는 바는 학생들이 지식을 '유연하게' 만들기 위해 주요 개념들을 다수의 맥락에서 적용하는 것을 배워야 한다는 것이다. ③ 그들이 자기 전공 연구 분야에 대해 더 많이 알고 집중할수록, 학생들이 이미 알던 것을 그 분야의 문제로 옮기는 게 더 쉬워진다. ④ 더 많은 수의 개념을 가진 다른 과학 분야들 또한 학생들이 개념들을 새롭고 다양한 상황들에 관련시키는 연습을 필요로 한다. ⑤ 이전에 언급되었던 것을 다시 해 보기 위해 다양한 맥락과 상황에 걸쳐 실습을 제공하는 것은 학습이 지속되도록 만드는 것이며, 이것이 바로 학습의 전이를 촉진하는 방법이다.

구문 [3행~9행] Research literature on the transfer of knowledge suggests // **that** when people acquire knowledge in one context **they can seldom apply** this knowledge to situations in *related contexts* [that look superficially different from the original context], but [which are related by the major idea that could be applied to solve or analyze them].

● that 이하는 명사절로 suggests의 목적어 역할을 한다. 명사절 내에서 주어는 they이고 동사는 can seldom apply이다. 두 개의 [ ] 부분은 관계사절로 둘 다 related contexts를 수식한다.

[12행~15행] **The more** they know about, and focus on, *their major area of study*, **the easier it** is **to transfer** what students already know to problems in that area.

● 「the 비교급 ~, the 비교급 …」 구문으로 '~하면 할수록, 더 …하다'의 뜻이다. their major area of study는 동사 know about과 focus on의 공통 목적어이다. it은 가주어이고 to transfer 이하는 진주어이다.

어휘 **a handful of** 몇 안 되는, 소수의　**context** 맥락　**literature** 문헌　**transfer** 전이　**acquire** 획득하다, 습득하다　**superficially** 외면적으로　**original** 본래의　**analyze** 분석하다　**implication** 함축, 암시　**fluid** 유연한, 가변적인　**transfer** 옮기다, 이동하다

5 요약문 완성 ③

해설 시를 반복해서 소리 내어 읽으면 상상력과 청각 감각과 교감하며 시를 더 잘 이해하게 된다. 즉, 이는 이해를 증가시키는(increases)데, 시를 읽어보면 읽어볼수록 그것에 대한 해석이 더 많이 변화될(altered) 수 있기 때문이다.

해석 읽을 줄 아는 사람은 누구라도 시를 읽을 수 있다. 시가 가진 힘의 일부는 말의 소리에 있으므로, 그것을 묵독한 후에는 소리 내어 다시 읽어야 한다. 한 번으로는 안 된다. 한 번이 넘는 소리 내어 읽기가 당신을 올바른 길로 인도해줄 것이다. 당신은 시를 다시 읽자마자 당신이 음성의 강세를 통해 의미를 전달하기 시작하고, 시의 문자 그대로의 그리고 비유적인 의미를 분석하기 시작하며, 당신의 상상력이 연상적 감정에 적극적으로 관여하는 것을 깨닫게 될 것이다. 그것은 실제로 시인과 함께 대화를 나누는 것과 같은데, 왜냐하면 그의 예술적 정신과 귀가 만들어낸 것이 당신의 상상력이 풍부한 정신과 귀와 교류하고 있기 때문이다. 더 많이 읽으면 읽을수록, 시에 단지 하나의 의미만이 있는 것은 아님을 더 많이 깨닫게 될 것이다. 독자들은 읽을 때 주관적이고 상상력이 풍부한 선택을 하며, 이는 시를 다시 읽자마자 변할 수 있다. 단지 한 번만 읽은 시는 완전히 읽은 것이 아니다.

↓

시를 소리 내어 읽는 것은 시의 의미에 대한 여러분의 이해를 (A) 증가시키는데, 이것은 시의 텍스트를 읽어보면 읽어볼수록, 그것에 대한 여러분의 해석이 더 많이 (B) 변화될 수 있기 때문이다.

구문 [5행~9행] You will find **upon re-reading** a poem **that** you begin to convey meaning through vocal stress, **that** you begin to parse the poem's literal and figurative meanings, and **that** your imagination actively engages in associative feelings.

● 「upon v-ing」는 '~하자마자'의 뜻이다. 세 가지 that은 find의 목적어 역할을 하는 명사절로, 콤마(,)와 and로 연결되어 병렬구조를 이룬다.

어휘 **spoken word** 구어　**upon v-ing** ~하자마자　**stress** 강조, 강세　**literal** 문자 그대로의　**engage in** ~에 참여하다　**associative** 연상의　**imaginative** 상상력이 풍부한　**subjective** 주관적인
[선택지] **alter** 변하다, 달라지다

1 빈칸 추론   ②

해설 본문에서 주관적 건강, 즉 본인 자신이 느끼는 건강이 어떠하다는 것인지를 찾아야 한다. 중병이거나 몸이 불편하여 객관적으로는 건강하지 않아도 열정적이고 활발하게 책임을 다했던 인물들과 또 그 반대가 되는 예를 통해, 주관적 건강은 ② '객관적 육체 건강만큼이나 중요하다'는 결론을 내릴 수 있다.
① 좋은 신체적 건강함에 영향을 받는다
③ 건강한 노인들에겐 잘 이해되지 않는다
④ 의학적 치료에 대한 사람들의 만족감이다
⑤ 사람마다 다른 의미를 지닌다고 알려진다

해석 우리는 건강에 대해 훨씬 더 잘 이해할 필요가 있다. 의사가 봤을 때 아픈 것과 당신이 아침에 일어났을 때 메스꺼움을 느끼는 것은 천지 차이다. 1948년에 세계 보건 기구(WHO)의 창립자들은 건강을 '질병이 없는 상태뿐만 아니라 육체의, 정신의, 그리고 사회적 행복'이라고 정의했다. 존 케네디와 드와이트 아이젠하워는 둘 다 중병과 싸웠지만, 그들은 지칠 줄 모르고 대통령직이라는 짐을 견뎠기 때문에, 그들을 포함한 누구도 그들이 아프다고 하지 않았을 것이다. 8년 동안, 절름발이인 루즈벨트 대통령은 활발하고 쾌활한 대통령이었다. 그러나 그의 절반 정도의 나이와 훨씬 나은 건강을 가진 어떤 사람들은 불행하게 침대에서 그들의 시간 대부분을 보낸다. 명백히, 주관적 건강은 객관적 육체 건강만큼이나 중요하다.

구문 [7행~10행] John Kennedy and Dwight Eisenhower both battled serious illnesses; // but nobody, (including themselves,) (**as** they tirelessly bore the burden of the presidency,) would have called them sick.
• 두 개의 ( )는 삽입구문이며, 여기서 부사절 접속사 as는 '~ 때문에'라는 의미이다.

어휘 **absence** 없음, 부재; 결석, 결근   **presidency** 대통령 직[임기]   **crippled** 절름발이의
[선택지] **fitness** 건강; 적합성

2 글의 순서   ④

해설 물속 물체가 왜곡되어 보이는 착시를 설명하는 내용이다. 주어진 문장에 이어서 빛의 굴절과 착시가 어떻게 이루어지는지를 설명하는 (C)가 오는 것이 알맞다. 그 다음으로 빨대로 예를 들어 다시 한번 빛의 굴절에 대해 설명하는 (A)가 나오고, 이어서 그로 인한 착시를 설명하는 내용인 (B)가 마지막으로 나와야 적절하다.

해석 물속에 있는 물체를 물 위에서 볼 때, 그것의 외형은 왜곡돼 보인다. 이것은 굴절이 그 물체로부터 나오는 광선의 방향을 바꾸기 때문이다.
(C) 이 광선이 관찰자의 눈을 발견하면, 눈 속의 신경이 관찰자의 뇌로 신호를 보낸다. 뇌는 그때 빛이 나온 것으로 보이는 곳을 근거로 하나의 상을 만든다. 그것은 굴절의 효과를 고려하지 않고 이렇게 하며, 그래서 그 물체의 외형은 일그러진다.
(A) 물 잔에 들어 있는 빨대를 볼 때 이런 효과를 쉽게 관찰할 수 있다. 빨대의 물속에 있는 부분에서 나오는 광선은 물과 잔 사이, 그리고 잔과 공기 사이의 표면들에서 굴절한다.
(B) 그 광선은 실제보다 표면에서 더 가까운 곳에서 나오는 것처럼 보이고, 빨대는 구부러져 보인다. 빨대를 물속으로부터 본다면, 물 위쪽 부분이 일그러질 것이다.

구문 [11행~13행] **If** the straw **were viewed** from underwater, the part above water **would be distorted**.

• 「If+S'+과거동사 ~, S+would+동사원형 ....」은 현재 사실의 반대 상황을 가정하는 가정법 과거 구문으로, '~한다면 …할 것이다'라는 의미이다.

어휘 **distort** 왜곡하다; 비틀다, 일그러뜨리다   **refraction** 굴절   **ray** 광선   **straw** 짚, 지푸라기; 빨대   **bent** 구부러진   **nerve** 신경   **take into consideration** ~을 고려[참작]하다

3 문장 넣기   ③

해설 누군가가 당신에게 친절을 베풀거나 당신을 좋아할 가능성을 높이려면 그 사람이 당신에게 호의를 베풀도록 해야 한다는 것을 정치가인 벤자민 프랭클린의 일화를 예로 들어 설명하는 내용이다. 주어진 문장의 agreed를 통해 주어진 문장 앞에 무언가를 요청했다는 내용이 나와야 하고 ③ 이후에 나온 that이 주어진 문장의 프랭클린의 말을 가리키므로 주어진 문장은 ③에 들어가는 것이 가장 적절하다.

해석 18세기 미국의 정치가인 벤자민 프랭클린이 한번은 펜실베이니아 주 의회의 한 까다롭고 시큰둥한 의원의 협조를 얻고 싶어 했다. 그 의원에게 굽실거리는 데 시간을 보내는 대신, 프랭클린은 완전히 다른 행동 방침을 취하기로 결심했다. 그는 그 의원이 개인 서재에 희귀 서적 한 부를 가지고 있다는 것을 알고 며칠간 그것을 빌릴 수 있는지 물어보았다. 그 의원은 승낙했고, 프랭클린에 따르면 "우리가 다음에 의회에서 만났을 때, 그는 언제든 나를 기꺼이 도와줄 마음을 보여 주었다"고 한다. 프랭클린은 그것을 "당신에게 한번 친절을 베푼 사람은 바로 당신이 도움을 준 사람보다 더욱 당신에게 또 다른 친절을 베풀 준비가 되어 있을 것이다"라는 한 단순한 원칙 덕으로 여겼다. 다시 말해서, 누군가가 당신을 좋아할 가능성을 높이려면 그 사람이 당신에게 호의를 베풀도록 만들어라. 한 세기가 지난 후, 러시아의 소설가인 레프 톨스토이는 "우리는 사람들이 우리에게 베푼 선의 때문이라기보다는 오히려 우리가 그들에게 베푼 선의 때문에 그들을 사랑한다"는 글을 써서 이에 동의하는 것 같았다.

구문 [13행~15행] ~: "*He* [that has once done you a kindness] will be more ready to do you **another** (kindness) / than *he* [whom you yourself have obliged]."
• 첫 번째 [ ] 부분은 주격 관계대명사가 이끄는 관계사절로 주어 He를 수식하고, 두 번째 [ ] 부분은 목적격 관계대명사가 이끄는 관계사절로 바로 앞의 he를 수식한다. another 다음에는 kindness가 반복을 피하기 위해 생략되었다.

[15행~17행] In other words, **to increase** the likelihood that someone will like you, get that person to do you a favor.
• to increase는 to부정사의 부사적 용법으로 목적을 나타낸다. 밑줄 친 the likelihood와 that someone will like you는 서로 동격 관계이다.

어휘 **manifest** (분명히) 보여 주다, 나타내다; 분명한   **readiness** 기꺼이 하기; 준비가 되어 있음   **serve** 도움이 되다; 제공하다   **occasion** 때, 경우; 행사, 의식   **politician** 정치가   **be eager to-v** v하고 싶어 하다   **cooperation** 협조, 협력   **apathetic** 시큰둥한, 냉담한   **state legislature** 주 의회   **bow and scrape** 굽실거리다, (머리를) 조아리다   **rare** 희귀한, 드문   **attribute A to B** A를 B의 덕[탓]으로 여기다   **principle** 원칙, 원리   **oblige** 도움을 주다; (도움을) 베풀다   **likelihood** 가능성   **favor** 호의, 친절; 지지(하다), 찬성(하다)   **novelist** 소설가, 작가   **not so much A as B** A라기보다는 오히려 B인

4~5 장문

4 ④ 5 ④

해설 4. 어떤 이유로 만들어졌던 전통이나 제도가 그 이유가 더 이상 쓸모가 없어졌는데도 불구하고 존속하는 예를 들면서 그것을 제거해 효율적이 되어야 한다고 말하고 있다. 그러므로 가장 적절한 제목은 ④ '끊임없이 낡은 가설을 재검토하라'가 적절하다.

① 자신을 과소평가하지 말라

② 전통적인 관습으로부터 배워라

③ 예상치 못한 조기 은퇴를 준비하라

⑤ 위험 지대에서 나와라

5. 이유가 더는 쓸모없게 되어도 확립된 태도나 신념은 계속 살아남는다고 했으므로 예상 수명이 훨씬 더 길어졌지만 이전에 정한 은퇴 연령이 존속한다는 것을 알 수 있다. 그러므로 ④는 persists 등이 되어야 한다.

해석 로스앤젤레스에는 신년 전야를 12월 30일 오후에 축하하는 전통을 가진 러시아 이민자 집단이 있다. 그들에게 이유를 물었을 때 그들 중 한 사람이 이렇게 대답했다. "우리가 젊고 돈이 별로 없었을 때 다음날보다는 30일 오후에 밴드를 구하는 게 (a) 더 저렴했어요. 그렇게 해서 우리 전통이 시작된 겁니다." 이상한 것은 이제 이 사람들 대부분이 쉽게 신년 전야에 여흥을 즐길 여유가 있지만 여전히 30일 오후에 축하하고 있다는 것이다. 중요한 점은 일단 어떤 태도나 신념이 확립되면 그것이 발전하게 된 원래 이유가 더 이상 존재하지 않음에도 불구하고 그것이 (b) 살아남는 경향이 있다는 것이다.

모든 상황이나 문제가 (c) 더 이상 쓸모가 없는 이유로 이렇게 '일찍 축하하는 사람들'을 약간씩 가지고 있다. 그것은 은퇴하기로 결정한 연령일 수 있다. 정말로 많은 서구 국가에서 은퇴 연령인 65세는 완벽한 하나의 예이다. 1870년대로 거슬러 올라가 독일 수상 오토 폰 비스마르크는 독단적으로 은퇴 연령을 65세로 정했다. 이 결정은 당시 평균 예상 수명이 그것보다 훨씬 짧았기 때문에 재정적으로 합리적이었다. 문제는 최근에는 예상 수명이 65세보다 훨씬 더 길어졌지만 여전히 그 연령은 재정적 사정이 다르게 영향을 줄지 모른다는 것에도 불구하고 (d) 사라진다(→ 존속한다)는 것이다.

어떤 것이든 효율적이기 위해서 우리는 항상 더 이상 쓸모가 없는 생각을 찾아 그것을 (e) 제거해야 한다. 정말로 이것이 창의적 사고의 기초이다.

구문 [11행~13행] The point: once *an attitude or belief* gets established, **it** tends to survive even though the original reason for **its** development no longer exists.

• it과 its는 모두 앞에 나온 an attitude or belief를 지칭한다.

어휘 **immigrant** 이주자, 이민 **curious** 특이한, 기이한; 호기심이 많은 **entertainment** 여흥, 오락 **chancellor** 수상, 재무 장관 **arbitrarily** 독단적으로, 마음대로 **life expectancy** 기대 수명, 평균 수명 **expire** 사라지다; 만료되다 **consideration** 고려, 사정 **dictate** 영향을 주다, 좌우하다 **obsolete** 더 이상 쓸모가 없는 **cornerstone** 초석, 토대, 기초

1 필자 주장 ②

해설 베르디, 세르반테스, 펄 벅과 같이 중년 이후에 인생의 정점에 이른 사람들의 예를 나열하고 마지막 부분을 통해 노령은 아무것도 하지 말라는 신호가 아니며 좋은 자질을 계속해서 계발하여 사회와 자신들을 위해 사용하자는 것이 필자의 주장임을 알 수 있다. 따라서 필자의 주장으로 가장 적절한 것은 ②이다.

해석 역사는 우리에게 중년 이후에 정점에 이른 사람들에 관해 이야기해준다. 베르디는 73세에 Othello를 썼다. 세르반테스는 중년에 Don Quixote를 썼다. 위대한 소설가인 펄 벅은 자신의 80번째 생일에 대해 얘기한 적이 있었다. 그녀는 쉰 살이나 마흔 살이었을 때보다 여든 살에 자신이 훨씬 더 훌륭한 사람이 되었다고 말했다. 그녀는 일흔 살 이후에 매우 많은 것을 배웠다고 말했다. 그녀는 다른 어떤 십 년의 기간보다 그 십 년 동안에 더 많은 것을 배웠다고 느꼈다. 사실, 펄 벅이 옳았다. 많은 연구들은 똑똑한 사람들은 나이가 들수록 더 똑똑해지는 경향이 있다는 것을 보여준다. 그러므로, 노령을 단순히 아무것도 하지 말라는 신호라고 생각하지 말아야 한다. 대신에, 사회와 당신 자신을 돕는 데 쓰일 수 있는 좋은 자질들을 계속 발전시켜야 한다.

구문 [8행~9행] She felt that she had learned **more** in those ten years **than** in any other ten-year period.

• 「more ~ than ...」 형태의 비교급 구문이 사용되었다.

[12행~14행] Instead, keep developing *your good qualities* [that can be used to help society and yourself].

• [ ]는 주격 관계대명사 that이 이끄는 관계사절로 앞의 your good qualities를 수식한다.

어휘 **peak** 정점, 최고조; (산의) 봉우리, 꼭대기 **period** 기간, 시기 **tend to-v** v하는 경향이 있다 **quality** (사람의) 자질, 특성; 품질 **cue** 신호, 단서; 신호를 주다

2 밑줄 함의 ③

해설 집필을 중단했던 소설을 나중에 출간한 두 작가의 사례를 들어 소설을 쓰는 것은 욕조를 타고 바다를 횡단하는 것과 같이 힘든 일이라고 표현하고 있으며 그 과정에서 때때로 '욕조가 가라앉는다'는 ③ '소설이 작가에 의해 버려지다.'를 나타낸다.

① 소설이 데드라인을 놓치다.
② 소설이 비평가의 호평을 받다.
④ 소설이 사실과 허구의 균형을 잡는 데 실패하다.
⑤ 소설이 독자의 기대를 충족시키지 못하다.

해석 때때로 오랫동안 죽었다고 생각되는 소설이 다시 살아나고 그 페이지에서 먼지를 쓸어내고 작가의 이력으로 뒤섞여 돌아갈 수 있다. 그리고 그것이 마이클 셰이본과 그의 소설 Fountain City에 일어났던 일인데 1992년에 5년 반의 작업 끝에 그는 그것을 없애버렸다. "그것은 날 지우고, 부수고, 생매장하고, 익사시키고, 계단 아래로 차버리고 있었어요."라고 그는 그 소설이 자신에게 끼친 영향에 대해 말했다. 그러나 셰이본은 2010년에 그것의 첫 4개의 챕터를 문학잡지에 게재하여 일생의 업무를 완수했다. 그리고 스티븐 킹도 있는데, 그의 최근 소설 Under the Dome은 30년 전 그의 미완성 소설의 완전한 정본이다. "등장인물 명단이 계속 늘어나자 등장인물들은 연결되지 않았고, 저는 제가 그만뒀던 지점에 이르게 되었죠."라고 킹이 회상했다. 그러나 30년 후 콘셉트의 새로운 시도는 마침내 효과가 있었다. 소설

을 쓰는 것은 욕조를 타고 보스턴에서 런던까지 노를 젓는 것과 같다. 때때로 <u>욕조는 가라앉는다.</u> 대부분의 욕조가 가라앉지 않는다는 것은 이상한 일이다.

구문 [10행~13행] And there's also *Stephen King,* // **whose** recent novel *Under the Dome* is a complete rewrite of his unfinished novel / from 30 years ago.

• whose 이하는 Stephen King을 부연 설명하는 계속적 용법의 관계대명사절로, 뒤의 명사 recent novel *Under the Dome*이 선행사의 소유이므로 소유격 관계대명사 whose가 쓰였다.

어휘 **shuffle** 뒤섞다 **impact** 영향, 충격 **literary** 문학의 **decade** 10년 **paddle** 노를 젓다

[선택지] **critical** 비평가들의; 비판적인 **acclaim** 호평, 갈채 **abandon** 버리다

3 빈칸 추론 ④

해설 빈칸 문장의 this fate는 예술가들이 흔히 목표를 성취한 뒤 더 나아가지 못하고 우울해하는 것을 말한다. 이는 목표 성취로 인해 더 이상의 목표가 없어진 데에서 기인하므로, 이러한 운명을 피하기 위해서 예술가들은 ④ '당신의 현재 목표가 유일한 목표가 되지 않도록 하는 것'이 필요하다는 것이 적절하다.
① 다양한 분야의 많은 친구들을 만들기 위해 노력하는 것
② 의도적으로 목적지에 도달하는 것을 지연시키는 것
③ 당신의 작품 전시회에 집착하지 않는 것
⑤ 일과 놀이 사이에 건강한 균형을 구축하는 것

해석 예술가들에게 흔히 나타나는 중대한 고비는 노력의 최종 목적지가 갑자기 사라졌을 때이다. 20년 동안의 유일한 목표가 그의 도시의 주요 미술관에서 개인전을 하는 것이었던 예술가를 떠올려 보라. 그가 마침내 그것을 성취했을 때, 그는 다시는 가치 있는 작품을 만들어내지 못했다. 얼마나 자주 그리고 쉽게 성공이 우울로 이루어질 수 있는지를 발견하게 되는 이와 같은 이야기에는 뼈아픈 역설이 있다. 이러한 운명을 피하는 것은 당신의 현재 목표가 유일한 목표가 되지 않도록 하는 것과 관련이 있다. 개인의 작품에 관하여, 이것은 앞으로 나아가고 다음 작품을 살피도록 하는 해결되지 않은 어떠한 사안을 남겨두는 것이다. 그리고 (춤과 같이) 일부 육체적으로 위험이 있는 예술 형태들에 관하여, 이것은 부상에 대비하여 다른 관심사를 개발해두는 것을 의미한다.

구문 [6행~8행] There's a painful irony <u>to stories like that</u>, <u>to discovering how frequently and easily success leads to depression.</u>

• 밑줄 친 to stories like that과 to discovering 이하는 동격 관계이다.

어휘 **moment of truth** 중대한 고비; 결정적인 순간 **single-minded** 한 가지 목표에만 전념하는; 성실한 **irony** 역설적인 점[상황]; 풍자, 반어법 **unresolved** 미해결의, 대답되지 않은

[선택지] **obsess** 집착하다; 강박감을 갖다 **cultivate** (관계를) 구축하다; (땅을) 경작하다

4 글의 순서 ②

해설 심리학과 개 훈련이 공통점이 많다는 주어진 내용에 이어, 개 심리학과 아동 심리학이 비슷한 길을 걸어왔다는 내용의 (B)가 오는 게 자연스럽다. (B) 후반부에서 긍정적 강화는 최근에야 생겼다고 했으므로, 그 이전 세대에는 어린이에게 처벌

이 용인되었다는 이야기를 제시하는 (A)가 이어서 와야 한다. 이어서 '마찬가지로 (Similarly)'로 시작하여 개 훈련도 처벌을 포함했다는 내용의 (C)가 마지막으로 오는 것이 자연스럽다.

해석 비록 심리학과 개 훈련이 매우 다른 분야인 것처럼 보일지 모르지만, 우리가 개와 그리고 사람과 긍정적인 방식으로 소통하는 방식에 관한 원리에는 실제로 공통점이 많다.
(B) 뿐만 아니라, 개 심리학과 아동 심리학의 발전은 둘 다 비슷한 길을 따라왔다. 긍정적 강화라는 개념은 20세기 초 이래로 존재해왔지만, 어린이의 좋은 행동에 대해 보상하고 그들의 자존감을 유지하는 것을 매우 많이 강조하는 것은 단지 최근 몇 년간의 일이다.
(A) 여러분은 이전 세대에는 어린이들에 대한 신체적 처벌이 더 용인되었고, '아이들은 보이는 곳에 있어야 하지만, 잠자코 있어야 한다'는 인식이 훨씬 더 흔했다는 것을 아마 알고 있을 것이다.
(C) 마찬가지로 전통적인 개 훈련 방법도 교정과 처벌을 포함하였고, 1970년대 초에 Gentle Modern Method of Dog Training이 소개될 때까지 긍정적 강화는 개 훈련 분야에서는 사실상 전례가 없던 것이었다.

구문 [2행~4행] ~, the philosophies of **how we interact with dogs and with people in a positive way** actually **have** much **in common**.

• how we ~ positive way는 전치사 of의 목적어 역할을 하는 관계사절이며, 여기서 have in common은 '공통점이 있다'라는 뜻이다.

[10행~15행] The concept of positive reinforcement has been around since the early twentieth century, // but **it** has *only* been *in recent years* **that** so much emphasis has been placed on rewarding the good behavior of children and on maintaining their self-esteem.

• 「It is ~ that ....」은 '…한 것은 바로 ~이다'라는 뜻의 강조구문이며, 이 문장에서는 only in recent years가 강조되고 있다. 밑줄 친 두 개의 전치사구는 병렬구조를 이룬다.

어휘 **profession** 분야; 직종 **philosophy** 원리, 철학 **acceptable** 용인되는, 받아들여지는 **evolution** 발전 **reinforcement** 강화 **place emphasis on** ~을 강조하다 **reward** 보상하다; 보상 **self-esteem** 자존감 **correction** 교정 **virtually** 거의, 사실상 **unheard of** ~의 전례가 없는 **circle** 분야, 집단

5 문장 넣기 ⑤

해설 ⑤ 앞에는 현대 소설의 단어의 용법 중 13%가 인쇄된 대형 사전에 없는 방식으로 사용되었다는 내용이고, in other words(다시 말해서)로 이어지는 ⑤ 뒤 문장은 물리적 공간의 제약(the limitations of physical space) 때문에 표준 사전에 진입하지 못한 현대적 용법이 있다는 내용이다. 주어진 문장에 전통적 사전에는 단어 용법 기입을 위한 제한된 공간(limited space)만이 있다는 단점을 서술했으므로 ⑤ 뒤의 문장의 in other words라는 표현으로 잘 연결된다. 따라서 주어진 문장은 ⑤에 들어가는 것이 적절하다.

해석 월드 와이드 웹과 같은 우리의 21세기 기술은 우리가 우리의 언어로 단어를 정의하는 방식에 깊이 영향을 끼친다. 인터넷 이전 시대에서는 인쇄된 사전이 항상 단어가 의미하는 바와 그것이 사용되는 방식에 대한 최종 권위의 역할을 했다. 사전의 저자들(사전 편찬자들)은 전통적으로 특정 단어가 사용되는 방식의 가능한 한 많은 예를 주의 깊게 분석함으로써 그것의 정의에 도달했다. 어떤 표준 탁상용 사전에서 발견되는 몇몇 복잡한 단어들이 9~10개의 가능한 용례를 가지고 있을 순 있지만, 이러한 정의조차도 가능한 모든 용법을 다루지는 못한다. 사전 편찬자 에린 맥킨에 따르면, 최근의 연구에서 현대 소설에서 무작위로 고른 여러 구절에서, 명사, 동사, 형용사의 13%가 대형 탁상용 사전에서 발견되지 않는 방식으로 사용되었음이 나

타났다. 전통적 사전의 주요 단점은 단어가 사용되는 방식의 표본 추출만을 제공할 제한된 이용 가능한 공간만이 있다는 것이다. 다시 말해서, 그 물리적 공간의 제약 때문에 표준 사전에 진입하지 못한 다수의 더 현대적인 용법들이 있다.

구문 [4행~6행] **Our 21st century technologies**, (such as the World Wide Web), **have** profound implications for *the way* [we define the words in our language].

• 주어는 Our 21st century technologies이고 동사는 have이다. [ ] 부분은 the way 를 수식하는 관계부사절이다.

[9행~12행] The authors of dictionaries (lexicographers) traditionally have arrived at their definitions by carefully analyzing **as** *many examples* **as possible** of **how a particular word is used**.

• 「as ~ as possible」은 '가능한 한, 될 수 있는 대로'의 뜻이다. how 이하는 of의 목적어 역할을 한다.

어휘 **shortcoming** 단점 **sampling** 표본 추출 **profound** 깊은, 심오한 **implication** 영향; 함축, 암시 **hard copy** 인쇄된 자료 **serve as** ~로서의 역할을 하다 **usage** 용법, 어법 **passage** 구절 **contemporary** 동시대의, 현대의 **limitation** 제한

1 글의 주제   ⑤

해설 단맛의 포도주를 선호하는 사람들은 성격이 충동적이고, 단맛이 없는 포도주를 선호하는 사람들은 솔직하다는 내용의 글이므로 이 글의 주제로는 ⑤ '성격과 와인 선택의 상관관계'가 가장 적절하다.
① 레드 와인이 심장 건강에 끼치는 영향
② 사람들이 다른 것보다 와인을 선호하는 이유
③ 확실히 좋은 품질의 와인을 선택하는 데 도움이 되는 조언들
④ 인간관계에 있어서의 와인의 보편적인 역할

해석 쇼비뇽 블랑과 샤도네이를 좋아하거나 보르도 또는 진판델을 좋아하는 것은 와인에 대한 단순한 선호도 이상의 것을 나타낼 수 있다. 그것은 성격적 특성을 보여줄 수도 있다. 호주와 영국의 과학자들에 의한 새로운 연구는 와인의 단맛을 선호한 사람들이 충동적일 가능성이 더 높은 반면 드라이한 품종을 선택한 사람들은 더 솔직했다고 보여 줬다. "단맛에 대한 선호를 가진 참가자들은 드라이한 맛에 대한 선호를 가진 참가자들보다 충동적인 면이 상당히 더 높았다."고 호주 와가와가에 있는 찰스 스터트 대학의 안소니 J. 살리바와 그의 동료들이 보고했다. 그들은 충동성과 솔직함을 제외하고, 다른 성격적 특성은 두 집단 간에 크게 다르지 않았다고 말했다.

구문 [4행~7행] *New research* (by scientists in Australia and Britain) **showed** // **that** *drinkers* [who preferred a sweet taste in wine] / were more likely to be impulsive, / while *those* [who chose dry varieties] had greater openness.
• that 이하는 동사 showed의 목적어 역할을 하는 명사절이다. ( ) 부분은 전명구로서 앞의 New research를 수식한다. 두 [ ] 부분은 주격 관계대명사절로 각각 앞의 선행사 drinkers와 those를 수식한다.

어휘 taste 좋아함, 기호; 맛이 ~하다   liking 애호, 좋아함; 취미   indicate 가리키다; 나타내다   preference 선호(도), 애호 *cf.* prefer 선호하다   reveal 드러내다; 나타내다   trait (성격상의) 특성, 특징   impulsive 충동적인 *cf.* impulsiveness 충동성; 충동적으로 행동하는 것   dry (와인이) 드라이한, 단맛이 없는; 마른, 건조한   variety 품종; 다양성   openness 솔직함; 편협하지 않음   participant 참가자; 참가하는   significantly 상당히, 크게   counterpart 상대, 대응 관계에 있는 사람[것]   apart from ~을 제외하고, ~외에는
[선택지] impact 영향(력); 영향을 주다   reliably 확실히; 신뢰할 수 있게   correlation 상관관계, 연관성

2 밑줄 어법   ③

해설 ③ 주어는 a travel information system이고 that ~ unrelated to someone's journey는 주어를 수식하는 관계대명사절이다. unrelated to someone's journey는 앞의 information을 수식한다. 따라서 밑줄 친 부분은 주어 a travel information system에 상응하는 동사 자리이므로 becoming을 becomes로 고쳐야 한다.
① 주어가 Existing travel information systems로서 복수명사이고 동사 design과 수동관계이므로 are designed는 수와 태를 적절히 사용하였다.
② 형용사 역할을 하는 과거분사 controlled를 부사 centrally가 적절하게 수식하고 있다.
④ 단수 주어 the reaction of drivers와 상응하여 수와 태를 적절히 사용하였다.
⑤ wrong or inaccurate information ~ information source가 완전한 절로서 앞의 Incidents를 수식하므로 관계부사 where가 쓰였다. where는 선행사가 물리적이고 구체적인 장소(house, city, place 등)가 아니더라도 본문의 incidents를 포함하여 point(점), case(경우), circumstance, situation(상황) 등 넓은 의미에서 장소로 생

각되는 말일 때에도 쓰일 수도 있다.

해설 고속도로의 전광판 같은 기존의 여행 정보 시스템은 여행자들을 어떠한 형태의 개별화된 정보 포맷과 전달도 없는 군중으로 여기도록 고안되어 있다. 게다가 대부분의 선진화된 교통 관리 시스템은 중앙 통제 기반 시설과 정보원에 의존한다. 이러한 두 가지 특징은 특정 시스템의 신뢰와 신용의 발달을 방해한다. 정말로, 누군가의 여정과 관련 없는 정보를 자주 전달하는 여행 정보 시스템은 여행자의 환경에서 점차 '소음'이 된다. 운송 연구의 전문가들에 따르면, 전광판 메시지에 대한 운전자들의 반응은 시간이 흐르며 감소한다고 하는데, 이는 전시된 메시지에 대한 잠재적인 불신을 나타낸다. 하나의 정보원에 의존하는 정보 시스템은 신뢰를 받지 못하게 될 위험에 처해 있다. 하나의 정보원에 의해 잘못된 혹은 부정확한 정보가 전달되어 일어난 사건들은 시스템에 대한 신뢰 수준을 전반적으로 손상시킬 것이다.

구문 [16행~17행] *An information system* [that relies on a single source of information] **is** at risk of becoming untrustworthy.
• 주격 관계대명사 that이 이끄는 [ ]은 주어 An information system을 수식하며 동사는 is이다.

어휘 motorway 고속도로   personalize 개별화하다   infrastructure 기반 시설   characteristic 특징   hinder 방해하다   credibility 신뢰성, 신용   more often than not 자주   transportation 운송, 수송   at risk 위험에 처한   untrustworthy 신뢰할 수 없는   incident 사건

3 빈칸 추론   ①

해설 정보 이동이 단계를 거치면서 효율성이 65퍼센트 미만으로 심지어 절반 정도보다 더 작을 수 있다고 했으므로 빈칸을 완성하면 정보 이동은 ① '실제로는 손해 보는 장사이다'가 된다.
② 상호 이익이 되는 결과를 이끈다
③ 훌륭한 의사소통 기술을 요구한다
④ 일시적인 불확실성의 효과를 만들어낸다
⑤ 실시간 의사소통이 있을 때 일어난다

해석 메시지는 사실에서 언어로, 언어에서 글로, 글에서 다른 사람의 마음속 언어로, 그리고 그 언어에서 저장 정보로 장소를 옮긴다. 이러한 단계들에서 그 과정이 얼마나 성공적인지는 아무도 알지 못한다. 또한 그 효율성을 알아내기 위한 실험을 고안하는 것도 거의 불가능할 것이다. 그럼에도 불구하고, 실제 현실에서 그런 이동의 효율은 결코 100퍼센트가 되지 못한다. 우리가 그 이동이 거의 90퍼센트와 다름없이 되게 한다고 해도, 그 네 단계들에서의 (메시지) 손실은 전체적인 효율성을 여전히 65퍼센트 미만으로 떨어뜨린다. 어림짐작으로는, 원래 메시지의 약 절반 남짓만 독자의 머리에 도달하며, 어쩌면 그보다 훨씬 적을 것이다. 책을 읽은 후나 강의에 참석하고 난 후에 여러분이 보유하는 전체 정보의 비율에 관해 그저 잠깐 생각해 보라. 정보 이동은 실제로는 손해 보는 장사이다.

구문 [12행~14행] Just think for a moment about *the proportion of the total information* [you retain] after **reading** a book [or] **attending** a lecture.
• [ ] 부분은 앞에 나온 the proportion of the total information를 수식하고 있고, 동명사구 reading ~과 attending ~은 병렬구조를 이루어 after의 목적어 역할을 한다.

어휘 transfer (장소를) 옮기다; 환승하다   devise 고안하다   determine 알아내다,

밝히다 **efficiency** 효율, 능률 *cf.* **efficient** 효율적인 **as good as** ~나 다름없는[마찬가지인] **overall** 전반적인 **rough guess** 어림짐작 **proportion** 비율, 균형 **retain** 보유하다

[선택지] mutually 서로, 상호 간에 **beneficial** 유익한, 이익을 가져오는 **temporal** 일시적인, 잠시의 **uncertainty** 불확실성, 불확정 **real-time** 실시간의; 동시의

4 무관 문장

해설 신석기 시대의 거석 건축 양식은 당대의 계층화된 사회를 반영하기도 하고 사회 결속 기능을 수행했다고 추정되기도 한다는 내용의 글인데, ④번 문장은 고대의 무덤이 당대인의 믿음과 일상생활을 보여준다는 내용으로 전체 글의 흐름과 무관하다.

해석 신석기 시대의 거대한 돌로 만든 육중한 무덤과 의식용 구조물들은 '크다(megas)'와 '돌(lithos)'에 대한 그리스어 단어에서 나온 거석 건축 양식이라고 알려져 있다. ① 고고학자들은 그것들을 만든 사회의 속성에 대해 의견이 다르다. ② 어떤 사람들은 거석 기념물들이 강력한 종교 혹은 정치 지도자들이 그것의 디자인을 지시하고 이러한 야심찬 공학 프로젝트를 성취하는 데 필요한 대규모 노동 인력을 장악했던 복잡하고 계층화된 사회를 반영한다고 믿는다. ③ 다른 해석자들은 이러한 거대한 사업이 사회 집단 내부의, 그리고 사회 집단들 사이에서의 협동적 협업에 대한 명확한 증거이며, (사회는) 지배층 엘리트의 통제 권력 없이 사회적 화합을 북돋우는 공동 프로젝트의 둘레에서 하나가 되었다고 주장한다. ④ 무덤 건축 양식은 복잡했고 채색의 형태, 조각, 그리고 문자에 나타난 무덤의 예술은 고대인들의 믿음과 일상생활을 엿보게 한다. ⑤ 많은 거석 구조물들은 죽음과 관련되어 있으며, 최근의 해석은 개인과 집단 정체성, 결속, 그리고 논쟁이 발생된 공공 연극 공연으로서의 죽음과 매장의 근본적인 역할을 강조한다.

구문 [6행~10행] Some **believe** // (that) megalithic monuments reflect complex, stratified *societies* [**in which** powerful religious or political leaders dictated their design / and commanded *the large workforce* (necessary to accomplish these ambitious engineering projects)].

● believe 뒤에 명사절 접속사 that이 생략되어 있다. [ ]은 '전치사+관계대명사' 형태인 in which가 이끄는 관계사절로 societies를 수식하고, 여기서 동사 dictated와 commanded가 and로 연결되어 병렬구조를 이룬다. ( )은 the large workforce를 수식한다.

[11행~15행] Other interpreters argue that these massive undertakings are clear evidence for cooperative collaboration within and among *social groups*, / **coalescing** around *a common project* [that fueled social cohesion] without the controlling power of a ruling elite.

● social groups는 전치사 within과 among의 공통 목적어이다. coalescing 이하는 능동의 의미를 가지는 분사구문이며, 의미상 주어는 social groups이다. [ ]는 주격 관계대명사 that이 이끄는 관계사절로 a common project를 수식한다.

어휘 **massive** 크고 육중한 **ceremonial** 의식의, 의례의 **Neolithic** 신석기 시대의 **megalithic** 거석의 **architecture** 건축 양식 **archaeologist** 고고학자 **monument** 기념비 **dictate** 지시하다, 명령하다 **command** 지휘하다, 장악하다 **workforce** 노동력[노동 인구] **ambitious** 야심 있는 **interpreter** 해석자, 설명자 **undertaking** 일, 프로젝트 **collaboration** 협업 **fuel** 연료를 공급하다, 부채질하다 **cohesion** 화합, 결합 **stress** 강조하다; 압박, 강제 **play out** ~을 발생시키다[유발하다]

5 요약문 완성 ④

해설 종이와 연필만 가지고 작곡을 하는 것이 작곡에 유용한데(useful), 상상 속에

서 잘 진행되던 작곡 과정에서 실제 악기의 음을 들으면 이것이 상상과의 괴리로 인해 작곡에 지장을 줄(disruptive) 수 있기 때문이다.

해석 믿건 안 믿건, 컴퓨터가 구비된 이 세상에서도 종이 한 장과 연필이 음악 작곡가에게 최고의 도구인 많은 상황이 여전히 존재한다. 권위 있는 많은 현대 작곡가들은, 특히 1940년 이전에 태어난 사람들은 종이와 연필 말고 무엇으로도 작업하지 않을 것이다. 그러므로, 이러한 변치 않은 도구들에 비해 당신이 너무나 고급 수준이라고 결코 생각하지 마라. 오직 종이와 연필로만 음악을 작곡하는 것에는 피아노나 다른 악기로 작곡하는 것에 비해 어떤 놀라운 이점이 있다. 우선 많은 작곡가들이 악기 자체의 실제 소리가 작곡 과정에 방해되는 것을 알게 된다. 당신이 머릿속으로 음표의 완벽한 이어짐을 들으며 생각에 깊이 잠겨 있는데 갑자기 당신의 손가락이 실제 건반을 건드리고, 그것이 정확히 당신이 상상한 것과 같은 소리가 나지 않는다고 상상해보라. 진짜 소리는 거칠며, 당신이 적기 전에 상상한 악구의 첫 음을 듣는 것조차 당신으로 하여금 음악 한 곡 전체를 잃게 할 수 있다.

↓

음악을 종이와 연필 같은 전통적인 도구로 작곡하는 것이 악기로 하는 것보다 더 (A) <u>유용한데</u>, 왜냐하면 진짜 소리는 작곡 과정에 (B) <u>지장</u>을 줄 수 있기 때문이다.

구문 [3행~6행] *Many important modern composers*, especially ***those*** (born before 1940), won't work with anything **but** paper and pencil.

● ( ) 부분은 과거분사구로 앞의 those를 수식하며, those는 many important modern composers를 지칭한다. 전치사 but은 '~을 제외하고'의 뜻이다.

[9행~11행] For one thing, many composers **find** *the actual sound of the instrument itself* **interruptive to the composition process**.

● the actual ~ itself가 동사 find의 목적어이고 interruptive 이하가 목적어를 설명하는 보어이다.

어휘 **computerize** 컴퓨터를 구비하다 **advanced** 선진의, 고급의 **humble** 겸손한, 변치 않은 **for one thing** 우선, 첫째로 **interruptive** 방해하는 **sequence** 연속, 순서 **note** 음표 **harsh** 거친, 가혹한
[선택지] disruptive 지장을 주는

1 빈칸 추론   ⑤

해설 이 글은 첫 문장이 주제문으로, 이야기가 우리의 삶의 거의 모든 면에 영향을 끼친다는 요지를 고고학자, 역사학자, 기업의 간부, 정치 분석가, 법학자의 사례로 열거한다. 즉 모두가 이야기를 만들어 내는 사람들이라는 내용의 글이므로 정치 분석가들 역시 대통령 선거를 ⑤ '그 나라에 관한 상반되는 이야기 간의 경쟁'으로도 간주한다는 것을 알 수 있다.

① 사람들이 자신의 권리를 행사할 아주 중요한 기회
② 민족 주체성을 설립하기 위한 정치 공약들 간의 경쟁
③ 보수적인 우파와 진보적인 좌파 간의 치열한 분쟁
④ 정부와 야당 간의 피할 수 없는 싸움

해석 인간은 이야기의 존재이므로 이야기는 우리 삶의 거의 모든 면에 관련된다. 고고학자들은 돌과 뼈에서 단서들을 캐내고 그 단서들을 짜 맞추어 과거에 관한 이야기로 만들어 낸다. 역사학자들 또한 이야기꾼들이다. 어떤 사람들은 콜럼버스의 아메리카 발견에 대한 일반적인 이야기와 같은 학교 교과서 속의 많은 이야기는 왜곡과 생략으로 너무 가득해서 역사보다는 신화에 더 가깝다고 주장한다. 기업체 간부들은 창의적으로 이야기하는 사람이어야 한다는 말을 점점 더 많이 듣는다. 즉, 그들은 자신들의 제품과 브랜드에 대하여, 정서적으로 소비자들의 관심을 끄는, 강한 흥미를 주는 이야기를 해야 한다는 것이다. 정치 분석가들은 대통령 선거를 유력한 정치인들과 그들의 생각 사이의 경쟁뿐만 아니라 또한 그 나라에 관한 상반되는 이야기 간의 경쟁으로도 간주한다. 법학자들 또한 재판을 이야기 경쟁으로 간주하는데, 여기서 서로 대립하는 변호인단이 누가 진짜 주인공인지를 두고 논쟁하면서 유죄와 무죄의 이야기를 구성한다.

구문 [15행~18행] Legal scholars regard a trial as a story contest, too, // **in which** opposing counsels construct narratives of guilt and innocence — arguing over who is the real protagonist.

• '전치사+which'는 이 자체가 전명구로 부사이며 이것이 이끄는 절은 관계부사절처럼 완전한 구조다. 선행사에 따라 where, when, why 등의 관계부사로 대체할 수 있으며, 이 문장에서는 where로 바꿔 쓸 수 있다.

어휘 archaeologist 고고학자 piece A together A를 짜 맞추다; 종합하다 distortion 왜곡 omission 생략 executive (기업의) 간부, 중역 spin (그럴듯하게) 이야기하다; 실을 잣다 compelling 강한 흥미를 주는 transport 관심을 끌다; 운송하다 analyst 분석가 opposing 서로 대립하는 counsel 변호인단; 상담
[선택지] exercise (권력을) 행사하다 pledge 공약; 서약 conservative 보수적인 liberal 진보적인 inevitable 피할 수 없는 conflicting 상반되는

2 글의 순서   ④

해설 주어진 글은 한 실험에서 참가자 절반에게 몸을 수그리게 했다는 내용이므로 반대로 나머지 참가자들에게는 자세를 똑바로 하게 한 후 두 집단에 퍼즐을 풀게 했다는 (C)가 먼저 나와야 한다. 그다음에 그 퍼즐들은 사실 풀 수 없는 것이었다는 내용과 실험의 목적이 나타나는 (A)가 나와야 한다. 마지막으로 실험의 결과(자세가 바른 집단이 두 배 더 오랫동안 끈기를 보임)를 설명하는 (B)가 나와야 적절하다.

해석 1980년대에 존 리스킨드는 자세가 끈기에 미치는 영향을 조사하기로 했다. 리스킨드는 참가자들을 두 자세 중 하나를 취하게 했다. 참가자들 중 절반은 푹 쓰러진 자세를 취하게 되어 등이 굽고 머리가 아래로 떨구어졌다.
(C) 대조적으로, 남은 참가자들은 어깨를 뒤로 하고 고개를 꼿꼿이 든 채로 똑바로 앉아 있으라는 말을 들었다. 약 3분 동안 구부리거나 똑바로 앉은 후에, 각 참가자들은 다른 방으로 보내졌고 연필을 페이지에서 벗어나지 않고 도표를 따라 그리는 것을 포함한 몇 개의 퍼즐을 시도하여 풀라는 요청을 받았다.
(A) 사실, 퍼즐 중 많은 것이 풀 수 없는 것이었고 리스킨드는 참가자들이 실패에 직면하여 얼마나 오랫동안 계속할 것인지에만 관심이 있었다.
(B) 그의 연구 결과를 한 논문에 기술하면서, 리스킨드는 전에 똑바로 앉아 있던 참가자들이 구부정하게 앉은 사람들보다 어떻게 해서 거의 두 배 오랫동안 견뎠는지를 기록했다.

구문 [10행~13행] ~ Riskind made a note of / **how** *the participants* [who had previously been sitting up straight] / endured for nearly **twice as** *long* **as** the slouchers.

• 밑줄 친 how 이하는 made a note of의 목적어이다. [ ] 부분은 the participants를 수식하는 관계사절이다. 「A twice as ~ as B」는 'A가 B보다 두 배 더 ~하다'의 뜻이다.

[14행~16행] In contrast, the remaining participants were told to sit upright, / with *their shoulders* **pulled back** and *heads* **held high**.

• 「with O p.p.」는 'O가 ~한 채로'의 뜻인데 '목적어+과거분사'에 해당하는 their shoulders pulled back과 heads held high가 and로 연결되어 병렬구조를 이루고 있다.

어휘 posture 자세 persistence 끈기 carry on 계속하다 in the face of ~에 직면하여 upright 똑바른, 꼿꼿한 hold high 높이 들다. (고개 등을) 꼿꼿이 들다 trace (선을) 그리다; 베끼다; 추적하다

3 문장 넣기   ⑤

해설 이 글은 과학은 과학자의 모국어와는 전혀 관련이 없는 그 자체의 언어를 지니고 있어 과학 논문을 쓸 때 모국어가 아닌 다른 언어로 쓰는 것이 장애가 되지 않는다는 내용이다. 주어진 문장의 In other words(다시 말해서)를 통해 영어를 잘하지 못하는 것이 논문을 쓰지 못하는 이유는 아니라는 것과 유사한 내용이 주어진 문장 앞에 언급되어야 함을 알 수 있다. 또한, ⑤ 이후에 In fact(사실상)를 통해 그 견해를 더 강조하여 오히려 원어민이 아닌 영어 사용자들이 이점을 가질 수도 있다는 내용이 나오고 있으므로 주어진 문장은 ⑤에 들어가는 것이 가장 적절하다.

해석 과학은 과학자의 모국어와는 전혀 관련이 없는 그 자체의 언어를 지닌다. 그것(과학의 언어)은 논리의 언어인데, 그 언어에서 잘 제시된 증거로부터 이치에 맞는 주장이 생겨나 타당하고 일관성 있는 결론으로 이어진다. 그 언어는 그것을 적는 사람의 출신과 그가 선호하는 언어와는 상관없이 같으며, 좋은 과학 저술은 주로 과학을 정확하고 명확히 표현하는 것에 달려 있다. 원어민이 영어 표현을 깔끔하게 정리하고 현대의 일상적 표현을 따르기 위해 그다음에 교정하는 것은 비교적 쉽고, 그 논문은 좋은 논문이 될 것이다. 과학의 표현이 보잘것없다면, 아무리 많은 양의 영어 교정도 그 논문을 만족스러운 논문으로 바꿀 수 없다. 다시 말해서, 영어의 제한된 유창성이 좋은 연구를 발표하기 위해 논문을 쓰는 것을 연기할 타당한 이유는 아니다. 사실상, 과학 저술에 관한 한 원어민이 아닌 영어 사용자들이 종종 뜻밖의 이점을 갖는다.

구문 [5행~8행] It is *the language of logic*, // **in which** reasoned arguments are developed from well-presented evidence and lead to sound and consistent conclusions.

- '전치사+관계대명사' 형태인 in which가 이끄는 계속적 용법의 관계대명사절이 앞에 있는 명사 the language of logic을 보충 설명해주고 있다.

[8행~10행] That language is the same regardless of *the origin and preferred tongue* (of *the person* [who writes it]), ~.

• ( )은 전명구로 the origin and preferred tongue을 수식하며, [ ]은 the person을 수식하는 관계사절이다.

어휘 **fluency** (언어의) 유창성, 능숙도 **valid** 타당한, 근거 있는; 유효한 **put off** ~을 연기하다[미루다] **article** 논문; 기사; 물품 **have nothing to do with** ~와는 전혀 관련이 없다 **native tongue** 모국어 **logic** 논리; 타당성 **reasoned** 이치에 맞는, 조리 정연한 **argument** 주장, 논거; 논쟁 **evidence** 증거; 증언 **sound** 타당한, 믿을 만한; 건강한; 소리 **consistent** 일관성 있는; 한결같은 **regardless of** ~에 상관없이[구애받지 않고] **precisely** 정확하게, 신중하게 **subsequent** 그다음의, 차후의 **edit** 교정하다, 편집하다 **native speaker** 원어민 **tidy up** ~을 깔끔하게 정리하다 **comply with** ~을 따르다, 준수하다 **relatively** 비교적 **correction** 교정, 정정 **when it comes to A** A에 관한 한

[24행~26행] You'll realize that *all those things* [they sell at the mall] are pretty useless in leading a happy life.

• [ ] 부분은 앞에 목적격 관계대명사가 생략된 관계사절로 all those things를 수식한다.

어휘 **introvert** 내성적인 사람 **and so on** 기타 등등 **small talk** 잡담 **resort** 휴양지, 리조트 **sip** 조금씩 마시다 **on the road** 여행 중인 **minimalist** 미니멀리스트, 최소한도 요구자

4~5 장문　　4 ④　5 ⑤

해설 **4.** 여행으로 인해 낯선 사람과 대화하는 데 능숙해지고 책에서 배울 수 없는 경험을 얻게 되고 덜 물질적이 된다고 했으므로 적절한 제목은 ④ '왜 여행이 당신을 더 좋은 사람으로 만드는가'이다.
① 더 소유하는 것 대 더 존재하는 것
② 경험을 사기 위해 해외여행을 하라
③ 여행을 더 즐겁게 만들어줄 방법
⑤ 여행은 숨 쉴 공간을 준다
5. 여행을 하면서 필요한 물건이 얼마나 적은지를 알게 된다고 했으므로 쇼핑몰에서 파는 것들이 행복에 무용하다는 것을 깨달을 것이다. 그러므로 ⑤는 useless 등이 되어야 한다.

해석 여행하는 동안 낯선 이들로부터 친구를 사귀고 새로운 사람들과 이야기하는 것에 익숙해지는 것을 배운다. 내가 처음 여행을 시작했을 때 나는 약간 (a) 내성적이고 모르는 사람들과 이야기하는 게 불편했다. 지금은 낯선 이들과 우리가 몇 년 알았던 것처럼 즐겁게 이야기할 것이다. 여행은 낯선 이들과 편안하게 이야기를 나누게 해줄 뿐 아니라 또한 그것을 더 잘하게 해준다. 항상 사람들과 이야기를 나눈 후 일상적인 질문들은 (b) 지루해진다. 잠시 후 여러분은 사람들이 어디 출신인지 어디로 갈지 얼마나 오래 여행하고 있는지 등등에 상관하지 않는다. 이런 종류의 질문들은 그 사람에 대해서 정말로 어느 것도 알려주지 않는다. 여러분은 잡담과 흥미로운 질문을 하는 것, 즉 (c) 중요하고 그 사람에 대해 더 잘 알려줄 질문들을 묻는 데 더 능숙하게 될 것이다. 여러분이 차가운 음료를 조금씩 마시면서 리조트에 앉아있지 않는다면 여행은 여러분에게 세상에 대해 가르칠 것이다.
여러분은 사람과 역사와 문화와 어떤 사람들은 단지 꿈꿀 수만 있었던 장소들에 대한 놀라운 사실들에 대해 배울 것이다. 그것은 책에서 배울 수 없는 것이고 여러분은 여행의 경험으로 그것을 알게 될 수 있다. 게다가 여행은 여러분을 (d) 덜 물질적으로 되도록 가르친다. 여행 중에 여러분은 사실 여러분이 필요로 하는 물건이 얼마나 적은지를 알게 된다. 쇼핑몰에서 파는 그 모든 것들이 행복한 삶으로 이끄는 데는 상당히 (e) 유용하다(→ 무용하다)는 것을 깨닫게 될 것이다. 고향으로 오면서 여러분은 무엇이 여러분이 살아가는데 필요하고 필요하지 않은가를 이해하기 때문에 자신이 미니멀리스트임을 발견하게 될 것이다.

구문 **[13행~16행]** You'll get better at small talk and asking underline{interesting questions} — *the ones* [that matter and tell you something about the person].
• the ones 이하 부분과 interesting questions는 서로 동격 관계이다. [ ] 부분은 관계사절로 the ones를 수식한다.

1 글의 요지 ⑤

해설 사소한 정보를 기억하려 노력하면 추상적 사고에 해가 되고, 많은 정보에 노출되는 것은 지적 능력을 낮춘다는 내용이다. 그러므로 글의 요지로 가장 적절한 것은 ⑤이다.

해석 당신의 두뇌는 시시각각 업데이트된다. 본질적으로, 당신은 새로운 처리 시스템을 빈번히 얻게 된다. 정말로 당신에게는 어느 정도 수준의 도전, 새로움, 혹은 다양함을 갖춘 당신이 행하는 모든 일로 당신의 두뇌를 바꿀 잠재력이 있다. 내 연구에서 한 가지 흥미로운 역설이 발견되었는데, 미미한 세부 사항을 기억하는 데 집중하면 그것이 더 전략적인 추상적 사고에 관여할 능력에 불리한 영향을 미칠지도 모른다는 것이다. 본질적으로, 가능한 한 많은 세부 사항을 기억하려고 애쓰는 것은 실제로 당신이 당신의 두뇌의 다락방에 들여보내는 것에 대하여 선별을 잘하는 데에 역효과를 낸다. 이러한 패턴은 더 많은 정보에 대한 접근이 왜 그 자체로 우리를 더 똑똑하게 만들어주지 못하는지를 설명하는 데 도움이 된다. 아마 정반대가 사실일 가능성이 더 높다. 대량의 정보에 대한 노출은 당신의 지능을 앗아가고 얼려버린다.

구문 [3행~5행] Indeed, you have *the potential* (to change your brain with *everything* [(that) you do] [that has some level of challenge, novelty, or variety]).
• ( ) 부분은 the potential을 수식하는 to부정사구이다. 두 [ ] 부분은 관계대명사절로 앞의 everything을 수식한다. you do 앞에는 목적격 관계대명사 that이 생략되었다.

[8행~11행] In essence, **trying** to remember **as** *many details* **as possible** can actually work against being selective about **what** you let into your brain's **attic**.
• 동명사 trying이 이끄는 밑줄 친 부분이 주어이며 「as ~ as possible」은 '가능한 한 ~하게'의 뜻이다. what 이하는 about의 목적어이다.

어휘 in essence 본질적으로 novelty 새로움 minute 극미한, 상세한 adversely 불리하게 engage in ~에 참여하다 strategic 전략적인 abstract 추상적인 selective 선별적인, 까다로운 attic 다락방 on one's own 혼자서, 단독으로

2 빈칸 추론 ③

해설 이 글은 하이퍼링킹과 같은 디지털 시대의 상호 작용식 읽기와 쓰기의 특징을 다루고 있다. 하이퍼링킹은 서로 다른 지문 안에서뿐만 아니라 다른 지문 사이에서, 여러 지문을 넘나들며 읽는다고 했으므로 지문 간의 연관성은 현저하게 ③ '확대된' 것이 가장 적절하다.
① 사소한 ② 무시된 ④ 공정한 ⑤ 변함없는

해석 현대의 읽고 쓰는 일은 우리 눈앞에서 변화하고 있다. 상호적 읽기와 쓰기는 현재 점점 더 우리의 관심을 끈다. 가상의 행간과 여백에 의견을 달거나 즉각적으로 서로의 의견을 읽고, 협력자가 이제 막 작성한 것에 어휘나 문장을 추가함으로써 실시간으로 문서를 같이 작성하면서, 우리는 멀리서도 다른 사람들과 함께 읽을 수 있다. 전체 문장 간의 경계는 말할 것도 없고, 자신의 표현과 다른 사람의 표현 사이의 경계가 빠르게 모호해진다. 하이퍼링킹은 별개의 지문 '안'과 '사이'에서뿐만 아니라 지문을 훨씬 더 활발하게 넘나들며 읽는 것을, 즉 통찰과 참고 문장을 상호 참조하고 상호 구성하는 것을 부추겨 왔다. 그 결과 지문들이 어떻게 연관되는지가 현저하게 확대되었고, 이는 지금까지 대체로 시야에서 숨겨졌던 것들을 가시화시킨다.

구문 [3행~8행] One can read together with others remotely, / **commenting** between the virtual lines and in the margins, / **reading** each other's comments instantaneously, / **composing** documents together in real time / by adding words or sentences to those just composed by one's collaborators.
• 주절 뒤에 세 개의 분사구문 commenting ~ margins, reading ~ instantaneously, composing ~ collaborators가 접속사 없이 콤마(,)로만 연결되었다.

어휘 contemporary 현대의; 동시대의 interactive 상호 작용하는 engage (주의·관심을) 끌다 remotely 멀리서 virtual 가상의 line (글의) 행 margin 여백; 가장자리 instantaneously 즉각적으로 collaborator 협력자 let alone ~은 말할 것도 없고 blurred 모호한, 흐릿한 discrete 개별적인 reference 참고하다 interweave 섞어 넣다[짜다] insight 통찰 dramatically 현저하게
[선택지] trifling 사소한 disregard 무시하다 magnify 확대하다 impartial 공정한, 공평한 invariable 변하지 않는

3 무관 문장 ④

해설 혁신적인 도시가 되기 위해 인간의 재능이 필요하다는 것을 언급한 글로서 '스마트 도시'라는 용어의 쓰임을 언급한 ④는 글의 흐름과 무관하다.

해석 도시의 혁신성은 인간 재능의 우수한 특질과 직접적인 관계가 있다. ① 중국의 해안 도시들은 우수한 특질을 기르고, 가장 재능이 있는 지식 노동자들 보유하고, 국내의 다른 지역 출신의 지식 근로자 중 최고를 끌어들이는 데 더 성공적이었기 때문에 상황 대처가 더 빨랐다. ② 그 해안 도시들은 또한 외부인에게 더 개방적이고 접근성이 있으며 전 세계의 지식 네트워크와 통합되었다. ③ 더 작은 내륙 도시가 혁신적인 스마트 도시가 되기 위해서는 전문화하고 전국에서 전문 분야에 있는 최고의 두뇌 중 일부를 견인할 필요가 있을 것이다. ④ 스마트 시티는 미래 도시에 대한 가장 인기 있는 용어가 되었고, 그 용어는 전 세계적으로 알려진 용어가 되어서 '지속 가능한 도시' 또는 '디지털 도시' 같은 다른 말로 된 용어를 대신하고 있다. ⑤ 결국 혁신의 생명선인 재능의 우수성을 기반으로 하여 구축되는 혁신적인 도시가 되기 위한 모든 진지한 시도는, 도시 설계와 재개발을 세계 정상급의 전문 기술을 갖춘 일부 핵심 분야의 개발에 대한 집중과 결합해야 할 것이다.

구문 [2행~7행] China's coastal cities have been quicker off the mark because they have been more successful in **nurturing** quality, **retaining** the most talented knowledge workers, and **attracting** the cream of the knowledge workers from other parts of the country.
• 전치사 in의 목적어로 nurturing, retaining, attracting로 시작하는 동명사구 세 개가 콤마(,)와 and로 연결되어 병렬구조를 이루고 있다.

어휘 innovativeness 혁신성 coastal 해안의 quick off the mark 상황 대처가 빠른 nurture 양성하다, 키우다 retain 보유하다, 유지하다 integrate with ~와 통합되다 inland 내륙의 pull in ~을 견인하다 replace 대신하다 sustainable 지속 가능한 life blood 생명선 urban 도시의 renewal 재개발 core 핵심적인 expertise 전문 기술[지식]

4 글의 순서 ③

해설 사람들이 음식을 선택하는 것은 알맞은 청중에게 알맞은 메시지를 전달하려는 의도가 있다는 주어진 글 뒤에 그 예가 될 수 있는 혼자 먹는 경우와 연인이 될

116

가능성이 있는 사람 앞에서 음식을 선택하는 것이 달라진다는 내용의 (B)가 이어져야 한다. 그다음 그러나(however) 이러한 음식마다 지니는 부호화된 메시지(its own coded message[it])를 상대방이 정확하게 이해하는 것만은 아니라는 내용의 (C)가 이어지고, 그에 대한 예가 (C)의 두 번째 문장에 나온다. 이후 마찬가지로(Equally) 비슷한 예를 더하고 있는 (A)가 이어져야 한다.

해석 물론, 사람들은 많은 다양한 종류의 식사를 하고, 알맞은 청중에게 알맞은 메시지를 전달하려는 의도로 그것들을 선택한다.

(B) 혼자 서두르며 먹는 일상의 음식을 위해서 사치스러운 재료에 거금을 쓰지 않는 것처럼, 연인이 될 가능성이 있는 사람에게 깊은 인상을 주려고 애쓸 때, 반 정도 먹다 남은 음식을 다시 데우지는 않을 것이다. 어떤 의미에서 모든 음식은 그 자체의 부호화된 메시지를 지닌다.

(C) 그러나 이것이 언제나 다른 사람에 의해 쉽사리 인식되거나 정확하게 이해된다고 말하는 것은 아니다. 식사를 준비하는 사람에게는 편안한 약식 행위로 의도될지도 모르는 것이 초대받은 손님에게는 게으름으로 해석될지도 모른다.

(A) 마찬가지로, 채식주의자에게 제공된 구운 소고기로 구성된 식사는 고의적인 모욕으로 해석될 수도 있다. 모든 언어에서처럼, 잘못된 전달이 있을 수 있다. 이것(잘못된 전달이 있음)에도 불구하고, 먹는 일을 관찰하거나 의견을 말하는 외부인은 아주 큰 어려움 없이 보통 의도된 메시지를 해독할 수 있다.

구문 [6행~9행] Despite this, *an outsider* (observing or commenting on an eating event) can usually decode the intended message without too much difficulty.

• ( ) 부분은 현재분사가 이끄는 분사구로 주어 an outsider를 수식한다.

[16행~19행] **What** may be intended as cozy informality to *someone* (preparing a meal) / **might be interpreted** as laziness / by an invited guest.

• 선행사를 포함하는 관계대명사 What이 이끄는 What ~ a meal이 주어, might be interpreted가 동사이다. ( ) 부분은 현재분사구로 someone을 수식한다.

어휘 naturally 물론, 당연히; 저절로   intention 의도 *cf.* intend 의도하다; 작정하다
roast 구운   calculated 고의적인, 계산적인; 계산된   insult 모욕(하다), 무례   observe 관찰하다; (의견을) 말하다; (법 등을) 지키다   comment on ~에 대해 의견을 말하다
leftover ((주로 복수형)) 남은 음식; 남은 (것)   impress 깊은 인상[감명]을 주다   spend a fortune 거금을 쓰다   extravagant 사치스러운, 낭비하는; 화려한   ingredient 재료   in solitude 혼자서, 외롭게   coded 부호[암호]화된   readily 쉽사리; 즉시; 선뜻   perceive 인식[지각]하다   interpret 해석하다; 이해하다   cozy 편안한, 안락한   informality 약식 (행위); 비공식   laziness 게으름, 태만

---

5 문장 넣기   ②

해설 주어진 문장의 '이것들(these)'이 가리키는 것이 정답을 찾는 단서가 된다. 예술 공연의 성공 여부를 판별하기 위해 고른음, 악구 나누기, 박자, 정확성, 속도, 음색의 맑음 등의 고려 사항들이 언급되는데, '그러나(But)'로 시작되는 주어진 문장에서 바로 피아니스트의 열 개의 손가락이 음을 만들어내는 것이라고 강조하므로 주어진 문장은 ②에 들어가는 것이 적절하다.

해석 예술 공연이 성공할지 실패할지를 아는 것은 우리가 어떤 공연 상황에서 무엇이 성공이나 실패로 간주되는지를 아는 것을 필요로 한다. 음악 비평가들은 피아니스트의 고른 음, 악구 나누기, 박자, 정확성, 그리고 멜로디를 유지하거나 최고조에 이르게 하는 능력을 고려할 것이다. 속도와 음색의 맑음은 중요한 고려 사항일 수 있는데, 이는 가장 빠른 연주가 최고일 것이라는 말이 아니다. 그러나 이것들의 이면에는 진술되지 않은 가정이 있는데, 그것은 그 음을 만들어 내는 것은 바로 한 사람의, '도움을 받지 않는 열 개의 손가락'이라는 것이다. 화려하게 쏟아내는 음들을 가지고 거장 피아니스트가 만들어 내는 흥분은 본질적으로 이 사실과 관계가 있다. 전

자 장치로 소리가 합성된 동일한 청각 경험은 결코 우리를 똑같이 경탄하게 할 수 없다. 전자 음향 합성 장치는 여러분이 원하는 만큼 빨리 개개의 음을 만들어 낼 수 있지만, 피아니스트는 그렇게 할 수 없다. 연주가 인간의 성취임을 보여 주는 것에 대한 감탄은 거장의 연주를 듣는 전율을 형성한다. 예술에서의 위조와 다른 형태의 속임수는 공연의 본질을 잘못 나타내고 그러므로 성취를 잘못 나타낸다.

구문 [1행~3행] But **behind these** is an unstated assumption: that **it is** *one person's ten unaided fingers* **that** produce the sounds.

• 전명구 behind these가 강조되어 문두에 나가 동사(is)와 주어(an unstated assumption)의 도치가 일어났다. an unstated assumption과 동격 관계인 that절에는 「it is ~ that ...(…하는 것은 바로 ~이다)」 강조구문이 쓰여 one person's *ten unaided fingers*를 강조한다.

[11행~13행] *The excitement* [(which[that]) a virtuoso pianist generates with a glittering shower of notes] **is** intrinsically connected with this fact.

• [ ] 부분은 목적격 관계대명사 which[that]가 생략된 관계사절로 주어 The excitement를 수식하고 문장의 동사는 is이다.

[17행~19행] **Built into the thrill of hearing a virtuoso** is <u>admiration for what</u>
　　　　　　　　　　　　　　　　　　　　　　　V　　　　　S
the performance represents as a human achievement.

• Built into ~ a virtuoso가 강조되어 문두에 나가 주어(admiration ~ a human achievement)와 동사(is)가 도치되었다.

어휘 unstated 진술[공표]되지 않은, 무언의   assumption 가정; 인수   unaided 도움을 받지 않는   count as ~로 간주되다   critic 비평가   tone 고른음, 악음 ((진동이 규칙적이고 일정한 높이가 있는 음))   phrase 악구를 구분하여 연주하다[부르다]; 악구   sustain 유지하다   line 멜로디, (일련의) 음   brilliance (음색의) 맑음; 탁월   glittering 화려한, 찬란한   shower 쏟아져 옴, 많음   note (악기의) 음, 음표   intrinsically 본질적으로   aurally 청각적으로   identical 동일한, 똑같은   synthesize 합성하다   dazzle 감탄시키다; 황홀하게 하다   build A into B A를 B로 만들다   admiration 감탄, 찬탄   fakery 속임수   misrepresent 잘못 나타내다

1 글의 제목 ④

해설 행동을 유발하기 위해서는 자신의 계획을 적어보라는 것이 이 글의 요지이므로, 제목으로는 ④ '행동에 동기 부여하기, 즉 결심을 적어라'가 가장 적절하다.
① 말하는 사람이 되지 말고 행동하는 사람이 돼라
② 일을 시작하는 것은 왜 항상 어려운가?
③ 당신이 확실히 할 수 있는 것만 약속하라
⑤ 행동 계기는 변화가 힘들 때에 일을 변화시킨다

해석 뉴욕 대학의 심리학자인 Peter Gollwitzer와 그의 동료인 Veronika Brandstatter는 행동 계기라는 것이 행동에 동기를 부여하는 데 매우 효과적임을 발견했다. 한 연구에서 그들은 크리스마스이브를 어떻게 보냈는지에 대해 보고서를 써서 제출함으로써 수업에서 추가 학점을 얻을 수 있는 기회가 있는 대학생들을 지켜보았다. 하지만 조건이 있었다. 학점을 얻기 위해서는, 그들은 그 보고서를 12월 26일까지 제출해야 했다. 대부분의 학생들이 보고서를 쓸 의향을 가지고 있었지만 그들 중 33%만이 마침내 보고서를 써서 제출했다. 그러나 연구에 참가한 일부 학생들은 행동 계기를 세우는 것, 즉 정확하게 언제 어디에서 보고서를 쓰려고 하는지를 미리 기록하도록 요구받았다. 그 학생들 중 75%가 보고서를 썼다. 그렇게 작은 정신적 투자에 비하면 그것은 꽤나 상당한 결과이다.

구문 [3행~6행] In one study, they followed *college students* [who had *the chance* (**to earn** extra credit in a class by writing a paper about how they spent Christmas Eve)].
• 주격 관계대명사 who 이하가 college students를 수식하고 있다. ( )는 to부정사의 형용사적 용법으로 the chance를 수식한다.

[10행~13행] However, some students in the study were required to set action triggers — to record, in advance, exactly **when and where they intended to write the report**.
• to record 이하는 to set action triggers와 동격 관계로 이를 부연 설명해주고 있다. when and where로 시작되는 간접의문문은 to record의 목적어 역할을 하고 있다.

어휘 trigger 계기, 동기; (총의) 방아쇠; 유발하다 credit 학점; 신용; 칭찬; 인정 turn in ~을 제출하다 (= submit) in advance 미리, 사전에 investment 투자(액)

2 밑줄 어휘 ④

해설 사람들은 새로운 관계에서 처음에는 일상적인 정보만을 공유하지만, 시간이 지나 서로를 더 많이 좋아하고 신뢰하게 되면 개인적인 정보를 점차 드러내게 된다는 내용이므로 오랫동안 알고 지낸 후에야 더 개인적인 일을 말하는 것을 편하게 느낀다는 내용이 알맞다. 따라서 ④ uncomfortable(불편한)은 comfortable(편한)로 바뀌어야 한다.

해석 새로운 관계에서, 사람들은 보통 처음에는 단지 몇몇 세부 사항만을 공유하고 그들이 서로 좋아하고 신뢰해야만 더 개인적인 정보를 제공하면서 서서히 자신을 ① 드러낸다. 예를 들어 친구가 되기 시작했을 때, Deepak과 Prasad는 자신들이 어디에서 성장했는지, 가장 좋아하는 팀은 무엇인지, 그리고 자신들의 직업이 무엇인지와 같은 주로 ② 일상적인 정보를 공유했다. 그들이 서로를 더 ③ 신뢰하게 되면서, 그들은 정치, 관계, 종교와 같은 것들에 관한 자신의 의견을 공유하기 시작했다. 그들이 꽤 오랫동안 서로를 알고 난 후에야 그들은 Prasad의 건강 문제나

Deepak의 결혼 생활의 어려운 점과 같은 더 개인적인 것에 관해 말하는 데 ④ 불편하게(→ 편하게) 느꼈다. 비록 몇몇 관계에서 사람들은 ⑤ 사적인 정보를 매우 빠르게 공유하기 시작하지만, 자기 노출은 보통 조금씩만 증가한다.

구문 [10행~14행] *Only after they had known each other for quite a while* **did they feel** comfortable talking about more personal things, such as Prasad's health problems or the challenges in Deepak's marriage.
• only after ~ while이 문두에 나와서 주어와 동사가 도치되어 「조동사(did)+주어(they)+동사원형(feel)」의 어순이 되었다. 밑줄 친 comfortable은 동사 feel의 보어로 쓰였다.

어휘 disclose 드러내다; 폭로하다 politics 정치; 정치적 견해 quite a while 꽤 오랫동안 intimate 친밀한; 사적인 self-disclosure 자기 노출

3 빈칸 추론 ②

해설 이 글은 사람들이 자신의 판단을 믿지 못할 때, 다른 사람들이 선택하는 것에 의존하고 강한 영향을 받는다는 내용이다. 이어지는 실험에서 상황이 모호하고 착시 때문에 움직이는 것처럼 보였기 때문에 실제로는 빛이 움직이지 않음에도 거의 모든 사람들이 집단의 평균치와 비슷하도록 자신의 추정치를 바꾸었다고 했다. 즉 ② '객관적으로 올바른 답이 없을' 때 자신을 의심하고 집단이 옳을 것이라 가정하는 상황이 일어나게 된다.
① 생각하고 답할 시간이 거의 없을
③ 외부 메시지의 일관성이 있을
④ 그들에게 반대하는 상당한 증거가 있을
⑤ 미리 발표된 어떠한 맥락이 있을

해석 사람들은 그들 자신의 판단을 믿지 못할 때, 다른 사람들이 올바르게 선택하는 방법에 대한 증거를 줄 것이라고 기대한다. 이러한 자기 의심은 터키의 사회심리학자인 무자퍼 셰리프에 의해 행해진 고전적인 일련의 실험에서처럼 상황이 모호하기 때문에 생기는지도 모른다. 셰리프는 어둡게 한 방의 벽에 한 점의 빛을 비추고는 실험 대상자들에게 그 빛을 보는 동안 그것이 얼마나 많이 움직이는지를 말해 달라고 부탁했다. 사실, 그 빛은 전혀 움직이지 않았지만, '자동운동 효과'라고 불리는 착시 때문에 비록 실험 대상자마다 정도의 차이는 있었지만 그것은 계속해서 움직이는 것처럼 보였다. 실험 대상자들이 집단 내에서 움직임에 대한 자신들의 추정치를 발표할 때, 이 추정치는 집단의 다른 구성원들이 추정한 것에 의해 강한 영향을 받았는데, 거의 모든 이들이 집단의 평균치를 향해 (자신의 추정치를) 바꿨다. 셰리프는 객관적으로 올바른 답이 없을 때, 사람들은 자신을 의심할 가능성이 있고, 따라서 특히 집단은 틀림없이 옳다고 가정할 가능성이 있다고 결론을 내렸다.

구문 [7행~8행] ~ and asked subjects to indicate **how much the light moved while they watched it**.
• how 이하는 indicate의 목적어 역할을 하는 명사절이다.

[8행~11행] Actually, the light never moved at all, // but because of *an optical illusion* (termed the *autokinetic effect*), it seemed to shift constantly about, ~
• ( )는 과거분사구로 수동의 의미로 an optical illusion을 수식한다.

어휘 look to A for B A가 B를 줄 것으로 기대하다 ambiguous 모호한 project 비추다, 투영하다 subject 실험 대상자 indicate 말하다; 나타내다 term 일컫다, 칭하다 estimate 추정치; 추정하다
[선택지] objectively 객관적으로 consistency 일관성 substantial 상당한

4 무관 문장 ④

해설 본문에서는 특별할 것 없고 일상적인 자연 경관을 보는 것만으로도 스트레스 회복의 효과가 있다는 실험을 소개하고 있는데, ④에서는 긍정적인 감정을 목표로 선정된 새롭게 만들어진 콘크리트 숲 경관을 논하고 있으므로 글의 전체적인 흐름과 맞지 않는다.

해석 대학생과 같은 비환자 집단에 대한 몇 가지 연구 결과는 단순히 일상적인 자연을 보는 것이 자연이 결여된 인공적인 경관에 비해 스트레스로부터의 회복을 촉진하는 데 상당히 더 효과적이라는 것을 보여준다. ① 한 초기 연구는 기말고사 때문에 가벼운 스트레스를 겪고 있던 학생들에게 초점을 맞추었다. ② 자연이 결여되어 있으면서 손상되지 않은 인공적인 경관의 다양한 슬라이드 샘플 또는 녹색 초목이 우세한 특별할 것 없는 자연 경관의 슬라이드 중 하나를 보는 것의 원기를 회복시키는 효과를 평가하기 위해 자기 평가 질문서가 사용되었다. ③ 결과는 공포와 분노/공격성과 같은 부정적인 감정의 더 큰 감소 및 훨씬 더 높은 수준의 긍정적인 감정에 의해 나타난 것처럼 자연 경치들이 더 큰 심리적 회복을 발전시켰음을 보여 주었다. ④ 이러한 감정을 목표로 선정된 새롭게 만들어진 콘크리트 숲 경관은 스트레스 회복을 제공하는 환경을 만드는 데 직접적인 도움이 되었다. ⑤ 또한 초목이 있는 경관이 자연이 없는 도시 경관보다 더 효과적으로 관심과 주의를 지속시켰다.

구문 [7행~12행] A self-ratings questionnaire was used to assess restorative influences of viewing **either** a diverse slide sample of *unblighted built settings* (lacking nature), **or** slides of *undistinguished nature settings* (dominated by green vegetation).

• 「either A or B (A나 B 둘 중 하나)」의 상관접속사가 사용되었고, 밑줄 친 두 부분이 각각 A, B 자리에 쓰였다. 첫 번째 ( )은 unblighted built settings를 수식하는 분사구이고, 두 번째 ( )은 undistinguished nature settings를 수식하는 분사구이다.

[19행~21행] Also, the scenes with vegetation *sustained interest and attention* **more** effectively **than did** the urban scenes without nature.

• 「비교급＋than」 구문이 사용되어 밑줄 친 두 대상을 비교하며, than 뒤에는 대동사 did와 비교 대상인 주어(the urban scenes without nature)가 도치되었다. 이때 did는 sustained interest and attention을 의미한다.

어휘 restoration 회복, 복원, 복구 *cf.* **restorative** (원기를) 회복시키는 **questionnaire** 설문지 **undistinguished** 특별하지 않은 **vegetation** 초목 **foster** 발전시키다, 조성하다 **aggression** 공격(성) **sustain** 지속시키다

---

5 요약문 완성 ②

해설 과체중인 만화 캐릭터에 노출된 아이들이 그렇지 않을 때보다 캔디와 쿠키를 두 배 정도 더 많이 먹었는데, 만화 캐릭터를 보기 전에 건강 지식에 관한 질문을 받은 경우에는 과체중 캐릭터에 영향받지 않았다고 했다. 따라서 비만인 만화 캐릭터에 노출된 아이들은 건강에 좋지 않은 음식에 탐닉할(indulge in) 가능성이 더 많은데, 이것은 건강에 관한 지식을 자극함으로써 고쳐질(modified) 수 있음을 알 수 있다.

해석 여러 세대의 아이들이 Winnie the Pooh와 Homer Simpson같은 통통한 만화 캐릭터들과 함께 자라왔으며, 이것은 아이들의 음식에 좋지 않을 수도 있다. 한 실험에서 6세에서 14세 사이의 아이들은 정상 체중이거나 과체중인 체형을 나타내도록 그려진 만화 캐릭터를 보았다. 그림의 특성에 관한 질문에 대답한 후, 아이들은 캔디나 쿠키를 제공받았다. 아이들은 분명하게 과체중인 캐릭터를 보았을 때, 더 마른 만화 캐릭터에 노출되거나 만화를 전혀 보지 않은 아이들보다 거의 두 배나 많은 캔디와 쿠키를 먹었다. 다른 연구에서, 아이들은 만화 캐릭터의 모습을 보기 전에 건강에 관한 지식에 대한 질문을 받았다. 이번에는, 아이들의 먹는 것과 관계된 선택이

더 이상 과체중인 캐릭터를 보는 것에 의해서 영향을 받지 않았다.

↓

비만인 만화 캐릭터에 노출된 아이들은 건강에 좋지 않은 음식에 (A) 탐닉할 가능성이 더 많은데, 이것은 건강에 관한 지식을 자극함으로써 (B) 고쳐질 수 있다.

구문 [3행~7행] In an experiment, *children* (between the ages of 6 and 14 years old) / viewed *cartoon characters* [that were drawn to represent / either normal weight or overweight physiques].

• ( ) 부분은 전명구로 children을 수식하고, [ ] 부분은 주격 관계대명사 that이 이끄는 관계사절로 cartoon characters를 수식한다.

[8행~12행] The kids ate almost **twice as** much candy or **as** many cookies // when they saw the apparently overweight character / **as** *those* (exposed to a thinner cartoon character or no cartoon at all).

• 「배수사(twice)＋as ~ as ...」 구문이 사용되어 '…보다 몇 배(두 배) ~한'으로 해석한다. ( ) 부분은 분사구로 those를 수식한다.

어휘 generation 세대, 대(代); 발생 **plump** 통통한, 포동포동한 **represent** 나타내다; 대표[대신]하다 **physique** 체형, 체격 **quality** 특성; 품질 **apparently** 분명히; 보아[듣자] 하니 **expose** 노출시키다 **impact** 영향을 끼치다; 영향 **obese** 비만인, 살찐 **stimulate** 자극하다, 격려하다

[선택지] indulge in ~에 탐닉하다[빠지다] **induce** 유도[설득]하다; 유발하다, 일으키다 **modify** 고치다, 수정[변경]하다 **be conscious of** ~을 의식하다[알고 있다] **reinforce** 강화[증대]하다 **be resistant to A** A에 저항하다 **optimize** 최고로[적합하게] 만들다[활용하다]; 낙관하다

1 빈칸 추론 ①

해설 기억은 과거의 사건을 정확하게 기록하는 게 아니라 유기체가 편리하고 자신의 이익을 도모하는 방식으로 계속하여 변하는 세계에 유동적으로 대처할 수 있도록 변화되는 것이며, 기억의 유동성은 불확실한 세계 속에서 생사가 걸린 결정을 내릴 수 있는 두뇌 설계에 내재된 도전을 반영하는 것이라는 내용이다. 이를 반영하여 빈칸을 완성하면 기억은 ① '생존에 관한 것이지, 정확성에 관한 것은 아니다'가 된다.

② 우리에게 잠재적 위험을 알려준다
③ 오해를 부르는 정보에 의해 왜곡된다
④ 과거의 사건이 이해되는 방식을 보여 준다
⑤ 현재의 경험에 따라 변화한다

해석 비록 우리의 기억 중 많은 것이 생생하고 몇몇 기억은 심지어 정확할지도 모르지만, 우리가 우리의 일상생활에 대해 기억하는 것의 대부분은 세부적으로 정확하지도 풍부하지도 않다. 진화는 우리의 기억이 우리의 매일의 경험을 충실하고 정확하게 녹화하는 비디오카메라가 되도록 고안하지 않았다는 압도적인 신경 심리학적 증거가 있다. 예를 들어, 두뇌의 핵심 기억 시스템은 유기체가 편리하고 자신의 이익을 도모하는 방식으로 그들을 둘러싸고 있는 계속하여 변하는 세계를 다루어 주는 무의식적인 규칙과 관념을 경험으로부터 추출하도록 명확하게 구조화되어 있다. 또한 우리가 기억을 떠올릴 때마다 다만 약간일지라도 우리가 우리의 기억을 변화시킬지도 모른다는 증거도 있다. 기억의 유동성은 시끄럽고 불확실하며 계속해서 변하는 환경 속에서 순간의 주목으로 생사가 걸린 결정을 내릴 수 있는 두뇌를 설계하는 데 내재된 도전을 반영하는 것일지도 모른다. 기억은 생존에 관한 것이지, 정확성에 관한 것은 아니다.

구문 [2행~3행] ~ $\underset{S}{\underline{most\ of\ what\ we\ remember\ of\ our\ daily\ lives}}$ $\underset{V}{\underline{is}}$ **neither** exact **nor** rich in detail.

• most of ~ daily lives가 주어이고 동사는 is이다. 「neither A nor B」는 'A도 B도 아니다'의 뜻이며, A와 B에 해당하는 자리에 모두 형용사가 위치하여 병렬구조를 이룬다.

[12행~13행] There is also <u>evidence</u> <u>that we may change our memories</u>, (if only a little), **each time** we recall them.

• evidence는 that 이하와 동격 관계이다. 삽입절 if only a little은 양보의 의미(~일지라도)를 갖는다. 접속사 each time은 '~할 때마다'의 뜻이다.

어휘 vivid 생생한, 선명한 in detail 세부적으로 overwhelming 압도적인 neuropsychological 신경 심리학의 faithfully 충실스럽게 specifically 명확하게 structure 구조화하다 extract 추출하다 abstraction 관념, 추상적 개념 ever-changing 늘 변화하는 self-serving 자신의 이익을 도모하는 manner 방식 recall 기억해 내다 fluidity 유동성, 가변성 inherent 내재하는 engineer 설계하다

2 글의 순서 ④

해설 주어진 문장에서 참가자들에게 4개의 다른 방식으로 소통해보라고 한 연구가 소개된다. 그다음에는 (C)에서처럼 각각의 소통에 나타난 정서적 유대감을 측정해 본다는 연구의 다음 목표가 소개된다. (A)에서는 디지털 소통 방식에서 정서적 유대감의 수치를 높이려는 참가자들의 노력이 나온다. But으로 이어지는 (B)에서는 그러한 노력의 무용함과 직접 대화의 효과를 실험의 결과로 제시한다.

해석 우리가 더 많은 것을 하는 순간을 살면서도 더 적은 것을 얻는 삶을 살아가고 있다는 생각은 몇 쌍의 대학생 나이의 친구들이 4개의 다른 방식으로 소통하도록 요청받았던 최근 연구에 의해 뒷받침되는데, 그 방식들은 직접 대면 대화, 화상 채팅, 음성 채팅, 그리고 온라인 인스턴트 메시징이었다.
(C) 그런 다음, 사람들이 어떤 기분인지를 묻고 그들이 서로에게 어떻게 행동하는지를 지켜봄으로써 이러한 우정에 있어서 정서적 유대감의 정도가 평가되었다. 결과는 명확했다. 직접 대화가 가장 정서적인 연결로 이어졌으며 온라인 메시지는 가장 적은 정서적 연결로 이어졌다.
(A) 학생들은 이모티콘을 사용하고, 웃음소리('하하하')를 타이핑하고, '전부 대문자로 타이핑하는 방식'을 이용하여 긴박함을 억지스럽게 나타냄으로써 자신들의 디지털 메시지에 '온기를 불어넣으려고' 노력했다.
(B) 그러나 이러한 기법들은 그 일을 해내지 못했다. 우리가 서로에게 가장 인간적이게 되는 것은 우리가 서로의 얼굴을 보고 서로의 목소리를 듣는 때이다.

구문 [11행~13행] **It is** *when we see each other's faces and hear each other's voices* **that** we become most human to each other.

• 「It is ~ that ....」 강조구문은 '…한 것은 바로 ~이다'의 의미로 It is와 that 사이의 말이 강조된다. 이 문장에서는 when ~ voices 절이 강조되고 있다.

[14행~16행] Then, the degree of emotional bonding in these friendships was assessed **both** by asking how people felt **and** (by) watching how they behaved toward each other.

• 「both A and B」는 'A와 B 둘 다'의 뜻이다. by asking ~ felt가 A에, (by) watching ~ each other이 B에 해당한다.

어휘 warm up ~을 따뜻하게 하다 urgency 긴급 cap 대문자 bonding 유대, 결합 assess 평가하다 in-person 직접의

3 문장 넣기 ④

해설 주어진 문장은 But으로 시작하여 내용 전환이 일어나며, they가 단순한 요소로 복잡한 것을 만드는 우주의 능력의 징후임을 서술하고 있다. ④의 앞부분까지는 우주가 탄생 직후에는 수소와 헬륨 등 단순한 구성 요소만 존재했다는 내용이다. 따라서 주어진 문장이 ④에 위치하고, 이후에는 항성들이 생물체를 포함한 더욱더 복잡한 독립체를 위한 기초를 세웠다는 내용이 와야 자연스럽다.

해석 우주는 그것이 생겨난 처음 순간에 너무 빠르게 식어서 수소, 헬륨, 그리고 (극소량의) 리튬보다 더 무겁거나 더 복잡한 원소를 만들어내는 것이 불가능했다. 초기 우주의 열기와 혼돈 속에서 더 복잡한 것은 아무것도 살아남을 수 없었다. 화학적 관점에서 초기 우주는 매우 단순했는데, 너무나도 단순하여 우리의 지구나 거기에 사는 생물체와 같은 복잡한 물체를 생성할 수 없었다. 최초의 항성들과 은하계들은 거의 수소와 헬륨에 지나지 않는 것으로 구성되었다. 그러나 그것들은 단순한 구성 요소로 복잡한 물체를 만드는 우리 우주의 정말 놀라운 능력의 징후였다. 항성들은 일단 생겨난 후, 생물체를 포함한 더욱 복잡한 독립체를 위한 기반을 다졌는데, 그것들의 불타는 핵에서 수소와 헬륨을 모든 다른 원소로 바꾼 연금술을 행했기 때문이다.

구문 [14행~18행] Once **(they were)** created, stars laid the foundations for even more complex entities, / including living organisms, // because in their fiery cores they practiced *an alchemy* [that turned hydrogen and helium into all the other elements].

• 부사절의 주어가 주절의 주어와 같고, 동사가 be 동사인 경우 '주어+be동사'의 생

락이 가능하기 때문에 once와 created 사이에 they were이 생략되었다. [ ] 부분은 an alchemy를 수식하는 관계사절이다.

- -

어휘 **building block** 구성 요소 **minute** 미세한 **hydrogen** 수소 **helium** 헬륨 **lithium** 리튬 **chaos** 무질서; 혼돈 **organism** 유기체 **inhabit** 살다 **galaxy** 은하계 **little more than** ~에 지나지 않는 **entity** 독립체; 실재 **fiery** 불타는; 불같은 **core** 핵; 중심

4~5 장문
4 ④ 5 ⑤

해설 4. 맑은 날보다는 비 오는 날에 사람들이 물건을 더 기억한 이유는 비 오는 날이 기분을 울적하게 하는데 이를 전환하려고 더 깊고 분명하게 생각한다는 것이 글의 요지이다. 그러므로 ④ '왜 비 오는 날씨가 우리를 더 분명하게 생각하도록 돕는가'가 제목으로 가장 적절하다.
① 맑은 날과 논리적 사고
② 날씨는 기분에 어떻게 영향을 주는가
③ 우울한 날은 쇼핑하기에 정말 좋다
⑤ 슬플 때 우리는 기억을 왜곡하는 경향이 있다
5. 비 오는 날에는 부정적인 기분이 들어서 기분을 행복하게 바꾸기 위해 주변을 살핀다고 했으므로 기분 상태는 환경 안에서 어떤 것이 한결같아야 할지를 알려주는 것이 아니라 어떤 것이 고쳐져야 할지를 알려주는 것으로 봐야 한다. 그러므로 ⑤는 fixed 등이 되어야 한다.

- -

해석 한 연구에서 사회심리학자들은 호주의 시드니에서 한 작은 잡지 가게를 떠나는 쇼핑객들에게 깜짝 기억 검사를 해줄 것을 요청했다. 쇼핑객들이 그 가게로 들어가기 전에 연구자들은 10개의 작은 장식품들, 즉 네 개의 플라스틱 동물, 한 개의 장난감 대포, 한 개의 돼지 저금통, 네 개의 성냥갑 자동차를 가게 계산대 위에 올려놓았다. 가게를 떠난 뒤, 쇼핑객들은 이 열 개의 품목을 최대한 많이 기억해보고, 그리고 또 열 개의 바른 품목과 열 개의 새로운 품목이 포함되어 있는 스무 개 품목의 목록 중에서 이 열 개의 품목을 골라보라고 요청을 받았다. 쇼핑객들은 햇빛이 밝게 빛나는 날보다 비가 내리는 날에 이 품목들을 세 배나 많이 기억해냈다. 그리고 스무 개 품목의 긴 목록 중에서 이 열 개의 품목을 고를 때도 거의 네 배나 더 정확했다. 연구자들은 (a) 어두컴컴한 날씨는 우리의 기분을 안 좋게 하여 우리가 더 깊고 분명하게 생각하게 한다고 설명했다.
인간은 슬픔을 피하려는 생물학적 성향을 지니고 있고 그래서 기분 전환의 기회를 찾게 되고 자신을 울적하게 만들 수 있는 온갖 것들에 맞서 주의하여 자신을 보호함으로써 울적한 기분에 반응한다. 반면에 행복은 모든 것이 잘되고 있으며 환경에 긴급한 위협 요인이 없고 (b) 주의 깊게 생각할 필요가 없다는 신호를 보낸다. 이런 (c) 대조적인 정신적인 접근법들은 비 오는 날에 쇼핑객들이 열 개의 자질구레한 품목들을 더 정확히 기억해낸 까닭을 설명한다. 비 오는 날은 쇼핑객들은 뭔가 부정적인 기분이 들게 되고, 쇼핑객들은 답답하고 우울한 기분을 더 행복한 대체물로 바꿀 정보를 위해 주변을 (d) 살펴보아 그 부정적인 기분을 극복하려 무의식적으로 시도를 했다. 여러분이 이것에 대해 생각한다면 이러한 접근방식이 이해가 될 것이다. 기분 상태는 우리에게 환경 안에서 어떤 것이 (e) 한결같아(→ 고쳐져)야 할지 아닐지를 말해주는 만능의 측정 장치들이다.

- -

구문 [7행~11행] After leaving the shop, the shoppers **were asked to remember** as many of the ten items as possible, and also **to choose** the ten items from *a list of twenty* [that included the ten correct items and ten new items].

- 밑줄 친 부분은 were asked에 이어지는 to부정사구로 and로 연결되어 병렬구조를 이루고 있다. [ ] 부분은 관계사절로 a list of twenty를 수식한다.

[19행~23행] Humans are biologically predisposed to avoid sadness, and they respond to sad moods by **seeking** opportunities for mood repair and

vigilantly **protecting** themselves against **whatever might be making them sad**.

- 전치사 by의 목적어로 두 개의 동명사구가 and로 연결되어 병렬구조를 이루고 있다. whatever ~ sad는 복합관계대명사절로 anything that might be making them sad의 뜻이다.

- -

어휘 **spring** 불쑥 묻다. 말하다 **ornamental** 장식용의 **piggy bank** 돼지 저금통 **identify** 확인하다 **gloomy** 어두컴컴한; 우울한 **hamper** 어지럽히다. 방해하다 **biologically** 생물학적으로 **predispose** ~하는 성향을 갖게 하다 **vigilantly** 주의하여 **pose** 태도를 취하다 **imminent** 절박한, 긴급한 **trinket** (값싼) 장신구 **dampen** 기를 꺾다 **all-purpose** 만능의, 쓸모가 많은 **measurement** 측정

● ANSWERS

	1	2	3	4	5			1	2	3	4	5
Day 01	①	④	③	③	④		**Day 31**	②	①	③	③	⑤
Day 02	⑤	⑤	②	③	②		**Day 32**	①	②	④	④	④
Day 03	②	⑤	③	①	④		**Day 33**	②	③	⑤	④	⑤
Day 04	③	④	④	④	④		**Day 34**	②	③	④	④	⑤
Day 05	③	④	⑤	③	①		**Day 35**	③	④	④	③	①
Day 06	①	②	④	②	③		**Day 36**	⑤	②	⑤	②	⑤
Day 07	④	②	③	③	⑤		**Day 37**	②	⑤	③	②	③
Day 08	⑤	③	①	③	①		**Day 38**	①	④	⑤	④	④
Day 09	④	②	⑤	①	④		**Day 39**	③	②	③	⑤	④
Day 10	④	⑤	②	⑤	③		**Day 40**	④	②	④	②	⑤
Day 11	④	②	③	④	①		**Day 41**	②	③	③	④	①
Day 12	③	③	③	⑤	④		**Day 42**	⑤	②	③	①	③
Day 13	⑤	②	③	⑤	②		**Day 43**	④	⑤	③	①	③
Day 14	②	③	①	④	⑤		**Day 44**	①	⑤	③	③	④
Day 15	②	④	②	⑤	②		**Day 45**	③	⑤	④	②	⑤
Day 16	②	⑤	③	⑤	⑤		**Day 46**	③	①	②	②	⑤
Day 17	⑤	⑤	③	④	②		**Day 47**	②	⑤	⑤	④	②
Day 18	①	③	⑤	②	④		**Day 48**	④	②	④	①	④
Day 19	⑤	②	③	③	④		**Day 49**	⑤	⑤	③	②	②
Day 20	③	⑤	②	③	②		**Day 50**	③	④	③	④	③
Day 21	④	⑤	③	②	⑤		**Day 51**	④	②	⑤	③	④
Day 22	②	②	①	④	④		**Day 52**	①	①	④	③	⑤
Day 23	③	⑤	⑤	④	②		**Day 53**	⑤	⑤	②	③	③
Day 24	②	⑤	③	⑤	⑤		**Day 54**	②	④	③	④	④
Day 25	③	③	⑤	②	③		**Day 55**	②	③	④	②	⑤
Day 26	②	③	②	④	①		**Day 56**	⑤	③	①	④	④
Day 27	②	③	①	⑤	③		**Day 57**	⑤	④	⑤	④	⑤
Day 28	③	④	③	⑤	④		**Day 58**	⑤	③	④	③	②
Day 29	⑤	⑤	①	④	④		**Day 59**	④	④	②	④	②
Day 30	③	⑤	②	⑤	③		**Day 60**	①	④	④	④	⑤

쎄듀 초등 커리큘럼

	예비초	초1	초2	초3	초4	초5	초6
구문		신간 천일문 365 일력 |초1-3| 교육부 지정 초등 필수 영어 문장		초등코치 천일문 SENTENCE 1001개 통문장 암기로 완성하는 초등 영어의 기초			
문법				초등코치 천일문 GRAMMAR 1001개 예문으로 배우는 초등 영문법			
		신간 왓츠 Grammar Start 시리즈 초등 기초 영문법 입문					
				신간 왓츠 Grammar Plus 시리즈 초등 필수 영문법 마무리			
독해				신간 왓츠 리딩 70 / 80 / 90 / 100 A / B 쉽고 재미있게 완성되는 영어 독해력			
어휘				초등코치 천일문 VOCA&STORY 1001개의 초등 필수 어휘와 짧은 스토리			
		패턴으로 말하는 초등 필수 영단어 1 / 2 문장 패턴으로 완성하는 초등 필수 영단어					
ELT	Oh! My PHONICS 1 / 2 / 3 / 4 유·초등학생을 위한 첫 영어 파닉스						
		Oh! My SPEAKING 1 / 2 / 3 / 4 / 5 / 6 핵심 문장 패턴으로 더욱 쉬운 영어 말하기					
		Oh! My GRAMMAR 1 / 2 / 3 쓰기로 완성하는 첫 초등 영문법					

쎄듀 중등 커리큘럼

	예비중	중1	중2	중3
구문		신간 천일문 STARTER 1 / 2		중등 필수 구문 & 문법 총정리
문법		천일문 GRAMMAR LEVEL 1 / 2 / 3		예문 중심 문법 기본서
		GRAMMAR Q Starter 1, 2 / Intermediate 1, 2 / Advanced 1, 2		학기별 문법 기본서
		잘 풀리는 영문법 1 / 2 / 3		문제 중심 문법 적용서
		GRAMMAR PIC 1 / 2 / 3 / 4		이해가 쉬운 도식화된 문법서
			1센치 영문법	1권으로 핵심 문법 정리
문법+어법		첫단추 BASIC 문법·어법편 1 / 2		문법·어법의 기초
문법+쓰기		EGU 영단어&품사 / 문장 형식 / 동사 써먹기 / 문법 써먹기 / 구문 써먹기		서술형 기초 세우기와 문법 다지기
				올씀 1 기본 문장 PATTERN 내신 서술형 기본 문장 학습
쓰기		거침없이 Writing LEVEL 1 / 2 / 3		중등 교과서 내신 기출 서술형
		개정 중학 영어 쓰작 1 / 2 / 3		중등 교과서 패턴 드릴 서술형
어휘		어휘끝 중학 필수편 중학 필수어휘 1000개	어휘끝 중학 마스터편 고난도 중학어휘 +고등기초 어휘 1000개	
독해		Reading Relay Starter 1, 2 / Challenger 1, 2 / Master 1, 2		타교과 연계 배경 지식 독해
		READING Q Starter 1, 2 / Intermediate 1, 2 / Advanced 1, 2		예측/추론/요약 사고력 독해
독해전략			리딩 플랫폼 1 / 2 / 3	논픽션 지문 독해
독해유형			Reading 16 LEVEL 1 / 2 / 3	수능 유형 맛보기 + 내신 대비
			첫단추 BASIC 독해편 1 / 2	수능 유형 독해 입문
듣기	Listening Q 유형편 / 1 / 2 / 3			유형별 듣기 전략 및 실전 대비
		쎄듀 빠르게 중학영어듣기 모의고사 1 / 2 / 3		교육청 듣기평가 대비